Vernunft und Erfahrung im Rechtsdenken der Gegenwart

Reason and Experience in Contemporary Legal Thought

IVR
11. Weltkongreß / 11th World Congress
Helsinki 1983
Verhandlungen / Proceedings

RECHTSTHEORIE

Zeitschrift für Logik, Methodenlehre, Kybernetik und Soziologie des Rechts

Beiheft 10

Vernunft und Erfahrung im Rechtsdenken der Gegenwart

Reason and Experience in Contemporary Legal Thought

Herausgegeben von / Edited by

Torstein Eckhoff / Lawrence M. Friedman
Jyrki Uusitalo

Vorwort von / Preface by

Ota Weinberger

DUNCKER & HUMBLOT / BERLIN

Zitiervorschlag:

Cees J. Bax, Two Functions of Legal Reasoning,
in: RECHTSTHEORIE Beiheft 10 (1986), S. 3 - 9

CIP-Kurztitelaufnahme der Deutschen Bibliothek

Vernunft und Erfahrung im Rechtsdenken der Gegenwart: [Helsinki 1983] = Reason and experience in contemporary legal thought / hrsg. von Torstein Eckhoff ... Vorw. von Ota Weinberger. — Berlin: Duncker und Humblot, 1986.
(Rechtstheorie: Beiheft; 10)
(... Weltkongress / IVR; 11)
ISBN 3-428-05894-1

NE: Eckhoff, Torstein [Hrsg.]; International Association for the Philosophy of Law and Social Philosophy: ... Weltkongress; Rechtstheorie / Beiheft; PT

Gedruckt 1986 bei Berliner Buchdruckerei Union GmbH, Berlin 61
Printed in Germany

ISBN 3-428-05894-1

Vorwort

Die Weltkongresse der Internationalen Vereinigung für Rechts- und Sozialphilosophie (IVR) haben sich nicht nur zu einem Treffpunkt der Rechtstheoretiker, Sozialwissenschaftler und politischen Denker aus Ost und West entwickelt, es scheint, daß sie darüber hinaus zum Markstein in der rechtsphilosophischen Entwicklung geworden sind. Nirgends läßt sich die Verlagerung der Forschungsschwerpunkte in den Rechts- und Sozialwissenschaften, der aktuelle Meinungsstreit der Schulen und philosophischen Richtungen sowie das Sprießen neuer Ideen und Gesichtspunkte besser verfolgen, als bei diesem Forum. Zweifellos kommen dabei nicht nur tragfähige Gedanken und perfekt ausgearbeitete Konzeptionen zum Vorschein; aber die Gedanken in statu nascendi wirken oft — wenn sie nur in ernster suchender Absicht vorgetragen werden — befruchtender als trockene Kompendien verstaubten Wissens. So gesehen erscheinen mir die umfangreichen Akten der Weltkongresse der IVR eine sehr wertvolle Orientierungshilfe und wichtige Anregung für die Fortsetzung unserer Forschungsarbeit zu sein.

Der XI. Weltkongreß für Rechts- und Sozialphilosophic fand vom 14. bis 20. August 1983 in der berühmten Finlandia-Halle in Helsinki statt. Das Generalthema „Die philosophischen Grundlagen der Rechts- und Sozialwissenschaften" steckte nicht nur einen breiten Rahmen für die Arbeit des Kongresses ab, sondern brachte auch implizit zum Ausdruck, daß in unserer Zeit gerade die philosophische Grundlagenproblematik eine neue eingehende Diskussion erfordert.

Die Arbeit des Kongresses war einerseits in Plenarsitzungen, andererseits in Arbeitsgruppen organisiert. Die Plenarsitzungen wurden durch einen vielbeachteten Eröffnungsvortrag von *G. H. von Wright* „Is and Ought" eingeleitet; weitere Sitzungen waren folgenden Themen gewidmet: „Rechtsphilosophie in den nordischen Ländern" (mit Referaten von *Stig Jørgensen, Jacob Sundberg, Hannu T. Klami* und *Mikael M. Karlsson*), „Recht und Moral" (mit Referaten von *Joel Feinberg, Michel Villey, Sergio Cotta*), „Die Grundlagen der Rechtskultur" (mit Referaten von *Franz Wieacker, Alice Erh-Soon Tay, Vladimir Tumanow*).

In den Sitzungen der sechs Arbeitsgruppen wurden täglich je ein Hauptreferat, ein oder zwei Koreferate und eine größere Anzahl kürzerer

Beiträge vorgetragen und eingehend diskutiert. Die Themen der Arbeitsgruppen lauteten:

1. „Recht und Gesellschaft“ mit den Sitzungsthemen:
   (a) Soziale Voraussetzungen der Rechtsphilosophie
   (b) Rationalität in der Gesetzgebung
   (c) Rechtsstaat und Wohlfahrtsstaat
   (d) Recht und Ökonomie
2. „Recht und Moral“ mit den Sitzungsthemen:
   (a) Verschiedene Naturrechtskonzeptionen
   (b) Die Bedeutung der Menschenrechte im Rechtssystem
   (c) Ziviler Ungehorsam
   (d) Strafe und Verantwortung
3. „Modelle des Rechtsdenkens“ mit den Sitzungsthemen:
   (a) Rechtsregeln und Prinzipien
   (b) Formale Logik und das Rechtsdenken
   (c) Argumentation in der juristischen Forschung und in der Rechtspraxis
   (d) Beweis und Plausibilität im Rechtsdenken
4. „System und Systematisierung im Recht“ mit den Sitzungsthemen:
   (a) Der Begriff des Rechtssystems
   (b) Die Systematisierung in der Rechtswissenschaft
   (c) Entwicklung und Fortschritt in der Rechtswissenschaft
   (d) Das Recht und die moderne Systemtheorie
5. „Wissen und Werte im Recht“ mit den Sitzungsthemen:
   (a) Die Voraussetzungen des juristischen Denkens
   (b) Wahrheit im Rechtsdenken — Korrespondenz, Kohärenz oder Konsens

(c) Probleme der materiellen Gerechtigkeit

(d) Die Grenzen der Rationalität im juristischen Denken

6. „Rechtstheorie und die Sozialwissenschaften" mit den Sitzungsthemen:

(a) Makrosoziologische Rechtstheorien

(b) Empirische Erkenntnis der Gesellschaft und die juristische Forschung

(c) Die Entstehung der Theorien des Rechts

(d) Der Rechtsrealismus und seine Grenzen

Außerdem gab es Sondersitzungen, und zwar über „Recht und Anthropologie" und über „Philosophische Probleme der Sozialwissenschaften".

In sehr verdienstvoller Weise hat ein Redaktionskomitee unter dem Vorsitz von *Georg Henrik von Wright* und *Werner Krawietz* die Herausgabe der Akten des Weltkongresses vorbereitet. Es wurde hierbei eine thematische Aufteilung der umfangreichen Materie des Kongresses durchgeführt. Die redaktionelle Bearbeitung der insgesamt sieben Bände der Akten für die Herausgabe wurde durch die finanzielle Unterstützung von seiten der Finnischen Kulturstiftung und der Finnischen Stiftung für die ökonomische Erziehung ermöglicht. Die Herausgeber und die IVR sind diesen Organisationen zu Dank verpflichtet.

Die Herausgeber des vorliegenden Bandes möchten dankbar erwähnen, daß bei der Vorbereitung der Texte für den Druck einige wertvolle Hinweise von *Alice Erh-Soon Tay* und *Carl Wellman* berücksichtigt wurden. Alle Beiträge wurden — wie bei den Kongreßakten der IVR-Kongresse üblich — nur im möglichst geringem Maße redaktionell bearbeitet.

Der vorliegende Band umfaßt Beiträge zum Problembereich „Vernunft und Erfahrung im Rechtsdenken der Gegenwart". Die Probleme der rationalen Strukturen und der wissenschaftlichen Begründungen sowie die Frage nach der empirischen Basis unseres Wissens sind heute nicht nur das zentrale Problem wissenschaftstheoretischer Untersuchungen, sondern Fragen dieser Art treten auch mit besonderer Dringlichkeit im Bereich der praktischen Philosophie und in der Theorie des juristischen Argumentierens auf. Es werden hier viele Probleme sprachphilosophischer, logischer und methodologischer Natur relevant, die die allgemeine wissenschaftstheoretische Problematik überschreiten. Es sind dies nicht nur die noch immer interessanten Fragen der logischen Strukturen als Basis des juristischen Denkens sowie die Probleme der Bestimmung des

Begriffes und der Methoden der rationalen Argumentation in der Jurisprudenz, sondern auch — und zwar in erhöhtem Maße — die Frage der Relevanz der Erfahrung als Grundlage praktisch-philosophischer Begründungen. Wichtig scheint es mir hier, zu unterstreichen, daß im Kontext der praktischen Philosophie Erfahrung nicht nur als Basis des Sachverhaltswissens auftritt, sondern auch als stellungnehmende Erfahrung, als Werterlebnis und als Element von spezifischen Prozessen des institutionalisierten Rechtslebens.

Das Buch enthält vier Abschnitte, deren Titel lauten:

1. Abschnitt: Systemische Grundlagen der Rechtsvernunft

2. Abschnitt: Systematisierung in Rechtsdogmatik und Rechtswissenschaft

3. Abschnitt: Das Rechtssystem und seine gesellschaftliche Basis

4. Abschnitt: Ökonomische Analyse des Rechts

Die Beiträge jedes Abschnittes werden jeweils in alphabetischer Reihenfolge abgedruckt. Die Beiträge von *Peczenik/Sajó* und *Raz/Tamayo* im ersten Abschnitt, von *Aarnio/Alchourrón* im zweiten Abschnitt, von *Krawietz/Friedman* im dritten Abschnitt und von *Summers/Tolonen* im vierten Abschnitt wurden als Hauptreferate/Koreferate in den Sitzungen 3 c, 4 a, 4 b, 4 d und 1 d gehalten. Die Koreferate sind jeweils unmittelbar nach den entsprechenden Hauptreferaten abgedruckt.

Ota Weinberger

Inhaltsverzeichnis

II. Systematisierung in Rechtsdogmatik und Rechtswissenschaft

III. Das Rechtssystem und seine gesellschaftliche Basis

I. Systemische Grundlagen der Rechtsvernunft

TWO FUNCTIONS OF LEGAL REASONING

By Cees J. Bax, Rotterdam

In continental legal systems it is not unusual for the administration of justice to be described as the use of syllogistic reasoning in the application of statutory rules to the facts of a case. After the facts are subsumed under the rule, a logical conclusion can be drawn to determine the legal consequences. Usually, in current legal writings, it is noted that various problems adhere to this apparently simple model. One problem is the difficulty of constructing a correct minor, partly because language provides a limited means of expression for representing a (given) state of affairs.[1] In this view, the foundation of the administration of justice is, after all, the possibility of true statements about the 'real' facts. By employing such true statements in the minor of the syllogism, logically correct conclusions are derived which entail the legal consequences belonging to the facts of the case.

In recent years this view has been criticized by various theoreticians. In a number of cases, linguistics and the philosophy of language have inspired their criticism.[2] In line with these developments, for my purposes here, I consider how in legal practice and in legal dogmatics, legal reasoning allows the supposition that the administration of justice is in essence the application of legal rules to facts. I will restrict myself to the rôle of facts and factual terms contained in legal texts.

I. Legal Practice

The first question which must be addressed on the basis of this view of the administration of justice, is the question whether it is indeed

[1] *K. Larenz,* Methodenlehre der Rechtswissenschaft, Berlin-Heidelberg-New York 1979, p. 255 pp.

[2] E. g. *A. Aarnio,* Linguistic Philosophy and Legal Theory, Some problems of legal argumentation, in: W. Krawietz e.a. (eds.), Argumentation und Hermeneutik in der Jurisprudenz, RECHTSTHEORIE Beiheft 1 (1979); *H. Brinckmann,* Rechtshandlung und Sprechhandlung, in: J. S. Petöfi e.a., Fachsprache — Umgangssprache, Kronberg 1975, p. 197—222; *C. Grzegorczyk,* Le rôle du performative dans le language du droit, in: APD 1974, p. 229—241; *J. H. Nieuwenhuis,* Drie beginselen van contractenrecht, Deventer 1979; *Th. M. Seibert,* Von Sprachgegenständen zur Sprache von juristischen Gegenständen, in: ARSP VIII (1972), p. 43—52; *J. Wróblewski,* Facts in Law, in: ARSP LIX (1973), p. 161 pp.

the facts, or at least descriptions of facts, which are utilized as the minor. The suggestion is, firstly, that the facts can be *described unambiguously* in language. Secondly, the assumption is, that preceding the judicial procedure such 'pure' facts are clearly established, *uncontaminated,* as it were, *by the law.* Both assumptions are theoretically untenable.

As early as the beginning of this century it was pointed out in the Netherlands by the psychologist, Van Eeden, the philosopher, Mannoury, and the poet and jurist, De Haan — who belonged to the so-called Significal Movement — that whenever we speak, we do *more than merely describe* what the case is: indeed our speech *creates* understanding.[3]

In this context, Van Eeden applied the term 'word-act', Mannoury and De Haan the term 'speech-act'. At that time, their approach was not adopted by others, at least not in the field of legal science and legal theory. In recent years, a revival in the interest for their ideas may be observed in the Netherlands.[4]

A similar approach has gained familiarity in the Netherlands and on the international level through the widely influential work of J. L. Austin.[5] His concept of 'performative speech-act' has also been adopted by jurists and legal theoreticians,[6] but still has not had the effect on legal theory which might have been possible.

Two reasons may be identified for this. In the first place, Austin's concept of 'performative' resembles the concept of 'act-in-law' ('Rechtshandlung') to a large degree.[7] It, therefore, can be (and has been) seen

---

[3] *F. van Eeden,* Redekunstige grondslag van verstandhouding, Utrecht-Antwerpen 1975; *J. I. de Haan,* Rechtskundige signifika, Amsterdam 1916. In a declaration in 1919, the Significal Movement stated: "the meaning of a speech-act for a speaker or a hearer is never fully clear out of the words and symbols that are used ..."

[4] See a. o.: *J. M. Broekman,* Betere taal is beter recht, in: Wijsgerig Perspectief 20 (1980), p. 48—55.

[5] *J. L. Austin,* How to do things with words, Cambridge (Mass.) 1975; *J. L. Austin,* Performative — Constative, in: J. L. Searle (ed.), The philosophy of language, Oxford 1971, p. 1—21.

[6] *Aarnio* (note 2); *Brinckmann* (note 2); *Grzegorczyk* (note 2); *Nieuwenhuis* (note 2); *Seibert* (note 2).

[7] Cf. *Austin,* How to do things with words (note 5), p. 7. Besides, Austin's work displays a remarkable resemblance to current legal writings on the application of rules. Just as the administration of justice is seen as the application of rules of law to arrive at judgments, in linguistics speech is generally regarded to be the correct use of the rules of language to form statements; cf. *J. M. Broekman,* Recht en taal, Deventer 1979. — The German term 'Rechtshandlung' may be translated into English as either 'act-in-law' or 'legally relevant act'. The first alternative is preferred in this essay.

as an *equivalent* to the concept of act-in-law (Rechtshandlung). In this way, the jurist gives the concept of performative speech-act a place in the legal-dogmatical system. Some implications and presuppositions of the legal-dogmatic concept of act-in-law can be elucidated in this way, *e. g.* the problem of determining which utterances can count as giving consent and, henceforth, give rise to obligation. The Dutchman Nieuwenhuis has done research in this field, but he restricts his attention to the level of substantive law.[8] Brinckmann proposes that only explicit performative speech-acts can serve as the basis for judicial decisions. This proposal seems unrealistic in present day Western society. Even in ancient Rome the idea of a closed system of *actiones* did not survive. He, however, is correct in stating that the meaning of utterances in the field of law rests not only upon their informative contents (the semantic meaning), but also is based upon the activity of speaking itself (the pragmatic meaning).[9]

The judicial procedure itself affects the determination of the facts; the judgment does not contain a mere description of the (relevant) facts of the case. The act of determining constitutes what afterwards is termed the 'facts'. This is generally not taken into account on the level of substantive law. Both the above authors, too, apparently did not take into account what here is seen as the further consequences of using the concept of performative speech-act in order to understand the rôle that the judicial procedure plays in determining the facts themselves.

Austin's conclusion that "to say something is to do something" is contained in the concept of act in law. This thesis is also valid for that which is said prior to and during the judicial procedure. *Speaking about* facts, including speaking about previously performed acts-in-law/speech-acts, *is in itself the performance of new speech-acts. The latter are no more 'constative' than the former.* A speaker always expresses a certain point of view with regard to what he describes.

With this conclusion, one problem remains. In the judicial procedure a relationship is presumed to exist between prior events and the 'image' the parties present to the judge in their narratives of earlier events. This may give rise to difficulties if the concept of speech-act is considered in depth. The narratives and texts which the judge has at his disposal all have a performative character.

As far as I know, in legal dogmatics only the Dutch jurist Eggens has reached similar conclusions. He pointed out that legal procedural (speech-)acts cannot be considered to be merely descriptions of the events

[8] *Nieuwenhuis* (note 2).

[9] *Brinckmann* (note 2), p. 201.

and circumstances, which gave rise to a dispute. The opening texts of the proceedings must meet certain requirements, which are imposed by legislation and by legal dogmatics. Proceedings cannot be initiated by means of texts which do not comply to these requirements. Consequently, Eggens argues, these (speech-)acts should be regarded as acts-in-law (Rechtshandlungen).[10]

Following Luhmann,[11] one could call this process a reduction of complexity. Positive law, in other words, employs a system of exclusions with regard to admissible texts. In addition, only some kinds of 'facts', *i. e.* sentences referring to some kinds of facts, are relevant to the proceedings. This is anticipated in a summons.

Subsequently evidence will have to be advanced to corroborate the facts formulated in this manner, which implies a further reduction of the 'facts'. The provision of evidence is also subject to legal requirements.[12] So, the 'facts' to which legal rules are applied, are *not fixed data,* existing prior to and independent of their 'description' by the parties to the dispute. On the contrary, they are *produced as texts* in and by a process consisting of an interplay of mutually defining speech-acts. In the context of existing laws and other legal texts, these speech-acts are performed by the parties to the dispute, their legal counsel and the judge(s). The outcome is the text of the judgement. A part of the text suggests to be a mere reference to pre-existing 'real' facts. Actually, it must be seen as a *transformation* of prior texts.[13]

On the basis of the text of a judicial decision, an underlying reality cannot be decided upon with certainty. The transformations are non-equivalent.[14] The text has congealed into an opaque unity.

II. Legal Dogmatics

Legal dogmatics, also, take texts into consideration, including those resulting from legal proceedings, as the representations of an underlying reality and of the legal consequences adhering thereto. The assumptions about the relationship between facts and reality are as follows: legal

---

[10] *J. Eggens,* De beginselen van het burgerlijk bewijs, in: J. Eggens, Verzamelde privaatrechtelijke opstellen, Vol. II, Alphen aan den Rijn 1959, p. 280—314.

[11] *N. Luhmann,* Legitimation durch Verfahren, Neuwied am Rhein und Berlin 1969.

[12] Cf. *Eggens* (note 10).

[13] *Broekman* (note 7); *A. Aarnio, R. Alexy, A. Peczenik,* The Foundation of Legal Reasoning, in: RECHTSTHEORIE 12 (1981), p. 133—158, 257—279, 423—448.

[14] *A. Peczenik,* Non-equivalent transformations and the law, in: RECHTSTHEORIE Beiheft 1 (1979), p. 163—176; cf. *Seibert* (note 2).

practice posits a correlation between facts and everyday language, everyday language and legal language, and thus between facts and legal language. Legal dogmatics posits not only a correlation between everyday language and legal language, but also an additional relation between the legal language of practice and the legal language of dogmatics, and thus between the latter and the facts. Legal dogmatics, in the end, denies the *transformational* relation between the different kinds of texts. Moreover, it transforms its object once again. Once again, texts are considered as *data* and not as *constructa*.

In legal-dogmatic reasoning, the genesis of the texts with which it is dealing, is ignored. An *a priori* correspondence is presumed to exist between facts in reality and 'legal facts' *(Rechtstatsachen)* to which legal texts should refer to.[15] Because legal dogmatics also operate according to the requirements of legal reasoning[16], an additional transformation process takes place. Thus, in my opinion, *legal dogmatic statements* also are themselves *never mere descriptions* of facts. They refer to other texts.[17]

One always expresses a certain point of view with regard to what one describes and so does the legal dogmatician. This is even more so if legal dogmatics include systematization of its object as one of its aims.[18]

The relationship between *dogmata* and *regulae* was problematic in classical thinking.[19] In the present day, too, there is no unanimity with regard to the relationship between legal dogmatic sentences and positive law, *i. e.*, sentences formulated by the legislator and/or the judge. It can be determined, however, that legal-dogmatic reasoning provides criteria for correct reasoning in the administration of justice. This is apparent in judicial decision-making in the final instance;[20] also sometimes tenets of legal dogmatics are incorporated in legislation. The new Dutch Civil Code contains various examples of the latter, as does the recently instituted new Dutch Constitution. Additionally, jurists play a central role in the drafting of legislation, operating inevitably according to the rules of their profession or *ars (technè)*.[21]

---

[15] *Th. M. Seibert*, Zur Fachsprache in der Juristenausbildung, Berlin 1977.

[16] *M. Herberger*, Dogmatik; Ius Commune Sonderhefte 12, Frankfurt am Main 1981.

[17] *J. M. Broekman*, Recht en antropologie, Antwerpen 1982; *Broekman* (note 7).

[18] *Aarnio* (note 2), p. 19.

[19] *Herberger* (note 16), p. 69.

[20] *Broekman* 1982 (note 17), p. 182.

[21] *Herberger* (note 16), p. 48.

III. Legal Reasoning

In legal practice, as in legal dogmatics, reasoning is primarily aimed at attaining and maintaining the *unity of law*. In other words, it produces a complex of coherent statements. At the same time, points of reference need to be found in (texts regarding) everyday reality, enabling such statements to be operative. These points of reference are formulated as *acts-in-law* and/or *legal facts* by means of concepts taken from everyday language. In this way legal reasoning produces texts which claim to be the *representation* of a legal reality which corresponds to everyday reality. This claim is based on the assumption that concepts of everyday language are identical to concepts used in legal language.[22]

Legal reasoning simultaneously fulfils two functions in the administration of justice, as well as in legal dogmatics:

— it produces a legal reality which is presented as a mere *reflection* of every-day reality;

— it denies, at the same time, its own contribution to this production-process by presenting itself as a neutral and objective *description* of a previously fixed reality.[23]

Actually, legal reasoning must be seen as a series of *performative speech-acts* interconnected by social, linguistic and legal principles.

Therefore, in agreement with Austin and Peczenik's observation, the question as to the nature of truth in legal reasoning cannot be answered on the basis of the notion of truth as *correspondence* to reality. Answers can only be based on the idea of a *coherence* of legal statements.[24]

The conclusion regarding legal reasoning requires that the question of how legal theoretical research on legal reasoning ought to be conducted be considered with great care. 'Perfect description' of legal reasoning in legal practice does not render a true model of the described object, but at most a *textual (re-)construction*. The question of what is truth in legal reasoning ought to be discarded. Instead, legal theory should address itself to those principles determining the organisation of legal texts which produce reality and truth, and to an understanding of the extent to which these principles also operate in proto-legal texts. The activity, *per se*, of reconstructing these principles on the basis of research of legal texts may possibly elucidate the activity of the process of legal reasoning to such an extent that the question of what is truth in

---

[22] *Broekman* (note 7).

[23] *B. Danet*, Language in the legal process, in: Law and Society Review 14 (1980), p. 445—564; esp. p. 540 pp.

[24] *Aarnio* e.a. (note 13).

legal reasoning can remain of secondary importance. Truth (in the sense of correspondence of text and reality) is the *product* of (legal) reasoning, not its foundation. In producing texts which present themselves as embodying *a priori* truth, legal reasoning seems to respond to a quest for truth in general in Western society. This is a separate problem which demands further consideration. Foucault raises the same point by stating: "[i]t seems that even the word spoken by the law can only be admitted in our society in a *true* discourse."[25]

[25] *M. Foucault,* L'Ordre du discours, Paris 1971.

"IS AND OUGHT" AS A LINGUISTIC PROBLEM

By Henk Jan M. Boukema, Amsterdam

The perennial controversy regarding the separation of law and morals comes down, for all practical purposes, to one distinct question: Is there a logical contradiction in the proposition "This is an evil legal rule"?

An adherent of natural law would say that the proposition is a contradictio in terminis. An evil rule cannot, in his view, be granted the qualification "legal". A positivist, on the other hand, would argue that a legal rule may be valid, even though it is evil. He would add that a disposition to obey or enforce such an evil rule is an entirely different matter.

Here we have a clear-cut controversy, for the standpoints of the believer in natural law and the positivist respectively are mutually exclusive. The controversy has a familiar ring and, to move into another province, it is an abiding source of dissension in aesthetics.

A work of art or other product of human inspiration which exhibits an affectionate regard for qualities or topics commonly regarded as repugnant, has frequently been denied the status of art. Lawrence's novel about the sexual relations of a highborn lady with a gamekeeper and its use of physical detail with all the forbidden words is a historic example of literary or artistic taboo. Art follows two paths — the moral and the aesthetic, and not infrequently they are in conflict with each other. Oscar Wilde believed that "no artist has ethical sympathies" (*The Picture of Dorian Gray*). Others, however, insist that the problems of our time can only be perceived from a moral angle and that art is subservient to moral, political or other ends.

The problematic cleft between the natural law supporters and the positivists is not as remarkable as it may seem. The gist of the controversy came to me at my sick-bed during childhood in the form of an argument between my mother and our doctor. A new film had just been released at the local cinema and was the subject of widespread discussion. My mother was of strict Protestant persuasion and disapproved wholeheartedly of Federico Fellini's *La Dolce Vita*. It was a bad film, she argued. The doctor, however, said it was a good film and pointed out various noteworthy aspects, such as the way in which it dealt with certain themes, how it was shot and directed, and the style of acting. My mother remained unimpressed. The doctor argued that the film gave a good picture of some of life's realities and added that, just as a good painting of a muck-heap was still a good painting, so *La Dolce Vita* was a good film. My mother did not agree. The subject was repulsive, she maintained, and therefore the film was not good.

To sum up, the doctor said *La Dolce Vita* was a good film about various evil aspects of life, while my mother insisted it was a bad film. In a way, they were both right and, what is more important, their attitudes may be reconciled. My mother expressed a blanket condemnation: the evil she detected compromised the film in its totality. This was a general judgment. The doctor, on the other hand, gave a conditional judgment.

The antagonism between positivism and natural law revolves, finally, around the question whether a rule may be called legal although it does not satisfy certain moral standards. It is submitted that the positivist gives a conditional judgment, whereas the supporter of natural law gives a general judgment. Both may be in agreement about the moral aspects of the rule.

THE ROLE OF PERSONAL VALUES IN LEGAL REASONING

By Jan M. van Dunné, Rotterdam

"Values spring from the immediate and inexplicable reaction of vital impulse, and from the irrational part of our nature. The rational part is by its essence relative; it leads us from data to conclusions, or from parts to wholes; it never furnishes the data within which it works."

George Santayana, The Sense of Beauty, 1896, p. 19.

I. Introduction. The Layman and the Judge Deciding Cases

Thinking of the role of personal values in legal reasoning in an impressionistic way one view of the cathedral would be the thought: what is the legal dimension of reasoning when solving a question of law, compared to a layman's reasoning in solving that same question? This is meant as a pragmatic, down-to-earth question which I would like to pose before turning to the more traditional jurisprudential views which are, by their nature, of a more abstract and lofty character. For the investigation of the layman's way of legal reasoning I will rely on a study which we carried out recently in The Netherlands, directed at judges and laymen.[1] Part of this research project on the role of personality traits in judicial decision making was the presentation of a number of legal cases decided by the participating judges to laymen. The last category consisted of law students and of faculty members of language departments of several universities. Before discussing the results, I would like to give some information on the set-up and the conceptual basis of this study.

---

[1] The project has been carried out by Peter J. Van Koppen, psychologist, and Jan Ten Kate, J. D. and psychologist, both of the Rotterdam Faculty of Law, Institute of Legal Decision Making, under the supervision of Willem K. B. Hofstee, Professor of Psychology at the University of Groningen, and the present author. The report of the project as presented to the Minister of Justice (January 1982, in Dutch) and an English version of it, in the Law and Society Review, 1984, p. 225, can be obtained from the authors, Van Koppen en Ten Kate (Erasmus University Rotterdam, Postbus 1738, 3000 DR Rotterdam, The Netherlands). The jurisprudential backgrounds of this research are treated by the present author in papers presented at the Oxford meeting of the Research Committee for Comp. Jud. Studies, of IPSA, 1981, and at the meeting of the Law and Society Ass., Toronto, 1982, which were published in 1984 (see Bibliography).

The basic philosophy was that in hard cases, where the personality of the judge counts most, there is the characteristic situation that the judge in making his decision has to choose between two positions: that of the one party having a strong position from the point of view of the law, or that of the other party having a strong position when considering his personal interest at stake. Therefore, there are good arguments to decide for either party: in a more formal, legalistic approach the first party will succeed, whereas in a more 'principled', result-oriented approach, the second party will win. For the purpose of our project the first party was labelled as having a stronger *'legal construction'* at her disposal (statutory rules, contractual rights, rules of precedent, etc.), the second party as having a stronger *'interest'* than her opponent, thus having equity on her side (principles of good faith, reasonableness, rules of equity, etc.).

On this basis nine cases were selected and presented to the judges; the cases were not too complicated (one-page length) and were derived from common practice (e. g. contract, tort, rent, unfair dismissal). In selecting the cases the interests of the one party were thought to be in balance with the legal construction (arguments) of the other party.

I will not go into the results regarding the correlation between personality characteristics of the judges and their decisions, but will return to the comparison between judicial and lay decision making. Surprisingly, although the cases had been so constructed that the interests of the one party were in balance with the legal construction (arguments) of the other party, in every case (with one exception, which can be explained), the judges agreed on which of the two parties should win, and with an approximately 4:1 majority. This outcome became even more puzzling, when we found that *the students and laymen tended to agree with the judges,* that is, they chose the same winning party. Apparently, in deciding these cases, where principles and rules of conduct were involved, it made no difference whether the judging person was a law-trained judge, a law student, or a layman with university training. In reflecting upon this outcome, one must keep in mind that the cases presented to the respondents all had to do with so-called 'open norms': the principles of good faith (contract), and duty of care (tort), which are also known as legal standards, a category a shade vaguer than the legal norms. Therefore, the decision asked for had much to do with what is thought to be fair and reasonable in the given case, with general principles of equity, norms of conduct, and the like.

II. Nine Theses on Legal Reasoning and the Role of Personal Values

The striking similarity we found in decision making by judges and laymen is a challenge to any student of the role of legal reasoning in the decision making process and its character. Thinking of a possible explanation of this phenomenon, several suggestions can be made. There seems to be, as a first impression, a certain form of intersubjectivity between persons judging legal cases. But then many questions are coming up, like: What basis is there for this intersubjectivity? Do people have the same value-system, for instance, when deciding these cases? Why has legal training so little to do with it all, and what role is played by legal reasoning anyhow?

Looking for a possible solution, I would like to present some theses:

1. General norms in private law, or as I would call them, *open norms,* are basically *norms of conduct,* that is to say, they can always be concretized into norms of conduct in a specific case. In disputes concerning rights (in the realm of property or of contracts) one finds a similar tendency to deal with rights as a problem of rules of conduct. In this sense the judge is not taking rights seriously.

2. A person asked to judge a situation and the legal controversy arising from it, in establishing the concrete norm(s) of conduct for the party or parties in question, is basing his judgment on his own value-system. This means that he is *taking his own personal norms of conduct as standard for the decision* ("What would I, as a reasonable man, do in this situation?").

3. The personal value-system of the judging person regarding rules of conduct is derived from two sources, which are being tapped in the dynamic process of decision making:

   a) *Person-originated values:* values provided by his subjective value-system, taken as part of an intersubjective system of his social group or society.

   b) *Situation-originated values:* values provided by the situation, the facts and circumstances of the case presented for judgment to him.

4. In the process of judging a legal controversy, of deciding legal questions, the process is essentially a two-way process, characterized by *dialectics:* in a confrontation of the person and the case, the concrete norms for decision stemming from the person judging, on the one hand, and from the case, on the other hand, are interrelated

and interdependent, influencing each other. (It thus is hard to say what comes first or what is dominating.) From this fusion the concrete norm(s) for the instant case is (are) born.

5. The finding of the concrete norm as a product of *Persona* and *Res* occurs in the confrontation of the judging person with the facts and arguments of the presented case, and can be seen by him in one flash, in an intuitive vision of the solution of the legal controversy. This insight can be characterized as a *Gestalt*. Thus, a basic similarity may be observed between the judging person and an artist, a scientist or a manager (or perhaps any person) looking for a solution of a complicated question. The Roman maxim, law as an 'ars aequi et boni', may hold a profound truth.

6. Intuition plays a central role in legal decision making, but is no antipode of reason. The separation of reason and intuition is an apriorism, arbitrary and unnecessary. Reason cannot do without intuition. (Compare the etymological relation between 'reason' and 'reasonable', the latter being the common description of normative rules of conduct.)

7. The solution found by the joint operation of reason and intuition, seen at the initial stage of the process as a *Gestalt,* does not have to be final. In addition to the flash-insight, further scrutiny is necessary, in a system of checks and balances. For the need for this procedure two reasons may be submitted:

   a) The average judging person is no philosopher-king or kadi, and usually is not accepted as such by society. He needs to give argumentations to support his decision, in order to live up to the expectations in regard to his role in the community. The character and extension of this legal argumentation depend on culture and traditions (compare the Continental style, e. g. Cour de Cassation, France, contra the Anglo-American style, e. g. the House of Lords, England).

   b) The decision has to fit into a system of law, considering the reasonable expectations in society regarding such a system. This will have an impact on the legal argumentation of the decision and on the checking of the (initial) solution as well. Policy reasons may influence the decision, e. g. security of the law, and bend it into a different direction.

8. The rational-intuitive reasoning involved in the legal judgment is not only operating in an (internal) value-based system, but simultaneously, in an (external) societal system.

Both systems are not strictly internal and external respectively, but are exposed to the contrasting sphere on the one hand, and, at the same time, influence each other in a dialectical process, on the other hand.

9. Thus, a legal judgment is the product of *Persona, Res and Societas.* The characteristic of a right judgment is that it shows an *intrinsic harmony* wherein all component parts are in balance. This is the common characteristic, as a matter of fact, of cognitive, ethical and aesthetic judgments. There may be a transcendental component involved too, being the source of this harmony.

III. Discussion of Some Theses

There is not much room left for discussing the above theses. I will concentrate, therefore, on three main issues: 1. the relation rationality-intuition, and as corollary, the *Is-Ought* dichotomy; 2. the situational values; 3. the flash or *Gestalt* part. With my brief remarks I will give some references which may be helpful in clarifying my views.

1. Rationality-Intuition. Is-Ought

Considering the famous debates in Jurisprudence (like Hart — Fuller of the late 1950s, and before that Frank — Salmond, Gray — Austin) or the prolific discussion of the philosophy of John Rawls of the last decade, one cannot but see one person at the centre of the stage: Kant. In essence, the Kantian division of Reason *(Vernunft)* and Understanding *(Verstand)* is at stake, concerning respectively, the intelligible and the empirical character of man. This well-known dichotomy is of crucial importance for the Kantian ethics and for law as well. Leaving aside the *jumelage* of both fields which is, to my opinion, only increasing in the last decades, we find in law the strongest Kantian influence in the well-known concept of the *Is-Ought* dichotomy. Looking for the underlying purpose of the use of this dichotomy, for instance in the work of Kelsen, one finds the need for the formulation of norms as objective standards of value, separated from subjective value-judgments. When explaining the distinction between positivism and natural law Kelsen states: in the first school of thought "[v]alue judgments are subjective and hence relative only, because they are not a description of facts, but, in the last analysis, the expression of wishes and fears" (*Kelsen* 1971, p. 174). Characteristic for a norm as an 'ought', is its being valuable for everybody and being determined by objectively verifiable facts (p. 229 seq.). As a consequence, "[j]udgments of justice cannot be tested objectively. Therefore a science of law has no room for them."

The remark once made by Fuller on Kelsen, seems appropriate: "His whole system might well rest on an emotional preference for the ideal of order over that of justice." Here we meet the core of positivism and Kantianism: an emotional and arbitrary preference for a certain form of rationality. At this stage I would like to refer to the citation of Santayana at the heading of this paper, on the relative character of rationality ('reason' is, by the way, rooted in 'relations'). The part which follows is even more interesting for our purpose:

> "The ideal of rationality is itself as arbitrary, as much dependent on the needs of a finite organization, as any other ideal. Only as ultimately securing tranquillity of mind, which the philosopher instinctively pursues, has it for him any necessity. In spite of the verbal propriety of saying that reason demands rationality, what really demands rationality, what makes it a good and indispensable thing and gives it its authority, is not its own nature, but our need of it both in safe and economical action and in the pleasure of comprehension" (o. c.).

There is no room in my paper to elaborate this theme,[2] and therefore I shall present only some concluding remarks. As far as the standpoint developed in my paper is concerned, my analysis of the needs for 'safe and economical action' in law, and the 'pleasure of comprehension' of the law-making process, makes some post-Kantian philosophers far more attractive than Kant. One may think of Schopenhauer, who, inverting the Kantian system, puts Understanding (discovered in intuition) on the first place, at the cost of Reason (for Schopenhauer, 'all intuition is intellectual'). (Compare *Whittaker* 1934/1977, p. 90.) Even more important is Hegel's contribution in this field, solving the subject-object split with a concept of dialectics in which the personality of the reasoning person has a central place. To my judgment the dialectic model for legal reasoning is best suited to our needs. We cannot here go further into this topic either (compare e. g. *Kubeš* 1980 a, p. 57, 1980 b, p. 201, discussing the view of Alfred Verdross).

It will be understood that in my opinion the traditional *Is-Ought* dichotomy is best criticized by authors using a dialectical method, albeit implicitly. (Compare *Fuller* 1940/1978, 1969, p. 145; *Brecht* 1954, p. 102, 1976, p. 320; *Jaffe* 1960, p. 30; *d'Amato* 1978, p. 513; *Van Dunné* 1984.)

Reason is a fascinating subject for lawyers. What should one think of Whittaker's view: reason divided into two categories, intuitive and discursive reasoning, restituting Kant's Reason and Understanding, respectively? The first category is seen as the total grasp, the 'synoptic' view of things; the second category as the procedure from point to point.

---

[2] Illustrative for the choice for rationality by authors of the school of Hart, is *MacCormick* (1978), p. 269 (also pp. 5, 239, 288, 292). By this choice he seeks to transcend Hume's dilemma of Reason and Passions.

The former is higher, but unavailable till it has been mediated by the latter (*o. c.*, p. 29). The 'practical reason' of the 'harmonious personality', developed by Hobhouse, is even more exciting. This process of 'mediation' is described as follows:

> "The problem of the practical reason is to develop the elements of a working consistency, mutual support, or, as I call it, Harmony, within the entire sphere of impulsive feeling, and the 'force' of the rational is the summed energy of the felt needs acting as an organized whole. Rational aims focus the felt wants of man so far as they are consistent. Reason operates on the primary impulses by purging them of mutual inconsistency and shaping them into contributory elements in a system of life by which in turn they are in their modified form sustained and furthered" (*Perry* 1926, p. 664).

The words of William James come to mind: "Consciousness is at all times primarily a selective agency." On the other hand, there is the reminiscence of Plato's philosopher-king whose knowledge of justice is derived from the balance and harmony of his personality. We will return to the aspect of harmony later (sub Section 3).

Insight in the character and functioning of reason and rationality may lead to a re-evaluation of the so-called 'intuitive law theories' or 'feeling-of-justice theories'. Special attention is deserved by the followers of Bergson ('creative intuition'), like Gény, Del Vecchio, Cardozo, and further the adherents of the *Wertphilosophie* of Scheler and Hartmann (*a priori* consciousness of values, structured in a hierarchy).

2. Situational Values

In the theses 3 and 4 I referred to values inherent in the facts and circumstances of the case presented for judgment, discovered in an intuitive way by the judging person. When looking for a backing in jurisprudence, the *Natur der Sache* ('nature of the thing') school, revived in post-war Germany, seems a natural ally. In this school, an offspring of the phenomenological value philosophy and a good neighbour of the natural law philosophy, the contribution of Maihofer is interesting for our topic. In his view the *Natur der Sache* serves as an extra standard bringing the abstract rules of law in accord with the norms of conduct prescribed by the social situation of a concrete legal condition ('concrete law of nature'). An illustration is found in general norms such as 'good faith' and 'reasonableness'. This view is helpful in our search for an explanation of the concurrence of lay and judicial judgments; as will be remembered, the cases presented for judgment dealt with open norms like 'good faith'. In this context, reference can also be made to Llewellyn's 'situation sense', a concept borrowed from the 19th century European *Natur der Sache*-adherents. It is interesting to note that a line of thought comparable to this has been developed in *Gestalt* theory in the Thirties: values are taken as a product of objective 'requiredness' in a definite situation or field (*Gestalt* = configuration). This is seen as a required response to a 'lacuna' in such fields, as a release of forces directed towards the 'right' filling of that lacuna, thus 'closing' the configuration, or perfecting the equilibrium (Wertheimer, Köhler, Koffka; see *Perry* 1926, p. 190; *Brecht* 1954, p. 110, 1976, p. 332).

The instrumentalist approach should also be mentioned, that is to say, the followers of Dewey. In their view it is the situation which supplies an implicit normative premise: that ought to be done which meets the requirements of the problem (*Jaffe* 1960, p. 30, and, in general, *Summers* 1981, p. 880). In this 'psychology of contextualism', that what solves the problem is also 'right' for the situation. In this way, the *Is-Ought* split is overcome. The ultimate end is the norm of self-development, the development of the individual as problem-solver (*Jaffe*, p. 102 seq.). Finally, support can also be found in hermeneutic theory. The hermeneutic re-definition of *Verstehen* by Gadamer, made accessible to jurists by Esser, presents an attractive view of the role of situational factors. The 'hermeneutic circle' stands for the balance, or the dialectic, between the prejudices we hold in approaching a case, and, on the other side, an openness for the object, allowing it to speak for itself (*Esser* 1970, p. 134; *Wolff* 1975, p. 104).

3. Flash or Gestalt

We have now several times come across the concept of *Gestalt* (configuration or wholeness). It is also used in the work of Gadamer; talking of aesthetic experience, he argues that any experience is united, by its intentional content, in an "unmediated relationship with the totality of life"; it is "the representation of the whole in a moment" (*Wolff* 1975, p. 127).

The concepts of 'the hunch', or 'the intuitive jump', and the like, used in jurisprudence in the description of judicial decision making, can be explained, to my judgment, as the appearance of a *Gestalt:* a lightning moment of insight in the legal question, in a flash of higher consciousness (comparable with the similar experience of composers, poets, scientists).

For a related view, the reader should consult Bihler's study on the feeling of justice, where reference is made to the work of Eberhard, a theory of value judgments based on developmental psychology. From early childhood on, objects obtain a certain 'Wertton' (value-tone); thus a sub-conscious value-structure is formed in the form of *Gestalts.* A paradigm for *Gestalt* here is the melody, which is more than the total of the notes involved (*Bihler* 1979, pp. 59, 121, 142).

Returning to the moment of illuminating insight, it has some relation to the discussion on truth as an immediately evident judgment (*Brentano* 1973, p. 129). Compare Leibniz' statement that certain truths establish themselves as valid "dans une manière lumineuse".

Many authors stress the relation between wholeness and harmony or balance. Essentially, this is a Stoic tradition: a thing of value must be in harmony with nature (Cicero). An example is Bosanquet's definition of the principle of value, as the 'character of wholeness and non-contradiction' (*Perry* 1926, p. 46; cf. also pp. 96, 120, on Bradley, McIntyre, and Meinong). The role of harmony in the view of Hobhouse has already been mentioned (*supra*, Section 1).

In conclusion, I would like to emphasize that it might be valuable for the science of law to reconsider the relation between the True, the Good and the Beautiful.

Bibliography

d'Amato, A. (1978), The Limits of Legal Realism, Yale L. J. 87, pp. 468—513.

Bihler, M. (1979), Rechtsgefühl, System und Wertung, Ein Beitrag zur Psychologie der Rechtsgewinnung, C.H. Beck'sche Verlagsbuchhandlung, München.

Brecht, Arnold (1954), The Myth of Is and Ought, in: The Political Philosophy of Arnold Brecht, N. Y. (orig. Harv. L. R. 54 [1941], pp. 811—831).

— (1976), Politische Theorie, Mohr, Tübingen (orig. 1959, Princeton Univ. Press).

Brentano, Franz (1973), The Foundation and Construction of Ethics, Routledge and Kegan Paul, London (orig. 1952, Bern).

Van Dunné, Jan M. (1984 a), Personality Influences on Judicial Decision Making in The Netherlands, part 1: The Personality of the Judge. Some Jurisprudential Remarks (orig. paper presented at the meeting of the Research Committee for Compar. Jud. Studies, IPSA, Oxford 1981), in: De dialektiek van rechtsvinding en rechtsvorming. Opstellen over rechtsvinding (Essays on the Dialectics of the Law-Making Process in Private Law), Arnhem, p. 172 (in English).

— (1984 b), The Personality of the Judge and Legal Decision Making in Private Law (orig. paper presented at the Annual Meeting of the Law and Society Association, Toronto, Canada, June 3—6, 1982), in: De dialektiek van rechtsvinding, op. cit., p. 181 (in English).

Esser, Josef (1970), Vorverständnis und Methodenwahl in der Rechtsfindung, Athenäum, Frankfurt/M.

Ewing, A. C. (1951), The Fundamental Questions of Philosophy, Routledge and Kegan Paul, London.

Fuller, Lon F. (1940), The Law in Quest of Itself, Chicago (also 1978).

— (1969), The Morality of the Law, rev. ed., Yale Univ. Press, New Haven, Connecticut.

Jaffe, Raymond (1960), The Pragmatic Conception of Justice, Univ. Cal. Press, Berkeley.

Kelsen, Hans (1971), What is Justice? Univ. Cal. Press, Berkeley.

Kubeš, Vladimir (1980 a), Das moderne Naturrecht und der Versuch um die rationale Bewältigung der rechtsvolitiven Sphäre, in: Juristische Blätter, 102 (1980).

— (1980 b), Freiheit des Willens, Sollen und Sein im Rechtlichen, in: RECHTSTHEORIE 11 (1980).

MacCormick, Neil (1978), Legal Reasoning and Legal Theory, Clarendon Press, Oxford.

Perry, R. B. (1926), General Theory of Value. Its Meaning and Basic Principles Construed in Terms of Interest, Longmans, Green Co., N. Y.

Santayana, George (1955), The Sense of Beauty. Being the Outline of Aesthetic Theory, Dover, N. Y. (1896).

Summers, Robert S. (1981), Pragmatic Instrumentalism in Twentieth Century American Legal Thought — A Synthesis and Critique of Our Dominant General Theory About Law and Its Use, Cornell L. R. 66, pp. 862—948.

Whittaker, Thomas (1977), Reason. A Philosophical Essay with Historical Illustrations, Greenwood Press, Westport, Conn. (orig. 1934, Cambridge Univ. Press).

Wolff, Janet (1975), Hermeneutic Philosophy and the Sociology of Art, Routledge and Kegan Paul, London.

EXPERIENCE AND LEGAL REASONING

By Elizabeth Flower, Philadelphia

Anyone interested in scientific method cannot but be impressed by the contrast between the treatment of evidence in the philosophy of science and the efforts to frame a model code or uniform rules of evidence or a case book on evidence in the law. The contrast generally entails a distance from scientific method. This and even the non-cognitive character of legal "reasoning" have been argued by appeal to such grounds as: that legal objectives in a trial seem only tangentially related to the discovery of the truth, hemmed in as they are by conventions about the burden of proof, constraints on admissibility, the enlistment of expert witnesses, and the general qualifications on probative value; the isolation of the legal vocabulary from ordinary language and its non-reducibility; the need for a decision in a sense that leads to the nonprobabilistic performative and prescriptive and signifies the practical character of judgment; jurisdictional relativity and its nesting in variant social custom; and a conserving weight on precedent that almost rules out self-conscious novelty. Doubtless this contrast was fed by the failures of inductive and deductive models for legal reasoning even in the nineteenth century, although it is not at all clear that the available resources for such models were adequately exploited. Additionally, the distinction between the normative and the descriptive, between fact and value as well as between the psychological and the logical, beguiled all fields from social and political theory to moral philosophy. While all such arguments are certainly of unequal persuasiveness, their collective weight is sufficient to put the topic 'Experience and Evidence in Legal Reasoning' on the philosophical agenda.

There is, however, an alternate view that more intimately ties the methods of science and law; by looking at knowledge in the broader context of human enterprises it widens the domain of relevance and hence of evidence. By employing a learning model that connects knowledge with action it opens the door to change and the criticism of funded knowledge, and the openness leads to canons of criticism and corrigibility. And the funded knowledge can embrace both technical advances and the growth of common experience.

We can trace the growth of such a view in the United States to the turn of the century, particularly in a group meeting in Cambridge, Mass., the Metaphysical Club, which included among its members the philosophers Peirce and James, and the lawyers Nicholas St. John Green, Joseph Warner, and Oliver Wendell Holmes, Jr. From the first there was an interplay of ideas from science and law, that was mutually instructive. There developed a philosophic perspective generally called *pragmatism*. Less a school than an outlook, it is far from both the "Yankee philosophy of the dollar" as Russell characterized it or the Nixonian etc. equation with mere expediency. In the law, its influence is clear not only in the explicit pragmatism of Holmes, but also in the social concerns of Brandeis and Cardozo, in the sociological jurisprudence of Pound, and even in the legal realism of Llewellyn and others. In the philosophy of science, its influence was somewhat eclipsed by the entry of logical positivism into American philosophy with its strong isolation of science from value and policy disciplines, although it has been a persistent force expecially in those epistemologists and philosophers of science who are concerned with decision (e. g., C. I. Lewis, Nelson Goodman, C. West Churchman).

The central features of pragmatism that enabled them to bring knowledge and action together were briefly these. Knowledge is functional; ideas are plans of action; a belief then is a rule of action which is not merely conservative and in some way funding the past, but is forward looking in the use of such wisdom facing the future (James's rowing a boat forward while looking backward or Llewellyn's precedent as Janus-faced). Doubtless the most decisive starting-point is Peirce's operational definition, which was directed more toward physical laws but which was quickly broadened to handle concepts in general, especially by James. It is clearly James's influence which more closely relates to method in the law. His use of a learning model assumes first that knowledge has a function; consciousness itself functions to make us at home in an alien world by categorizing or organizing knowledge in terms of likeness classes or "samenesses". Unlike Kant, whose categories are rigid, for James these categories or likenesses are open to change in the light of continuing experience. Unlike the associationists, for whom experience is merely aggregated, James has an organized funding in which we try to incorporate the novel into the familiar, but always with some stretching of the concept (the organized precedent). When the fit is too difficult we often break the bounds and forge new concepts to address the novel, but which at the same time reorganize our past constructions. Thus a criterion of adequacy comes to regulate change.

The intellectual connection between the philosophic pragmatists and developments in legal philosophy is incontestable. There were personal contacts and friendships, acknowledgments, reviews of one another's books, and participation in joint seminars. Doubtless the influence was reciprocal, but the influence on the philosophers is not our present concern. Doubtless too, they shared a general social outlook inasmuch as both were confronting similar problems. They saw Social Darwinism and laisser-faire economics as both enshrined in the law and blocking social experimentation, and they generally shared a melioristic attitude toward the growth of democracy; all this gives the picture of an attitudinal, if not a substantive, liberalism in the tradition of J. S. Mill and as radical as the Philosophical Radicals. Finally, they came to recognize the importance of the social sciences from psychology to sociology and economics as critical features which need to be taken into account in at least three ways in judicial decision. They help us understand what in fact influences decision (the prejudices of the judge, the changing social context of a problem, the prevailing theories). These provide the necessary knowledge and information at any given time for what the consequences of the decision will be, and so provide warrant for the decision itself (as in the role of the "Brandeis brief" or the appeal to psychiatric evidence in criminal cases). And they affect the general method of the law (as in the supplementing of deductive with inductive methods, and currently stimulating a more sophisticated use of models and paradigms, with a conception of rationality that is geared to problem-solving). And there is a marked exploration, though with varying outcomes, of the place of morality in law.

The characteristics that the pragmatic philosophers assigned to knowledge are readily discerned in the judgments of their legal brethren. Holmes is the central figure, but well supported by St. John Green and John Chipman Gray. The suspicion (perhaps earliest voiced by Green) that *stare decisis* with its reliance on past experience does not provide ready-made formulae or axioms for the new case grew into an appreciation of the complexities of alternative interpretations and the novel features that a new case always offers. Gray is explicit that law is an open-textured system, with change as well as continuity; and his analysis of fictions shows that change is in concepts also, not merely rules. Judges through their decisions make law, for decision always covers a class of cases, and a particular case can strain as well as reinforce the classification. These concerns are the setting for Holmes' more popular and quotable sentence, "The life of the law has not been logic; it has been experience." This was not an anti-intellectual thrust, for the sentence before suggests that logic is only *one* tool. Emphasis should rather fall on the *life* of the law, and by experience he meant the cumulative experience of a tradition and the need for experimentation. "The law embodies the story of a nation's development ... it cannot be dealt with as if it contained only the axioms and corollaries of a book of mathematics." Among its determinants are "the felt necessities of the time, the prevalent moral and political theories, intuitions of public policy, avowed or unconscious, even the prejudices which judges share with their fellow-men."[1] By prejudice, Holmes intends not merely the pejorative sense but an acknowledgment that custom, beliefs, and values are woven into the fabric of the law; it is not quarantined from ordinary experience, nor from the changes that take place in that experience, for the beliefs which are the incontrovertible truths of one age may be challenged in the next.

While many of the Peircean and Jamesian themes appear in Holmes' work, he is not simply translating them into a legal context. On the contrary, his view of the judicial process, his use of functional definition, and his prospective approach enlarge the pragmatic insights in an institutional setting — all of which qualifies him as one of pragmatism's architects.

Precedent is not *the* law, it is not an implacable constraint, but a funding of legal experience that provides a resource for facing the problems at hand. Holmes gives an experimental cast to the law that goes beyond the merely predictive. The latter is manifest in his view that the law at a given time is that for which there is a remedy or the prophesy of what the courts will do. The experimental means that a decision must take into account the probable social consequences, convenience and efficiency as well as the economic. Legal objectives are social utilities; consequences are not merely the inevitable or foreseeable ones, but those that we can learn through experimentation that can be avoided or realized. Thus experimentation functions as a rational way of adapting our ideas to an unknown but not unknowable environment and transforming it to serve perceived needs and interests. This adds to prediction of consequences their evaluation in the light of social ideals used as standards. As we come to a better understanding of the content of those standards they enter integrally into the processes of verification and justification.

But social interests and needs change (and in fact are changed by changes in the law). The "same" social formula has a different meaning as the context changes. The Constitution of 1789 is not the same as that of the 1860s, and it is altered with each industrial, technical, and social revolution. The problem is whether such change can be channeled. Thus we need to rely on the best understanding of needs and circumstances, the most effective predicting and evaluating of consequences that science

[1] *O. W. Holmes*, The Common Law, Boston 1881, chapter 1.

can provide. Holmes has given a new breadth to legal relevance and legal evidence.

The impetus provided by Holmes seems to have flowed through two rather different channels. His most influential impact on social practice lay through the Supreme Court, which as the final umpire defines the framework of American living and by its decisions modifies precedent. Brandeis joined him on the Court in 1916 and Cardozo succeeded him on the Court in 1932. While only the latter could properly be regarded as a card-carrying pragmatist, Brandeis, despite disclaimers of being either a pragmatist or a social reformer, agreed so often with Holmes on critical matters that for our purposes he is at least a fellow-traveller. He agreed above all that the Common Law does not contain within it the principles adequate to meet the challenges of the conflicts and inequities that radical changes and social conditions had produced (pace Langdell). He emphasized as well the need to understand the actual situation that gives rise to the strains and inequities, and thus he insisted on the relevance of economics and sociology, but he explored further the specific influences of social life — from health conditions, life insurance, public utilities, to labor-management relations. In his effort to correct particular problems, he was led to a newly sophisticated analysis of the structures which often made the legal system itself a partner to particular interests. He saw legal institutions thoroughly integrated into the life of the community. Thus the courts have responsibility to allow and to guide the forces of social experimentation that makes evolution, not revolution, possible. In particular here he also is opposing the Social Darwinist efforts to uphold the legal barriers which restricted the government's power to regulate the economy. Thus he writes:

> There must be power in the States and the Nation to remold, through experimentation, our economic practices and institutions to meet changing social and economic needs ... This Court has the power to prevent an experiment ... as arbitrary ... but we must be ever on our guard lest we erect our prejudices into legal principles.[2]

> ... legal science — the unwritten or judge-made laws as distinguished from legislation — is largely deaf and blind [to revolutionary economic and social change]. Courts apply complacently eighteenth century concepts of the liberty of the individual and the sacredness of private property. Early nineteenth century scientific half-truths, like "The Survival of the Fittest", which in practice mean "The devil take the hindmost", are erected by judicial sanction into a moral law.[3]

Cardozo is attentive to both continuity and change. Looking to the psychological factors in decision-making, Cardozo in Jamesian fashion

---

[2] *L. Brandeis*, New State Ice Co. v. Liebmann, 285 U.S. 262, 1932, p. 311.

[3] *L. Brandeis*, Business, A Profession, Boston 1925, p. 349.

looks to the process of 'matching colors'; that is, often enough an almost mechanical application of precedent will yield the *ratio decidendi.* But even then there are options with respect to the relevant likenesses: as in MacPherson v. Buick, "precedents drawn from the days of travel by stagecoach do not fit the conditions of travel today. The principle that danger must be imminent does not change, but the things subject to the principle do change. They are whatever the needs of a life in a developing civilization require them to be."[4]

When constitutional precedents are not clear, or when there are gaps, ambiguities and conflicts, and above all when changes in conditions change some aspects of the case, then creative measures are needed, or resourceful adapting of old ones. In those cases, the judge may turn to guides or resources in analogy, in historical development, or he may search the lines of the customs of the community, or he may turn to the larger question of justice, morals, and social welfare. The final cause of the law is social utility, the welfare of society, and the law must serve human needs. Hence statutes are not isolated pronouncements of abstract principles for an ideal community, but always have the setting of present-day conditions to which the insights of economists, social scientists, etc. are relevant. "It is too late today for the argument to be heard with tolerance that in a crisis so extreme the uses of the moneys of the nation to relieve the unemployed and their dependents is a use for any purpose narrower than the promotion of the general welfare."[5]

The influence of pragmatism in philosophy and law was modified in a second generation, especially as it was channelled through academia. But Harvard, especially in the developing epistemology and formal logic, followed a non-social path. It remained for Dewey in philosophy and Pound in legal theory to turn to the social and the social sciences, not only for evidence to diagnose and respond to present conflicts, but to understand how institutional growth and social change generate the problems. Doubtless both were responding to developments in European social thought, but even more immediately to the burgeoning of the social sciences at Chicago, where Pound had participated in a seminar of Dewey's.

For Pound it is not enough to acknowledge that particular social needs should be invoked in legal decisions. For behind these lies a background of the requirements for a civilized society as well as the multiplicity of interests to be served — individual, public (governmental), and social (the claims and values of society). Law-making involves the balancing

---

[4] *B. Cardozo,* MacPherson v. Buick Motor Co., 217 N.Y. 382.

[5] *B. Cardozo,* Steward Machine Co. v. Davis, 301 U.S. 548, 1937, p. 587.

of interests and the reconciling of claims; and because such processes and techniques are instrumental and functional, law is a kind of social engineering, one among many institutions exerting social control.[6]

Such control has its own history, and by examining the development and social history of the law we can mark out the different stages in the dominant ends and thus map the cumulative objectives. Thus, for example, in the seventeenth and eighteenth century law was perceived in terms of equity and a morality of natural law; while the twentieth century is bringing social rather than individual interests to the fore, and so the predominance of social over individual and governmental interests. It is not a matter of ends to be attained so much as ends already funded into rules and institutions. And so we find postulates, not as an axiom set for deduction, but rather as empirical generalizations of fundamental expectations and values gained by reflection on the law. They serve normatively to help evaluate how effective the law can be and what is dead and what is viable at a given time.

It is obvious that a theory of the breadth of Pound's has as a counterpart (or consequence) a broadened theory of what is relevant to, hence what constitutes evidence for, legal judgment or decision. Only in such light can we discern the judicial logic that derives constantly new forms of property rights (whether intricate corporate rights or new welfare rights) from old principles, or new safeguards (against economic as well as physical coercion) from older formulae of liberty, new concepts (whether of privacy or of "external costs") that bring in their train revolutionary treatments in matters of sex and abortion or in the control of pollution, and so on. The narrow view of the law and its functions could see changes only as causes that led logic astray or as explicit legislation that alone could justify new premises in an unchanging logic. The broader view of law and logic can accomodate within its criteria and its processes the growth of the law.

Dewey and Pound share much of this approach to social change, to the importance of the social sciences, and to the importance of the normative. But from Dewey's point of view Pound was faint-hearted insofar as he worried whether the system could bear the tax of the emerging socialization, a worry clearly related to the perpetuation of the interests already established rather than to the creative role that law can play in institutional reconstruction in the face of emerging needs and interests.

Dewey's approach both to intellectual method and to law is essentially prospective. In contrast, say to C. I. Lewis, who tended to think of

[6] *R. Pound,* Interpretations of Legal History, Cambridge, Mass. 1946.

knowledge as a systematic structure tested on its periphery until the strains of experience and testing force a revision, Dewey envisages the whole of our funded wisdom marshalled at the point of the problematic situation with all its conflicts and indeterminacy.[7] This formulation of problems may be cast in individual or in institutional terms. The recognition that there is a problem can begin in uncertainties, in perceived conflicts of interest affected by the consequences of people's action, queries about the social utility of custom, or a crisis arising from social and technological change. But the diagnosis of the problem includes the funded lessons of experience and tradition, the values which are embedded in institutions and a sense of the tasks and functions they perform, an exploration of alternatives in prospective action together with the resources to be found in the social and natural environment. Reflection is turned toward innovative proposals and possible changes, thus not simply compromising existing interests but reorienting needs and modes of action. Decisions made in such a way are a kind of experiment whose adequacy is to be tested by consequences and subsequent experience.

In such a broadly pragmatic approach, objectives have entered integrally into the evidential and warranting process. What is relevant, what is to count as evidence, is seriously constrained by the increasingly explicit understanding of functions, goals, values, objectives, and their interrelations.

The fact that the objectives of logic and of science are generally implicit or tacitly accepted while those of law and ethics are agonizingly debated often leads us to exaggerate in the first and overlook in the second what is an essentially shared cognitive task.

---

[7] *J. Dewey,* The Quest for Certainty, New York 1960, chapters 5 and 6.

ARBITRARINESS, LEGALITY, AND DISCRETIONARY POWERS

By Denis J. Galligan, Southampton

I.

A common theme in modern legal writing is that the nature of legal authority in contemporary western societies has shifted in various noticeable and important ways from a system based around something approximating Max Weber's ideal type of formal rational authority to one more closely resembling his notion of substantive rational authority.[1] These ideal types of authority should briefly be explained. Weber noticed a distinct tendency in the development of modern societies away from traditional and charismatic modes of authority towards the rational use of power. Rational authority, however, may be formal or substantive. It is formal when decisions are made by officials applying given abstract rules according to logical analysis of their meaning. It is substantive when decisions are made in order to achieve specified goals or values in a manner relatively unmediated by precise rules of general application. Rules may of course be directed towards achieving particular ends and goals, but Weber's point is that as decision-making comes to depend on the application of rules, those rules tend to become ends in themselves with consequential diminution in concern for underlying purposes. Substantive rationality on the other hand suggests a relatively direct correlation between the goals and purposes to be achieved, and specific decisions.[2] In his later work Weber moved away from earlier suggestions that those modes of authority could be related to distinct historical trends, and came to consider them more as ideal types of authority which could be identified as having greater or lesser prominence in any context of decision-making.[3]

However various contemporary jurists have noticed a dominant trend in modern societies towards substantive rationality. It is often suggested

---

[1] See *Max Weber*, Economy and Society (Eds. G. Roth and C. Wittich), Vol. 1, Part 1 Ch. III, and Vol. 2, Part 2 Ch. VIII, New York 1968.

[2] For discussion of Weber's models of authority, see: *R. Bendix*, Max Weber: An Intellectual Portrait, Methuen 1966, Ch. XII and XIII; *Alan Hunt*, The Sociological Movement in Law, Macmillan 1978; *D. Trubek*, Max Weber on Law and the Rise of Capitalism, in: Wisconsin L.R. 3 (1972), 720.

[3] See: *W. Mommsen*, The Age of Bureaucracy, Blackwell 1974, Ch. IV.

that one important source of evidence for this tendency is the increasing delegation of discretionary powers to government authorities for the achievement of broadly specified goals and purposes, guided by only the most abstract and open standards. Now of course what may look like wide discretion from one point of view may be tightly rule-governed from another point of view, and indeed on Weber's own account there are considerable institutional pressures within administrative organisations towards formal rationality.[4] Nevertheless it may be both the intention and the practice within areas of discretionary power that decision-making should not centre around the articulation and application of precise rules, but rather should maintain an openness more akin to substantive rationality. One question of considerable interest that arises is what part the notion of legality, or the rule of law, has to play within such contexts. This matter might be approached from various points of view, but in this paper I am concerned with only one specific aspect of legality, and that is the notion of arbitrariness.

There is a long and vocal tradition of criticism of discretionary powers on the grounds that they inherently are tainted with arbitrariness. Many have echoed Dicey's famous contrast between a system of authority where the powers of officials are governed by general legal rules, and one in which powers are "wide, arbitrary or discretionary."[5] It is arguable that Dicey did not mean that discretion is a synonym for arbitrariness, but he certainly suggested that where there is discretion there is a high risk of arbitrariness. My purpose is to consider various aspects of this concept and to see how it bears upon the exercise of discretionary powers.

II.

In its clearest sense arbitrariness relates to the reasoning process whereby decisions are made and is a way of criticising particular kinds of defects or omissions in that process. Arbitrariness in this sense is the antithesis of rationality. An action is rational if it is believed by the actor to be a means to a predetermined end; an action is arbitrary if the actor does not have such a belief. It seems, however, that in order to give the notion of rational action a sharper analytical sense, a certain objective element may be required, so that not only must the action be a means to the required end, but also it must be a reasonably economical and efficient means to that end. In order to act rationally in this

---

[4] *Weber* (note 1), Ch. XI.

[5] *A. V. Dicey*, The Law of the Constitution, Macmillan 1961, p. 188. An even stronger association between discretion and arbitrariness can be seen in *Lord Hewart*, The New Despotism, 1929, Ch. IV.

narrower sense the decision-maker must consider possible alternative courses of action to that end, and then choose between them.[6] It is clear then that actions are more or less rational, depending on how closely they achieve an optimum realisation of purpose. Correspondingly, arbitrariness as a negative function of rational action is also a matter of degree.

These general observations may be translated into the context of officials exercising public power. Rational decision-making in this context requires (a) that decisions be based on reasons, and (b) that those reasons be intelligibly and objectively related to the purposes of the power.[7] According to the first of these conditions a decision will be arbitrary if it is made without reasons; it will also be arbitrary if made without reasons even where the same decision could have been reached according to good reasons. The second condition implys that not all reasons are good reasons and provides the basis for distinguishing the good from the bad. The general criterion is relevance to purpose and this eliminates reasons based on whim, caprice, ritual, or by tossing a coin. It also eliminates reasons directed towards the private ends of the decision-maker. Whether any reasons are good reasons can be tested against the general requirement that they be relevant to the purpose for which powers have been granted.

These requirements do not remove the official's discretion but they do impose some restrictions by insisting that the official exercise his discretion according to reasons of a certain kind. Nor do they mean that there is only one set of satisfactory reasons in respect of any decision; it is often implicit in a grant of power that there are various options open in achieving the purposes of the power, and that it is for the power-holder to settle both the substantive policies to be followed and the strategies for doing so. His decisions will escape the charge of arbitrariness if those choices can be seen to be related in a reasonably objective way to the purpose of his powers.

While an action which satisfies those requirements of rationality may escape any charge of arbitrariness, the position becomes more complicated when an official is required to pursue a course of decision-making. Here the principle of consistency must be considered. Consistency embodies the idea that the reasons for one decision be uni-

[6] For further discussion, see: *J. Ladd,* The Place of Practical Reason in Judicial Decisions, in: C. J. Friedrich (Ed.), Rational Decision, Nomos VII, Atherton 1964, p. 126.

[7] For discussion, see: *J. L. Jowell,* The Legal Control of Administrative Discretion, in: Public Law, 1973, pp. 186—192; *Joseph Raz,* The Authority of Law, Oxford 1979, pp. 219—220; *P. Selznick,* Law, Society and Industrial Justice, Sage 1969, pp. 12—16.

versalised at some level of abstraction and applied generally to situations that come within their terms.[8] When a parole board, for example, releases one prisoner on licence because he is no longer a threat to the community, the implication is that that is a good reason for releasing any prisoner, assuming the absence of conflicting considerations. Stronger versions of the consistency principle claim that the parole board is bound in future cases by its past rulings.[9] Now while it would normally be expected that past rulings will be applied to future cases, the reasons for doing so are not the fact of having made that ruling in the past, but that the reasons for the ruling are considered still to be good. It is not arbitrary to change one's mind because the past ruling was mistaken or no longer holds good, and accordingly to decide future cases differently. There may of course be other kinds of reasons for continuing to apply past rulings quite apart from their merits; these may relate to the notions of fairness that often are linked to expectations, or they may be reasons of a very practical kind, such as those that occur in institutional decision-making.

Moreover, it is often the case in discretionary decisions that the reasons for one decision are of little guidance in other decisions, since the circumstances may vary so greatly. Indeed it might be argued that any attempt to forge links between decisions and to generate general standards in the interests of consistency would be to prevent the decision being reached which best serves the purposes of the power. An excessive striving for consistency may itself create arbitrariness in the sense that the specific case is not given adequate consideration in the light of specified goals.

In order to avoid arbitrariness, therefore, a difficult course must be taken between extreme individualisation on the one hand, and over universalisation on the other hand. With regard to the first, a commitment to principles of rational decision-making requires links to be sought between one decision and another, so that each decision can be seen not just as the solution to a particular problem but also as involving a set of reasons with some general application. In this way general standards of decision-making develop, if not by express formulation, but at least by incremental accumulation.[10] With regard to the second, that same commitment requires that general standards do not become precise and detailed rules to be applied in a formal and literal manner. There

---

[8] On the principle of consistency, see: *Neil MacCormick,* Legal Reasoning and Legal Theory, Oxford 1978, pp. 72—86, 106, 179, 266, 270—271.

[9] Ibid.

[10] For discussion of the idea of incremental accumulation, see: *R. Cyert* and *J. March,* A Behavioural Theory of the Firm, 1963, and *D. Braybrooke* and *C. Lindblom,* A Strategy of Decision, 1963.

must be space within the framework of standards for account to be taken of the diversity and complexity of the situations that arise for decision. In other words, rationality requires that a constant interaction and equilibrium be maintained between the general framework of standards and the particular case. Rationality reaches its optimum as decision-making approaches that point of equilibrium, and correspondingly the degree of arbitrariness diminishes.

All rational decision-making is concerned with a balance between settled general standards and achieving the best result in the particular case. The primary object of discretionary decision-making is to achieve the purpose for which power has been conferred; but that itself requires some refinement and generalisation as to what the purpose is and how it is to be achieved. This very process of stipulation tends to limit the purpose by giving it a more precise meaning. If one adds to that the imperfections of decision-makers and the world they inhabit — their limited training and expertise, and lack of time and facilities, and the scarcity of resources — then one can see further reasons for the balance tilting towards settled ways of doing things. Here we have a good illustration of Herbert Simon's bounded rationality;[11] in an imperfect world there can be no perfect realisation of purpose. But one can aim at a form of rationality which seeks to accommodate in the best way the inevitable limitations and imperfections. Thus the balance between settled patterns and individualisation will shift and change along an infinitely variable line, guided by purpose, and by the closely related and double-edged notion of arbitrariness.

III.

To return now to Weber's distinction between formal and substantive rationality, it is clear that even if the perceived trend of authority towards substantive rationality is well-founded there is no cause for associating this with any inherent arbitrariness. The progress of western societies towards rational authority may be seen as part of a cultural tendency to overcome the sense of arbitrariness associated with premodern political organisations, that is, the arbitrariness associated with personal patronage in the disposal and exercise of official positions. But while formal rational authority may overcome arbitrariness in that sense, it contains within itself another sense of arbitrariness to which reference has already been made, that is, the arbitrariness that accompanys the exercise of authority according to fixed and abstract rules without adequate concern for congruence between the particular case

[11] See *Herbert Simon*, Administrative Behaviour, Free Press 1945.

and the justifying purpose. A tendency towards the ideal type of substantive rationality may be seen as a response to the limitations of formal rationality and an attempt to achieve that congruence. The argument here is that in so far as the prevalence of discretionary powers are part of that tendency, they can be seen as a cultural advance towards a heightened sense of rationality. And provided that the reasons for any decision can be seen to serve and advance the purposes of power in an intelligible and reasonable manner, and provided that the principle of consistency is applied conscientiously and in a reasonable way, then whatever criticism may justly be made about discretionary powers, arbitrariness is not one of them. If the increased dependence upon discretionary powers is taken as evidence of a tendency towards substantive rationality, then there can be no natural association between the latter and arbitrariness.

However, not only Dicey, but various other writers, of whom F. A. Hayek has been perhaps the most influential,[12] have perceived a natural link between discretionary powers and arbitrariness. This alleged link appears to be based on two premises: (a) that discretion and rules are incompatible with each other, so that where there is discretion there is an absence of rules guiding the citizen and controlling the official; (b) that where power is exercised in the absence of clear decision rules the official may choose among a range of possible actions which creates a state of uncertainty and unpredictability, which in itself constitutes a sense of arbitrariness. With regard to the first of these premises it is sufficient to note that the relation between rules and discretion is complex and variable, and that unless one takes an exceptionally narrow view of the concept of a rule, there is no inherent compatibility between the two, and one should not assume that a grant of discretionary power is a licence for the random and subjective preferences of officials. The second premise however does raise more interesting questions. It might be taken in two different ways: the first and stronger assertion is that unless there are clear rules governing the exercise of powers they will be arbitrary. Here arbitrariness is being used in a different sense from that considered in the preceding discussion; there arbitrariness is linked to purpose, here however arbitrariness is linked to the absence of authoritative decision rules. Arbitrariness in this latter sense is not removed by showing that the official acted conscientiously and based his

---

[12] See *F. A. Hayek*, The Road to Serfdom, 1946; The Constitution of Liberty, 1960; Law, Legislation and Liberty, 3 Vols, 1972—79; New Studies in Philosophy, Political Economy and the History of Ideas, 1978. For critical discussion, see: *A. de Crespigny*, Freedom for Progress, in: A. de Crespigny/K. Minogue (Eds), Contemporary Political Philosophers, Methuen 1976; *R. Haromwy*, Law and the Liberal Society, in: J. of Libertarian Studies 2 (1978), 11; *Raz* (note 7), Ch. 11.

action upon considerations squarely within the purposes of his power; rather arbitrariness in this sense will be removed only by the formulation and application of authoritative decision rules.

We may accept the importance of the guidance that standards provide, and of general stability in the relations between citizen and state; we may also recognize, however, that there are other ends to be served in government regulation and these may better be served by a system of authority based not on strict rules but on a network of more open standards. One does not have to choose between settled rules and chaos, but rather the object is to reach a reasonable balance between certainty and predictability on the one hand, and openness and adaptability on the other, a balance which must be sought in the context of particular powers. Perhaps the real significance of the claim that discretion is inherently arbitrary is to remind us in a forceful way that some interests are of such personal value that if the state is to assume power to limit, curtail, or reduce those interests, then it should do so in a way that is clearly regulated by clear standards. Much of the contemporary criticism of decision-making within the criminal justice system is founded on precisely this point:[13] here the vital interest at stake is personal liberty in a most fundamental sense, and yet decisions affecting that liberty are riddled with discretions which are inevitably hard to control. The contemporary urge for precise and inflexible sentencing codes owes much of its momentum to precisely this criticism. It should also be remembered that Dicey's own criticisms were directed primarily at the increase in discretionary powers in matters of arrest and detention; but the undoubted legitimacy of his claim in those areas should not be inflated into condemnation of discretionary powers in general.[14]

This leads us to the second and weaker sense in which discretion might be seen as linked to arbitrariness. Here the point of criticism might be not that there is some inherent arbitrariness in decision-making which does not proceed according to set rules, but just that there will always be the appearance of arbitrariness. By providing an objective basis for scrutiny, rules help to eliminate the risk that officials will use their powers for the wrong purposes or even for their own private purposes. Even the conscientious officials may find it difficult in making a discretionary decision to confine himself to clearly relevant considerations, and to maintain the high level of argumentation and reflection that rational decision-making requires. And even where the official does meet these demands, it might still be difficult in the absence

---

[13] See *A. von Hirsch*, Doing Justice, New York 1976; and *American Friends' Service Committee*, Struggle for Justice, New York 1977.

[14] *Dicey* (note 5), Ch. IV.

of clear rules to convince those directly affected of the legitimacy of the decision and its supporting reasons. Rules provide comfort not just for the decision-maker but also on occasions for those to whom the decision is directed.

This criticism of discretionary powers shows the importance of the principle that powers not only should be exercised rationally but also should be seen to be. It suggests, rightly I think, the existence of deep psychological reasons for any power to be exercised in an environment of reasonably clear and settled standards; it also suggests that these reasons are at their strongest when personal liberty is at stake. Nevertheless these considerations do not show that decision-making according to precise rules is the only adequate way of overcoming the appearance of arbitrariness that may be associated with discretionary powers. Tightly rule-governed action represents one particular conception of rationality, but as we have seen, it has its costs. Above the threshold of rational and purposive activity there are various ways of co-ordinating a concern for consistency, certainty, and adaptability, and the interesting question in exercising discretionary powers is always to find a strategy which achieves these concerns in the most satisfactory way. This is another way of saying that the task within discretionary powers is to find the most rational strategy and thereby reduce elements of arbitrariness.

MODELE DEDUCTIF, MODELE INDUCTIF ET MODELE RHETORIQUE DE RAISONNEMENT JURIDIQUE

Par Letizia Gianformaggio, Siena

1. L'élaboration de modèles de raisonnement juridique s'inscrit dans le domaine des recherches de logique juridique. 'Logique juridique' est une locution intensionnellement et extensionnellement équivoque. Intensionnellement équivoque parceque l'adjectif peut indiquer un domaine d'application de la logique, ou bien une espèce particulière de logique. Extensionnellement équivoque parceque le substantif 'logique' peut se réferer aux relations (règles d'inférence) entre les éléments d'un système juridique, ou bien aux relations (règles d'inférence) entre les éléments d'un raisonnement juridique.

Les deux sens intensionnels s'excluent réciproquement; au contraire les deux signifiés extensionnels sont ensemble exhaustifs du champ des études de logique juridique. C'est-à-dire que seulement l'option pour l'un ou l'autre des deux sens entraine une prise de position théorique qui, en tant que telle, demande à être justifiée rationnellement; tandis que entre les deux signifiés aucun choix ne s'impose et, par conséquent, aucune justification; on doit simplement spécifier, chaque fois que l'on emploie la locution, l'acception dans laquelle on l'emploie. Pour cela il suffirait d'employer, pour les deux différentes acceptions, deux différentes locutions. Par exemple, ainsi qu'on l'a déjà proposé, 'logique du droit' pour la première et 'logique des juristes' pour la deuxième.[1]

2. L'élaboration de modèles de raisonnement juridique est une tâche propre aux recherches de logique des juristes. Au début de mon exposé sur ce sujet je dois préciser, d'après ce qui vient d'être dit, que en parlant de logique des juristes et de raisonnement juridique je ne me réfère pas à une espèce particulière de logique ou à une forme spécifique de raisonnement, mais seulement au domaine juridique d'application de la logique; en particulier à la logique qui a été employée pour contrôler les raisonnements des juristes: c'est-à-dire à l'objet spécifique des méthodologies juridiques.

---

[1] Cf., à ce sujet, *N. Bobbio*, Diritto e logica, dans: Rivista Internazionale di Filosofia del Diritto 39 (1962); *N. Amato*, Logica simbolica e diritto, Milano 1969, p. 331—346.

Or, les lois logiques et les schémas d'inférence (c'est-à-dire le sujet spécifique des recherches de logique du droit en tant que logique déontique) sont une donnée préliminaire à l'élaboration des modèles de raisonnement juridique.

3. Que doit-on entendre par 'modèles de raisonnement juridique'? Je distingue trois acceptions de 'raisonnement juridique'.

(a) 'Raisonnement juridique' *lato sensu:* il s'agit d'un discours ayant pour objet des questions juridiques ou, en tout cas, du ressort du domaine juridique qui, d'après notre culture juridique, doivent être traitées d'une façon rationnelle; ou bien aussi, chaque raisonnement développé par ceux qui exercent une activité juridique quelconque.[2]

(b) 'Raisonnement juridique' *stricto sensu:* il s'agit d'un discours qui traite d'une question juridique posée par le droit existant, c'est-à-dire un discours dont la conclusion est un énoncé prescriptif, une norme qui est justifiée par le recours au droit existant, en tant que tirée de lui, fondée sur lui.[3]

(c) 'Raisonnement juridique' *strictissimo sensu:* il s'agit de la justification d'une décision juridique (c'est-à-dire d'une norme) prise par un organe auquel le droit confère une compétence spécifique à décider; en particulier la justification produite en obéissant à un devoir étroit de justifier: un cas exemplaire d'un raisonnement juridique *strictissimo sensu* est la motivation du jugement ou de l'arrêt d'une Cour.[4]

Quant au terme 'modèle' dans la locution 'modèle de raisonnement juridique', je pense qu'on peut certainement l'entendre plutôt génériquement, comme synonyme de 'structure', 'schéma', 'forme'. Mais il est peut être plus stimulant de l'entendre dans un sens plus proche de celui de l'*analogue model* de Max Black.[5] Le modèle de raisonnement juridique serait, d'après cette interprétation, la forme ou structure qu'on reconnait propre et essentielle au raisonnement juridique, car il s'agit de la structure typique au domaine de raisonnement le mieux étudié ou le plus privilégié à l'égard du domaine juridique. Dans ce sens, déterminer

[2] Cf. *J. Wróblewski,* Justification of Legal Decisions, dans: Revue Internationale de Philosophie 127—128 (1979); *R. Alexy,* Theorie der juristischen Argumentation, Frankfurt a. M. 1978.

[3] Je voudrai souligner, en me rattachant à ce que j'ai écrit au début de ce texte, qu'on n'aborde pas içi la question des règles d'inférence entre normes d'un système juridique donné (qui est, à proprement parler, une question de logique du droit), mais la question des règles d'inférence suivant lesquelles les méthodologues ont analysé les discours des juristes.

[4] Cf. *Ch. Perelman,* Le raisonnement juridique, dans: *Id.,* Droit, morale et philosophie, Paris 1968.

[5] Cf. *M. Black,* Models and Metaphors, Ithaca 1962, p. 25—47.

ou élaborer un modèle de raisonnement juridique signifie accorder une certaine idée de scientificité ou de rationalité au domaine du raisonnement juridique; avec le double résultat de placer, d'un point de vue épistémologique, ce domaine au niveau des autres envisagés comme exemplaires, et de fournir un critère pour évaluer les arguments particuliers de ce domaine.

4. Dans les pages qui suivent je proposerai une évaluation comparative de trois logiques des juristes, de trois modèles de raisonnement juridique *strictissimo sensu* que la méthodologie juridique a élaboré. J'appelerai les trois modèles: modèle déductif, modèle inductif et modèle rhétorique; et l'évaluation comparative que j'en proposerai s'appuira sur la mise en évidence de l'espèce de contrôle de la décision par le modèle prefiguré.

En effet, on oblige un organe qui a la compétence à décider de motiver ses jugements de telle façon qu'il ne peut pas s'empêcher de reconnaitre des pouvoirs ou des instances supérieures, et de façon qu'il est aussi plus facile de contrôler la conduite de cet organe.[6] Or, dans les systèmes juridiques contemporains, les organes obligés de motiver leurs décisions ont le pouvoir en même temps que le devoir de décider sur le cas qu'on leur présente; et ils sont encore obligés, lorsqu'ils décident sur un cas, d'appliquer une norme juridique, c'est-à-dire de fonder la décision sur une norme juridique positive.

Or, on peut distinguer les modèles suivant le rôle que chacun d'eux attribue à la production de la norme en tant que raison de la décision, et par conséquent suivant le rapport que chacun d'eux institue entre détermination de la norme de droit positif à appliquer (reconnaissance d'un pouvoir supérieur) et motivation de la décision (présentation des appuis de la décision pour les passer au crible de la discussion).

5. Le modèle déductif, élaboré à l'intérieur d'une philosophie rationaliste et d'une culture juridique jusnaturaliste et transmis par cette dernière au positivisme juridique, retrouve dans le raisonnement juridique la même structure que la solution d'un problème de calcul, élevé à modèle de raisonnement. Essentiellement ce modèle considère la norme à appliquer comme une donnée, une prémisse de l'argumentation à laquelle il réduit tout ce qui est jugé, dans la motivation, comme juridiquement remarquable; et puisque la conclusion descend de cette prémisse comme dans un syllogisme parfait, la motivation en ligne de droit s'épuise avec la détermination de la norme à appliquer. Quand on a déterminé la norme et référé le fait, la décision s'impose avec la force de la logique, et aucun autre argument n'est requis. L'organe qui décide et motive est

[6] Cf. *T. Sauvel*, Histoire du jugement motivé, dans: Revue du Droit Public et de la Science Politique en France et à l'Etranger LXXI (1955).

la bouche de la loi; et il est peut-être même impropre de dire qu'il motive: il ne fait que répéter la norme, pas plus.[7]

La construction du modèle déductif du raisonnement juridique a eu une fonction politique très remarquable; mais la sphère politique dans laquelle ce modèle a exercé son influence a été celle du balancement des pouvoirs publics; dans l'horizon politique à l'intérieur duquel il a été élaboré il n'y a en effet aucun intérêt pour la question du contrôle démocratique de la jurisprudence. Ceux qui soutiennent ce modèle veulent seulement que le pouvoir judiciaire soit soumis au pouvoir législatif, et cette soumission est admise, et chaque fois confirmée, par la déclaration de la Cour que la décision particulière se fonde sur le texte de la loi générale; que, en donnant raison, la Cour répète seulement la volonté du législateur, c'est-à-dire la loi, qui est déjà d'elle même raison. Mais au moment où, après le XVIIIème siècle, la confiance des lumières dans l'équivalence volonté = raison = loi s'est éteinte, le modèle déductif ne signifie plus que cela: en donnant raison, la Cour répète seulement la volonté du législateur qui, de son côté, n'est pas obligé de déclarer ses raisons.

6. Le modèle inductif, au contraire, n'attribue pas à la norme de loi générale, dans le contexte de la justification de la décision juridique, un rôle de tout premier ordre en tant que raison de la décision même. En adoptant ce modèle, on ne nie pas qu'on passe de la norme à la décision par une inférence déductive; on ne conteste pas le fait qu'une partie au moins de la justification d'une décision consiste dans le recours à une norme générale, c'est-à-dire qu'elle est constituée moyennant l'application de la norme générale; mais on retient que d'autres phases, d'autres moments de la motivation sont plus centraux, plus essentiels, plus spécifiques du raisonnement juridique; et que, dans ces phases, l'espèce de raisonnement qu'on emploie est le raisonnement qu'on appelle «induction amplifiante». Le raisonnement juridique suivant le modèle inductif procède d'une prémisse particulière à une norme générale, la norme à appliquer, qui n'est pas à la disposition de l'organe qui doit décider lorsqu'il s'apprête à accomplir sa tâche; qui n'a pas été prédisposé auparavant pour lui avec rigueur et précision par le législateur, mais que l'organe même doit forger. Le raisonnement juridique, donc, se développe du particulier au général, et cela peut avoir un double sens.

---

[7] Cf. *Th. Hobbes*, Leviathan, in: The English Works of Thomas Hobbes, reprint Aalen 1966, vol. III, chapt. XXVI, p. 250—277; *Ch. L. Montesquieu*, L'esprit des Lois, in: Oeuvres complètes de Montesquieu, Paris 1950, vol. I, VI 1—8 p. 96—109, XI 6 p. 207—222; *C. Beccaria*, Dei delitti e delle pene, Torino 1965, cap. IV p. 15—17.

a) Le premier étant que de la norme générale forgée par le législateur on ne considère pas le *contenu* (général) de la prescription autant que le *fait* (particulier) de la statuition, que l'on regarde comme un effet, ou un symptôme, ou une manifestation d'une volonté, ou d'une dynamique d'intérêts, ou d'une conscience juridique matérielle répandue dans la société. Cette volonté, cette dynamique d'intérêts, cette conscience juridique sont le droit, c'est-à-dire la *ratio*, c'est-à-dire la vraie norme juridique générale que la Cour doit trouver pour l'appliquer au cas.[8]

b) Le second étant que le cas particulier à propos duquel on doit décider est la prémisse; et de cette prémisse on infère une norme fondée sur la *ratio* = nature du cas (nature de la chose).[9]

Le domaine de raisonnement considéré comme exemplaire est évidemment, dans ce cas, le domaine des sciences de la nature. On sait bien que la jurisprudence sociologique est un fruit de l'âge du positivisme.[10]

Or, c'est désormais une donnée acquise que, dans le domaine des sciences empiriques, la conclusion du raisonnement ne découle pas analytiquement de la prémisse ou des prémisses; dans ce domaine la simple énonciation des prémisses ne suffit à fonder rigoureusement aucune conclusion. On sait que la conclusion d'une inférence inductive doit être vérifiée, ou du moins soumise à essais de falsification. Mais la conclusion du raisonnement juridique n'est pas une assertion, c'est une norme; et une norme, à laquelle on ne peut pas appliquer les valeurs du vrai et du faux, ne peut pas être «prouvée» empiriquement, c'est-à-dire vérifiée ou falsifiée. La conclusion du raisonnement juridique ajoute donc quelque chose aux prémisses: la *ratio* de la norme ou du cas particulier, le droit, la norme juridique générale de laquelle la décision sera déduite; et cela leur est ajouté par une opération qui n'est pas, sur la base de ce modèle, contrôlable. Celui qui juge trouve le droit. La recherche qu'il accomplit à telle fin est libre: c'est une *libre recherche du droit.*

Ce modèle est de toute évidence proposé lorsqu'on croit de ne plus pouvoir s'en remettre à la loi pour le contrôle de l'activité des Cours. L'élaboration du modèle inductif du raisonnement juridique est, en conséquence, l'essai de soustraire l'activité des Cours aux contrôles: non seulement au contrôle démocratique, qui n'est même pas favorisé par le

[8] Cf. F. *Gény*, Méthode d'interprétation et sources en droit privé positif, Paris, 1919, vol. II p. 221: «La loi écrite, par exemple, sur laquelle notre science juridique positive prévent aujourd'hui édifier tout son système, ne peut être tenue pour autre chose, qu'une *information*, très limitée, du droit.»

[9] Cf. C. *Gangi*, Il problema delle lacune nel diritto privato, dans: Archivio Giuridico Giuseppe Serafini LXXXIX (1923), p. 163.

[10] K. *Larenz*, Methodenlehre der Rechtswissenschaft, 3. Aufl., Berlin-Heidelberg-New York 1975, chap. III.

modèle déductif, mais aussi au contrôle bureaucratique. Les Cours pour le sociologisme du début du XXème siècle sont par définition interprètes fidèles de la volonté et des intérêts des citoyens, comme l'était le législateur pour le rationalisme du XVIIIème siècle. La conduite des Cours pour le sociologisme du début du XXème siècle n'a aucun besoin de contrôles, tout comme n'en avait pas la conduite du législateur pour le formalisme du XIXème siècle.

7. Le modèle rhétorique lui-même ne nie pas que la justification de la décision juridique consiste, du moins en partie, dans le recours à (c'est-à-dire dans l'application de) une norme générale. Mais, sur la base de ce modèle, ce qui est essentiel, spécifiquement juridique dans la justification, n'est pas l'application déductive de la norme au cas particulier; ce n'est pas néammoins l'inférence inductive d'un particulier (que ce soit une norme ou un cas) à la norme générale. Ce qui est essentiel c'est la justification de l'assomption d'une *ratio,* justification qui consiste dans l'évaluation comparative des arguments qu'on a proposés dans le débat, ou qui sont considerés proposables dans la culture juridique à l'intérieur de laquelle l'organe opère. Le juge, qui au point de vue du modèle déductif est celui qui applique le droit au cas particulier, et au point de vue du modèle inductif est celui qui produit le droit pour le cas particulier, au point de vue du modèle rhétorique est celui qui résout une controverse juridique;[11] il n'existe, pour le juge, aucune donnée objective méta-discursive sur laquelle se fonder, comme il n'existe aucun *prius* absolument certain de l'argumentation; ni la norme générale à appliquer, ni l'événement qui s'est vérifié ne sont des entités réelles que la justification discursive d'une décision puisse seulement assumer, et ne pas manipuler. La donnée, le *prius,* est seulement l'existence d'un problème constitué par la collision de deux différentes façons d'évaluer ce qui est juste, convenable, équitable à propos d'un cas particulier.

L'évaluation comparative des arguments est accomplie d'après des assomptions qu'on croit partagées ou partageables par les défenseurs des différentes thèses. En ce qui concerne la structure de la dérivation du jugement de ces prémisses, le modèle n'en préfigure pas seulement une; il reconnait diverses structures d'argumentation, dont la force relative dépend de la culture juridique ainsi que de la question envisagée.

Le présupposé épistemologique du modèle en question se trouve dans la reconnaissance de la liaison étroite qui existe entre la *raison* et le *fait* de l'adhésion à une thèse ou de l'acceptation d'un procédé. Il n'existe aucun procédé obligeant, comme il n'existe aucune prémisse indiscutable.

---

[11] *Ch. Perelman,* Logique juridique. Nouvelle rhétorique, Paris 1976, p. 135 ss.

N'est indiscutable que ce qu'on envisage de ne pas devoir discuter. N'est obligeant que ce par quoi on se croit obligé. Les règles d'après lesquelles on accomplit l'inférence dans le raisonnement juridique selon le modèle rhétorique, c'est-à-dire les schémas argumentatifs, les procédés adoptés, sont les lieux *(topoi)* spécifiquement juridiques.[12] L'adoption de l'une ou de l'autre de ces règles d'inférence *(ad impossibilia nemo tenetur*, le silence n'oblige à rien, la confiance mérite protection, etc. ...) signifie l'option en faveur d'une valeur, le choix d'un point de vue duquel envisager les circonstances qui constituent le cas en question.

Or, si, malgré la multiplicité des règles d'inférence, on parle d'*un* modèle rhétorique, c'est en raison du fait qu'il réconnait le noyau de l'argumentation, le clou du raisonnement juridique d'après une précise idée de la fonction de juger. Cette fonction, peut-on dire avec une métaphore, est celle de débrouiller un écheveau embrouillé. Le juge doit seulement mettre de l'ordre. Il ne produit aucun matériau pour la déliberation; il n'est dépositaire d'aucun savoir privilégié, mais seulement d'une sagesse supérieure. A la lumière de cette sagesse il *trouve* la raison, c'est-à-dire le droit, d'un côté ou de l'autre. La raison, qui ne se trouve ni dans la loi ni dans le fait: elle se trouve dans les mots de l'une ou de l'autre partie ou, peut-être plus souvent, en partie dans les mots de l'une, en partie dans les mots de l'autre. Les mots du juge, le raisonnement juridique, decouvrent cette raison cachée: le juge est le *vir bonus dicendi peritus* de la tradition rhétorique.

Ou mieux «il doi l'être». Il y a, içi, un modèle de juge. L'admission d'un modèle rhétorique du raisonnement juridique signifie, en effet, non seulement l'admission que le juge évalue, choisit, soupèse, outre que calcule et déduit; elle signifie aussi la propension à soumettre à un contrôle ses évaluations: contrôle par les instances supérieures (bureaucratique) et contrôle diffusé par l'opinion publique (démocratique).

8. L'aperçu d'analyse et d'évaluation critique des trois modèles que je viens d'accomplir a eu ce double but:

(1) montrer que la méthodologie juridique a toujours envisagé le raisonnement juridique en tant que cas particulier du raisonnement tout court, et construit le modèle déductif suivant la conception du raisonnement en tant que calcul basé sur des axiomes; le modèle inductif suivant la conception du raisonnement en tant qu'inférence basée sur les données de fait; le modèle rhétorique suivant la conception du raisonnement en tant qu'argumentation à l'appui de l'une des nombreuses thèses opposées.

---

[12] *G. Struck*, Topische Jurisprudenz, Frankfurt a. M. 1971; *Id.*, Zur Theorie juristischer Argumentation, Berlin 1977.

(2) montrer que le choix d'un modèle, c'est-à-dire le choix d'un domaine de raisonnement privilegié et par conséquent de critères d'évaluation et de contrôle, n'est pas lui-même évaluable et controlable en termes de correspondance à l'objet (au raisonnement juridique); et que au contraire le choix d'un modèle est chargé d'implications idéologiques et politiques.

A mon avis, cette façon d'aborder le problème de la méthodologie juridique a deux conséquences remarquables:

(1) elle permet de séparer le côté logique du côté idéologique de la vieille querelle sur le syllogisme judiciaire;

(2) elle permet de réunir le côté récognitif (descriptif) et le côté propositif (prescriptif) de la fonction des modèles, en soulignant comment la distinction entre méthodologie descriptive et méthodologie prescriptive, convenable au niveau analytique, ne peut pas être retrouvée, aussi précise, au niveau phénoménologique.

NORMATIVE AND PURPOSIVE-RATIONAL REASONING

A Case Study of the Norwegian Petroleum Directorate*

By Hans Petter Graver, Oslo

I. Introduction

Theories on legal reasoning have traditionally concentrated on the judge's decision in individual cases.[1] Typical of legal reasoning in this sense is that it is normative, meaning that it consists of applying a general norm to the specific instance.

There are, however, decisions made within a legal system which at least on the surface differ from the judicial decisions above described. One example is the decision of the legislator.[2] The legislator is assumed to take an ends-means approach to a problem: when an act is passed, the legislator presumably chooses the solution that is preferable as a means of reaching the specific goal which the legislator has.

The cognitive structures of the judicial decision and such purposive decisions are dissimilar.[3] The purposive decision is seen as a causal factor giving rise to future events, while the judicial decision is seen as the best way of complying with a given set of norms or values.

The majority of the decisions made in our modern legal system are not those made by the judge or the legislator, but by the administration. It is therefore of interest to analyse the structure of the administrative

---

* Since the submission of this article, the legislative framework for the off-shore activities has been revised in the 1985 Petroleum Activity Act and in the 1985 decree on safety. The main regulatory principles as described in this article are, however, unchanged by the new legislation.

[1] Good examples are found in *V. Aubert*, The Structure of Legal Thinking, in: Legal Essays, a Tribute to Frede Castberg, Oslo 1963, and *L. M. Friedman*, The Legal System — A Social Science Perspective, New York 1977, pp. 234—247.

[2] For theories on legal reasoning in legislation see *P. S. Lauridsen*, Studier i retspolitisk argumentasjon (Studies in Reasonings of Legal Policy), København 1974, and *J. Hellner*, Argumentation de lege ferenda (*De lege ferenda* reasoning), in: Svensk Juristförening, 1975, pp. 401—419.

[3] *T. Eckhoff*, Justice, Efficiency and Self-Made Rules, in: Eckhoff, Justice and the Rule of Law, Oslo 1966, pp. 66—90.

decisions. We may call an administrative decision legal if it directly affects the rights, duties or obligations of members of the society.

An administrative body may have powers to enact *rules* which are generally binding on everyone within a set category of subjects. (*Viz.* everyone, all oil companies, everyone connected with the activity of exploration for or production of petroleum etc.) Other bodies have powers to issue individual binding *orders*. Some bodies have the power to do both.

We would expect a decision to enact rules to be similar in structure to that of the legislator. On the other hand, we cannot presuppose any similarity between a decision to give orders and the judicial decision. Here we must distinguish between an authority which is fixed and one which is open (discretionary).

The authority to give orders can be fixed in the sense that a decision has to be made when certain conditions are met, or in the sense that the contents of the decision have been established by law, or both. In the latter case the decision is purely normative. Once we bring in a discretionary element there is a possibility of a causal approach. However, not all discretionary powers open for a causal approach because the decision may be governed to a greater or lesser extent by normative guidelines.

When confering discretionary powers on a body, the intention may be that the body shall apply a general statute to specific cases in a judicial way. The intention may, however, also be that the body should take a causal approach in its regulating activity. This will often be the case with technical agencies with expertise in the fields of economics, medicine, engineering etc.

Although an open, causal approach may be ideal for certain types of administrative decisions, experience shows that administrative decisions tend to be normative. Open powers may be substituted for by "home made" rules.[4] Such rules need not be the result of an open policy decision, but may arise from a tendency to decide new cases in the same way as previous ones. They may also be the result of conflicting groups of experts within an agency not being able to decide which causal approach is the correct one. To decide according to a given set of rules or principles may be the compromise which enables the agency to make decisions at all.[5] Furthermore, the judicial decision has certain advantages for the decision-maker. It frees him from directly taking the side of one

---

[4] *Eckhoff* (note 3), p. 88.

[5] *V. Aubert,* Rettens sosiale funksjon (The Social Function of Law), Oslo 1976, p. 293.

party if there are several parties with conflicting interests and it makes him less liable to criticism in the event of the facts or the future turning out wrongly.[6] It seems reasonable to suppose that the tendency towards judicial decisions will be strongest in an agency which also has powers to give general rules. There the purposive decisions can be made once and for all in a way which legitimates a future normative approach.

Obviously this tendency in administration arises partly from tradition, administration in Norway being founded on a strong legal tradition. In addition, the theories of administration do not tell us how an agency with powers to enact general rules solves the problems of conflicting interests and criticism when exercising this power. For this reason it is of interest to look closer at a recently established agency with powers to enact both general rules and individual orders. My work has enabled me to study the regulatory functions of the Norwegian Petroleum Directorate (NPD).

II. The Legal Position of the Norwegian Petroleum Directorate

The Norwegian Petroleum Directorate is the main institution in Norway with administrative functions concerning the off-shore petroleum industry. Its functions can be divided into three categories.[7] Firstly, it exercises control by ensuring that the activities on the continental shelf are in accordance with current statutes and regulations and the conditions stipulated in the licence. This includes safety aspects connected with production and drilling, but not with the operation of mobile rigs for exploration which are covered by the Norwegian Maritime Directorate. Secondly, the NPD has a role in connection with the allocation of licenses. Thirdly, it has an important planning function in collecting and evaluating information from the shelf activities, in making plans for future activities. Here I shall deal only with the functions of the NPD regarding the regulation of and control with *safety*.

The powers of the Norwegian Petroleum Directorate in this respect are laid down in the Royal Decree of 9. 7. 1976 relating to Safe Practice for the Production etc. of Sub-marine Petroleum Resources. This Decree establishes duties for the industry to comply with safety requirements, to submit relevant information, to apply for and receive permissions or licences before certain steps or measures are taken and to establish plans for the line of command on the units and the people working there, on contingency and emergency situations etc. Apart from such specific

---

[6] *Aubert* (note 1), p. 59.

[7] *H. J. Bull*, Norwegian Offshore Petroleum, The Legal and Administrative Response, in: Scandinavian Studies of Law, 1981, pp. 33—50.

duties, the Decree outlines safety requirements in a general and unspecified way. It is however a presupposition that detailed requirements be laid down in rules issued by the administration.

Section 3 outlines the main part of the powers given to the NPD as the authorised representative of the Ministry. Here it is stated that "The Ministry may issue such regulations and orders as may be necessary to enforce the provisions of this decree." Seeing that many of the provisions in the Decree are quite general and require that operations be safe, this is quite a substantial delegation of power. The NPD may also grant exemption from the requirements under the same provision.

As we see, the NPD has a wide range of traditional administrative powers. Its function as regards control of safety is two-sided: on the one hand giving norms for the industry to comply with, and on the other hand actually controlling that the activity is in compliance with the set requirements. To fulfill its functions, the NPD may issue universally binding rules and/or individually binding orders. In addition it may of course make statements as to recommended procedures, guidelines and specifications of the general safety requirements in the Decree. The actual control may be undertaken directly through inspections during construction on-shore and off-shore, and of the activity in general off-shore. It may also be undertaken indirectly by evaluation and assessment of information submitted by the operators and by evaluating concepts and plans before issuing permissions required under the Decree.

III. The Way in Which the NPD has Exercised its Powers[8]

A comment often heard about Norwegian policy as regards control with the petroleum industry is that the industry is over-regulated. On the surface this may very well seem to be true also for the NPD policy on safety. Since it came into being in 1973, the NPD has issued 13 regulations directly concerned with safety.

These are by date of issue: regulations on the structural design of fixed structures (15. 4. 77), regulations on cranes on production installation (25. 5. 77), guidelines for the inspection of primary and secondary structures (1. 4. 78), regulations on production and auxiliary systems (3. 4. 78), provisional regulations on diving (1. 7. 78), regulations on instrumentation recording and processing of environmental and platform data (1. 8. 78), regulations concerning fixed means of access, stairs, ladders and railings (2. 4. 79), regulations on transfer of personnel to and from production installations (2. 4. 79), provisional regulations on living quarters (2. 4. 79), guidelines for the licencees' internal control (15. 8. 81), guidelines for safety

[8] A more complete presentation is given in *H. P. Graver*, Sikkerhetsstyring og reguleringsteknikk (Safety Management and Control Policy), Oslo 1983.

evaluation of platform conceptual design (1. 9. 81), regulations on drilling etc. (23. 9. 81), and regulations on drilling installations and equipment on mobile drilling platforms (23. 9. 81).

The bulk of the regulations are issued in the period from 1977 to 1979. If we look closer at the regulations issued later than 1979 we see that these are mere revisions or formalising of requirements applied before 1979. The internal control guideline is a revision of a guideline from 1979. The concept of internal control was applied from 1975—76. The guidelines for safety evaluation of platform concepts are a formalisation and codification of requirements applied from 77—78. The drilling regulations are a revision of the previous regulations from 1975 (revised also in 1978). It is fair to say that there is a shift in the NPD policy in 1979 in the sense that issuing regulations has become a less important part of the work of the Directorate.

The statement that a shift of policy can be observed needs some further attention. The statement could possibly be contested on the grounds that by 1979 all the necessary regulations were stipulated so that further activity along these lines was no longer required. However, this does not explain the change. It is not difficult to point to areas and parts of the activity not covered by any regulation. Safety and job training is one, general working conditions another, requirements as to maintenance yet a third. This does not mean that the NPD has not shown any interest in these aspects. What it implies is that control over these areas has been exercised through other means than formal regulations.

Interesting observations may be made if we look closer into the background and revisions of the regulations stipulated, into the control policy developed by the NPD and into the regulation of fields not covered by formal regulations.

The background of all the regulations but one, i. e. the regulations concerning fixed means of access etc. is to be found in documents presented by the Ministry and the Government to the Parliament. This implies that for all the regulations but one the NPD was actually requested by the controlling political institutions to issue formal regulations. What it also implies, and perhaps what in our context is more interesting, is that apart from the regulation on fixed means of access etc. the NPD has not issued any regulations on its own initiative. This seems to indicate that when the NPD has a choice as to how to regulate and control a specific field or area of the activity, it avoids using formal regulations.

Looking at the contents of the revisions of the regulations undertaken after 1979 we see a tendency to deregulate. This is also an explicit policy of the Directorate. Both by the Directorate itself, and by the controlling political institutions it has ever since the beginning been stated that the regulations must be flexible and allow the industry itself to come up with new and better solutions as the technical progress continues. The last couple of years have seen this policy put into practice by the NPD in its revisions of the regulations.

Thirdly, the control policy of the NPD is of interest. From 1975—76 the internal control of the licensees has gradually become more important and the direct control of the NPD through inspections less important.

Here the content of the concept of internal control needs a few comments.

It is a fundamental principle in Norwegian law that anyone subject to duties and obligations is alone responsible for the fulfilling of these obligations and duties. In some areas of public control, currently in fact, as regards the control of the agency for the workers' health and safety, it has been contested that the government by its control also has taken over part of the responsibility for the consequences of legal requirements not being met. A central issue in public control as regards safety aspects in the petroleum industry has been that the responsibility for safety must lie with the industry and the industry alone. Partly for this reason, and also surely due to the limited resources of the governmental agencies concerned, a unique control system has been established for the supervision of safety aspects of the off-shore drilling and production of petroleum.

Internal control, as devised by the NPD, is legally founded upon the duty to meet legal requirements as mentioned above. However, it reaches much further than that. In its guidelines for internal control the NPD requires of the operators that they set up an administrative system in the company, with a direct line of command to the company management, to deal with safety aspects. This system has to be approved in each case by the NPD. The function of the safety section thus established is partly by inspections and partly to ensure otherwise that the activity is in compliance with governmental safety requirements. In addition to this, internal control, as outlined by the NPD, includes application of general requirements to the specific instance. This means that in all instances where the governmental requirements are vague, ambiguous or simply not directly adequate, it is up to the operating company to come up with the right legal solution to the problem. The role of the NPD in this system is to check that the internal control is functioning by going through inspection reports submitted by the operator, and by occasional spot checks on the installation.

Lastly we must point to other ways in which NPD has approached the safety question. Issuing regulations is only one form of making decisions when it comes to regulating safety. A study of the NPD regulating policy shows that other types of decisions are becoming increasingly important. In several areas we find decisions which in their consequences are much like regulations in the sense that they are generally legally binding. The requirements as regards safety training are an example of this. First the NPD asked the industry to come up with acceptable solutions. When this failed they sent a letter to the different operator companies stating that the training programme outlined in a report by a governmental task force on training for the petroleum industry (Leiro committee) in the opinion of the NPD satisfied the general requirements of the Decree as to "necessary qualifications" (section 23). When the industry still lagged behind, the NPD threatened to issue formal regulations. We also find opinions and recommendations expressed by the NPD which could not be regarded as formal and binding rules. A common technique is to recommend that certain fields or areas of the activity be given special attention. Another is to issue statements specifying the contents of the general safety standard of section 5 of the Decree. Yet another way to express priorities is to concentrate the NPD inspections on specific areas to increase the level of safety in this area. An example of this can be seen concerning general working conditions, diving equipment and maintenance.

IV. Conclusions

These findings may be summed up as follows:

The structure of reasoning when enacting general rules seems to be more normative than purposive.[9] And on the other hand, the structure of the individual decisions and the control policy is increasingly purposeful, not judicial.

We have seen that establishment of rules takes up a very small part of the NPD regulating policy. Formal rules have been enacted only where directions to do so have been issued by higher authorities (with one exception). In some instances the enactment of rules has been used as a sanction towards an uncooperative industry, as may be seen from the case of safety training. The NPD apparently hold formal rules as being counter-productive to the goal of achieving better safety.

One may point to several possible causes of the development which has taken place in the regulating policy of the NPD. Apart from explanations connected with the internal organization of the NPD such as the lack of

[9] This is in accordance with theories presented by *P. S. Lauridsen* and *J. Hellner* (note 2) on the reasoning of legal policies. But regarding the fact that the NPD is a body with highly qualified *technical* expertise the result is surprising.

tradition and the dominant position of engineers, I will point to certain connections with the conditions under which the NPD operate.

The role of the managing political institutions is important when it comes to explaining the development. The oil industry is a very technical field, the management of which is difficult without technical expertise. Even if this is not true when it comes to evaluations of which risks to allow and which not to allow, how much money to spend on safety, what level of risks and injuries to the workforce should be accepted etc., the politicians seem to avoid expressing definite views on such matters. Instead, certain issues have been given priority by the political institutions in such a way that they may be regarded as goals for the work of the NPD. The problem is, however, that none of these goals as such can be attained from the rationality of a technical, purposive approach. Goals like "improving safety", "efficient control programmes", "giving detailed regulations for the activity" all have to be redefined to be implemented in the technical rationality of the NPD. For instance, an aim to improve safety may easily become a goal to decrease the rate of injuries recorded in the statistics and to make certain that the NPD cannot be blamed should a major accident occur. Likewise, "efficient control programmes" may become "manageable" control programmes by limiting the object of control in such a way that reasonable efficiency is possible. The history of the NPD gives several examples of such redefinitions of goals in order to make them operational within the technical rationality of the NPD. Furthermore, we see that such redefinitions are fully accepted by the political authorities.

There are, however, certain disadvantages for the oil companies in the present development. Firstly, the NPD requires the establishment of a safety organisation which perhaps is unfamiliar to traditional company organisation. On the other hand, the companies in return are left pretty much alone when it comes to checking that the safety requirements actually are met. Secondly, where there are no fixed rules, there is no rule of law. This is the other side of vague regulations, general requirements and recommendations from the NPD and of leaving the actual implementation of the measures to the companies themselves. This is perhaps more of a problem for other parties in the activities, such as contractor firms and workers, but it is also a problem for the operator company. The reason for this is that noncompliance with the general requirements of the Decree is subject to criminal liability. In event of something going wrong, someone in the company is likely to have to pay. There are so many vague legal and semi-legal obligations floating about that the prosecution and the courts in most cases are likely to find that some duties have not been fulfilled. The oil companies nevertheless seem to be happy about the development.

There are also grounds for arguing that the oil companies have a particularly strong position when it comes to getting their viewpoints across to the NPD. The development in NPD policy indicates that it is certainly more in favour of the oil companies than in favour of other participating interests. Moreover, the oil companies have a near-monopoly when it comes to furnishing the NPD with information and highlighting aspects of importance. The oil companies are also consulted more both on a formal and informal basis than are representatives of other participating interests. The links to the oil industry are at least as close as the links to the ministry to which the NPD is answerable.

Finally, there is the question of protection from criticism. The mandate of the NPD is so wide that it would be difficult for the NPD to avoid criticism on the grounds that they have just followed instructions. A judicial approach could in fact prove hazardous. If the NPD confined itself to making formal rules, criticism in connection with an unwanted occurrence would easily be raised on the grounds that the rules were not good enough, that the situation should have been anticipated, etc. Now the uncertainty of the purposive approach may function as an excuse. One of the factors legitimating this approach is the technical uncertainty we are faced with when exploring the limits of technology during deep-sea drilling and producing under very difficult conditions. Although most accidents cannot be explained in this way,[10] the impression of uncertainty tends to justify the position of the industry and the government in any case.

Control and licensing might have been exercised by the NPD under a traditional judicial rationality, limiting itself to seeing that precedent was followed and formal norms applied. The size of the activity on the continental shelf makes it impossible for any governmental body to actually control the operations without spending much more money than the government seems willing to do at present. One way out of this could be to standardize licenses and control programmes in order to show the politicians and the public that the NPD was acting according to its obligations. As regards the policy of internal control the NPD has, however, chosen a different approach. What they have to ensure is that company structure and procedures comply with the requirements of the NPD. If something unwarranted happens, the responsibility is already placed on the operator.

The study of the case of the Norwegian Petroleum Directorate shows that a shifting from purposive decisions towards judicial decisions is not a universal tendency. In my view an important factor here is that the

[10] *W. G. Carson,* The Other Price of Britain's Oil, Oxford 1982, pp. 47—49.

NPD has found an alternative way of protecting itself from criticism. I also think it is fair to say that the NPD has been reasonably successful in regulating the oil industry in view of improving safety. I think there is no doubt about the fact that the oil companies have been forced to give safety a higher priority than they would have done having their interest in an economic outcome only. There is, however, a price to pay. Safety has very much become a concern of one professional group, the engineers. The result of this is that the balancing of safety interests against other interests of the society at large is undertaken by experts and not by politicians who have a responsibility to the voters. Another result is that technical safety is given a higher priority than are other aspects of safety such as organisational set-ups and working procedures on the installations, long-term effects on the workers' health etc. Furthermore the purposive approach has not shown much success in solving the conflict of interests between different participants in the activities, such a conflict being hardly recognized at all.

THE GENESIS AND LIMITS OF ABSTRACT REASON IN JURIDICAL THOUGHT

By Martín Laclau, Buenos Aires

I.

Law participates in the fast transformation that the human world, in all its aspects, is undergoing. While long-standing institutions have reached a critical point in their existence, others crumble down and some others, not yet born, start rising in the horizon. We are thus witnesses of the uncertain steps that announce a new stage in the history of mankind. For the first time we do not think in terms of nations or cultural circles: the diagnosis covers the whole of our planet. Perhaps at no other time have we been able to ascertain the truth of the phrase uttered by Terence's character, which conveyed that nothing human remains alien to us for the mere reason that we are human beings: *homo sum: humani nil a me alienum puto*. But the crisis we find ourselves immersed in not only affects the non-essential aspects of our existence, but also manifests itself intensely in the fact that it influences our vision of reality, that is, the mental instruments whereby we come into contact with the world around us.

The relation that man establishes with the reality he faces is not direct, since between both is inserted the cultural world that man himself creates and which constitutes an interpretation of the reality he intends to perceive. Man differs in that aspect from the rest of the animals. Modern biology has succeeded in determining that there is not a world common to all living species, but, on the contrary, the conformation of each organism makes it possible for some of them to perceive portions of reality which remain unknown to others. Anatomical structure establishes a distinction in the experiences of differently constituted organisms. The world will thus be experienced differently by a fly or by a sea-urchin. But what characterizes all species is that there is in them a marvellous adjustment between the organism and the medium where it lives: each organism receives external stimuli and, automatically, reacts to them. If we take the case of man, we shall see that the human individual does not establish a direct relation with external reality, but between both is interposed the cultural world that man creates by means of the values inherent in his behaviour. Life is, unavoidably, an assessment of circumstances. We must all the time choose among various possibilities offered to us and, in order to do so, we must evaluate them. The perception of reality, therefore, does not appear as something inseparable from the axiological context characteristic of human life. An animal is biologically conditioned, it reacts mechanically to external stimuli. Man, instead, as a free being, finds his action determined by an emotional intuition, by means of which he values the various possible behaviours within his circumstances.

It is worth pointing out that — contrary to Kant's ideas — the mental categories used by man in his perception of reality are not always the same. These vary, following in this sense the temporal flow that every existence consists in and on which its essential historic condition is based.

Man is not a ubiquitous being; on the contrary, he is always in a certain situation, which imposes its own perspective to the perception of reality. This reality is inexhaustible: it only offers each of us some of its facets. It is impossible to seek the integral perception of an object. We see the world in front of us from a given perspective: certain aspects are obvious, but others remain unrevealed. Every individual vision gives us a fragmentary knowledge of the objects, a partial perception, which does not mean, however, that this perception is false. These differences, that might be found among people considered individually, acquire greater importance insofar as we speak about different societies or different periods of time. The changing situation, that is part and parcel of human life, ensures a continuous enrichment of its apprehension of reality: each period of time, each individual, is capable of perceiving by intuition aspects of reality that remained hidden for other people or at other times.

II.

All this having been made clear, I think that our times offer new possibilities for legal research. Our law has shaped itself, over centuries, by making use of the rational categories inherited from Greek philosophy. Nowadays we face a global crisis of the heritage handed down by our predecessors; but at the same time the road is open for new possibilities of improvement if we become conscious of the fact that the instrument that we jurists have been using for centuries is a rational, abstract, and generalizing thought, fit for the apprehension of natural reality, but unfit for the perception of human life, which appears as an individual concrete reality, marked by the historic and temporal mobility that is its main constituent.

Our apprehension of reality has inherited the conceptual patterns of Greek thought, whose unquestionable prevalence has lasted to these days, when we are likely to perceive the limitations of the remarkable rational apparatus forged in ancient times. In Parmenides we may clearly observe the beginnings of rationalism. Parmenides aims at the apprehension of being, that is, of things insofar as they are, leaving aside the changing world of sensations. Sensation faces us with the world of appearances, while thought, νοῦς, gives us access to being. Now, being presents predicates opposed to the changing world of appearances: it is unique and not subjected to variation. The nature of the thing apprehended by νοῦς is fixed, static, self-contained. And these features will be sustained in the subsequent development of philosophy. Things stand before our senses as endowed with multiple qualities: their colours vary, they are hard or soft, big or small, they appear at a given moment and then disappear. But in the eyes of thought all these divergencies are effaced and their being appears as what is common to all of them. The qualitative diversity given by sensations disappears and, before νοῦς, what is plural and changeable becomes unique and immovable. Thus, when we attempt to find the being of an object, our thought should aim at the apprehension of something fixed, permanent; we should consider that that object has an invariable consistency, granted once and for good. Parmenides denies the reality of the world perceived through sensations. This world is constituted by an endless multiplicity of things in perpetual change. All movement, consisting in the transition from one state to another, is a mere appearance, for it implies a twofold reality contrary to the unity of being. The Parmenidean conception of being cannot explain any movement, for this cannot exist in a theory that considers that being shows properties such as uniqueness, immutability and eternity.

The compatibility between movement and the Eleatic conception of being is achieved by Aristotle, who succeeds in explaining movement without conflicting with the Parmenidean conception of being. The Greek had conceived change as a passing from a beginning to an end, and this dual nature made it incompatible with that of being as conceived by Parmenides. But Aristotle changes the terms of the problem by saying that, even if movement implies a passage from being to not-being, it is not a change to absolute non-being, but to another form of being: mutation takes place from being in potentiality to being in actuality (*Met.*, 1069 b 15—20). Underneath this change to which all things are subjected we should look for what — according to Aristotle — does not vary, for their immutable essence that can only be perceived by means of our reason.

In this way we can observe, in Aristotelian philosophy, the presence of the traditional Hellenic conception of reason that binds it with a substantialistic idea of reality. Parmenides had already expressed it: being and νοῦς are so closely related that it is possible to state that both are, in a certain sense, the same thing: τὸ γὰρ αὐτὸ νοεῖν ἔστιν τε καὶ εἶναι. Νοῦς puts us in contact with actual reality, with being insofar as it is; sensations, instead, do not go beyond the realm of mere appearances. Even since Greek times, when referring to substance, Western tradition has spoken about a fixed, static entity, whose merely accidental variation will only imply the change of one way of being to another way of being of the substance whose core does not vary.

Now, the Greek conceived not only the idea of an abstract reason that puts us in contact with true reality, but also the peculiar form that scientific knowledge has adopted in the Western world. The Presocratic philosophers conceived knowledge as a discerning, a separating of what appears to be from what actually is. One of the remaining fragments of Heraclitus' says, precisely, that nature enjoys hiding itself (frag. 123). True reality is concealed and the scholar's mission will consist in disclosing it, in making it perceptible to our mind, in distinguishing the things that actually are from those that only appear to be. This notion of knowledge dominates Parmenides' poem. According to him, as we have seen, the function of νοῦς lies in opening a road towards immutable, unique, eternal being, leaving aside the veils with which multiple appearances attempt to hide it when they show a being which, in fact, these appearances lack. That is why the Greek understood truth as αλήθεια, an unveiling of a hidden reality.

With Socrates Greek thought will take a significant turn. Now knowledge will consist not so much in distinguishing but in defining. We attain knowledge of something when we limit that something, apprehending it in its essence. Socrates will wonder about the *what* of things, that is, about their definition, about the features that characterize them, that are essential to them. We cannot here enlarge upon all the implications of this transformation; it is sufficient to say that from this new way of conceiving knowledge will arise Plato's philosophy and his theory of ideas as substantial forms in which participate the different individual objects offered by our everyday experience.

If we consider Aristotle, we will see that according to him σωφία, wisdom, is the supreme knowledge that enables us to get to know the cause of things, their *why*. According to Aristotle, knowledge will not consist so much in discerning, as the Presocratic philosophers thought, or in defining, as understood by Platonic philosophy, but in a knowledge of the causes. It is not sufficient to know the *what* of things; it is necessary to seek their *why*. Scientific knowledge is demonstrative knowledge, ἐπιστήμη, which guides our steps to deduce things from their first principles. Now these do not derive from anything. There is no possible demonstration of them: they can only be perceived intuitively by νοῦς. Thus, scientific reason implies the use of two faculties: νοῦς, which apprehends intuitively the first principles, and ἐπιστήμη which, from these principles, follows a discursive reasoning (*Met.*, 981 b 25—982 a 4; *An. Post.*, 72 b 18—22). In this way, according to Aristotle, scientific knowledge starts from a limited number of obvious statements, from which it is possible to deduce the rest of the statements that constitute the science in question. This theory of science, which achieved its first complete formulation in Euclid's geometry, dominated European thought throughout twenty-four hundred years, and has reached a critical point only in our times.

III.

We have seen how the two notions originated that give Western thought its distinctive features: abstract rationality and systematization. Both have been present ever since Western thought was born and contribute to creating a certain vision of reality, dominated by the notion of substance, which is regarded as a fixed, self-contained entity, which serves as a support of multiple and variable accidents.

In *De Jure Belli ac Pacis* (1625), which marks the beginning of modern juridical thought, Hugo Grotius explains, in its first pages, the method followed, establishing a relation between it and that used by mathematicians: just as the latter consider figures making an abstraction of bodies, so the jurist must dispense with any individual and contingent fact: *Injuriam mihi faciet si quis me ad ullas nostri saeculi controversias, aut natas aut quae nasciturae praevideri possunt, respexisse arbitratur. Vere enim profiteor, sicut mathematici figuras a corporibus remotas considerant, ita me in jure tractando ab omni singulari facto abduxisse animum.* This exercise of reason that abstracts the unique, peculiar features of the objects that it apprehends, gives us unavoidably a substantialistic vision of reality, which is the one that has prevailed to our days.

Ever since ancient times man has been conceived as a substance. This idea was well received in modern times and thus Descartes conceived man as *res cogitans*, as a thinking substance. And if we inquire into what Descartes understands by substance we will see that his concept does not go far from that put forward by Hellenic philosophy: *Per substantiam nihil aliud intelligere possumus, quam rem quae ita existit, ut nulla alia re indigeat ad existendum* (*Principia philosophiae*, I, 51). We always find the notions of invariability, of independence; the same that appear in Spinoza's *Ethica: Per substantiam intelligo id quod in se est et per se concipitur; hoc est, id cujus conceptus non indiget alterius rei a quo formari debeat.* Even in our century, and within this tradition, Wittgenstein will tell us that substance is what exists independently of what happens (*Tractatus logico-philosophicus,* 2.024).

This abstract reason, that makes man perceive the world as a whole of substances, proceeds on the basis of a systematic, deductive thinking. What it is interested in is not the unique, that which gives its peculiarity to objects, persons or situations, but the global whole within which the various individual notions are inserted. In this way, when we are confronted with problems, these are faced as parts of a previously conceived whole, and when they are incompatible with the system that is our starting-point, they are regarded as wrongly posed.

Now, can law adopt an abstract, systematizing way of thinking? Taking into account the fact that norms are mental patterns whereby we can give juridical sense to certain human conducts, is it possible to use a reason that conceives the objects it attempts to apprehend as substantial, fixed, self-contained entities that are susceptible of being placed within the rigid determinations of a conceptual system? Will law not need, on the contrary, a reason different from that used for the knowledge of nature, since it does not intend to conceptualize physical beings but human behaviour, which offers peculiarities that render it so different from the former?

The systematic ideal of our legal science had its origin in Greece: it springs — as was seen — from the conception of knowledge created by Aristotle. But this ideal has not always prevailed in the development of law. According to the dominant tradition in Rome, law was created on the basis of the decisions that the judges and jurists made for the solution of each concrete case. It was so to such a degree that Pomponius admits that *jus civile* did not have its origin in written texts, but in the interpretations of the learned men: *proprium jus civile, quod sine scripto in sola prudentium interpretatione consistit* (*Dig.*, I, 2, 12).

Not until the first century B. C. did the idea of system make an appearance in Rome, as a product of the influence gained by Greek philosophy in the learned classes of society. It seems that it was Quintus Mucius Scaevola, consul in the year 95 B. C., who for the first time attempted to group the arguments of *jus civile* according to genera: *jus civile primus constituit generatim in libros decem et octo redigendo* (*Dig.*, I, 2, 41). Connected with this movement there is a work by Cicero, which has not come down to us, but whose title *De jure civile in artem redigendo* speaks for itself. From these times onwards, Roman jurisprudence will make attempts at definitions and classifications into genera and species. The systematizing approach will become more and more obvious in the didactic works, as an attempt to organize the juridical subject matter with the aim of making its teaching easier. Thus, in the second century, Gaius' *Institutas* will offer a threefold systematization into *personae-res-actiones,* which will later become widespread in legal science. The idea of system will prevail until the end of antiquity and will be present in the juridical task performed by Emperor Justinian. It is necessary to point out, however, that the systematization in question does not consist in the derivation of new juridical norms coming from previously established ones; it is rather a question of gathering in a coherent whole the traditional juridical material that was scattered.

IV.

The first medieval centuries witnessed the desuetude of the systematic ideal. Thus, when in the 12th century the renaissance of legal science takes place in Italy, the Glossators will study the Roman legal texts trying to avoid the contradictions that might exist between them, and trying to render applicable their solutions to the various disputes arising in everyday life. Irnerius and his followers limited themselves to writing marginal or interlinear notes in the classical texts. The order of the exposition was that of the texts themselves, with no application of principles or axioms. Not until the appearance of the school of the Post-Glossators did the situation begin to change. By means of a series of logical operations the Post-Glossators sought *ratio legis* in *Corpus Juris.* They conceived the former as a fragment of natural reason. Cino da Pistoia clearly expresses this: *multum est consideranda mens et ratio legislatoris et ubi possit colligi mens et ratio, quae est idem, ab ea est concludendum.* Finally, in 16th century France the attempt to elaborate a juridical system is once again made, and this tendency spreads throughout the European continent, paving the road for the school of Hugo Grotius and his followers.

The natural law jurists of the 17th and 18th centuries conceived law as a rational product, in which no element deriving from historic experience could be found. Rationalistic metaphysics was characterized by the use of the mathematical method. Law was the expression of human reason as translated by the legislator, who had to elaborate the juridical subject matter with the elegance and precision used by a mathematician for the demonstration of a theorem. Starting from certain given principles, the jurist, by means of the deductive and rational method, could derive the rest of the constitutive norms of law. The notion of system as applied to the juridical field was at its height; but system was not regarded in the sense given to this concept by Roman jurists, that is, as an ordering factor of previously existent matter, but as a rigid structure based on deduction, and in which all the conditions are given of scientific knowledge as conceived since Aristotle's time.

At the beginning of the 19th century the advent of the Historical School conceived law as belonging to the world of experience. This, however, did not imply that systematizing reason should be set aside. According to Savigny, *Volksgeist* is the original source of law; but, as the spirit of the people, its performance is not rational, but intuitive: concrete human behaviours are perceived by intuition, and these form the *juridical relations* between individuals, which as a whole constitute *juridical institutes*. The *juridical institute* has an organic nature, made up of a group of human relations. Every particular *juridical relation* is always a part of *juridical institutes*, and, in turn, the institutes do not exist independent of each other; on the contrary, they have an organic relation, thus forming a unique system. The conscience of the people perceives these *juridical institutes*, and, by the means of a subsequent rational process, the various rules in their logical form begin to develop. The sort of balance between an empirical element and a rational one that we find in Savigny's work is set aside by Puchta, according to whom system loses its organic character and adopts a decidedly abstract aspect. Propositions intertwine forming a pyramid, in which some of them derive from others and condition each other. Savigny speaks about *juridical institutes* and organic connection; Puchta will deal with *juridical propositions* and logical connections. Rather than an actual process, whereby society gives impulse to the development of law, what matters is the internal development of juridical concepts. The historic development of law takes place within the system as it unfolds itself. From this moment onwards, with *Begriffsjurisprudenz* and the conceptualistic orientations that succeeded it on the one hand, and the sociological tendencies that fought against them on the other, the problem posed is that of the relationship between juridical reason and experience. Analyzing this one step further, we could state that the question ultimately lies in wondering about the limits of the abstract reason that has traditionally been used by juridical science, and in discovering how far its use has conditioned the development of law.

V.

Abstract reason is an adequate instrument for the knowledge of physical objects, which present the features of independence and immutability typical of beings like those conceived by the Hellenic mind. This abstract reason, which puts us in contact with a world understood as a group of various substances, is an analytical and discursive reason that separates the elements to reconstruct artificially the whole. The idea of system is inherent in it.

Now, ever since the Greeks, man had been conceived as substance, and for that reason jurists, in their attempt to apprehend his essence, made use of abstract reason, which they considered an adequate instrument to have access to this essence. But man is not a self-contained substance, like stones, animals, or the various objects that surround him. His essence lies in a perpetual task: he is forever interrelating with his environment. All the other beings present a fixed nature, but in man nothing is stable. For that reason it has been rightly said that man is not a fixed substance that always remains the same underneath, notwithstanding accidental and successive changes. He is essentially an open being, which always comes out of itself, projecting itself towards the future. As was previously said, Wittgenstein held the view that substance is what exists independently of what happens. In this definition we find the two features that have characterized the notion of being ever since Greek times: its stability and its independence. Both features may be applied to natural objects, but not to human reality, which is inseparable from the behaviour of a human being.

Legal norms are conceptual structures by way of which we perceive the sense that a certain human behaviour has for law. Now behaviour does not admit of being divided into its constituent elements. Far from it, an adequate understanding of every human act involves the perception of its sense, which implies the global intuition of that conduct. Man is a totality of sense that unfolds itself throughout time, the different moments of its trajectory not being separable. These moments influence each other, forming a continuity.

The Western mind has attempted to apprehend the essence of man by means of abstract reason, which can provide access to an immutable, substantial reality; but it has not perceived that man is not a ready-made, immobile, self-contained being; pervaded with temporality, he is in a constant flow; his essential mutability cannot be ignored. It is therefore imperative to set aside from our field this abstract conceptualization of reality, since it is not adequate for the correct understanding of human behaviour, to which legal norms unavoidably must refer. Abstract reason must be replaced by a concrete reason that takes charge of the peculiarities granting each individual and each historical period their uniqueness within their temporal mutability. Legal thought must free itself from the prevalence of abstract, systematizing reason, which often binds it to anachronic solutions, and must open itself to the joyful spectacle of flowing human life, trying to reflect it as it is, and thus reclaiming the meaning that knowledge had in the origins of Western thought: an unveiling factor of a hidden reality.

A MODEL OF LEGAL REASONING

By Aleksander Peczenik, Lund

The purpose of this paper is to describe and justify some particular features of reasoning in legal practice and in legal research.

I. Legal Practice and Legal Dogmatics

All jurists know that some legal cases are "hard". Justification of them involves other reasons than those referring to the enacted law and description of the case; *inter alia,* it involves moral evaluations.

Legal essays, handbooks and monographs often include comments on such cases. In Continental Europe, such comments belong to *legal dogmatics* ("doctrinal study of law", "analytically-evaluative study of the substance of law".[1] The German word for it is *Rechtsdogmatik).* Legal dogmatics consists in the interpretation and systematization of legal norms. It is often connected with such kinds of "legal science" as legal history, sociology, jurisprudence, comparative law, etc. Legal dogmatics is more systematic and less case-oriented than Anglo-American analysis. Yet, both legal dogmatics and its Anglo-American counterpart use methods in principle similar to judicial method, although the legal scholars have no power to decide cases. The differences are secondary: Legal dogmatics deals with changing examples of many real and imaginary cases. Its orientation is general, abstract and often hypothetical: it says that *if* a value-statement *W* is accepted, one should do *X*.

Legal dogmatics constructs various sorts of "theories".[2] Some "theories" develop general principles, for example the principle that punishment shall serve the purpose of reforming the criminal; of retribution; of deterring the criminal or others from committing crimes, and so on. Other "theories" develop fundamental concepts, for instance those of causation in the law;[3] describe legal institutions, for example marriage;

[1] *Robert S. Summers* has suggested the latter term.

[2] Concerning this classification, cf. *R. Dreier,* Zur Theoriebildung in der Jurisprudenz, in: Recht und Gesellschaft. Festschrift für Helmut Schelsky, Berlin 1978, p. 106 ff.

[3] Cf. *A. Peczenik,* Causes and Damages, Lund 1979, passim.

perform systematizations of a whole branch of the law, for example civil law, etc.

II. Criteria of Law, Norms of Legal Reasoning and Evaluations

European legal scholars often assume the distinction between three different operations (or stages) involved in legal reasoning, that is, (a) establishing the fact that a given norm system as a whole, for example the Swedish law, is a *legal* system (not merely a system of conventional habits or extra-legal norms); (b) establishing legal validity of the sources of the law in a given legal system; and (c) establishing the content of legal norms. Each operation involves both an application of socially established criteria *and* an evaluative justification, but the relative importance of the established criteria seems to be greatest as regards the first stage while the relative importance of evaluations is greatest as regards the third.

Neither judges nor legal dogmaticians have given much attention to the first step. Yet, their reasonings *assume* this step. A legal system they discuss must thus fulfil many (although not all) of the following established criteria. This system is hierarchical: its higher-order norms partly determine how the lower-order norms must be created[4]; the legal system is by and large operational; it claims to be the supreme norm system[5] with the sole right to the physical exercise of force in its territory[6] and with the authority to regulate any type of behavior[7]; it is frequently interpreted by professional lawyers, using noticeably technical methods; and so on. Yet, if the norm system fulfils many criteria of law but is *strikingly immoral*, many people would not recognize it as legal. This shows that an evaluative step is needed to pass from the established criteria of law to the conclusion that a norm system is legal.

The role of evaluations is greater concerning the second and especially the third step. In the context of justification, reasonings in legal practice and legal dogmatics can be criticised or defended, found to be right or wrong. There are not only repeated acts of reasoning but also some norms of legal reasoning. One can classify these norms in the way presented in Figure 1.

---

[4] Cf. *H. Kelsen*, Reine Rechtslehre, 2nd ed., Wien 1960, p. 228 ff.

[5] Cf. *J. Raz*, The Authority of Law, Oxford 1979, p. 118 ff.

[6] Cf. *Kelsen* (note 4), p. 34 ff.; *K. Olivecrona*, Law as Fact, 1st ed., Copenhagen-London 1939, p. 171 ff. and 2nd ed., London 1971, p. 271 ff.; *A. Ross*, On Law and Justice, London 1958, p. 34.

[7] See note 5.

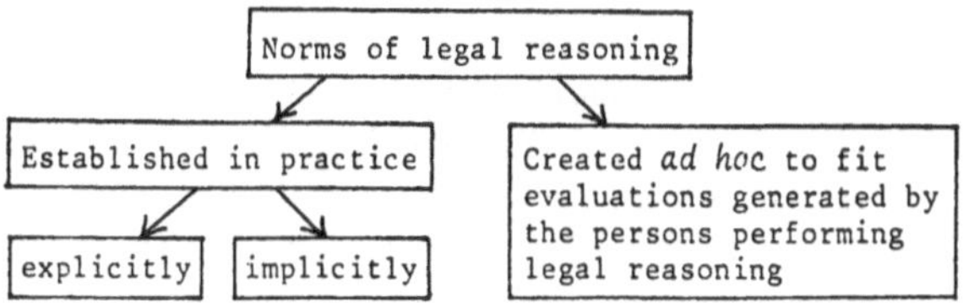

Fig. 1

Some of these norms are thus established in practice, either explicitly, that is, formulated in statutes, precedents, juristic literature, etc., or implicitly, that is, as assumed when one creates a model (an idealization, a construction) that aims at expressing legal practice as a coherent totality. Let me mention two types of such norms.[8]

1. The *source norms* help to identify the sources of the law (the second step of legal reasoning, see *supra*). Some examples: All courts and authorities *must* use statutes in the justification of their decisions, if any are applicable. They *should* use applicable precedents and legislative preparatory materials. In some cases, they *should* pay attention to custom. They *may* use, *inter alia,* the following material: custom, draft statutes, repealed statutes, foreign statutes; juristic literature, decisions of private or semiprivate organizations such as Swedish Press Council; etc.

2. The *reasoning norms* help to derive non-written legal norms from the sources of the law, or to derive concrete legal judgments from the legal sources and non-written legal norms (the third step of legal reasoning, see *supra*). Let us discuss three kinds of these.

a) *Interpretation norms.* Examples: One must not interpret similar words occurring in different parts of the same statute in different ways unless strong reasons for such an interpretation exist. One must not interpret words occurring in a statute in a way conflicting with the ordinary usage unless there are strong reasons for such an interpretation.

b) *Construction norms.* Examples: Only very strong reasons can justify a reasoning by analogy leading to the conclusion that an error exists in a statute. One should construe restrictively provisions imposing burdens or restrictions on a person unless strong reasons require another interpretation.

c) *Collision norms.* Examples: Whenever one discovers a *prima facie* collision of legal norms one should eliminate it either by reinterpreting

[8] Cf. *A. Peczenik*, Rationality of Legal Justification, in: Archiv für Rechts- und Sozialphilosophie LXVIII (1982), p. 143 ff.; *Peczenik*, The Basis of Legal Justification, Lund 1983, p. 36 ff. and 54—69.

these norms or by arranging a priority order between them. Whenever one reinterprets or ranks legal norms one should do so in a manner which one can repeatedly use when confronted with relevantly similar collisions between other norms. The *must*-sources of the law have a *prima facie* priority before the *should*-sources and these before the *may*-sources. When a higher norm is incompatible with a norm of a lower standing, one must apply the higher. If one abandons the priority orders in a concrete case, one should justify one's departure with strong reasons.

There are a great number of reasoning norms. Most of them express *socially established moral evaluations.* At the same time, they have *a weakly analytic* (conceptual) character, in the following sense:[9] One who is *simultaneously* trying to refute or reject many such norms and yet also trying to perform a *legal* reasoning is likely either to be thinking *incoherently,* or else deviating from the mode of *interpretation* of such concepts as "legal reasoning", "legal sources", "construction of statutes", etc. that most *jurists* would find *acceptable.*[10] On the other hand, one can disregard some of the norms and formulate new ones, if there are important reasons for doing so. Such norms are thus partly embedded in the legal practice and partly re-made *ad hoc* in order to fit evaluations generated by the persons performing legal reasoning. When disregarding or modifying an established norm of legal reasoning, one relies upon one's evaluations. Evaluation thus has a decisive role in legal reasoning.

III. The Quasi-Descriptive Character of Contextually Sufficient Legal Justification in "Hard Cases"

Juristic conclusions, judicial decisions etc. can be either justified (a) within the system of legal reasoning or (b) outside of it. The former I call a *contextually sufficient legal justification.* The latter can be either (b 1) a *deep (fundamental) justification* which provides support or criticism to the premises the jurists take for granted or (b 2) a justification of another type, e. g., historical or sociological. Contextually sufficient legal justification *presupposes* some support from the legal sources, source norms and reasoning norms. Various parts of it may, however, require deep justification in various contexts, for example if one wishes to convince moralists, philosophers, political opponents, and so on. The question "Why shall we follow the Swedish Constitution?"

---

[9] Cf. *Peczenik,* Rationality (note 8), p. 149; *Peczenik,* The Basis (note 8), pp. 73—76.

[10] Cf. *A. Aarnio,* On Truth and the Acceptability of Interpretative Propositions in Legal Dogmatics, in: RECHTSTHEORIE Beiheft 2 (1981), p. 46 ff.

makes no sense if asked during a legal trial but may be well-motivated at an Anarchist meeting.[11]

The problem, now, is how to deep-justify the contextually sufficient legal justification (that is, legal reasoning). Legal reasoning involves two different ideally distinguishable components. The first one is a true *description* of the legal sources, established evaluations, source norms and reasoning norms. The second is a continual *creation* of new evaluations that tell one whether to follow or not these sources and norms.[12] Yet, legal reasoning is expected to give us *knowledge* of "the law", often identified with the legal sources. Courts and authorities in many countries have a legal duty to *apply* the law. Most jurists thus interpret the ambiguous phrase "legal reasoning" in such a way as to imply that had the court made most of its decisions without support from the pre-existing legal sources, then the reasoning behind them would not, by definition, have been legal.[13] Neither would it have been "legal", had the court systematically neglected the established norms of legal reasoning (see section II *supra in fine*) that assure, among other things, the backing-up of judicial decisions by legal sources (see section V *infra*). Legal reasoning is *quasi-descriptive*.[14] One *claims* to base the conclusions on the sources of the law but in fact one makes a compromise between these sources, established source norms and reasoning norms, and own evaluations. This situation is presented in Figure 2.

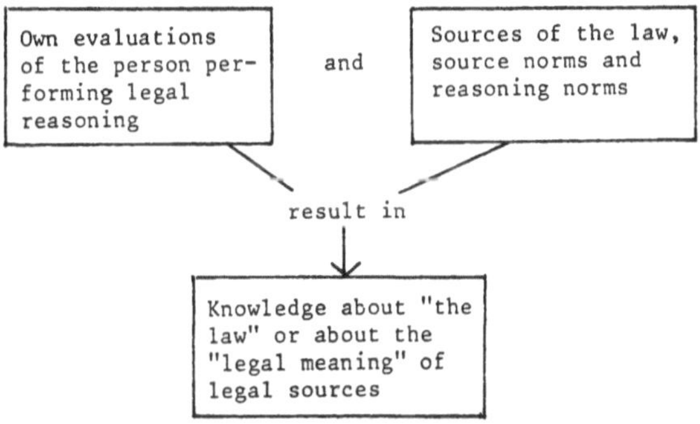

Fig. 2

[11] Cf. *Peczenik*, Rationality (note 8), p. 139; *Peczenik*, The Basis (note 8), p. 1. The terms "contextually sufficient" and "deep" are suggested by Robert S. Summers.

[12] Cf. *Peczenik*, Wartość naukowa dogmatyki prawa, Kraków 1966, p. 72; Doctrinal Study of Law and Science, in: Österreichische Zeitschrift für öffentliches Recht XVII (1967), p. 138; Rationality (note 8), p. 138; The Basis (note 8), p. 76 ff.

[13] Cf. *N. MacCormick*, Legal Reasoning and Legal Theory, Oxford 1978, p. 53.

[14] Cf. *Peczenik*, Rationality (note 8), p. 138 ff.; The Basis (note 8), p. 76 ff.

Consider, for example, Section 4 of the old Swedish Instrument of Government *(Regeringsformen)*, derogated as late as 1969. According to this constitutional norm, "the King has the right to govern the realm alone ...". The actually applied norm was rather, "The *Government* has the *executive* power". Can one *read* the word "the King" as meaning "the Government, responsible to the Parliament", and the words "right to govern the realm alone" as meaning "executive power"? Legal reasoning in hard cases does not merely produce true descriptions of the literary sense of the enacted law. One must thus choose one or more of the following ways to characterize legal reasoning:

1. Legal reasoning is *unjustifiable,*[15] wrong, irrational, and so on.
2. The jurists *discover* the special *expert-meaning* of the legal sources.[16]
3. The jurists *discover* the *real valid law* which is not identical with the legal sources.[17]
4. When the jurist tells us what the "valid law" is, he actually formulates his *own moral opinion,* telling himself or others what to do. He justifies his opinion by *weighing* his individual value-intuitions, general principles he endorses, and the established sources, source norms and reasoning norms, and presenting a *reflective equilibrium* of these reasons.[18]
5. The jurists *transform* the established sources, source norms and reasoning norms into something else,[19] that is, into the *interpreted* "valid law".

Some comments to these:

1. The thesis that there is something fundamentally wrong with legal reasoning is not acceptable, since it contradicts centuries of social practice.

[15] Cf. e.g. *Ross* (note 6), pp. 135—6 and 155 ff.

[16] When the "expert meaning" changes, most jurists would *not* say that the statutory norm has changed but merely that its interpretation (and perhaps the inference rules) have changed. Cf. *C. E. Alchourrón/E. Bulygin,* Normative Systems, Wien/New York 1971, p. 92.

[17] *R. Dworkin,* Taking Rights Seriously, London 1977 (quoted from 6th printing, Cambridge, Mass. 1977, with Appendix), p. 87, formulates "the rights thesis, that judicial decisions enforce existing political rights" (cf. pp. 82—90, 31—5 and 68—71). The rights are "described" by principles (p. 90), and these express "a sense of appropriateness developed in the (legal) profession and the public over time" (p. 40). In brief: the jurists use their sense of appropriateness to discover the legal rights.

[18] Cf. *Dworkin* (note 17), p. 159 ff. On reflective equilibrium in general, cf. *J. Rawls,* A Theory of Justice, Oxford 1971, p. 20 ff.

[19] Cf. *A. Aarnio/R. Alexy/A. Peczenik,* The Foundation of Legal Reasoning, in: RECHTSTHEORIE 12 (1981), pp. 136—158. Cf. *Peczenik,* Non-equivalent Transformations and the Law, in: RECHTSTHEORIE Beiheft 1 (1979), p. 163 ff., and *Alchourrón/Bulygin* (note 16), p. 92 ff.

2. The thesis that the jurists discover the "expert-meaning" of the legal sources implies either that the same words and expressions have an "expert-meaning" when occurring in the law and a different meaning when occurring elsewhere or that they have both meanings in all contexts. Moreover, all evaluative considerations, influencing legal reasoning, would by definition affect the "expert-meaning" of the legal sources.

3. The thesis that the jurists discover the "real valid law", not identical with the legal sources, implies a controversial ontology and epistemology, according to which one uses *evaluations* to *discover* something.

4. The thesis that the jurist develops his own moral opinion and ascribes it to the "valid law" implies that he means one thing, that is, "I, or you, ought (morally) to do *X*", and says another, that is, "The valid law says: do *X*!".

5. The thesis that the jurists *transform* the established material into the interpreted law contradicts the jurists' claim that they merely *discover* or describe the pre-existing law.

In my opinion, the combination of the fourth and fifth theses is *necessary* to understand and deep-justify legal reasoning. Affirming these theses, one *may* also adopt the second or the third opinion, if one's philosophical views permit this.

IV. Transformations in the Law

Legal reasoning thus involves *transformations,* that is, either changes of a "theory" about valid law, or proposed changes of the valid law itself. One backs up these transformations with non-deductive steps ("jumps") involving either a precise interpretation or a change of original premises, such as statutes, precedents, other legal sources, source norms and reasoning norms embedded in legal practice, etc.[20, 21]

A "jump" from *p* to *q* is performed if and only if the following conditions are fulfilled:

---

[20] One can classify justifiable inferences in the law as follows: (1) *deductive* inferences, (2) *"jumps"*. The "jumps" in the law can be (a) ordinary, (b) specifically legal. The reasons for performing a legal "jump" may be manifold, for example the vagueness of language and the controversiality of problems discussed; but the foremost reason is the fact that the jurist tends to adapt his own evaluations as well as the established legal sources, source norms and reasoning norms to mutually correspond with one another.

[21] "Jumps" occur not only in the law. For example, the step from observational data to any scientific theory is a "jump".

a) The truth (or rightness, etc.) of *p* is a sufficient reason for the truth (or rightness) of *q*; and

b) *p* does not deductively entail *q*.[22]

I try to present here as large a part of legal reasoning as possible as a form of logical deduction. This mode of presentation helps to remove concealed contradictions, ambiguities and other errors. Moreover, it shows that the premises and inference rules of legal reasoning, on which the deduction is based, may require justification. One can thus convert a "jump" into a deductive reasoning by adding or changing some premises or inference rules.[23]

By definition, the added or changed premises or inference rules cannot be analytic (logically necessary). Yet, they *can be certain (evident) from the point of view of contextually sufficient legal justification.* Jurists can thus reformulate their reasoning in a *complete* manner, that is, arrive at a formulation of premises and inference rules that needs no deeper support as far as the legal audience is concerned. The existence of "jumps" in the contextually sufficient legal justification is thus a contingent fact: Jurists do not formulate their reasoning in a complete manner but they could do so. On the other hand, the existence of "jumps" is *logically necessary* within deep justification. One can thus question and modify the *legally* certain premises or inference rules. For example, a philosopher can doubt the legally indubitable new interpretation of the old Swedish Instrument of Government (see section III *supra*). In particular, no *evaluative* premises and inference rules can be indubitable. When one doubts the added inference rules or premises, one can support them by others. One can then reformulate one's reasoning, thus *replacing* the previously added premises or inference rules with new ones constituting their justification. But the latter are not evident, either. Since the supporting premises and inference rules themselves require a backing-up, this process of reformulating one's reasonings has no logical end. The set of premises and inference rules may change and grow indefinitely. *One cannot convert a "jump" into a deductive reasoning by adding*

---

[22] For earlier versions of this definition, see *Aarnio/Alexy/Peczenik* (note 19), p. 137; *Peczenik*, Rationality (note 8), pp. 140—1; *Peczenik*, The Basis (note 8), p. 3.

[23] On inference rules cf. *Peczenik*, The Basis (note 8), pp. 1, 4 ff. and 73 ff. Cf. *Toulmin*, The Uses of Argument, Cambridge 1958 (paperback 1976, pp. 98 and 109 ff.). In principle, an inference rule can be replaced by a corresponding premise; cf. *E. Nagel*, The Structure of Science, New York 1961, p. 138.

One can often replace a premise by a corresponding inference rule, especially if the premise is (a) on the meta-level, (b) normative, (c) presupposed by most jurists (and disputable only in the context of deep justification), and (d) used in many different legal reasonings.

a finite number of premises or inference rules that are certain from the point of view of deep justification.

Moreover, one has some room for a choice between many possibilities of adding or changing premises or inference rules. The conclusion of a "jump" follows from any member of a family of sets, each containing some originally accepted premises and inference rules together with some added ones. For example, one can back up a given interpretation of a statute by adding premises either about the "will of the legislator" or about the value of the consequences of the statute. Since such sets include a great number of premises or inference rules, some of them occurring at a remote place in the chain of justification of the originally adopted ones, they may be mutually incompatible. One may be unable to arrange them into a non-arbitrary priority order.[24] To justify an ordering of the sets of added or changed premises, one may need another "jump", convertible to a deduction by means of another set of added or changed premises, and so on. In effect, one obtains in this way a "tree" of premises presented in Figure 3.

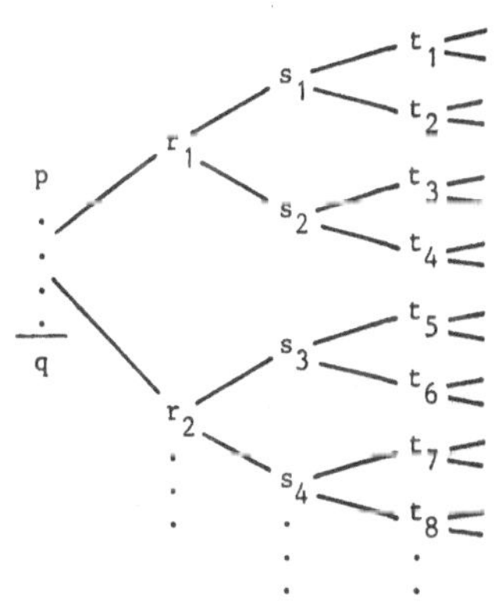

Fig. 3

[24] Cf. *Peczenik,* The Basis (note 8), pp. 70—1. Similar problems occur as regards implicit rejection of norms; cf. *C. E. Alchourrón/E. Bulygin,* The Expressive Conception of Norms, in: R. Hilpinen (ed.), New Studies in Deontic Logic, Dordrecht 1981, p. 109 ff.

When a non-arbitrary priority order is impossible, one must create an arbitrary one, *ad hoc.* One does this in a manner that *O. Weinberger* (Die Pluralität der Normensysteme, in: Archiv für Rechts- und Sozialphilosophie LVII (1971), p. 399 ff.) calls *Zusammenschluss.* Cf. *Weinberger,* Analytisch-dialektische Gerechtigkeitstheorie, in: RECHTSTHEORIE Beiheft 3 (1981), p. 329: "Begründungsstrukturen, die nicht in Form *einer* 'Prämissen-Konklusion'-Kette dargestellt werden können", and p. 330: "...keine Regeln, welche die Gerechtigkeitsüberlegung algorithmisierbar machen würden". These remarks concern reasonings about justice but are applicable to legal reasoning as well.

In this "tree" r_1 and r_2 designate sets of premises making the passage from p to q deductive; $s_1 \ldots s_4$ and $t_1 \ldots t_8$ indicate sets of premises of different orders, deductively justifying r_1 and r_2.

The following classification of "jumps" corresponds to the classification of evaluative operations in legal reasoning (section II *supra*). (a) The *transformation into the law* is needed in order to know that the norm system as a whole is a legal system and ought to be observed from the legal point of view.[25] (b) The *source transformation* is needed to derive the conclusion about validity of some legal sources (e. g. precedents) from other sources.[26] (c) The *norm transformation* is needed to derive non-written legal norms and concrete legal judgments from the legal sources.[27] (I have called the source transformation and the norm transformation *transformations inside the law*.[28])

One can classify the inference norms of legal reasoning in a similar manner: (a) the *Grundnorm*, corresponding to the transformation *into* the law;[29] (b) the source norms; (c) the legal reasoning norms; see section II *supra*.

One may single out the following ways to provide a deep justification of transformations in the law:

a) The transformations follow, to some extent, a set of established inference norms. This set, taken as a whole, is in a weak sense analytic (see section II *supra in fine)*.

b) The transformations are rational in a weak sense (see section V *infra*).

c) The structure of legal reasoning involving these transformations is, to some extent, analogous to the structure of science (see section VI *infra*).

d) The transformations are supported by moral reasons (see section VII *infra)*.

e) The transformations are supported by what I call our form of life (defined in section VIII *infra*).

---

[25] Cf. *Aarnio/Alexy/Peczenik* (note 19), p. 142 ff. My concept of a "legal point of view" is less "detached" than *Raz*'s (Legal Validity, in: Archiv für Rechts- und Sozialphilosophie LXIII (1977), p. 346) and refers to a compromise between one's own evaluations and socially established norms and meta-norms. Cf. *Peczenik*, The Basis (note 8), pp. 28—9.

[26] See note 8.

[27] See note 9.

[28] See notes 8 and 9.

[29] Cf. *Aarnio/Alexy/Peczenik* (note 19), p. 142 ff. and a much more complete discussion in *Peczenik*, The Basis (note 8), pp. 25—31. The *Grundnorm* is a bridging principle that establishes a link between the legal and the moral 'ought'; cf. *H.-N. Castañeda*, Thinking and Doing, Dordrecht 1975, p. 333.

V. Rationality of Legal Reasoning

Legal reasoning, involving transformations, is rational in a weak sense.

A necessary condition of rationality is the practice of *giving reasons.* All reasons can be reconstructed from the following "atomic constituents": facts, values and logical inferences. In legal reasoning, the class of facts includes the legal sources and the socially established source norms and reasoning norms. The class of values includes evaluations that the person who interprets and applies the law endorses and recommends for others. The class of logical inferences includes inferences that are correct in all or in some interpretations of vague words (see section II *supra in fine*). "Giving reasons" for a conclusion is the same as "supporting" it. If *p* is a reason for *q*, *p supports q*. Legal reasoning thus receives support from both *legal sources* and *moral considerations.* The former is expressed in all reasoning norms demanding respect for statutes, precedents, etc. Another example: Only very strong reasons can justify a reasoning by analogy leading to the conclusion that an error exists in the text of the statute. Morality also supports juristic conclusions, in three different ways. Some moral principles may support a specific cluster of legal norms. For example, the principle "promises ought to be kept" supports a large part of the law of contracts. Second, many norms of legal reasoning are oriented towards generality (see below), and thus towards universalizability and justice, that is, towards important aspects of morality. Finally, I will argue (see section VII *infra*) that morality is capable of justifying even the fact that a concrete legal reasoning may be morally doubtful.

Reasons can be more or less *good. Sufficient* conditions for the conclusion that a given reason is good, that is, sufficient conditions of rationality, may vary across different fields. *Necessary* conditions for a reason's goodness are of the following sort. Good reasons fulfil the demands of logical *consistency* and are oriented towards two regulative ideas, the idea that one should be able to produce a *coherent* totality of reasons, in which a number of statements support a number of others in a complex system, and the idea that one should be able to express both description and evaluation in *general* terms. The regulative idea of generality manifests itself in the use of *concepts* and *theories,* and in *morality.* When using concepts, we put the same label on a *class* of things. Theories are often general. Morality requires *universality* of norms and evaluations. One should here mention *Kant*'s categorical imperative, *Hare*'s idea of universalizability,[30, 31] several conceptions of formal justice, etc.

Let us now return to *legal* reasoning. It is oriented towards *consistency*, as all the collision norms (section II *supra*) amply show. Legal reasoning is also oriented towards *generality*. One must mention the following source norms and reasoning norms: All courts and authorities must use statutes, and these are general. They should use precedents and thus promote generality through treating similar cases similarly. One must not interpret similar words in legal sources in different ways. One should treat any collision between legal norms in a manner which one can repeatedly use in similar situations. The very idea of statutory analogy also promotes generality, since it demands that like cases be treated alike; all the reasoning norms about the use of statutory analogy thus tell the lawyer to what extent he is supposed to promote generality. Every concrete legal judgment must be derivable from a universal normative premise, along with further premises and inference rules. Moreover, legal reasoning is oriented towards *coherence*, that is, towards a many-sided and complex support from legal sources and moral evaluations (see *supra*).

According to *Robert Alexy*, not only consistency, coherence and generality but also efficiency, testability and sincerity are principles of practical rationality.[32] The requirement of efficiency is quite complex, but its important part, the "goal-rationality" *(Zweckrationalität)* is a special case of coherence, that is, coherence of goals and means. The demand that one's views must be (intersubjectively) testable is related to the requirement of support: *A* can test *B*'s opinion only if good reasons support it. Sincerity is, finally, a condition of consistency and coherence between two levels: that of belief and that of speech. Efficiency, testability and sincerity are thus *conceptually* less fundamental than the ideas of consistency, generality and coherence. Yet they certainly make our insight into the nature of rationality richer. Moreover, they may be very important when one weighs various principles in order to solve a legal or moral case. In many contexts, I would thus impart rather more significance to the principle of efficiency than to the principle of generality.

---

[30] Cf. e. g. *R. M. Hare*, Principles, in: Proceedings of the Aristotelian Society 73 (1972), p. 4. Universalizability requires that ethical precepts shall not use proper names and definite descriptions.

[31] According to *Hare* (Moral Thinking, Oxford 1981, e. g. pp. 226—7), the requirement of universalizability compels us to adopt utilitarianism, that is, the view that morality demands maximal satisfaction of other persons' preferences. In my opinion, however, a moral person does not adapt his judgment to other persons' *actual* preferences. To be moral, he must adopt the internal point of view and weigh his own actual preferences against the *hypothetical* preferences that *he* would have in the other persons' situations.

[32] Cf. *Aarnio/Alexy/Peczenik* (note 19), p. 266 ff.

Robert Alexy has given several examples of the role of the above-mentioned principles in legal reasoning. Moreover, he has elaborated 22 rules and 6 forms of argument, defining rationality in a more precise manner.[33] Alexy's theory is thus *stronger* than the analysis of rationality that I have presented above but seems to be consistent with it. Generally speaking, the more precisely one formulates a theory of rationality, the closer will be its connection with one's own culture, and the more alien it will be for people belonging to some other traditions. One can thus develop a theory of rationality as a "pyramid" of more and more culture-bound ideas (Figure 4).

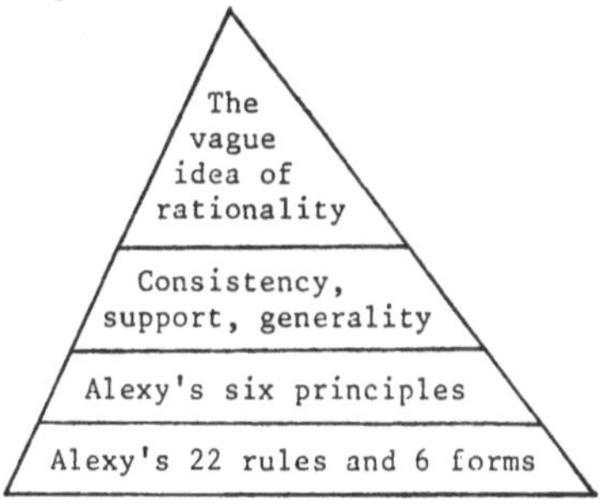

Fig. 4

We must, however, interrupt here our discussion about rationality and state the main point: The jurist combines the established legal materials with his own evaluations, and *rationally transforms* this mixture into the interpreted "valid law", or into the legal "expert-meaning" of the sources of the law; or into his own justified opinion what to do from the legal point of view. This is graphically presented in Figure 5.

Rationality, that is, consistency combined with an *optimum* of generality and coherence, is thus a complex yardstick of deep-justifiability of legal reasoning. The *total practice* of legal reasoning fulfils, *to some extent,* the demands of rationality. On the other hand, these demands are *vague.* One cannot say how general and how coherent good legal reasons should be. Neither can one say what stronger demands of rationality are embedded in our culture here and now. This means that one cannot state precisely *how great* the rationality of a given particular legal reasoning is. No algorithm of rational legal reasoning, that is, of rational legal transformations, exists.

---

[33] *R. Alexy,* Theorie der juristischen Argumentation, Frankfurt a. M. 1978, passim.

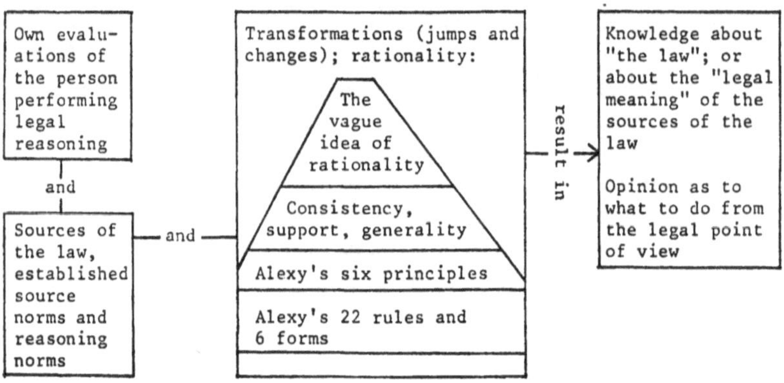

Fig. 5

VI. Legal Reasoning and Theory of Science

Science is the most rational form of human activity. Let us thus put the question whether the theory of science provides a deeper justification of the thesis that legal reasoning is rational. Many competing views about scientific rationality exist in modern theories of science. According to the so-called *inductionism,* a theory is sound if it constitutes an inductive generalization of the observed data.[34] According to *Karl Popper,* the proper method of science consists in formulating bold hypotheses; one should try to falsify hypotheses and accept them as long as they are not falsified.[35] I *assume* that induction is sufficient to *reconstruct* all scientific reasonings[36] *and* that *if* there is an order that rules the universe, induction is the only method of discovering this order.[37] At the same time, I *assume* Popper's view that the idea of *truth* gives purpose to the activity of science[38] *and* his view that science evolves by trial and error. But one needs not only the logical reconstruction of science and the insight into its purpose but also *effective criteria* of its progress. Popper has argued that induction does not provide such a criterion.[39] But Popper's theory does not do this either. Assume that theoretical physics combined with the hypothesis of expanding universe implies a given

[34] An old theory; cf. *J. S. Mill,* A System of Logic Ratiocinative and Inductive, 8th ed., Book III, Chs. 8—10, London 1866.

[35] Cf. *K. R. Popper,* The Logic of Scientific Discovery, New York 1959, p. 40 ff. and passim.

[36] Cf. *H. Reichenbach,* The Theory of Probability, Berkeley 1949, p. 429 ff.

[37] Cf. *Reichenbach,* On the Justification of Induction, in: The Journal of Philosophy 37 (1940), p. 97 ff.

[38] Cf. *K. R. Popper,* Objective Knowledge, Oxford 1972, pp. 29—30.

[39] Cf. *Popper,* The Logic (note 35), p. 28 ff.

position of a star but the observed position is different. In such a situation, an astronomer rather assumes that the observation is unreliable or that some auxiliary hypotheses would explain the contradiction. Only seldom does he challenge theoretical physics. How can one then falsify a theory?[40] Several sociologically oriented philosophers of science have formulated various criteria of scientific progress. According to *Thomas Kuhn,* one should judge scientific theories as parts of a broader totality called a paradigm. A *paradigm* includes a concrete scientific achievement, imitated by scientists in subsequent research, and a network of evaluations, norms, symbolic generalizations, basic beliefs, etc., shared by a group of scientists.[41] The idea of paradigms fits the deep philosophical insight that all experience is *holistic:* All data and theories affect each other. At the same time, it fits the practical necessity that a scientist cannot discuss everything at once, he must take some things for *granted* and thus *isolate* the part of universe he studies. For example, he takes for granted *Einstein's* relativity theory or, let us say, the basic idea that the purpose of science is to give true knowledge that corresponds with reality. According to *Aulis Aarnio,* the lawyers in a similar manner take for granted some philosophical assumptions concerning legal validity, a list of legal sources, source norms and reasoning norms, and some established evaluations.[42]

One can also express similar thoughts from another point of view, developed by *Imre Lakatos.*[43] A scientific *research program* (a series of theories) contains a *hard theory core* protected by auxiliary hypotheses; one ought to direct counter-examples against the auxiliary hypotheses, never against the theory core. Within the program, one develops increasingly complex theories. *Aart de Wild* has applied Lakatos's ideas to the *descriptive* component of legal reasoning.[44] Let us now apply them to its *evaluative* component. I shall assume that the *evaluations* continually created by the person performing legal reasoning are *analogous to*

---

[40] Cf. e. g. *N. Koertge,* Towards a New Theory of Scientific Inquiry, in: G. Radnizky/G. Andersson (eds.), Progress and Rationality in Science, Dordrecht-London 1978, p. 255.

[41] Cf. *T. S. Kuhn,* The Structure of Scientific Revolutions, 2nd ed., Chicago 1970, passim.

[42] Cf. *A. Aarnio,* On Paradigm Articulation in Legal Research, in: RECHTSTHEORIE Beiheft 3 (1981), p. 51 ff.; *E. Zuleta Puceiro,* System and Function in Legal Dogmatics, in: RECHTSTHEORIE Beiheft 2 (1981), p. 349 ff.; *J. Dalberg-Larsen,* Retsvidenskaben som samfundsvidenskab, Copenhagen 1977, passim.

[43] Cf. *I. Lakatos,* Falsification and the Methodology of Scientific Research Programmes, in: Lakatos/A. Musgrave (eds.), Criticism and the Growth of Knowledge, Cambridge 1970, p. 132 ff.

[44] Cf. *A. H. de Wild,* De Rationaliteit van het rechterlijk Oordeel, Deventer 1980, p. 55 ff.

observational data. Of course, we must pay attention to the epistemological and semantical difference between the practical evaluations and value-statements and, on the other hand, theoretical data and data-propositions. This difference is, however, compatible with the analogy between the position of evaluations in the *structure* of legal reasoning and the position of data in the structure of science. If evaluations are analogous to observational data, then the *sources of the law* are analogous to *theories.* Some of these sources, namely the *must-* and *should-*sources, such as statutes and precedents, are analogous to the *theory core* of the legal "reasoning program". When a jurist produces new "theories", or when he generates new evaluations (analogous to data), these "theories" and evaluations may affect the interpretation of the *must-* and *should-*sources (analogous to the theory core). Of course, the literal texts of these sources are fixed and may be changed only by the lawgiver or precedent-establishing courts. A scientist tries to interpret the theory core in such a way that apparent incompatibilities within it disappear; similarly, a jurist explains away incompatibilities in the sources of the law. At the same time, however, the *descriptive* component of legal reasoning implements various theories developed in social sciences, concerning, for example, the linguistic meaning of words used in the legal sources; causal correlations between judicial decisions and other social facts; attitudes prevailing in the society or in its "ruling circles", etc. These theories are based on the societal data in the usual sense. Consequently, a jurist treats the sources of the law in two different ways. If he regards his activity as a description of the sources, then the sources are analogous to observational data. But if he regards his activity as adaptation of the sources to his evaluation of the "demands of the life",[45] then the sources are analogous to a theory core.

The overall description of legal reasoning ensuing from this account is given in Figure 6.

Socially established sources and norms, analogous to socially established paradigms and theory cores, *support* the normative component of legal reasoning, thus increasing its coherence, testability and, generally speaking, rationality.

VII. Moral Justification of Legal Reasoning as a Whole

The comparison with science reveals also the following problem. Legal reasoning involves transformations whose result has a *dual nature.* From the theoretical point of view, the result is the interpreted *valid*

[45] Cf. *J. Wróblewski,* Zagadnienia teorii wykladni prawa ludowego, Warsaw 1959, p. 167 ff., on dynamical theories of statutory construction.

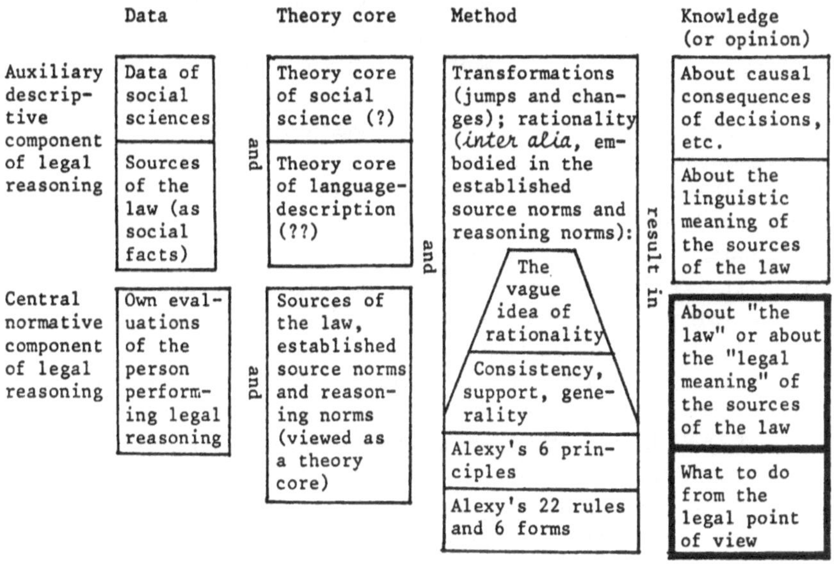

Fig. 6

law; or the legal *expert-meaning* of the sources of the law; or the *knowledge* about valid law and expert-meaning respectively. In the practical perspective, the result is the jurist's conclusion *what to do* from the legal point of view, that is, how to decide a case, how to advise a decider, etc. One must now answer two questions:

1. Why do the established sources, source norms and reasoning norms have any significance for the jurist's justified opinion about what to do? One may answer that the established sources and norms increase *certainty,* that is, both predictability and material justifiability of practical conclusions.[46] One can rely on others, that is, on legislators, precedent-creating judges and other jurists who endorse the source norms and reasoning norms. They probably have more accumulated skill, time and information, necessary to justify practical judgments. It is thus morally better for the society to establish an institutional system of legal sources, source norms and reasoning norms, even though it leads sometimes to morally doubtful conclusions, than to force societal actors to evaluate all the complex social situations autonomously.[47]

[46] Cf. *Peczenik,* The Basis (note 8), pp. 78 and 168; cf. also note 12.

[47] Cf. R. *Alexy,* Die Idee einer prozeduralen Theorie der juristischen Argumentation, in: RECHTSTHEORIE Beiheft 2 (1981), p. 186 ff. on "Notwendigkeit des Rechts"; cf. *Aarnio/Alexy/Peczenik* (note 19), p. 273 ff.

This justification of legal reasoning is coherent with the view that *all knowledge* needs some socially established starting points, paradigms, research programs, etc. (see section VI *supra* on *Kuhn*'s and *Lakatos*'s theories). Moreover, one can find an additional reason for the fact that *legal reasoning* relies upon established sources. A moral reasoning that pays no attention to the socially established sources and norms is, at least in the modern Western societies, much *less certain* than scientific reasoning. The history of modern moral opinions gives an impression of ad-hocness.[48] Assume that an evaluative moral "theory" is a system of more general and less general statements supporting each other. Now, the following phenomenon often occurs. Some statements, expressing one's evaluation of a concrete case (or, in a utilitarian view, describing some persons' preference in this case) are often incoherent with the "theory", that is, either inconsistent with it or insufficiently supported by it. If one tries to avoid these counterexamples, the level of precision of the whole "theory" tends to be low. If one tries to adapt the moral "theory" to the counterexample and to preserve the high level of exactitude, the changed "theory" tends to be incoherent with some other evaluations (or preferences). A gain of coherence at one end leads to a loss at the other.[49] It seems that, at least in our culture, moral justification can be protected against convincing counter-examples only if it approaches the *optimal balance achieved via* reflective equilibrium between *individual* values such as individual standards of action (e. g. justice, moral rights, inoffensiveness, benevolence, care or love) and individual goals (e. g. self-fulfillment, virtue, pleasure or happiness) and, on the other hand, *transpersonal* values, for example social goals (e. g. protection of freedom, order, welfare, or progress).[50] The "moral good" is not easily reducible to a single formula or principle. Each of the above-mentioned values can be a good reason of action. But when good reasons conflict with each other, one needs good reasons to choose between them. The same kind of values can be quoted on the "ground-floor" of moral discourse, at its meta-level, at a meta-meta-level, etc. One thus obtains a "tree" of reasons, that is, the "tree" of premises of a justificatory "jump" (see section IV *supra*). The "tree" changes over time, and one must construct and reconstruct it *ad hoc*, from case to case. This is the reason why we have so many competing theories of justice. If one, for example, emphasizes the connection between justice and *equality*, one tends to forget both the protection of ownership or other *entitlement* and *the needs of the*

---

[48] Cf. *A. Edel*, Ethical Judgment, pb. ed. London 1964, p. 28 ff.

[49] Cf. *Peczenik*, Rationality (note 8), p. 150 ff.; The Basis (note 8), p. 80 ff.

[50] Cf. *Peczenik*, Rationality (note 8), p. 151; The Basis (note 8), p. 112. On individual values, collective values and *Werkwerte* cf. e. g. *G. Radbruch*, Rechtsphilosophie, Stuttgart 1950, p. 147 ff.

"*weakest*" members of the society. If one respects entitlement, one tends to disregard both equality and the needs of the "weakest". Finally, if one respects the needs of the "weakest", one tends to disregard both equality and entitlement.[51] I cannot prove that moral "theories" *must* have this property of ad-hocness. But already the contingent fact that they actually have it in modern societies justifies the conclusion that *legal* reasoning needs more certain, socially established, starting-points than moral "theories" can give. This need of socially established basis of legal reasoning gives the sources of the law and the norms of legal reasoning their justificatory force.

2. But why is it better to establish the quasi-descriptive, and half-moral, legal discourse than to follow the enacted law literally, regardless of its moral quality? The *Western tradition* in fact speaks against the latter solution. This tradition is a complex and unique mixture[52] of such legal factors as the protection of an individual's entitlement and demand of an individual responsibility; such political factors as the existence of many competing states from which a dissident always could emigrate; religious and philosophical factors, like respect for human person; economic factors, like decentralized market economy; and administrative factors, such as development of relatively fair and impersonal bureaucracy. The quasi-descriptive legal reasoning is coherent with this tradition. The possibility of its progress depends on the progress of the tradition as a whole.[53]

Metaphorically speaking, a good jurist is not only an *egoist* following his own preferences, but also both a *moral person* whose conscience creatively decides how to pay attention to needs of others, and a *social person* who follows the established opinions expressed, *inter alia,* in the enacted law. The Western cultural tradition makes it possible for one to be all these three persons at once.

VIII. Justification and Form of Life

I have discussed five ways of providing a deep-justification of transformations in the law. None of them, however, is *complete.*

a) Transformations in the law follow, to some extent, a set of established inference norms which, taken as a whole, are in a weak sense analytic (section II *supra in fine*). But one cannot say to *what* extent the transformations should follow these norms.

[51] Cf. *Peczenik,* Rationality (note 8), p. 151 ff.; The Basis (note 8), p. 113 ff.

[52] Cf. *E. L. Jones,* The European Miracle, Cambridge 1981, p. 225 ff. and passim.

[53] Cf. *Peczenik,* The Basis (note 8), pp. 116—7, on the notion of *cultural progress.*

b) Transformations in the law fulfil, to some extent, the demands of rationality, *inter alia*, generality and coherence. But one cannot say *how* general and how coherent good legal reasons must be. Moreover, a rational justification of the very theory of rationality would involve a circle.[54]

c) Transformations in the law are, to some extent, analogous to transformations in science. But one cannot say whether this analogy is close enough to make legal dogmatics a "legal science".

d) Legal reasoning as a whole is supported by moral reasons. In particular, it increases the certainty of practical conclusions, and thus creates an order which, in principle, is better than chaos. But one cannot state precisely what kind of order is immoral to such a degree that it is worse than chaos.

Deep-justification of a transformation in the law is completed when it *follows to a satisfactory degree* the transformation norms, demands of rationality, analogies with science and moral arguments. What is 'satisfactory'? To answer this question, one needs an individual and unique insight,[55] embedded in one's form of life.[56] Although unclear,[57] the concept "form of life" is definable as our world picture that manifests itself in action.[58] Common form of life is a precondition of rational discourse, *inter alia* rational legal reasoning. Two persons thus belong to the same form of life if their actions, intentions, concepts, beliefs, evaluations and prescriptions stand in such a relation of causal dependence and relevant similarity with each other that these persons can rationally discuss, respectively, the central topics of their lives.[59] But one cannot say *precisely* what our form of life is. Neither can one say

---

[54] Cf., however, *Alexy*, Theorie (note 33), pp. 221—33: One can *empirically* establish that people ask for argumentative *support*, formulate *general* theories and norms, etc. One can *analytically* establish that the *concept* of rationality is vaguely related to consistency, support, and generality. One can show how consistency, generality and support are *preconditions* of knowledge, understanding, intersubjective communication and efficient realization of the *goals* people have.

[55] A remark made by *Aulis Aarnio*.

[56] Cf. *L. Wittgenstein*, Philosophical Investigations, Oxford 1953, par. 23: "The *speaking* of language is part of an activity, or of a form of life." Cf. *Wittgenstein*, On Certainty, Oxford 1969, par. 204, and *Aarnio*, On Legal Reasoning, Turku 1977, p. 126 ff.

[57] Cf. *M. Black*, "Lebensform" and "Sprachspiel" in Wittgenstein's later work, in: Wittgenstein and His Impact on Contemporary Thought. Proceedings of the 2nd International Wittgenstein Symposium, Vienna 1978, p. 330.

[58] Action constitutes "the practical, non-propositional 'phase' of the *Weltanschauung*" (*A. Aarnio*, Linguistic Philosophy and Legal Theory, in: RECHTSTHEORIE Beiheft 1 [1979], p. 34).

[59] Cf. *Peczenik*, The Basis (note 8), p. 102.

precisely that the deep-justification is here-and-now completed *in virtue of this-and-that*. If one could do so, then "this-and-that" would have to be added to this very justification, which thus could *not* have been complete already before this addition.

At the end of the deep-justification of legal reasoning lie things that cannot be said. But much can be said before we reach the end.[60]

[60] In addition to the theses developed above one can e. g. discuss the following view: "Auf dem Hintergrund des Verhältnisses von Recht und Kultur betrachtet, ist [...] jede 'deep justification' noch 'contextually sufficient', d. h. an die Wirkung der Dogmatik gekettet. Erkennt man diese Sachlage, dann eröffnet sich das Vorfeld einer Erkenntnistheorie, die Ideologiekritik einschliesst." (*J. M. Broekman*, Die Rationalität des juristischen Diskurses, in: W. Krawietz/R. Alexy [eds.], Metatheorie juristischer Argumentation, Berlin [W] 1983, p. 115.)

TRANSFORMATIONS INSIDE THE LAW

Some Comments on Peczenik

By András Sajó, Budapest

> "The meaning lies in what they are as they seem to be, and the dark you note within, although I did not plan it so or put it there, may be thought of as an attribute ..."
>
> Bernard Malamud

Obscure texts and bright axiomatic statements both invite comment. Professor *Peczenik*'s paper, "A Model of Legal Reasoning", is inspiring because of its brightness. It is an extremely interesting presentation of an ancient, recurring, and timely problem. Professor Peczenik offers a very conclusive solution to a puzzle haunting today's legal development and legal science.

A model of legal reasoning cannot be elaborated without our facing a(n unfortunately highly practical) problem. That is, what is considered as law by the subject who reasons about law? The fact that this reasoning is part of the realization of the law makes the puzzle even more complicated. A sound model of legal reasoning should be welcome in a world of rule scepticism, particularly because even non-sceptics have to confess that we work only with pale (or perhaps on the contrary, too vivid) *Rechtssätze* instead of legal norms. The problems of legal reasoning are fundamental to, and dependent upon, the objective existence of the law.

The purpose of the present paper is to find an answer to this question. The comments of the present author on *Peczenik*'s statements concerning the problem of *legal transformations* are those of a sociologist; therefore, my perspective is necessarily somewhat different from that of Professor Peczenik.

I.

"Legal reasoning [...] involves *transformations*", which one backs up "with non-deductive steps ('jumps') involving either a precise interpretation or a change of original premises, such as statutes, precedents, other legal sources, source norms and reasoning norms embedded in legal practice, etc."[1]

Legal transformations resulting in a change of the original premises mentioned above are empirical facts in the law of every historical period or legal system. The occurrence of these changes is not only different in each system but it also varies with the criteria accepted as measures of legal change.

Any empirical observation of the above changes requires some criteria. The following criteria may be offered as the most general and neutral ones for a description of jumps. They are:

(a) The jump results in a solution different from an earlier solution for the same case. Unfortunately there are only similar cases!

(b) The solution is one embarrassing to contemporary lawyers. At least, one supposes that there is such a feeling among law users and that one feels himself obliged to present a motivation in favour of the jump.

Jumps in modern law have a more definite significance. In *Peczenik*'s formulation a jump is not deductive reasoning or if it entails deductive reasoning then the premises are "new".

It is useless to deny the empirical fact of open or hidden implicit jumps, even if many legal ideologies and legal norms do so. The problem is of a normative character, viz., are the results of jumps acceptable as parts of the law? Deviant acts and law-breaking are present in our everyday life, yet we are not supposed to accept these phenomena as lawful, even if they are widely spread. Mere realization does not amount to law. The same holds true of "jumps": their existence is not an *a priori* guarantee of their legal nature.

Many lawyers have denied and would still deny the legal character of the results of jumps. This denial occurs particularly in older traditions of legal reasoning, for example:

1. Existing legal texts, especially those of the Roman law, were idolized from the glossators onwards.
2. The idea of a *more geometrico* legal system and legal reasoning (commonly associated with *Leibniz*) has favored deduction.
3. The modern state has produced a whole social group that is supposed to operate as a deductive device putting into effect the abstract norms of a centralized will. *Max Weber* emphasized the relation between

[1] *A. Peczenik*, A Model of Legal Reasoning (in this volume), section IV.

bureaucracy and the idea of a paragraph-automaton-like law-application.[2]

Enacted legal sources in socialist law and the majority of socialist legal scholars are against the admissibility of jumps. Many scholars in this tradition consider the spread of open jumps as a loosening of legality. According to the traditional doctrine of the socialist theory of law, the application of law is a series of syllogisms. Law application is delimited from deduction by the application of dialectic logic. As *Imre Szabó* stated, "[l]aw application is not simply the application of the legal rule to the individual case but the concretization of the abstract rule and, at the same time, the abstraction of the individual case."[3] Other Marxist scholars recognize the law-making capacity of the judiciary or the Supreme Court, which implies the acceptance of jumps as legitimate forms of *legal* reasoning.

Certainly, there are techniques of legal change in every legal system. These often go unnoticed in systems not admitting jumps. Changes in this case are less openly problematic than in the case of transformation by jumps. A transformation becomes problematic if the charge of its earlier non-occurrence cannot be refuted without further proof. The problematic nature of the jump is obvious when its results clearly contradict earlier solutions. But when a new social relation is subsumed under a rule aimed at governing other or different relations, the chances of the subsumption's becoming problematic are few.

I should like to mention only two transformational techniques used in anti-jump, traditional systems: manipulation of words (notions) and of (relevant) facts. The latter is widely used by judges and other decision-makers in each and every system of legal reasoning. It means a hidden change in the decision due to different consideration of the facts of the case. Being a privileged tool of the legal practice, this goes nearly unnoticed by legal theories oriented to legal reasoning and not to practical legal activity (among the few examples, see the work of *Jerome Frank*). The failure to take into consideration the given facts of the case does not require a legitimization, particularly if the decision is socially acceptable otherwise. The omission of taking into consideration certain facts proving, say, negligence might amount to a failure in legal reasoning or to breach of legal norms (e. g. the imperatives of the law of evidence). As most facts remain hidden from the "audience", the decision will lead to transformations that remain within the framework of the deductive system. In this case there is no reason for a particular ulterior

---

[2] *M. Weber*, Wirtschaft und Gesellschaft, Tübingen 1925, p. 662.

[3] *I. Szabó*, Jogelmélet (Theory of Law), Budapest 1977, p. 254.

justification. The law remains "the same", yet the social reality has been changed in a happy though somewhat miraculous way.

The other traditional solution to the problem of legal transformation manipulating the text is certainly more interesting for a theory of legal reasoning. In the last century, an important school of German legal science devoted itself to *Begriffsbildung*. As a matter of fact, the theory reflected to a great extent the practical legal activities of the time. (One may cite the French *exegetes*, too.) The considerable differences in French and Belgian *jurisprudence* are clear examples of the great freedom of movement implicit in textual analysis without jumps.

Accelerating social changes make legal adaptation without jumps increasingly difficult. The crisis at the beginning of the 20th century does not, however, prove the impossibility of an adaptation of the traditional methods. The conservatism of the judiciary in interpreting the texts more "freely" is more a sign of their socially conditioned reluctance to accept new social values and interests than of an inherent insufficiency of the text-manipulating methods of transforming the law. Today, when judges are more prepared to accept *certain* social changes *and* when legal texts are changed and full of open textures and undetermined notions, the likelihood of a *transformation* not based on jumps is increasing. The growing reliance of the legislators on the judiciary means that some of the legitimation of legal transformation has been taken away from legal reasoning and legal dogmatics. The legitimation comes from the legislation and is done in reference to the textual formulation of the legal norm explicitly or implicitly (by vague formulation).

The legitimacy of jumps does not seem to depend on the codified or judge-made nature of the law.

"It is trite legal history that (individualized justice) suffered a marked decline in the 18th and 19th centuries. In the last two decades or so the trend has been reversed; there has been a perceptible shift in judicial attitudes from principle to pragmatism, what is sometimes unflatteringly referred to as 'ad hockery'."[4]

Whatever the importance of traditional techniques might be, juridical and scientific tendencies strive to put an end to fictitious or hypocritic

---

[4] *A. I. Ogus*, Quantitative rules and judicial decision-making, in: P. Burrows/C. Veljanovski (eds.), The Economic Approach to Law, London 1981, pp. 216—217. An alien such as the present writer might be inclined to think that the English judicial reasoning (as e. g. *Mansfield* has us understand) is hardly inclined to admit the role of jumps. They seem to prefer to hide transformations not by (faulty) deductions but through surprising analogies and by means of distinguishing. Cf. *R. David*, Le droit anglais, Paris 1965, p. 21.

deductions that have become increasingly widespread in countries of codified law. It would be very instructive to conduct international comparative research on the spread of jumps, which are very probably becoming more and more common in juridical activities. And, what is even more important, one discovers new techniques of legitimation to save the results of these transformations for the legal realm. One of the most important ways of legitimation consists of the growing acceptance of new forms of legal reasoning.

Sometimes the growing concern with new forms of legal reasoning and their inner problems fortunately comes into contact with modern trends in the philosophy of language. Thus Professor *Hart* insists on a transposition of general methods of ordinary language philosophy.[5]

Instead of endeavoring to arrive at definitions of legal terms, one should look at the range of expressions within which the legal terms are characteristically being used. A further element of this approach is the concept of rule-governed action. To a certain extent this search for secondary rules signals the efforts on the Continent to develop a rule-oriented "modern" legal dogmatics.

For about two decades a conspicuous effort has been discernible in legal philosophy and perhaps in the theory and practice of judicial decision-making as well. This effort is aimed at bridging the gap between traditional (deductive) legal reasoning and discretionary decision-making including jumps without contextually sufficient legal justification. A middle-way effort to this effect is present in *Dworkin*'s theory advocating principles against policy.[6] *Aarnio, Alexy* and *Peczenik* present a somewhat similar and very clear effort in the same general direction.[7]

This effort to create legal justification for jumps may rely upon the sympathies of the legal profession, as it safeguards the legal profession's power to sanction the new legal solutions. It also promises that lawyers (judges) should not be bound by external criteria handled by other professional groups and power holders. It is highly promising for the legal scholar, too, as it opens a field of activity that is indispensable for the functioning of the law. Therefore, it offers a good claim for the important intellectual role of legal scientists, not to speak of the intellectually interesting aspects of the approach itself.

---

[5] *H. L. A. Hart,* Definition and Theory in Jurisprudence, in: Law Quarterly Review 70 (1954), p. 37.

[6] *R. Dworkin,* Taking Rights Seriously, London 1978.

[7] *A. Aarnio/R. Alexy/A. Peczenik,* The Foundation of Legal Reasoning, in: RECHTSTHEORIE 12 (1981).

Nevertheless, the outlook for this approach is not very bright. The principles of interpretation of statutory laws on the Continent are lenient enough to cope with and welcome jumps. In *Peczenik*'s words, courts and authorities in many countries have a legal duty to *apply* the law.[8] For instance, they are supposed to refer to the legal sources and to base their decisions on them. The vague phrase "to base" indicates receiving some justificatory support from the sources. As a matter of fact, the "some" amounts to "quite a lot" even if many legal texts are open (i. e., the idea is to facilitate their use as support by the application of an open terminology, e. g. *Generalklauseln*). A recent survey of European sources of law shows that in written positive law the primacy of the traditional sources (enacted law) prevails, and this primacy is based on a very limited concept of interpretative activities and a narrow concept of valid law.[9] In the Federal Republic of Germany, Par. 60 of the preamble of the Preussisches Allgemeines Landrecht — "No new laws can be made by customs, opinions of legal science, decisions of the judiciary, nor can existing laws be repealed in this way" — is considered to be "not changed".[10]

The limited inclination of the legislation to enlarge the powers of the judiciary is sometimes supported by the traditionalism of the judiciary. On the other hand, as the number of the legally untrained among legal decision-makers increases (especially in the law-application of public administration), legal justification becomes increasingly vulnerable to extra-legal evaluations and criteria of effectiveness. At present, there are also considerable differences in the social cohesion and intellectual and social openness of the judiciary and the legal profession. This increases the diversity of the value system of the "legal" audience.[11] In many cases, fields (branches) of law, even legal systems, are under the influence of non-legal professional groups, elites, power-holders, and so forth. Lawyers have to accept extra-legal legitimations (socio-economic "efficiency", moral theories, etc.) rather than the rationality of the legal system. This holds true even if one fully accepts *Peczenik*'s dictum that legal reasoning needs more certain, socially established starting points than can be given by moral "theories".

---

[8] *Peczenik* (note 1), section III.

[9] *C. Kourilsky/A. Rácz/H. Schäffer* (eds.), The Sources of Law, 1982. There are notable exceptions, as Norway, for example, where *standards of value* are accepted as a method of interpretation (p. 222), although this is not based on legal texts but on the practice of legal reasoning.

[10] *D. Merten*, Sources of Law in the Federal Republic of Germany, in: Kourilsky/Rácz/Schäffer (note 9), p. 82.

[11] *A. Aarnio*, Denkweisen der Rechtswissenschaft, Wien/New York 1979, p. 166.

II.

The above sociological considerations may have only indirect relation to the basic problem of jumps, viz., do jumps transform law or is their result but a form of appearance of the already existing law?

What is the legal status of jumps? Are these a constituent part of legal reasoning; are they to be placed somewhere else; or does only the justification of jumps pertain to the domain of extra-legal reasoning? Legal reasoning is governed by norms. Many authors are probably inclined to apply or accept *Noam Chomsky*'s definition of language to legal reasoning. In Chomsky's understanding, language is that set of propositions described by the grammar.[12] Proceeding along this line, legal reasoning would be whatever conforms to the norms of legal reasoning. A possible further inference might be the following: only those *Rechtssätze* that are elaborated or generated according to the norms of legal reasoning are in keeping with the legal norms.

Certainly, *Peczenik* does not hesitate to emphasize the importance of norms in legal reasoning. In his opinion, however, inference norms of legal reasoning established in practice include others, too, namely, those created *ad hoc*. And *ad hoc* norms would contradict a Chomskyan approach, as *ad hoc* norms *per definitionem* depart from the established norms. (This would amount to a breach of grammar and to non-language, i. e. non-law.) A net advantage of Peczenik's point is that it escapes the riddle of the creation of new norms and the mess of innate grammar. An *ad hoc* norm might be accepted as a norm *a posteriori* when it is generalized and fits the system of reasoning or is accepted. The normative problem may still haunt one: are *ad hoc* norms justified?

Whatever the similarity between jumps and *ad hoc* norms may be, *Peczenik* does not discuss the former in connection with the latter.[13]

Legal reasoning is one of the possible ways of justifying juristic conclusions. If justification is a "contextually sufficient legal justification", then it remains "within the system of legal reasoning".

Peczenik chooses the following way of characterizing legal reasoning:

"(...) When the jurist tells us what the 'valid law' is, he actually formulates his *own moral opinion* [...] The jurists *transform* the established sources, source norms and reasoning norms into something else, that is, into the *interpreted* 'valid law'."[14]

---

[12] *N. Chomsky*, Rules and Representations, New York 1980, p. 220.

[13] However, his remarks at the end of section II (see also his Fig. 1) seems to suggest that there is some connection between the both.

[14] *Peczenik* (note 1), section III.

In *Peczenik*'s opinion, "the combination of [the above and certain other theses] is *necessary* to [...] deep-justify legal reasoning."[15]

In my understanding, this means that

a) outside the legal reasoning as a context-bound activity there is another form of justification, the deep one;

b) transformation is legal reasoning;

c) (b) is a condition for deep reasoning.

Another possibly surprising conclusion is that reasoning involves transformations, yet transformation is also the transformation of reasoning norms into 'valid law'. Legal reasoning contains its *own* transformation. *Peczenik* expressly states that legal reasoning involves jumps (the *par excellence* transformations). Certainly "to involve" does not equal "to consist of". I surmise that this is also the standpoint of Peczenik.[16]

In *Peczenik*'s formulation, the main reason for performing a jump is that "the jurist tends to adapt his own evaluations as well as [*inter alia*] the established [...] reasoning norms to mutually correspond with one another."[17] There remains some ambiguity, though, as to the status of jumps in legal reasoning: they are described as if parts of the legal realm were or might be contraventions or modifications of the legal reasoning norms — although Peczenik, if my understanding is correct, seems inclined to leave this role to *ad hoc* norms. In the positive description of jumps one cannot find reference to change in reasoning *norms:* jumps are dealt with as problems of inferences from different *premises.*

Are jumps justifiable by ordinary legal reasoning or do they require deep justification? The reader might be inclined to accept the latter position. One rarely finds a sufficient legal (or contextual) justification for a jump. In my opinion, this is usually done according to norms of reasoning; but this is not sufficient. The reliability of the jump rests on the premises and I would have been happier with an explanation for the acceptance of adding or changing a premise. Certainly, if one is inclined to consider the different sets of premises as equifunctional, the possibility of a sociological theory of acceptance is virtually lost. The choice of the premises remains a matter of the jurist's evaluations. Consequently, choice needs deep justification ("rationality"). *Peczenik*

[15] Ibid.

[16] In an earlier version of his paper Peczenik calls jumps "justifiable inferences performed *in legal reasoning*" (his italics). Cf. also his classification of jumps that "corresponds to the classification of evaluative operations *in* legal reasoning" (in: section IV of his paper in this volume; italics mine).

[17] *Peczenik* (note 1), note 20.

already stated that even various parts of the contextually sufficient legal justification may require deep justification in various contexts.[18] Unfortunately, these contexts are non-legal contexts for Peczenik (they aim at "convincing moralists [*et al.*]"). Consequently, deep justification would be necessary for the legal acceptability of the jump, but deep justification does not serve justification in legal contexts. Does this mean that "criticism of the premises" will not be admitted in legal activities? Is there no contextually sufficient legal justification in hard cases? Is legal development left to extra-legal spheres and, perhaps, forces?

A differentiation between two sorts of premises might be helpful at this point, that is, a distinction between those premises that are criticizable within the legal context and using deep justification in this process and those that are exempt from this criticism. In the latter case legal criticism is impossible *a posteriori* at least. When criticism is refuted, it makes no sense in the legal context in view of juristic conclusions. As a matter of fact, a legal system is a set of *taboos* for the jurist, and, accordingly, good comparative law is nothing more than a comparison of taboos and their consequences.

III.

For *Peczenik,* the justification of *hard cases* involves reasons other than those referring to enacted law. For other writers, the problems of hard cases consist of admitting borderline cases that fall within the objectives of the rule and excluding those inconsistent with such objectives.[19] Many lawyers and scholars would search and find the missing premises for the solution of a hard case in the enacted laws and their penumbra. To put it more cautiously: The premises to be applied for a jump with contextually sufficient legal justification are to be found "elsewhere" *in* the legal system or there is an authorized link in the legal text, e. g. a norm that might justify the application of new premises. Most demands for rationality might be interpreted as requirements for a justified choice between premises already existing in the legal system.

The "objectives of the rules" as sources of premises have often been misused. But misuse is a clear sign of existence, and a considerable number of legal scholars believe in these objectives. The personal evaluations of a jurist are thoroughly conditioned by the law. Moreover, legal reasoning is a phenomenon of the Durkheimian "collective conscience" rather than an individual reasoning. It has an objectivity that cannot be explained in interpersonal terms. This is clearly so as regards

[18] *Peczenik* (note 1), at the beginning of section III.
[19] *Ogus* (note 4), p. 212.

the acceptance of jumps. *First*, jumps are not individual mental acts of a single jurist; they become meaningful when accepted by the audience. This audience is delimited and partly determined by law, through rules on or requirements concerning legal education, professional rules, and so on.

Second, acceptance by the audience is a practical act. The practice of this audience evolves in accordance with law. The jumps should be embedded in the structure of this activity. Normative communication plays only a secondary role in the validation of the jump; the jump is validated mainly by the complex set of practice.

For a more objective understanding of legal reasoning one should bear in mind that the point of reference for a jurist is not just another jurist. Yet this might be the case when the lawyer would like to please the judge deciding on his instance. The audience is not important as a set of individuals. We must consider at least two audiences, the more important one being that constituted by the legislators and the related ruling circles (even though this audience is, in this form, imaginary). The second important audience is constituted by the legal community or other reference groups that intellectually control lawyers' activities. Both audiences are relevant through their objectified forms, namely through legal norms and legal decisions. The legal-intellectual community might have non-legal emanations as well, e. g. doctrines and scientific papers.

As to the legal norms, according to *Vilmos Peschka*, their central influence is due to the fact that "they distillate through *Widerspiegelung* a social content which guarantees a considerable social support for the norm."[20]

Only this social nature of the norms explains why jurists work with the *paradigm* of legal sources etc. Intellectual needs are necessary but not sufficient reasons for the acceptance of the "enacted law" paradigm.

IV.

Does our emphasis on the objective nature and priority of the law facing the lawyer amount to negation of the importance of legal reasoning and especially of its subjective elements? *Peczenik* considers legal reasoning a mental activity of the jurist. This viewpoint is correct if it refers to empirical facts. Peczenik certainly would not deny that the norms and other elements of legal reasoning exist above the individual level. At least one has to accept this if one does not wish to dispute the

[20] *V. Peschka*, Die Theorie der Rechtsnormen, Budapest 1982, p. 232.

following statement: the mental activity of the jurist does not constitute a "legal reasoning" if it remains unaccepted. The acceptance of the results of his mental activity, as mentioned earlier, is normatively bound. The enacted law has an eminent role in this norm-boundedness. Peczenik himself emphasizes the importance of established sources, source norms and reasoning norms "for the jurist's justified opinion about what to do".[21] Their importance is due to the fact that these elements "increase certainty" in the sense that it is morally better for society to avoid forcing societal actors to evaluate autonomously all the complex social situations.[22] In my opinion, this anti-moralistic statement applies to jurists' personal evaluations as well. One should remember that these personal evaluations were seen to be the sources of the "tension" that leads to jumps.

For a sociologist, however, the main reason for jurists' acceptance of the established sources etc. and their tendency to include the results of jumps and their justification in the legal system or the legal reasoning, respectively, is not that in this case one may rely on (other) jurists. To adhere to enacted norms and accepted rules, including those of legal reasoning, means reliance on others who share power. The social links or relations of law and lawyers with power seriously question the neutrality of rationality. For this reason I would accept *André-Jean Arnaud*'s dialectic evaluation of the creative importance of legal reasoning.[23] The function of legal reasoning lies in the perpetuation of society, perpetuation in the sense that it does not necessarily mean the reproduction of society in the stereotypes. These are the social limits of legal jumps and this is the reason for their growing acceptance.

[21] *Peczenik* (note 1), section VII.
[22] Ibid.
[23] *A.-J. Arnaud,* Critique de la raison juridique, Vol. 1, Paris 1981, p. 32.

THE INNER LOGIC OF THE LAW

By Joseph Raz, Oxford (U.K.)

Lawyers, both academic and practising, are fond of talking of the life of the law, its spirit, or its inner logic. In part these expressions refer to the unwritten conventions of the legal profession. These extend beyond habits and manners, and affect the presentation of argument. They include conventions of interpretation and a sense of propriety in the conduct of cases which may be decisive in determining their outcome. There is no doubt that because of the importance of the legal profession and its conventions in contemporary legal systems any study of the law which disregards them is liable to produce a distorted picture. Often, however, references to the logic of the law have a different and a more ambitious purpose. It is sometimes claimed that legal thought or legal reasoning are subject to a special legal logic. This is sometimes taken to mean that legal reasoning is not subject to logical laws. But more often it indicates a belief that there are additional rules of logic which apply to legal reasoning only.

Although I will assume that both these claims about legal logic are false, I will consider neither of them here. My purpose is to examine another view often expressed by talk of the inner logic of the law, a belief in the inner dynamism of the law, its internal momentum for development. My purpose is to clarify and explain this belief, in as much as there is truth in it.

I. Clarifications

The conventional picture is reasonably clear. Legal positivism is held to present a static view of the law. Legal positivists, such as Kelsen and Hart, regard the law as a system of rules, or norms. The rules may be changed from time to time. But they are changed by external political intervention "from outside" the law. So far as one is concerned with legal reasoning as such its point and purpose can only be the interpretation of existing law. Any change or development in the law requires an extra-legal injection. It requires input from outside the legal system.

This, it is claimed, is a one-sided picture. It is true that legislation is typically an effecting of a change in the law which, though authorized by law, is motivated by extra-legal considerations. Legislation typically reflects political concerns, be they social, economic, technological or bureaucratic. But, the claim goes, the same is not true of the so-called judge-made law. The courts do indeed develop the law but they do so not as political agents but by working out the implications of internal legal considerations. Courts in developing the law do not give expression to their personal views nor do they reflect external social or political forces. Rather, they unravel the spirit of the law, unfold its hidden force and reveal its meaning.

Though the conventional picture is clear, its meaning and validity are not. How can the law provide the impetus for its own development? If the law itself points to a certain rule as the right legal rule, is not that rule a legal rule now? If it is, then recognising it and acting on it is merely acting on existing law. It is not a case of developing and changing the law. But, on the other hand, if acting on, recognising or enforcing the rule does change the law, if the rule is not yet a legal rule but will be made legal by its recognition, then how can it be that existing law points to it as the correct legal rule to adopt? Must all law be explicitly enacted? Surely one can enact by referring to certain rules and dictating that they should be deemed valid law. What is the difference between enactment by reference which makes the referred to binding and a pointing to a rule as the right one without making it thereby into a binding law? Unless supporters of the view of the inner dynamics of the law can resolve this puzzle their thesis cannot even be held to be false. It is merely incoherent.

The puzzle may be thought to be easy to solve, but some solutions are too easy. The law is, for example, an inspirational source for its own development. Ideas embodied in the law may suggest solutions to new social or legal problems. Knowledge of how certain legal institutions, or legal solutions, have fared in practice may suggest ways of improving them. These facts are not in contention. We all know that reflection on the law and its practical impact has been a major source of proposals and ideas for reform and improvement. In a sense this is a way in which the law provides an impetus for its own development but this is not a sense relevant to the argument between legal positivists and their opponents. Clearly neither side has any difficulty in accounting for these facts, for this sense of the dynamism of the law.

As a source of ideas for its own development the law suggests what reasons for action (i. e., for reforming action) there are. It does not itself constitute a reason for its own development. But the very existence of the law, or of certain parts of it, is a reason for introducing certain changes in the law. The existence of, e. g., a local property tax and of a national income tax is a reason for not introducing a separate system of local income tax. To do so would duplicate existing bureaucracies and would lead to inefficiencies and to a great increase in complaints from the public. Similarly, the existence of a duty to pay income tax is a reason for instituting a duty to report one's income to the authorities. Failing to do so will lead to large scale tax evasion which is harmful to the exchequer, unjust towards honest tax-payers, and which undermines respect for the law and for the government.

These are examples of one legal rule or institution providing a reason for instituting or for maintaining another legal rule or institution. This way of pointing to possible or desirable changes in the law is of major importance for the understanding of legal history generally and of the development of judge-made law in particular. Elsewhere I have argued that considerations of this kind explain one of the most important differences between the role of the courts and the role of Parliament in their activities as law-makers. (I. e. it is sufficient to explain why they behave differently when they have power to change the law. It does not explain the differences between the occasions on which they have power to change it.) Because of the importance of the point to our present purpose let me briefly summarise that argument.

Suppose that rules *C* and *D* are currently the law. The court believes that replacing them with rules *A* and *B* respectively will be a great improvement. It is sitting in a case which involves *C* but not *D*. Let us further assume that the court has power to replace rule *C* with rule *A* (suppose, e. g., that both *C* and *D* are common law rules, and that the court involved is the House of Lords). The court believes that rule *A* is far better than *C* and yet it may rightly conclude that it should not change it. The reason may be that though *A* is better than *C*, *A* and *D* are worse than *C* and *D*. It is true that in such a situation there is likely to be another rule, e. g., *B*, such that *A* and *B* are better than *C* and *D*. But since a court can only change rules the application of which is possible in the case before it, our court cannot replace *D* with *B*. Not knowing when an opportunity to do so will arise, it may well judge, and judge correctly, that it should not replace *C* with the better rule *A*. Sometimes in such circumstances the court may find another rule, *A'*, which though inferior to *A* is such that it with *D* is an improvement over *C* and *D*. If so the court will choose to replace *C* with *A'*. To do so is in a sense to settle for a second best. But it may be the best course of action open to the court in the circumstances.

It would be wrong to suggest that considerations of this character never apply to legislation by Parliament. But since the courts have little control over the cases coming before them and since therefore they cannot control the opportunities available to them for changing the law, their reasoning is often dominated by considerations of this kind, i. e. by what I have called the dilemma of partial reform. I have claimed that the dilemma of partial reform explains why the development of the law in the hands of the judges tends to be gradual and organic. For radical reform in a short period of time one has to look to Parliament.

The dilemma of partial reform, despite its fundamental impact on the law, is simple in structure. Because the courts lack control over their opportunities for changing the law the existence of the rest of the law, which is currently beyond their reach, is a major constraint on their reforming activities. The existence of the law is a reason for or against the acceptability of certain possible reforms.

Elsewhere I have distinguished between two kinds of reasons, operative and auxiliary. Put loosely, operative reasons are those which, if accepted, provide the motivating force. They point to the need for action in pursuit of a certain goal. Auxiliary reasons connect a certain course of action to that goal by showing it to be a route to its achievement. That getting wet and cold is bad for one is an operative reason. That by leaving the house one will get cold and wet because there is a storm outside, is an auxiliary reason, which in combination with the operative reason just mentioned points to staying at home as the thing to do. Similarly, a promise to convey certain information to a friend is an operative reason. The fact that he is now at home and reachable by phone is an auxiliary reason. Both together point to telephoning the friend as the thing to do.

These explanations beg many questions and require much refinement. But they will do for our purpose. It seems clear that the existence of legal rules and institutions is, as explained above, an auxiliary reason for certain legal reforms, and against others. Given certain operative reasons which set certain goals of social justice or welfare to be achieved, the existence of certain legal rules or institutions points to the conclusion that certain legal changes would or would not be desirable. Can the existence of legal rules and institutions ever constitute an operative reason for the development of law? Even though it is true that legal theorists have often been guilty of neglecting the many important ways in which the law serves as an auxiliary reason for its own development, it has to be admitted that the main theoretical problem is whether it can form an operative reason for its own development.

II. Directed Powers

Consideration of ordinary legislative powers suggests a sense in which the law can provide reasons for its own development. Legislative powers are granted by laws which may confer limited or unlimited legislative powers, that is they may make any rule made by the designated authority valid, or they may make only rules which meet certain conditions valid. One special kind of condition may be that the rule was made in order to promote certain designated objectives or that it does in fact promote certain designated objectives. But the possession of legislative powers, be they limited or not, is no reason for using them. If I possess a certain power then I can use it (at least on certain occasions). This raises the question whether I should do so and how, a question which would have been out of place had I lacked the power. Possessing the power cannot in itself provide an answer to this question. Even if I have the power only if I use it for a certain purpose (as when a knight in shining armour can defeat his enemy only if he fights to defend the honour of his lady) it is no reason to use it for that purpose. The law can, however, combine the grant of a power to legislate with the imposition of a duty to use it in a certain way.

Most commonly we are free to use legal powers as we please. Indeed often it is the purpose of the grant of a legal power that its holder shall use it as he wishes. The power to make contracts is an obvious example of such a power. Yet legal powers can be coupled with duties concerning their exercise. In some countries (e. g. Australia) the power to vote in elections is coupled with a duty to do so. This duty does not dictate how one should use one's vote. But duties concerned with the exercise of other legal powers do precisely that. Agents ought to use their power to represent their principals in accord with their instructions, company directors are duty bound to use their powers in the interests of the shareholders, and there are detailed rules specifying some of the particular duties this involves, etc.

Subordinate legislators are often subjected to legal duties as to how they should exercise their legislative powers. Just as the conditions limiting legal powers can be of many shapes or forms, so the duties regulating their use can vary greatly in content. I am concerned with one kind of duty. It is a duty to legislate and to legislate rules which promote or protect certain ends and none other. We have already seen that there could be a limitation on a legislative (or any other) power which has an analogous form. The legislation may be valid only if it does or if it is undertaken in order to promote some specified aims. Very often both the limitation of a legislative power and the duty concerning its use are imposed by one and the same enactment. Often the same words used in a statute are interpreted to have the dual meaning and effect of limiting the legislator's power and of directing him to use it to achieve a certain purpose. All this is common enough but it should not obscure the distinction between a limitation on a power and a duty concerning its exercise.

For our present purpose we want to concentrate on a law-making power coupled with a duty to use it and to use it to achieve certain objectives and only them, regardless of whether or not this power is limited in the corresponding way. I shall call such a power and the duties attached to it a *directed power*.

Directed powers are the paradigmatic case of the law providing for its own development. Here we find the law providing reasons for the introduction of new legal rules yet those are not part of the law until enacted by the empowered authority. It is important to understand the reason why in such cases the rules the authority is directed to make are not legally binding, are not law, until enacted by it. The reason is not that the direction as to which rules to enact is imprecise and therefore cannot be said to identify a specific rule as the one to be enacted. The directions can but need not be imprecise. They can be as precise as, for example, a law that "the Secretary of State for Social Welfare shall, by regulation, increase old age pensions and unemployment benefits annually by the rate of inflation during the preceding year". Even in such a case the new rate of the specified benefits does not come into force until the Secretary of State approves the required regulation.

The general function of directed powers is to introduce and maintain a certain division of power and of labour between various authorities. In my example Parliament could have enacted for automatic augmentation of old age pensions and unemployment benefits according to its chosen formula. It chose to make such increases dependent on ministerial regulation, thus sharing some of its legislative power with the Secretary of State. The law of the E.E.C. provides an interesting illustration of this point. Many provisions in the Treaties of Rome which were drafted and ratified with the intention that they shall constitute directed powers requiring action by the member states were, especially since the second decade of the existence of the Community, interpreted by the European Court of Justice as directly applicable, that is as complete rules already in force, rather than as directives to the member states to introduce new rules. The purpose and effect of this development in the jurisprudence of the court was to diminish the power of the governments of the member states, in order to reduce their ability to frustrate the goals of the Community as set out in the Treaties of Rome.

The general function of laws creating directed powers is to effect a certain division of power and of labour. The reasons why such a division is thought desirable are many and varied and need not detain us here. It is important, however, to distinguish between two kinds of directed power. The one kind includes all those cases where the directions for the use of the legislative power may require the exercise of some moral judgment on the part of the authority. The second kind includes all the other cases, i. e. those where the legal directions as to how the legislative power is to be exercised can always be followed without the empowered authority resorting to any moral propositions or arguments. A case where power is given to make rules for the protection of public safety and the freedom of the individual belongs to the first kind. In making such rules the legislator may have to settle conflicts between public safety and individual liberty and this cannot be done other than by the exercise of moral judgment. Furthermore, even the question of what actions affect individual liberty is a moral question. The definition of one's concept of individual liberty is in itself a moral issue.

It may be thought that my earlier example of increasing social benefits in line with inflation is a case of the second kind. The duty imposed on the legislator is to enact a rule the content of which can be calculated without resort to any moral reasoning. But this is a mistake. Though in this case there is less room for the legislator to exercise moral judgment he may yet have to do so. The question of what is the best measure of inflation is more than a purely factual question. It may well involve moral jugdment. (In Britain after the 1979 election the government introduced a new index which reflects the change in the combined level of prices plus taxes as a truer measure of inflation than the ordinary cost of living index.) Even questions of how much evidence is required to establish a point of fact may well be a moral question, a point familiar to anyone who reflects on the difference in the level of proof required by law in criminal and civil cases.

Though directed powers of the second kind can exist, it is perhaps not surprising that they are rather rare. Administrative powers whose use is subject to duties which do not require the exercise of moral judgment are much more common. An example of such a power is that of certain officials to issue licences for holding TV receivers. Those officials are under a duty to issue the licence upon payment of a fixed fee and then only. All they have to do to follow their instructions is to collect the fee. They are not called upon to exercise any moral judgment. Indeed it is precisely the exclusion of any moral judgment which marks these powers as a special class known as mandatory powers which is contrasted with discretionary administrative powers. The latter are not to be confused with absolute powers. Their use is subject to legal duties (the minimal duty imposed on all administrative discretionary powers in English law is that they be exercised in good faith). But these are duties whose discharge requires moral judgment.

III. The Directed Powers of Courts

Directed powers of both kinds mentioned above are the model for the law's ability to provide for its own development. It is by an analogy with legislative directed powers that one can understand the often discussed inner logic of the law, i. e. the ability of the courts to change the law by following guidelines set by the law itself. This analogy also solves the puzzle mentioned at the outset: How can the law provide for a new rule without that rule being already part of the law in virtue of the fact that it is legally provided for.

Let us use as examples two legal doctrines. First, a contract that tends to corruption in public life is illegal. Second, a person owes a duty of care to another "where the circumstances of the time, place and person would create in the mind of a reasonable man in those circumstances such a probability of harm resulting to other persons as to require him to take care to avert that probable result" (*Nova Mink Ltd. v. Trans Canada Airlines* [1951] 2 D.L.R. 241 at 254). Consider the following two hypothetical decisions which (purport to) apply these doctrines:

1. A contract wherein a property developer agrees to contribute to the election campaign funds of a candidate in a local election in return for a commitment that if elected the candidate will propose the construction of a road connecting two housing estates is held to be illegal.

2. It is held that surveyors owe a duty of care to anyone who commissions a survey and to anyone whom they authorise to use it, but to no one else.

Two points I will take for granted. *First,* that the decision in the first case, though couched in specific language referring to a particular case, is based on a general proposition which applies to a class of cases. This much is entailed by the universal requirement that judicial decisions be reasoned. (This requirement should not be confused with the duty to give reasons. Juries are not required to give reasons but they are required to reach reasoned decisions.) *Second,* that in all legal systems judicial decisions are a source of law, i. e. that the legal propositions in the two examples will become part of the law of the land if a judicial custom to follow them is established. In some countries, e. g. in England, there is a formal doctrine of precedent which allows for a short cut, i. e. judicial decisions can establish binding rules of law even before they crystallize in a judicial custom. Doctrines of precedent often enable a single decision of a superior court to establish a new rule of law. But in all legal systems, even those which do not have a doctrine of precedent, judicial custom is a source of law.

Many theorists, myself included, have argued that the law is an institutionalized normative system administered by judicial institutions and have explained why this entails that courts have law-making powers, even where none are expressly granted. Let me just note that this does not deny that courts can make mistakes in law. It is well known that customs can emerge by action which itself offends against the previously existing customs. To revert to our E.E.C. example: The European Court of Justice may well have been acting against the law when it declared Article 119 of the Treaty of Rome to be directly applicable. But since its decision has now hardened into a customary rule of the Court, and of the national courts when applying Community law, it has become a rule of the Community.

Let us return to my two examples of the illegality of some contracts fettering administrative discretion and the duty of care of surveyors. Do the decisions described in them change the law? The two points I am taking for granted establish only that the decisions can change the law, not that they do so. They can change the law because being reasoned they are based on a general rule or principle, and because it is necessarily the case that judicial decisions, at least once they harden into a judicial custom, are a source of law. But these points do not establish that the decisions, even if they crystallize a judicial custom, do in fact change the law. It could be that they merely reflect the way the law has been all along. Remember that the same is true of parliamentary legislation. It is a source of law, but not every Act of Parliament changes the law. Some Acts are consolidation Acts merely re-enacting in one statute provisions previously found in several. To establish that the decisions in our examples change the law we have to establish not just that they are sources of law but also that they do more than simply repeat existing law.

In arguing that these decisions do change the law I am assuming that they either set a binding precedent or crystallize a judicial custom. I am also assuming that apart from the general doctrines set out above which they (purport to) apply there are no other legal rules directly determining the outcome of the issues decided in these cases. Given these assumptions any argument to the effect that the instanced decisions do not change the law will have to claim that they merely reiterate what is implicit in the two general doctrines set out above. It is of course possible that the two decisions misapply the doctrines which they purport to apply. They may have reached conclusions which are at odds with these doctrines. In that case given that they are sources of law, it has to be admitted that they change the law. They do so by mistake, but nevertheless they do so. The interesting case, however, is the one in which the courts do not fail to apply the doctrines correctly.

This case opens up two possibilities. The decisions of the court may have been the ones required by the general doctrines or the doctrines may have been indeterminate on the issue in question. For the sake of argument let us assume that the first doctrine, that contracts which tend to corruption in public life are illegal, dictates the result in the first case, i. e., that a contract exchanging contributions for an election campaign for a commitment how to behave when elected is illegal. And let us assume that the second doctrine, that one's duty of care is determined by what a reasonable man would have judged right in the circumstances, is indeterminate on the question of whether a surveyor owes a duty of care to people whose reliance on the survey was not authorized by him.

In making these assumptions we are not assuming that the first doctrine is not indeterminate in any way. All that is assumed is that it gives a definite answer to the case in our first example. The second doctrine, it is assumed, fails to give an answer to the second case. This does not mean that it is indeterminate on all cases. By dictating that the duty of care follows the judgment of the reasonable man it determines the fate of many cases in which there are sound arguments to establish what the view of a reasonable man would have been. It is merely assumed that it is indeterminate on the case in the second example, i. e. there is no sound argument as to what the reasonable man would think in *that* case.

If the doctrine in the second case is indeterminate on the issue of the case then it neither entails the rule decided upon in it nor does it entail its negation. Since the rule is established in the case and since it was not established law before it, the second case does, given our assumptions, develop the law. It is true that one is intuitively more hesitant to say that the law was changed in the case. This is because 'a change' is often used to convey a change of direction, or an alteration to the existing situation which is significant enough to make the changed object substantially or significantly different from before. In this sense no change occurred. The law was modified in a matter of detail which merely develops it in the same direction and in the same spirit it had before.

This is shown also by the fact that we are willing to refer to the court in this case as applying the doctrine even though it does not dictate the result of the case. We do so because the decision is not only consistent with the doctrine but was designed to be so and because either no rival doctrine has been avowed by the court as guiding it in reaching its decision or if one was avowed it was taken to be lexically subordinate. Yet the decision changes the law if this means just that as a result of the decision the law on one particular point is not exactly as it was before. Where it was indeterminate it is now determined.

The more difficult case is the first one. A correct application of the doctrine that contracts that tend to corrupt public life are invalid does yield the rule that a contract securing a contribution to an election fund in return for a promise how one would use one's powers if elected is illegal. It yields these rules through a chain of reasoning concerning the likely effects of recognising the validity of such contracts and of their moral desirability. I shall assume that in that chain of reasoning two considerations are prominent. First, that it is undesirable that office holders will assume their powers while under legal obligations which stop them from changing their views on issues of public concern once they assume office. Second, that ideally one's wealth should not determine one's political influence.

My argument is that in such a case the new decision does change and develop the law. The rule it establishes is a new rule and there was no law to that effect before. In saying that I mean to say nothing more than what is the common view of the legal profession, i. e. I am merely repeating generally acknowledged facts. (The reasons why the views of the legal profession should be taken as determining such legal facts cannot be explored here.) This is clear both when we survey a course of such decisions and when we anticipate them. When we survey the development of the American Supreme Court decisions on, say, freedom of expression, and even when we confine our attention to those which correctly apply the First Amendment of the American Constitution, we are aware that the general view is that those decisions have greatly developed the legal protection of freedom of expression in the U.S. and that many of the doctrines which govern freedom of expression have become part of the law in recent times. They correctly apply the First Amendment. But they were not legally binding until enshrined in the jurisprudence of the court.

Similarly when we anticipate such a decision in a case of first impression we are aware that we anticipate a new development in the law. An attorney advising a client as to the legality of the contract in our example before the case comes to litigation for the first time will tell him of the general doctrine and will advise him that this means that the court ought to declare that such contracts are illegal. But he would also warn his client that this is a case of first impression, that there is no legal authority on the issue, and that given that the law is as yet unsettled much depends on the political and moral convictions of the judges. The case, he may say, will set an important new precedent, and may help develop a dormant legal doctrine in new directions.

I have dwelt on these familiar reactions for they are the foundation of the assertion that decisions like the one in our example change the law. But these common perceptions though very persuasive are less than decisive in themselves. They may be susceptible to different interpretations and in any case we may refuse to follow them if we believe that they do not reflect any distinction of importance or that they are confused or incoherent. But the described reactions reflect a distinction which is both cogent and important.

Clearly many general legal statements are true even though they do not repeat verbatim the contents of statutes or precedents. They are true because they are entailed by other legal statements which do directly describe the contents of enactments or of precedents perhaps together with some further true factual premises. A statement that contracts such as the one in our example are illegal was not true until the decision to that effect was given. It is not entailed by an existing legal doctrine with the addition of further true *factual* premises. Its justification calls for and relies upon moral reasoning, especially on the propositions concerning the undesirability of allowing one's wealth to affect one's political power and of having public officials assume office shackled with prior legal undertakings as to the way they will exercise this power. In other words the reactions we have described reflect a belief in what I have elsewhere dubbed the Sources Thesis, i. e. the view that the law is capable of being identified by social facts without resorting to moral argument. Prior to the decision establishing the illegality of such contracts there was no way of arguing that there was a legal rule rendering the contracts illegal except by relying on moral argument. Therefore there was no such law.

Does the sources thesis capture an important fact about the law? The general importance of the divide between moral and non-moral discourse (and its importance does not presuppose that the distinction is sharp or that the categories are entirely exclusive) suggests that a distinction based on it is likely to be viable and important. But its importance is often misinterpreted by its own supporters. They often see it as based on certainty and regard moral arguments as inherently uncertain. This, I think, is a mistake. At best there is here a complex difference of degree. Many moral propositions are more certain and less controversial than many factual ones (that murdering a healthy and innocent person is wrong is much more certain and uncontroversial than any economic theory). The insight embodied in the sources thesis is the importance of the distinction between those (valid or invalid) moral considerations which have received authoritative public endorsement and those which have not. But as I and others have discussed this point before let us leave it here and return to our main problem.

I have spent a long time arguing that the decision in my example changes and develops the law because once this point is established the similarity between the courts' legal situation in such cases and that of a subordinate legislator subject to a directed power is evident and striking. We have already mentioned that both have power to make law. In the situations illustrated by the example the courts' powers are directed, i. e. they are subject to duties prescribing the ends which alone must be served by the exercise of the powers and enjoining the courts to use their powers to those ends. The ends are embodied in the general doctrines, e. g., declaring the illegality of all contracts tending to corruption in public life. In dealing with cases falling under this doctrine the courts may develop the law but only in order to achieve the end set by the doctrine. We expect the courts to be guided by the general doctrines applicable when developing the law to meet the circumstances of different cases. We judge their efforts by their success in doing so. And we regard them as having failed in their duties if their decisions fail to serve the governing doctrines.

It has been suggested by R. M. Dworkin, and accepted by many who disagree with his views on almost all other points, that courts can change the law only where the pre-existing law fails to indicate one solution as the uniquely correct solution to the legal question in litigation. Elsewhere I have shown that this is a misconception which overlooks the fact that the courts may have power not only to fill in gaps in the law but also to reserve a valid legal rule and replace it with another. The prevalence of directed legislative powers points to another misconception in Dworkin's suggestion. A subordinate legislator subject to a directed power often has a legal duty to enact one particular rule. If he fails to do so or if he enacts a different rule he is guilty of breach of duty. Most commonly there are no legal remedies against such breach of duty. But occasionally legal remedies are available and they may include an order of mandamus or a positive injunction demanding that the legislator shall enact the rule he has a duty to enact. What is not in doubt is that despite the fact that in a sense this is a situation in which the law points to one uniquely correct rule, that rule is not law until enacted.

That much is uncontroversial. What is overlooked is the fact that the same is often true of the courts when they are subject to a directed power. There is then a uniquely correct solution to the case but it is not law until given legally binding force by the court. Until then it may be the case that the law imposes a duty on the court to establish a new legal rule, but that rule is no more legally valid prior to the courts' decision than is a piece of subordinate legislation, which an official has a legal duty to enact, legally valid before its enactment.

IV. Directed Powers and Defeasible Rules

Our task is largely complete. We have in the notion of a directed power the key to the way in which the law provides (operative) reasons for its own development. Directed legislative powers are confined to subordinate legislation and their existence normally depends on specific statutory provisions which expressly or implicitly direct the exercise of the legislative power. Directed judicial law-making powers are much more pervasive. They exist in all cases in which judicial decisions are a source of law (either as precedent or as judicial custom) and in which the courts are legally required to apply certain moral considerations to the determination of the case. They then have a power to make law and a duty to do so in accord with those moral considerations. Indeterminacy may result in the law failing to single out any specific rule as the one the courts ought to establish. But many cases are not affected by indeterminacy and there the courts' duty uniquely points to one specific rule as the one they ought to establish. But it is not law until established as such by the courts. And thus it is that we have here a legal reason for changing the law.

To leave the subject at this point, however, would suggest that doctrines such as "Contracts tending to corruption of public life are invalid" are instructions to the courts and nothing more. This is a mistake. It is true that a statutory provision establishing a directed legislative power is addressed to the relevant legislator and to him alone. But general legal doctrines which call for the exercise of moral judgment in their application, while they do confer directed powers on the courts, do also address themselves to the public. They also confer rights, duties, powers, status, etc., or deny them to members of the public.

The doctrine of the illegality of certain contracts which we have been examining determines, even before any decision applying it, that people do not have the legal power to make contracts tending to corruption in public life. The first Amendment to the American Constitution that "Congress shall make no law ... abridging the freedom of speech ..." establishes everyone's right to free expression. In this respect these judicial directed powers differ from legislative powers. If Article 119 of the E.E.C. Treaty were not directly applicable it would have established a directed legislative power. This would have meant that women workers in the Community would have had a right that their government enact laws guaranteeing them equal pay. But they would not have had a right to equal pay until such laws were enacted. The ECJ decision in *Defrenne v. Sabena* 43/75 (1976) that the Article is in part directly applicable has two direct results: First, women workers have a right to equal pay even prior to specific state legislation. Second, the courts (as well as the states' legislatures) have a directed power to make rules implementing the doctrine.

The legal significance of holding women workers to have a legal right to equal pay is self-evident. It means, first, that they enjoy those particular rights which can be derived from the general right without relying on moral argument. Thus a woman has a right not to receive half the pay enjoyed by a man employed under the same conditions to do the same job. Secondly, it means that they can approach the courts and demand that they use their directed powers to make rules for the implementation of the right to equal pay which will be applied in their case. They cannot do so if Article 119 is not directly applicable. That is the reason for holding that if the Article is not directly applicable and merely grants directed legislative powers then it only grants women a right against the state to adopt equal pay legislation. Since, however, it is directly applicable it not only establishes directed powers in the courts but also, and for the reason stated, grants women a right to equal pay against their employers and a duty on the latter to respect it.

In Common Law jurisdictions, and perhaps in all precedent-recognising legal systems, legal doctrines governing the use of the directed powers of the courts are defeasible to a particularly high degree. All legal rules are defeasible in at least three ways. First, they may be overridden by other conflicting legal rules. Secondly, they are overridden by the specific decrees rendered in final judicial judgments purporting to apply them to the parties before the court, which in fact misapply them through a judicial mistake. Thirdly, they are overridden, in circumstances similar to those of the second case, by general rules adopted by the courts which have the force of precedent (or which have hardened into a judicial custom). Common Law systems restrict defeasibility of the third kind. The fact that a judicial decision misinterpreted or misapplied a statute, or even a Common Law doctrine, may deny it its binding force, or at any rate weaken it (in a case in which the judicial mistake may not have been decisive in determining the rule adopted in the case. Cf. *Conway v. Rimmer* [1968] A.C. 910 on the misunderstanding of Scottish law in *Duncan v. Cammell, Laird & Co. Ltd.* [1942] A.C. 624). No such restrictions on the force of a decision as a binding precedent apply when its misapplication of the existing law consists in faulty moral reasoning, or in accepting the wrong moral premises. This is the clear implication of, e. g. *Miliangos v. George Frank (Textiles)* [1975] 3 All E.R. 801. Therefore, legal doctrines directing the law-making powers of the courts are particularly defeasible.

The structure which emerges is therefore this. The law provides for its own development by granting directed powers. The typical case is of directed judicial law-making powers governed by a general doctrine, which applies to ordinary law-subjects as well, and therefore provides them with access to the courts.

V. The Systematic Nature of Law

What is it that makes a legal system into a system rather than a haphazard collection of legal rules? To this ancient question there are two kinds of answers. The first refers to the criteria of membership in the system which determine what belongs to it and what does not. These criteria determine the formal unity of the system. They are presupposed by any discussion of what may be called material unity. But they do not themselves account for it. They cannot explain the way in which one legal system has a certain character which marks it off from other legal systems.

One should not be carried away by talk of the spirit or character of a particular legal system. Many modern legal systems are far from being all of a piece. They reflect different and often conflicting attitudes to human life and to social cooperation as well as to the legal methods of handling them. Furthermore, to a large extent talk of the distinctive character of one legal system is but a flowery reference to the fact that its arrangements and institutions are different from those found in other legal systems. But there is more to it than that. Talk of the nature of the Common Law legal systems as against those based on the Roman law tradition, of their different character and different approach to legal problems, means more than the obvious fact that they differ in their legal institutions. It also refers to their tendency to develop along different routes, their tendency to provide different solutions to similar problems.

In this article I have touched on the three main factors which account for these facts. First, there are the traditions, conventions and practices of the legal profession. These do extend to style of argument and the kind of arguments allowed in court. They thus have a very significant impact on the role of the court in developing the law. An example of such a factor is the willingness of American courts to admit arguments based on social research and to take note of social statistics. Such arguments are not allowed in English courts. Therefore decisions such as *Brown v. Bd. of Education* 347 V.S. 483 (1954) or many apportionment cases could not have been reached, at least not on the same grounds, in England.

The second factor is the impact of the existence of certain legal institutions and arrangements on the desirability of introducing certain reforms, and of avoiding others. This factor, i. e. the law as an auxiliary reason for its own development, explains, I have claimed, the importance of the widespread use of analogy in judicial reasoning. It thereby explains why the courts are essentially a conservative force, conserving existing institutions by gradually modifying their details to conform to the perceived social and economic conditions.

Lastly, the law provides operative reasons for its own development. It does so primarily by conferring directed judicial powers which are reasons for the courts to develop the law in certain ways and not in others.

All three factors help to explain the feeling that different legal systems have a different character by explaining how they tend to perpetuate their own institutions and legal traditions. The importance of such factors is great but it is exaggerated by those who regard it as sufficient by itself to explain the development of judge-made law.

I started the article by referring to a view common in certain quarters that while legislated developments in the law reflect political, social and economic forces, developments in judge-made law are not to be explained by reference to such forces but by the inner logic of the law. I have done my best to explain this view (by reference to the three above-mentioned factors) and to defend it in as much as it is defensible. For at the end of the day it has to be rejected as a distorting exaggeration.

This is particularly clear in so far as the impact of directed powers on the development of the law is concerned. Those, as I have argued above, require the courts to use extra-legal considerations in developing the law. They refer them to moral considerations and thus open them to the influence of social and political considerations. The degree to which this is so depends on the extent to which the courts have power to develop the law at all and the degree of discretion they are given and the kind of direction in its use they are provided with. These are empirical matters which vary between different legal systems. But as it is a necessary fact that courts have law-making powers it is also a universal fact that in exercising them their actions are based on moral and political tendencies, and that they are directed by law to do so.

THE INNER LOGIC OF LAW AND LEGAL HERMENEUTICS

Some Comments on Raz

By Rolando Tamayo, Mexico City

The expression 'the inner logic of law' (as other English expressions) refers to the functioning of law (in particular to the functioning of courts) and presupposes somehow the idea of a specific coherence within legal systems. Dr. Raz correctly claims that this expression applies to what he dubs "the unwritten conventions of the legal profession". A clear comprehension of these conventions is of major importance for our understanding of the functioning of legal systems. As Dr. Raz says, "any study of law which disregards them is liable to produce a distorted picture". It is plain that the sharing of legal traditions (myths and prejudices included), the common possession of canons of interpretation, and the similarity of legal training, *inter alia,* do affect the development of legal systems. There is sufficient evidence to prove that the same legal institutions develop differently when implanted in different systems. The Roman Law of Justinian developed differently under the manner and habits of the Bolognese School. I can think of an example much closer to me: Mexico, after 1824, adopted the United States' constitutional structure and copied practically *verbatim* the United States' judiciary. Notwithstanding the same model, Mexico developed a different procedure of judicial review — the *Amparo* — which was molded to the constraints imposed by the Civil Law tradition. In the end, the Mexican Amparo resembles the French cassation more than it resembles any judicial procedure under United States' law.

It is clear from Dr. Raz' paper that the inner logic of the law is not a part of the analysis of the structure of the system. Nor is it a part of the description of the internal relations of its components (it is not a part of the individuation of laws). In his essay Dr. Raz intends rather to determine the main factors and rules that guide the internal development (the judicial development) of any system. How far is this enterprise connected with legal hermeneutics? Is it a meta-theory of legal hermeneutics? Is it descriptive hermeneutics?

Legal hermeneutics is concerned with the *correct* application of legal rules; it seeks to establish the canons of the interpretation of laws. The term 'legal hermeneutics' has come to designate the general theory of interpretation of all spoken or written legal expressions and the principles and procedures that lead to an appropriate use of them in adjudication. Legal hermeneutics (or hermeneutics, for short) is concerned with the meaning of legal rules and *all* their normative implications; it focuses on the constitutive and performative function of legal language. The hermeneutic approach is not satisfied with a surface (or ordinary) interpretation of legal language; it seeks to reach its hidden or latent meanings. Legal hermeneutics searches not only for the expressed intentions of the lawgiver but also for the unexpressed intentions; it seeks to go beyond the manifest statement of a legal rule to a (judicial) interpretation that reveals the possibilities of the meaning latent in the rule. H. L. A. Hart says:

> ... judges are only "drawing out" of the rule what, if it is properly understood, is "latent" with it.

Legal rules, which are necessarily formulated in terms of language, have implicit meanings that the judge, in the exercise of his directed powers, has to draw out. Is this not what the inner logic of the law designates or implies?

Further on, Dr. Raz points out that legal positivism presents a static view of law. Legal positivism regards the law as a system of existing rules. Does the idea of the inner logic of law necessarily contradict the main thesis of positivism? Does the idea of the inner logic of law presuppose a sort of rule-scepticism? Apparently there is nothing inconsistent in working out new rules from others already in existence. Legal positivism may perfectly well describe the law-creating acts of the law-applying organs. In any case, the mention of Kelsen in relation to this static view of positivism is rather severe and does not do justice to Kelsen's nomodynamics.

Raz is not concerned here with changes in the law by means of legislation (which, he says, though authorized by law are motivated by extralegal considerations). He is not concerned with a development where the impetus for changes comes from outside. Raz' concern is the *inner dynamics of law* as it is shown in the daily operation of courts. Courts do indeed develop the law. The question is: How can the law provide the impetus for its own development?

The way in which Dr. Raz approaches the problem is attractive enough to merit a brief summary. He distinguishes between operative and auxiliary reasons. He accepts that the existence of legal rules (and institutions) is an auxiliary reason made to implement a given operative (political or moral) reason. This is clearly manifest in legislation. But the problem is whether the law (*i. e.* the legal rules) can constitute an operative reason for its own development. Dr. Raz' answer is plainly 'yes'. He introduces the notion of directed powers (powers coupled with directions — duties — to use them solely to achieve certain objectives) to illustrate how the legal rules can form an operative reason for the development of law. Raz claims that directed powers are the paradigmatic case of the law providing for its own development.

It is worth noticing that, consistently with his own sources thesis, Dr. Raz maintains that the new rules (those created because of the power so conferred) are not part of the law until created by the empowered authority.

It is through this notion that Dr. Raz intends to explain the inner logic of the law (*i. e.* the ability of courts to change the law) by following the guidelines set out by the law itself.

Raz uses as examples of directed powers two legal doctrines and two hypothetical decisions (one for each doctrine) which purport to apply them. Through these examples, Dr. Raz shows that courts, when developing the law, do change it. Courts — he states — do more than simply repeat existing law; they do not merely reiterate what is implicit in the law (*i. e.* in the doctrines). Besides the case of misapplication, Dr. Raz points out two possibilities: (1) the decision may have been the one required by the doctrine, and (2) the doctrine may have been indeterminate on the issue in question. It seems to me that, as to the first case, it is somehow paradoxical to assert at the same time that the decision may have been the one required by the doctrine and that the decision does not merely apply what is implicit in the law.

If, in developing the law, courts do not reiterate something that is already law (though implicit), how can we state that they follow the doctrine? How can we assert that courts do develop the law in compliance with the directions set out in the doctrine? If courts in developing the law do not reiterate what is implicit in some rules (or doctrines) that constitute an operative reason set out by law for its own development, how can we determine that the law has been developed a step forward along the course foreseen by the law itself?

It is clear that the compliance with a doctrine or rule does not mean mere compatibility. A decision can be consistent with many rules and doctrines without purporting to apply either those rules or those doctrines. The decision that develops the law has to be somehow connected with the different possibilities covered by the directed powers. (Furthermore, this argument helps us in distinguishing changes in the law when developed by courts from all other changes in which courts act on the basis of other [extra-legal] operative reasons [introducing, for instance, revolutionary changes].)

In stating this, I mean to say nothing more than what is generally acknowledged by the legal profession. Why do courts seek to reach the implicit meaning or latent implications of a rule (or doctrine)? Why do courts search not only for the expressed intentions and aims of the "legislator" but for the unexpressed and presumptional ones as well? In doing this, courts search for a legal justification, a legal ground for developing the law along the direction foreseen by the law itself. Courts do not take legal rules and doctrines as merely sources of inspiration.

Of course I agree, as many legal theorists do, on the fact that the decision that develops the law does change it. I also agree that there is no doubt that despite the fact that some changes are implicit in the rule (or doctrine), no implicit change, even if we can anticipate it, is law until given legally binding force by the court. Is it not a kind of legal scepticism to deny that courts, when developing the law, apply what is latent in the rules?

Since the legal rules which constitute operative reasons set out by the law for its own development are meant to program court action, I can dub them, as other legal scholars do, 'programmatic rules' (particularly in the field of constitutional law). Programmatic rules are developed by courts when circumstances favor going on with the program (or part of it). Courts may be absolutely convinced of the benefits of developing the law as *programmed*, but prudential reasons (*e. g.* absence of consensus) may advise them to maintain the law as it has been till then. The decision introducing a change in the law shall have to wait.

Dr. Raz — as I have said — distinguishes between operative and auxiliary reasons. He correctly states that the existence of rules is an auxiliary reason made to implement certain operative (political or moral) reasons we find outside the legal system. On the other hand, Dr. Raz claims that legal rules can form an operative reason when they confer directed powers on some social institutions (subordinate legislature, courts). It seems to me that the existence of legal rules which confer directed powers can be described as an auxiliary reason made to implement (legally) some political goals (which form an operative reason). When some legal rules confer directed powers on some institutions (*e. g.* courts), they pursue defined political goals already accepted; they connect certain courses of action, *i. e.* the investing of directed powers, to the accepted goal. Legal rules, in such a case, provide a route to the goal's achievement. Law, then, implements specific political goals by creating directed powers.

Are legal rules solely auxiliary reasons? Is the law a specific social technique intended to implement political goals, as some legal theorists have claimed? It is clear that directed powers do not emerge spontaneously. They respond to some accepted political ideals. When some directed powers are conferred on courts, law establishes a particular régime with a particular judiciary. Do we duplicate (operative) reasons when we say that directed powers form an operative reason?

Perhaps the law constitutes an auxiliary reason only, made to serve operative reasons of a political or moral nature.

It is clear that when a goal is legally established, that fact does not mean only a legal recognition of the goal in question. It constitutes the first step in its legal achievement. Furthermore, the legal establishment of certain goals not only indicates (and initiates) the course of action towards its achievement; it also grants legal authority to that matter. The legal establishment of a goal converts any operative reason into a legal reason. And we have a vivid idea of how legal reasons operate. Certainly legal reasons are not weightier than any other reasons; nor are they more important. A legal reason excludes all other reasons. It is a characteristic feature of law that it claims (legitimate) authority. The essential exclusionary character of a legal reason provides a course of action submitted to the severity of legal mechanics.

VALUE RELATIVITY AND LEGAL INTERESTS

By Matti Sintonen, Helsinki

Several philosophers have defended what may be called a contextualist view of causal judgments and causal explanations of singular events. Thus R. G. Collingwood held that certain practical considerations, such as ability to produce or prevent an event, determine the selection of its cause, and Samuel Gorovitz has argued that judicial contexts focus on potentially punishable human action. The general judicial goal of preventing such actions rules some types of causes as type-inappropriate. Take an example. If we ask why a person *A* died, the judicial goal may require the selection of a person *B*'s act of installing a bomb in *A*'s car as *the* cause, while some other (e. g. merely technical) interest might select *A*'s turning of the ignition key.[1]

Gorovitz does not advocate any form of relativism, for according to him scientific inquiry is not interested in the inescapably contextual search for causes. Therefore his view allows for the classic division of labour between scientists who provide disinterested information and policy makers who provide the contextual — and often biased — values.

A more radical contextualist view has been recently propounded by Alan Garfinkel who holds, as against Gorovitz, that scientific inquiry is interested in causes, but secondly, that all causal claims are practically and even ideologically loaded.[2] For instance, assuming that both a rise in wages and no fall in the profits are necessary conditions for a rise in prices, there is no disinterested choice to be made between the explanations and causal claims (1) "The prices rose because there was a rise in wages", and (2) "The prices rose because there was no fall in the profits." According to Garfinkel the assumption that profits are not allowed to fall is a built-in presupposition in the question "Why did the

---

[1] See *R. G. Collingwood*, An Essay in Metaphysics, Oxford 1940, and *S. Gorovitz*, Aspects of the Pragmatics of Explanation, in: Nous 3 (1969), pp. 61—72. A similar contextualist view can also be found in *H. L. A. Hart/A. M. Honoré*, Causation in the Law, Oxford 1959. For discussion, see also *T. R. Girill*, Explanatory Pragmatics: A Critical Analysis, in: Philosophy Research Archives, Vol. III, pp. 1—50.

[2] *A. Garfinkel*, Forms of Explanation. Rethinking the Questions in Social Theory, New Haven and London 1981.

prices rise?", as intended by some queriers. Therefore they rule out, *a priori*, some potential answers as inappropriate or illegitimate. And since there are, pace positivism, no presuppositionless questions, there are no disinterested explanations and causal claims.

Applied to legal theory or argumentation the radically contextualist view would also entail the denial of a division of labour. Judicial questions contain practical or perhaps even ideological built-in presuppositions which rule out some explanations and causal claims as irrelevant from the point of view of legal interests. Again, since there are no presuppositionless questions, there is no one right or correct answer to the question "Why did *A* die?".

I. The Logic of Questions

The key notion in the contextualist argument is that of the presupposition of a question. To put the argument into perspective I shall sketch a question-theoretic proposal which draws a distinction between the logical presuppositions of a question and the pragmatic presuppositions of an inquirer in a context. My argument will be that the pragmatic presuppositions in the judicial and the economic examples are of an entirely different nature.

According to a classic analysis by Belnap and Steel, a statement *S* is a presupposition of a question *Q* if and only if the truth of *S* is a logically necessary condition for there being some true answer to *Q*.[3] To use the above examples, if *A* did not die and if the prices did not rise there are no true answers to the questions "Why did *A* die?" and "Why did the prices rise?".

Belnap and Steel also note that inquirers may impose certain completeness- and distinctness-conditions on potential answers. Such conditions are pragmatic in that they cannot be read from the question sentences. I propose to generalize this observation. There always is more to a question than meets the ear. The background knowledge — and possibly interests — of inquirers (queriers) lay further strictures on what answers are acceptable in a pragmatic context.

The radical contextualist proposal now hinges on the nature of these pragmatic presuppositions. In the price-wage example, Alan Garfinkel argues, any inquirer must have his choice from among the contextually necessary antecedent conditions. There are no such things as complete causes or explanations which would list all causal antecedents, for such

[3] *N. Belnap/T. B. Steel,* The Logic of Questions and Answers, New Haven and London 1976, p. 113.

lists are necessarily relative to a contrast class or specific question. As a consequence any putative list ends up with a regress or "bad infinity" of causes.[4]

Garfinkel's claim in fact is that causal judgements themselves are value laden, for the following reason. Any putative causal law of the form "All *F*'s are *G*'s" must have counterfactual force to count as lawlike. Counterfactuality in its turn means that the law retains its validity not just in the actual world but also in circumstances which differ to some extent from the actual ones.

The trouble arises when we try to determine the range of the possible worlds within which the lawlike statement is supposed to hold. To count as lawlike the putative law "If wages rise, prices will also rise" must hold in certain possible worlds different from but sufficiently similar to the actual one. But the range of possible worlds cannot be that of logically or physically possible worlds, for that would include too much. Rather, inquirers have views about "economically feasible" possibilities and "live" economic options.

II. The Intertwinement Thesis

This is where the thesis of the intertwinement of facts and values comes in. According to Garfinkel, a possible world in which wages rise but prices do not is deemed unrealistic because in it profits fall — or perhaps because it is not a market economy at all.[5] The judgment is covertly ethical (Garfinkel speaks of "the ethics of explanation") or ideological, the intertwinement argument goes, for some physically and economically possible worlds are excluded on the grounds of their unpalatable practical consequences. Behind such *a priori* constraints there may be the view that shareholders *ought to have* (fair) profits or that profits are necessary for economic growth and we *want* growth.

However, there are reasons to think that such relativity is rather innocuous and does not jeopardize the classic division of labour between suppliers of information and of values. Granted that a selection of live options depends on value impregnated pragmatic presuppositions, it does not follow that facts and values are inseparably intertwined.

To put the issue in question-theoretic terms, an inquirer may build into his question pragmatic *a priori* limitations on admissible answers. Such constraints may well be ethically or ideologically motivated. However, an answerer need take such limitations at face value. Quite simply,

---

[4] *Garfinkel* (note 2), pp. 145—146.

[5] Ibid., p. 150.

just as he can correct the questioner's logical presupposition ("But the prices did not rise") he can correct the questioner's pragmatic presupposition which rules out, illegitimately in his view, economically possible alternatives ("But, sir, you take it for granted that profits cannot fall!")

I am not proposing that there can be a knock-down argument for or against the feasibility of a counterfactual economic possible world, only that such disagreements are ordinary factual ones. In fact the intertwinement example is so spelled out that we can incorporate the presuppositions into the causal laws and get the relatively more neutral "If wages rise and profits do not fall, prices will rise". The example is still overly naive, for there are innumerable other boundary conditions (presuppositions) for the validity of the causal statement. But of course such a state of affairs is the rule in all causal research, social scientific and natural scientific alike. Notice that with the caveat about idealization (and *ceteris paribus* conditions) the statement can no doubt support counterfactuals and the explanation (3) "The prices rose because there was a rise in wages and no fall in the profits."[6]

How about radical contextualism and legal interests? Take the example of the person *A*'s dying as a result of an explosion in his car. The two alternative causal claims and explanations are (4) "*A* died because *B* installed a bomb in *A*'s car" and (5) "*A* died because he turned the ignition key". There are more candidates, such as (6) "*A* died because his chest was injured", but these should suffice.

The examples should make it clear that there need be no factual disagreement between a lawyer who offers (4) and a medical doctor who opts for (6), for both can agree about the causal chain which leads to *A*. Interest-relativity here boils down to the selection of different stretches of the causal chain. Judicial interests pick out judicially relevant causal chains which may be irrelevant for merely technical or medical purposes. For instance a causally relevant necessary condition may be too remote to establish liability. But the judicial principles of assessing and establishing liability do not unravel a notion of causation distinct from that of ordinary causation. Rather, they enter into the causal queries as pragmatic presuppositions which restrict the possible answers to those causal antecedents which are judicially relevant.[7]

---

[6] John Mackie has coined the notion of a *causal field* to mark the assumptions taken for granted in a given context. In Mackie's terminology explanation (1) may be unacceptable for an inquirer who does not include the assumption of no fall in the profits within the causal field. See *J. Mackie*, The Cement of the Universe: A Study in Causation, Oxford 1974, pp. 34—35.

[7] I have discussed these questions in greater detail in *M. Sintonen*, Causation and the Legal Point of View, in: *U. Kangas* (ed.), Essays in Legal Theory in Honour of Kaarle Makkonen, Vammala 1983.

III. Two Divisions of Labour

It should be clear that there is a fundamental difference between the alleged interest-relativity of the two types of queries. In the economic example there is room for ideology criticism, so to say, which brings tacit epistemic background assumptions and the underlying practical interests into the open. In the simplified example at least factual disagreements, based on different epistemic assumptions, and the values can be disentangled. And although it may well turn out that one cannot make all boundary conditions of causal statements explicit, they nevertheless are conditions which pertain to knowledge.

The interest-relativity of the second example is of a different nature. For behind the principles governing assessment of liability there are straightforwardly legal and moral principles of protecting the interests of people, of compensating for and preventing harm, of promoting moral order, etc. Such principles are irreducibly legal or moral for they are not (exclusively, or at all) concerned with what states of affairs or courses of events are possible but what indeed is legally and morally desirable, just, or whatever. One can perhaps eliminate the judicial presuppositions — but only on the pain of changing the topic or abandoning the subject matter. The claim is not that the details of such presuppositions are above criticism, but that some such presuppositions are constitutive of legal discourse.

An interesting fact emerges at this point. Garfinkel's radical contextualism is, in his own words, designed to undermine the positivist assumption of value-free science, and the concomitant division of labour. But if I am right it is not this division of labour that must go, for even in the judicial example we can draw, in principle at least, a distinction between the legal scholars' personal interests and the more anonymous values constitutive of legal discourse.[8] Rather, the principle that there is but one type of discourse must be jettisoned.

The logical positivist movement of the 1920's and 1930's was also known as the unity of science movement. Roughly, logical positivists believed that there is a unified empiricist (phenomenal or physical) language, and that all (cognitively) meaningful sentences (statements) were translatable into this language. It follows from this picture that there is essentially but one type of discourse and one science, governed by the purely scientific (if not scientist) interest in maximum predictive power and intellectual economy. The differences between various

[8] I want to emphasize that by drawing attention to the contrast between the two types of inquiry I do not wish to claim that ideology criticism cannot take place in legal research or debate.

domains of inquiry were thought to be matters of application and division of labour.

In question-theoretic parlance, the positivist ideal excludes pragmatic presuppositions which incorporate interests other than knowledge. Why this limitation? The fear was that pragmatic interests would jeopardize the fundamental scientific values of intersubjective testability and objectivity.[9] But of course the fear was about subjective or personal stakes, and not the stakes of the judicial system.

To the extent there are irreducible disciplinary interests of the type sketched above, the comforting picture must be radically altered. Indeed, there are field-specific presuppositions which require that the world, or a portion thereof, be sliced in a certain way.[10] These presuppositions enter into the very questions asked. It is not just that it is impossible to give purely physicalist translations of certain types of discourse. In the positivist picture only purely epistemic division of labour was allowed. However, judicial presuppositions bring in non-epistemic moral and legal interests.

---

[9] For this, see *M. Sintonen*, The Pragmatics of Scientific Explanation, Acta Philosophica Fennica Vol. 37, Helsinki 1984, Sections I. 4. and IV. 4.

[10] *Gorovitz* (note 1), p. 70.

ZUM PROBLEM EINER TRANSZENDENTALEN DEDUKTION DES BEGRIFFS DES RECHTS

Von Johannes Strangas, Komotini/Hamburg

I.

Die Tatsache, daß im Titel meines Referats der Ausdruck „transzendentale Deduktion" enthalten ist, bewirkt, daß ich als erstes im Rahmen meines Referats klarzumachen habe, in welcher Bedeutung dabei der Terminus „transzendental" verwendet ist. Und dies um so mehr, insofern die Absicht besteht, diesen Terminus in der klassischen, nämlich in der von *Kant* geprägten Bedeutung desselben zu benutzen. Denn diese Bedeutung gilt heute im allgemeinen als überholt, derart, daß, wenn heute noch — was immer seltener der Fall ist — der Terminus „transzendental" verwendet wird, seine Verwendung in aller Regel die von *K.-O. Apel*[1] formulierte Annahme, daß die Frage nach den transzendentalen Möglichkeitsbedingungen mit der Frage nach der Deduktion von Theoremen im Rahmen eines selbst wieder zu begründenden axiomatischen Systems nicht identisch sei, impliziert. Diese Annahme gründet Apel auf diejenige These *Alberts*, die dieser[2] mit dem Namen „Münchhausen-Trilemma" versehen hat.

Albert hat nämlich die These aufgestellt[3], daß, wenn man für alles eine Begründung verlange, man auch für die Erkenntnisse, auf die man jeweils die zu begründende Auffassung zurückgeführt hat, wieder eine Begründung verlangen müsse, was zu einem Trilemma, nämlich zu einer Situation führe, in der man vor die Wahl zwischen einem regressus ad infinitum, einem logischen Zirkel und dem Rekurs auf ein Dogma stehe. In Anlehnung an diese These möchte Albert dann[4] das „Begründungsprinzip" — welches an dem Satz vom zureichenden Grunde „orientiert ist"[5] — zugunsten des „Prüfungsprinzips" — welches an

[1] *K.-O. Apel*, Die Kommunikationsgemeinschaft als transzendentale Voraussetzung der Sozialwissenschaften, in: *ders.*, Transformation der Philosophie, Bd. 2, Frankfurt/M. ²1981, S. 220 f.

[2] *H. Albert*, Traktat über kritische Vernunft, Tübingen ²1969, S. 13.

[3] Ebd., S. 13 f.

[4] Ebd., S. 33 f.

[5] Ebd., S. 11 f., 29 f., 35 f.

dem „Satz vom ausgeschlossenen Widerspruch“ (d. i. dem principium contradictionis) „orientiert ist“[6] — verlassen.

II.

Die erwähnte These *Alberts* vermag indessen, wie näheres Zusehen zeigt, der Kritik nicht Stand zu halten:

Albert weist das „Begründungsprinzip“ mit dem Argument zurück, daß es auf ein Trilemma, dessen Glieder logische Fehler ausmachen, hinauslaufe. Die vorsichtige Betrachtung dieser drei Fehler ergibt, daß sie insofern miteinander verwandt sind, als sie gleichermaßen in eine Verletzung des principium contradictionis auszumünden scheinen: der logische Zirkel läuft auf eine dahingehende contradictio in adjecto hinaus, daß etwas als Grund von etwas anderem und zugleich als Folge, d. i. nicht als Grund von diesem letzteren fungiere; der regressus ad infinitum auf eine dahingehende contradictio in adjecto, daß in Anwendung des „Begründungsprinzips“ keine Begründung erfolge bzw. erfolgen könne; und der Rekurs auf ein Dogma, indem er einen Abbruch des Begründungsverfahrens bedeutet[7], auf eine dahingehende contradictio in adjecto, daß die Anerkennung bzw. Verwendung des „Begründungsprinzips“ notwendig mit der Verletzung desselben verbunden sei. Die Zurückweisung des „Begründungsprinzips“ und die durch sie implizierte Verneinung der Gültigkeit des demselben zugrundeliegenden Satzes vom zureichenden Grunde erfolgen somit in Anwendung des principium contradictionis; und sie hängen daher von der Gültigkeit dieses letzteren ab.

Die Gültigkeit desselben kann, da das auf demselben beruhende „Prüfungsprinzip“ den Ausgangspunkt des Verfahrens der Überprüfung der Wahrheitsgemäßheit von Erkenntnissen bzw. Auffassungen bildet, nicht etwa durch die „Erfahrung“ „bestätigt“ werden (weil der Versuch einer derartigen „Bestätigung“ auf eine petitio principii bzw. auf einen circulus vitiosus hinausliefe, indem die „Erfahrung“ als bereits hinsichtlich der Wahrheitsgemäßheit derselben gewiß betrachtet würde). Sie muß daher irgendwie eine Rechtfertigung „besitzen“ (sollte sie „vermeiden“, daß sie als das „Produkt“ einer willkürlichen Setzung auftritt, in welchem Falle das „Prüfungsprinzip“ die demselben von *Albert*[8] zuerkannte Aufgabe, als Instrument der Überprüfung der Wahrheitsgemäßheit von Erkenntnissen bzw. Auffassungen zu dienen, nicht erfüllen könnte). Und es lassen sich insb. zwei Arten von Rechtfertigung

[6] Ebd., S. 43.

[7] Zum letzteren siehe auch ebd., S. 13—14.

[8] Ebd., S. 35 f., 41 f.

denken, nämlich einerseits die Rechtfertigung des principium contradictionis durch Rekurs auf ein anderes Prinzip und andererseits eine Rechtfertigung desselben aus sich selbst.

Die erstgenannte denkbare Rechtfertigungsart scheidet hierbei deswegen aus, weil sie in einer Begründung bestünde und somit die Verwendung des „Begründungsprinzips" implizieren würde, welches jedoch nach dem oben Gesagten von *Albert* eben in Anwendung des principium contradictionis zurückgewiesen wird.

In Frage käme also nur die zweitgenannte denkbare Rechtfertigungsart. Diese ist aber jedenfalls nicht etwa als dahingehend zu konzipieren, daß die Gültigkeit des principium contradictionis auf dem Als-evident-Erscheinen desselben beruhen würde (weil das letztere die Verwendung des „Begründungsprinzips" implizieren würde, indem das Als-evident-Erscheinen als zureichender Gültigkeitsgrund behandelt würde). Also ist sie dahingehend zu konzipieren, daß die Verneinung der Gültigkeit des principium contradictionis unmöglich ist (was gerade den einzigen Fall bildet, in dem seine Gültigkeit nicht auf Grund des Rekurses auf ein anderes Prinzip gerechtfertigt würde); und in der Tat kann die Verneinung des principium contradictionis gar nicht gedacht werden, weil sie für ihre Richtigkeit (= Gültigkeit) gerade die Gültigkeit desselben bzw. des aus demselben abgeleiteten[9] Satzes vom ausgeschlossenen Dritten impliziert[10, 11].

Ob eine solche Rechtfertigungsart die Gültigkeit des principium contradictionis zu sichern vermag, mag in diesem Zusammenhang dahingestellt bleiben. Vielmehr interessieren in diesem Zusammenhang die

---

[9] Dazu siehe etwa *Sigwart*, Logik, Bd. I, Tübingen [5]1924, S. 202; *Freytag Löringhoff*, Logik, Bd. I, Stuttgart [5]1964, S. 19.

[10] Die Tatsache, daß *Alberts* Theorie für ihr Sinnvoll-Sein die derartige Rechtfertigung des principium contradictionis notwendig voraussetzt, wird klar durch die kritische Analyse der Stellungnahmen Alberts zu der Frage, ob auch die seinen universalen Fallibilismus beinhaltende Überzeugung diesem Fallibilismus nicht entgeht, d. h. nicht unanzweifelbar ist, und zu der Frage, ob es unaufgebbare Bestandteile der Logik gibt. Siehe *Strangas*, Bemerkungen zum Problem der Letztbegründung, in: Archiv für Rechts- und Sozialphilosophie LXX (1984), S. 477, Fußn. 11.

[11] Auf die Tatsache, daß man bestimmte logische Regeln — darunter auch das principium contradictionis — nicht verwerfen kann, ohne daß man diese Regeln zugleich anwendet, weist auch *H. Lenk*, Philosophische Logikbegründung und rationaler Kritizismus, in: Zeitschrift für philosophische Forschung 24 (1970), S. 202 f. hin, der diese Regeln dann für unverzichtbare Bestandteile der Theorie des kritischen Rationalismus — d. i. eben der auch von *Albert* vertretenen Theorie — erklärt. Zwischen der einschlägigen Argumentation *Lenks* und der im Text entwickelten Argumentation bestehen jedoch zwei wichtige Unterschiede, die in meiner Studie „Bemerkungen zum Problem der Letztbegründung" (Fußn. 10 oben), Fußn. 12 (S. 478) analysiert sind.

Implikationen einer solchen Rechtfertigungsart, die das Problem, ob neben dem principium contradictionis weitere principia logica anzunehmen sind, betreffen, welches Problem hier anhand der Beantwortung der Frage nach der Gültigkeit des Satzes vom zureichenden Grunde zu erörtern ist:

Die Tatsache, daß *Alberts* Zurückweisung des „Begründungsprinzips", wie oben dargestellt wurde, letzten Endes „mittels" des principium contradictionis erfolgt, bedeutet, da diese Zurückweisung die Verneinung der Gültigkeit des Satzes vom zureichenden Grunde impliziert, gerade, daß Albert stillschweigend anzunehmen scheint, daß das principium contradictionis auf andere denkbare logische Prinzipien Anwendung finde. Eine solche Annahme wäre indessen widersprüchlich — d. h. gerade dem principium contradictionis zuwiderlaufend — und zwar deswegen, weil sie impliziert, daß die anderen angeblich denkbaren logischen Prinzipien Anwendungsfälle des principium contradictionis, diesem also nicht ranggleich und daher keine eigenständigen principia logica seien. Es ist also das principium contradictionis selbst, welches die Möglichkeit ausschließt, daß dasselbe zum ausschließlichen Kriterium der Gültigkeit bzw. Ungültigkeit anderer logischer Prinzipien dient.

Darüber hinaus ist es aber auch das principium contradictionis, welches „fordert", daß Sätzen, die in gleicher Weise wie es selbst zu rechtfertigen sind, die Eigenschaft, principia logica zu sein, zuerkannt wird. Wenn sich nämlich z. B. zeigen ließe, daß die Verneinung der Gültigkeit des Satzes vom zureichenden Grunde bzw. die Zurückweisung des auf diesem Satze beruhenden „Begründungsprinzips" für ihre Richtigkeit (= Gültigkeit) gerade die Gültigkeit dieses Satzes impliziert, könnte diesem Satze die Eigenschaft, principium logicum zu sein, nicht abgesprochen werden; denn die etwaige Gegenannahme würde dem principium contradictionis zuwiderlaufen (weil sie der Annahme gleichkäme, daß ein und dieselbe Eigenschaft, d. i. das Nicht-verneinbar-Sein, einmal — nämlich im Falle des principium contradictionis — die genannte Eigenschaft rechtfertige, das andere Mal — nämlich im Falle des Satzes vom zureichenden Grunde — hingegen die genannte Eigenschaft nicht rechtfertige). Und die Tatsache, daß für die Richtigkeit (= Gültigkeit) der Verneinung der Gültigkeit des Satzes vom zureichenden Grunde die Gültigkeit desselben vorausgesetzt ist, wird z. B. anhand der Argumentation klar, mit welcher *Albert* das „Begründungsprinzip" zurückzuweisen versucht. Denn Albert beruft sich dabei auf das notwendige Ausmünden des „Begründungsprinzips" in das „Münchhausen-Trilemma", d. h. letzten Endes in die Verletzung des principium contradictionis; somit behandelt er aber die Verletzung des principium contradictionis als zureichenden Grund für die Zurückweisung des „Begründungsprinzips"[12], welche Zurückweisung auch die Verneinung der Gültigkeit des Satzes vom zureichenden Grunde impliziert[13].

Kann also dem Satze vom zureichenden Grunde die Eigenschaft, principium logicum zu sein, nicht abgesprochen werden, dann ist man gezwungen, auch dem „Begründungsprinzip" Gültigkeit zuzuerkennen. Damit wird der oben erwähnten Annahme, daß die Frage nach den transzendentalen Möglichkeitsbedingungen mit der Frage nach der Deduktion von Theoremen im Rahmen eines selbst wieder zu begründenden axiomatischen Systems nicht identisch sei, und der mit dieser Annahme zusammenhängenden Zurückweisung der klassischen (d. i. der von *Kant* geprägten) Bedeutung des Terminus „transzendental", das Fundament entzogen.

III.

Die somit erfolgende Wiederherstellung der Gültigkeit der klassischen Bedeutung des Terminus „transzendental" legt es aber nahe anzunehmen, daß mit deren Gültigkeit zugleich die Gültigkeit derjenigen philosophischen Lehren wiederherzustellen ist, durch die sie erzeugt bzw. weiterentwickelt wurde, nämlich vor allem der Lehren *Kants* und *Fichtes;* und wenn die Gültigkeit dieser Lehren wiederherzustellen wäre, wäre eine erneute Beschäftigung mit dem Problem der transzendentalen Deduktion des Begriffs des Rechts — welche ja das Thema dieses Referats bildet — nur insofern als sinnvoll anzusehen, als sich etwa erweisen würde, daß jene Lehren entweder keine transzendentale Deduktion des Begriffs des Rechts oder eine der Kritik nicht Stand haltende transzendentale Deduktion dieses Begriffs enthalten. Ob die Gültigkeit der genannten Lehren im allgemeinen wiederherzustellen ist, hängt freilich davon ab, ob sie die Voraussetzungen erfüllen, deren Erfüllt-Sein-Müssen durch die klassische Bedeutung des Terminus „transzendental" bzw. durch den Satz vom zureichenden Grunde, dessen Gültigkeit sie ja „beansprucht", impliziert wird. Welches diese Voraussetzungen sind, ergibt die Analyse der Implikationen der Anerkennung des Satzes vom zureichenden Grunde als eines logischen Prinzips:

Würden der Satz vom zureichenden Grunde bzw. das „Begründungsprinzip" in einer Weise konzipiert, auf welche sie in das „Münchhausen-

[12] Was könnte denn besser als zureichender Grund fungieren als ein principium logicum, d. h. etwas, dessen Gültigkeit nicht verneint werden kann?

[13] Daß die Zurückweisung des „Begründungsprinzips" die Verneinung der Gültigkeit des Satzes vom zureichenden Grunde impliziert, geht gerade daraus hervor, daß das „Begründungsprinzip" nichts anderes als die „Anordnung" der Anwendung des Satzes vom zureichenden Grunde beinhaltet (genauso wie das „Prüfungsprinzip" nichts anderes als die „Anordnung" der Anwendung des principium contradictionis beinhaltet).

Trilemma", mithin letzten Endes in eine Verletzung des principium contradictionis ausmünden, so würde die Logik (als Inbegriff der principia logica verstanden) als einen logischen Fehler, nämlich eine Verletzung des principium contradictionis enthaltend auftreten. Da das letztere jedoch auf die Verneinung der Gültigkeit des principium contradictionis hinausliefe, welche indessen nach dem oben sub II Gesagten unmöglich ist, ist es die Logik selbst, die „fordert", daß der Satz vom zureichenden Grunde bzw. das „Begründungsprinzip" in einer Weise aufgefaßt werden, auf welche der erwähnte Fehler vermieden wird. Und eine derartige Auffassung „beinhaltet" notwendigerweise die Annahme, daß die Logik den Begriff eines „Letzten" impliziert, welches keiner Begründung bedürftig bzw. zugänglich ist und zum Ausgangspunkt jeglicher Begründung dient bzw. zu dienen hat.

Welches nun dieses „Letztes" ist, dies zu bestimmen stellt kein Problem der Logik (= der Formalphilosophie), sondern ein Problem der Materialphilosophie[14] dar. Dieses Problem kann in diesem Zusammenhang keine vollständige Erörterung erfahren. Es kann nur in dem Maße erörtert werden, in dem seine Erörterung in der Kritik der Lehren, durch die die klassische Bedeutung des Terminus „transzendental" erzeugt bzw. weiterentwickelt wurde, und zwar in der Kritik derselben unter dem Gesichtspunkt der Frage besteht, ob das durch dieselben aufgestellte „Letzte" sich zu einer erfolgreichen transzendentalen Deduktion des Begriffs des Rechts eignet. Daher werden wir im folgenden auch auf die Suche nach einer angemessenen Bezeichnung desjenigen, dessen Begriff die Eigenschaft, Begriff des „Letzten" zu sein, zuzuerkennen ist, verzichten und uns weiterhin einfach des Terminus „Letztes" bedienen.

IV.

Als „Letzes" fungiert im Rahmen der kantischen praktischen Philosophie die sittliche Einsicht, als „Faktum der reinen Vernunft" aufgefaßt. Und insofern die sittliche Einsicht, so aufgefaßt, als ein Wissen auf der „Ebene" der Dinge an sich selbst betrachtet auftritt[15], scheint ihre Erhebung zum „Letzten" aus der Sicht der praktischen Philosophie gerechtfertigt zu sein. Wohlgemerkt: aus der Sicht der praktischen Philosophie. Denn die Möglichkeit, daß die so aufgefaßte sittliche Einsicht auch für die theoretische Philosophie als „Letztes" fungiert, ist im

---

[14] Zur Unterscheidung zwischen Materialphilosophie und Formalphilosophie (= Logik) siehe *I. Kant*, Grundlegung zur Metaphysik der Sitten, Riga [2]1786, S. III.

[15] Vgl. *Strangas*, Die Billigkeit und ihr Standort im Rechtssystem (Hamburger Jur. Diss.), Athen/Hamburg 1976, S. 188.

Rahmen des kantischen philosophischen Systems ausgeschlossen. Und der Ausschluß dieser Möglichkeit bedeutet gerade, daß in jedem der beiden Zweige der Philosophie etwas anderes als „Letztes" zu konzipieren sei, was jedoch mit dem Begriff des „Letzten" als solchen unvereinbar ist[16]. Doch sei davon in diesem Zusammenhang abgesehen!

Darüber hinaus spricht *Kant* im Falle des Rechtsbegriffs[17] nicht von „transzendentaler Deduktion"; und er hat auch in der Tat keine transzendentale Deduktion, d. i. keine rein apriorische Ableitung dieses Begriffs geleistet: Er bemerkte zwar schon in der „Kritik der reinen Vernunft"[18], daß das Recht gar nicht erscheinen könne, sondern sein Begriff in dem Verstande liege und eine Beschaffenheit der Handlungen darstelle. Aber es ist ihm nicht gelungen, den Unterschied zwischen moralischem und rechtmäßigem Handeln transzendental, d. i. rein apriorisch, zu deduzieren. Dies ist auch daran zu erkennen, daß er diesen Unterschied in die „Ebene" der Neigungen zu „versetzen" suchte, indem er bemerkte[19], daß die Triebfeder der rechtmäßigen Handlungen, nämlich der äußere Zwang, von den pathologischen Bestimmungsgründen der Willkür der Neigungen und Abneigungen und unter diesen von denen der letzteren Art hergenommen sei, und daraus z. B. folgerte, daß die Erfüllung eines Versprechens in den Fällen, in denen kein Zwang besorgt werden darf bzw. kann, ein Beweis der Tugend sei[20]. Auch hat

[16] In der Tat impliziert der Begriff der Zweiheit das Gleich-Sein der sie zusammensetzenden Dinge im Hinblick auf etwas, mithin das In-Beziehung-zu-diesem-Etwas-Stehen derselben und folglich auch das Aus-diesem-Etwas-abzuleiten-Sein derselben. Und das Aus-etwas-anderem-abzuleiten-Sein ist mit dem Begriff des „Letzten" überhaupt unvereinbar.

[17] *Kant*, Metaphysische Anfangsgründe der Rechtslehre, Königsberg ²1798, S. 14 ff., 31 ff.

[18] *Kant*, Kritik der reinen Vernunft, Riga ¹1781, S. 44; ²1787, S. 61.

[19] *Kant*, Metaphysische Anfangsgründe der Rechtslehre (Fußn. 17), S. 15.

[20] Es ist jedoch zu bedenken, daß die alltägliche Erfahrung des Soziallebens uns vielfach lehrt, daß viele Menschen unabhängig von der Bedrohung durch staatlichen Zwang bzw. trotz des Fehlens eines solchen rechtmäßig und dennoch nicht etwa aus Tugendhaftigkeit handeln. So bietet etwa die Praxis des Handels- bzw. Wirtschaftsrechts und des Völkerrechts zahlreiche Beispiele von Versprechenserfüllungen, die keineswegs aus Tugendhaftigkeit bzw. zum Zwecke der Vermeidung staatlichen Zwangs, sondern infolge anderer Zweckmäßigkeitserwägungen (etwa im Falle des Handels- bzw. Wirtschaftsrechts unter Berücksichtigung von Gesichtspunkten wirtschaftlicher Spekulation bzw. im Falle des Völkerrechts zum Zwecke der Förderung irgendwelcher nationaler Interessen) erfolgen. Aber auch aus der sozusagen alltäglichen zivilrechtlichen Praxis ist der Fall bekannt, daß der Schuldner die Leistung korrekt bzw. rechtzeitig bewirkt, obwohl gegen ihn entweder kein staatlicher Zwang überhaupt (z. B. wegen Verjährung des gegen ihn bestehenden Anspruchs) oder aber mit sehr großer Verzögerung staatlicher Zwang besorgt werden könnte, und er dennoch nicht aus Tugendhaftigkeit handelt, sondern etwa um seinen sozialen Ruf nicht zu schaden oder um der schönen Gläubigerin Gefallen zu tun.

Kant keine transzendentale Deduktion des Person-Seins als Eigenschaft mehrerer unvollkommener Wesen vorgenommen, welche Deduktion es gerade erlaubt, das Bestehen rechtlicher Verhältnisse anzunehmen.

Der Umstand, daß *Kant* keine transzendentale Deduktion, d. i. keine rein apriorische Ableitung des Rechtsbegriffs vorgenommen hat, vermag freilich weniger zu befremden, wenn man bedenkt, daß auch dort, wo Kant von „transzendentaler Deduktion“ sprach — etwa im Falle der Kategorien[21] bzw. im Falle des Begriffs der Erwerbung durch Vertrag[22] — er keine transzendentale Deduktion im eigentlichen Sinne, d. h. keine rein apriorische Ableitung geleistet hat[23]. Der genannte Umstand vermag aber noch weniger, ja überhaupt nicht mehr zu befremden, wenn man bedenkt, daß Kant eine transzendentale Deduktion des Begriffs des Rechts wegen innerer Mängel seines Systems gar nicht leisten könnte:

Den Grundbegriff der kantischen praktischen Philosophie bildet der Begriff der Freiheit, den *Kant* aus dem Begriff des mittels der sittlichen Einsicht zu „erfahrenden“ Sollens ableitete, indem er behauptete[24], daß „der Handelnde urteilt, daß er etwas kann, darum, weil er bewußt ist, daß er es soll, und erkennt die Freiheit, die ihm sonst unbekannt geblieben wäre“. Um aus dem Begriff der Freiheit weitere rein apriorische Begriffe abzuleiten (d. h. transzendental zu deduzieren), bedürfte freilich Kant — da jede Einteilung außer dem Gegebensein des einzuteilenden Begriffs das Gegebensein eines Einteilungskriteriums voraussetzt, und dieses Kriterium bei einer Einteilung, auf deren Weg eine rein apriorische Ableitung (d. i. eine transzendentale Deduktion)

---

[21] *Kant,* Kritik der reinen Vernunft, 2. Aufl. (Fußn. 18), S. 124 f., 129 f.

[22] *Kant,* Metaphysische Anfangsgründe der Rechtslehre (Fußn. 17), S. 99 in fin.

[23] In der Tat gewinnt *Kant* in der „Kritik der reinen Vernunft“ die Begriffe der Kategorien aus den Begriffen der Urteilsarten, die in seiner Urteilstafel enthalten sind (vgl. charakteristisch [Fußn. 18], 2. Aufl., S. 105 in fin. und S. 159), wobei er seine Urteilstafel — wie auch von *Tonelli* (Die Voraussetzungen der kantischen Urteilstafel in der Logik des 18. Jahrhunderts, in: Festschrift für Heimsoeth, Berlin 1966, S. 150 ff.) gezeigt wurde — nur einigermaßen originell entwickelt hat, zumal er sich z. B. im Falle der Urteilsarten der Qualität und der Quantität der Majorität der damaligen Logik angeschlossen hat. Und in den „Metaphysischen Anfangsgründen der Rechtslehre“ verhält es sich mit der „transzendentalen Deduktion des Begriffs der Erwerbung durch Vertrag“ so, daß — wie von *G. Lübbe-Wolff* (Begründungsmethoden in Kants Rechtslehre untersucht am Beispiel des Vertragsrechts, in: R. Brandt (Hrsg.), Rechtsphilosophie der Aufklärung, Berlin 1982, S. 297/298) bemerkt wurde — diese „Deduktion“ nicht den Charakter eines Beweises der Vereinbarkeit des Vertragsinstituts mit dem allgemeinen Rechtsgesetz hat, weshalb man sich nach einer Auskunft über die rechtliche Möglichkeit bzw. Notwendigkeit des Vertragsinstituts außerhalb dieser „Deduktion“ umsehen muß.

[24] *Kant,* Kritik der praktischen Vernunft, Riga 1788, S. 54.

zu erfolgen hätte, in seinem Begriff rein apriorisch bestimmt sein muß — eines zusätzlichen aus dem Begriff des mittels der sittlichen Einsicht zu „erfahrenden" Sollens unmittelbar abzuleitenden Begriffs, welcher das Einteilungskriterium bildete, bzw. aus dessen Verbindung mit dem Begriff der Freiheit das Einteilungskriterium zu gewinnen wäre. Als solcher zusätzlicher Begriff läßt sich nur der (rein apriorische) Begriff der Unvollkommenheit denken[25], der, wie näheres Zusehen zeigt, aus dem Begriff des mittels der sittlichen Einsicht zu „erfahrenden" Sollens quasi mit demselben Denkschritt, mit dem aus diesem letzteren Begriff der Begriff der Freiheit abgeleitet wird, abzuleiten ist, indem der Handelnde daraus, daß er etwas soll, nicht nur darauf, daß er es kann, sondern auch darauf, daß es nicht notwendig erfolgt, schließen kann. Kant hat jedoch den (rein apriorischen) Begriff der Unvollkommenheit nicht aufgestellt und infolgedessen seine praktische Philosophie der Möglichkeit beraubt, ihre Begriffe — darunter auch den Begriff des Rechts — auf dem Wege rein apriorischer Ableitungen, d. h. transzendentaler Deduktionen derselben zu gewinnen.

V.

Anders als bei *Kant* ist bei *Fichte* von einer „transzendentalen Deduktion" des Begriffs des Rechts die Rede.

Die Unterscheidung zwischen Ich und Nicht-Ich, d. h. zwischen den beiden Grundbegriffen, von denen die gesamte philosophische Theorie *Fichtes* und somit auch der fichtesche Versuch jener transzendentalen Deduktion ihren Ausgang nehmen, wurde von Fichte freilich nicht transzendental deduziert[26]; und dies bewirkte, daß auch der Versuch der genannten transzendentalen Deduktion zwangsläufig unbegründet ist. Davon sei aber in diesem Zusammenhang abgesehen.

Fichte argumentiert bei seinem Versuch einer transzendentalen Deduktion des Begriffs des Rechts folgendermaßen[27]: Der Grund der Unmöglichkeit, das Selbstbewußtsein zu erklären, ohne es immer als schon vorhanden vorauszusetzen, liege darin, daß, um seine Wirksamkeit setzen

[25] Aus dem Begriff des mittels der sittlichen Einsicht zu „erfahrenden" Sollens ist neben den Begriffen der Freiheit und der Unvollkommenheit kein weiterer Begriff unmittelbar abzuleiten. Denn die Freiheit und die Unvollkommenheit stellen gerade die Position und die Negation der vollkommenen Freiheit; und tertium, welches weder die Position noch die Negation von etwas darstellt, non datur.

[26] Vgl. auch *Strangas*, Kritik der kantischen Rechtsphilosophie. Ein Beitrag zur Herstellung der Einheit der praktischen Philosophie (im Druck), sub IV 9.

[27] *Fichte*, Grundlage des Naturrechts nach Prinzipien der Wissenschaftslehre, De Gruyter-Ausgabe der Werke Fichtes, Bd. III, S. 31 f.

zu können, das Subjekt des Selbstbewußtseins schon vorher ein Objekt, bloß als solches, gesetzt haben müsse, wodurch man aus dem Moment, in welchem man den Faden anknüpfen wolle, zu einem vorherigen getrieben werde. Der genannte Grund sei nur so zu heben, daß angenommen werde, die Wirksamkeit des Subjekts sei selbst das wahrgenommene und begriffene Objekt, das Objekt sei kein anderes als diese Wirksamkeit des Subjekts, und so seien beide dasselbe. Es sei aber Charakter des Objekts das Hemmend-Sein, Charakter der Wirksamkeit des Subjekts hingegen das Absolut-Frei-Sein, womit eine Antinomie entstehe, die dadurch zu überwinden sei, daß man annehme, daß das Objekt in etwas Gefordertem bestehe, nämlich in einer Aufforderung an das Subjekt, sich zu einer Wirksamkeit, d. h. zum Handeln zu entschließen. In dieser Weise bekomme das Subjekt den Begriff seiner freien Wirksamkeit nicht als etwas, das im gegenwärtigen Moment sei, sondern als etwas, das im künftigen sein solle. Andererseits wäre die etwaige Annahme, daß das Subjekt sich irgendwie zur freien Wirksamkeit, d. i. zum Handeln genötigt finde, mit dem Begriff des Frei-Seins des Subjekts unvereinbar, so daß nichts anderes widerspruchslos anzunehmen übrig bleibe, als daß das Subjekt sich in der Weise als Objekt, d. h. als zur Wirksamkeit bestimmt finde, daß es sich als etwas finde, das hier wirken könnte, zum Wirken aufgefordert sei, aber es ebensowohl unterlassen könne. Der somit aufgestellte Begriff einer freien Wechselwirksamkeit beinhalte — wenn er scharf bestimmt sein solle —, daß Wirkung von Gegenwirkung sich gar nicht abgesondert denken lassen müsse, daß vielmehr Wirkung und Gegenwirkung die partes integrantes einer ganzen Begebenheit ausmachten. So etwas werde nun zu einer notwendigen Bedingung des Selbstbewußtseins in dem Sinne, daß das Subjekt unter dieser Bedingung sich als freiwirkendes Wesen setzen könne und müsse; setze sich aber das Subjekt als solches, so könne und müsse es[28] eine Sinnenwelt setzen, um sich selbst ihr entgegenzusetzen.

Und somit gelangt *Fichte* zu Ende seiner „erläuternden" Analyse der von ihm vorgenommenen Synthesis von freier Wirksamkeit und Objekt derselben. Er wendet sich nunmehr[29] einer „folgernden" Analyse zu, nämlich einer Analyse, auf Grund deren aus dem notwendigen Faktum, daß die oben erwähnte Einwirkung auf das Subjekt notwendige Bedingung alles Selbstbewußtseins sei, Folgerungen gezogen werden: Insofern die erwähnte Einwirkung ein Empfundenes sei, sei sie eine Beschränkung des Ich. Da nun aber keine Beschränkung ohne ein Beschränkendes denkbar sei, müsse das Subjekt etwas außer sich als den Bestimmungsgrund der erwähnten Einwirkung genauso wie diese setzen.

---

[28] Gemäß dem von *Fichte*, S. 23 f. Bewiesenen.

[29] Ebd., S. 35 f.

Aber diese Einwirkung sei ein Bestimmtes, nämlich eine Aufforderung an das Subjekt zu einer freien Wirksamkeit, und jede Aufforderung ist Materie des Wirkens. Nun müsse die zu setzende Ursache der Aufforderung wenigstens die Möglichkeit voraussetzen, daß das Subjekt überhaupt verstehe und begreife (denn sonst wäre die Aufforderung als solche gar nicht möglich). Folglich müsse die genannte Ursache den Begriff von Vernunft und Freiheit haben, also selbst ein der Begriffe fähiges Wesen (eine Intelligenz), und — da dies ohne Freiheit nicht möglich sei — auch ein freies, also ein vernünftiges Wesen sein.

Das Ergebnis dieser „folgernden" Analyse formuliert nun *Fichte*[30] in folgender Weise: „Der Mensch (so alle endliche Wesen überhaupt) wird nur unter Menschen ein Mensch ... — sollen überhaupt Menschen sein, so müssen mehrere sein ... Sobald man den Begriff des Menschen vollkommen bestimmt, wird man von dem Denken eines Einzelnen aus getrieben zur Annahme eines zweiten, um den ersten erklären zu können. Der Begriff des Menschen ist sonach gar nicht Begriff eines Einzelnen, denn ein solcher ist undenkbar, sondern der einer Gattung."

Der soeben angeführten Beweisführung von *Fichte* ist aber Vielfaches entgegenzuhalten:

Erstens enthält die Beweisführung *Fichtes* einen logischen Fehler: Fichte will hier aus der Annahme, daß das endliche Vernunftwesen sich als Subjekt nicht setzen könne, ohne ein anderes, auf es einwirkendes endliches Vernunftwesen zu setzen, auf die Annahme schließen, daß, wenn es überhaupt endliche Vernunftwesen geben solle, diese mehrere sein müßten[31]; sodann schließt er aber aus der letztgenannten Annahme darauf, daß die mehreren endlichen Vernunftwesen als mit denselben in einem Rechtsverhältnis stehend anzusehen seien[32]. Somit läuft aber Fichtes Beweisführung auf einen circulus vitiosus hinaus. Denn wenn Fichte das endliche Vernunftwesen als Objekt einer notwendig bestehenden Einwirkung eines anderen endlichen Vernunftwesens konzipiert, so tut er damit nichts anderes, als das In-einem-Rechtsverhältnis-Stehen dieser beiden endlichen Vernunftwesen anzunehmen. Dies wird übrigens auch daran klar, daß die Materie dieser Wirkung nach Fichte in einer Aufforderung — d. h. letzten Endes in dem Geltend-Machen von etwas Gesolltem — besteht (kann doch ein Sollen nur derjenige geltend machen, gegen den die durch das Sollen ausgedrückte Pflicht besteht).

---

[30] Ebd., S. 39.
[31] Ebd., S. 35 f.
[32] Ebd., S. 41 f.

Zweitens gibt es eine Lücke in dem von *Fichte* geführten Beweis, daß daraus, daß das endliche Vernunftwesen sich als Subjekt nicht setzen könne, ohne ein anderes, auf es einwirkendes endliches Vernunftwesen zu setzen, auf die Annahme, daß, wenn es überhaupt endliche Vernunftwesen geben solle, diese mehrere sein müßten, zu schließen sei. Die Lücke besteht darin, daß dabei nicht bewiesen wird, daß die „vernünftige Ursache", die auf das sich als Subjekt setzende endliche Vernunftwesen einwirkt, ein anderes endliches Vernunftwesen ausmacht. Das letztere kann jedoch nicht als von jedem Zweifel frei angesehen werden. Denn bis zu diesem Punkte der Beweisführung war Fichte nicht dazu gekommen, wenigstens die prinzipielle Möglichkeit bzw. Notwendigkeit des Bestehens einer Vielzahl endlicher Vernunftwesen zu beweisen; sondern er setzt diesen Beweis in einen viel „späteren" Punkt der Beweisführung an (worauf sich übrigens der oben formulierte erste Einwand gegen die Beweisführung Fichtes bezieht).

VI.

Die Tatsache, daß *Kant* eine transzendentale Deduktion des Begriffs des Rechts nicht geleistet hat und *Fichte* eine der Kritik nicht Stand haltende transzendentale Deduktion des Begriffs des Rechts vorgenommen hat, hat zur Konsequenz, daß ein neuer Versuch transzendentaler Deduktion des Begriffs des Rechts alles andere als überflüssig anzusehen ist. Wie ein solcher Versuch auszusehen hat, habe ich in meiner Schrift „Kritik der kantischen Rechtsphilosophie. Ein Beitrag zur Herstellung der Einheit der praktischen Philosophie" (im Druck) dargestellt.

ÜBERLEGUNGEN ZU METAMETHODOLOGIEN DER RECHTSWISSENSCHAFT

Von Jyrki Uusitalo, Helsinki

I. Metamethodologie als Bindeglied zwischen Philosophie und Einzelwissenschaft

Gegenstand dieser Bemerkungen[1] ist die Problematik des internen philosophischen Systemelementes der Rechtswissenschaft.

Was bei Erörterungen solcher Art naturgemäß immer als Gefahr lauert, ist eine allzu abstrakte Weise des Herangehens. Vor dieser Gefahr warnt uns die Bemerkung *Hegels*, daß menschliches Denken oft dazu neigt, eng miteinander verbundene Sachen als voneinander getrennt zu betrachten[2]. Z. B. ergibt sich in der Rechtstheorie diese Gefahr dann, wenn „Philosophie" (Wissenschaftsphilosophie) als Analyse und Empfehlung solcher Normen der Forschung aufgefaßt wird, die in der Rechtswissenschaft als abstrakte Prinzipien schlechthin erfüllt werden sollen.

Auch abstrakt wäre es, davon auszugehen, daß eine bestimmte Methodologie der Rechtswissenschaft bloß aus dem Grunde anzunehmen sei, weil sie eine „Verallgemeinerung der tatsächlichen Verfahrensweisen der Wissenschaft" darstellt. Versuche dieser Art würden schon daran scheitern, daß stets mehrere Kandidaten einer solchen „tatsächlichen Methodologie" vorhanden wären. Es würde dann offenbar keine eindeutige Referenz geben, um einen dieser Kandidaten vor den anderen präferieren zu können. Gäbe es aber eine solche, würde sie vermutlich „tatsächliche rechtswissenschaftliche Forschungspraxis" heißen. Es wäre aber ein höchst problematisches Unterfangen, zu unterstellen, daß ein Methodologiemodell bestimmter Art vermittels eines „direkten" Hinweises auf die Natur der Wissenschaftspraxis für gültig bzw. nichtgültig angesehen werden könnte.

Das Problem kann konkreter angegangen werden, wenn wir eine besondere Betrachtungsebene heranziehen, um die Gültigkeit verschie-

---

[1] Der Artikel geht zurück auf einen Diskussionsbeitrag in einer Arbeitssitzung des Kongresses. Für die sprachliche Durchsicht danke ich Herrn *Peter Wagner*, M. A.

[2] *G. W. F. Hegel*, Vorlesungen über die Geschichte der Philosophie, Einleitung.

dener methodologischer Modelle der Rechtswissenschaft diskutieren zu können. Eine solche Ebene wird u. a. in *Ernan McMullins* Studien über die sogenannten *Metamethodologien der Wissenschaft* expliziert[3]. Im Unterschied zu *methodologischen* Programmen, die beschreibende und präskriptive Darstellungen der gängigen Methodik gegebener Wissenschaftszweige sind, sind *Metamethodologien* theoretische Verstehensweisen jener Grundlagen, auf welchen bestimmte Methodologien zu verteidigen sind, Verstehensweisen der Natur der durch diese Methodologien gewonnenen Erkenntnis, sowie Darstellungen der Beziehungen dieser Erkenntnis zu anderen Formen der wissenschaftlichen u. a. Erkenntnis (z. B. zu Erkenntnissen anderer Wissenschaftszweige)[4].

Methodologische Stellungnahmen betreffen die Anwendung der wissenschaftlichen Methode als ein Mittel zu einem kognitiven Zweck. *Metamethodologische* Stellungnahmen explizieren das philosophische Element der tatsächlichen wissenschaftlichen Arbeit: sie betreffen die „Gegebenheitsweise" des Gegenstandes im Hinblick auf die wissenschaftliche Betrachtung. Die metamethodologische Ebene bringt stets auch metaphysisch-heuristische, transzendentale u. a. ä. Annahmen über den Gegenstandsbereich der jeweiligen Disziplin mit sich. Metamethodologien der Forschung können z. B. empiristische, phänomenologische, sprachanalytische oder kritisch-realistische — im Sinne des „wissenschaftlichen Realismus" — sein. McMullin und andere Autoren vertreten die Meinung, daß die beste Darstellung der „tatsächlichen" wissenschaftlichen Arbeit durch solche Metamethodologien gewonnen werden kann, die verschiedenerlei argumentative Gründe etwa bei der Auswahl der Theorie mit der besten Erklärung anbieten: neben den rein logischen Gründen z. B. auch den Grad des wissenschaftsgeschichtlichen Erfolgs der bisherigen Erklärungen einer gegebenen Theorie, und auch wie realistisch die Modelle der jeweiligen Theorie sind.

II. Metamethodologien in der Rechtswissenschaft

In der Entwicklung jeder Rechtstheorie, die der Erforschung des geltenden Rechts und der Rechtsfindung als Richtschnur gedient hat, können wir eine Reihe verschiedener Metamethodologien unterscheiden. Mit verschiedenen Argumenten verteidigen sie stets denselben Grundgedanken: daß das geltende Recht ausfindig zu machen der Kern des methodologischen Systems der Rechtswissenschaft ist. In der Entwicklung der Rechtswissenschaft scheint dabei eine innere Abfolge der

---

[3] *E. McMullin*, Philosophy of Science and Its Rational Reconstructions, in: G. Radnitzky/G. Andersson (Hrsg.), Progress and Rationality in Science, Dordrecht 1978, S. 221—250.

[4] Ebd., S. 224.

Metamethodologien zu unterscheiden zu sein. Wie ich sehe, markiert dieser „rote Faden" die Entwicklung einer zu Beginn noch undifferenzierten Idee der Rationalität der Rechtserkenntnis über ihre, sagen wir, dialektische Antithese in Richtung einer reifen (aber ihrerseits künftigen Entwicklungen gegenüber offenen) Auffassung von Rechtswissenschaft und ihren Zwecken. Die Lektüre des nun folgenden geschichtlichen Abrisses soll uns zeigen, daß die Rechtswissenschaft den besten Nutzen aus einer solchen Metamethodologie ziehen kann, die bei der Erforschung des geltenden Rechts fruchtbringend sowohl rationale als auch historisch-soziale Bewertungsmaßstäbe anlegt[5].

Das jeder Metamethodologie der Rechtswissenschaft inhärente philosophische Element ist mit der tatsächlichen Erforschung des Rechts stets aufs engste verschmolzen. Ein zentrales philosophisches Problem ist dabei, wie das Recht jeweils als ein der Erforschung des geltenden Rechts „vorgegebener" Forschungsgegenstand betrachtet wird. Metamethodologische Stellungnahmen in der Rechtswissenschaft beziehen sich im wesentlichen auf diese Frage.

Die metamethodologischen Ansätze, die in ihrer geschichtlichen Reihenfolge m. E. unterscheidbar sind, wären etwa:

1. Die klassische Metamethodologie der *Vernünftigkeit des Rechts.*
2. Die Metamethodologie der *Wirklichkeit des Rechts.*
3. Die Metamethodologie der *vernünftigen Wirklichkeit des Rechts.*

Die hier benutzten Hegelschen Ausdrucksweisen sind kein bloßes Wortspiel. Die drei Modelle bilden zusammengenommen eine idealisierte Darstellung der Problemstellungen und deren Wandel, die in der Entwicklung der Rechtstheorie zutage zu treten scheinen. Jede dieser Metamethodologien verteidigt den Primat *bestimmter* Theorienwahl-, Erklärungs- bzw. Problemlösungskriterien in der Erforschung des geltenden Rechts. (Ich halte den Terminus „Metamethodologie" auch darum für gut, damit man schon auf der rein terminologischen Ebene die Problematik der Philosophie der Rechts*wissenschaft* und die Problematik der systematischen Rechtsphilosophie unterscheiden kann. Freilich darf man nicht übersehen, daß Metamethodologien auch den Gehalt rechtsphilosophischer Probleme in den Relevanzbereich der Rechtswissenschaft selber vermitteln[6].)

---

[5] Damit wäre der Begriff der Rationalität selber zu „historisieren", ohne damit in einen Relativismus zu verfallen. Vgl. etwa den von *W. H. Newton-Smith* vorgeschlagenen „moderaten Rationalismus" (The Rationality of Science, Boston/London/Henley 1981). Deutlich in dieser Richtung bewegt sich die von *W. Krawietz* vorgeschlagene „Rahmentheorie des Rechts"; vgl. etwa *Krawietz,* Recht als Regelsystem, Wiesbaden 1984.

Die Unterscheidung und Beziehungsstruktur zwischen der metamethodologischen und der methodologischen Ebene der Rechtswissenschaft wären ihrerseits in folgender Weise vorzuführen[7]. Dabei sind die zwei erstgenannten Ebenen metamethodologisch und die dritte ist methodologisch:

(i) *Philosophische Methodologie:* die explizite oder — öfters! — implizite rechtstheoretische, philosophisch fundierte Auffassung von der Zugangsweise der Rechtswissenschaft zu ihrem Gegenstand;

(ii) *Analyse der theoretischen Grundbegriffe:* Frage nach dem epistemischen Gehalt und den logischen Eigenschaften von Begriffen wie „geltendes Recht", „Rechtsordnung", „Rechtsquelle" u. dgl.

(iii) *Methodologie der rechtlichen Erkenntnisgewinnung:* Explizite Prinzipien der Ausarbeitung, Bildung und Prüfung von Sätzen, die über das geltende Recht etwas sagen, sowie explizite Prinzipien des rechtlichen Argumentierens im allgemeinen und im besonderen.

Die maßgebende historische und theoretische Spannung zwischen verschiedenen Methodologiemodellen entsteht vornehmlich auf der Ebene (i), und dies hat einen entscheidenden Einfluß auf die Standpunkte auf den Ebenen (ii)—(iii). Die Ebene (i) ist entscheidend eben darum, weil die philosophische Analyse und Methodologie des Rechts stets danach strebt, gedankliche Klarheit für unser Verständnis des Gegenstandbereichs zu verschaffen. Sonst wäre dieses Verständnis selbst allzu „selbstverständlich", und folglich wären wir außerstande, den Gehalt unseres Verständnisses ausdrücklich formulieren zu können[8].

Der nun folgende theoriengeschichtliche Abriß der metamethodologischen Modelle hat, zugestanden, einen gewissen tendenziösen Ansatz. Meine Absicht ist dabei, darzulegen, wie sich die systematische Leitidee der Rationalität des Rechts in ihrer Entwicklung aus einem ursprünglich undifferenzierten Ganzen in einer Art Antithese desselben zu einer differenzierteren Form entwickelt hat. Ich schlage vor, den berühmten Leitsatz der Hegelschen „Rechtsphilosophie" in diesem Zusammenhang im Sinne zu behalten: „Was vernünftig ist, ist wirklich; und was wirklich

---

[6] Diese Funktion der Metamethodologien der Rechtswissenschaft geht deutlich aus den Ausführungen von *J. W. Harris*, Law and Legal Science, 2. Aufl. Oxford 1982, hervor.

[7] Die Unterscheidung ist durch die etwas ähnliche Unterscheidung von *R. M. Hare* inspiriert, in: N. Daniels (Hrsg.), Reading Rawls, Oxford 1975, S. 81.

[8] Diese Funktion der philosophischen Reflexion hat u. a. *E. Tugendhat* betont, im Anschluß an „Confessiones" von Augustinus und „Philosophische Untersuchungen" von Wittgenstein; vgl. *Tugendhat*, Vorlesungen zur Einführung in die sprachanalytische Philosophie, Frankfurt a. M. 1976, S. 19.

ist, ist vernünftig[9]." Die drei metamethodologischen Modelle stellen drei Linien der Auseinandersetzung mit dem Gehalt dieses Prinzips dar: in theoriegeschichtlicher Abfolge zuerst mit Betonung auf der „ersten Komponente" (das Vernünftige als das Wirkliche), dann mit Betonung auf der „zweiten Komponente" (das Wirkliche als das Vernünftige), und schließlich als Theorie der Rechtsvernunft in ihren historischen und sozialen Bestimmungen[10].

1. Das klassische Modell der Vernünftigkeit des Rechts

Dieses Modell hat, wie ich sehe, von den Anfängen der Neuzeit bis zur Wende des letzten Jahrhunderts als eine Art gemeinsamer Nenner verschiedener Traditionen des Rechtsdenkens fungiert: in den Theorien des Naturrechts, in der Historischen Rechtsschule, in der Begriffsjurisprudenz und in den klassischen Formen des Rechtspositivismus. Die Denkrichtungen, die im Bereich dieses Modells vorkommen, sehen in ihrer *philosophischen Methodologie* (d. h. in ihrer Metamethodologie) die Rechtswissenschaft als ein innerlich „tendenziös" philosophisches Vehikel einer vorgegebenen Idee der rechtlichen Rationalität. Es gilt zu bemerken, daß die Metamethodologie, die hinter diesen Richtungen steht, natürlich erst nachträglich rekonstruierbar ist. Rekonstruktionen solcher Art kommen vornehmlich dann vor, wenn die Tragweite dieser klassischen Rationalitätsmodelle des Rechts im Hinblick auf die gegenwärtige Rechtsforschung zum Problem wird[11].

Was vernünftig ist, ist (wird) wirklich; so lautet der Grundgedanke der klassischen Modelle. Verschiedene klassische Richtungen haben gewiß

---

[9] *G. W. F. Hegel*, Grundlinien der Philosophie des Rechts, Theorie-Werkausgabe Bd. 7, Frankfurt a. M. 1970, S. 24. Die von der neueren Hegel-Forschung angedeutete Originalversion dieses Satzes (nämlich: „Was vernünftig ist, wird wirklich; und was wirklich ist, wird vernünftig") würde auch im Einklang mit der vorliegenden Deutungsperspektive sein.

[10] Vgl. *B. Liebrucks*, Recht, Moralität und Sittlichkeit bei Hegel, in: M. Riedel (Hrsg.), Materialien zu Hegels Rechtsphilosophie, Bd. 2, Frankfurt a. M. 1975, S. 13—51. „Philosophie lebt immer nur in der Gegenwart. Eine nichtgegenwärtige Philosophie, also eine Philosophie, die sich aus der Wirklichkeit herausreflektiert hat und nicht zu ihr zurückgekehrt ist, was sie *als Philosophie zu leisten hat*, ist tot" (ebd., S. 20). Diese Formulierung scheint den — spätere Denkformen antizipierenden — metamethodologischen Imperativ Hegelscher Rechtsphilosophie und seine impliziten historisch-sozialen Ansätze vortrefflich zu explizieren.

[11] Zur Rekonstruktion und Problematisierung des Naturrechts vgl. z. B. *A. Aarnio*, Eternal and Changing Law: Problems in Modern Natural Law Theory, in: Aarnio, Philosophical Perspectives in Jurisprudence, Acta Philosophica Fennica Bd. 36, Helsinki 1983, S. 76—93. Zur Rekonstruktion der Begriffsjurisprudenz vgl. z. B. *J. Tolonen*, Om begreppet rättshandling inom det traditionella rättssystemets ram, in: Tidskrift utgiven av Juridiska Föreningen i Finland 109 (1973), S. 340—364.

diese „universelle Idee“ des Rechts und der Rechtswissenschaft auf unterschiedliche Weise gesehen. Die metamethodologische Grundeinstellung scheint aber bei allen im wesentlichen gleich zu sein. Am klarsten ist dies in den Doktrinen der Rechtsquellen und des rechtlichen Schließens zu erkennen[12]:

Nach den Theorien des Naturrechts spiegelt das positive Recht der Menschen die „natürlichen“ Zwecke der Menschheit wider, und diese Prinzipien des Naturrechts sind als universell gültig angesehen.

Der Historischen Rechtsschule zufolge ist die einzige wahre Quelle des geltenden Rechts der von der Gesetzgebung unabhängige „Volksgeist“.

Die Begriffsjurisprudenz geht davon aus, daß der universelle Gehalt des Rechts in den durch Rechtsdogmatik zu erschließenden, die veränderliche Rechtsordnung transzendierenden immutablen Rechtsfaktoren gegeben ist.

Gemäß dem klassischen Rechtspositivismus (*Bentham* und *Austin*) ist das Recht wesentlich ohne Bezug auf seinen Gehalt zu definieren, d. h. als Vorschrift des Souveräns, die mit Sanktionen untermauert ist. Diese klassisch-positivistische Einstellung findet sich mit etwas verschiedener Akzentuierung auch in der Begriffsjurisprudenz.

Die genannten Denkrichtungen zeigen eine Art „Familienähnlichkeit“ untereinander. Sie können funktionell mit den metaphysischen Ideen der Philosophie der Wissenschaften des 19. Jahrhunderts verglichen werden, Ideen wie z. B. die neuhegelianische Theorie der Entfaltung der erkennenden Vernunft durch ihre Negation, *Comtes* Glaube an die Kraft der „positiven Fakten“ der Physik des Sozialen, der Platonismus der „Denkformen“ im Marburger Neukantianismus, *Machs* Prinzip der Denkökonomie, *Peirces* Idee einer schrittweisen Approximation der Wirklichkeit durch die Wissenschaft — um nur einige der herausragendsten Denkmodelle zu nennen[13]. Die klassischen Rationalitätsmodelle des Rechts haben sich deutlich auch von diesen allgemeineren metaphysisch-heuristischen Denkansätzen inspirieren lassen.

Entscheidend bei der Entwicklung der rechtswissenschaftlichen Metamethodologien ist, daß gerade die Undifferenziertheit der klassischen Modelle dadurch zu einem vorwärtsweisenden Faktor wurde, daß seit Ende des 19. Jahrhunderts die Kritik an der aprioristischen Natur dieser Modelle einsetzte. Diese Kritik sollte ihrerseits Voraussetzungen für eine

[12] Eine ausgezeichnete Studie dazu: *Harris* (FN 6).

[13] Eingehender: *M. W. Wartofsky*, The Relation between Philosophy of Science and History of Science, in: Wartofsky, Models, Representation and Scientific Understanding, Dordrecht-Boston-London 1979, S. 119—139 (128).

neue philosophische Methodologie schaffen. In den klassischen Modellen waren die vorgegebene (prästabilisierte) Rationalitätsidee und die Problematik der genuinen Rechtsforschung noch in einer genauso harmonischen wie auch undifferenzierten Weise verschmolzen. Wir sehen hier etwa einen wissenschaftsgeschichtlichen Fall des Anaximandrischen *apeiron*: etwas, das die konstitutiven Elemente in ihrer voneinander noch nicht deutlich ausdifferenzierten, also in einer bestimmungslosen Form enthält[14].

2. Die Metamethodologie der Wirklichkeit des Rechts

Dieser metamethodologische Ansatz wurde als Kritik an der obenerwähnten „bestimmungslosen Harmonie" vorgebracht. Bei dieser Kritik der klassischen Rechtsvernunftsmodelle werden nun die Beiträge bestimmter, an Bedeutung zunehmender, empirisch fundierter „Korrelatwissenschaften" beim Herangehen an die rechtliche Realität und Rechtswirklichkeit wichtig: empirische Psychologie, Sprachwissenschaft, die frühe empirische Soziologie und Wirtschaftswissenschaft. Der Beitrag dieser Disziplinen hat also nun seine Bedeutung für die Entwicklung der philosophisch reflektierten Problematik der Rechtswissenschaft.

Wissenschaftssoziologisch können wir die neue Einstellung auch als Modell der *streitigen Beziehungen* zwischen Philosophie und Rechtswissenschaft bezeichnen (im Gegensatz zu den klassischen Modellen der „bestimmungslosen Harmonie" der Philosophie/Rechtswissenschaft-Konstellation)[15]. Diese ausdrücklich so genannte „Antiphilosophizität" ist freilich gegen eine *solche* „Philosophizität" gerichtet, die der neuen Richtung als unnützer Ballast auf dem Wege der Rechtsforschung erschien. Natürlich ist auch die neue Richtung von philosophischer Signifikanz; diese liegt darin, daß dieses Modell die Voraussetzungen für die Entwicklung des dritten Modells geschaffen hat, und zwar überwiegend ohne selbst als eine Metamethodologie der systematischen Rechtsforschung zu fungieren. Bei dem zweiten Modell geht es also um „den Samen seiner eigenen Transformation".

Die kritische Attitüde dieses Modells gegen die klassischen Rationalitätsmodelle des Rechts weist in ihrer Motivierung Ähnlichkeit mit der Kritik des logischen Empirismus an den vom 19. Jahrhundert überlieferten „metaphysischen" Wissenschaftskonzeptionen auf. Die Denkrichtungen der *Wirklichkeit des Rechts* brachten zum ersten Mal u. a.

---

[14] Das *apeiron*-Gleichnis ist durch *M. W. Wartofsky* inspiriert (vgl. ebd., S. 127).

[15] Die Termini „streitige/harmonische Beziehungen" sind von *Wartofsky* inspiriert (vgl. ebd., passim).

soziologische Gesichtspunkte in die Analyse des Rechts hinein. Auch begegnet man jetzt Hinweisen auf die Bedeutung der „inneren" Zweck- und Wertkonstellationen der Juristen: der amerikanische Realismus entfaltet sich als eine soziologisch-pragmatische Theorie der richterlichen Entscheidung in common law-Rechtskulturen; der skandinavische Realismus betont die psychologische Rechtserfahrung und die Zweckbezogenheit der juristischen Entscheidung; die deutsche Interessenjurisprudenz entwickelt sich als Kritik der Begriffsjurisprudenz und strebt nach einem gesellschaftstheoretisch abgesicherten Begriffsrahmen der Rechtserfahrung.

Einer der wesentlichsten Berührungspunkte zwischen diesen Rechtsrealismen und dem logischen Empirismus ist, daß die Realisten den Begriff der „rechtlichen Realität" im Bezugsrahmen der empirisch fundierten Wissenschaft definieren. Obwohl die Realisten ansonsten nicht ohne weiteres das Programm des logischen Empirismus unterschreiben, sind sich die Grundgedanken der Kritiken bei beiden ähnlich, und theoriegeschichtlich ist dies sicherlich kein Zufall. Bei den Realisten gewinnt die „zweite Komponente" des Hegelschen Prinzips an Bedeutung: Bei der Erforschung des geltenden Rechts ist davon auszugehen, was *wirklich* ist (i. e. „was wirken kann", d. h. was in der sozialen Welt für das Rechtsgeschehen kausal relevant ist).

Die Rechtsrealisten (oder Rechtsskeptizisten; diese von *Harris* für den skandinavischen Realismus gebrauchte Bezeichnung eignet sich zur Beschreibung der ganzen jetzt diskutierten Denkweise[16]) waren also nach ihrem Selbstverständnis dazu geneigt, den Anteil von Philosophie in der Rechtsforschung kritisch zur Debatte zu stellen. Paradoxerweise trägt dies aber dazu bei, eine philosophisch reflektierte Dimension in die Analyse der „Gegebenheitsweisen" des Rechts als Gegenstand einzuführen. Die bekannten Worte von *Alf Ross* sind für das Selbstverständnis dieser metamethodologischen Richtung symptomatisch: „Der Gegenstand der Rechtsphilosophie ist nicht das Recht oder irgendeiner seiner Teile bzw. Seiten, sondern ihr Gegenstand ist die Rechtswissenschaft. Die Grenze zwischen Rechtswissenschaft und Rechtsphilosophie ist fließend (...). Diese Relativität zeigt uns auch, daß es nicht zweckmäßig ist, von ‚Rechtsphilosophie' zu reden, weil dieser Terminus unvermeidlich die Vorstellung von einem gehaltlich abgegrenzten Forschungsgebiet hervorruft. Ich halte es also für das Beste, von *rechtsphilosophischen Problemen* zu reden[17]."

---

[16] Vgl. *J. W. Harris*, Olivecrona on Law and Language — the Search for Legal Culture, in: Tidskrift for Rettsvitenskap 94 (1981), S. 626.

[17] *A. Ross*, Om ret og retfaerdighed, København 1953, S. 35.

Die von Ross und anderen Realisten vertretene Richtung suchte vor allem die Auffassung der klassischen und, wenn man will, auch „vorkritischen“ Modelle zu widerlegen, denen zufolge eine vorgegebene Idee der rechtlichen Rationalität sozusagen einen direkten Königsweg zur Erkenntnis des „Wesens des Rechts“ aufweisen kann. Die neue Metamethodologie hat damit in einer fruchtbaren Weise die Frage problematisiert, unter welchen Bedingungen der Gegenstand der Rechtsforschung als „gegeben“ angenommen werden kann — insoweit dies möglich ist. Damit wurde diese Richtung primär eine Art Sprungbrett für die Entwicklung einer neuen systematischen Metamethodologie. Symptomatisch in dieser Hinsicht ist, daß die Realisten letzten Endes keine Schulen der tatsächlichen Rechtsforschung geschaffen haben; meistens gehen die Realismen in die Geschichte der rechtswissenschaftlichen Metamethodologien ein als interdisziplinäre Bestrebungen, Rechtswissenschaft mit Informations- und Theorieansätzen anderer Human- und Gesellschaftswissenschaften zu bereichern.

3. Das Modell der vernünftigen Wirklichkeit des Rechts

Teils im Geiste des vorigen Modells und teils als Kritik einiger seiner Unzulänglichkeiten ist eine Denkweise entstanden, die man mit Recht als die Metamethodologie der *vernünftigen Wirklichkeit* des Rechts bezeichnen kann. In unserem vorliegenden Abriß bildet die Entfaltung und Konsolidierung dieser Richtung sozusagen den Schlußpunkt. Dies ist aber zugleich ein neuer Anfang, weil damit die Ausgangspunkte für ein Verständnis der Rechtswissenschaft vorliegen, welches unterscheidungsfähig genug ist, um kognitiv jene Faktoren beherrschen zu können, von denen die Erforschung des geltenden Rechts im sozialen Kontext abhängt.

Die zentrale Einsicht dieser Denkweise ist die Erschließung und Ausarbeitung des sogenannten inneren Gesichtspunktes bzw. Aspekts des Richters und Juristen. Bekanntlich hat *H. L. A. Hart* diese Problematik mit seiner Unterscheidung zwischen primären Rechtsregeln und den sekundären Regeln, die zum Erkennen dieser Regeln verhelfen, erschlossen[18]. Dieser Ansatz ermöglicht die Analyse der in der juristischen Gemeinschaft tatsächlich angewandten Auslegungs- und Entscheidungsregeln, und damit wird es möglich, alle diese Formen und Ebenen der Regel einer kritischen Diskussion zu unterziehen und der Rationalität

[18] Vgl. *H. L. A. Hart*, The Concept of Law, Oxford 1961. Zur Bedeutung des Hartschen Ansatzes vgl. etwa *N. MacCormick*, H. L. A. Hart, in der Reihe: „Jurists: Profiles in Legal Theory“, London 1981. MacCormick diskutiert auch die Möglichkeiten einer kritischen Weiterentwicklung des Hartschen Ansatzes. Offensichtlich stellt die Reine Rechtslehre *Kelsens* ein anderes maßgebendes Forschungsprogramm im Rahmen des dritten Modells dar.

juristischer Tätigkeit einen historischen und sozialen Gehalt zu verleihen. Eine philosophische Methodologie dieser Art ist dazu geeignet, sowohl den „vernunftgemäßen“ als auch den „wirklichkeitsbezogenen“ Dimensionen der Rechtsforschung Genüge zu leisten: z. B. können jetzt die Möglichkeiten der rechtsdogmatischen Auslegung, dem gesellschaftlichen Ziel des Rechtsschutzes (Rechtssicherheit) und der gleichwertigen Behandlung der Rechtssubjekte näherzukommen, in die Analyse einbezogen werden. Dabei ist von Vorteil, daß dieser Aspekt im Prinzip mit den Kriterien der Hypothesenbildung und -annahme in der wissenschaftlichen Forschung im allgemeinen vergleichbar ist[19] und gegebenenfalls durch Vergleich mit diesen Kriterien auch expliziert werden kann.

III. Metamethodologien und Rechtsphilosophie

Das Ende des vorliegenden geschichtlichen Abrisses bringt uns auch sozusagen wieder zurück an den Anfang — in die Problematik der klassischen Modelle der rechtlichen Rationalität. Es scheint nämlich ein entscheidender Verdienst des dritten Metamethodologie-Modells der (modernen) Rechtswissenschaft zu sein, daß mit seiner Hilfe auch die Tragweite der Traditionen der klassischen Rechtsvernunft stets aufs neue eingeschätzt werden kann — retrospektiv, aber sicherlich niemals zu spät. Dabei erweisen sich diese Denkweisen als Forschungstraditionen (etwa im Sinne von *Laudan*[20]), deren inhärente Möglichkeiten und Grenzen als eine Art von abgelagerten Elementen in der Gegenwart und Zukunft der Theorie des Rechts fortbestehen. Damit können diese Elemente stets gegenüber möglichen Neueinschätzungen offen bleiben[21].

Gleichzeitig scheint es aber auch, daß eben die dritte — wenn man so will, „reife“ — Metamethodologie des Rechts uns am besten in den Stand versetzen kann, auch das Problemgefüge der systematischen Rechtsphilosophie in die tatsächliche Rechtsforschung einzubeziehen. Zum Beispiel die Frage, was es eigentlich bedeutet, daß sich der Richter bei seinem Handeln von der Gerechtigkeit leiten läßt und folglich die Gerechtigkeit eine „Quelle“ seines Entscheidens, nicht nur einfach einen teleologischen Zweck seines Handelns bildet[22], wäre vielleicht in dem-

---

[19] Erhellende theoretische Bemerkungen und vorwiegend strafrechtliche Modellanalysen findet man in *E. von Savigny et al.*, Juristische Dogmatik und Wissenschaftstheorie, München 1976.

[20] Vgl. *L. Laudan*, Progress and Its Problems, London 1977.

[21] Die in FN 11 erwähnten Studien sind m. E. repräsentative Beispiele der Auseinandersetzungen mit dem klassischen Erbe der Rechtstheorie unter den Bedingungen der modernen Problematik.

[22] Diese beiläufige Problemstellung ist durch *M. Stocker* inspiriert: Values and Purposes. The Limits of Teleology and the Ends of Friendship, in: The Journal of Philosophy, LXXVIII (1981), S. 747—765.

selben Sinne zu behandeln wie die Frage nach der „Wahrheitsähnlichkeit" der empirischen Ergebnisse der Natur- und Sozialwissenschaften als die Quelle oder Grundlage der praktischen Wirksamkeit dieser Ergebnisse. Dieses Beispiel verdeutlicht uns die interne wissenschaftstheoretische Dimension des dritten metamethodologischen Modells[23]. Zugleich aber steht fest, daß diese Dimension durch moral- und rechtsphilosophische Fragestellungen ergänzt werden muß, damit das dritte Modell nicht selbst eine neue aprioristische Rationalitätsidee wird, sondern als Basis der Forschung im Dienste aufgeklärter Theorie und Praxis juristischer Erkenntnis- und Entscheidungstätigkeit dienen kann.

[23] Diese Dimension tritt deutlich zutage z. B. in der Debatte zwischen *A. Aarnio* und *I. Niiniluoto* über den kognitiven Status rechtsdogmatischer Aussagen, in: RECHTSTHEORIE Beiheft 2 (1981) u. Beiheft 3 (1981).

ARGUMENTATION ET MORALE EN DROIT PENAL BELGE AU XIXe SIECLE

Par Jacques Vanderlinden, Bruxelles

Le droit pénal offre à l'argumentation un champ intéressant d'application en ce que ce champ et limité en droit belge, comme en nombre d'autres systèmes contemporains, par le principe *nullum crimen sine lege;* celui-ci apparaît dans la constitution belge du 7 février 1831 à l'article 7 qui dispose, entre autres, que «nul ne peut être poursuivi que dans les cas prévus par la loi». Il en résulte qu'au cas où les juges souhaiteraient réprimer un comportement qui n'entrerait pas strictement dans le cadre légal, ils n'ont comme seule ressource que l'argumentation; celle-ci bien employée, leur permet en effet de déclarer «normale» ou «évidente» l'inclusion d'un comportement condamnable à leurs yeux dans ceux prévus par la loi pénale. Cette tentation est d'autant plus grande que le droit pénal est l'outil par excellence de la transposition dans le champ du droit des principes moraux qui sous-tendent la norme juridique. En outre, et peut-être en conséquence de l'intérêt des techniques interprétatives en droit pénal, il existe dans la Belgique du XIXe siècle un intérêt considérable pour ces techniques. Nombreux sont les ouvrages publiés sur le sujet. S'ils sont le plus souvent brefs, ils n'en fournissent pas moins aux juristes des règles à appliquer systématiquement de manière à permettre une interprétation «satisfaisante» ou encore »convaincante« de la loi. Enfin la matière de l'interprétation de la loi est dominée à l'époque et jusqu'en 1865 par le principe selon lequel, en cas de conflit entre les cours d'appel et la cour de cassation, l'interprétation devient le fait du législateur statuant par voie de loi interprétative; on possède trois exemples de pareille intervention entre 1830 et 1865, l'un d'entre eux faisant particulièrement l'objet de mon propos.

L'article 334 du code pénal français de 1810, maintenu en vigueur en Belgique en 1830, portait que «quiconque a offensé les bonnes moeurs en excitant, favorisant ou facilitant régulièrement la débauche ou la corruption de jeunes personnes de l'un ou l'autre sexe sous l'âge de 21 ans» sera puni des peines prévues par la loi. Pendant près de vingt-cinq ans la pratique judiciaire française et belge fit entrer dans le champ de cet article tout outrage aux moeurs qui n'était pas public, violent ou contraire au droit du mariage, ces trois cas étant prévus dans d'autres articles qui couvraient respectivement l'outrage public aux moeurs, le viol et l'adultère. La rupture dans la jurisprudence se produisit en 1842, lorsqu'en deux décisions successives la cour d'appel de Gand déclara que l'article 334 visait uniquement les cas de proxénétisme; cette décision s'opposait à l'avis du ministère public rendu en ces deux causes. Le pourvoi introduit par ce dernier devant la cour de cassation n'étonna donc pas. Plus surprenant furent sans doute pour les contemporains la confirmation des deux jugements par les cours de renvoi, celles de Bruxelles et Liège. La cour de cassation, toutes chambres réunies, cassa à nouveau les arrêts des cours d'appel et, entrée en conflit avec toutes les juridictions de ce niveau dans le pays, introduisit un référé au législatif. Le gouvernement élabora un projet de loi soutenant l'opinion de la juridiction suprême, mais ne fut pas suivi par le parlement qui se prononça en faveur de la solution préconisée par les cours d'appel; mais, quelques années plus tard, il déposa un nouveau projet de loi modifiant l'article 334 et fournissant au problème une solution intermédiaire entre celle de la cour de cassation et celle des trois juridictions d'appel. Cette solution fut ultérieurement incorporée dans la révision du code pénal belge en 1867.

Dans le cours des débats en justice et devant le parlement et dans les décisions rendues par les diverses juridictions, diverses règles d'interprétation furent invoquées qui, appliquées à l'article 334, devaient, aux yeux des interprètes, fournir une réponse «logique», «nécessaire», «évidente» rendant en fait inutile le recours au législateur puisqu'aussi bien, soutenaient les uns comme les autres, il n'y avait guère problème. Parmi ceux-ci figuraient le recours:

— à la «vraie» signification des mots. Les cours d'appel soutenaient que exciter, encourager et faciliter la débauche n'était pas s'y livrer soi-même. La cour de cassation estimait par contre que ces mots recouvraient toutes espèces d'actes licencieux aboutissant à pousser vers le vice des jeunes gens sans expérience et que le terme corruption ne pouvait en aucun cas signifier seulement «prostitution».

— aux travaux préparatoires. Les cours d'appel faisaient observer qu'ils ne se référaient jamais à ceux qui corrompent afin de satisfaire leurs propres passions, mais la cour de cassation soulignait que les discours préliminaires n'étaient pas nécessairement complets et ne faisaient que mettre en évidence des points importants sans en exclure d'autres.

— aux textes antérieurs au Code pénal de 1810. Les cours d'appel montraient qu'ils étaient différents dans leur formulation car ils parlaient directement de corrompre la jeunesse et non de l'exciter, l'encourager ou la faciliter, tandis que la cour de cassation affirmait sans sourciller que le texte de l'article 334 était semblable aux précédents.

— aux travaux préparatoires des textes antérieurs. Les cours d'appel y découvrent que ces textes visent «particulièrement» le proxénétisme. Ce à quoi la juridiction suprême réplique que «particulièrement» ne veut pas dire «exclusivement» mais «spécialement» ou encore «exactement». Nous rejoignons ainsi l'argument du sens exact des mots.

— à la spécialisation des termes juridiques. La cour de cassation estime en effet que l'on n'utilise pas dans un même texte des mots différents pour désigner la même infraction surtout lorsqu'il existe un terme non-ambigu. Si on visait uniquement le proxénétisme, c'est ce terme spécialisé qu'il fallait utiliser et pas d'autres. Les cours d'appel ne répondent pas à cet argument.

— à l'homogénéité des articles du code. Les cours d'appel semblent en effet accueillir l'argument selon lequel le législateur n'incorpore pas deux infractions distinctes dans un même article. La cour de cassation répond que l'article 334 est au contraire un texte général qui couvre toutes les incitations à la débauche indistinctement.

— à la localisation des articles dans le Code. Les cours d'appel semblent également se rallier au fait que dans le Code pénal de 1810 l'article 334 se situe après 4 articles relatifs à la débauche pour son propre plaisir et avant un autre qui concerne, comme l'article 334, le plaisir d'autrui, tandis que l'article 336 vise un cas tout à fait particulier. La cour de cassation objecte qu'en fait ce dernier concerne le plaisir de l'auteur de l'infraction et devrait donc précéder l'article 334.

— aux conséquences illogiques qui peuvent résulter des interprétations. Les cours d'appel considérent que les sanctions de l'article 334 sont relativement légères et que la généralisation de son application entraînerait pour des infractions sérieuses des peines illogiques alors que d'autres infractions spécifiques, de toute évidence moins graves, seraient sanctionnées très sévèrement. La cour de cassation ne répondit pas à cet argument.

— à l'intention du législateur. Ce dernier argument ne fut pas invoqué par les cours d'appel, mais bien, en sa faveur, par la cour de cassation.

Au delà de ces considérations relevant de la technique d'interprétation, chacun des adversaires fit appel à des principes. Le Parquet de cassation fonda ainsi son argumentation sur le principe que l'existence d'un comportement hautement immoral doit être sanctionnée même s'il n'est pas érigé en infraction; dans ce cas, la cour devrait suppléer au silence de la loi. La cour s'érige ainsi en gardien de la morale publique et les cours d'appel ont beau jeu de lui répondre qu'il existe dans toute société des actes profondément immoraux qui ne sont pas sanctionnés. Les cours d'appel invoquent de leur côté deux principes qu'elles estiment fondamentaux. D'une part le caractère nécessairement strict de l'interprétation de la loi pénale qui, s'il n'existait pas, permettrait de tourner le principe constitutionnel de l'article 7 de la constitution belge. D'autre part, celui selon lequel tout doute (il s'agit en l'occurrence d'un doute sur la portée du droit et pas d'un doute sur le fait) doit bénéficier à l'accusé. A l'un comme à l'autre, la cour de cassation répond qu'en l'occurrence il n'y pas de problème qu'il s'agisse d'interprétation ou de doute: la première n'est pas nécessaire et le second n'existe pas. Il faut remarquer par ailleurs qu'aucun de ces principes n'est formulé dans un texte législatif.

En conclusion, face à des convictions profondes des juridictions, convictions reflétées dans les principes qu'elles invoquent, l'argumentation apparaît comme un habillage technique recouvrant une réalité culturelle et sociale qui est, tous comptes faits, le moteur essentiel de la décision judiciaire. L'habillage technique n'est là que pour donner l'illusion de la rationnalité au justiciable et aussi au législateur hostile au «gouvernement des juges».

II. Systematisierung in Rechtsdogmatik und Rechtswissenschaft

ON CHANGES IN THE SYSTEMATICS OF LAW

By Aulis Aarnio, Helsinki

I.

In their well-known and eminent work *Normative Systems*, Carlos Alchourrón and Eugenio Bulygin characterize legal systems as normative systems whose bases are composed of legal sentences.[1] The authors use the term 'legal sentence' instead of the expressions 'legal norm' or 'legal rule' because of its neutrality as far as e.g. the definition of the concept of norm is concerned. Characterized in this way, the notion of legal system is *more general* than the concept of legal order. The legal order consists of all those legal sentences (norms) that are valid according to certain criteria of identification. In this respect, legal order as the totality of valid legal sentences is an outcome of the exercise of societal power. Legal order is, as Otto Brusiin called it, a power-order.[2] In the ordinary legal language, legal systems are usually understood as products of legal scientific work (research). The standard definition concerning legal dogmatics, i. e. the analytic-dogmatical study of law, consists of two different elements:

(a) The central task of legal dogmatics is to clarify the contents of the legal order. This activity is usually called *interpretation*. As will be seen later on, the term 'interpretation' refers also, in its usual sense, to other activities than to the linguistic interpretation only. Due to the common use of the term in legal contexts, it has been accepted for the purposes of my paper as well.

(b) Another perspective on the legal order focuses on the *systematization* of legal norms. In this view, the systematization of norms serves to provide a more comprehensive and more outlined view on the legal order than does a mere detailed interpretation of legal norms.[3]

---

[1] *C. Alchourrón/E. Bulygin*, Normative Systems, Wien-New York 1971, p. 43 ff., especially p. 50 ff. Cf. also chapters I—III.

[2] *O. Brusiin*, Tuomarin harkinta normin puuttuessa, 1938, p. 117 ff.

[3] *Alchourrón/Bulygin* (note 1), p. 78 pp. Cf. also *A. Aarnio*, Denkweisen der Rechtswissenschaft, Wien-New York 1979, p. 52 ff. and *Aarnio*, On Legal Reasoning, Turku 1977, p. 272 ff.

The kernel of the problem lies, however, in the *distinction* between interpretation and systematization. As is the case with scientific approach in general, we face here the question of how the practical and theoretical elements are interwoven in human thinking. In other words: Can the systematization of norms be carried out *regardless* of the (detailed) knowledge of the norms? What does it mean to say that a legal scholar constructs a legal system?

The main thesis of the present study is that systematization and interpretation have a *reciprocal relation* with each other. With regard to change and dynamics in law and the growth of legal knowledge in general, systematization provides a framework for (legal) interpretation and, vice versa, every act of interpretation must be carried out within a certain systematization. Hence, every change *of* legal systems also brings about a change *in* the content of the part of the legal order which is the subject-matter of the systematizing activity. This means that after any change of the first-mentioned sort, our conception of the content of the legal order will be different from that based on the system which was seen as prevailing before the change took place.

According to Alchourrón and Bulygin changes of the legal system may take place and in fact do take place quite often in society. All legal systems are bound to some particular time, i. e. they are *momentary* systems. As an example Alchourrón and Bulygin refer to the French law. It is not "one legal order, but a temporary and discrete succession of (momentary) legal orders". This side of the dynamics of the legal order is, however, the concern of lawyers and jurisprudents involved in practical affairs. From this point of view, the most important "creator" of the system is — besides the legislator — the judge, especially the judges of the Supreme Court. The scientific (legal dogmatic) systematization involves quite another viewpoints. It involves replacing the basis of a certain legal system in such a way that the normative consequences of the system remain the same. The scientific system is always axiomatic in nature. Therefore, the reformulation of the system comprises that the extensional basis of the original system will be replaced by another that is more restricted but deontically equivalent. The system thus becomes simpler and more general.

II.

This characterization of legal systematization will be questioned later in this contribution. To begin with, let us recall certain basic viewpoints presented by Alchourrón and Bulygin.[4] In their opinion,

[4] Here I generally refer to *Alchourrón/Bulygin* (note 1), p. 51 ff.

an important part of the kind of activity that is called "interpretation" can be understood "as a determination of the normative consequences of a set of legal sentences for a certain problem or topic". Legal scholars simply aim at making explicit what is already hidden in the legal order. For Alchourrón and Bulygin this is the same as the construction of an axiomatic system. Here can also the cornerstone of the systematizing activity be found. The precondition of systematization is the identification of the system. "This presupposes the existence of certain elements which are the starting points for the systematization. These elements are: (1) a problem or a group of problems (a topic) whose regulation by the law is of interest to the jurist; (2) a set of legal sentences relevant to the topic in question; (3) a set of rules of inference used by the jurist in the derivation of the consequences."

The basis of the system consists of valid legal sentences. Thus, the identification of those valid sentences is the first stage in the systematization. The identification can be carried out by means of certain (material) criteria of validity. The role of the rules of inference is to define the notion of consequence. Using these (logical) rules the scholar can derive the consequences of the basis. As was mentioned above, the derivation of the consequences involves merely discovery, but no creation (in the proper sense of the word). Referring to this Alchourrón and Bulygin write: "The three elements (topic, legal sentences and rules of inference) determine the content of a normative system and the task of jurists consists in formulating it explicitly and, eventually, in reorganizing it."

The importance of the derivation of all the consequences of the legal sentences lies in the fact that any defects such as gaps, inconsistencies and redundancies will be made explicit. The significance of the reformulation of the system, on the other hand, is based on the principle of economy: the basis of a legal system should be as restricted as possible. The final outcome of the reformulation task is less extensive and more general than the original one.

From the theoretical point of view, the requirement of deontic equivalence is of special importance. Alchourrón and Bulygin put it as follows: "Only if the new basis has the same normative consequences as the original can we regard the result as the same system reformulated." Slightly in other words, the systematizing activity does not modify the system at all; it only provides us with a new way of *presenting* the system. As regards the scholarly work, this means that the (genuine) modification of the system takes place outside of the system's own framework. The creation of a new systemic basis belongs to the legislator and — in everyday practice — to the judge.

Hence, in order to be scientific the work of a legal dogmatician has to be logically coloured. The derivation of the consequences from the basis sentences is a problem of logical inference, because the rules of inference are logical rules. On the other hand, the relation of the original basis to the new one is a matter of logical implication. The scholar gets the general principles which belong to the new basis by means of deductive inference using the original basis as the starting point. Yet, for Alchourrón and Bulygin systematization is not merely a mechanical activity. The discovery of the general principles requires "a considerable degree of creative activity", as does also the drawing of a logical or mathematical conclusion from a given set of premises. This kind of activity presupposes creative imagination, too. The same holds true of the proof which shows that the new basis is deducible from the sentences of the original basis. The authors add, however, that the creative side of legal dogmatics does not involve the creation of totally new basic norms. This societal function is not involved in legal science.

III.

In terms of legal philosophy, the viewpoint presented by Alchourrón and Bulygin can be called formalistic.[5] Part of what is meant by formalism in this context is this: all sound normative consequences can be derived from the basis by means of valid deductive operations. The only task left to legal dogmatics (as a scientific approach) is to find out what is hidden in the legal system and, in addition to that, to present the results in a simple and general language.

This is not only important but also acceptable in many respects. However, that kind of characterization does not cover all the essential features of everyday legal dogmatics. Let us examine the matter in terms of some concepts introduced by Thomas Kuhn.

For Kuhn, science is essentially the use of conceptual instruments. In the concrete scientific work, scholars learn how to use these instruments in practice. As a product of this learning procedure, scientists adopt a certain uniting framework which in Kuhn's terminology is called a "paradigm". Every scientific paradigm is *articulated* in scientific theories. In legal dogmatic practice, however, the current usage of the concept of *theory* is ambiguous in many respects. The ambiguity is revealed e. g. in civil law, where the concept 'theory' may sometimes refer to general (legal) principles, sometimes to a certain way of solving individual (legal) problems, and sometimes to a doctrine, like

[5] On the formalistic attitude, see *D. Lyons*, Legal Formalism and Instrumentalism — A Pathological Study, in: Cornell Law Review, 1981, p. 949 ff.

the doctrine of ownership, that of authorization, etc. Thus, the fairly loose concept of theory as such is applicable neither to the paradigmatic analysis of legal dogmatics nor to the analysis of change in legal systems. Therefore, an effort at conceptual specification is needed. In what follows, this concept, i. e. the concept of theory *in* legal dogmatics (theory in law), is defined by means of the notion of systematization.

Def.: A theory in legal dogmatics is a set of concepts and statements used for systematizing legal norms in a certain way.[6]

Hence, a theory in law (as distinguished from a theory *of* law) is the outcome of the systematizing activity. Legal systematization, in other words, is a (partial) articulation of the legal dogmatic paradigm. The theories in legal dogmatics, in this respect, can easily be compared with theories in other scientific disciplines. The systematizing activity is the theoretical part of legal dogmatics, whereas interpretation fulfills the practical function in the scholarly work. The interaction between the two, i. e. systematization and interpretation, is thus much the same thing as the widely discussed interaction between the theoretical and practical approaches in the legal science.

As an example of a theory in legal dogmatics I shall take the theory of ownership. According to Alf Ross[7] and Simo Zitting[8] the concept of ownership — equally with any other concept comparable with it — is a (practical) instrument in presenting a very complex totality of legal norms. Instead of describing a vast number of different norms one can communicate by means of a few general concepts.[9]

An abstract scheme of that kind of theory can be presented as follows:

[6] *A. Aarnio,* On the Paradigm Articulation in Legal Research, in: RECHTSTHEORIE Beiheft 3 (1981), p. 53.

[7] *A. Ross,* On Law and Justice, New York 1960, section VI.

[8] *S. Zitting,* An Attempt to Analyse the Owner's Legal Position, in: Scandinavian Studies in Law, 1959, 3, p. 227 ff.

[9] Cf. what *Alchourrón/Bulygin* (note 1) write about this (p. 79): "The advantages of a system with a small but general basis are manifest: the relatively small number of sentences makes it easier to grasp the structure as a whole and to apply it in practice."

Theory T_1

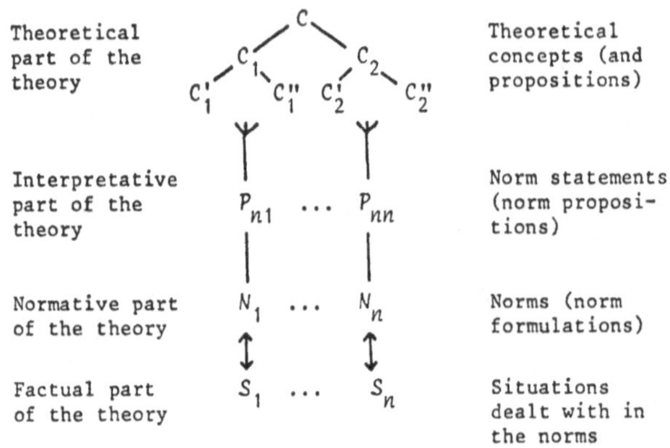

IV.

Let us accept the theory T_1 as an illustration of a theory in legal dogmatics. The concept C may refer to any kind of legal concepts: ownership, authorization, guardianship etc. What does it mean to say, in accordance with this, that a legal system undergoes a change? What is the *reformulation* of a legal system?

Behind every legislative act there is a many-sided set of elements:

(a) *Generalizations,* formed upon everyday experience, about the prevailing states of affairs and about the existence and character of given phenomena in society.

(b) *Theory-like totalities* of propositions regarding the reasons for and the consequences of certain phenomena, the structure of institutions, and so on. Good examples of this are the configurations of assumptions in economic theory analyzed in an illuminative way by Juha Tolonen.[10] Various legal doctrines and theories, such as the doctrines of authorization and of contract, also belong to this group.

(c) *Normative and axiological views* of how things should be in society. In this connection, reference is often made to ideology.

The list is not exhaustive. Even so, it gives a first indication of the background elements on which every legislative act is based. I shall

[10] *J. Tolonen,* Der allgemeine Erklärungshintergrund der wirtschaftlichen Ordnung und seine Anwendung auf das Aktiengesellschaftsrecht, Helsinki 1974, *passim.* Tolonen examines the relation of certain economic theories (presented e. g. by Smith and Keynes) with various conceptions of the structure of companies-limited-by-shares. His theoretical aim is to establish an internal connection between these theories and the content of law.

call this totality *the pre-theory of legislation (PT)*. This term can be defended on two grounds. The viewpoints formulated in the process of legislation are not in spurious contact with each other; instead, they form a whole that already is systematized to some extent. This whole also includes factors which can be regarded as pure theory. On the other hand, the viewpoints do not form a theory which were based on scientific criteria. The systematization is sufficient from the *legal point of view* in general, but for example from the point of view of *legal dogmatics*, it is only "pre-theory". It is first of all in this sense that we say that the legal system is a (pre-) systematized power-order. Legislation is the use of power based on a certain systematized preconception.

An everyday societal situation, however, is *tied to a certain tradition*. The reform of legislation does not start from a vacuum. New legislation either changes, supplements or clarifies the old one. The legislator, in other words, does not *create* the system in its totality. He only transforms and modifies it. Legal tradition consists of normative structures that are independent of any individual lawgiver. Thus, one must add one more element to the above list:

(d) Previous legislation and its systematics make up the *framework* for new legislation. Special mention must be made of the systemic analysis that legal dogmatics has directed at the then prevailing legislation. The drafters of the new legislation receive the basic concepts for their legal thinking from the ways of thinking prevailing at that time. I shall denote the system including these concepts by S_i.

Generally speaking, the use of legislative power is based on pretheoretical thought. The latter has many elements and its general function is described above. An important role in it is played by normative and axiological points of view, but the other factors mentioned in the above list are significant as well. *Law texts* are the outcome of the exercise of legislative power. As linguistic expressions they carry certain *meanings*. These meanings form a system which is in accordance with the pre-theoretical systematization. This can be called the *basic system* (S_b). It is precisely the *developing* of the basic system S_b that can be called the *systematization* of legal norms. The result of this activity — a scientific legal system — will be denoted here as S_j. In this respect S_j has the same function as (e. g.) S_i in legislation.

That is what is meant when one distinguishes between legal *order* and legal (scientific) *system*. As we could notice, one of the main tasks of legal dogmatics is the formulation of a scientific system. To this end, legal norms belonging to S_b are rearranged, and the system itself is thus developed.

Theoretically, systematization has been regarded as the *replacement* of the basic system with an identical (scientific) system. This is how the matter has been presented by Alchourrón and Bulygin. As was noted above, their basic idea is that systematization does not bring anything new to the contents of the basic system. It is merely a question of describing the basic system in a more workable way. The *normative solutions* produced by the two systems are the same. The basic system and the replacing system are *identical.*

There are certain difficulties ensuing from this view. Its particular problem is the concept of identity. It would appear that research praxis frequently shows that the result of systematization is *not* identical with the basic system. On the contrary, systematization is, in a true sense, a *creative* procedure. System S_j is something "more" than the basic system S_b. There is, however, a need for further clarification of this statement.

When the basic system (S_b) is reformulated, it is made by means of a certain *theory in law.* Let us recall Figure 1 and the theory of ownership as an illustration of it. The conceptual structure of the theory is the basis on which the individual legal norms in question are reorganized. Hence, the key to systematization lies entirely in the change of this kind of *systematizing theory.* Let us denote this theory by *ST*. The conceptual structure of *ST* is like a lens through which the set of individual legal norms is being observed.

A view in the philosophy of science which has been much repeated and referred to is that every observational statement (to a certain extent) is theory-laden. There are no pure observations, in the sense that it would be possible to purify them of all theoretical understanding in advance. Therefore, we speak of theory-laden observations.[11] In legal dogmatics, this finds its application in the concept of *theory-laden interpretations.* This concept calls for preliminary clarification. Systematization theory *ST* provides a set of basic concepts within the limits of which every problem concerning the contents of legal norms must be set, i. e. systematization theory defines the limits of interpretation. But it also marks the boundaries of something more. Systematization theory organizes legal norms in a certain way *in their relation to one another.* The placement of norm N_i in the systematic connection created by norms N_j and N_k affects the way in which the *content* of norm N_i is understood. It is not merely a question of their relative order; it is at the same time a question of the content of every

---

[11] See e. g. *N. R. Hanson,* Perception and Discovery, ed. by Willard C. Humphreys, 1969. Cf. also *Aarnio,* 1977 (note 3), p. 277 ff. and *Aarnio,* 1979 (note 3), p. 25 and 60—61.

single element which enters the unit in question. In other words, we are dealing with an example of the way in which *the whole affects its parts*. We must, however, notice also the feed-back effect: the reinterpretation of the contents of the norms may force us to test and rectify the systematization theory. This re-examination has an effect on the interpretation of the norms, and so on and so forth. There is thus an interrelationship between systematization theory and the interpretation of legal norms.

The *meanings interpreted* on the basis of the systematization theory form the replacing system S_j referred to above. Already the term 'interpreted meaning' shows that the system S_j is *not* identical with the basic system. The original system is based on the legislator's subjective interpretations and, through this, is tied to a pre-theoretical view. Even though the pre-theoretical view may, and often does, have a connection with the systematization theory *ST*, the systematization that follows *ST* is not identical with pre-theoretical systematization. It is not merely a question of raising the level of abstraction, or something like that. The systematization theory changes our view of the relationship between norms, and as a consequence it is possible to pose new questions, which in turn make it possible to give answers of a new sort.

It is important to note that within the framework of system S_j it is possible to pose new problems which were not known under the basic system S_b or under the previous reformulation of the basic system. Every systematization opens up new possibilities for interpretation. Some principles, however, cannot even in theory turn up within a certain system, if the set of terms necessary to present the problem is lacking.

The relations between pre-theory and the systematization theory, the relation between the basic system and the replacing system, and the shaping role of interpretation can be presented in the following manner:

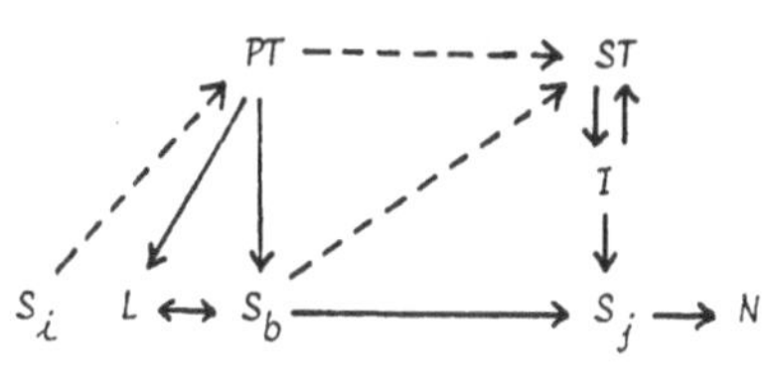

In the figure, *PT* = pre-theoretical systematization, *ST* = the systematization theory, S_i = the scientific systematization presented before legislation *L*, S_b = the basic system or the system of the intended meanings expressed by the law texts, I = interpretation in legal dogmatics, S_j = the replacing system or the scientific systematization, and N = legal norm interpreted in legal dogmatics.

The figure is intended to express the view already mentioned: that the interpretation arising from the law text (the interpretative standpoint) makes it possible to present the standpoint on the contents of the legal norm (the norm standpoint). This procedure is shown by the path from L to N.

On the other hand, it is important to emphasize that at the same time or at different times there can be given two or more alternative replacing systematizations *of the same basic system* (S_b), for example S_j and S_k. They each include their own systematization theory. For this reason, replacing systematizations can never be identical. S_j and S_k form two *separate* (non-identical) pictures of the legal order interpreted on theoretical grounds.

This observation entitles us to once again return to the concept of identity. As noted earlier, the point of departure taken by Alchourrón and Bulygin is that the basic systematization and the replacing system are identical. If the basic system is defined as the intended system, as presented above, the view of Alchourrón and Bulygin is not correct. The pre-theoretical view (*PT*) and the systematization theory (*ST*) are two different ways of systematizing the legal order. When we add to this the interaction between the systematization theory and interpretation, the replacing system (S_j) receives of necessity a different content than does the basic system (S_b). However, despite this, we can speak of a "weak" identity. The replacing system attempts to present an interpretation which is *in accordance with law*. It "describes" the valid legal order. Even though it is not identical with the intended system, it still represents the meanings expressed by law. Finnish law (Finnish law texts) *has* the content shown by S_j. The same applies also to other replacing systems, for example to system S_k. It does not give the same outcome as the original intended system does, but it gives us in any case a valid interpretation of the given law text. Both S_j and S_k involve a *creative* element: the replacing system shapes the intended system so that the content of the law becomes rational and acceptable at the time of systematization.

SYSTEMATIZATION AND CHANGE IN THE SCIENCE OF LAW

By Carlos E. Alchourrón, Buenos Aires

I. Introduction

One of the classical topics of jurisprudence is the characterization of the functions of legal science. Legal dogmatics, as ordinarily conceived, performs at least two important tasks: the identification of the conceptual content of existing legal orders and the systematic and organized presentation of the solutions offered by the law for possible conflicts in a given society. But once the issue is presented in this way there appear a lot of questions the answers to which depend on the conceptual scheme used in the analysis. For example the questions of whether the systematizing activity does or does not entail a change in the conceptual content of the legal order, and whether it is possible to have different non-equivalent systematizations of the law of a country. In relation to these questions Aarnio maintains the following theses:

(i) The systematizing activity involves always a creative element, in the sense that when a system S_b is reformulated (systematized) by a system S_i then both systems are not logically equivalent.

This is so because

(ii) The systematizing task of legal dogmatics is to shape and enrich the basic system. It involves a reformulation that entails different normative consequences.

These assertions, and others related to them, are contrasted to what is stated in *Normative Systems*,[1] where it is stated that:

(i') Although the systematizing activity requires creative imagination, the reformulation of set of norms S_b by means of S_i is such that both sets are logically equivalent.

(ii') The systematizing task of legal dogmatics aims to present the normative content of the basic set of norms in a new perspective. But the reformulation of a system must preserve the whole of its normative consequences.

---

[1] *C. E. Alchourrón/E. Bulygin*, Normative Systems, Wien-New York 1971.

Presented in this way both points of view seem to be completely opposite. But we must not jump too soon to conclusions. In order to appreciate whether and where there are real and not merely verbal disagreements we must first give an explanation about the meaning of the main concepts involved in the discussion.

According to the conception put forward in *Normative Systems* three aspects of the activity of legal science can be distinguished: (1) the identification of legal norms, (2) the systematization of a set of normative sentences, and (3) the modification or change of legal systems. The main motivation for this classification was to isolate the empirical, the conceptual and the axiological elements that are required for the justification of the statements of legal science.

Aarnio's account of the functions of legal dogmatics starts from a twofold distinction: (1) the interpretation (formulation) of a legal system, and (2) its systematization or reformulation. So he says, "In this view the traditional task of legal dogmatics becomes crystallized on the one hand as the formulation of system (determination of the content) and on the other, as its reformulation (systematization)."[2] From this standpoint Aarnio presents an apparently different picture of the tasks of legal dogmatics.

In what follows I am going to sketch out my conception of legal science in order to compare it with that of Aarnio.

II. Norms and the Empirical Identification of a Basic Set

The identification of a legal order requires, as a preliminary step, the determination of its elements. In so far as legal orders are designed to qualify human behaviour as obligatory, permitted or prohibited they must contain, in addition to other elements, at least a set of norms. For reasons of terminological clarity it is convenient to start with a brief account of the nature of norms.

We must distinguish first between *norms* and *norm-formulations*. Norm-formulations are sentences, i. e. linguistic entities, used to indicate what must, may or may not be done in certain cases, i. e. to present normative solutions for the cases considered. In order to be able to perform this function it must be possible to identify the factual situations and the actions referred to in the normative sentences; hence only meaningful sentences can be recognized as norms. The conceptual content associated with the norm-formulation is essential for the

[2] *A. Aarnio*, On Legal Reasoning, Turku/Loimaa 1977, p. 288.

identification of a norm, because the same sentence endowed with a different meaning will express a different norm as far as the cases and/or the actions referred to in it are not the same. What, then, is a norm and in what does it differ from a norm-formulation? There are in the literature two not incompatible answers to this question. According to the first, the norm is the meaning associated to the normative expression. This seems to be the standpoint of Aarnio when he states that "the norm is the idea-content which is *expressed* by means of the norm formulation."[3] The second answer identifies the norm with the normative sentence plus a definite meaning. This was the position adopted in *Normative Systems* and it seems to be also admitted by Aarnio when he says that a norm is a function of the norm formulation and the idea-content. For our present purpose both answers are equally satisfactory. In this paper I am going to consider 'norm' as a normative sentence plus a definite meaning.

Anyway, whenever a norm is conceived as a meaningful sentence or as the meaning of a normative formulation it is senseless to speak of the interpretation of a norm. Only normative formulations can be interpreted, and their interpretation consists in the identification of the norm associated with the expression. In this sense when jurists say, for example, that a legal norm has been given different judicial interpretations, it must be understood that they are referring to norm-formulations. The assertion amounts to the statement that different norms have been associated with one and the same legal sentence. When the term 'norm' is used in this way it means just norm-formulation. I have the impression that many times Aarnio uses 'norm' as a synonym of norm-formulation. This is clearly the case when he says in his book: "Usually two or more alternative interpretations may be suggested for a certain norm."[4] I understand this statement as an assertion to the effect that frequently the same law text is associated with different norms, i. e. that we have a common norm-formulation endowed with different meanings. Later on we shall see how this ambiguity may cause certain difficulties to understand Aarnio's concept of legal order and systematization.

But there is no doubt that one of the main tasks of legal dogmatics consists in the identification of legal norms and consequently in the interpretation of law texts and other kinds of norm-formulations. In order to achieve this goal the scientist must perform several activities: First, he must be able to single out the set of norms that forms the basis of the legal order. Second, he must be able to state the consequences

---

[3] *Aarnio* (note 2), p. 12.

[4] *Aarnio* (note 2), p. 275.

and the principles that follow from the basic sentences. The first step is what we called the identification of the basis of a legal order and the second forms part of what we understand by its systematization. In this section I am going to refer only to the first task.

For the identification of the sentences of the basis certain criteria are used. These criteria of identification establish what requirements legal sentences must satisfy in order to be introduced to or removed from the basic set. The criteria consist of conceptual rules that indicate the various sources of law. The process of identifying of the basic set is, of course, complicated and difficult. Take for example the simplest case: the identification of the norms contained in a statute. The simplicity of the case derives from the fact that in it there is no problem of identifying the norm-formulations. Moreover it is natural, though many times unrealistic, to think that the legislator has endowed each sentence of the law text with a definite meaning. In such situations it is possible, in principle, to discover empirically the meaning of the norm-formulations and so to identify the norms contained in the statute. However, sometimes it may be impossible to find the empirical evidence necessary for the identification of the norms pertaining to the statute.

In other circumstances there does not even exist a unique meaning attached to a legal sentence. Think of the case in which several members of a legislative body understood the promulgated expressions with a definite meaning without noticing that others had intended to pass a different norm.

For one reason or other the scholar may find that he cannot identify by empirical means a unique set of norms. In such a case what he will do subsequently depends on the guiding purpose of his research. If he just wants to describe the result that comes out from the empirical investigation based on the sources of law then he will finish his work showing the alternative sets of norms that can be associated to the same norm formulations. But even if his purpose is more ambitious and he wants to evaluate the different possibilities, he will begin his critical research by taking into account all the alternative sets of norms. We must not forget that the identification process is the logical precondition for the systematizing activity and for the critical activity. Therefore after this preliminary step, designed to determine the material to be systematized, the jurist may find himself facing a set of norms or a plurality of alternative sets of norms. In any case his discoveries are empirically grounded and may be contested by empirical reasons.

The standard situation in which a scholar will be forced to start his systematizing activity from a plurality of alternative sets of norms is that in which the law text is ambiguous. Sometimes the same effect is attributed to vague expressions, but this is a mistake, because an unambiguous vague expression has a unique meaning. Von Wright has correctly observed that "[i]t is important to distinguish between vagueness and ambiguity. The first is a feature of some *concepts* or, as one could also say here, *meanings*. The second is a characteristic of some *words* (and phrases)."[5] Hence vagueness does not present any problem at the identification level.

III. Systematization and the Conceptual Content of a Set of Norms

Usually jurists are concerned with determining the normative status conferred by law to certain actions by means of an adequate description of the consequences that follow from a previously identified set of meaningful legal sentences. In general any set of sentences determines the set of its logical consequences; the latter is what we call the *system* determined by the former. The importance of the notion of system comes from the fact that it represents the full conceptual content of a set of sentences. Two or more different sets of sentences may determine the same system, so that each of them can be used to present the system. When we start from a definite set of sentences, then any other set that determines the same system amounts to a *reformulation* of it. From a practical point of view some formulations are more valuable than others, and for this reason legal science tries to find the most perspicuous reformulation.

The doctrinal study of law is not limited to a simple restatement of the legal rules in force. A legal scholar must be able to show the consequences that follow from several norms of the system. The knowledge of the consequences for some area of problems brings to light the particular features of the identified set of legal sentences. As this knowledge progresses, the jurist may come to discover that the original set was unnecessarily complicated, and hence that it is possible to present the system in a simplified manner. The whole system is then reorganized in order to show how the sentences of the original set can be derived from some general principles that make explicit the evaluational grounds for the solutions contained in the system. No critical evaluation is possible before the investigation of the conceptual interconnections between the different elements of the system. But only when the modification is performed preserving the conceptual content of the original set we refer to it as a *reformulation* of the normative system determined by the basic set of sentences. In this technical sense a re-

[5] *G. H. von Wright,* The Varieties of Goodness, London 1963, p. 13.

formulation is a replacement of a set of norms by another logically equivalent set. Alf Ross[6] has shown how some theoretical concepts like ownership are used in legal discourse to present a large group of directives by means of a simpler totality of norms. Theoretical concepts are one of the technical tools used by legal science to conceptualize rules in such a way that they are reduced to systematic order and by this means to give an account of the law in force as plain and convenient as possible. One of the motives for the reformulation of a normative system is to give satisfaction to the requirement of Jhering's principle of economy.

More often than not a system will contain some consequences that are inadequate from an axiological point of view. These consequences may remain unnoticed until some scholar discovers a hidden implication of the basic set of sentences. In legal science like in any other science deductive inference plays an important role in the identification of the defects contained in a set of premises. When the fault is axiological, one may think that the reformulation of the system by means of an equivalent set of sentences is a pointless activity because the new set will have the same defects as the old one. Nevertheless it may be very useful to have an equivalent basis in which all the axiologically inadequate consequences are derived from an independent set of norms. This kind of isolation of the bad principles that are responsible for the bad consequences is part of the normal activity of legal science. Hence the significance of the reformulation of normative systems is independent of any judgment about their axiological properties. Moreover, assessment of the merits of large groups of legal rules presupposes the knowledge of its consequences. The reformulation of a normative system is designed to increase that knowledge. For this reason it is important to preserve its conceptual content.

In general, by systematization we understand those operations that aim to present, as clearly as possible, the conceptual content of normative systems.

IV. Substantial Transformations of Normative Systems (Changes)

It is well known that positive law is in permanent change and that legal systems do not remain the same in the course of time. These plain truths are susceptible of different analyses. From the point of view of the theory contained in *Normative Systems* the historical evolution of the law of a country is represented by means of a sequence of momentary legal orders. We use the notion of change to conceptualize the modifi-

[6] *A. Ross*, On Law and Justice, London 1958, Chapter 6.

cations that take place in the historical evolution. Nevertheless our concept of change does not necessarily presuppose a temporal reference. A change will be any transformation that affects the content of a normative system.

"When a jurist says that a system has changed — because some of its normative consequences have been modified — what he intends to assert, or at least what he is entitled to assert, is that it is no longer the same system, that it has become another system different from the former. This is a direct consequence of our definition of system: the criterion of identity is provided by its consequences. Therefore, expressions like 'change in a system' or 'change of a system' must be taken to mean not a modification of the same system (which would retain its identity despite the change), but the substitution of a new and different system for the original one. This is a perfectly natural meaning of the term 'change'."[7]

A change of a system amounts to a substantial transformation of its content. The new and the old system may have many elements in common but there must be a norm that belongs to one of them and not to the other. In this sense change must be carefully distinguished from the operation called systematization in which the identity of the system is preserved.

Many times a change of legal order is concealed by what is called the interpretation (or reinterpretation) of law texts. This is the case when the interpretation gives rise to a new normative correlation, i. e. when we have a different norm even though the norm-formulation remains the same.

Behind any change of a legal order there is a creative element that requires axiological grounds for its justification. One of the functions of legal science consists in providing us with the theoretical tools necessary for those evaluative justifications.

The evaluative elements of legal science become evident when we focus our attention on the nature of a scholar's arguments relative to normative changes. More often than not those arguments involve recommendations for or against normative changes. Of course, when legal science merely describes or predicts actual or possible changes there is no particular moral or ideological commitment. The creative element — in Aarnio's sense — appears only in those statements that imply a recommendation. In actual legal practice we find both kinds of statements. Moreover we expect from legal dogmatics some guidance to overcome the deficiencies of the law in force.

---

[7] *Alchourrón/Bulygin* (note 1), p. 88.

V. Aarnio's Conceptual Scheme

In order to appreciate Aarnio's criticism of our position we must first analyze the kernel of his conceptual scheme, in particular, his concepts of system, systematization and interpretation.

Aarnio's example of systematization starts from a *basic system* S_b, which is also called legal order, constituted by the intended meanings of certain law texts. The result of the systematizing activity is a legal (scientific) system, denoted by S_j. It is important to observe that the scientific system S_j and the legal order S_b must have different contents, because "systematization is, in a true sense, a *creative* procedure. System S_j is something 'more' than the basic system S_b."[8] Aarnio explains this difference in his book by saying that "the *creative* nature of the new systematics lies in the fact that the view concerning *the content of the legal order has changed* [...] between these two system variations there can never prevail any relationship of identity. The new system differs from the old in the very fact that it manifests the legal order in a new way, in a way within which the normative consequences need not be the same."[9]

The legal order and the scientific system are two meaningful totalities that differ in their conceptual content; one must have at least one norm, i. e. a correlation between a case and a deontic solution, that is not derivable from the other.

On the other hand, one and the same legal order S_b may be transformed into a plurality of different systems. This point is emphasized by Aarnio's assertion that "at the same time or at different times there can be given two or more alternative replacing systematizations *of the same basic system* (S_b), for example S_j and S_k."[10] This observation seems to reflect the fact that quite often we find in legal science different suggestions for changing a legal order. Each of the rival normative systems tries to give better solutions for practical problems by means of different norms. Any choice among them must be grounded on evaluative considerations. Legal science must offer for its proposals adequate axiological justifications.

Up to this point it seems clear that for Aarnio legal orders, as well as legal systems in general, are sets of norms, i. e. classes of pure meanings or meaningful expressions. But this is not the only way in which he uses the key terms. Commenting the above theoretical example he

---

[8] *Aarnio*, On Changes in the Systematics of Law (in this volume), Section IV.

[9] *Aarnio* (note 2), p. 280. Italics mine.

[10] *Aarnio* (note 8), Section IV.

asserts that each of the replacing systems S_j and S_k attempts to present an interpretation which is *in accordance with law*, so that each of them somehow "describes" the legal order. But when we recall that for Aarnio interpretation is the activity that aims to clarify the contents of legal orders, the question arises of whether the basic system S_b — which in the example is the legal order — is the object of these different interpretations. An affirmative answer seems to be contained in Aarnio's statement "that only in few cases it is possible to give one and only one consistent interpretation of a norm belonging to the basic system."[11] According to this assertion, S_j and S_k would be different interpretations of the norms contained in the basic system S_b.

But then, as E. Bulygin has correctly observed, commenting this part of the book, the elements of S_b cannot be norms but only norm-formulations (law texts). Bulygin's interpretation is confirmed by Aarnio's actual assertion "Finnish law (Finnish law texts) *has* the content shown by S_j. The same applies also to other replacing systems, for example to system S_k."[12] Hence, it is clear that Aarnio sometimes uses the expressions "legal order" and "basic system" as referring to sets of norm-formulations (i. e. mere law texts and not meaningful sentences) instead of sets of norms.

This ambiguity gives rise to a conceptual problem when we try to understand his distinction between interpretation and systematization under the assumption, made at the beginning of his paper, that both activities refer to the same kind of entities, viz. legal orders. When the legal order is a set of norm-formulations, then it seems impossible to distinguish interpretation from systematization. For this reason Bulygin concludes: "Given Aarnio's use of the term 'systematization', the difference between systematization and interpretation is indeed not only problematic, but simply non-existent."[13] Both processes are directed to the identification of the norms expressed by certain texts.

I believe that these difficulties have a new answer in Aarnio's present paper. Interpretation is — at least in the light of examples like the one he is considering — a process referred to a set of norm-formulations (law texts), and systematization, on the other hand, is an operation on sets of norms.

This amounts to a rejection of the thesis that both activities refer to entities of the same kind. The source of the plausibility of the thesis lies in the ambiguity of the terms involved in it.

[11] *Aarnio* (note 2), p. 275.

[12] *Aarnio* (note 8), Section IV.

[13] E. *Bulygin*, Legal Dogmatics and the Systematization of Law (in this volume), Section V.

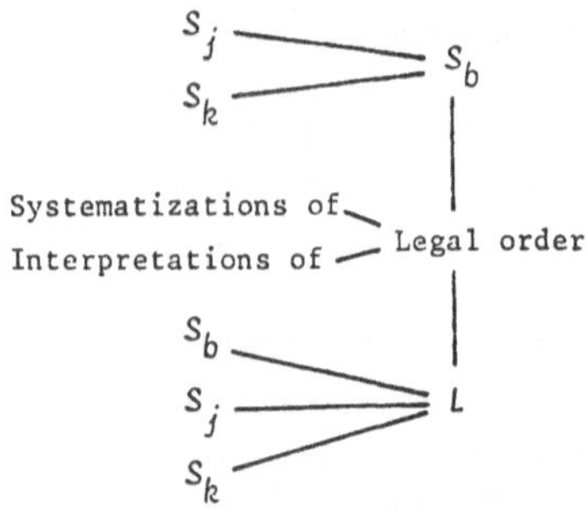

Here S_b, S_j and S_k stand for sets of norms with different consequences, and L is a set of norm-formulations (law texts)

The following diagram depicts the ambiguity of "legal order" in relation to "systematization" and "interpretation".

Once the ambiguity is removed, the two operations become clearly distinct, and we are in a position to ask for their reciprocal relations.

As a preliminary step it must be noticed that although each of these sets of norms is an interpretation of L, not all of them require the same kind of justification. This is so because the assertion that S_b is the intended interpretation of L, presupposes empirical arguments based on the factual evidence that can be found in the sources of law according to some common criteria of identification. It is convenient to observe that this kind of interpretative statements are identifications (in our terminology) of the basic set of norms expressed by some law texts.

The situation is completely different in relation to S_j and S_k. They are not presented by legal science — in Aarnio's example — as the intended interpretation (or as the interpretation in force) but as suggestions to modify S_b. Hence their justification requires the same kind of evaluative reasons needed for the acceptance of any normative change. As pointed out before, any change of interpretation amounts to a change (systematization in Aarnio's sense) of a normative system.

In legal scientific practice both kinds of interpretation are not always clearly distinguished. The creative feature involved in many of them is often concealed by means of different devices. In order to make explicit these evaluative elements contained in many interpretative processes we should distinguish between creative and non-creative interpretations. In the example, S_b is the only non-creative interpretation of L. On the other hand we may assert that S_j and S_k are creative interpretations because they change the conceptual content of S_b. The change is performed by means of the process of systematization (in Aarnio's sense of the term) that opens the possibility for new and different interpretations. For this reason Aarnio asserts that systematization gives a framework for legal interpretation. The creative element of systematization is transmitted to the corresponding interpretation. In this way systematization and interpretation are closely related activities.

This brief sketch of Aarnio's concept of systematization shows that any systematization is a substantial transformation (change, in our sense) of a basic system. But the converse is not always true, for not every normative change amounts to a systematization. The reason for this asymmetry lies in the role played by legal theories. A systematization is a modification made by means of a certain theory of law.[14] The theory is the uniting framework that gives scientific character to the whole process. It is a complex totality whose main function is to organize and present a large number of norms by means of few general theoretical concepts. To understand the internal structure of a theory we may divide its elements into two categories: (1) the norms contained in the theory (its normative content), and (2) the elements used to organize them (the systemic component of the theory). Hence systematization is for Aarnio a substantial transformation of a basic system by means of the normative content of a legal theory. But it is important to emphasize that if the normative content of a theory is the same as that of the basic system then this theory will not change the system but only its presentation, no matter how different its systemic component may be. Transformations of this last kind are not, of course, systematizations in Aarnio's sense, although they are reformulations (systematizations) in our sense. Aarnio admits the importance of such operations, but he seems not to be particularly interested in them.

Aarnio's example shows how a legal theory can be used to give a particular interpretation to some law texts. Interpretations of this kind are linguistic interpretations. But Aarnio observes that "the term 'interpretation' refers also, in its usual sense, to other activities than to the linguistic interpretation only."[15] Legal theories can be used to interpret not only norm-formulations but also social reality. The legal significance of human behavior depends upon the normative theory used to appreciate the deontic and evaluative properties of social transactions. In this way a legal theory is like a picture that enables us to understand human action from an evaluative perspective. One and the same activity may receive different interpretations according to the nature of the theory

[14] Terms 'theory of law' and 'legal theory' in my paper mean, of course, the same as Aarnio's term 'theory *in* law' in his paper here. Theories of/in law as cognitive entities serving scientific systematization are to be distinguished from 'legal theory' in its broad sense.

[15] *Aarnio* (note 8), Section I.

used to conceptualize social relations. In his book Aarnio shows how the traditional and the analytical theories of ownership give different legal significance to actual transactions concerning the transference of real estate. In this sense legal theories are the conceptual tools that provide the framework for interpreting the (legal) significance of social situations. The object of the interpretation is not any more a linguistic entity but real human behavior. We have now a new sense of interpretation that explains the practical societal relevance of legal science.

I am not sure whether Aarnio will accept the above construction in the way I have presented it, but I believe that it is somehow implicit in some of his statements. Anyhow it brings to light the practical importance of the creative-evaluative elements contained in legal theories, which is one of the main points in Aarnio's paper.

VI. Concluding Remarks

With these elements at hand we are in a position to appreciate the force of Aarnio's criticism of our approach.

The first objection is concerned with our notion of identity. According to our point of view a basic set of legal sentences and any of its reformulations must have the same normative consequences. Aarnio thinks that this statement is false because "research praxis frequently shows that the result of systematization is *not* identical with the basic system."[16] Hence he looks for a weaker concept of identity. In this objection Aarnio falls victim to two related misinterpretations: (i) he misunderstands our statement — which is a definition of "reformulation" — as a factual assertion about legal dogmatic practice; (ii) he does not notice that his notion of reformulation (systematization) corresponds to our notion of change which is completely different from our concept of systematization. Once the ambiguity is detected it becomes clear that both his and our statements are true, because they refer to different and incompatible processes.

The second objection is related to what Aarnio calls the formalistic nature of our point of view, which would amount to the following: "all sound normative consequences can be derived from the basis by means of valid deductive operations. The only task left to legal dogmatics (as a scientific approach) is to find out what is hidden in the legal system and, in addition to that, to present the results in a simple and general language."[17]

[16] *Aarnio* (note 8), Section IV.

[17] *Aarnio* (note 8), Section III.

To this Aarnio objects that it "does not cover all the essential features of everyday legal dogmatics."

I can easily concede this point, but is it really an objection to what has been said in *Normative Systems*? What is indeed essential is to distinguish between two radically different tasks: the description of the law prevailing in a certain community at a given time, and its critical evaluation. In our book we were mostly, though not exclusively, concerned with the first task, but this does not mean denying the fact that legal theorists also perform the second task; they do indeed evaluate critically the legal order and they formulate proposals for its change, proposals that once accepted by the legal community lead to the substitution of another legal system for the existing one. The importance of the descriptive task lies in the fact that (i) it allows us to identify the existing law, which will be the object of critical evaluations (if we do not identify what we want to evaluate, this last task becomes pointless), and (ii) it shows the properties and possible deficiencies of a legal system, such as gaps, inconsistencies and lack of justice, which will provide reasons for the criticism and eventually will lead to the change of the system. So the description of the law is a previous and basic task, without which a rational evaluation of law is impossible.

The difference between the two tasks, description and evaluation, is reflected in the different kinds of reasons used to justify the corresponding assertions. In order to support critical or evaluative assertions about the legal order, we must resort to certain values and to moral arguments.

The focus of Aarnio's interest seems to lie in the justification of the extension of a legal system to new cases (which are inadequately solved or not solved at all by the basic system). This is why his notion of systematization implies a *change* of the system: he states explicitly that the replacing system is not and cannot be identical with the basic system. On the other hand, in our book the notion of systematization is restricted to those operations that make explicit what already is there or modify the presentation of the system without affecting its identity. So the difference is more a question of emphasis than of substance. But we never denied the importance of that aspect of legal science that consists in advocating and justifying a change of a legal system. All we wanted was to stress the difference between these two operations, mainly because they are supported by different reasons, and because, as experience shows, it is not as easy to achieve the same degree of objectivity in moral arguments as in empirical or logical ones.

The search for objectivity implies the need to resort to certain general principles from which the proposed solutions can be derived; so the role of deductive inference is important even for the task of justification, as has been already stressed in *Normative Systems*. One of the conditions of rational acceptability linked to the requirements of universalization of evaluative judgments and of justice as fairness is precisely the justification of particular cases by means of general rules. But even in the realm of description and systematization (in our sense) of a legal system, where the deductive reasoning occupies the key position, one must not forget that the mere fact that a solution can be inferred from a system does not justify its acceptability. Moral justification of solutions requires moral justification of the system, and this task needs arguments of a different kind. So the distinction between description and justification is a basic one, for evaluative arguments are used not only in advocating or rejecting a change, but also for the general acceptability of any given system and its particular solutions. To stress this difference was one of the main purposes of our book.

DIE SYSTEMATISIERUNG DER REGULIERUNGSMETHODEN

Von Jiří Boguszak, Prag

I.

Folgende Thesen befassen sich mit der Teilfrage des Themas „Systematisierung der Rechtswissenschaft" unter Stellungnahme zum Problem der Gliederung des Rechts und der Rechtswissenschaft. Sie beanspruchen nicht eine allgemeine Gültigkeit. Aus der ganz allgemeinen, rein formellen Sicht gehen sie aus dem kontinental-europäischen Typ der Rechtstechnik aus, deren Anfänge gewöhnlich von dem Code Civil (Code Napoléon) aus dem Jahr 1804 datiert werden. Im übrigen knüpfen sie vor allem auf die Erfahrungen aus der Entwicklung des sozialistischen Rechts an, namentlich in der Tschechoslowakischen sozialistischen Republik (= ČSSR).

Die Gestaltung der *Rechtswissenschaftszweige* zeichnet sich durch den logischen und den historischen Aspekt aus.

II.

Aus der logisch-systematischen Sicht kommt es darauf an, was für ein Kriterium als principium divisionis angewandt wird. In der marxistischen Rechtstheorie werden als grundlegender Ausgangspunkt gesellschaftliche Verhältnisse betrachtet, die zum Objekt der Rechtsregelung werden. So entstehendes System der Rechtsnormen deckt sich nicht mit dem Komplex der Rechtsquellen, da es im Laufe des legislativen Verfahrens aus verschiedenen praktischen Gründen nicht selten zur Verbindung ungleichartiger Normen (z. B. der arbeitsrechtlichen und der verwaltungsrechtlichen) in einer und derselben Vorschrift oder umgekehrt kommt. Die Klassifizierung des Rechts dient also eigentlich zur Gliederung der Rechtswissenschaft; sie wird zum Leitsatz für die Gestaltung einer Systematik, mit deren Hilfe die Rechtswissenschaft das Recht verarbeitet.

III.

Aus historischer Sicht hängt die Gestaltung der Rechtswissenschaftszweige von den gesellschaftlichen Bedingungen und Bedürfnissen ab; sie ist durch die Interessen dieser oder jener sozialen Klassen oder

Gruppen in der gegebenen Entwicklungsetappe des betreffenden Landes bedingt. Dieses oder jenes Modell des Rechtszweiges gehört zu den Formen des gesellschaftlichen Bewußtseins. Soziale Ursachen seiner Entstehung und seine Funktionen kann man soziologisch untersuchen. Zu den mitspielenden Faktoren gehören wissenschaftliche Traditionen wie auch die Stabilisierung einzelner Disziplinen auf den Hochschulen, was u. a. auch durch pädagogische Gründe beeinflußt wird.

Das sich historisch gestaltende „System" der Rechtswissenschaft unterscheidet sich meistens von dem System, das bei einer konsequenten Einhaltung der formell logischen Klassifizierungsregeln installiert würde[1]. Einzelne Zweige haben sich sukzessiv — in verschiedenen Etappen, unter verschiedenen gesellschaftlichen Bedingungen ausgegliedert. Es geht tatsächlich um einen Komplex, der eine strikte logische Analyse kaum erträgt, da darin das Recht bzw. die Rechtswissenschaft nicht aufgrund eines einheitlichen Kriteriums aufgeteilt sind und einzelne Zweige gegenseitig nicht völlig disjunktiv sind. Desto wirklicher ist das Wirken dieses „historischen Systems" im Rechts- und Gesellschaftsleben, da seine Zweige durch Institutionen repräsentiert sind (Institute, Katheder, Assoziationen, Editionen usw.).

Die angedeutete Divergenz des formal Logischen und des Historischen ist ein mehr oder weniger unvermeidliches Phänomen. Die Frage der „Anerkennung" eines Zweiges aufgrund dieses oder jenes Kriteriums für logische Gliederung wird in der Theorie zum Gegenstand schleppender Diskussionen und Streite. Dahinter figurieren jedoch tatsächliche soziale Interessen, die sich letztenendes auch ohne Rücksicht auf die formell logische Reinheit der Rechtswissenschaftsgliederung meistens durchsetzen.

[1] Als Beispiel der Divergenz zwischen dem logischen und dem tatsächlich im Rechtsleben wirkenden System kann das Hybridephänomen des Wirtschaftsrechts dienen. Respektiert man konsequent logische Verfahren (und auch wissenschaftliche Traditionen) ist es wohl notwendig, seine Konstituierung abzulehnen und darauf zu verweisen, daß die „horizontalen" (Obligations-) Wirtschaftsverhältnisse zwischen den sozialistischen juristischen Personen zu den Bürgerrechtsverhältnissen gehören, wogegen die „vertikalen" Leitungsverhältnisse zwischen den Staatsorganen (z. B. den Wirtschaftsministerien) und den staatlichen Wirtschaftsorganisationen (oder ihren Gruppierungen) in die Verwaltungsrechtsverhältnisse einschlagen. Nichtsdestoweniger hat sich in der ČSSR schon anfangs sechziger Jahre schrittweise die Richtung durchgesetzt, welche die Erlassung eines selbständigen Wirtschaftsgesetzbuchs und die Konstituierung des entsprechenden Rechtszweiges — des Wirtschaftsrechts — forderte. Zweifellos hat dazu u. a. die Tatsache beigetragen, daß sich in der Praxis der Kreis der „Nutzer" des Wirtschaftsrechts (Staatsarbitrage, Betriebsjuristen, Wirtschaftsministerien) beträchtlich von den „Abnehmern" des Zivilrechts (Gerichte, Anwaltschaft) oder des Verwaltungsrechts (Organe der Staatsverwaltung, die die Verwaltungsprozeßordnung anwenden) differenziert. (In einigen anderen sozialistischen Staaten überwiegt jedoch in dieser Hinsicht weiterhin die ursprüngliche, wissenschaftliche Klassifikation.)

Es ist wenig praktisch, Musterklassifizierungen zwecks der Besserung der im Rechtsleben verankerten institutionalisierten Rechtswissenschaftszweige bloß im Interesse der logischen Echtheit durchzuführen.

Die Unterscheidung der *Regulierungsmethoden,* welcher folgende Thesen gewidmet sind, verfolgt einen anderen Zweck.

IV.

Jede Rechtsregulierung kennzeichnet sich durch folgende Aspekte:

a) die inhaltlichen Aspekte, d. h. diejenigen, welche die Entstehung, die Entwicklung, bzw. das Erlöschen der Rechtsregelung bedingen, und zwar

aa) die objektiven, d. h. die gesellschaftlichen Verhältnisse, die zum Gegenstand der Regelung werden und die primäre, bestimmende Rolle spielen (vom Standpunkt der Noetik und im Sinne der historischen Determination) und

ab) die subjektiven, d. h. den Zweck (oder das Ziel) der Regulierung, welche durch die Widersprüche in den gesellschaftlichen (vor allem ökonomischen) Verhältnissen, durch die Bedingungen und Bedürfnisse ihrer Lösung und durch das Interesse der herrschenden Klasse bestimmt werden;

b) die methodischen Aspekte[2]. Samt den Zwecken (bzw. den Zielen) gehören sie zu den subjektiven Aspekten der Regelung.

Für die Wahl der Methode ist der Inhalt (das Objekt und der Zweck) der Regelung entscheidend. Die Angemessenheit der Methode dem Inhalt gehört zu den Voraussetzungen der Effektivität der Regulierung. Die Erreichung der Zwecke bzw. der Ziele hängt von den angewandten Methoden ab. Die von den Zwecken oder Zielen abgeleiteten Werte der Zweckmäßigkeit werden zu den Kriterien für die Wertung der Regulierungsmethoden als Mittel zur Erzielung jener Zwecke.

Die Klassifizierung gilt als Ausgangspunkt für die Charakteristik der Verwendbarkeit einzelner Regulierungsmethoden mit Bezug auf diese oder jene Art der gesellschaftlichen Verhältnisse und auf diese oder jene Zwecke.

---

[2] Zu den methodischen Aspekten der Regelung zählen auch formelle Aspekte, die sich auf die Rechtsquellen (im formellen Sinne des Wortes) und ihre Gliederung, wie auch die Verfahrensregeln der Normensetzung beziehen. Den Gegenstand der folgenden Darlegung bilden jedoch nur die methodischen Aspekte der Normensetzung, welche in materiell-rechtlicher Hinsicht die Gestaltung und die Natur der entsprechenden Rechtsverhältnisse beeinflussen.

Der Sinn der nachfolgenden Unterscheidung von Regulierungsmethoden steckt also nicht darin, die bestehenden gesellschaftlich etablierten Rechtswissenschaftszweige zu ändern, sondern im Rahmen der allgemeinen Rechtstheorie Kenntnisse zu formulieren, welche eine heuristische Bedeutung für die Praxis der Rechtsetzung und der Rechtsauslegung auf verschiedenen Gebieten haben könnten.

Die Regulierungsmethoden können zur Gliederung der Rechtswissenschaft schon deswegen praktisch nicht dienen, da in den reellen gesellschaftlichen Entwicklungsprozessen komplizierte Interferenzen zwischen Methoden, Objekten und Zielen der Regulierungen notwendigerweise entstehen.

Die gesellschaftlichen Verhältnisse von einer und derselben Art werden zum Gegenstand der Regulierungen, wodurch mehrere (häufig heterogene) Zwecke und damit verbundene Werte verfolgt werden. Einen und denselben Zweck kann man vielfach mittels dieser oder jener Methode erreichen, jedoch mit unterschiedlichem Tempo und mit unterschiedlichen Auswirkungen im Hinblick auf andere Zwecke und Werte.

Die Rechtsregulierungen bedeuten die Stufen der Lösung verschiedener gesellschaftlicher Widersprüche. Elementare Widersprüche ergeben sich schon daraus, daß es in der sozialistischen Periode der gesellschaftlichen Entwicklung bei weitem noch nicht möglich ist, alle Bedürfnisse völlig zu befriedigen, die zum Grunde für die Formulierung der Zwecke und der Werte werden.

Die Funktion der Rechtsregelung besteht also darin, die Proportionen bzw. die relativen Präferenzen oder Prioritäten in der betreffenden Entwicklungsetappe zu bestimmen und festzuhalten.

Die Rechtsinstitute als Komplexe der die gleichartigen gesellschaftlichen Verhältnisse regulierenden Normen kennzeichnen sich deshalb vielfach durch Kombinationen verschiedener Regulierungsmethoden. Bei der Rechtsetzung wird u. a. die wichtige Frage gelöst, inwieweit diese oder jene Methode zur Regulierung bestimmter gesellschaftlicher Verhältnisse auszunutzen sei.

Im Rahmen dieses Beitrages kann man nicht eine erschöpfende Klassifizierung versuchen, sondern das angedeutete Herangehen nur auf drei Beispielen demonstrieren, die sich auf verschiedene Ebenen der Klassifikation beziehen und sich daher auch auf unterschiedliche Gliederungskriterien stützen.

V.

Ein Kriterium besteht in der logischen Struktur der Normen, wonach man unterscheiden kann: a) Normen, die sich durch die Struktur der *Implikation* auszeichnen („wenn p ist, darf q_1 und soll q_2 sein"), b) *Finalnormen* (teleologische Normen: „damit t ist, darf q_1 und soll q_2 sein").

Meritorische Behandlung der Unterschiede und der Beziehungen zwischen den beiden Methoden wurde in meinem Beitrag für den in Basel abgehaltenen 9. Kongreß der IVR gegeben[3]; hier genügt es also bloß allgemeine Randbemerkungen hinzufügen, die mit der (oben ad IV.) vorhergehenden Thesis zusammenhängen, und zwar in bezug nur auf die wirtschaftlich-organisatorische Funktion des sozialistischen Staates.

Die Betätigung verbindlicher Finalnormen — insbesondere Plannormen — ist charakteristisch für die Dynamik, die Verwandlungen und die Extension der Staatsverwaltung im Sozialismus auf Grund der Vergesellschaftung der Produktionsmittel. Die Finalnormen sind die Form der direkten Leitung im Rahmen der Rechtsverhältnisse, die die sozialistische Staatsverwaltung mit den untergeordneten (namentlich wirtschaftlichen) Organisationen zu einem System verbinden.

Für das Fungieren desselben Systems sind die Regulierungen unentbehrlich mittels der Normen des traditionellen Typus (mit der Struktur der Implikation) als Instrument der indirekten Leitung. Sie dienen u. a. zur Gestaltung der Stimuli der materiellen Interessiertheit an der Erreichung der durch die Finalnormen festgelegten Ziele.

Die Realisierungsentscheidungsprozesse in der Praxis, die von Normen mit der Struktur der Implikation ausgehen, unterscheiden sich in gewissen Hinsichten wesentlich von denen, für welche die Finalnormen als Ausgangspunkt auftreten.

Das System der staatlichen Wirtschaftsleitung stellt Kombinationen der beiden Methoden dar. Die Projekte und die Maßnahmen zu seiner Vervollkommnung zielen u. a. auf die Bestimmung des optimalen Maßes der Betätigung der ersten und der zweiten Methode im Hinblick auf den Charakter der zu regulierenden gesellschaftlichen Verhältnisse, auf die jeweiligen Bedingungen, Bedürfnisse und Ziele. Jedenfalls ist es wesentlich, eine harmonische Wirkung der beiden Regulierungsarten zu erreichen, was nicht einfach ist.

---

[3] *J. Boguszak*, Rechtsauffassungen und Regulierungsmethoden, in: Archiv für Rechts- und Sozialphilosophie, Supplementa, vol. I, part 3 (1983), S. 43 ff.

VI.

Die Rechtsgliederung in öffentliches und privates Recht gehört längst der Vergangenheit an aus Gründen, die notorisch sind.

Die Unterscheidung der *„öffentlichrechtlichen"* und der *„privatrechtlichen"* Regulierungsmethoden behält jedoch eine bestimmte heuristische Bedeutung, ohne die Konstituierung beliebiger Rechtswissenschaftszweige im Sinne zu haben.

Die Terminologie ist übrigens nicht angemessen und wird hier mangels anderer, mehr passender bündiger Termini verwendet. Im Sozialismus werden die Grenzen der „privatrechtlichen" Dispositionsautonomie mit Hilfe der öffentlichrechtlichen Methoden so bestimmt, daß darin nur solche individuellen bzw. Gruppen-Interessen zur Geltung kommen, auf deren Schutz das öffentliche Interesse vom Standpunkt der Bedürfnisse der sozialistischen Gesellschaftsentwicklung besteht.

Die angeführte Unterscheidung hat eine Reihe von Dimensionen. Erinnern wir hier wenigstens brachylogisch bloß einige in der Gestaltung und im Charakter der subjektiven Rechte auftretenden Differenzen. (Beide Methoden vermischen sich jedoch in einzelnen Rechtsinstituten, so daß das subjektive Recht eventuell einen Hybridecharakter haben kann.)

Privatrechtliche subjektive Rechte sind — in dem öffentlichrechtlich abgegrenzten Rahmen — auf dispositiven Rechtsnormen begründet. Die Subjekte können über sie durch ihre privatrechtlichen Handlungen verfügen, welche beim Übertreten der im Gesetz festgelegten Grenzen der privaten Dispositionsautonomie ungültig sind. — Öffentlichrechtliche subjektive Rechte beruhen auf den kategorischen (zwingenden) Normen. Sie werden ausschließlich durch die Rechtsakte der Staatsorgane instituiert (entweder direkt ex lege oder durch die rechtsanwendenden Akte), deren rechtliche Wirkungen unabhängig von den Willen der Adressaten sind und denen die Voraussetzung der Richtigkeit verleiht wird (so daß auch ein mangelhafter Akt gültig ist, solange er nicht annuliert oder geändert wird). Sie sind unveräußerlich; ihre Subjekte können über sie nicht rechtsgültig verfügen; sie werden festgelegt und beschützt unabhängig von dem Willen des konkreten Subjektes.

Private subjektive Rechte entstehen meistens gegen Entgelt; in der Regel werden sie durch den Grundsatz der Äquivalenz (also durch das Marktprinzip) beherrscht. Wenn sie relativ sind, zeichnen sie sich meistens durch die Reziprozität der Rechte und der Verpflichtungen aus (jedes Subjekt des betreffenden Rechtsverhältnisses hat sowohl relative Rechte wie auch koherente Verpflichtungen). — Öffentliche subjektive Rechte entstehen dagegen entweder unentgeltlich oder unabhängig von dem Äquivalenzprinzip und sind unilateral, was die Rechte und Pflichten anbelangt.

Die Entwicklung der Korrelationen beider Methoden widerspiegelt die geschichtlichen Fortschritte in der Lösung des klassenwidersprüchigen Problems der Freiheit und der Gleichheit. Sie kennzeichnet sich durch öffentlichrechtliche Eingriffe, welche die Sphäre der privatrechtlichen Dispositionsfreiheit einschränken, und zwar verengen und damit auch ein zweckmäßiges Fungieren dieser Sphäre im Interesse der betreffenden Gesellschaftsordnung gewährleisten. Historische Stufen dieser Beschränkungen als Resultate der Klassenkämpfe waren die öffentlichrechtliche grundgesetzliche Festlegung der gleichen persönlichen Freiheiten (und damit ihre Entnahme der privaten Disposition) und zuletzt auch der gleichen politischen Rechte und — in der sozialistischen Revolution — die Herausnahme der Produktionsmittel aus der Privatsphäre und damit auch die Beschränkung des Äquivalenzprinzips auf die Arbeitsäquivalenz (die Verhinderung des arbeitslosen Gewinns), die überdies durch die außerordentlich breiten sozialen Rechte reduziert wird.

Die spezifische Differenz der *sozialen* Rechte gegenüber den traditionellen Grundrechten impliziert eine besondere Regulierungsart im Rahmen der öffentlichrechtlichen Methoden. Die traditionellen öffentlichen Rechte gehören sämtlich zu den absoluten subjektiven Rechten. Besondere Verpflichtungen des Staates betreffen erst ihren Schutz, sie treten bei ihrer Verletzung an, jedoch im Stadium ihrer Verwirklichung haben alle Subjekte nur die Pflicht non facere: nicht stören. Die Ungleichheit der realen Möglichkeiten in Betreff der Ausnutzung der traditionellen Grundrechte wird jedoch durch die sozialistische Gesellschaftsordnung in dem Maße überwunden, welches der im Sozialismus erreichten Stufe der sozialen Gleichheit entspricht.

Die sozialen Rechte berühren direkt die materiellen Lebensbedingungen. Sie stellen deshalb relative öffentliche subjektive Rechte dar; im Rechtsverhältnis, das sich auf die sozialrechtliche Regulierungsart stützt, entspricht dem sozialen Recht eines Subjektes die Verpflichtung eines anderen individuell bestimmbaren Subjektes, etwas bestimmtes zu geben oder zu tun. In der ČSSR kennzeichnet sich die Regulierung der sozialen Rechte zugleich durch alle angeführten Attribute der öffentlichrechtlichen Regelungsmethode.

Indem sie die Sphäre der privatrechtlichen Dispositionsautonomie einschränken, erfüllen die öffentlichrechtlichen Regulierungsarten ausgeprägt Egalisierungsfunktionen. Eine extreme Publizisierung würde jedoch die Stimuli der materiellen Interessiertheit eliminieren oder schwächen, die für die effektive Entwicklung der gesamten Volkswirtschaftszweige in der sozialistischen Gesellschaft unentbehrlich sind. Im Rahmen des ganzen Komplexes der diesbezüglichen normsetzenden Verfahren handelt es sich also wieder um womögliche optimale Korrelationen bzw. Kombinationen der beiden Methoden. Die Gestaltung der Hybriderechtsinstitute wird dabei eher zur Regel als zur Ausnahme. Die betreffende Klassifikation der Regulierungsmethoden hat nun zwar die angedeutete heuristische Bedeutung für die Rechtsetzung und Rechtsauslegung; es wäre jedoch immer mehr ungangbar und unpraktisch, das Recht und die Rechtswissenschaft nach diesen Methoden zu gliedern.

VII.

Im Rahmen der öffentlichrechtlichen Regulierungsmethoden eine solche Bedeutung gebührt der Gliederung nach dem, ob die Regelung ein freies Ermessen bei der Rechtsanwendung ermöglicht, sowie der Klassifizierung der das *Ermessen* vermittelnden oder vermeidenden Regulierungsarten. Außer den klassischen Gesichtspunkten (einerseits die Sicherstellung der Gleichberechtigung der Bürger und der Rechtssicherheit, andererseits die Vermeidung der Härten, die mit der unvermeidlichen Schablonenmäßigkeit jeder Rechtsregelung zusammenhängen: „summum ius summa saepe iniuria"), zeugt für die praktische Wichtigkeit dieser Lehre am neuesten noch ein anderer Grund. Gegenwärtig kann man die Rechtsanwendung nur dann automatisieren, wenn es sich um Entscheidungsprozesse handelt, die das Ermessen nicht einschließen. Meritorische Thesen zur erwähnten Klassifikation enthält der schon oben (sub V.) zitierte, für den Baseler Kongreß der IVR 1979 bestimmte Beitrag[4].

[4] *Boguszak* (FN 3).

LEGAL DOGMATICS AND THE SYSTEMATIZATION OF LAW

By Eugenio Bulygin, Buenos Aires

I. Preliminary Remarks

Aulis Aarnio's theory of legal reasoning is one of the most important contributions to legal philosophy in recent years. In successive publications, many of which are unfortunately not accessible yet to the non-Finnish world, Aarnio has developed a comprehensive theory of judicial decision making and of legal dogmatics. It is with the latter topic that I will be concerned in this paper. I intend to discuss some of Aarnio's views on the task of legal dogmatics and the systematization of legal norms, comparing them with the ideas presented in *Normative Systems*.[1] Aarnio's account of systematization differs considerably in some important respects from the picture outlined in NS and it might be of some interest to compare both theories in order to trace the origin of the differences, which — I hope — will shed some light on different aspects of legal dogmatics and the different tasks performed by legal dogmatists. At the same time I will take into account the forceful criticism (both of Aarnio and of NS) put forward in two highly illuminating papers by another distinguished Finnish scholar, Ilkka Niiniluoto.[2]

Legal dogmatics is a complex activity, in which at least three different stages can and should be distinguished: (i) the identification of legal norms, (ii) the systematization of legal norms, and (iii) the modification or transformation of legal systems. Not all of these activities are theoretical or cognitive in nature; legal dogmatics fulfils also an important practical function. This is why it is so difficult to classify the so-called legal science[3] into any of the well defined categories of

[1] *C. E. Alchourrón/E. Bulygin,* Normative Systems, Wien-New York 1971; in the text henceforth NS for short.

[2] *I. Niiniluoto,* On Truth and Argumentation in Legal Dogmatics, in: RECHTSTHEORIE Beiheft 2 (1981); On the Truth of Norm Propositions, in: RECHTSTHEORIE Beiheft 3 (1981). The page numbers in the text and subsequent footnotes refer to the first of these articles, unless indicated otherwise.

[3] The term 'legal science' is not usual in the English-speaking world. One reason why Anglo-American writers refuse to use this term in connection with the typical activity of legal scholars is the practical or normative aspect of it.

science, as it is equally impossible to single out one scientific method characteristic of legal dogmatics.

In this paper I intend (i) to characterize briefly the three aspects of legal dogmatics mentioned above, and (ii) to argue that both Aarnio's and Niiniluoto's criticism of NS is mainly due to the lack of a clear distinction between these different tasks performed by legal dogmatists. Particularly, I have the impression that in spite of using the same term 'systematization', Aarnio's main interest is directed to a problem different from the one that has been focussed in NS, so that our views are not necessarily incompatible.

II. Identification of Legal Norms

The step that leads from the various *sources* of law (legislation, precedents, custom, etc.) to legal *norms* is what I shall call the *identification* of legal norms. (Another more usual but for this very reason more ambiguous term for this activity is 'interpretation'.) G. H. von Wright's distinction between the *norm-formulation* as the sentence expressive of a norm, the *norm* expressed by that sentence, and *norm-proposition* as a proposition descriptive of a norm, is useful in this connection. Both Aarnio and Niiniluoto make use of it, and both conceive norms — contrary to von Wright[4] — as *meanings* of norm-formulations, i. e. a certain kind of (prescriptive) propositions.[5] As meanings are rather elusive entities which cannot be directly observed, Aarnio conceives the identification of legal norms as an operation that, starting from norm-formulations (law texts), leads to the formulation of norm-propositions descriptive of the meaning of those law texts, that is, of legal norms themselves (pp. 16 ff.).

---

[4] Cf. *G. H. von Wright*, Norm and Action, London 1963, p. 94. In recent years von Wright has adopted an even more radically "expressivist" position: cf. his Norms, Truth and Logic, in: A. A. Martino (ed.), Deontic Logic, Computational Linguistics and Legal Information Systems, Amsterdam-New York-Oxford 1982; Norms, Truth, and Logic, in: *G. H. von Wright*, Practical Reason, Oxford 1983, pp. 130—209.

[5] *Niiniluoto*, p. 63. Aarnio's position appears to be less clear, at least in *A. Aarnio*, On Legal Reasoning, Turku 1977. He seems to oscillate between three different senses of the term 'norm':
(a) as the meaning expressed by a norm formulation ("This sentence ... is however not a norm; ... it *expresses* a norm"; "It can also be said that the norm is the idea content which is *expressed* by means of the norm formulation" (p. 12). The page numbers here and elsewhere in my essay refer to On Legal Reasoning.
(b) as norm formulation plus its meaning, i. e. as a meaningful sentence ("... the norm (N) is a function of the norm formulation (N_f) and the idea-content (N_{ic})" (p. 12), and
(c) as a mere norm formulation (pp. 275 ff. — cf. below section V). Still it seems to me that the sense (a) is dominant.

In NS norms are defined in syntactical terms as sentences whose function is to correlate cases with solutions. This definition gave rise to a sharp criticism by Niiniluoto. In his opinion the conception of norms as sentences is perhaps the main shortcoming of what he calls the logistic approach [p. 62, points (e) and (f), and p. 63]. His main charges are: (i) The conception of norms as sentences and of legal order as a set of sentences is unintuitive, because "all purely linguistic changes in the statutes which are irrelevant to the content of the laws have to be counted as creating a new legal order. And a country which has two official languages, so that all statutes are written in two languages, seems to have two legal systems." (ii) In the case of a change of interpretation of legal texts, there is no change of any *sentence* — "at least the statutes remain here the same as before, and it is difficult to point out any sentence in set *S* which has changed" — and so the claim that the legal order has changed "seems to be false". (iii) The "definition of legal systems as sets of sentences does not give a realistic picture of the practice of legal dogmatics." Particularly, it does not account for "the fact that legal theorists are concerned with the *meaning* of legal statutes."

Consequently, Niiniluoto proposes to define norms as propositions of a certain kind, considering it as an alternative account destined to improve the "logistic notion of legal order" (p. 63).

Niiniluoto's criticism is based on a misinterpretation of the conception presented in NS.[6]

This misinterpretation is due to the fact that Niiniluoto seems to disregard the fact that the syntactical approach adopted in NS does not imply that meanings are not taken into account. It only means that linguistic expressions have a univocal and constant meaning, which does not change in the course of analysis.[7] It would be absurd to claim that this condition is actually satisfied by legal regulations; they must first be reconstructed or interpreted in a definite way. This is illustrated in chapter I of NS, where such a reconstruction of certain dispositions of the Argentine Civil Code and of the Freitas' Code takes place as a step previous to the systematization of those dispositions. So in NS norms are not uninterpreted linguistic entities, but *meaningful sentences*, i. e.

[6] This misinterpretation is probably due to a not sufficiently accurate formulation of our ideas; e. g. there is no explicit statement in NS that norms are meaningful sentences, though it should be clear from the context that it is so. The very fact that such a lucid and careful thinker as Niiniluoto (who gives an otherwise excellent account of the main lines of thought of NS) should incur in this mistake already shows that something is rotten in the state of Denmark ...

[7] Cf. *R. Carnap*, The Logical Syntax of Language, London 1937.

sentences endowed with a definite and constant meaning. Thus, two structurally identical sentences with different meanings, that is, sentences which do not correlate the same cases with the same solutions, would count as two different norms (exactly as for Aarnio and Niiniluoto) and two different sentences with identical meaning would also be two different, though equivalent, norms (whereas for Aarnio and Niiniluoto they would express the same norm).

As to the objection that for NS there are two legal orders in a bilingual country, we must distinguish first between a legal *system* as the set of all logical consequences of a given set of norms and a particular *formulation* of the axiomatic basis or code of a system. I firmly believe that to say that in Finland there are two (and in Switzerland even three) different formulations of (an axiomatic basis of) a system, far from being unrealistic, is the only correct way of describing the situation. Of course, these formulations claim to be different formulations *of the same system*, but whether this claim is justified or not is an empirical question. It is by no means warranted a priori that the two formulations are indeed logically equivalent. If they are, no problem arises, for then we have two formulations of one and the same system. If they are not, two situations must be distinguished: (i) Suppose that only one of them is "authentic", e. g. because the Finnish parliament votes only the Finnish and not the Swedish version. Now if the two versions are not equivalent, i. e. there are some consequences of the Finnish text which are not derivable from the Swedish text or vice versa, then jurists would say that the Swedish version is a bad translation and should be amended. (ii) It might also be the case that both versions are authentic, e. g. because the parliament votes both. Then there are not only two different formulations, but two different legal systems, which is a politically highly undesirable but not logically impossible situation.

Nor is it true that in case of a change of interpretation the statutes remain the same: if by "statutes" we understand certain legal norms and this in the terminology of NS means sentences correlating cases with solutions, then a change of interpretation entails a change of such correlations and so a change of statutes, i. e. of legal norms. The statutes would not change only if they were mere norm-formulations without meaning. The fact that jurists sometimes use the term 'norm' in this restricted sense, does not entitle Niiniluoto to ascribe this use to us. (As we shall see below, even Aarnio — in spite of his explicit definition of norm as proposition or meaning — uses on many occasions the term 'norm' as synonymous with norm-formulation, i. e. a mere text without any fixed meaning.)

Therefore Niiniluoto's objection that our definition of 'norm' does not give a realistic picture of the practice of legal dogmatists seems to have no support. On the other hand, if a norm is a sentence with a definite meaning, then the identification of legal norms (or interpretation of law texts[8]) consists in the determination of the meaning of norm-formulations, that is, sentences occurring in law texts. Thus, the process of identification will be described in the same or very similar terms by a theory that defines norms as propositions or as meaningful sentences. It is important to bear in mind that no detailed account of this process is actually given in NS, for the very prosaic reason that the problem of identification lies outside the scope of the book, whose main concern is with the second task of legal dogmatics (systematization):

"It is particularly important to draw a sharp distinction between *logical problems,* which arise in the course of the activity of jurists that we call the *systematization* of legal sentences and *empirical problems* which arise in the course of the prior activity of identifying these sentences. (This division does not claim to exhaust the whole set of problems of the science of law.)"[9]

To sum up: Niiniluoto's proposal to treat norms as propositions can hardly be regarded as a more satisfactory alternative; for many purposes it is substantially equivalent to the account given in NS and in some respects it is less advantageous: there are certain problems (posed above all by the phenomenon of *derogation*) which cannot be solved at the level of propositions (i. e. the conceptual content of a system), but require that a particular formulation of the system be considered (cf. below, section III).

The assertion quoted above that problems of identification are empirical stands in need of clarification. It is, I think, an overstatement, for these problems are not purely empirical. But to a certain extent they are indeed empirical.

In this connection it is important to distinguish between the discovery of an existing meaning and the assignment of a (wholly or partially) new meaning. The first activity is empirical in spite of the fact that meanings are not empirical entities. The meaning of an expression is given either by the *common usage* in ordinary language or in the legal discourse, or by the *intention* of the author of the expression (in our case, the norm-authority). Both can be investigated and eventually

[8] By 'law texts' I understand not only statutes, but also judicial decisions, legal drafts or any other relevant text.

[9] NS, pp. 65—66.

determined by empirical methods.[10] This is why, unlike Aarnio, I am sceptical about the need of a special (hermeneutical) method for determining the meaning of legal sentences.

However, in certain circumstances it may prove impossible to discover the meaning of an expression (e. g. if it is very obscure or hopelessly ambiguous). In such cases it may be necessary to *assign* a meaning to it. Jurists usually do this by means of stipulative definitions that play the role of proposals. Once such a stipulative definition is generally accepted by the legal community or auditory, it becomes a descriptive definition: descriptive of prevailing linguistic usage.[11]

This process of giving a meaning is not cognitive; it is a matter of decision which of course may be backed by more or less convincing reasons. So the activity consisting in the identification of legal norms is not entirely cognitive, insofar as jurists do not only aim at discovering the meaning of norm-formulations, but also — at least in certain cases — propose to assign new meanings.

The distinction between discovery and assignment of a meaning sheds some light on the relation between norm-propositions and norms. Aarnio is not exceedingly clear on this topic: he speaks e. g. of a "creation of norm propositions" (p. 17), of their validity instead of truth (p. 16) and he even claims that "there exists nothing to which the norm proposition could directly be compared to determine its validity" (p. 16). This last sentence is only true of those cases in which legal dogmatists assign a new meaning to an expression; in such cases the norm-proposition is indeed neither true nor false in the sense of correspondence and here something "softer" than the correspondence theory of truth is in fact needed. But it would be a mistake to think that this occurs always; situations in which jurists give a new meaning to a legal sentence are relatively rare. In many cases norm-formulations have a more or less precise meaning and it is perfectly possible to determine it by observation either of the prevailing linguistic usage or of the intentions of the norm-authority. Here Niiniluoto's contention that norm-propositions are either true or false and that we need the correspondence theory of truth is correct. To *this* extent his criticism of Aarnio's conception of truth in legal dogmatics is justified. But I think that he exaggerates when he says that "the only notion of truth which is needed in connection with legal dogmatics is the correspondence theoretical

---

[10] Cf. *Alf Ross*, On Law and Justice, London 1958, pp. 121—123, on subjective and objective interpretation, and *C. E. Alchourrón/E. Bulygin*, Definiciones y normas, in: Bulygin/M. D. Farrell/C. S. Nino/E. A. Rabossi (eds.), El Lenguaje del Derecho. Homenaje a Genaro R. Carrió, Buenos Aires 1983.

[11] *Niiniluoto*, pp. 66—70.

one."[12] There is a grain of truth in Aarnio's claim for a coherence or consensus theory of truth in the field of legal dogmatics.

III. The Systematization

The second stage of the typical activity of legal dogmatics is the systematization of legal norms. According to NS the systematization includes two different activities: (a) the solution of generic cases by means of the derivation of consequences of the set of legal norms, and (b) the reformulation of the legal system.

(a) In order to determine the content of a legal system, the legal dogmatist must be able to tell what legal consequences (solutions) it correlates with different kinds of situations (generic cases). So he must first determine the range of legal problems the norms in question are destined to solve, which involves the identification of all relevant cases (Universe of Cases: *UC*) and of the actions regulated by the norms (Universe of Actions which in its turn gives rise to the Universe of Solutions: *US*). The next step is purely deductive for it consists in displaying the logical consequences of the legal norms which function as the axiomatic basis of the system. In this way certain formal or structural properties of the system, such as completeness, consistency and independence come to light. To put it in negative terms: the displaying of logical consequences of the system (relative to a certain *UC* and a certain *US*) enables the legal dogmatist to uncover some formal faults or defects of the system (inconsistency, lack of completeness, i. e. normative gaps, and redundancy) which otherwise might remain concealed.

It is important to stress that it is only possible to perform this task, *once the problem of identification of legal norms is solved.* This is explicitly stated in NS: "No matter what procedure is used to identify the sentences [i. e. the legal norms] of the basis, we cannot speak about a system or systematization unless a set of legal sentences has been delimited and identified." (p. 69). So the identification of legal norms is a previous and necessary step without which no systematization is possible. This is so because a normative system is a system of norms and not a system of norm-formulations. In other words, a legal system is not a purely formal, non-interpreted system, but a system with a definite interpretation.

(b) Another task of legal dogmatics is the reformulation of the system which consists in finding a new but equivalent axiomatic basis, i. e. without changing the system itself. This new basis must be — according

[12] *Niiniluoto,* On the Truth of Norm Propositions (note 2), p. 172.

to the principle of economy (Jhering) — smaller and simpler, i. e. more general and independent, but at the same time it must be normatively equivalent to the original basis, i. e. its logical consequences must be the same. Niiniluoto calls this operation conservative extension of the legal order (p. 60); however, it looks more like a *conservative contraction of the basis* of the system.

The importance of the reformulation of the system is twofold:

(i) By reducing the number of norms pertaining to the basis it makes it easier to grasp the structure as a whole and to handle it in practice. This aspect of reformulation has been stressed in NS.

(ii) It may improve the formulation of the system, for in an important sense one formulation of a system may be better than another, even if both are normatively equivalent.

This second aspect of reformulation has not been considered in NS. As far as I know it was Erik Stenius who first drew attention to the importance of the formulation of a system.[13] Using the term 'codex' for what is called 'axiomatic basis' in NS, i. e. a finite set of regulations from which all other norms of the system are derivable, Stenius stipulates that a codex is well-formed if it is independent, that is, if it does not contain any regulation which is a logical consequence of other regulations of the codex. Let us call, following Hilpinen,[14] such a well-formed codex a *normative code* of the system.

Hilpinen has convincingly shown that two normatively equivalent codes may be, nevertheless, *essentially different*. The difference comes to light in connection with *derogation*.

It has been shown that in certain circumstances a derogation of a norm or set of norms can lead to the so-called logical indeterminacy of the system[15], i. e. it does not transform a system into another well-defined system. Hilpinen calls *infelicitous* an act of derogating that leads to this, certainly undesirable, result. Now, it may occur that a derogation of the same norm(s) is felicitous regarding a given code and infelicitous in respect to another, normatively equivalent, code.

---

[13] In an unpublished but nevertheless influential paper called Ross' Paradox and Well-Formed Codices, which Prof. Stenius kindly sent me.

[14] *R. Hilpinen,* On Normative Change, in: E. Morscher/R. Stranzinger (eds.), Ethics: Foundation, Problems and Applications (Proceedings of the 5th International Wittgenstein Symposium), Wien 1981.

[15] Cf. *C. E. Alchourrón/E. Bulygin,* Unvollständigkeit, Widersprüchlichkeit und Unbestimmtheit der Normenordnungen, in: A. G. Conte/R. Hilpinen/G. H. von Wright (eds.), Deontische Logik und Semantik, Wiesbaden 1977; also by the same authors, Sobre la existencia de las normas jurídicas, Valencia (Venezuela) 1979, and The Expressive Conception of Norms, in: R. Hilpinen (ed.), New Studies in Deontic Logic, Dordrecht-Boston-London 1981.

Let me illustrate this with an example adapted in a slightly simplified form from Hilpinen.

Consider two normative systems *Q* and *R*. The code of *Q* is formed by the following two norms:

Q_1: John ought to work every day between 10 a.m. and 6 p.m.

Q_2: John ought not to drink while he works.

The following two norms constitute the code of *R*:

$R_1 = Q_1$

R_2: John ought not to drink between 10 a.m. and 6 p.m.

Though the two codes are different, the systems *Q* and *R* are normatively equivalent: they correlate exactly the same solutions with the same cases; in other words, the same actions in the same situations are obligatory or prohibited according to both systems. Nevertheless the two systems are different. What does this difference consist in?

Suppose the norm-authority (in this case John's employer) decides to lift the prohibition to drink on Saturdays. He can do it by issuing a permissive norm *M*: "John may drink on Saturdays between 10 a.m. and 6 p.m." As this permission is incompatible with some of the prohibitions, it is supposed that it derogates (at least partially) those prohibitions.

Now if the permission *M* is added to *R*, the derogation generates another well-defined system *R'*, which differs from *R* in one respect, viz. the norm R_2 is replaced by the norm

R'_2: John ought not to drink between 10 a.m. and 6 p.m., except on Saturdays.

The exception clause lifts exactly that part of the prohibition established by R_2 which is inconsistent with *M*. So the new system *R'* is consistent and the act of derogation is felicitous regarding the system *R*. This is so because *M* is inconsistent with R_2, but consistent with R_1.

But if the same permission *M* is added to *Q* the result will be quite different. For *M* is consistent with each of the two norms of the code *Q*, but is inconsistent with the conjunction of Q_1 and Q_2. So *the conjunction* Q_1 & Q_2 must be derogated. This entails that at least one of the two conjuncts (Q_1 or Q_2) must be eliminated from the system, but we have no criterion to decide which of the two should be removed. (Eliminating both would certainly be too much.) Hence the act of derogation is infelicitous, for it gives rise to two alternative systems:

$Q' = (Q_1$, John ought not to drink while he works except of Saturdays)

and

$Q'' =$ (John ought to work every day except on Saturdays, Q_2)

and there is no way of deciding which of the two is the "right" one.

This example shows that the felicity of a derogation is not relative to a normative system or theory, but rather to a particular formulation or code of the system.

Hilpinen's example proves that normative codes do not satify the so-called principle of intensionality: logically equivalent codes may be essentially different. This shows the importance of the reformulation of a system, for even if this operation preserves the equivalence (being no more than a conservative contraction of the code), it nevertheless may *improve* the system not only from the point of view of practical handling, but also in the sense that the new code *represents better or more directly the intentions of the norm-authority or the grounds (values) on which the system is based.*[16] And the new code might not give rise to infelicity of derogation acts, where the old code does.

Suppose that the intention of John's employer was to prohibit John's drinking by daytime because it would somehow disturb other people, but not because drinking would impair John's ability to work. In such a case Q_2 is merely an unintended consequence of *R*. So the code *R* represents better the intentions of the norm-authority. This is not an explanation why the derogation produced by the permission *M* is felicitous regarding *R* and infelicitous regarding *Q*. For in that case the same derogation should be felicitous regarding *Q* if *Q* were a better or more direct representation of the norm-authority's intentions. Unfortunately this is not so. Suppose the motivation of John's employer was to prohibit John's drinking during working hours (e. g. because it would impair John's ability to work). In this case *Q* would represent better his intentions and R_2 would be a merely unintended consequence of *Q*. However the derogation produced by *M* would still be infelicitous regarding *Q* and felicitous regarding *R*. In order to make the act of derogation felicitous regarding *Q*, one must introduce a hierarchical order between the norms Q_1 and Q_2. If one of them were in some sense more important than the other, then the exception clause would be introduced in the less important norm. But as long as both norms are equal we have no criterion for removing one instead of the other.[17]

---

[16] *R. Hilpinen* (note 14).

[17] Cf. *C. E. Alchourrón/D. Makinson*, Hierarchies of Regulations, in: R. Hilpinen (ed.), New Studies in Deontic Logic (note 15).

We might sum up the foregoing discussion:

a) It is convenient to discuss the problem of derogation not in relation to normative systems, but in relation to a particular formulation of a system, i. e. a code.

b) The conservative contraction (reformulation) of the code of a system may lead to important improvement, for

c) A given code may express better the intentions of the legislator or the values on which the system is grounded than another code, even if they are normatively equivalent.

All this suggests that, contrary to Niiniluoto, it is more convenient to define a norm as a meaningful sentence, i. e. as norm-formulation plus its meaning and not as meaning alone. For logically equivalent formulations may nevertheless be different in an important respect.

IV. Modifications of a Legal System

It is well known that legal systems are dynamic in character; this means that they are subject to change in the course of time. If a legal system is a set of norms (closed under the operation of logical consequence), then it is clear that any change of a system is a replacement of a system by another one. In this sense, a legal order may be conceived of as a temporally ordered sequence of successive systems.[18]

There are three ways in which a normative system can change: (i) by addition of a set of norms *(expansion)*, (ii) by subtraction of a set of norms *(contraction)*, and (iii) by a combination of (i) and (ii), i. e. by successive expansions and contractions.

Normally expansion takes place when a new norm or set of norms is generated by the sources of law; contraction is a consequence of derogation. Replacement of a norm by another different norm can be described as contraction and expansion.

Legislation is in modern times by far the most important source of law (at least in countries with Roman law tradition) and it consists of creation (promulgation) and annihilation (derogation) of norms. So legislation is the main factor of legal change and it is widely accepted that the proper task of the legislative authorities is to modify legal systems. Moreover, there is a widespread belief among jurists that it is

---

[18] This terminology has been introduced in *C. E. Alchourrón/E. Bulygin*, Sobre el concepto de orden jurídico, in: Crítica 8 (1976), pp. 3—23.

not the task of legal theorists and of legal dogmatics in particular to change the law: legal dogmatics is often conceived of as a purely descriptive science, whose function is to describe the existent law, not to modify it.[19]

In spite of this belief, it cannot be denied that legal dogmatics as a matter of fact fulfils an important normative function which goes far beyond the mere cognition of the law.[20] Legal dogmatists often make proposals to change the existing system and when these proposals are accepted by the legal community they produce important changes. Of course, the modifications of law introduced by legal dogmatics are usually more subtle and more restricted than those produced by the legislative authorities. But it is important to bear in mind that such modifications are *changes*, i. e. substitutions of a new system for the old one, and as such they must be sharply distinguished from the operation called systematization, which does not transform a system into another, not equivalent with the first.

Legal dogmatists rarely if ever change the law in a straightforward way, as the legislator does; what they do is to *adequate* or *adjust* the system to certain requirements. The most important among them are the *rational requirements of completeness and consistency* and the *moral requirement of justice.* Moreover, usually legal dogmatists do not perform their normative function overtly; they try to disguise it by means of different rhetorical devices. This is a tribute to a political ideology, according to which only the parliament (as representative of the people) can change the law; neither the judge, nor even less the legal theorist, should invade the proper sphere of legislation. But in actual practice things are different. In order to adequate the system to the requirements of completeness, consistency and justice, legal dogmatists modify the system, presenting their proposals as if they were direct consequences of the system itself.

I call the requirements of completeness and consistency rational, because they do not depend on any moral, political or ideological commitment; if they are not satisfied the system cannot perform its main task, viz. to regulate human behaviour. The situation is different in respect of the moral requirement of justice. Here the system can work even if it does not satisfy this requirement; but it would work badly.

[19] Cf. *H. Kelsen,* Reine Rechtslehre, 2nd ed., Wien 1960, and *Alf Ross,* On Law and Justice (note 10).

[20] Cf. *C. S. Nino,* Algunos modelos metodológicos de 'ciencia' jurídica, Valencia (Venezuela) 1979, capítulo 6.

Completeness is a relative notion; it means that the system provides a solution for each case of a relevant Universe of Cases.[21] The lack of completeness may stem from two different sources: (i) the system does not correlate a generic case with a solution *(normative gap)*, or (ii) the characterization of a case is so vague that an individual or generic case cannot be subsumed under it *(gap of recognition)*. (Niiniluoto rightly points out that in NS we did not pay sufficient attention to the subsumption of generic cases under other generic cases.[22])

Consistency means that no generic case has two or more incompatible solutions. Two norms that provide incompatible solutions to the same cases are *conflictive*.

It is clear that both in case of a normative gap or a gap of recognition, as well as in case of inconsistency the system fails to perform its regulating or evaluating function.

Legal dogmatists use different techniques to obviate these deficiencies of a legal system. Sometimes they try to solve these problems at the level of identification of norms: if there are several possible interpretations of a text, they prefer the one that does not give rise to gaps or normative conflicts. So the ideals of completeness and consistency function as criteria for selecting one out of several possible interpretations of a norm-formulation. When this is not possible (e. g. because the text admits not more than one interpretation or there is already one accepted interpretation), other techniques are used. Normative gaps are closed by analogical reasoning (argumenta a pari and argumenta a fortiori),[23] which consists in extending the scope of a norm in order to cover the case in question. But we should not forget that this means exactly to replace a norm by another: only the bare text remains identical, the norm expressed by it has changed!

In case of inconsistency a much used technique is the *hierarchical ordering* of norms. A norm for some reason regarded as higher or more important prevails thus over an inferior norm. Things become more difficult when sets of norms are to be compared. Some forms of this technique have been thoroughly studied by Alchourrón and Makinson.[24] An important result of their investigations is the proof that the imposing of an ordering on a system (or any modification of the existing ordering) is tantamount to a derogation of certain norms (that is, those norms

[21] Cf. NS, chapters 1 and 4.

[22] *Niiniluoto*, p. 61. There are some few remarks on this point in NS, pp. 60—61.

[23] Cf. *C. E. Alchourrón*, Juristische Schlüsse a fortiori und a pari, in: ARSP, Beiheft 41 — Neue Folge 4, 1965.

[24] *Alchourrón/Makinson* (note 17).

that are discarded as inferior). So ordering and derogation are substantially equivalent (though not quite identical) operations, in the sense that to each ordering corresponds a derogation and to each derogation corresponds an ordering.

This shows, by the way, that a normative system is not just a set of norms (closed under deduction) — as it was defined in NS — but an *ordered* set of norms. Any change of the ordering gives rise to a new system, even if the elements (norms) of the system remain the same, because the correlations of cases with solutions are different. As the normative status of an action can change as a result of a different ordering of the same set of norms, one and the same set (code) gives rise to different systems if it is ordered differently.

So the term 'legal system' is ambiguous; this ambiguity enables the legal dogmatists to claim that they do not change the system as long as they do not change the norms, even if they do change the hierarchical order of these norms. This claim is much subtler than the claim that the law does not change just because the texts remain the same, but both claims are based on fallacies of ambiguity: the ambiguity of the term 'norm' whose sense shifts from meaning expressed by a text to the bare text, or the ambiguity of 'legal system' whose meaning changes from 'ordered set of norms' to 'set of norms' (disregarding the ordering).

The *moral requirement of justice* means that a legal system must satisfy certain minimal criteria or standards of justice. As has been emphasized by Nino,[25] this does not only mean that jurists try to adjust the system to the standards of justice prevailing de facto in a given society, but that they, as moral agents, should and often in fact do adequate the existing system to the standards of a critical or ideal morality.

It is true that legal dogmatists do not often advocate that a legal regulation should be discarded because it fails to satisfy the minimal conditions of justice; this happens only in very exceptional cases. A more usual procedure is to argue that the legislator did not foresee the case in question, for if he had foreseen it, he would have introduced a relevant distinction which would lead to another solution (which in many cases may be true). Consequently, the legal dogmatist proceeds to close this "gap", making the relevant distinction and applying by analogy some other norm which gives a more just solution. This is what we called *axiological gaps* (cf. NS, chapter VI).

---

[25] Cf. *C. S. Nino*, Legal Ethics: between Metaphysics and Futility, in: U. Kangas (ed.), Essays in Legal Theory in Honor of Kaarle Makkonen, Vammala 1983, pp. 189—220, and by the same author, Los límites de la responsabilidad penal, Buenos Aires 1980.

V. Concluding Remarks

There are no clear-cut limits in the practice of legal dogmatists between the three different activities I have so far described. The distinctions between identification, systematization and transformation are purely conceptual; in practice the three tasks are often performed at the same time, so that it is extremely difficult to separate them. However, conceptual distinctions are very important: without them it would be impossible to outline a clear picture of the complex activity corresponding to legal dogmatics.

The main charge I can raise against Aarnio and Niiniluoto is that they not always clearly distinguish between identification of legal norms, their systematization and the transformation of a legal system.

Aarnio's main (if not exclusive) interest seems to be directed toward the *problem of identification* of legal norms, or as he puts it, the "determination of the content of legal regulations". Even when he speaks of systematization he has in mind something utterly different from what is understood under this heading in NS. This comes clearly to light in chapter 4, Part III, of *On Legal Reasoning*, especially in 4.1.: "The Systematizing Task of Legal Dogmatics".

The starting point for the systematization is, according to Aarnio, a *basic system* (S_b), which — as Aarnio states explicitly — is a system of valid *norms* (p. 273). I think it is worth while to quote in full what Aarnio says about the systematization (or reformulation) of the basic system.

> "When the basic system S_b now is substituted by another system S_1 identical with it, the manner of organizing (O_1) must be such that the new system S_1 provides every case also covered by the system S_b with a solution similar to that provided by S_b. In other words, the systematization must not change the content of the basic system; also in the new system, every norm belonging to the basic system must have the same content as before. However, here lies a difficult and noteworthy problem.
>
> It has been already established above that *only in few cases it is possible to give one and only one consistent interpretation of a norm belonging to the basic system.* Usually two or more alternative interpretations may be suggested for a certain norm (N_i). The matter may be expressed also by saying that *it is possible to formulate the basic system S_b in more than one way.* However, this raises the problem, what the identity of the basic system S_b and the system S_1 substituting it means.
>
> Alchourrón's and Bulygin's way of thinking seems to imply that we know the content of the basic system as though beforehand and independently of the new system S_1. The new system only expresses (more accurately) the things that already are contained in the basic system and/or puts the matter in a more compehensive form. However, this is the very point that

> turns out to be problematic. Is it on the whole possible to think that an interpretation of the basic system S_b is given independently of the systematization (the reformulation S_1) by means of which the set of norms is organized? [...]
>
> In regard to our topic the question naturally concerns the fact whether it is possible to uphold the distinction between systematization (reformulation) and interpretation (formulation) in the way Alchourrón and Bulygin think. That is to say, *if the systematization (e.g. the reformulation S_1) affects the way the basic system is being interpreted, also the identity assumption comes to a new light.* A quite specific content must be given to the latter in order to ascertain its validity in the form sketched above ..." (p. 275, all italics mine).

The problem for Aarnio is that "every norm can be endowed with one or more contents ('interpretations')." So for each norm of the basic system there are several possible interpretations. Now if the system S_1 reproduces all the conceivable interpretations, then it will be in a way "empty". So it must pick up one particular interpretation of S_b, sayS_{bi}. And here

> "the problem is exactly *whether it is possible to determine the content of the system S_{bi} irrespective of the system S_1 or are the interpretation of the basic system (the formulation) and the new system (the reformulation) intertwined in such a way that the difference between systematization and interpretation gets problematic*" (p. 276, italics mine).

Taken literally this text is utterly inconsistent. If by a norm we understand, as Aarnio does (pp. 12, 274), the *meaning* of a norm formulation, i. e. a correlation of a case (legal fact) with a solution (legal consequence), then it simply does not make sense to talk about interpretation of *norms*. To say that two interpretations are different entails that the correlations they establish between cases and solutions are different, so they are *different norms*, not just two different interpretations of one and the same norm. Only norm-formulations can be interpreted in different ways; each interpretation associates a different norm to the same norm-formulation. Therefore when Aarnio speaks of interpretation of a norm, by 'norm' we must understand the norm-formulation and not its meaning. So his use of the term 'norm' is inconsistent with his own definition.

One way of making Aarnio's text coherent (which as I hope reproduces Aarnio's actual intentions) is to accept that what he calls the basic system S_b is not a system of norms, but a set of norm-formulations. Then it makes sense to say that each element of S_b can be endowed with one or more contents or interpretations. But then it becomes clear that Aarnio's concern is not with systematization or reformulation of a legal system (as it is defined in NS), but with the *identification of the norms* expressed by a certain text (i. e. the norm-formulations of S_b). In other words, the step from S_b to S_1 has nothing to do with what has been called reformulation; it is instead a step previous to identifying the norms to be systematized. Given Aarnio's use of the term 'systematization', the difference between systematization and interpretation is indeed not only problematic, but simply non-existent.

So Aarnio's criticism of NS is misplaced. As systematization starts in NS with an already interpreted set of norms, no wonder that the knowledge of the content of these norms is given "as though beforehand and independently of the new system S_1". As a matter of fact, systematization (in our sense) does not start with Aarnio's basic system S_b (which is a set of mere norm-formulations), but with the set that Aarnio calls S_1, i. e. a set of interpreted norm-formulations, that is, a set of norms.

Both problems, that of identification of norms with which Aarnio is concerned and that of the systematization of norms discussed in NS are important, but we must bear in mind that they are different problems which should not be confused. In this sense, the results of Aarnio's investigations, far from being incompatible with the analyses of NS, are complementary.

In a similar way Niiniluoto's criticism of NS is based to a large extent on a lack of conceptual distinction between the cognitive function of systematization and the normative ("creative") function of legal dogmatics, viz. the modification of the system. As NS is primarily concerned with the first of these two different functions of legal dogmatics, much of the criticism put forward by Niiniluoto is also misdirected. This happens with three of the six points of his criticism: (a) *Legal induction*, (b) *Legal systematization*, and (c) *Sources*.

The reconstruction of legal induction as "decision making (or 'choice') with 'judicial utilities'" (p. 60) and the closure of gaps by some sort of inductive inference belong to the normative function of transformation of a legal system and not to systematization. On the other hand, systematization is by definition conservative; it preserves the normative equivalence. It was never our intention to deny that legal dogmatists perform creative activities as well, but our interest was focussed on the purely cognitive aspect of legal dogmatics. Legal theorists do, of course, close all kinds of gaps and remove inconsistencies, but this activity is different from the mere systematizing, as it is characterized in NS.

Nor do I see why the assumption that the sources of law "are used only once as *inputs* to the legal order" (p. 61) should be unrealistic. Niiniluoto thinks it "more appropriate to assume that the various sources can be directly employed at any time to any issue at hand" (p. 61). Unless there is some misunderstanding on my part, I do not see why both assumptions should be incompatible. One thing is the description of what legal dogmatists really do in practice (here Niiniluoto's assumption is quite correct: of course, they can employ the sources at any time to any issue). A quite another matter is a rational reconstruction of their activity: here we must distinguish between different stages of this activity or different operations performed by them. The fact that such operations are fused in practice does not entitle us to confuse them in thought.

Niiniluoto also complains that the deductivist view in his Fig. 1 (in which he admirably resumes the main ideas of NS regarding systematization) is too narrow, for the structure of argumentation in legal theory is more complex than it is suggested in it. This is quite true, but one must bear in mind that NS does not pretend to give a full characterization of legal dogmatics; its concern is only with one aspect of it, viz. the systematization and there the deductive reasoning is indeed dominant.

The points (e) *Changes in Interpretation* and (f) *Sentences vs. Propositions* have already been dealt with in section II; here too Niiniluoto's criticism is based on a misunderstanding (of which the authors of NS are probably responsible). So only the point (d) *Subsumption and Generic Cases* marks — as has been already acknowledged — a valid criticism of the model developed in NS. But it is not sufficient to sustain the claim that the approach, that Niiniluoto for some inscrutable reasons calls "logistic", is unrealistic and should be replaced by a different one.

Of course, the *formulation* of the ideas put forward in NS is very defective and stands in need of many amendments and clarifications. But the general approach still seems to me to be basically sound.

LA CAUSE DANS LA SYSTEMATIQUE DES ECHANGES

Par Pierre Dauchy, Rouen

La géométrie euclidienne, qui fait de l'espace un ensemble de points juxtaposés, sans liaison entre eux, a influencé à partir du seizième siècle la conception de la société aussi bien que celle du cosmos. Il ne faut pas chercher ailleurs que dans la conception moderne, atomistique, de la société l'origine des difficultés rencontrées par les théoriciens et les praticiens du droit pour mener une critique de la notion de cause qui apparaît centrale dans la théorie générale du subjectivisme moderne du contrat et de l'obligation.

Si l'on part des choses telles qu'elles se donnent à l'observation, on ne peut concevoir une nature inorganisée où les individus créent une société par le moyen du contrat. Le monde se donne comme toujours déjà organisé, notamment le monde qui a trait à l'homme, nous entendons: la société. Le donné social nous apparaît comme une base de départ nécessaire, où viennent s'inscrire subsidiairement les actions de tel ou tel homme.

Il existe ainsi une conception ancienne du donné social: nous devons à Aristote d'avoir exposé clairement les observations auxquelles il s'est livré sur la société et d'en avoir rendu compte grâce au concept de justice distributive, distribution proportionnelle des biens et des charges, ce qui permet de décrire la société comme un tout organique, structuré selon un ordre non pas artificiel et créé par la volonté de l'homme, mais inscrit dès le départ dans la nature.

L'ordre social, sous-jacent et caché dans la société qu'il anime, est sous-tendu par les valeurs et doit permettre à l'homme d'accomplir le plus parfaitement possible sa nature d'être raisonable. L'ordre social, toujours présent, fait découler la *praxis* humaine de l'ontologie. Dès lors le donné social tel qu'il se présente dans sa structuration conditionne l'activité sociale elle-même, et ceci de trois façons. Il est en effet impossible de concevoir le contrat comme un acte d'échange entre deux individus étrangers l'un à l'autre. Bien au contraire, ces individus sont saisis dans un faisceau de relations sociales préexistantes au contrat.

On remarquera ensuite que ce donné social non seulement fournit un cadre aux actes d'échange, mais encore qu'il les produit. En effet, il n'y aurait pas d'échange si les parties à cet échange ne se trouvaient pas dans des situations différentes. Reprenons l'exemple du cordonnier et de l'architecte tel que le donne Aristote:[1] c'est la distribution sociale des tâches qui nécessite en contrepartie les échanges des produits élaborés et des services rendus. Du point de vue du fonctionnement des échanges dans la société, les conceptions aristotéliciennes nous renvoient à l'image de la machine thermique avec ses différences de potentiel: il y a en quelque sorte une différence de potentiel entre les acteurs sociaux, qui entraîne entre eux des flux d'échanges analogues à la circulation de l'énergie entre l'entrée et la sortie d'un moteur thermique. Enfin le donné social conditionne les échanges (ou les contrats — et l'on voit ici que le contrat n'apparaît que comme le moyen juridique des échanges —) en ce qu'ils doivent nécessairement s'inscrire dans une finalité sociale, qui est celle du fonctionnement de la société. Le contrat n'est pas l'affaire des parties; le contrat répond à une finalité, qui est de maintenir la société.

La notion d'information peut être ici utilement mise en oeuvre. Il y a d'abord une information-structure, au sens où la structure est informée, munie d'une forme. Chaque échange se fait selon des formes, des règles générales imposées par la société et qui sont à rattacher à l'ordre social. On peut dire que la justice distributive se reflète dans la structure contractuelle au travers de l'information-structure (ordre public, règles supplétives, règles interprétatives, qualifications).

Il y a ensuite une autre information, que nous appellerons circulante, celle-ci, dans la mesure où elle n'est pas déterminée par le donné social, ne ressortit pas du domaine des finalités profondes de la société, mais se trouve remise aux parties et évolue continuellement avec le contrat lui-même. En ce sens, il ne s'agit pas de forme, mais de renseignements que s'échangent les parties et qui correspondent au particularisme vécu de chaque contrat.

Si l'on prend l'exemple d'un bail à location, il y a une information que s'échangent les parties concernant l'offre et l'acceptation, la qualification du contrat (c'est-à-dire l'énonciation de la volonté de se placer dans telle ou telle situation juridique impliquant l'information-structure correspondante), et une série d'informations concernant l'évolution du contrat (par exemple le prix, diverses dispositions particulières, les échéances, les faits nouveaux). Parallèlement à ces informations sont échangés les biens (remise d'une maison, de sommes d'argent pour le loyer, pour d'éventuelles cautions et assurances).

---

[1] *Aristote,* Ethique à Nicomaque, 1132 b.

Ceci comporte des conséquences fondamentales sur notre conception de la cause. En effet, nous avons vu que le contrat permet la circulation des biens dans la société. Les modalités de cette circulation constituent une information. Nous dirons que lorsqu'un bien est déplacé il apparaît un trou dans le patrimoine qu'il a quitté, et qu'à ce manque est liée l'obligation de rendre une prestation équivalente. Aristote parle du juste correctif: si telle personne m'a pris, acheté ou endommagé mon véhicule, et que la valeur de ce véhicule est de 10 000 Francs, elle devra me verser cette somme de façon à rétablir la juste distribution des patrimoines. Le juste correctif ne peut apparaître que lorsqu'il y a quelque chose à corriger; c'est le manque d'un bien à sa place qui l'actionne. Ce manque est proprement ce que nous appelons «case vide» par référence aux analyses de Gilles Deleuze et de Claude Lévi-Strauss.

On voit donc apparaître un manque dans la série purement factuelle des échanges de biens, et une obligation de rétablir l'équilibre dans la série de l'information. Un manque d'un côté, un excès de l'autre, car l'idée d'obligation suppose bien autre chose qu'une simple information. Le juste correctif renvoie en effet au juste distributif, qui relève de fins qui ne sont pas immédiatement sensibles aux acteurs sociaux.

La case vide, en ce sens, renvoie aux fins de la société sans que ces fins soient exprimées dans la structure, ou plus exactement elle permet à ces fins de se traduire dans la structure contractuelle sous forme concrète (non pas comme principe général de réciprocité, mais comme nécessité de donner *hic et nunc* telle contrepartie précise à un échange). De cette façon, les fins peuvent être réinsérées dans un modèle de rationalité circulaire comme pièce d'un ensemble formel.

La case vide renvoie donc à un ordre extérieur au contrat. Le principe de cet ordre, c'est le juste, qui est une tension dans les choses (juste distribution) et non pas dans les âmes (sentiment d'obligation).

On opposera alors la conception individualiste-volontariste et la conception structuraliste du contrat. Si le contrat est production, création d'obligation entre des individus qui n'avaient auparavant aucun lien entre eux, comme le prétendent les tenants des théories individualistes, il est nécessaire d'expliquer le lien d'obligation par quelque chose situé dans le contrat, puisqu'on ne se donne que le contrat; mais si le contrat est seulement actualisation de rapports préexistants, et s'il y a un ordre dans la société, le lien d'obligation n'est plus nécessairement intrinsèque au contrat, mais peut dépendre de l'ordre externe.

Par exemple, lorsque les romains sanctionnent une partie qui n'a pas fourni de contreprestation dans le contrat, ce n'est pas en recourant à l'idée de cause (cause interne: l'obligation d'une partie est cause de l'obligation de l'autre partie), mais en recourant à l'idée d'enrichissement sans cause, c'est-à-dire d'enrichissement socialement injustifié (cause externe au contrat, liée à l'ordre juste de la répartition des biens dans la société).

On voit que le concept de case vide ne peut être précisé qu'à l'occasion de son application à des exemples concrets de structure. Il nous semble particulièrement riche dans le domaine de l'analyse structurale du contrat, où il permet de formuler une théorie structurale de la cause, qui vient elle-même éclairer par sa valeur démonstrative le concept de case vide.

Il est tentant ici d'évoquer les réflexions du Doyen Carbonnier:[2]

> «Pourquoi en effet le primitif qui a reçu un don se sent-il obligé à rendre? Parce que, nous explique Marcel Mauss, il sent dans la chose donnée une force, une potentialité, un esprit (mana, han). Mauss lui-même a suivi cette idée d'une force enfermée dans la *res* à travers les droits antiques; ainsi en droit romain, dans le système des droits réels, ou des contrats innomés. Mais nous avons encore des contrats réels. Et justement, on peut mettre en doute que, dans notre analyse civiliste du contrat, nous ayons fait une place suffisante à cette catégorie de contrats réels, pourchassée comme un archaïsme au nom de l'autonomie de la volonté, et peut-être plus vivante que nous ne pensons, parce qu'elle répond à une donnée primitive du droit contractuel.»

Ce texte nous apparaît remarquable en ce qu'il décèle dans les objets une potentialité, une force qui en fait non plus seulement des choses matérielles, mais les porteurs d'une signification. Dans le mana, dans le han, plus généralement dans la potentialité dont sont investis les objets, nous voyons se croiser la série purement factuelle, signifiante, et la série juridique, signifiée. Deux choses apparaissent au regard de l'observateur: d'abord ce mana, cette potentialité, est ce qui provoque le respect du contrat et de la mécanique des échanges par les parties, d'autre part cette pontentialité se dérobe à l'analyse.

Affinant davantage l'intuition du Doyen Carbonnier, il nous semble qu'il faille opérer une distinction: le mana, la potentialité, n'est pas incorporé à l'objet déplacé, mais apparaît à l'occasion du déplacement de l'objet. Nous dirons que le déplacement de l'objet dans la série factuelle de l'échange de biens laisse apparaître un vide dans la série de l'échange d'information. En d'autres termes, si un bien quitte un patrimoine pour un autre, il apparaît un manque dans le patrimoine initial tant qu'une contre prestation n'a pas été fournie.

---

[2] Dans son article: Sociologie et droit des contrats, Annales de la Faculté de Droit de Toulouse, T. VII, 1959, p. 116.

Ce manque nous semble être le moteur essentiel des échanges, dans la mesure où il dépasse le factuel pour signaler un manque à l'être, une incomplétude. En effet, nous avons vu que le donné social est toujours premier, et que les patrimoines ne résultent pas d'une appropriation individualiste mais d'une répartition juste des biens de manière à permettre l'épanouissement de la communauté et de ses membres. L'information qui indique le manque d'un bien à sa place renvoie donc immédiatement à ce faisceau de finalités.

On voit l'importance capitale du concept de cause (case vide), car il intervient aussi bien au niveau de la description de la structure contractuelle (assignant à chaque acteur son rôle), qu'au niveau du fonctionnement de la structure contractuelle (comme principe dynamique qui articule la série des échanges de biens et celle des échanges d'information). Enfin, le concept de cause (case vide) relie l'individu à la globalité de la structure contractuelle et sociale parce qu'il lui assigne une place et un rôle et qu'il lui impose un certain comportement.

La cause (case vide) apparaît ainsi non seulement comme principe de fonctionnement des échanges, mais comme principe d'autorégulation de la structure contractuelle: en effet, la mesure de la contreprestation à fournir est ce qui rétablit l'équilibre proportionnel des patrimoines, qui lui-même rend compte de certaines fins, et du juste. La cause (case vide) réinsère les fins dans la logique contractuelle; il y a bien une régulation de l'état initial par l'état final, une autorégulation inséparable du fonctionnement même de la structure. C'est ainsi que l'on peut, dans la systématique des échanges, opposer la rationalité circulaire de la structure à la rationalité linéaire des systèmes hypothético-déductifs triomphant dans la pensée occidentale à partir du seizième siècle.[8]

---

[8] Pour de plus amples développements sur la systématisation dans le droit, voir, du même auteur, Essai d'application de la méthode structurale à l'étude du contrat, Paris 1979, et ses contributions dans Archives de philosophie du droit, Sirey, Paris, tomes 26 à 29.

LA SYSTEMATISATION DANS LA DOGMATIQUE JURIDIQUE

Par Mark Van Hoecke, Bruxelles

Le but de cet article est de donner un aperçu de l'activité du juriste lorsqu'il systématise le droit dans le cadre de la dogmatique juridique, et de discuter de quelques problèmes méthodologiques lors de cette systématisation.[1]

I. La Matière

Au sein du matériau utilisé par les juristes pour construire la dogmatique d'un système juridique concret, on peut distinguer des éléments d'une triple nature:

a) des *textes juridiques normatifs:* législation, traités, principes généraux de droit (reconnus comme tels dans des textes juridiques: jurisprudence, dogmatique juridique), clauses usuelles dans des contrats ou factures, etc.

b) le *langage juridique.* Dans ce langage juridique comme matière de base de la dogmatique juridique, une place dominante est occupée par les *concepts* juridiques.

Ces concepts ne sont pas uniquement un moyen de communication dans le sens où chaque mot a comme fonction de traduire une idée, de transmettre un message. La construction de concepts juridiques est le résultat même de l'activité dogmatique du juriste. Un concept juridique de base, comme par exemple le concept de propriété[2], constitue en lui

---

[1] *Bibliographie.* En dehors de la litérature citée dans les notes infrapaginales qui suivent, nous voudrions encore mentionner: *T. Ascarelli,* Hobbes et Leibniz et la dogmatique juridique, dans: Th. Hobbes et G. W. Leibniz, avec une étude introductive de Tullio Ascarelli, Collection 'Philosophie du droit' 10 (1966), pp. 3—69; *D. De Lazzer,* Rechtsdogmatik als Kompromißformular, dans: R. Dubischar e. a., Dogmatik und Methode. Josef Esser zum 65. Geburtstag, Kronberg 1975, pp. 85—112; *W. Krawietz,* Rechtssystem und Rationalität in der juristischen Dogmatik, dans: A. Aarnio e. a., Methodologie und Erkenntnistheorie der juristischen Argumentation, RECHTSTHEORIE Beiheft 2 (1981), pp. 299—335; *F. von Hippel,* Zur Gesetzmäßigkeit juristischer Systembildung, dans: F. von Hippel, Rechtstheorie und Rechtsdogmatik, Frankfurt am Main 1964, pp. 13—46.

[2] Voyez par exemple l'analyse d'Aulis Aarnio dans son livre Denkweisen der Rechtswissenschaft, Vienne-New York 1979, p. 52.

même tout un ensemble de normes juridiques. La systématisation dans la dogmatique juridique consiste entre autre dans une telle construction de concepts, 'de synthèse' à divers niveaux d'abstraction.

c) *l'application concrète du droit.* Cette application peut être analysée en référence à un des cas réels ou fictifs.

Des cas réels d'application de règles de droit à une réalité concrète peuvent être trouvés dans la jurisprudence ou évidemment ailleurs: par exemple dans la pratique notariale, la pratique commerciale, etc. Là où la jurisprudence publiée est accessible à tous, la connaissance de la réalité même (dont la jurisprudence ne reste toujours qu'un reflet partiel) dépendra des voies d'information et de la pratique juridique du dogmaticien lui même, ainsi que de la disponibilité de données scientifiques utilisables (statistiques, résultats de recherches sociologiques, psychologiques, économiques, etc. ...). Outre les exemples pris dans la réalité, le jurisconsulte emploie aussi des cas juridiques fictifs pour les confronter avec les données normatives, indiquant ainsi certains problèmes, certaines lacunes dans (l'application) des règles juridiques, et avertissant ainsi les intéressés avant que des problèmes similaires réels ne se posent dans la pratique juridique.

d) enfin le jurisconsulte s'inspire aussi de temps à autre du matériel et des résultats de la *dogmatique juridique des systèmes de droit étrangers.* Ceci comprend aussi bien les autres systèmes de droit dans l'espace (le *droit comparé)* que les systèmes de droit qui, dans le temps, ont précédé le système de droit actuel *(l'histoire juridique).*

Avec ce matériau la dogmatique juridique opère de deux façons différentes, opposées même l'une à l'autre.

D'une part la dogmatique juridique *systématise* le droit. Cette activité se développe plutôt à long terme: chaque jurisconsulte, chaque génération ajoute de nouveaux éléments à l'élaboration dogmatique du système juridique. D'autre part la dogmatique juridique *concrétise* le droit, en ce sens que dans l'interprétation et l'application du droit elle développe des règles plus concrètes à partir de normes juridiques formulées d'une manière plutôt générale, qu'elle donne des exemples, qu'elle indique des problèmes qui peuvent surgir dans la pratique, qu'elle cherche des solutions pour résoudre ces problèmes, etc.

Cette activité est un travail à court terme: chaque juriste peut à lui seul entreprendre cette mission, par exemple dans un commentaire sur une nouvelle loi, sans qu'il soit obligé de s'inscrire dans une tradition dogmatique (ce qui évidemment ne signifie pas que cette activité concrétisante pourrait se dérouler sans tenir compte des concepts, des divisions, etc. de la dogmatique juridique actuelle).

M. Aarnio a comparé, à juste titre, ces deux approches différentes de la matière par la dogmatique juridique à l'activité des autres sciences. L'activité concrétisante consiste en fait dans la construction *d'hypothèses* vis-à-vis de la signification de textes juridiques, tandis que l'activité systématisante est comparable à l'élaboration de *théories* dans d'autres disciplines.[3]

Dans notre article nous n'envisagerons que l'activité *systématisante* de la dogmatique juridique.

II. Objectifs

D'un point de vue historique la dogmatique juridique a longtemps eu comme objectif principal la systématisation d'un droit coutumier et d'une jurisprudence fragmentaire et hétérogène. Les grandes codifications, comme par exemple le Code civil français de 1804, ont d'ailleurs été le travail d'éminents jurisconsultes. A un certain degré ces codifications ont été le couronnement d'une longue tradition de dogmatique juridique.

Cette systématisation avait alors comme but *l'unification du droit*. Actuellement la compétence pour créer des normes juridiques est devenue quasi intégralement un monopole d'autorités politiques ou juridiques. Le droit est devenu, au moins en Europe continentale, quasi totalement un droit de législateur(s).

Pourtant on constate que l'objectif d'unification du droit, dans le sens mentionné, reste actuel, quoique sur un autre plan: en utilisant le droit comparé on tend en effet aujourd'hui à une unification du droit par delà les frontières. Ceci est le cas pour le travail législatif (voyez par exemple les législations européennes concernant l'émission de chèques, ou les diverses initiatives au niveau du Benelux), mais aussi pour la jurisprudence et pour la dogmatique juridique.

Ainsi la jurisprudence et la doctrine belge ont longtemps utilisé la jurisprudence et la doctrine française pour interpréter des articles du Code civil, aussi bien lorsqu'il s'agissait de textes identiques[4], que lorsqu'il ne s'agissait que de textes plus ou moins comparables. Cette référence a atteint un tel degré qu'actuellement encore un arrêt de la cour de cassation française aura souvent une plus grande valeur argumentative devant un tribunal belge que par exemple un jugement isolé d'un juge de paix belge.

---

[3] *Aarnio* (note 2), pp. 49—50 et pp. 66—68.

[4] Après 1830 la Belgique a conservé le Code civil français, introduit en 1804 lorsque la Belgique faisait partie de la France. Une grande partie des articles du Code est restée inchangée jusqu'à ce jour.

On pourrait dire que la dogmatique juridique actuelle a en premier lieu un *objectif didactique* vis-à-vis du praticien du droit, de l'étudiant en droit et du non-juriste. La première tâche de la doctrine est d'informer les juristes aussi bien que les non-juristes des règles de droit en vigueur à un moment donné et en un lieu donné.

Toutefois il s'avère impossible de décrire les règles de droit en vigueur d'une manière complètement neutre. Chaque 'description' du droit est en même temps, d'une manière explicite ou implicite, une théorie concernant l'interprétation des règles de droit, la systématisation du droit, l'hiérarchie des sources du droit, la solution de problèmes juridiques, etc.

D'ailleurs, la littérature juridique comporte d'innombrables vues divergentes sur une foule de règles et de problèmes juridiques.

La doctrine juridique doit donc avoir des fonctions et des objectifs qui dépassent de loin cet objectif didactique.

La systématisation dans la dogmatique juridique s'avère en effet être nécessaire pour:

a) une rationalisation et une simplification du système juridique, et

b) l'élaboration de solutions pour des problèmes juridiques non prévus dans le droit (dans la loi).

La rationalisation et la simplification du système juridique, *la réduction de la complexité du système juridique* peuvent en effet être considérées comme *l'objectif primordial* de la systématisation dans la dogmatique juridique. Comme il a déjà été mentionné plus haut, la création de concepts juridiques a, notamment, comme fonction de désigner tout un ensemble de normes par le moyen d'un seul mot.

> "It is one of the essential functions of the law to reduce the multitude, variety, and diversity of human actions and relations to a reasonable degree of order and to promulgate rules or standards of conduct applicable to certain circumscribed types of action or behavior. In order to accomplish this task successfully, the legal order must undertake the formation of technical notions and concepts designed to aid in classifying the multifarious phenomena and events of social life. It thereby lays the basis for subjecting equal or essentially similar phenomena to a unified and consistent regulation or treatment. Legal concepts may thus be viewed as working tools used for the purpose of identifying, by a shorthand description, typical situations which are characterized by identical or common elements."[5]

Toutefois il ne s'agit pas seulement de 'classement' ou de 'description' d'un certain nombre de caractéristiques. Les concepts juridiques ont toujours un aspect normatif et l'utilisation de ces concepts dans la

---

[5] *E. Bodenheimer*, Jurisprudence, Massachusetts 1962, p. 325.

systématisation a un caractère normatif par excellence. Prenons comme exemple la qualification d'un bien comme mobilier ou comme immobilier. Cette activité n'est pas du tout comparable, par exemple, au classement d'un dossier dans le tiroir de gauche ou de droite. Une fois qu'un bien en droit belge est qualifié d'immobilier il peut être hypothéqué, il doit obligatoirement être vendu par acte notarié, il est soumis à d'autre taxes qu'un bien mobilier, etc. Ce classement, à première vue neutre, conditionne par conséquent l'application de toute une série de normes juridiques, qui peuvent différer d'une manière assez substantielle selon le choix que l'on fait.

Vu le grand nombre de règles juridiques, la construction et l'élaboration de tels concepts juridiques s'avère nécessaire en vue d'une simplification du système juridique.

De même, la dogmatique juridique doit rechercher des règles générales et des principes généraux à différents niveaux d'abstraction en vue d'une réduction de la complexité des règles juridiques.

Ainsi la dogmatique juridique présente non seulement un intérêt théorique mais également un intérêt pratique. La réduction de la complexité du système juridique par la dogmatique juridique a finalement aussi une fonction didactique vis-à-vis des praticiens de droit. Sans la dogmatique juridique chaque système de droit développé, comme le sont par exemple les systèmes de droit européens, aurait inévitablement une allure kafkaïenne.

L'élaboration de concepts juridiques et la recherche de principes généraux dans l'ensemble de règles juridiques fournissent aux juristes les moyens pour *trouver une solution à des problèmes juridiques non explicitement prévus dans les règles juridiques* du système de droit actuellement en vigueur. La recherche de telles solutions peut être considérée comme un second objectif essentiel de la systématisation dans la dogmatique juridique.

En guise de conclusion on pourrait dire que la systématisation du droit est inévitablement une tâche pour une science juridique. Ce n'est que de temps en temps que les juristes peuvent créer de grandes codifications et encore n'est ce possible qu'après une longue période de préparation. Normalement, et actuellement davantage, la promulgation de règles juridiques par le législateur est une activité pragmatique qui opère cas par cas. L'élaboration du système juridique et des concepts généraux est nécessairement le travail d'une science juridique, in casu de la dogmatique juridique. Evidemment il n'y a pas une séparation totale entre le travail dogmatique et le travail législatif. Comme le jurisconsulte travaille avec le matériel legislatif, de même le législateur travaille avec le matériel dogmatique: il utilise par exemple les concepts élaborés dans la dogmatique juridique. En plus, on peut constater, au moins dans la technique législative actuelle en Belgique, que le législateur s'efforce de faire des lois, qui, du moins prises séparément, forment un ensemble logique et systématisé de règles juridiques. Néanmoins, même en présence d'un législateur très consciencieux, voire qui s'approcherait même de la perfection, il restera toujours une tâche importante de systématisation pour la dogmatique juridique.

Ainsi on constate par exemple que la dogmatique juridique fonctionne comme facteur dirigeant pour une resystématisation par le législateur de la législation, devenue ou restée dispersée. La doctrine ne se contente donc pas d'une systématisation en déans les limites des règles juridiques promulguées par le législateur. On trouve un bel exemple de cet activité doctrinale dans plusieurs pays de l'Europe orientale où la dogmatique juridique propose la création d'un droit économique autonome, qui se dégagerait du droit civil classique.[6]

III. Niveaux de Systematisation

Dans la dogmatique juridique on peut distinguer trois niveaux de systématisation. Deux niveaux se situent sur le plan interne du système juridique, le troisième sur le plan externe.

1. Sur le Plan Interne

Un premier niveau de systématisation peut être qualifié de '*technique*'. C'est le travail de base de la dogmatique juridique: le recueil et la classification des règles juridiques en vigueur.

A ce premier niveau de systématisation la dogmatique juridique se soumet intégralement aux données du système juridique. On se contente d'une simple classification de la matière. Le but de cette forme de systématisation est de décrire et de classifier les règles de droit en vigueur selon la hiérarchie des sources de droit généralement acceptées, en vue de construire une base légitime pour l'interprétation de ces règles.[7] La systématisation technique est élaborée principalement à l'aide des textes législatifs et des travaux préparatoires, et, accessoirement, à l'aide de la jurisprudence et d'autres oeuvres doctrinales.[8]

---

[6] Voyez: *Th. Vondracek*, Nieuwe begrippen in het Tsjechoslowaaks burgerlijk wetboek en hun socialistische karakter, La Haye 1981, pp. 12—17.

[7] *L. Lehtimaja*, Systematization in the study of particular crimes, dans: RECHTSTHEORIE Beiheft 2 (1981), p. 341.

[8] Comparez le schéma dans l'article cité de Lehtimaja, à la page 346.

Le second niveau de systématisation sur le plan interne du système juridique peut être qualifié de *téléologique.*

Ici la dogmatique juridique travaille d'une manière dialectique: après une systématisation technique le juriste repense et remanie, dans un premier temps, son matériel en fonction du système 'technique' et provisoire pour, dans un second temps, reconstruire le système juridique d'un point de vue téléologique. A ce niveau la dogmatique juridique systématise vraiment le *contenu* du droit, là où la systématisation technique se contente d'une simple classification des règles et des concepts juridiques sans que leur contenu soit modifié dans ce processus de systématisation.

On peut faire la comparaison avec la distinction entre une coordonnation de la législation et une codification. La coordonnation ne fait que classer des textes dispersés, tandis que la codification repense et modifie les règles et les concepts. A côté de codifications 'officielles' du droit, la dogmatique juridique travaille constamment à une telle codification 'officieuse' en systématisant le droit d'un point de vue téléologique.

Comme dans l'interprétation téléologique de textes législatifs la signification à première vue du texte peut changer après une confrontation du texte avec le but de la loi, de même la confrontation de règles et de concepts juridiques avec la structure de base, les valeurs et les concepts fondamentaux du système juridique peut mener le juriste à redéfinir et reformuler ces règles ou ces concepts.

Jusqu'à un certain degré la systématisation téléologique peut être réalisée de lege lata en redéfinissant certains concepts et en réinterprétant certaines règles juridiques. Les limites d'une telle opération dépendent intégralement de la théorie d'interprétation, explicitement ou implicitement adoptée par le jurisconsulte en question.[9] Si selon sa théorie d'interprétation les modifications nécessaires ne sont plus possibles de lege lata il formulera des propositions de lege ferenda, adressées au législateur.

2. Sur le Plan Externe

L'activité de la dogmatique juridique, aussi bien dans l'interprétation que dans la systématisation, ne se déroule pas uniquement à l'intérieur du système juridique. La systématisation n'a pas seulement pour but de classer et de moduler les règles et les concepts juridiques pour

[9] La question se pose naturellement d'une manière différente dans le droit fiscal ou le droit pénal où la marge d'interprétation est nettement plus étroite (voyez au sujet du droit pénal: *Lehtimaja* [note 7], pp. 343—346).

arriver à un système juridique bien structuré, avec une construction logique sans antinomies et sans lacunes. La dogmatique juridique essaie aussi *d'intégrer au maximum le système juridique dans la société, constamment en évolution, de même que dans le système de valeurs et de normes qui domine dans cette société.* Ainsi pendant les années dernières les pays de l'Europe occidentale ont connu plusieurs conflits où les travailleurs occupaient leur usine après sa fermeture définitive par le propriétaire. Ce dernier se basait sur son droit de propriété pour demander aux tribunaux d'interdire la continuation de la production par les travailleurs à l'aide des machines et des bâtiments du propriétaire. Cette situation incite les jurisconsultes à reconsidérer le concept de propriété en fonction des nouvelles conceptions relatives aux rapports entre travailleurs et propriétaires au sein d'une entreprise.[10]

Luhmann a plaidé en vue d'une réorientation de la dogmatique juridique traditionelle, laquelle s'occupe quasi exclusivement de la systématisation interne, vers une nouvelle dogmatique qui s'occuperait en premier lieu de la systématisation externe, de l'intégration du droit dans la société:

„Der Primat der Input-Orientierung soll durch einen Primat der Output-Orientierung ersetzt werden, das Rechtssystem soll auf seine gesellschaftlichen Folgen ausgerichtet, durch seine Folgen kontrolliert werden. Wertungen und Rechtssätze seien, so wird gesagt, nur durch ihre Folgen begründbar. Aber ist das möglich? Ist eine solche Wendung mit der Funktion des Rechts und mit der Ausdifferenzierung des Rechtssystems zu vereinbaren? Und kann sie durch Korrekturen an der herkömmlichen Dogmatik — etwa im Sinne von neuen juristischen Erfindungen — erreicht werden, oder erfordert sie ein völlig anderes Instrumentarium, das nicht aus der vorhandenen Dogmatik entwickelt werden kann? Und liegt gar hier der Ansatzpunkt für eine juristische Verwendung sozialwissenschaftlicher Forschungsergebnisse?“[11]

Luhmann se voit pourtant obligé de reconnaître qu'il est en fin de compte impossible de développer une dogmatique juridique qui élabore uniquement, ou au moins principalement, une systématisation extérieure qui s'oriente en premier lieu aux *effets* du droit dans la société en négligeant les valeurs et les principes internes du système juridique:

„Als Fazit können wir festhalten, daß wir keine überzeugende Möglichkeit gefunden haben, eine Rechtsdogmatik zu empfehlen, die Folgen als Kriterien für Recht und Unrecht verwendet.“[12]

---

[10] Voyez p. ex. pour la doctrine belge: *W. Van Gerven,* Bedrijfsbezetting en verkoop in eigen beheer door werknemers van de onderneming, in: Rechtskundig Weekblad 1976—77, col. 65—78.

[11] *N. Luhmann,* Rechtssystem und Rechtsdogmatik, Stuttgart 1974, pp. 29—30.

[12] *Luhmann* (note 11), p. 48.

IV. Méthodes

Comme il apparait que la systématisation dans la dogmatique juridique peut se dérouler sur plusieurs niveaux et peut avoir des buts différents, il va de soi que parallèlement plusieurs méthodes différentes peuvent être utilisées.

Dans la dogmatique juridique actuelle la systématisation joue en effet un rôle important pour:

a) la systématisation d'une jurisprudence et d'une pratique juridique, qui opèrent cas par cas;

b) l'intégration de cette jurisprudence dans le système de droit en vigueur (déterminé d'une part par la législation et d'autre part par la doctrine dominante);

c) la systématisation d'interprétations de textes législatifs isolés;

d) l'intégration dans le système juridique de solutions juridiques élaborées pour des situations et des problèmes nouveaux (par exemple l'intégration du contrat de leasing, créé par la pratique, dans les types de contrats classiques: vente, louage etc.).

Bien que sur le plan théorique on peut faire une nette distinction entre les deux activités de la dogmatique juridique, notamment l'interprétation et la systématisation, en réalité ces deux activités sont fort liées entre elles. *L'interprétation* peut en effet être utilisée *comme instrument de la systématisation*. C'est précisément grâce à l'interprétation que les textes législatifs peuvent obtenir la souplesse, qui est nécessaire pour l'intégration d'éléments divergents et même parfois contradictoires dans un système juridique qui doit conserver un maximum d'unité logique. C'est peut être ici que l'aspect *idéologique* du travail dogmatique apparait de la façon la plus claire. En effet, selon les résultats désirés par le jurisconsulte, il peut interpréter des lois nouvelles d'une manière restrictive, afin que les valeurs visées par le système juridique traditionnel restent inaltérées au maximum, ou il peut au contraire réinterpréter les règles traditionnelles dans le sens des valeurs visées par la nouvelle loi. Un exemple de cette idéologie conservatrice peut être trouvé dans la règle, créée par la dogmatique juridique, selon laquelle les dérogations au 'droit commun' doivent être interprétées d'une manière restrictive. En considérant le droit civil comme le droit commun on a longtemps contrecarré par exemple le développement du droit social, qui fût qualifié de 'dérogation au droit commun'.

La systématisation même se déroule alors par des voies d'ordre logique (dans un sense large). Ici on peut distinguer trois méthodes différentes:

la méthode logique 'pure', la méthode typologique et la méthode téléologique.

La *méthode logique 'pure'* est étroitement liée à la nature du processus de systématisation. Systématiser le droit signifie: créer une structure logique pour une masse de règles de droit dispersées. Le processus de systématisation implique inévitablement un classement logique. Dans le cadre de ce classement logique plusieurs procédés peuvent être utilisés.[13] Citons à titre exemplatif l'analyse à l'effet de retrouver les éléments constitutifs de solutions complexes; le recours aux principes de la logique formelle, comme les principes de non contradiction ou d'identité; l'emploi de raisonnements para-logiques, comme les raisonnements par analogie, a contrario ou a fortiori; la synthèse, c'est-à-dire le processus d'abstraction dans lequel un nombre de règles détaillées sont réduites à une ou à quelques règles plus générales (ce qui mène à la fin aux principes généraux de droit); la déduction, par laquelle des concepts ou des règles générales sont appliqués à des situations ou des problèmes nouveaux; l'induction, qui mène par exemple à la modification d'un concept ou d'un principe après leur confrontation à des problemes pratiques ou à d'autres éléments.

A côté de la méthode logique pure on peut utiliser la *méthode 'typologique'*. Avec cette méthode on n'essaie pas de créer des concepts ou des règles générales recouvrant des concepts, situations ou règles plus détaillés, mais on essaie de construire un concept ou une règle qui peut fonctionner comme 'type normal' pour une série de situations différentes. Cette méthode peut s'avérer utile lorsque la matière que le jurisconsulte doit systématiser contient tant de nuances qu'il est presque impossible de construire un concept de base ou une règle générale qui retient toutes les caractéristiques de chaque élément qu'on veut rassembler dans un même groupe. Avec la méthode typologique on construit un type normal qui peut être considéré comme représentatif pour ce groupe d'éléments, parce que chaque élément diffère peu du type normal, même s'il n'y a aucune caractéristique qui soit commune à tous les éléments du groupe.[14]

Enfin on peut aussi utiliser la *méthode téléologique,* qui est étroitement liée au second niveau de systématisation interne du système juridique (la systématisation téléologique du contenu des règles juridiques). Dans cette méthode ce ne sont ni les textes législatifs comme tels, ni les

---

[13] Voyez: *J. Renauld,* La systématisation dans le raisonnement juridique, dans: Logique et Analyse, 1958, p. 179.

[14] Cette méthode a été élaborée entre autre par le jurisconsulte néerlandais E. M. Meijers. Voyez à ce sujet: *A. R. Bloembergen,* Over de methode van Meijers, dans: Weekblad voor Privaatrecht, Notariaat en Registratie, 5504, p. 46. Voyez aussi: *K. Larenz,* Methodenlehre der Rechtswissenschaft, Berlin 1975, pp. 443—457.

mots et les concepts utilisés par le législateur, qui forment la base du travail de systématisation, mais les valeurs et les buts qui se situent derrière les textes législatifs en question. Dans sa forme la plus prononcée la méthode téléologique systématise les règles juridiques à partir d'une idée ou d'une valeur centrale:

> "To take the particular character of actual cases into consideration, recourse must be had to valuation under the idea of law. But the legal norms cannot be apprehended without the idea of law; on the other hand, the idea of law cannot be apprehended without the legal norms. The idea of law gives meaning and value to legal norms. But this meaning and value is meaningless and devoid of value without an object which the legal norm regulates. A legal system is constituted when legal construction is built around a legal order whereby non-contradiction and self-sufficiency of every legal provision in relation to one area of law or the entire legal order is developed from the idea of law. The above mentioned work of dogmatic legal science is done at three stages; it starts from the recognition of the content of concrete value of positive law and its system and arrives, in the end, at the understanding of this law as it is. Therefore dogmatic legal science must start from building up its subject matter, positive law or a positive legal order, as one logically arranged normative system."[15]

En réalité les systèmes de droit actuels, au moins en Europe occidentale, ne sont pas construit à partir d'une seule idéologie uniforme. Pour des raisons historiques ces systèmes de droit contiennent plusieurs sous-systèmes lesquels fonctionnent avec une autonomie relative. Ainsi le droit civil est basé principalement sur l'idéologie libérale du dix-neuvième siècle, tandis que le droit social est plutôt la concrétisation de l'idéologie «socialiste» du vingtième siècle. Mais aussi à l'intérieur de ces branches de droit on peut dire que chaque partie, chaque institution juridique a sa logique propre, c'est-à-dire ses propres buts et valeurs. Ainsi on peut se trouver face à des divergences dans le langage juridique, dans la terminologie employée par le législateur, ou à des règles juridiques qui sont à première vue incompatible l'une avec l'autre, sans qu'on puisse parler d'antinomie ou de contradiction logique. En droit belge par exemple le concubinage est «favorisé» dans le droit social et dans le droit fiscal, tandis qu'il est déconsidéré dans le droit civil.

La systématisation ne peut avoir comme but une unité logique parfaite du système de droit dans son ensemble. Par contre cette unité logique apparaît réalisable pour des parties de ce système juridique (par exemple le droit de famille).

En ce qui concerne la systématisation du droit au niveau externe, c'est-à-dire l'intégration du droit dans le système social et son adaptation permanente aux changements sociaux, d'autres méthodes s'imposent à

[15] *T. Minemura*, Dogmatic Legal Science and Sociology of Law, dans: Archiv für Rechts- und Sozialphilosophie (ARSP), 1970, pp. 358—359.

côté des méthodes logiques. Ce sont les *méthodes sociologiques,* ainsi que les méthodes psychologiques, historiques, économiques, etc.

Dans la pratique la systématisation externe est élaborée en général d'une manière peu scientifique, c'est-à-dire qu'elle est basée uniquement sur l'information concernant la réalité que le jurisconsulte trouve dans la jurisprudence publiée, ainsi que sur sa propre expérience, professionnelle ou extra-professionnelle. Même les recherches qui prennent comme point de départ la jurisprudence non publiée sont très rares pour ne pas parler des recherches qui étudient la réalité même à l'aide de techniques scientifiques.

V. Rapports entre la Dogmatique et la Pratique Juridique

La dogmatique juridique est fort liée à sa matière, c'est-à-dire aux éléments de base du système de droit que sont notamment les textes législatifs. Une grande partie du système est ainsi déjà donnée et construite par *la législation.* Par contre les concepts et les structures utilisés par le législateur sont à leur tour influencés par la dogmatique juridique.

Vis-à-vis de *la jurisprudence,* la dogmatique juridique est plus influente. On peut dire que normalement c'est à travers la dogmatique juridique que les juges s'informent sur le système de droit et les règles qu'il contient. Si les interprétations et les théories sont élaborées par la jurisprudence, dans un second temps ces interprétations et théories seront décrites dans la dogmatique juridique comme s'il s'agissait d'une donnée objective, d'une 'réalité juridique' et non plus comme des interprétations et des théories discutables qu'il faut motiver et argumenter. Ainsi, à travers la jurisprudence, des hypothèses et des théories dogmatiques se métamorphosent en une réalité juridique, en apparence certaine.

Dans certains cas ceci peut même fausser *le droit* par une collaboration, consciente ou inconsciente, entre dogmatique juridique et pratique judiciaire. On constate que dans certains domaines spécialisés du droit (p. ex. le droit de la construction), où il n'y a que quelques spécialistes et parfois même une seule 'autorité' parmi les jurisconsultes, et où il n'y a qu'un périodique spécialisé, la jurisprudence publiée dans ce périodique est sélectionnée selon qu'elle est favorable ou non aux interprétations et théories défendues par ce(s) jurisconsulte(s) (p. ex. des décisions uniquement favorables aux entrepreneurs). Ceci est par ailleurs rendu possible parce que généralement ces spécialistes sont ceux qui précisément constituent le comité de rédaction de telles revues.[16]

---

[16] Une situation comparable s'est présentée lorsqu'à un moment donné presque tous les professeurs de droit pénal en Belgique étaient membre du parquet. Ainsi s'est développée une doctrine favorable aux poursuites et

Par après ces jurisconsultes peuvent se référer à cette 'jurisprudence constante' pour prouver la validité de leurs thèses. Ceci influencera inévitablement les juges qui bien qu'au départ favorables à d'autres interprétations ou d'autres théories, seront induits en erreur par ces jurisconsultes.

Heureusement une telle influence par quelques jurisconsultes sur le système de droit n'est possible qu'en déans des limites assez restreintes. La pratique juridique et judiciaire n'acceptera pas n'importe quelle interprétation ou n'importe quelle théorie. Si la solution prônée par la doctrine n'est pas adaptée à la réalité ou est considérée comme injuste, elle sera repoussée par la pratique et par les juges.

Je crois que si Uusitalo considère que la dogmatique juridique *'explique'* dans un certain sens la *'réalité juridique'*[17], cette théorie paraît inexacte parce qu'il ne s'agit pas de l'explication de l'une ou de l'autre réalité en dehors de la dogmatique juridique, une réalité que cette dogmatique devrait reproduire fidèlement. En effet il n'y a pas question de deux réalités séparées: d'une part la 'réalité' de la dogmatique juridique et d'autre part la 'réalité' de la pratique juridique. La dogmatique juridique est élaborée et les règles juridiques sont systématisées dans une *action réciproque* entre dogmatique et pratique juridique. Ces deux activités ne sont pas séparées l'une de l'autre, mais elles ne coïncident pas non plus l'une avec l'autre. Chacune d'elles a ses propres buts. La dogmatique juridique a en premier ordre *une finalité logique* (dans le sens large du mot), tandis que la pratique juridique a en premier ordre une *finalité pratique:* résoudre des problèmes juridiques concrets.

La dogmatique juridique *décrit* le droit jusqu'à un certain degré, mais pour une partie importante elle *construit* également le droit, par l'interprétation et par la systématisation des règles de droit. Cette construction n'est pas une activité neutre, mais une vraie *création* de droit. La pratique juridique se conforme à la dogmatique juridique jusqu'à un certain degré, c'est-à-dire la pratique consulte la doctrine comme source d'information pour le droit en vigueur et elle considère cette doctrine comme une description objective de ce droit. Mais la pratique a elle aussi sa propre finalité: trouver la solution la plus adaptée pour chaque cas, éventuellement au détriment de la systématique et de la cohérence logique du droit.

---

aux condamnations. En plus ces magistrats/professeurs pouvaient par après s'appuier sur cette doctrine dans leur réquisitoires et ainsi influencer la jurisprudence dans le sens désiré.

[17] *J. Uusitalo,* The representation of the legal system in legal dogmatics, dans: A. Peczenik/J. Uusitalo (éds.), Reasoning on Legal Reasoning, Vammala 1979, p. 186.

La dogmatique juridique peut donc très bien évoluer de manière autonome par rapport à la pratique juridique (comme ceci a été le cas en Allemagne pendant les siècles précédants). Ce n'est que pour être utile et utilisable que la dogmatique juridique doit être adaptée à la pratique juridique. Cependant elle doit être *acceptée* par cette pratique.

SYSTEMATIZATION IN LEGAL DOGMATICS AND JUDICIAL DECISIONS

By Roberto J. Vernengo, Buenos Aires

I. The Systematization Function in Legal Dogmatics

Traditionally, legal dogmatics, in its continental sense, tries to describe and to explain the contents and the hierarchical structure of a positive legal order. To describe norms and to explain a legal order are rather intricate activities; it is not at all clear what we must understand under those terms. The very simple and naive ordering of normative materials, as was done by the early French Civil Code commentators, is one way to accomplish that descriptive and explanatory task. But the very subtle and complicate job of reformulating and reconstructing the contents of legal norms according to some general theoretical concepts is also considered a form of scientific description and explanation. With these two words — description and explanation — we refer, therefore, to different kinds of theoretical activity: from some very primitive form of classification of norms depending on their contents and in view of some practical purpose, to a refined and strict logical analysis of their syntactical structure and their semantical interpretation. In general terms, legal scientists agree on this goal for their theoretical undertakings.

Kelsen, for instance, maintains that "die Rechtswissenschaft hat das Recht zu erkennen und auf Grund ihrer Erkenntnis zu beschreiben", or, more emphatically: "die Rechtswissenschaft kann das Recht *nur* beschreiben"[1], although there is no clear indication of the procedure by which law (Recht), as a set of positive norms, can be the object of a description. Description has a clear sense when it refers to an individual empirically given: a set of norms cannot be ontologically characterized that way. Nevertheless, the description thesis about jurisprudence can be found, with variations derived from different preconceptions about what law is, in other writers. Hart's attitude on that matter has been defined as a sort of "analytical description of legal systems"[2]; for him, legal science should be a "descriptive jurisprudence"[3], even though

---

[1] *H. Kelsen*, Reine Rechtslehre, 2nd ed., F. Deuticke, Wien 1960, p. 74.

[2] *N. MacCormick*, H.L.A. Hart, London 1981, p. 25.

[3] *MacCormick* (note 2), p. 43.

what must be described by the sentences of jurisprudence is something more complex than Kelsenian norms. Scandinavian realist jurisprudence has always accepted, with its philosophical realist trend, that the proper task of a legal science must consist in an objective description of the law, done in similar ways as descriptions in other empirical sciences; again, it must be pointed out that law, for Ross or Olivecrona — to mention legal thinkers who have had important influence outside Scandinavia —, is another kind of phenomena than Kelsenian norms or the mixture of rules Hart has in mind when speaking about the law. I do not wish to enter here any further in the question of the proper scope of the descriptive endeavour of legal science, whatever be the forms it borrows.

As regards the other function ascribed to legal science — the systematization function —, it is striking to notice that Kelsen, following in that matter a strong tradition of German dogmatics, specifies that the systematization function is, for legal science, as essential as the descriptive function.[4] On this point, Alchourrón and Bulygin observe that "legal philosophers seem to agree that the task or, at least, the most important task of legal science consists in describing the law and presenting it in a systematic way, thus making possible the knowledge of the law and facilitating its application by individuals subject to the legal order, specially those who must deal with it for professional reasons (lawyers, judges, officials)"[5]; they understand systematization as "the determination of the normative consequences of a set of sentences for a given topic".[6]

From a purely theoretical point of view, that asseveration is right. But it gives a rather unilateral view of the real activity legal scientists accomplish when they systematize their scientific discourse about the law. The systematization activity, in fact, is a way of rationalizing our prescientific experience of legal phenomena. To nourish the thesis about the systematization function of legal dogmatics, as an essential part of its theoretical task, is to sustain tacitly the thesis that the job of the jurist consists in a rationalization effort. It is for that reason — an essential reason for considering what the jurist does with the normative material in his scientific activity — that legal dogmatics not only studies the content of legal rules, but also the systemic order of those rules, as A. Aarnio has pointed out.[7] Other social sciences, having to do with

[4] Cf. *H. Kelsen*, General Theory of Law and State, Harvard University Press 1945, p. 1.

[5] *C. Alchourrón/E. Bulygin*, Normative Systems, Springer Verlag, Wien-New York 1971, p. 67.

[6] *Alchourrón/Bulygin* (note 5), p. 68.

[7] *A. Aarnio*, On Legal Reasoning, Turku-Loimaa 1977, part III.

norms or social rules, do not regard the normative systematization of their material as something that the scientist must do. Sociology, for instance, although taking into account the order in which social rules are given, takes that order as something given: the systemic order of rules is a fact more to be taken into consideration and not an order that the scientist is supposed to impose on the material.

As soon as the methodological question of the systematization function appears, legal scientists differ on their theoretical posture. It seems clear to us nowadays that the normative material (orders, prohibitions, derogations, authorizations, etc.) that the legislator issues pretends to be ordered systematically by itself; we naturally tend to expect that a rational legislator will not issue norms randomly. The apparent order given to norms by the legislator, as in the case of a codification, does not constitute a system in any interesting scientific sense of that word. It is on something done by the jurist on that material where the result of the systematization function is to be found. Legal norms — and also other constituents of legal orders, which must be taken into consideration when describing the contents and structure of a dynamic system — are, therefore, the data on which the ordering or systematization efforts of the legal scientist converge. It is not however at all clear how norms — and the other ingredients indicated — are given, as data, to the legal scientist.

Instead of thinking of norms as something given in a sort of legal or moral experience, it seems more reasonable to take them as the theoretical (conceptual) reconstruction of some kind of utterances or, even, as the translation in some set of conventional symbols of utterances or gestures used for accomplishing the social function of controlling human behaviour. But even then, norms do not appear as evident data; not only their ontological status is doubtful, but it looks as if we do not make explicit to ourselves the use that is made of them. This means that nothing can be decided so far regarding their ontological classification.

Let's admit, for argument's sake, that norms, as linguistic entities, are a class of (i. e.: are apt to be construed as) expressions signifying deontic propositions referring obliquely to human actions, employed institutionally by state organs to control conduct or define behavioural situations. What the legal scientist systematizes is clearly not the normative material issued by the legislator with some pragmatical purpose in view, but what he conceptually understands as "norms" according to the set of categories he applies. More precisely, one would say that what is systematized is the theoretical discourse of legal science itself. By extension, it is possible to assert that law itself (the legal order composed of norms and other elements) is thus indirectly systematized:

the legal order appears as a prima facie ordered set of normative sentences. Law is thus rationalized, as Max Weber said. The question is now: what are the theoretical and the practical functions of this systematization effort done by legal scientists?

II. Systematization and Rationalization

In consequence, legal systems (being systematic orderings of the theoretical propositions of legal dogmatics) are not given, but brought forth through scientific activities. It is only norms that, so to say, are given. Systems, on the other hand, are created by methodical efforts of the legal scientists. The systematization effort is a contingent fact in the history of legal knowledge. There may be some types of legal lore without the pretension of scientific knowledge; there have been, and still are, societies where no legal science was produced at all and even societies where law is not distinguished from other forms of normative motivations. In those cases — generally mentioned in relationship with primitive societies, but also, as is well known, in relationship with international law viewed as mere custom or morality —, as there is no socially recognized scientific knowledge of the law, it is not possible to speak strictly of a "legal order".

From an outsider's point of view, any set of social rules can be characterized as law. A more cautious attitude, as would be the one adopted by a social scientist, would be that no such set can be defined if we do not possess a group of cognitive categories (rules of recognition or gnoseological categories in the Kantian sense as Kelsen would have it), allowing us to recognize some social data (perhaps, recurrent social actions or recurrent interpretations of social actions given by the group itself) as legal norms or as law.

This necessary set of cognitive categories would normally appear as a consistent set of general concepts (defining properties and relations); it must be adequate to effect a sufficient reformulation of the normative material, in such a way that at least that reformulation could be taken, by the scientific community, as a description of the law. That reformulation constitutes already a sort of systematization, an incipient legal science.

At what moment in its development would legal science have attained the systematic stage? The question itself, asked of many other sciences, would be difficult to answer if system is understood in a very strict or rigorous way. The rearrangement and reformulation of normative materials — authoritative orders, rules of custom, traditions, value judgments, moral principles, technical definitions in the law itself, etc. —

are a very important part of what legal science, in its dogmatic form, in effect does, with various degrees of refinement. Perhaps the most elementary form of that initial systematization task is done professionally by the bureaucratically organized personnel of state administrations, with the pragmatical purpose of an easier retrieval of normative materials and, consequently, of a simpler and ordered application of its prescriptions. It is supposed that the jurist, as a scientist, would accomplish a more refined form of systematization of the same normative material with a pure theoretical interest in view. Perhaps it happens so, although normally jurists are not so purely theoretically inclined, nor so politically naive. In any case, the systematization effort made by bureaucrats or by legal scientists has a practical effect on the application of the law to cases. To inquire what kind of practical effect, in the resolution of cases, the systematization effort of legal science has, is the question that this paper tries to answer.

It has to be admitted, in principle, that a systematic reformulation of the legal order of a state, in a coherent and systematically ordered theoretical discourse, would not, if true, increase in any way the normative information given by the normative sentences (of various kinds) that constitute the legal order. By normative information, I understand that information received by the receptor of the normative function (in Kelsen's sense) about the deontic character of an action, activity or situation.

But that is an ideal situation. In practice, legal dogmatics performs its systematization task with an implicit practical purpose in view: to restrict the decision criteria applicable to concrete cases and, thus, to eliminate some sets of possible solutions. This restriction function of systematization remains obscure even to a critical examination of dogmatics, because the supposed identity, as regards normative information, between the legal material issued by the legislator and the systematic reformulation done by legal scientists is taken for granted. Strictly, once a certain set of norms to be accepted as the basis of a systematic construction is established, the consequence set of its derived norms is also — theoretically at least and when the derivation rules are precisely defined — circumscribed. But the systematization effort never pretends to establish more than a limited subset of the norms of the legal order, defined for a common content or for practical reasons. Systematization, then, is always of a very restricted and limited scope; as a result, legal science offers a number of so-called theories concerning different topics of legal interest. Those so-called theories may strike one as being completely independent: it would be difficult to find, for instance, clear connections between the penal theory regarding delictual intention (dolus, culpa), as developed by continental dogmatics, and the old Roman doctrine about civil responsibility, where dolus and culpa again reappear. Furthermore, legal dogmatic theories are in some way or another arranged in certain logical orders: some theories imply others, others are considered more general or particular (as the case may be) than others. So we find theories about some contracts (for instance: "real" contracts) jointly with more general theories concerning civil contracts, civil obligations in general, legal agreements, etc.; according to the practical interest taken into account, each of those theories is accepted by legal scientists and legal practitioners, as a closed field. Some of them even pretend to be autonomous branches of legal science. The legal order, as an ideal totality covering all promulgated and derived positive norms, is construed as a sort of quarry where one is supposed to look for the norms necessary to justify some decision; the legal order is, therefore, an imprecise horizon where potentially new principles and norms may appear if the restricted systematized legal order reformulated by legal science proves to be insufficient as a justification to the solution the judge wants to arrive at. The judge — the decision authority — resorts to legal theories (i. e.: partial systematizations of normative material) as a recognized source of justification principles for his decision. They may be also other kinds of justification principles. But, as such, legal theories, as defined, are used purposely, and not merely as subject to theoretical evaluation.

If the (normative) meaning of a norm may be interpreted as the set of its logical (compatible) normative consequences, the systemic relationships established between norms by the systematization efforts of legal science somehow determine the possible meaning of the norms taken into account for the resolution of a case. According to the extension of the set of norms systematized, the meaning of each norm may be altered as its logical relationships with other norms are modified. Norms are not applied in isolation; their effective meaning is determined by the set in which it is included. Systematization, therefore, operates as a restriction in the semantic domain of the set included in the ordered set called a "legal system"; pragmatically, the possible solutions those norms admit are restricted by those systemic limitations. It is clear that if a set of norms is not rationally ordered (systematized), the field of possible solutions remains imprecise or all possible solutions are not excluded (which is the same thing). Lack of systemic order implies, tacitly, a widened discretionary power conferred to the judge. But if the judge has the duty to give reasoned decisions, he must refer to a set of norms logically ordered as a partial coherent whole; the possible solutions attainable by the judge are thus limited.

The restriction that every (partial) systematized set of norms imposes on the judge has a counterpart that must be given the necessary attention. The point is this: there is no unique systematization of any given set of norms. According to the criteria of derivation and the ordering procedures chosen, any set of norms can be systematized differently. From a strictly theoretical point of view, one should say that if the basis of the systems and its derivation rules are equivalent, the different systems arrived at would also be equivalent (i. e. the same set of normative consequences could be derived from them); therefore, in principle it would be indifferent to the judge and the political circumstances where the judge acts, which of the possible systems is effectively used as normative justification of the judgment.

In practice, nevertheless, that rigorous equivalence between different systematizations is no more than a theoretical supposition, not a proven logical equivalence. Jurists elaborate different theories on some normative materials identified as ones that concern the same topic or problem; those theories, which have different purpose and different theoretical depth, cannot be said to be equivalent from a logical point of view; they do no have strictly the same normative consequences and, therefore, strictly speaking, they would not be used as equivalent in the justification of judicial decision. But, in practice, their character of "theories", accepted as such by a scientific and professional community, permits that they be used as an acknowledged reasoned justification of judgements. So, judges do not take into account theories in virtue of their intrinsic theoretical merits, but only inasmuch as they are effectively recognized by the scientific and professional community as "correct" partial systematizations of a subset of norms. When we speak of legal "theories", we do not by this term understand the same as other scientists do in other fields of scientific activities: in law, a theory is a reformulated and coherent set of norms that the judge can refer to as a valid justification of its decision. In a way, it is rhetorically supposed (but not logically proven) that the theory referred to must be such that its sentences imply the solution the judge wants to attain. As there are several theories, equivalent in their pragmatical utility, the judge can refer to any one of those theories without having to worry about some ideal theoretical cogency. Recourse to different theories opens the possibility of different decisions.

Systematization in legal science and practice, therefore, is not only a problem of theoretical constructions; it is, in a way, a matter of choice between different possible interpretations of the normative material available. Systematizations are alternative options for non-uniform solutions of practical cases.

It is a traditional thesis of sociology of knowledge that the erection of a systematic discourse on a topic, or the employment of more refined techniques of exposition, like axiomatization, represent a trend towards rationalization in the management of the topic or problem. As concerns law, Max Weber introduced the notion of "rationalization of law", not only to typify different historical kinds of legal organizations and societies, but also to describe hermeneutically the evolutions of legal orders. Law rationalization does not always imply an effective systematization of the legal material by legal science; however, the converse of this does seem to be true. In that sense, therefore, the systematization task done by legal sciences has always practical consequences for the decision making behaviour of judges and must be taken into account in the description of the law itself, because systematization is an operation that modifies the structure and the content of the law.[8]

III. Legal Systems and Closed Criteria of Decision

Lawyers do not work with "haphazard collection of legal rules", as J. Raz describes one possible situation, nor with a "rhapsody" of norms, as Kant perhaps would have said. They work with partial systematized subsets of norms. In some circumstances and for some specific purposes, which are not easy to define, lawyers refer to some particular set of norms which have been the object of a sort of prescientific systematization. That is, perhaps, what the lawyer understands when he speaks of the unity of the norms constituting an institution: family matters, for instance, or commercial undertakings and contracts. The classificatory criteria for those distinctions are vague, as the notion of a prescientific system itself is a concept in need of a more precise conceptual definition or explanation. It seems plausible to think that a prescientific systematization is nothing more than an intuitive approximation to an ideal theoretical systematization. Both notions — ideal theoretical systematization and prescientific systematization — resemble ideal conceptual types much more than real descriptions of the result of the scientific and practical work of the jurist.

If a legal order were a mere haphazard collection of rules, every case would be decided unpredictably, that is, on *ad hoc* normative basis. The decision criteria, then, would have to be interpreted as an open model of decision making. That is, action and its results could be foreseen, but there is no social (or even theoretical) interest in this foresight. The decision making action is then taken as unique, in the sense that it is not evaluated in its relationship with other alternatives. Furthermore, there would be no accepted preference criteria between the eventual

[8] Cf. *S. I. Benn/G. W. Mortimore* (eds), Rationality and the Social Sciences, London 1976.

possible alternatives. The decision making would, therefore, lack what Max Weber called a *Zweckrationalität;* it is not a purposeful rational action; it expresses only the axiological attitude of the judge.

If the legal order appears as a haphazard collection, the selection of the subset of norms required to justify the decision is, in principle, random: any subset could be referred to by the judge according to his own personal and value-laden criteria. The logical relationships that could be established among the haphazard collection of norms are not taken into account; there is no reason to reject a decision as contradictory to the selected set of norms, as these can always be reshuffled at will. It is not possible to formulate a cogent and not ad hoc set of objectives to be attained through the decision making; objectives are always particular and specific for the concrete case. Therefore, the decision making action of the judge is permanently influenced by changing circumstances and it is not possible to assert that judicial judgments are implied by express general principles or norms. Open models of decision making are adopted in specific social situations: not only in primitively structured societies or social groups, but also in situations of emergency or urgency.

The systematization task accomplished by bureaucratic officials or by legal scientists makes it possible to limit the application of the open model of decision making and, thus, to restrict the discretionary powers of decision authorities.[9] Although systematization does not determine univocally a certain possible alternative as a solution of a case, it restricts stringently the subsets of norms and principles that can be used as rational justification of a decision. As the number of alternatives is thus limited, and as the decision must be logically compatible with the set of norms chosen, decisions become much better foreseeable. Judicial decision making approaches thus a model of closed decision.

---

[9] Cf. *S. S. Nagel/M. G. Neef,* Decision Theory and the Legal Process, Toronto 1979.

III. Das Rechtssystem und seine gesellschaftliche Basis

IDEALTYPEN FÜR EINE THEORIE DER KONSTITUTIVEN REGELN

Von Amedeo G. Conte, Pavía

„Die reale Erklärung des realen Geschehens interessiert mich nicht. [...]
Mich interessiert das geistig Typische, [...] das Gespenstische des Geschehens."

Robert Musil

Einführung

Was ist eine konstitutive Regel?

Diese Frage ist falsch (sie „irrt in bezug auf die Antwort, welche sie erwartet"[1]). Sie ist falsch, weil sie die falsche Präsupposition hat, daß es *einen einzigen* Begriff der konstitutiven Regel gibt. Wie ich in früheren Arbeiten belegt habe, hat man in wenigstens *zwei* verschiedenen Sinnen von konstitutiven Regeln (*constitutive rules, règles constitutives, regole* oder *norme costitutive, konstitutiva regler, konstitutiiviset säännöt*) geschrieben. Für diese beiden Sinne habe ich die Bezeichnungen '*eidetisch*-konstitutive Regel' und '*thetisch*-konstitutive Regel' eingeführt.

Im vorliegenden Referat bestimme ich das Verhältnis zwischen *eidetisch*-konstitutiven und *thetisch*-konstitutiven Regeln, und von diesen beiden Regeltypen unterscheide ich eine dritte Art konstitutiver Regeln: die Regeln, die ich *anankastisch*-konstitutive Regeln nenne. Die eidetisch-konstitutiven Regeln untersuche ich im Abschnitt I, die anankastisch-konstitutiven Regeln im Abschnitt II, die thetisch-konstitutiven Regeln im Abschnitt III[2].

I. Eidetisch-konstitutive Regeln

1. Die eidetisch-konstitutiven Regeln (*eidetic-constitutive rules, règles éidético-constitutives, regole eidetico-costitutive*) sind Regeln, die in dreifachem Bedingungsverhältnis zur durch sie konstituierten Praxis

[1] Vgl. *Hertz* (1894), S. 9: „Aber offenbar irrt die Frage in bezug auf die Antwort, welche sie erwartet."

[2] Ich danke Tecla Mazzarese und Giampaolo M. Azzoni für ihre zahlreichen Kommentare.

stehen: Sie sind (eidetische) *Denkbarkeits*bedingung, (alethische) *Möglichkeits*bedingung, (noetische) *Wahrnehmbarkeits*bedingung.

Der paradigmatische Fall der eidetisch-konstitutiven Regeln sind die Regeln vom Schachspiel. (Beispiele: 'Der Läufer soll diagonal gezogen werden'; 'Die Rochade ist verboten, wenn der König unter Schach ist'; 'Schachmatt liegt vor, wenn der König unter Schach ist und durch keinen Zug dem Schach entzogen werden kann'.)

Die Praxis: Schachspiel und ihre Einheiten (die Steine, z. B. der Läufer; die Pragmeme, z. B. der Läuferzug und die Rochade; die ludischen Status, z. B. das Schach und das Schachmatt) bestehen nicht vor (und unabhängig von) ihren Regeln. Erst und nur die Spielregeln konstituieren das Spiel und (im Spiel) die Spieleinheiten (Steine, Pragmeme, ludische Status).

2. Die eidetisch-konstitutiven Regeln sind 1964 von John R. Searle im Rahmen seiner Theorie der „*constitutive rules*" thematisiert worden. Aber weder der *Begriff*, noch die *Bezeichnung* 'konstitutive Regel' stammen eigentlich von Searle.

Der *Begriff:* konstitutive Regel ist schon vor Searle belegt. Die Konstitutivität der eidetisch-konstitutiven Regeln war schon von mehreren Autoren (Johannes Thomae, Max Weber, Czesław Znamierowski, Ludwig Wittgenstein, Ernst Mally, Antonino Pagliaro, Alf Ross, John Rawls) eingesehen worden. Insbesondere:

— Die Idee, daß die Identität der Steine im Schachspiel durch die Spielregeln bestimmt wird (d. h. die Idee, daß eine Figur der deontische Ort ihrer Regeln ist), ist bei mehreren Autoren vorhanden. Johannes Thomae schreibt davon schon 1898; Ludwig Wittgenstein 1934 (er verwendet sogar ein Paronym von 'eidetisch', nämlich '*idea*', und das Verb '*to constitute*' dort, wo er schreibt, daß „the rules constitute the idea" des Königs im Schachspiel[3]); Ernst Mally (der erste der Erfinder von 'Deontik' und 'deontisch') um 1943.

— Die Idee, daß die Züge im Schachspiel durch die Regeln ermöglicht werden, ist schon bei Czesław Znamierowski (1924) vorhanden.

— Die Idee, daß ein Zug erst und nur durch die Vermittlung der Spielregeln wahrnehmbar und also solcher erkennbar ist, ist bei Max Weber (1907) und Alf Ross (1953) belegt.

Nicht nur der Begriff, sondern auch die *Bezeichnung* 'konstitutive Regel' ist schon vor Searle belegt, und zwar bei Antonino Pagliaro, der 1951 von „*regole costitutive*" des Schachspiels geschrieben hat.

[3] Vgl. *Wittgenstein* (1979), S. 86—87.

Nach dieser schematischen philosophischen Bestandaufnahme werde ich jetzt Searles Begriff *constitutive rule* einer immanenten Kritik unterziehen.

3. Searles Begriff *constitutive rule* ist in zweifacher Hinsicht undifferenziert.

a) *Erstens* unterscheidet Searle nicht zwischen *deontischen* eidetisch-konstitutiven Regeln (Beispiele davon sind: 'Der Läufer soll diagonal gezogen werden'; 'Die Rochade ist verboten, wenn der König unter Schach ist'; 'Der König soll dem Schach entzogen werden') und *ontischen* eidetisch-konstitutiven Regeln.

Der Begriff: ontische eidetisch-konstitutive Regel mag selbstwidersprüchlich erscheinen. Paradoxerweise aber sind die paradigmatischen Fälle der *constitutive rules* von Searle Regeln, die nicht deontisch, sondern ontisch sind ('To make a promise is to undertake an obligation'; 'A checkmate is made when the king is attacked in such a way that no move will leave it unattacked'; 'A touchdown is scored when a player has possession of the ball in the opponents' end zone while a play is in progress').

Es ist nun nicht so, daß Searle ontische und deontische eidetisch-konstitutive Regeln gleichsetzt: Vielmehr trifft er einfach keine Unterscheidung. Dagegen halte ich die Unterscheidung für notwendig.

Zwar ist es möglich, eine deontische eidetisch-konstitutive Regel wie 'Der Läufer soll diagonal gezogen werden' in eine ontische (etwa 'Notwendige Bedingung, damit ein Läuferzug erfolgt, ist die diagonale Versetzung der Figur') zu übersetzen. Aber es ist unmöglich, eine ontische eidetisch-konstitutive Regel wie 'A checkmate is made when the king is attacked in such a way that no move will leave it unattacked' in eine deontische zu übersetzen.

b) *Zweitens* trifft Searle keine Unterscheidung (innerhalb seiner ontischen eidetisch-konstitutiven Regeln) zwischen den Regeln, die ich *X-Regeln* nennen möchte, und den Regeln, die ich *Y-Regeln* nennen möchte. Ein Test, der sich dazu eignet, die Heterogenität dieser Regeln zu zeigen, ist mir paradoxerweise durch eine Stelle bei Searle selbst suggeriert worden. Nach Searle können die *constitutive rules* auf die standardisierte Form '*X* counts as *Y* ('*X* gilt als *Y*') zurückgeführt werden. Nun zeigt ausgerechnet die Übersetzung in die standardisierte Form, daß Searles ontische *constitutive rules* nicht homogen sind: Einige sind *X*-Regeln, andere sind *Y*-Regeln.

— *X-Regeln:* Searles *constitutive rule* über das Versprechen ('To make a promise is to undertake an obligation') bestimmt, *als was* das Versprechen gilt, d. h., welchen Wert das Versprechen hat. Ihre Übersetzung in die 'X counts as Y'-Form ist: 'Das Versprechen gilt als Pflichtübernahme'. In dieser Übersetzung nimmt das Wort 'Versprechen' die *X*-Stelle ein. Daher die Bezeichnung '*X*-Regel'.

— *Y-Regeln:* Searles *constitutive rule* über das Schachmatt ('A checkmate is made when the king is attached in such a way that no move will leave it unattacked') bestimmt nicht *als was* das Schachmatt gilt, sondern *was als* Schachmatt gilt. Ihre Übersetzung in die '*X* counts as Y'-Form ist: 'Die Lage, in der sich der König durch keinen Zug dem Schach entzogen werden kann, gilt als Schachmatt'. In dieser Übersetzung nimmt das Wort 'Schachmatt' die *Y*-Stelle ein. Daher die Bezeichnung '*Y*-Regel'[4].

4. Von den *eidetisch*-konstitutiven Regeln (die notwendige Bedingung dessen *sind,* was sie regeln) unterscheide ich andere, andersartige konstitutive Regeln, und zwar die Regeln, die eine notwendige Bedingung *setzen:* die *anankastisch*-konstitutiven Regeln[5].

[4] Die von mir eingeführte Unterscheidung zwischen *X*-Regeln und *Y*-Regeln ist eine strukturelle. Selbstverständlich ist es möglich, daß es eine Regel über das Schachmatt gibt, in der 'Schachmatt' die *X*-Stelle einnimmt (z. B.: 'Das Schachmatt gilt als Verlieren'). Und symmetrisch ist es möglich, daß es eine *Y*-Regel über das Versprechen gibt (z. B.: 'Die Äußerung des Satzes "Hiermit verspreche ich, *p* zu tun" gilt als Versprechen').

[5] Zwei erkenntnistheoretische Fragen über eidetisch-konstitutive Regeln. Die *erste* betrifft die Erkenntnis *von* eidetisch-konstitutiven Regeln, die *zweite* die Erkenntnis *durch* eidetisch-konstitutive Regeln.

Erste Frage. Können eidetisch-konstitutive Regeln aus der regelkonformen Handlung erschlossen werden? (Z. B.: Können die Schachregeln aus der Beobachtung von Zügen erschlossen werden?)

Die *Antwort* ist eindeutig. Die eidetisch-konstitutiven Regeln (z. B. die Schachregeln) können nicht aus der Erfahrung der regelkonformen Handlung (in unserem Beispiel, aus der Erfahrung von Zügen) erschlossen werden, weil die Regeln selbst notwendige Möglichkeitsbedingung jener Erfahrung sind.

Es ist unmöglich zu erkennen, daß eine gewisse Bewegung ein Zug ist (und *a fortiori* ist es unmöglich zu erkennen, um welchen Zug es sich handelt), wenn man die Regeln nicht schon kennt, die jenen Zug konstituieren. (Z. B.: Die Erfahrung einer Rochade ist erst und nur dann möglich, wenn man über das εἶδος: Rochade verfügt. Erst und nur in bezug auf die Regeln ist es möglich, eine Bewegung als *token* vom *type:* Rochade zu deuten.)

Es ist ein ὕστερον πρότερον, eidetisch-konstitutive Regeln aus einer Erfahrung zu erschließen, die durch die Regeln selbst vermittelt und ermöglicht worden ist.

Zweite Frage. In welchem Sinne (wenn überhaupt) ermöglichen eidetisch-konstitutive Regeln die Erkenntnis der regelkonformen Handlung?

Die *Antwort* ist nicht eindeutig. Die eidetisch-konstitutiven Regeln gestatten zwar, *tokens* der durch sie konstituierten *types* zu erkennen, aber sie gestatten nicht, das Individuelle in seinem eigenen Individualsein (dieses Wortspiel hat mir Hans-Georg Gadamer suggeriert), das ἴδιον, idiographisch zu erkennen.

Mit einem Wortspiel, das auf der Assonanz von ἴδιον und εἶδος (die mit 'idiographisch' bzw. 'eidetisch' zusammenhängen) beruht, kann man folgendes

II. Anankastisch-konstitutive Regeln

1. Die anankastisch-konstitutiven Regeln (*anankastic-constitutive rules, règles anankastico-constitutives, regole anankastico-costitutive*) sind Regeln, die eine notwendige (ἀνάγκη = Notwendigkeit) Gültigkeitsbedingung setzen. Ich gebe zwei Beispiele.

Eine *erste* anankastisch-konstitutive Regel ist der Art. 602 des italienischen Bürgerlichen Gesetzbuches: „Das holographe Testament soll [...] vom Erblasser eigenhändig unterzeichnet werden." Nach der geläufigen Interpretation setzt diese Regel eine notwendige Gültigkeitsbedingung des holographen Testaments. Sie schreibt die eigenhändige Unterzeichnung nicht an sich, sondern als notwendige Bedingung dafür, daß ein Akt als holographes Testament gilt, vor.

Eine *zweite* anankastisch-konstitutive Regel ist der Art. 782 des italienischen Bürgerlichen Gesetzbuches: „Die Schenkung soll mittels öffentlicher Urkunde erfolgen"[6].

2. Wie verhalten sich die anankastisch-konstitutiven Regeln zu den eidetisch-konstitutiven? Den Unterschied zwischen eidetisch-konstitutiven und anankastisch-konstitutiven Regeln habe ich versuchsweise anhand der Unterscheidung von *connotation* und *denotation* im Sinne John Stuart Mills formuliert.

Eidetisch-konstitutive Regeln und anankastisch-konstitutive Regeln stehen nicht im selben Verhältnis zur *connotation* des Praxeonyms (des *nomen actionis*), das den Akt bezeichnet, den sie betreffen. ('Praxeonym' im Sinne von '*nomen actionis*', 'Name einer Handlung, eines Aktes', habe ich nach dem Muster von 'Toponym' usw. geprägt.)

Die *eidetisch*-konstitutiven Regeln bestimmen die *connotation* der Praxeonyme. (Z. B.: Im Falle des Schachspiels bestimmen sie die *con-*

---

sagen: Die eidetisch-konstitutiven Regeln gestatten zwar die Erkenntnis nach einem εἶδος, aber sie gestatten keine Erkenntnis des ἴδιον. Sie sind kein Werkzeug idiographischen Verstehens des ἴδιον; sie sind Werkzeug eidographischen Deutens nach einem (durch sie konstituierten) εἶδος.

[6] 'Anankastisch' hat Georg Henrik von Wright in die heutige philosophische Sprache eingeführt. Vgl. *von Wright* (1963 a), S. 10 und *von Wright* (1963 b), S. 157. Während von Wright '*anankastic*' auf *apophantische Sätze* über das Bestehen notwendiger Bedingungen und auf (alethische) *Modalverben* bezieht, verwende ich 'anankastisch' in bezug auf *Regeln*. In *Conte* (1983 b) habe ich nämlich den Begriff: anankastische Regel eingeführt, und in *Conte* (1985) spreche ich zum ersten Male von anankastisch-konstitutiven Regeln.

'Anankastisch' in bezug auf Regeln zu verwenden, ist kein willkürlicher Schritt. Einen Präzedenzfall meines Sprachgebrauchs habe ich bei Platon entdeckt, bei dem (zwar in einem ganz anderen Sinne) ἀναγκαστικός in Verbindung mit νόμος (Regel, Gesetz) vorkommt.

notation der Termini, welche die Pragmeme des Spiels bezeichnen: 'Läuferzug', 'Rochade', ...) Die *anankastisch*-konstitutiven Regeln bestimmen dagegen nicht die *connotation*, sondern die *denotation* der jeweiligen Praxeonyme. (Z. B.: Die oben erwähnte Regel über Schenkung setzt voraus, daß das Praxeonym 'Schenkung' schon eine *connotation* hat und bestimmt seine *denotation*, grenzt sie dadurch ab, daß sie eine notwendige Bedingung dafür setzt, daß ein Akt als Schenkung gilt.)

3. Die Heterogenität von eidetisch-konstitutiven und anankastisch-konstitutiven Regeln erklärt, warum die eidetisch-konstitutiven Regeln (im Gegensatz zu den anankastisch-konstitutiven Regeln) nicht in Antinomie zueinander stehen können.

Die eidetisch-konstitutiven Regeln können nicht in Antinomie zueinander stehen, eben weil sie die *connotation* der Praxeonyme bestimmen, welche die jeweiligen Pragmeme bezeichnen.

Nehmen wir an (es ist ein Gedankenexperiment), daß es über die Rochade zwei Regeln gibt: 'Die Rochade ist verboten, wenn der König unter Schach ist' und 'Die Rochade ist erlaubt, wenn der König unter Schach ist'. Stehen diese beiden Regeln in Antinomie zueinander? Paradoxerweise nicht, wenn es sich um zwei eidetisch-konstitutive Regeln handelt. Sind sie eidetisch-konstitutiv, dann bestimmt jede der beiden Regeln je eine *connotation* des Praxeonyms 'Rochade', so daß 'Rochade' in der einen Regel nicht dieselbe *connotation* hat, die (das homonyme Praxeonym) 'Rochade' in der anderen Regel hat.

III. Thetisch-konstitutive Regeln

1. Die thetisch-konstitutiven Regeln (*thetic-constitutive rules, règles thético-constitutives, regole thetico-costitutive*) sind Regeln, die kein Verhalten vorschreiben, sondern einen institutionellen Sachverhalt unmittelbar setzen (θέσις = Setzung).

Beispiel: der Art. 45 des italienischen Bürgerlichen Gesetzbuches: „Der Entmündigte teilt den Wohnsitz des Vormunds." Im Gegensatz zur *präskriptiven* Regel, die dem Professor *vorschreibt*, am Universitätsort zu wohnen (Art. 7 des Gesetzes Nr. 311 vom 18. März 1958), *schreibt* die *askriptive* Regel über den Wohnsitz des Entmündigten einen Wohnsitz thetisch *zu*.

Die Theorie der thetisch-konstitutiven Regeln gehört zur Theorie der Performativität: Diese Regeln sind nämlich eine Untermenge der Menge der performativen Sprechakte, die ich thetische Sprechakte genannt habe. Die Bezeichnung 'thetisch-konstitutive Regel' weist eben auf den

Begriff: thetischer Sprechakt hin, den ich 1975 in meinem Referat „Aspekte der Semantik der deontischen Sprache“ eingeführt habe[7].

2. Wie verhalten sich die Begriffe: thetisch-konstitutive Regel, anankastisch-konstitutive Regel, eidetisch-konstitutive Regel zueinander? Das Verhältnis dieser drei Idealtypen für eine Theorie der konstitutiven Regeln stelle ich schematisch anhand des Begriffes: Bedingung dar.

Sowohl die *thetisch*-konstitutiven als auch die *eidetisch*-konstitutiven Regeln *sind* Bedingung dessen, was sie konstituieren. Was sie voneinander unterscheidet, ist die *Art der Bedingung.*

Die *eidetisch*-konstitutiven Regeln sind *notwendige* Bedingung der durch sie konstituierten Praxis[8]. Die *thetisch*-konstitutiven Regeln dagegen sind *hinreichende* Bedingung des durch sie konstituierten Sachverhalts[9].

Was die *anankastisch*-konstitutiven Regeln von den eidetisch-konstitutiven und von den thetisch-konstitutiven Regeln unterscheidet, ist nicht die *Art der Bedingung,* sondern das *Bedingungsverhältnis,* und zwar die Tatsache, daß die anankastisch-konstitutiven Regeln keine (notwendigen bzw. hinreichenden) Bedingungen *sind,* sondern (notwendige) Bedingungen *setzen.*

Bibliographie

Carcaterra, G. (1974), Le norme costitutive, Giuffrè, Milano.

Conte, A. G. (1977), Aspekte der Semantik der deontischen Sprache, in: A. G. Conte/R. Hilpinen/G. H. von Wright (Hrsg.), Deontische Logik und Semantik, Athenaion, Wiesbaden, S. 59—73.

[7] Das Referat „Aspekte der Semantik der deontischen Sprache“ habe ich beim Kolloquium „Deontische Logik und Semantik“ im Zentrum für interdisziplinäre Forschung, Universität Bielefeld, am 21. März 1975 vorgetragen. Der dort eingeführte Begriff: thetischer Sprechakt weist auffällige Ähnlichkeiten mit dem von John R. Searle gleichzeitig eingeführten Begriff: *declaration* auf. Vgl. *Searle* (1975). Mein Begriff: thetisch-konstitutive Regel entspricht nur teilweise dem Begriff: *norma costitutiva,* den Gaetano Carcaterra in einem wichtigen Buch thematisiert hat. Vgl. *Carcaterra* (1974).

[8] Jede einzelne eidetisch-konstitutive Regel ist notwendige Bedingung der jeweiligen Praxis; erst die Gesamtheit der eidetisch-konstitutiven Regeln ist auch hinreichende Bedingung der durch sie konstituierten Praxis.

[9] Das Bedingungsverhältnis der thetisch-konstitutiven Regeln zum durch sie thetisch konstituierten Sachverhalt kann man durch die elegante Paronomasie von 'Bedingung' und 'Ding' formulieren, die in *Friedrich Wilhelm Joseph Schellings* Frühschrift „Vom Ich als Princip der Philosophie“, 1795, vorkommt: „*Bedingen* heißt die Handlung, wodurch etwas zum *Ding* wird, *bedingt,* das was zum *Ding* gemacht ist.“ Eine thetisch-konstitutive Regel ist nämlich *Bedingung* des konstituierten Sachverhaltes in dem Sinne, daß durch sie „etwas zum *Ding* wird“.

— (1981 a), Konstitutive Regeln und Deontik, in: E. Morscher/R. Stranzinger (Hrsg.), Ethik. Akten des V. Wittgenstein-Symposiums, Hölder-Pichler-Tempsky, Wien, S. 82—86.

— (1981 b), Variationen über Wittgensteins Regelbegriff, in: R. Haller (Hrsg.), Sprache und Erkenntnis als soziale Tatsache, Hölder-Pichler-Tempsky, Wien, S. 69—78.

— (1983 a), Paradigmi d'analisi della regola in Wittgenstein, in: R. Egidi (Hrsg.), Wittgenstein, Guida, Napoli, S. 37—82.

— (1983 b), Regola costitutiva, condizione, antinomia, in: U. Scarpelli (Hrsg.), La teoria generale del diritto. Studi dedicati a Norberto Bobbio, Comunità, Milano, S. 21—39.

— (1985), Phénoménologie du langage déontique, in: G. Kalinowski/F. Selvaggi (Hrsg.), Les fondements logiques de la pensée normative, Editrice Pontificia Università Gregoriana, Roma, S. 179—193.

Hertz, H. (1894), Die Prinzipien der Mechanik, Barth, Leipzig.

Mally, E. (1971), Logische Schriften, Reidel, Dordrecht.

Pagliaro, A. (1951), Le regole del giuoco, in: Idea, vol. 3, 22, S. 1 und S. 6.

Rawls, J. (1955), Two Concepts of Rules, in: The Philosophical Review, vol. 64, S. 3—32.

Ross, A. (1953), Om ret og retfaerdighed, Nyt Nordisk Forlag A. Busck, København.

Searle, J. R. (1964 a), How to Derive 'Ought' from 'Is', in: The Philosophical Review, vol. 73, S. 43—58.

— (1964 b), What Is a Speech Act?, in: M. Black (Hrsg.), Philosophy in America, Allen and Unwin, London, S. 221—239.

— (1975), A Taxonomy of Illocutionary Acts, in: K. Gunderson (Hrsg.), Language, Mind and Knowledge, University of Minnesota Press, Minneapolis, S. 344—369.

Thomae, J. K. (1898), Elementare Theorie der analytischen Functionen einer complexen Veränderlichen, Nebert, Halle.

Weber, M. (1907), R. Stammlers „Überwindung" der materialistischen Geschichtsauffassung, in: Archiv für Sozialwissenschaft und Sozialpolitik, Bd. 24, S. 94—151.

Wittgenstein, L. (1979), Wittgenstein's Lectures, Cambridge, 1932—1935, edited by A. Ambrose, Blackwell, Oxford.

von Wright, G. H. (1963 a), Norm and Action, Routledge and Kegan Paul, London.

— (1963 b), The Varieties of Goodness, Routledge and Kegan Paul, London.

Znamierowski, Cz. (1924), Podstawowe pojęcia teorji prawa, I, Fiszer i Majewski, Poznań.

PROZESSRECHT UND MATERIELLES RECHT ALS TEILSYSTEME EINER RECHTSORDNUNG

Von Hilmar Fenge, Hannover

I.

Viele Rechtsordnungen kennen eine deutliche Ausgrenzung des Prozeßrechts aus dem Bereich des gesamten Rechts. Es gibt insoweit nicht nur jeweils besondere gesetzliche Kodifikationen dieser Rechtsmaterie. Auch im Lehr- und Wissenschaftsbetrieb wird Prozeßrecht gesondert dargestellt und bearbeitet. Lehrstühle und Forschungsinstitute an den Universitäten sind ausdrücklich, allein oder jedenfalls in Verbindung mit anderen Fachbezeichnungen, dem Prozeßrecht gewidmet, die Prozeßrechtslehrer in besonderen Vereinigungen zur gemeinsamen wissenschaftlichen Fortentwicklung des Prozeßrechts zusammengeschlossen, spezielle Fachtagungen, Zeitschriften und Publikationsreihen mit der Erörterung prozessualer Fragen befaßt. Und in der Rechtspraxis wird wiederum die so betriebene Arbeit nutzbar gemacht für die Entscheidung zahlreicher Einzelprobleme. Die Grenzziehung zwischen Prozeßrecht und materiellem Recht selbst dient als Argumentationstopos bei der Begründung richterlicher Urteile.

Das in dieser Weise ausgegrenzte Prozeßrecht läßt sich als ein „System" auffassen. Umfassende Lehrdarstellungen verwenden diesen Ausdruck in ihrem Titel[1] oder benutzen ihn wenigstens zur Kennzeichnung des Hauptteils des Werkes.[2] Auch einzelne Abhandlungen machen ausdrücklich spezielle Teile des Prozeßrechts unter der Bezeichnung eines „Systems" zu ihrem Gegenstand. So wird etwa — um einige Beispiele aus dem Bereich des Zivilprozeßrechts zu nennen — das „System der Beweisaufnahme und der mündlichen Verhandlung"[3], die „Systematik des Wiederaufnahmeverfahrens"[4], die „Systematik der Revisions-

---

[1] *Hellwig/Oertmann*, System des Deutschen Zivilprozeßrechts, 1912/1919; *Carnelutti*, Sistema del diritto processuale civile, 1936/1939; *Rammos*, Σύστημα πολιτικῆς δικονομίας, 1931/1940.

[2] *Prieto-Castro*, Tratado de derecho procesal civil, libro tercero: Sistema del derecho procesal civil, 1982.

[3] *Rammos* (griechisch) AID 1934, S. 35 ff. u. 238 ff.

[4] *Gilles*, in: ZZP 78 (1965), S. 466 ff., 80 (1967), S. 391 ff.

gründe“[5], oder das „Rechtsbehelfssystem der Zwangsvollstreckung“[6] behandelt.

Systematisch ist insoweit zunächst die Anordnung des Stoffes in seiner äußeren Darstellung. Das Prozeßrecht wird als ein Zusammenhang verschiedener Begriffe vorgeführt, die ihrerseits wiederum in nach bestimmten Prinzipien Gemeinsamkeiten aufweisende Gruppen zusammengefaßt sind. Klassifikation und Prinzipienbildung bestimmen das Bild einer Systematisierung mit dem Ziel, Wissenschaft im Sinne Kants, d. h. „ein Ganzes der Erkenntnis als System und nicht bloß als Aggregat“[7] zu erreichen. Wechselnde Prinzipien kennzeichnen den jeweils persönlichen Stil der Darstellung, dokumentieren aber auch einen allgemeinen Erkenntnisfortschritt, der freilich nicht immer als geradlinige Entwicklung, sondern manchmal eher als Kreisbewegung erscheint.

Die systematischen Ordnungsleistungen erfüllen eine unbestreitbar notwendige didaktische Aufgabe. Sie dienen nicht nur der Unterrichtung des in den Stoff erstmals eindringenden Studenten, sondern geben auch noch dem mitten in der Berufspraxis stehenden Juristen Übersicht und fortwährende Orientierung über das, was in seinem Bereich möglich ist. Indem hier Grenzen in einem dogmatisch verfestigten Bezugsrahmen gezogen werden, verschafft sich eine selbstbewußte Wissenschaft darüber hinaus Einfluß auf die Entwicklung der Rechtspraxis. Das wissenschaftliche System tritt in Konkurrenz zu dem Rechtssatzsystem des Gesetzgebers; seine Erkenntnisfunktion geht über in eine Regelungsfunktion.

II.

Im folgenden soll zunächst der Wirkungsmechanismus prozeßrechtlicher Systematik im innerprozessualen Bereich beschrieben werden. Welche Überlegungen setzt wissenschaftliches Denken den Normen des Gesetzes entgegen, und mit welcher Argumentation wirkt es auf die Praxis ein? Drei Beispiele aus dem deutschen Zivilprozeßrecht[8] mögen unterschiedliche Formen dieses Vorgehens verdeutlichen:

a) Nach den Vorschriften der Zivilprozeßordnung (ZPO) unterliegt ein durch rechtskräftiges Urteil abgeschlossenes Verfahren in bestimmten Fällen der Wiederaufnahme. Die Wiederaufnahme muß durch eine Klage (Nichtigkeits- bzw. Restitutionsklage) erwirkt werden. § 589 I ZPO

[5] *Rimmelspacher*, in: ZZP 84 (1971), S. 41 ff.

[6] *Gaul*, in: ZZP 85 (1972), S. 251 ff.

[7] *Kant*, Logik § 95, Akademie-Textausgabe 1968, Bd. IX, S. 139.

[8] Die Beispiele sind dem Themenbereich der Abhandlungen zu Fußn. 4—6 entlehnt, ihre Behandlung deckt sich jedoch nicht in vollem Umfang mit der Auffassung der zitierten Autoren.

bestimmt hierzu: „Das Gericht hat von Amts wegen zu prüfen, ob die Klage an sich statthaft und ob sie in der gesetzlichen Form und Frist erhoben sei. Mangelt es an einem dieser Erfordernisse, so ist die Klage als unzulässig zu verwerfen." In den §§ 579, 580 ZPO sind im einzelnen die Gründe aufgeführt, nach denen eine solche Klage „stattfindet". Und in § 590 I ZPO heißt es dann: „Die Hauptsache wird, insoweit sie von dem Anfechtungsgrunde betroffen ist, von neuem verhandelt."

Bei unbefangener Betrachtung scheint also der Gesetzgeber hier ein Verfahren vorgesehen zu haben, das unter gewissen Zulässigkeitsvoraussetzungen eine erneute — und zwar von der ersten abweichende — Entscheidung des alten Rechtsstreits erlaubt. Wissenschaftliche Analyse trennt jedoch den Gang des Verfahrens rigoros in drei verschiedene Abschnitte. In einem stufenförmigen Aufbau seien Zulässigkeit und Begründetheit der Wiederaufnahmeklage sowie die „Hauptsache" nacheinander zu prüfen und entscheiden. Da jede Entscheidung über den nachgeordneten Verfahrensabschnitt die positive Erledigung des vorhergehenden voraussetze, müsse vor Eintritt in die erneute Prüfung der Hauptsache in jedem Fall zunächst das angefochtene Urteil aufgehoben werden. Möglicherweise sei dann ein zweites Urteil mit dem gleichen Inhalt zu erlassen. Absurde Konsequenzen dieser Ansicht zeigen sich etwa bei Anfechtung eines Scheidungsurteils gegenüber dem erneut verheirateten Partner: Liegt ein Wiederaufnahmegrund vor, so führt die Aufhebung des Scheidungsurteils auch dann zur Nichtigkeit der Zweitehe wegen Bigamie, wenn die Erstehe letztlich doch zu scheiden ist.

b) Gegen die Endurteile der Oberlandesgerichte findet in bürgerlichen Rechtsstreitigkeiten das Rechtsmittel der Revision zum Bundesgerichtshof in Karlsruhe statt. Gemäß § 549 I ZPO kann die Revision „nur darauf gestützt werden, daß die Entscheidung auf der Verletzung des Bundesrechts oder einer Vorschrift beruht, deren Geltungsbereich sich über den Bezirk eines Oberlandesgerichts hinaus erstreckt". § 550 ZPO bestimmt: „Das Gesetz ist verletzt, wenn eine Rechtsnorm nicht oder nicht richtig angewendet worden ist." Und § 551 ZPO nennt schließlich eine Reihe von Tatbeständen, bei deren Vorliegen eine Entscheidung „stets als auf einer Verletzung des Gesetzes beruhend anzusehen" ist.

Demnach wären nach der gesetzlichen Regelung zwei verschiedene Gruppen von Revisionsgründen voneinander zu unterscheiden: die in § 551 ZPO aufgeführten sogenannten „absoluten Revisionsgründe", auf denen stets, und die übrigen Gründe, auf denen im Einzelfall bei Erfüllung der gesetzlichen Voraussetzungen die angefochtene Entscheidung „beruht". Die wissenschaftliche Systematik der Revisionsgründe geht jedoch von einer Dreiteilung aus, indem sie innerhalb der relativen Revisionsgründe noch einmal differenziert: „Fehler des materiellen

Rechts" müßten die falsche Entscheidung „verursacht" haben in dem Sinne, daß diese bei richtiger Rechtsanwendung nicht getroffen worden wäre; bei „Verfahrensfehlern" genüge es dagegen, daß „ohne die Verletzung möglicherweise anders erkannt wäre". Praktisch wirkt sich diese Unterscheidung dahin aus, daß im Falle einer begründeten Verfahrensrüge, die nicht einen absoluten Revisionsgrund betrifft, dem Revisionskläger die Darlegung eines hypothetischen Kausalverlaufs zum Erfolg verhilft, während umgekehrt im Falle einer materiellen Rechtsverletzung dem Revisionsbeklagten hypothetische Erwägungen über eine zum gleichen Ergebnis führende Urteilsfindung bei anderer prozessualer Behandlung nicht zugute kommen.

c) Das Zwangsvollstreckungsrecht kennt verschiedene Rechtsbehelfe, die es dem Schuldner ermöglichen, gegen ihn eingeleitete Vollstreckungsmaßnahmen durch gerichtliche Entscheidung einstellen oder aufheben zu lassen. Einzelne dieser Rechtsbehelfe betreffen spezielle Bereiche der Zwangsvollstreckung. So kann das Vollstreckungsgericht nach § 813 a ZPO die Verwertung gepfändeter Sachen bis zu einem Jahr aussetzen, „wenn dies nach der Persönlichkeit und den wirtschaftlichen Verhältnissen des Schuldners sowie nach der Art der Schuld angemessen erscheint und nicht überwiegende Belange des Gläubigers entgegenstehen." Die Zwangsversteigerung eines Grundstücks kann nach § 30 a ZVG zweimal auf die Dauer von je sechs Monaten einstweilen eingestellt werden, „wenn Aussicht besteht, daß durch die Einstellung die Versteigerung vermieden wird, und wenn die Einstellung nach den persönlichen und wirtschaftlichen Verhältnissen des Schuldners sowie nach der Art der Schuld der Billigkeit entspricht." Darüber hinaus darf nach § 765 a ZPO das Vollstreckungsgericht ganz allgemein eine Vollstreckungsmaßnahme „ganz oder teilweise aufheben, untersagen oder einstweilen einstellen, wenn die Maßnahme unter voller Würdigung des Schutzbedürfnisses des Gläubigers wegen ganz besonderer Umstände eine Härte bedeutet, die mit den guten Sitten nicht vereinbar ist".

Die systematische Abgrenzung des zuletzt genannten allgemeinen Rechtsbehelfs zu den beiden anderen speziellen Rechtsbehelfen läßt sich unterschiedlich vollziehen. Entweder ordnet man alle Rechtsbehelfe unter dem gemeinsamen Wertungsgesichtspunkt des richterlichen Schuldnerschutzes zu einer Gruppe zusammen, in der dann die Regelung des § 765 a ZPO als eine Generalklausel erscheint, die durch die jeweilige Spezialregelung normativ verdrängt wird. Oder aber man sieht in ihrer Schutztendenz zur Abwehr sittenwidriger Härten ein besonderes Prinzip verwirklicht, das gleichrangig neben andere Prinzipien tritt, die, wie etwa die Förderung gesamtwirtschaftlich bedeutsamer ökonomischer Interessen, in den übrigen Normen zum Ausdruck kämen. Die verschiedenartige Systematisierung führt u. a. zu gegensätzlichen Antworten auf die Frage, ob aufgrund der allgemeinen Regel auch Vollstreckungsmaßnahmen im Bereich der Spezialregeln über die dort angegebene Zeit hinaus eingestellt werden können.

Die drei hier vorgeführten Argumentationsmuster bringen Systematik in unterschiedlicher Qualität zur Geltung. In dem ersten Beispiel geht es um eine rein begriffliche Abgrenzung nach einer nahezu willkürlich erscheinenden Konstruktion. Warum die Voraussetzungen für einen Erfolg der Wiederaufnahmeklage gerade so und nicht anders gruppiert werden und daß sie in der gewählten Anordnung nicht nur einen Denkzusammenhang, sondern einen Handlungszusammenhang bilden sollen, wird nicht einsichtig. Das zweite Beispiel verweist auf eine sachbezogene Struktur. Die Differenzierung der Revisionsgründe nach Verletzungen materieller und prozessualer Vorschriften erklärt sich daraus, daß das Revisionsgericht die materielle Rechtslage aufgrund eines verfahrensmäßig korrekt festgestellten Sachverhalts ohne weiteres selbst ermitteln kann, während es hinsichtlich der Auswirkungen verfahrensmäßig inkorrekter Feststellungen mangels einer entsprechenden eigenen Kompetenz auf Vermutungen angewiesen bleibt. Freilich wird insoweit nicht plausibel, d. h. hier: wertender Betrachtung nicht einsichtig, warum derartige Vermutungen zur Begründung relativer Revisionsgründe bei Verfahrensfehlern zugelassen, hypothetische Erwägungen über die ebenso wenig sicher feststellbaren Auswirkungen materieller Fehlvorstellungen auf prozessuale Verfahrensabläufe dagegen versagt werden. Für das dritte Beispiel systematischer Ordnung sind umgekehrt Wertungen grundlegend. Die Entscheidung über das Konkurrenzverhältnis der verschiedenen vollstreckungsrechtlichen Rechtsbehelfe wird nach ihrer Ausrichtung auf bestimmte Wertmaßstäbe getroffen, die ihrerseits vorausgesetzt werden. Wiederum fehlt dem systematischen Argument volle Überzeugungskraft, und zwar diesmal deswegen, weil die Exposition der hervorgekehrten Begriffe „gute Sitten" und „ökonomischer Nutzen" ohne einen die jeweilige Zuordnung notwendig bestimmenden Realitätsbezug bis zu einem gewissen Grade subjektive Beliebigkeit zuläßt.

Erst eine Verbindung der rein begrifflichen Formalisierung mit sachhaltigen und wertbezogenen Strukturen macht Systematik zu einem vollkommen einsichtigen Ordnungsfaktor mit handlungsbestimmender Kraft. Systembildungen, die diese Voraussetzungen erfüllen, folgen einer Methode, die sich als „Rechtfertigung" von bloßer regelorientierter „Begründung" oder dezisionistischer „Planung" abhebt[9]. Für ein System

[9] Vgl. *Fenge*, Systemvorstellungen über Begriff, Theorien, Konzeptionen und Methoden des Rechts, in: Zeitgenössische Rechtskonzeptionen, ARSP Supplementa Vol. I Part 2 (1982), S. 141/148.

des Prozeßrechts gilt insoweit nichts anderes als für jede andere Systematisierung im Rechtsbereich.

III.

Was ist nun die spezifische Differenz zwischen Prozeßrecht und materiellem Recht, die es erlaubt, die beiden Bereiche insgesamt als Teilsysteme einer Rechtsordnung anzusprechen? Schon ihre formale Relationsbeziehung ist nicht einfach zu bestimmen. Offenbar handelt es sich hier nicht um ein reines Verhältnis der Inklusion. Prozeßrecht ist nicht in dem Sinne ein Teil der gesamten Rechtsordnung, wie das System des Wiederaufnahmeverfahrens einen Teil des Prozeßrechts bildet. Prozeßrecht und materielles Recht stehen aber auch nicht derart als Teilgebiete nebeneinander, wie etwa Öffentliches Recht und Privatrecht oder weiter spezialisierte Fächer wie Verfassungsrecht, Verwaltungsrecht, Strafrecht, Bürgerliches Recht usw., die in ihrer Vereinigung zusammen als Rechtsordnung gedacht werden. Die ihnen eigentümliche Relation läßt sich eher als ein „Zusammenhang" beschreiben, in dem Sinne, daß „eine Veränderung des einen Objekts von einer entsprechenden Veränderung des anderen Objekts begleitet wird"[10]. Jedenfalls ist es einsichtig, daß einschneidende Umgestaltungen des Prozeßrechts die Qualität des materiellen Rechts beeinflussen, wenn auch in umgekehrter Richtung Abhängigkeiten weniger deutlich in Erscheinung treten[11]. Immerhin zeigt die Tatsache, daß der Gesetzgeber in speziellen Verfahrensordnungen für verschiedene Rechtsgebiete je nach deren besonderen Eigenheiten Prozeßrecht unterschiedlich auszugestalten pflegt, grundsätzlich beachtliche Züge einer Interdependenz.

Der Substanz nach muß die Unterscheidung in den drei Dimensionen angesetzt werden, in denen Recht allgemein theoretisch erfaßt und handelnd zur Entstehung gebracht wird, nämlich in den Dimensionen der Formen, Fakten und Werte:

a) Schon von der sprachlichen Bezeichnung her liegt es nahe, Prozeßrecht als formelles Recht dem materiellen Recht gegenüberzustellen. Auf die überragende Bedeutung von Formen im prozessualen Geschehen ist oft hingewiesen worden[12]. Formvorschriften sichern gerade im Prozeß eine rechtsstaatlichen Geboten entsprechende Gleichbehandlung, und zwar sowohl im Verhältnis der rechtssuchenden Bürger gegenüber den

---

[10] *Klaus/Buhr*, Philosophisches Wörterbuch, 8. Aufl. 1972, Stichwort „Relation", S. 934.

[11] Dazu *Jauernig*, Materielles Recht und Prozeßrecht, in: JuS 1971, S. 329 ff.

[12] *Radbruch*, Rechtsphilosophie, 6. Aufl. 1963, S. 280 ff.; *Mitsopoulos*, 'Η θεωρία τοῦ ἀστικοῦ δικονομικοῦ δικαίου, 1970, S. 19 f.; *Vollkommer*, Formenstrenge und prozessuale Billigkeit, 1973.

rechtsprechenden Organen der Rechtsgemeinschaft als auch im Verhältnis dieser Bürger untereinander. Aber Formalismus ist nicht das alleinige und nicht ausschließliches Merkmal des Prozeßrechts. Es gibt Verfahrensabläufe, die zweifellos dem Prozeßrecht zuzuordnen sind und gleichwohl — wenn nicht gerade regellos, so doch weitgehend ungesteuert von gesetzlichen Vorschriften — richterlichem Ermessen überlassen bleiben. Ein Beispiel hierfür bietet etwa der sogenannte „Freibeweis" zur Feststellung von Prozeßvoraussetzungen im Zivilprozeß. Andererseits machen stark formalisierte Regelungen, wie etwa von einer Bank für die Einräumung von Krediten eingeführte Bewilligungsverfahren, einen rechtlich bedeutsamen Handlungszusammenhang noch nicht zu einem Teil des Prozeßrechts.

Sofern man vom Standpunkt einer analytischen Rechtstheorie aus Recht insgesamt als ein System von Normen beschreibt, müßte der Gegensatz zwischen Prozeßrecht und materiellem Recht in einer unterschiedlichen Struktur der Normen beider Bereiche hervortreten. In dieser Richtung ist die Unterscheidung Harts zwischen „Primärregeln" und „Sekundärregeln" grundlegend[13]. Verfahrensrechtliche Normen sind in diesem Schema den Sekundärregeln zuzuordnen[14], also Regeln, welche nicht unmittelbar Pflichten auferlegen, sondern Macht einräumen. Und zwar würden Sekundärregeln in allen drei Unterarten das Prozeßrecht bilden. Die große Masse der die Gerichtsverfassung und den Verfahrensablauf bestimmenden Normen ist nach Harts Einteilung als „Entscheidungsregeln" aufzufassen. Normen über das Wiederaufnahmeverfahren wären etwa zu den „Abänderungsregeln" zu zählen. Und die richterliche Gewalt effektiv begründende Voraussetzungen des Prozeßrechts gehörten zu einer „Anerkennungsregel". Allerdings bleibt die Abgrenzung der insoweit Prozeßrecht konstituierenden Regeln zu den übrigen Sekundärregeln im Sinne Harts, insbesondere den private Macht übertragenden Sekundärregeln, einer rein analytischen Rechtsbetrachtung verborgen.

b) Prozeßrecht hat es ferner sicherlich in besonders ausgeprägter Weise mit Praxis zu tun. Es ist kein Zufall, daß die Lehre von den Prozeßhandlungen in den Lehrdarstellungen des Prozeßrechts einen festen Platz behauptet, mag auch die Verwendung formaler Ordnungselemente unter der Bezeichnung eines „Verhältnisses" oder eines „Gegenstandes" bisweilen in den Vordergrund gerückt werden. Auch das Wort „Prozeß" verweist unmittelbar auf einen in der Realität sich vollziehenden Handlungsablauf: ein Fortschreiten in einer bestimmten Richtung, in ver-

---

[13] *Hart*, The Concept of Law, 1961, S. 78 ff.

[14] Vgl. *Eckmann*, Rechtspositivismus und sprachanalytische Philosophie, 1969, S. 63; Zweifel bei *Singer*, Hart's Concept of Law, in: The Journal of Philosophy 60 (1963), S. 197—209.

schiedenen Abschnitten und gegen einen gewissen Widerstand. Der so angedeutete dynamische Charakter des Prozesses, den namentlich Goldschmidt zur Grundlage einer umfassenden Prozeßrechtstheorie gemacht hat, darf wiederum nicht verabsolutiert werden. Vorgänge des materiellen Rechts, z. B. der Abschluß und die Abwicklung eines Kaufvertrages und erst recht die Durchführung von Dauerschuldverhältnissen wie Miete und Pacht, führen ebenso wie ein gerichtliches Verfahren über verschiedene Stationen zu einem angestrebten Resultat. Goldschmidts Kennzeichnung des Prozesses als „Rechtslage“ hebt demgegenüber den besonderen Aspekt der Ungewißheit des im Entwicklungsgang des Erkenntnisverfahrens zu gestaltenden Rechts hervor[15]. Ein in neuerer Zeit von Henckel unternommener Abgrenzungsversuch führt zu einer Trennung nach „Lebensbereichen“[16].

Nicht irgendwelche Handlungen, sondern in einem inneren Zusammenhang stehende Handlungen bilden also einen Prozeß. Ob es sich dabei um Kauf, Miete oder Gerichtsverfahren handelt, wird durch jeweils besondere Deutungsschemata entschieden. Sofern man zum Zwecke einer solchen Abgrenzung wiederum auf die Kategorien von „Normen“ oder „Regeln“ zurückgreift, muß man sich freilich darüber im klaren sein, daß dann diese Ausdrücke anders gebraucht werden, als wenn es um bloße Subsumtionsmaßstäbe ginge. Das Handlungsgeflecht des Prozeßrechts setzt sich in dieser Sicht in der Ausdrucksweise von Searle[17] aus „institutionellen Tatsachen“ zusammen, die ihrerseits durch „konstitutive Regeln“ im Gegensatz zu „regulativen Regeln“ bestimmt, d. h. im eigentlichen Sinn erst hervorgebracht werden.

c) Den Wertungen des Prozeßrechts wird gewöhnlich die geringste Aufmerksamkeit geschenkt. Sieht man im Prozeß nichts anderes als einen Weg zur Ausübung von materiellen Rechten, so finden die allgemeinen Wertkategorien ohne weiteres auch Anwendung auf prozessuale Handlungen[18]. Differenzen zwischen Prozeßrecht und materiellem Recht könnten insofern gar nicht auftreten. Meiner Ansicht nach unterschätzt eine solche Auffassung die Eigengesetzlichkeit derart fest im allgemeinen Bewußtsein verankerter Institutionen wie des Gerichtsverfahrens.

---

[15] *Goldschmidt*, Der Prozeß als Rechtslage, 1925, insbes. S. 255.

[16] *Henckel*, Prozeßrecht und materielles Recht, 1970, S. 408.

[17] *Searle*, Speech Acts, 1969; vgl. auch schon *Rawls*' Auffassung von Regeln als Definitionen einer Praxis: Two Concepts of Rules, in: Philosophical Review 64 (1955), S. 3 ff., insbes. Fußn. 1, S. 24.

[18] Für eine solche Rückbindung des Prozesses an materiellrechtliche Wertungen *Henckel* (Fußn. 16), S. 61 ff. und schon: Vom Gerechtigkeitswert verfahrensrechtlicher Normen, 1966; dazu kritisch: *Bötticher*, Prozeßrecht und materielles Recht, in: ZZP 85 (1972), S. 1 ff.

Nach anderer Meinung scheinen prozeßrechtliche Wertungen hinter der allgemeinen Wertordnung des Rechts zurückzutreten, wie es ein oft zitierter Ausspruch von Stein formuliert: „Der Prozeß ist für mich das ‚technische Recht' in seiner allerschärfsten Ausprägung, von wechselnden Zweckmäßigkeiten beherrscht, der Ewigkeitswerte bar[19]." Freilich läßt sich das verschieden interpretieren: Einmal könnte damit Wertung aus dem Prozeß völlig ausgeblendet, zum anderen aber auch in ihm beschränkt anerkannt sein, eben nicht auf ewig festgelegt, sondern mit wechselnden zweckbezogenen Inhalten. In letzterer Richtung würde die Funktionalität prozeßrechtlicher Handlungen spezielle Wertungsgesichtspunkte in Erscheinung treten lassen. Hierhin zielen neuere Überlegungen, die im Anschluß an Luhmann[20] dem Prozeß eine eigene „Systemrationalität" zuerkennen wollen, die etwa in der Legitimation von Entscheidungen mit Hilfe einer „Umstrukturierung des Erwartens durch den faktischen Kommunikationsprozeß" gesehen wird.

Abschließend bleibt festzustellen, daß die Ausgrenzung des Prozeßrechts aus der Rechtsordnung keineswegs als eindeutig geklärt gelten kann. Nur einer auf den ganzen Wirkungszusammenhang des Rechts gerichteten Anstrengung kann es gelingen, methodische Regeln[21] zur allgemeinen Begriffsbildung zu entwickeln und sie für die konkrete Rechtsanwendung in systematischer Argumentation nutzbar zu machen.

---

[19] *Stein,* Grundriß des Zivilprozeßrechts, 1921, S. III.

[20] *Luhmann,* Zweckbegriff und Systemrationalität, 1968; Legitimation durch Verfahren, 1969, S. 37.

[21] Dazu *Fenge,* Juristische Methodenlehre und Prozeßrechtswissenschaft, in: Festschrift für Weber, 1975, S. 135/145 ff.

SIX CONCEPTS OF 'CONSTITUTIVE RULE'

By Riccardo Guastini, Genoa

Something named 'constitutive rule' (or *'norma costitutiva'*) has been made a subject of philosophical analysis by two authors (among others), namely the American philosopher of language John R. Searle and the Italian legal theorist Gaetano Carcaterra.[1] However, each of these authors uses the same phrase 'constitutive rule' as to designate quite different things.[2] As a matter of course, this is a source of conceptual confusion.

My purpose, in this paper, is just to outline a tentative analysis of these various concepts of 'constitutive rule'.

I.

J. R. Searle tries to sketch the concept of 'constitutive rule' in two different ways.[3]

In the first place, he claims that constitutive rules are those rules which create or define new forms of behaviour, viz. kinds of behaviour which do not exist previously and independently of the rules themselves. Hence, 'constitutiveness' in this sense seems to be not just a particular mark of some rules among others, but a peculiar relationship between some rules and the behaviour governed by them.

In the second place, he claims that constitutive rules are those rules which are not imperative in character and can be smoothly reduced into the standard form 'x counts as y in the context c'. Constitutive rules in this sense are rules which do have a specific logical structure. Therefore, 'constitutiveness' in this sense seems to be the particular logical character of some rules.

---

[1] I am not directly concerned here with Amedeo G. Conte's important works on this subject, although I am indebted to him for many suggestions. Cf. his contribution in the present volume.

[2] A preliminary analysis of Searle's and Carcaterra's ideas is in *Guastini* (1983a).

[3] Cf. *Searle* (1964a), (1964b), (1969, pp. 33 ff.), (1972).

Now let me consider closer these two kinds of constitutiveness.[4]

1. As regards to the first kind of constitutiveness, two remarks seem to be convenient.

First: the relationship, pictured by Searle, between constitutive rules and the behaviour dependent on them is not entirely clear. Rules are but language entities, and there is something magical in the suggested idea that certain linguistic utterances are able to bring into existence some new part of the non-linguistic world. Perhaps, one could better say that constitutive rules (in the first sense of this phrase) are but conditions of possibility for new forms of behaviour.[5]

Second: I take it for granted that, by the phrase 'new forms of behaviour', Searle does not mean such conducts as 'moving a bishop (in chess)', or 'castling (in chess)', but he means practices like 'playing chess', 'voting', 'adjudicating', or 'legislating'. If this is correct, one could say as a matter of course that there is no single rule being a condition of possibility for a new form of behaviour. 'Constitutiveness' in this sense is not a property of isolated rules: it is a property of sets of rules.

Accordingly, I should define a 'constitutive rule' in its first sense as follows: a rule is constitutive (whatever its logical frame can be) when belonging to a set of rules which (as a whole) is a condition of possibility for a new kind of behaviour.

2. As regards to the second sort of constitutiveness,[6] consider the following examples (all suggested by the standard model 'x counts as y in the context c'):

(1) The situation so-and-so on chess board counts as checkmate.

(2) Checkmate counts as victory.

(3) The happy utterance of the sentence *s* counts as undertaking an obligation.

(4) Taking off one's hat in certain circumstances counts as a greeting.

The rules of the preceding examples do not seem to be constitutive in the same sense (or in the same way) as the rules of chess as a whole are. They are no condition of possibility for the behaviours they direct. E. g., taking off one's hat is a behaviour which certainly is possible independently of the rule of greeting.

---

[4] On this subject cf. *Guastini* (1983b).

[5] This point has been made quite clear by A. G. Conte in a number of essays. Cf. *A. G. Conte* (1981a), (1981b), (1981c), (1983a), (1983b).

[6] On this subject see especially *Ransdell* (1971), *Cherry* (1973), *Raz* (1975, pp. 108 ff.).

Furthermore, the phrase 'counts as' seems to have at least two different meanings in the preceding rules. In the first rule, it seems to stipulate a semantical equivalence between the subject (x) and the predicate (y) of the sentence. Indeed, I consider the first rule to be but a stipulative definition of 'checkmate' (although its formulation is somehow peculiar). One should notice that such a definition belongs to a system of rules, just as legal definitions do.

In normative systems, stipulative definitions fulfil the task which immediately results from the connection of the first rule and the second one. That is, they are rules aiming at directing the behaviour of judges and referees, by controlling their interpretation of other rules. In a sense, one also could say that such "legal" definitions are but fragments of every other rule of the same system, in which the term defined occurs.[7]

Otherwise, in the other rules (2 to 4) the phrase 'counts as' fulfils the function of conferring a 'sense' or 'value' to the subject of the sentence. Strictly speaking, these rules do not concern new forms of behaviour, but rather ascribe new senses or values to independently possible behaviours.

3. The preceding one is but a sketch of analysis. Anyway, if the analysis just suggested is right (or at least plausible), one should no more talk about constitutive rules without any detailed characterization. One should better distinguish among the following subjects:

(i) Systems of rules which (as a whole) are condition of possibility for new forms of behaviour. Such normative systems usually consist of several rules of various kinds. They can include obligation-rules, permission-rules, competence-rules, etc. They can include rules of the two following kinds as well:

(ii) Stipulative ("legal") definitions of terms used in other rules of the same normative system.

(iii) Rules which confer a (new) sense or value to some pre-existing behaviour. One could use for these rules the name of 'sense-conferring rules' (shortly 'sense-rules').

If one prefers to speak in terms of 'constitutiveness', then one could say that: some systems of rules are constitutive of new forms of behaviour; some rules are constitutive of the meaning of terms; some rules are constitutive of senses or values.

---

[7] Cf. *Ross* (1958).

II.

G. Carcaterra, in his turn, outlines the concept of 'constitutive rule' in three stages.[8]

At the first stage, Carcaterra defines 'constitutive rule' as follows: constitutive rules are propositions which neither describe nor prescribe any behaviour whatsoever, but immediately produce a normative (institutional) state of affairs.

A paradigmatic example is a legal rule repealing another legal rule, such as: 'Hereby, the rule *r* is repealed (derogated).' Derogatory rules plainly neither describe an already performed derogation, nor prescribe anyone to bring it into effect: they directly accomplish their own effect, i. e. the derogation itself.[9] Yet, derogatory rules are but an example. Legal definitions too fall into the same class: they neither describe nor prescribe the meaning of the *definiendum,* but ascribe it that meaning. Similarly, power-conferring or right-conferring rules neither describe nor prescribe the power or right just conferred, but ascribe it to someone. And so on. The only rules which cannot be called constitutive in this sense are the prescriptive ones. And the reason for this is obvious: prescriptive rules (do not describe, of course, but) prescribe or command.

Accordingly, at the second stage, Carcaterra outlines constitutiveness only *ex negativo* as non-imperativeness. Those rules are constitutive, which are not prescriptive in character. Any rule which cannot be shaped in imperative or deontic form is a constitutive one.

However, one could argue that there is no logical difference between prescribing and ascribing. Indeed, prescribing just seems to amount to ascribing obligations. Thus, at the third stage, Carcaterra does not speak any more of particular constitutive rules (as contrasted with prescriptive rules), but rather of the 'constitutiveness' (or 'constitutive force') which is inherent to every rule. For, according to him, every rule is constitutive of some normative entity. Such entities are institutions, rights, powers, derogations, as well as obligations and prohibitions.

Hence, Carcaterra draws up not just one but (at least) three concepts of 'constitutive rule'.

1. In the first sense, constitutive rules are no rules of behaviour; they do not bear upon behaviour. Therefore, as Carcaterra just points out,

---

[8] *Carcaterra* (1974), (1979).

[9] About derogatory rules, see *Kelsen* (1962), (1979, pp. 84 ff.). A prescriptivist construction of derogatory rules is presented by *Bobbio* (1980), and *Guastini* (1982a).

they are susceptible neither of compliance nor of infringement. Indeed, in a sense, they have no addressee at all; there is no subject to whom they are directed.

This class of rules includes validity-conferring rules (e. g., Hart's recognition rule and Kelsen's *Grundnorm*), validity-repealing rules (derogatory rules), as well as legal definitions. It is true that all these rules do not directly bear upon any behaviour, but the reason why this is so has nothing mysterious in it. Of course, such rules just bear upon other rules of the normative system to which they belong. (It should be emphasized that rules about rules are to be distinguished from rules about rule-creating acts, such as Hart's rules of change and adjudication. Rules of this kind just deal with acts, hence with behaviour.)

2. In the second sense, only imperative rules are not constitutive. Thus, from the class of constitutive rules only obligation-rules and prohibition-rules are excluded. But that class includes a lot of different rules of behaviour, such as permission-rules, power-conferring and right-conferring rules, etc.

Perhaps, this second concept of constitutive rule is too wide as to be useful in the analysis of normative language. Anyway, it does not seem to increase the common knowledge of it. This feature of Carcaterra's theory is but a new tentative account of the distinction between prescriptive and ascriptive language: a distinction already used by Hart in the analysis of legal systems and legal language.[10]

But the main trouble with the concept of 'ascription' is that the nature of the mentioned distinction is not clear at all. Carcaterra seems to maintain that the difference between ascription and prescription is a matter of meaning. Yet, as to me, the prescriptive meaning of ascriptive sentences is self-evident. As a matter of course, ascriptive sentences do not express propositions (in the logical sense of the term). Hence, they express but norms, i. e. prescriptions *lato sensu. Tertium non datur.*[11]

If this argument is correct, one could better distinguish not between ascriptions and prescriptions, but among the various syntactical forms of prescriptive language. A norm can be expressed by means of imperative, deontic, evaluative, as well as ascriptive sentences.

3. In the third sense, every rule is a constitutive one. Thus, the concept of 'constitutive force' is not useful as to single out any particular

---

[10] Cf. *Hart* (1948—1949), *Legault* (1977), *MacCormick* (1981), *A. G. Conte* (1981a).

[11] Cf. *Ross* (1968), (1972).

class of rules. In this wide sense, 'constitutiveness' denotes no peculiar logical framework of any rules. It rather is a peculiar point of view about rules, a special way of representing all of them. Carcaterra's suggestion can be made clear as follows.

On one hand: from the syntactical point of view, every prescriptive utterance can be construed as an explicit performative.[12]

On the other hand: from the pragmatical point of view, every prescriptive utterance counts as the performance of a particular speech act, namely an act of setting up a certain normative or institutional state of affairs.[13]

In my view, however, such states of affairs have no independent "existence" beyond the normative language itself. They are but language entities.[14]

III.

From the preceding analysis I draw a set of suggestions for further inquiry:

(1) Some systems and/or sub-systems of rules are conditions for new forms of behaviour. As a consequence, there are human behaviours which cannot be properly described without reference both to facts and rules.[15]

(2) The enacting of legal rules can be represented as the performance of a special class of speech acts, such as commanding, prohibiting, permitting, ascribing rights, derogating, and so on.[16]

(3) Imperative and deontic sentences are not the only ways of expressing rules. Rules can be expressed by means of ascriptive, evaluative, and sense-conferring sentences as well.

(4) Rules about behaviour and rules about rule-creating acts do not exhaust the realm of legislative language. Among legal rules one should also include rules about rules: e. g., definitions, validity-conferring rules, derogatory rules. Each of these rules performs a peculiar function in normative systems.

---

[12] This thesis has been argued also by *Opałek* (1972), (1974).

[13] On this subject cf. *A. G. Conte* (1977), (1983a).

[14] Cf. *Ross* (1972).

[15] Cf. *Searle* (1969, ch. 8), *MacCormick* (1974), *A. G. Conte* (1981c), *Guastini* (1983b).

[16] Cf. *Opałek* (1972), (1974); *Legault* (1977).

Bibliography

Agazzi, E. (1980), Sulla possibilità di una fondazione razionale delle norme, in: Miscellanea filosofica, Le Monnier, Firenze, pp. 7—23.

Baker, G. P./*Hacker*, P. M. S. (1966), Rules, Definitions, and the Naturalistic Fallacy, in: American Philosophical Quarterly, vol. 3, pp. 299—305.

Bobbio, N. (1980), Norma, in: Enciclopedia, vol. IX, Einaudi, Torino, pp. 876—907.

Boër, E. S. (1974), Speech Acts and Constitutive Rules, in: The Journal of Philosophy, vol. 71, pp. 169—174.

Carcaterra, G. (1974), Le norme costitutive, Giuffré, Milano.

— (1979), La forza costitutiva delle norme, Bulzoni, Roma.

Castignone, S. (1981), Le "parole del fare". Austin, Olivecrona, Ross, e la "fallacia performativa", in: Materiali per una storia della cultura giuridica, vol. 11, pp. 439—458.

Cherry, C. (1973), Regulative and Constitutive Rules, in: The Philosophical Quarterly, vol. 23, pp. 301—315.

Conte, A. G. (1977), Aspekte der Semantik der deontischen Sprache, in: A. G. Conte/R. Hilpinen/G. H. von Wright (eds.), Deontische Logik und Semantik, Athenaion, Wiesbaden, pp. 59—73.

— (1978a), Deux questions en réponse à une critique de Georges Kalinowski, in: Logique et analyse, vol. 21, pp. 111—120.

— (1978b), Parerga leibnitiana, in: A. A. Martino/E. Maretti/C. Ciampi (eds.), Logica, informatica, e diritto, vol. I, Le Monnier, Firenze, pp. 217—255.

— (1981a), Konstitutive Regeln und Deontik, in: E. Morscher/R. Stranzinger (eds.), Ethik. Akten des Fünften Internationalen Wittgensteins-Symposiums (Kirchberg am Wechsel, 1980), Hölder/Pichler/Tempsky, Wien, pp. 82—86.

— (1981b), Variationen über Wittgensteins Regelbegriff, in: R. Haller (ed.), Sprache und Erkenntnis als soziale Tatsache, Hölder/Pichler/Tempsky, Wien, pp. 69—78.

— (1981c), Regola costitutiva in Wittgenstein, in: F. Castellani (ed.), Uomini senza qualità. La crisi dei linguaggi nella grande Vienna, U. C. T., Trento, pp. 51—68.

— (1983a), Paradigmi d'analisi della regola in Wittgenstein, in: R. Egidi (ed.), Wittgenstein. Momenti di una critica del sapere, Guida, Napoli, pp. 37—82.

— (1983b), Regola costitutiva, condizione, antinomia, in: U. Scarpelli (ed.), La teoria generale del diritto. Problemi e tendenze attuali. Studi dedicati a Norberto Bobbio, Comunità, Milano, pp. 21—39.

Conte, M.-E. (1983), La pragmatica linguistica, in: C. Segre (ed.), Intorno alla linguistica, Feltrinelli, Milano, pp. 94—128.

Di Bernardo, G. (1983), Le regole dell'azione sociale, Il Saggiatore, Milano.

Dickey, A. (1980), The Concept of Rules and the Concept of Law, in: The American Journal of Jurisprudence, vol. 25, pp. 89—116.

Ferrari, G. (1981), Regole costitutive e validità, in: Materiali per una storia della cultura giuridica, vol. 11, pp. 507—526.

Filipponio Tatarella, A. (1978), E' sanzionabile il potere?, in: Rivista internazionale di filosofia del diritto, vol. 55, pp. 908—917.

— (1980), Sulla teoreticità delle norme costitutive, in: Rivista internazionale di filosofia del diritto, vol. 57, pp. 238—281.

Geach, P. (1960), Ascriptivism, in: The Philosophical Review, vol. 69, pp. 221—225.

Grzegorczyk, C. (1974), Le rôle du performatif dans le langage du droit, in: Archives de philosophie du droit, vol. 19, pp. 229—242.

Guastini, R. (1982a), Performativo, normativo. In margine ad un saggio di Ross, in: R. Guastini, Lezioni di teoria analitica del diritto, Giappichelli, Torino, pp. 103—140.

— (1982b), Variazioni su temi di Scarpelli, in: Materiali per una storia della cultura giuridica, vol. 12, pp. 545—565.

— (1983a), Teorie delle regole costitutive, in: Rivista internazionale di filosofia del diritto, vol. 60, pp. 548—564.

— (1983b), Cognitivismo ludico e regole costitutive, in: U. Scarpelli (ed.), La teoria generale del diritto. Problemi e tendenze attuali. Studi dedicati a Norberto Bobbio, Comunità, Milano, pp. 153—176.

Hart, H. L. A. (1948—49), The Ascription of Responsibility and Rights, in: Proceedings of the Aristotelian Society, vol. 49, pp. 171—194.

Hedenius, I. (1963), Performatives, in: Theoria, vol. 29, pp. 115—136.

Kasher, A. (1977), Foundations of Philosophical Pragmatics, in: R. E. Butts/J. Hintikka (eds.), Basic Problems in Methodology and Linguistics, Reidel, Dordrecht-Boston, pp. 225—242.

Kelsen, H. (1962), Derogation, in: R. A. Newman (ed.), Essays in Jurisprudence in Honour of Roscoe Pound, Bobbs-Merril, Indianapolis-New York, pp. 339—361.

— (1979), Allgemeine Theorie der Normen, Manz, Wien.

Legault, G. (1977), La structure performative du langage juridique, Presses de l'Université de Montréal, Montréal.

Leonardi, P. (1983), Sulle regole, Libreria Universitaria Editrice, Verona.

MacCormick, N. (1974), Law as Institutional Fact, in: The Law Quarterly Review, vol. 90, pp. 102—129.

— (1981), H. L. A. Hart, E. Arnold, London.

Miller, D. (1981), Constitutive Rules and Essential Rules, in: Philosophical Studies, vol. 39, pp. 183—197.

Olivecrona, K. (1971), Law as Fact, Stevens, London.

Opałek, K. (1972), Les normes, les énoncés sur les normes, et les propositions déontiques, in: Archives de philosophie du droit, vol. 17, pp. 355—372.

— (1974), "Doing Things with Words" and the Law, in: Anuario de filosofìa del derecho, vol. 17, pp. 233—243.

Pattaro, E. (1982), You Cannot Do Things with Words (The Concept of a Legal Transaction according to Axel Hägerström), in: P. Trappe (ed.), Contemporary Conceptions of Law. Proceedings of the 9th World Congress of I.V.R., Steiner, Wiesbaden, pp. 153—161.

Pollastro, P. (1983), Fenomenologia delle regole costitutive, in: Materiali per una storia della cultura giuridica, vol. 13, pp. 233—262.

Ransdell, J. (1971), Constitutive Rules and Speech Acts-Analysis, in: The Journal of Philosophy, vol. 68, pp. 385—400.

Rawls, J. (1955), Two Concepts of Rules, in: The Philosophical Review, vol. 64, pp. 3—32.

Raz, J. (1975), Practical Reason and Norms, Hutchinson, London.

Ross, A. (1958), Definition in Legal Language, in: Logique et analyse, vol. 1, pp. 139—149.

— (1968), Directives and Norms, Routledge & Kegan Paul, London.

— (1972), The Rise and Fall of the Doctrine of Performatives, in: R. E. Olson/A.M. Paul (ed.), Contemporary Philosophy in Scandinavia, Johns Hopkins, Baltimore-London, pp. 197—212.

Savoini, G. P. (1982), Performatività e validità in Alf Ross, in: Materiali per una storia della cultura giuridica, vol. 12, pp. 343—407.

Searle, J. R. (1964a), How to Derive 'Ought' from 'Is', in: The Philosophical Review, vol. 73, pp. 43—58.

— (1964b), What Is a Speech Act?, in: M. Black (ed.), Philosophy in America, Allen & Unwin, London, pp. 221—239.

— (1969), Speech Acts. An Essay in the Philosophy of Language, Cambridge U.P., Cambridge.

— (1972), Theories of Meaning and the Uses of Language, in: J. Rachels/ F. A. Tillman (eds.), Philosophical Issues. A Contemporary Introduction, Harper & Row Publishers, New York, pp. 294—303.

Smith, J. C. (1976), Legal Obligation, The Athlone Press, London.

Stoljar, S. (1980), Moral and Legal Reasoning, MacMillan, London.

Urban Coyne, M. (1981), Beyond Rules: Mapping the Normative, in: American Philosophical Quarterly, vol. 18, pp. 331—337.

ESSAI D'IDENTIFICATION DE LA TOTALITE SOCIALE DU PHENOMENE JURIDIQUE EN TANT QUE SYSTEME

Par Nikolaos G. Intzessiloglou, Thessaloniki

I. Introduction

L'évolution des relations sociales telle qu'elle s'effectue au niveau tant de la production que de la consommation de biens économiques est accompagnée par certains signes manifestant un changement du droit, que l'on pourrait qualifier de «diffusion sociale du droit». Comme le capitalisme individualiste montant, moyennant le développement du positivisme juridique, a érigé la volonté de l'individu-sujet de droit en source de l'obligation, de même et en se différenciant, le capitalisme avancé des groupes (groupes d'entreprises, syndicats, associations de consommateurs, etc), tend à créer des conditions sociales nouvelles de naissance des obligations (par négociations entre groupes sociaux dans le cadre d'une planification et par contrat d'adhésion ou de simple acceptation des clauses déjà négociées par d'autres, etc) et plus généralement des formes nouvelles d'existence du phénomène juridique. Celles-ci obligent à un dépassement du positivisme juridique au sein d'une perspective plus large correspondant à la réalité «socialisée» du phénomène juridique.

Le vecteur de ce dépassement peut être la philosophie sociale du Droit ou la sociologie juridique au moyen d'une méthode globalisante et synthétique telle l'analyse systémique[1]. Mais en dehors même de cet objectif ambitieux qui consiste à substituer l'objet d'étude du dogmatisme juridique par un autre, l'identification du phénomène juridique en tant que système social est à moyen terme un procédé intéressant, utile et instructif dans le cadre de la seule philosophie sociale du droit.

---

[1] Voir *N. Intzessiloglou*, L'apport de l'analyse systémique dans le domaine juridique, Université de Droit, d'Economie et de Sciences Sociales de Paris, Paris 1980, pages 816.

II. Problèmes de Méthode

1. La Problématique de l'Utilisation de l'Analyse Systémique dans le Domaine Juridique

Le choix de l'analyse systémique comme instrument de méthode est justifié par le fait que le phénomène juridique n'est pas un objet simple et analysable en diverses parties-éléments dont l'étude pourrait, au moyen d'une démarche analytique, aboutir à la connaissance de la totalité du phénomène. La méthode analytique mène au démentèlement du phénomène juridique et aboutit à une perte d'information précieuse tant pour la compréhension du phénomène juridique que pour son étude opérationnelle. Cette information n'est pas perdue lorsqu'on saisit d'emblée le phénomène juridique dans sa totalité, à savoir lorsqu'on l'identifie au moyen du concept de système.

Cette identification doit servir de support à la conceptualisation globale, à la description organisée ou même à l'explication des diverses manifestations du droit en tant que phénomène social dans son sens le plus large possible. Ce droit doit être identifié de telle manière qu'il soit assez général pour se modifier en tant que modèle, et évoluer avec les nouvelles connaissances, et assez souple pour s'adapter aux particularités des cas concrets et singuliers, se transformant ainsi en vecteur du mouvement dialectique par lequel s'effectue l'enrichissement et le développement du concept de système juridique qui passe de la généralité de la théorie générale des systèmes à la singularité du phénomène juridique concret.

L'analyse systémique est une appellation d'un ensemble de procédés appliqués dans diverses branches scientifiques, ayant comme caractéristique commune le fait que l'objet d'étude y est considéré en tant que système. Le système, en général, est un ensemble d'éléments en interaction, organisé en totalité réagissant à ces interactions, de telle sorte que tant au niveau des éléments qu'au niveau de la totalité, apparaissent des qualités nouvelles.

Au sein de cet immense champ systémique, une solide base heuristique interdisciplinaire est constituée par la Théorie générale des systèmes, telle qu'elle est élaborée par Ludwig von Bertalanffy[2]. Il s'agit d'une construction théorique qui traite des principes et des lois concernant toute sorte de systèmes dans n'importe quelle branche scientifique, et qui vise la formalisation mathématique des relations et des

---

[2] Voir *L. von Bertalanffy*, General Systems Theory, Braziler, New York 1969.

fonctions isomorphes caractéristiques de l'ensemble des systèmes du monde matériel et immatériel. En utilisant les connaissances acquises par d'autres procédés interdisciplinaires, tels la théorie des organisations, la cybernétique et la théorie des jeux, Ludwig von Bertalanffy et ses collaborateurs (A. Rapoport, K. E. Boulding, R. Gérard et d'autres) ont enrichi et développé la Théorie générale des systèmes.

Parallèlement, d'autres efforts de justification épistémologique et philosophique de la Théorie générale des systèmes et du systémisme en général ont visé la constitution d'une méthodologie alternative à celle de la pensée analytique dont le paradigme a trouvé sa meilleure incarnation dans la physique mécanique. Les oeuvres de chercheurs tels E. Laszlo, J.-W. Sutherland, J. Miller et d'autres, illustrent de la manière la plus brillante cette recherche philosophico-épistémologique.

L'ensemble de ces élaborations théoriques s'appuie sur des isomorphismes structurels constatés dans les diverses branches scientifiques, et fonde une perspective interdisciplinaire synthétique refusant toute sorte de réductionisme du réel à une seule de ses dimensions: biologique, physique, chimique ou autre.

2. L'Adaptation Méthodologique de l'Analyse Systémique aux Particularités du Phénomène Juridique

Le paradigme théorique de système élaboré par la Théorie générale des systèmes comporte, dans sa potentialité synthétique, les composantes suivantes: (1) une composante logique, analogique ou déductive (notions, principes et catégories systémiques telles le système, les éléments, la totalité, l'environnement, l'organisation, la variété, la finalité, la rétroaction, etc); (2) une composante empirique ou inductive (la constitution des principes ci-dessus, à partir des isomorphismes constatés dans diverses branches scientifiques); (3) une composante heuristique (le modèle analogique facilite l'intuition et permet de substituer à l'observation ou à l'expérience impossible ou malaisée, soit des observations et des expériences possibles ou aisées, soit le raisonnement ou le calcul).

Au travers de ces composantes se réalisent les processus qui mènent du concept de système tel qu'il est élaboré dans la Théorie générale des systèmes jusqu'à la singularité d'un phénomène juridique concret considéré en tant que système; ces processus peuvent être représentés par le schéma suivant (p. 274).

Les flèches montrent les directions de l'influence exercée par chacun des facteurs participant à ces processus; la flèche en tiretés indique

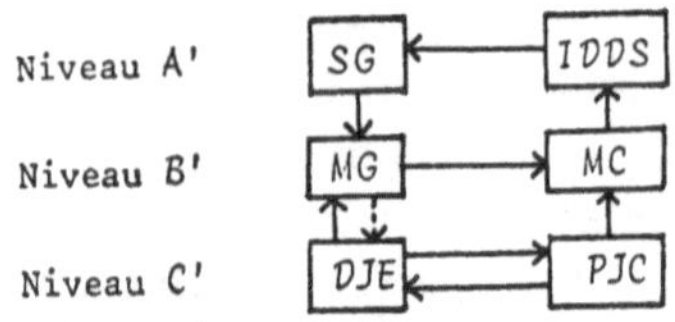

SG = Système général élaboré par la Théorie générale des systèmes.

MG = Modèle général du phénomène juridique.

MC = Modèle d'un phénomène juridique concret.

IDDS = Isomorphismes constatés dans divers domaines de la science.

DJE = Doctrines, jurisprudences et expériences juridiques vécues (c'est-à-dire l'idée que les spécialistes ou/et les profanes se font du droit en général).

PJC = Phénomène juridique concret étudié dans sa totalité sociale.

Schéma 1er

le caractère éventuel de l'influence exercée par *MG* sur *DJE*. Cette éventualité deviendra une certitude à partir du moment où l'approche systémique proposée dans cet exposé sera généralement acceptée. Sur les niveaux *B'* et *C'* s'ébauche la phase qui concerne plus directement la philosophie sociale du droit; c'est-à-dire la spéculation et la recherche philosophique sur le droit en tant que phénomène social. Etant donné que notre instrument méthodologique est procuré par l'analyse systémique (et surtout par la Théorie générale des systèmes), la mise en relief du système des processus concernant directement la philosophie sociale du droit aboutit à la transformation du schéma 1er dans le schéma suivant:

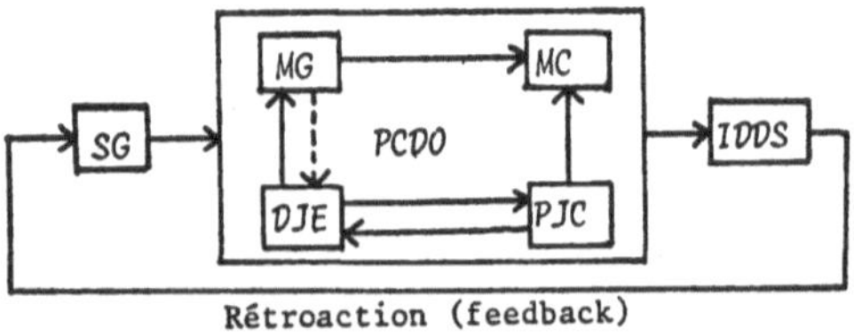

Système *PCDO* = Système des processus concernant directement le phénomène juridique en tant qu'objet de la philosophie sociale du droit.

Schéma 2ème

Les éléments *DJE* et *PJC* sont extérieurement imposés au chercheur et constituent donc des contraintes dont il doit tenir compte en construisant le *MG* et le *MC*. Mais puisque le premier constitue la cause co-productive de second, c'est sur l'élaboration du *MG* que doit se concentrer l'attention du chercheur, étant en plus donné que le *MG* constitue la variable invariante donc structurelle du système *PCDO*.

En même temps, le *MG* doit représenter le concept générique qui permet de définir le genre commun dont les transformations, les développements et les dérivations produisent la diversité des états de totalité concrets et singuliers du phénomène juridique.

III. La Structure de la Totalité du Système Juridique

1. Les Trois Sous-systèmes

Ayant l'intention de saisir le phénomène juridique dans sa dimension sociale la plus large possible, et faisant un effort pour se débarasser de tout a priori doctrinal, le chercheur jette un «regard naïf» sur l'ensemble des donnés socio-juridiques (démarche de phénoménologie perspectiviste). Ces données peuvent être organisées en trois catégories que conventionnellement on peut appeler: a) sous-système normatif, b) sous-système judiciaire, c) sous-système de comportement.

Dans la première catégorie on ne classe pas le comportement lui-même, mais: a) ce que les acteurs sociaux pensent du comportement, tel qu'il doit être, et b) l'ensemble des structures et processus qui participent directement à la formation de ces messages-étalons de mesures des comportements humains. La troisième catégorie comporte toute action humaine saisie dans une perspective d'alternative raisonnable au niveau de l'évolution historique qualifiant la société concrète étudiée[3]. La deuxième catégorie comprend l'ensemble des structures, processus ou mécanismes sociaux, au travers desquels un ou plusieurs comportements sont mesurés par une autorité[4].

Chacune des trois catégories de données constitue un sous-système du système phénomène juridique total. La nature de ces sous-systèmes, comme celle du système juridique dans sa totalité est double: a) ils constituent de simples catégories analytiques de classification de données concernant le droit, et b) ils correspondent à des ensembles con-

---

[3] Sont ainsi exclus de la catégorie du sous-système de comportement juridique les comportements visant à la satisfaction des besoins organiques et biologiques pour lesquels il n'y a pas d'alternative de satisfaction.

[4] L'autorité peut avoir ses sources dans la sagesse, dans l'âge, dans la pratique magique ou religieuse, dans la capacité personnelle, dans la force, dans l'institutionnalisation, dans le pouvoir en général. L'autorité constitue en fait une modalité du pouvoir, les deux autres étant la puissance et la direction (v. *J. Baechler,* Le pouvoir pur, Calmann-Levy, Paris 1978, pp. 22—23).

crets de normes ou de comportements singuliers participant à l'émergence d'un phénomène juridique concret.

Dans sa qualité d'entité réelle et concrète, le sous-système normatif comporte un modèle idéalisé du comportement juridique; il est caractérisé par une certaine clôture informationnelle, et sa position peut être qualifiée de dominante au sein du système juridique puisque: (1) c'est la norme-mesure qui fixe les limites du système juridique considéré; (2) l'unité et le degré d'intégration d'un ensemble de régulations juridiques dépendent de la cohérence et du niveau d'intégration du sous-système normatif; (3) le sous-système normatif constitue la «surface» du système juridique car c'est là que les messages circulant au sein du système juridique sont les plus figés, et les échanges avec l'environnement social les moins nombreux.

Pour délimiter un sous-système de comportements concret, il faut «opérationnaliser» les concepts des normes-mesures correspondant. Il s'agit de déterminer dans quelle mesure un concept s'applique à une situation ou à un comportement en fonction de la présence d'une série de traits ou de caractéristiques observables et concernant le comportement.

Dans un sous-système judiciaire (ou de jugement, ou juridictionnel, ou de juges) sont inclus toutes sortes de juridictions et d'arbitrages, depuis les conseils de personnes âgées des diverses tribus jusqu'aux juridictions bureaucratiques et hiérarchisées des sociétés modernes.

Au sein de chaque société, les données ci-dessus se trouvent en interactions. Ces interactions résultent des mesurages successifs de comportements. Ces mesurages, dans leur ensemble, forment le phénomène social de la régulation juridique. Celle-ci est donc le résultat de la mise en interaction d'au moins une règle-mesure avec le comportement sémantiquement isomorphe à cette règle-mesure, sous la contrainte que constitue l'éventualité d'intervention d'une autorité garantissant l'application de la règle-mesure.

La totalité des interactions entre une ou plusieurs règles-mesures, un ou plusieurs comportements à mesurer et l'éventualité d'intervention d'une autorité garantissant le mesurage, forme un système juridique. Ce dernier peut donc être représenté par le schéma suivant (p. 277).

C'est seulement au sein de ce système et en raison de nouvelles qualités systèmiques qui en émergent que les éléments-sous-systèmes s'investissent de leur caractère juridique qui nous permet de les distinguer des autres règles, comportements et jugements moraux, éthiques, artistiques, axiologiques, hygiéniques, etc. Ainsi le critère «eïdétique» du phénomène juridique n'est intrinsèque à aucun de ses éléments

Système juridique

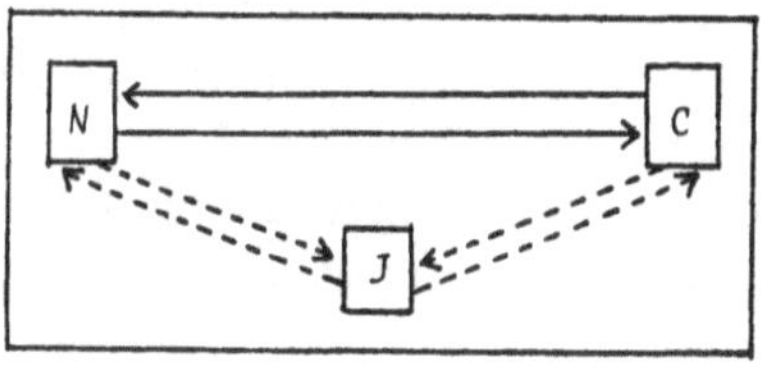

N = Sous-système normatif
C = Sous-système de comportement
J = Sous-système judiciaire (ou de juridiction)

Schéma 3ème

constitutifs mais apparaît au niveau de la totalité du système juridique et permet la distinction entre la régulation juridique d'une part et les autres formes de régulation, morale, religieuse, politique, économique, culturelle, etc de l'autre.

2. La Finalité de Dikaiosûne et la Formation du «Topos» Juridique

L'organisation des trois sous-systèmes s'effectue autour d'une fin, la «justice» (= Dikaiosûne). La finalité d'un système est une causalité interne commandant les performances du système. La performance est définie comme la capacité d'atteindre un but déterminé, en dépit des perturbations et aléas qui surgissent en cours d'action[5]. La meilleure, la plus complète des analyses qui n'ait jamais été faite de la finalité du système juridique est, selon notre avis, celle d'Aristote qui distingue entre «Dikaiosûne générale» et «Dikaiosûne particulière»[6] qui sont deux manières d'être de la «Dikaiosûne».

En s'appuyant sur l'analyse aristotélitienne nous constatons, en termes d'analyse systémique, que la finalité «Dikaiosûne» (= justice) désigne un état de la totalité du système juridique correspondant au niveau des acteurs sociaux, au comportement de l'homme, «dikaios», de l'homme vertueux dans son sens le plus achevé. Dans cet état de la totalité du système juridique l'intervention d'une autorité n'apparaît pas comme nécessaire, de telle sorte que la régulation juridique se confond avec la régulation morale et l'harmonie sociale en général (dikaiosûne générale). La «... justice ainsi entendue n'est pas une partie de la vertu; c'est la vertu toute entière ... tant que la vertu regarde autrui c'est la justice»[7].

---

[5] Voir *E. Morin,* La méthode, Tome I: La nature de la nature, Ed. du Seuil, Paris 1977, pp. 259 et ss.

[6] Voir surtout *Aristote,* Ethique à Nicomaque, Chap. V.

[7] *Aristote* (note 6), L.V.C.C. I, 2.

Cette justice générale constitue l'objectif à atteindre vers lequel tendent les divers mécanismes de socialisation de l'individu dans n'importe quelle société. Le droit, tel qu'il s'applique, contribue à la poursuite de cet objectif général en fonctionnant sous la forme de la «Dikaiosûne particulière», qui désigne une certaine manière de distribuer les biens matériels et les honneurs. Cette justice particulière, impliquant une égalité proportionnelle («jussuum quique tribuere»), doit être saisie dans son contexte social culturel, politique, économique, etc, puisque c'est sous la contrainte de ce dernier que se concrétise le contenu sémantique singulier tant de la dikaiosûne-morale sociale que du juste partage. Dans cette perspective réaliste un partage apparaît comme juste lorsqu' il correspond aux valeurs, aux normes, aux statuts et aux rôles organisés au sein des structures hiérarchiques sociales concrètes.

Les finalités du système juridique («juste partage», «dikaiosûne générale», régulation sociale) représentent les variables dites essentielles du système, et leur poursuite s'effectue au moyen des actions appliquées sur les «variables de commande»[8] (ces actions sont l'interprétation et/ou l'application des normes par le juge, par la doctrine et par les justiciables), les effets de ces actions sur l'état des variables essentielles étant dépendants de l'état du système social environnant.

L'espace social couvert par chacune et par l'ensemble des interactions des éléments impliqués directement au fonctionnement interne du système juridique (tels les sous-systèmes des normes, des comportements et des juridictions, le juste partage) forment un «topos» où, sous les contraintes de l'environnement social, le message et la signification juridique naissent par transformation des messages sociaux, politiques, culturels, religieux, psychologiques, économiques, etc.

Cette transformation s'effectue par le traitement, au sein du système juridique, de flux d'informations tels par exemple: (1) l'information normative véhiculant un message concernant la partie programmée des rôles des acteurs sociaux; (2) l'information normative à propos des systèmes de valeurs, tels qu'ils se manifestent au travers de l'organisation hiérarchique du sous-système normatif; (3) l'information normative véhiculant des messages semi-programmés ou non programmés de rôles concrets; (4) l'information de provenance du sous-système de comportements.

L'ensemble de ces flux est processé par trois sortes de «processeurs»: a) les processeurs de commande: tels les sources formelles du droit, la

[8] Les variables de commande sont les règles juridiques qui «commandent» une norme-mesure.

volonté des personnes juridiques sous certaines conditions, et les procédés de création des normes juridiques. Il s'agit de toute structure formulant et/ou émettant un programme et/ou une commande précisant certains objectifs, finalités et/ou moyens; b) les processeurs décisionnels: tels les diverses juridictions et la bureaucratie administrative en général, lorsqu'elle a un pouvoir discrétionnaire. Il s'agit de toute structure mettant en place des moyens prévus par la commande et reliant les variables de mémoires (par exemple, la jurisprudence) aux variables de projet (par exemple, la finalité de la loi); c) les processeurs opérants: il s'agit de toute sorte de structure réalisant effectivement les décisions ou les commandements émis soit directement des processeurs de commande, soit des processeurs décisionnels.

IV. Remarques Finales

Par son fonctionnement, le phénomène-système juridique forme un champ d'organisation des relations sociales. Dans ce champ, les fonctions sociales de régulation, de reproduction, d'intégration et de résolutions de conflits sont remplies dans le sens, la direction et le niveau de profondeur sociale que l'idéologie inspirant le modèle juridique dominant (celui du positivisme juridique à l'époque du capitalisme montant) le permet et l'impose.

Le modèle systémique du droit qui semble répondre le mieux aux exigences de la réalité juridique «socialisée» du capitalisme avancé (= capitalisme des groupes économiques et sociaux), impose une perspective globale du phénomène juridique dans sa dimension sociale. L'adoption de cette perspective est lourde de conséquences politiques car tôt ou tard elle contraint les juristes à repenser les relations existantes entre le pouvoir de promulguer les normes juridiques d'une part, et les conditions dans lesquelles les sujets de droit sont obligés d'y obéir.

En refusant aux normes juridiques l'exclusivité de véhiculer le message juridique, le modèle systémique du droit est capable de contribuer à un déplacement de pouvoir vers le bas des hiérarchies sociopolitiques. Ce déplacement signifie en fait l'amorce d'un processus long, de plus en plus conscient et systématique, conduisant à long terme vers un état d'autodétermination et d'autogestion des groupes sociaux d'une part, et d'imposition de règles-messages juridiques à l'issue des négociations entre groupes sociaux, d'autre part. Il s'agit de l'aboutissement de la période actuelle de transition d'un droit individualiste vers un droit de groupes sociaux.

RECHT UND MODERNE SYSTEMTHEORIE

Von Werner Krawietz, Münster

I. Notwendigkeit und Möglichkeiten einer Zusammenarbeit von Rechtstheorie und Systemtheorie

1. Seit Begründung der modernen Systemtheorie, die sich zunächst als *allgemeine* Systemtheorie (general systems theory)[1] und erst relativ spät als allgemeine Theorie *sozialer* Systeme zu etablieren vermochte, das heißt als eine Theorie, deren Forschungsfeld sich auf alle sozialen Institutionen, Organisationen und sonstigen Handlungs- und Sinnsysteme erstreckt, die das menschliche Erleben und Handeln mitbestimmen[2], ist ungeklärt geblieben, welchen praktischen und theoretischen Stellenwert eine derartige *Systemtheorie für das Recht und die Rechtswissenschaft* besitzt[3]. Offensichtlich fehlt bis auf den heutigen Tag ein einheitliches, in sich kohärentes und konsistentes *Handlungs- und Forschungsparadigma,* das für sich beanspruchen könnte, die inter- und multidisziplinäre Zusammenarbeit von Juristen, Soziologen und Philosophen mit und am Recht anzuleiten. Ein derartiges Paradigma müßte zumindest die Arbeit an drei Aufgaben hinreichend orientieren können, nämlich (i) einen praktisch brauchbaren Begriffs- und Bedeutungsrahmen für alles normengeleitete Rechtshandeln bieten, (ii) auch die Grundlage und eine Basistheorie für wissenschaftliche Aussagen über das Recht abgeben, das heißt, einen geeigneten Bezugsrahmen für die rationale Deutung und Erklärung des am geltenden Recht orientierten menschlichen Erlebens und Handelns schaffen und damit zugleich (iii) auch die spezifischen Existenz- und Erkenntnisbedingungen des Rechts und der hier

---

[1] Hierzu: *Kenneth E. Boulding,* General Systems Theory: The Skeleton of Science, in: General Systems 1 (1956), S. 11—17. Der deutsche Name stammt bekanntlich von: *Ludwig von Bertalanffy,* Allgemeine Systemtheorie: Wege zu einer neuen Mathesis Universalis, in: Deutsche Universitätszeitung 12 (1957), 5/6, S. 8—12. Vgl. ferner: *Russel L. Ackoff,* General System Theory and Systems Research: Contrasting Conceptions of Systems Science, in: General Systems 8 (1963), S. 117—121.

[2] Dazu vor allem: *Walter Buckley,* Sociology and Modern Systems Theory, Englewood Cliffs, N. J. 1967; *Frederick Kenneth Berrien,* General and Social Systems, New Brunswick, N. J. 1968; *Niklas Luhmann,* Soziale Systeme. Grundriß einer allgemeinen Theorie, Frankfurt am Main 1984.

[3] Eingehend hierzu: *Werner Krawietz,* Recht als Regelsystem, Wiesbaden 1984, S. 145 ff., 148 f., 152 f.

schon präsupponierten Rechtstheorie reflexiv aufzuhellen suchen. Letztlich geht es darum, die gesellschaftlichen *Beziehungen, die mit Mitteln des Rechts geordnet* werden, durch eine Verknüpfung, Verbindung und Fusion von rechtstheoretischen, rechtssoziologischen und rechtsphilosophischen Überlegungen zu erfassen und zu einer *Rahmentheorie des Rechts* zu integrieren, die in dieser Form — wenn ich recht sehe! — wohl neu ist.

a) Die moderne Systemtheorie bietet nach Auffassung von *Ludwig von Bertalanffy*[4], eines der Gründerväter heutiger Systemforschung, sowie nach Ansicht mancher Anhänger, wie beispielsweise *Ervin Laszlo*, nicht mehr und nicht weniger als ein „New Paradigm" wissenschaftlicher Forschung[5]. Die Computer-Weltmodelle, die im Auftrage des Club of Rome auf Grund von Systemanalysen ausgearbeitet wurden, haben systemtheoretische Denkansätze und Betrachtungsweisen in breitesten Kreisen der Öffentlichkeit bekanntgemacht. Mit der wachsenden Technisierung und den gesteigerten Möglichkeiten einer Informationsverarbeitung in unserer mehr oder weniger industrialisierten Gesellschaft macht sich im vorwissenschaftlichen Bereich die Einsicht breit, daß wir in einer immer stärker von Systemzusammenhängen geprägten, durch wechselseitige Systemverflechtungen[6] bedingten Welt leben.

b) Auf der anderen Seite, d. h. auf seiten der mit diesen Gegebenheiten befaßten Wissenschaften, korrespondiert mit ihrer zunehmenden Einsicht in das Geflecht von politischen, ökonomischen, kulturellen, rechtlichen, ökologischen und sonstigen Daten und Faktoren, die für das wissenschaftliche Verstehen unserer Lebenswelt als irgendwie charakteristisch erscheinen, die Erfahrung, daß es sich dabei um kaum noch überschaubare Wirkungsverflechtungen handelt. Sie überfordern die Problemerfassungs- und Problemverarbeitungskapazität *jeder* der beteiligten *Einzelwissenschaften* bei weitem[7].

c) Diese Umstände legen es nahe, (i) schrittweise — zunächst ganz pragmatisch — eine mehr oder weniger sporadische Zusammenarbeit einzelner, am Recht und seiner Erkenntnis wie auch immer beteiligter wissenschaftlicher Disziplinen zu betreiben, sodann (ii) eine Phase immer

[4] *Ludwig von Bertalanffy*, The History and Status of General Systems Theory, in: George J. Klir (Hrsg.), Trends in General Systems Theory, New York 1972, S. 21—28, 36.

[5] Hierzu statt anderer: *Ervin Laszlo* (Hrsg.), Introduction to Systems Philosophy. Toward A New Paradigm of Contemporary Thought, New York — London — Paris 1972.

[6] Dazu und zum folgenden: *Hans Lenk*, Wissenschaftstheoretische und philosophische Bemerkungen zur Systemtheorie, in: ders., Pragmatische Philosophie, Hamburg 1975, S. 247—267, 247 f.

[7] Ebd., S. 248 f.

dichter werdender inter- und multidisziplinärer Kooperation aller mit dem Recht befaßten Einzelwissenschaften ins Werk zu setzen, insbesondere der Rechtswissenschaft, Soziologie und Philosophie, um (iii) schließlich zu einer *rechts- und systemtheoretischen Integration* derjenigen Erkenntnisse zu gelangen, die für den Aufbau einer allgemeinen *Theorie des Rechts* von Belang sind.

2. Im folgenden geht es mir zunächst einmal darum, im Hinblick auf das Recht und die Rechtswissenschaft *problemaufschließende Bezugspunkte* zu gewinnen, die eine Zusammenarbeit der Rechtswissenschaft sowohl mit *allgemeiner* Systemtheorie als auch mit der allgemeinen Theorie *sozialer* Systeme gestatten. Voraussetzung dafür ist, daß man alles Recht nicht bloß als durch Serien sprachlicher Zeichen symbolisierte und repräsentierte Wortnormen begreift, deren Bedeutung (Sinn) systematisch zu erforschen ist, sondern es zugleich als *subsistente* Norm, d. h. in seiner normativen *Tiefenstruktur*, zu erfassen sucht, die stets eingebettet ist in soziale Beziehungen und daher als *Teil der jeweiligen Gesellschaftsstruktur* verstanden werden muß[8]. Was die Möglichkeiten einer Zusammenarbeit von Rechtstheorie und Systemtheorie angeht, die ich noch näher ausloten werde, so sind die hier anzustellenden Überlegungen zunächst nach zwei Seiten hin abzusichern, nämlich (i) gegenüber der Rechtswissenschaft und (ii) gegenüber der Systemtheorie.

a) Nur zur Klarstellung sei angemerkt, daß es *die* allgemeine Systemtheorie ebensowenig gibt, wie *die* soziologische Systemtheorie[9]. Im Hinblick auf das Recht und die Rechtswissenschaft halte ich eine Zusammenarbeit mit Systemtheorie, so wie ich sie verstehe, auf *allen* Ebenen einer *Theoretisierung des Rechtsdenkens* durchaus für möglich[10]. Ich bin der Auffassung, daß systemtheoretische Denksätze und das zugehörige begriffliche Instrumentarium sowohl (i) auf der Ebene dogmatischer Rechtswissenschaft als auch (ii) auf der Ebene der ihr zugehörigen Juristischen Methodenlehre oder, etwas modischer formuliert, auf der Ebene der juristischen Argumentationstheorie als Erkenntnishilfe eingesetzt werden können[11]. Jedoch werde ich mich im folgenden auf einem weiteren, noch abstrakteren Level des Theoretisierens (iii) ausschließlich

---

[8] Noch immer grundlegend: *Theodor Geiger*, Vorstudien zu einer Soziologie des Rechts, 2. Aufl., Neuwied 1970, S. 58 f., 62 f. et passim.

[9] Hierzu die treffende Kritik von: *Hans Lenk*, Wissenschaftstheorie. Zehn Thesen zu Paradigma und Wissenschaftsprogramm des Systemansatzes, in: Ders./Günter Ropohl (Hrsg.), Systemtheorie als Wissenschaftsprogramm, Königstein/Taunus 1978, S. 239—269, 244 f.

[10] Zu den verschiedenen Levels einer Theoretisierung des Rechtsdenkens: *Werner Krawietz*, Zum Paradigmenwechsel im Juristischen Methodenstreit, in: RECHTSTHEORIE Beiheft 1 (1979), S. 113—152, 114 f., 130 ff.

[11] *Werner Krawietz*, Rechtssystem und Rationalität in der juristischen Dogmatik, in: RECHTSTHEORIE Beiheft 2 (1981), S. 299—335, 301 f., 303.

auf die Erörterung der *Möglichkeiten einer Verbindung von allgemeiner Rechtslehre/Rechtstheorie und Systemtheorie* konzentrieren, da diese Problematik auf seiten der Rechtswissenschaft von der konventionellen allgemeinen Rechtslehre bislang stark vernachlässigt worden ist. Diese Überlegungen haben selbstverständlich ihrerseits auch Rückwirkungen auf eine zeitgemäße Konzeption der dogmatischen Rechtswissenschaft und der juristischen Methodenlehre, doch kann ich hier nicht näher darauf eingehen.

b) Was das Verhältnis von Rechtstheorie und Systemtheorie angeht, so werde ich meine Überlegungen auf die Theorie *sozialer* Systeme beschränken[12]. Jedoch darf ich daran erinnern, daß die moderne Systemtheorie sich vor allem in den Vereinigten Staaten als ein Gebiet entwickelt hat, das in seinen Problemstellungen und Zielsetzungen erheblich breiter angelegt ist als das Problemfeld, um das es der modernen Rechtstheorie in ihren fortgeschrittensten Forschungsrichtungen heute geht, doch kann die Rechtstheorie auf bestimmte Einsichten der *allgemeinen* Systemtheorie nicht verzichten. Ich kann und muß die Kenntnis der dabei präsupponierten grundlegenden Vorstellungen der allgemeinen Systemtheorie (general systems theory) und ihres Wissenschaftsprogramms in diesem Kreise jedoch ebenso voraussetzen[13] wie die soziologische Systemtheorie von *Talcott Parsons*[14]. Ich nehme sie hier auf in der durchaus eigenständigen westdeutschen Rezeption und Fortentwicklung durch *Niklas Luhmann*[15]. Letztere wird hier im Anschluß an Luhmann verstanden als *eine* Theorie sozialer Systeme und des Rechtssystems, ohne daß damit ein Exklusivitätsanspruch erhoben wird.

c) Was das rechtstheoretische *und* systemtheoretische Fundament meiner Überlegungen angeht, so stütze ich mich einerseits auf die Theorie des Rechts von *Lawrence M. Friedman*[16], vor allem auf seinen Begriff

---

[12] Noch immer grundlegend: *Niklas Luhmann*, Moderne Systemtheorien als Form gesamtgesellschaftlicher Analyse, in: Jürgen Habermas/Niklas Luhmann, Theorie der Gesellschaft oder Sozialtechnologie — Was leistet die Systemforschung?, Frankfurt am Main 1971, S. 7—24, 11 ff., 16 ff. Vgl. ferner: *Niklas Luhmann*, Wie ist soziale Ordnung möglich?, in: ders., Gesellschaftsstruktur und Semantik. Studien zur Wissenssoziologie der modernen Gesellschaft, Band 2, Frankfurt am Main 1981, S. 195—285, 198 f., 252 ff., 184 f.

[13] *Ludwig von Bertalanffy*, General Systems Theory. Foundations — Development — Applications, New York 1968; *Fred Edmund Emery* (Hrsg.), Systems Thinking, Harmondsworth 1978; *Hans Lenk/Günter Ropohl* (Hrsg.), Systemtheorie als Wissenschaftsprogramm, Königstein/Ts. 1978.

[14] Eingehend zur Normentheorie von Talcott Parsons: *Reinhard Damm*, Systemtheorie und Recht, Berlin 1976, S. 41 ff., 111 ff., 141 ff., der freilich nicht hinreichend zwischen dem bloß analytischen „Realismus" von Parsons und dem Rechtsrealismus Niklas Luhmanns unterscheidet.

[15] Bezogen auf das Rechtssystem vgl. vor allem: *Niklas Luhmann*, Ausdifferenzierung des Rechts, Frankfurt am Main 1981.

des Rechts und des Rechtssystems[17], andrerseits auf die soziologische Theorie des Rechtssystems von *Luhmann*[18]. Ich kann eine Darstellung der Theorie des Rechtssystems, so wie sie von beiden Autoren vorgelegt wurde, hier nicht ersetzen, sondern muß deren Kenntnis voraussetzen. Ich werde im folgenden nur einige, mir grundlegend und wichtig erscheinende Probleme herausgreifen und diskutieren, die im Verhältnis von Rechtstheorie, Rechtssoziologie und soziologischer Systemtheorie nach wie vor umstritten sind.

3. Im Zentrum meiner Überlegungen steht durchgängig eine für die heutige Entwicklung der Rechtstheorie zentrale Problematik, nämlich die Frage, ob und gegebenenfalls welchen Beitrag die moderne Systemtheorie, letztere hier verstanden als Theorie sozialer Systeme, insbes. als *Theorie staatlich organisierter Rechtssysteme*[19], für den Aufbau einer normativ-realistischen und soziologisch reflektierten *Strukturtheorie des Rechts* zu leisten vermag. Ich werde diese Problematik in vier Schritten behandeln:

(1) Zunächst werde ich versuchen, einige Hindernisse auszuräumen, die auf Seiten der Rechtstheorie einer *Kooperation und Integration mit der Systemtheorie* gegenwärtig noch entgegenstehen (Abschnitt II).

---

[16] Hierzu: *Lawrence M. Friedman*, The Legal System. A Social Science Perspective, New York 1975, dtsch. Übers.: Das Rechtssystem im Blickfeld der Sozialwissenschaften, Berlin 1981, S. 1 f., 16 ff., 22 ff.

[17] Sehr treffend weisen: *Lawrence M. Friedman/Stewart Macauly*, Law and the Behavioral Sciences, Indianapolis 1969, S. VII auf die Notwendigkeit hin, „to see the legal system as an integral part of the larger social system rather than as a set of rules, procedures and activities of officials sealed off and isolated from the rest of society". Im Anschluß hieran auch: *Werner Krawietz*, Juristische Methodik und ihre rechtstheoretischen Implikationen, in: Jahrbuch für Rechtssoziologie und Rechtstheorie 2 (1972), S. 12—14, 41 f.

[18] Zum Verhältnis von Rechtswissenschaft und Soziologie vor allem: *Niklas Luhmann*, Rechtssoziologie, Reinbek 1972, S. 354 ff. Die in seinen „Fragen an die Rechtstheorie" gebotene Antwort (und sein in ihr vorausgesetzter Vorschlag einer Arbeitsteilung!), daß die Rechtswissenschaft sich „mit der Realität des Rechts befaßt", „aber nicht mit seiner sozialen, sondern mit seiner symbolischen Realität", d. h. mit dem Recht als einer „Sinnkonstellation für sich", vermag freilich weder die Rechtswissenschaft, letztere hier verstanden als Rechtsdogmatik, noch die Rechtstheorie zufriedenzustellen. Sie trägt auch dem durchaus sinnkritischen Rechtsrealismus der deutschen Interessen- und Wertungsjurisprudenz keinerlei Rechnung, die sich bereits am Ausgang des 19. Jhdts. von derartigen Bereichsabgrenzungen befreite und sich selbst bis auf den heutigen Tag als eine Form soziologischer Jurisprudenz versteht!

[19] In diesem Punkt unterscheidet sich meine Zugangsweise zur Theorie und Soziologie des Rechts von derjenigen Luhmanns, der (i) den praktischen und theoretischen Stellenwert der Staatsorganisation für das Rechtssystem der modernen Gesellschaft und für die Intersystembeziehungen (Gemeinschaftsrecht, Völkerrecht) unterschätzt und (ii) die Relevanz des frühen deutschen Rechtsrealismus (Ihering, Max Weber u. a.) für den Aufbau einer Strukturtheorie des Rechts ignoriert.

(2) Im Anschluß daran werde ich die systemische *Struktur der staatlich organisierten Rechtssysteme* näher charakterisieren, insbesondere den Begriff des Rechtssystems, wie er sich in rechts- und systemtheoretischer Perspektive heute darstellt (Abschnitt III).

(3) Sodann werde ich der Frage nachgehen, welche *Konsequenzen* sich aus der jüngsten Entwicklung der soziologischen Systemtheorie *für die Integration von Rechts- und Systemtheorie* und für den *Aufbau einer Strukturtheorie des Rechts* ergeben (Abschnitt IV).

(4) Abschließend werde ich, wenn auch nur kurz, auf einige Fragen eingehen, welche die erkenntnis- und wissenschaftstheoretische Problematik einer *Fusion von Rechts- und Systemtheorie* betreffen (Abschnitt V).

II. Hindernisse einer Kooperation von Rechts- und Systemtheorie

1. Der Zusammenarbeit von Rechtstheorie und Systemtheorie stehen auf seiten der Rechtstheorie, soweit sie selbst sich als rechtspositivistisch versteht, vor allem drei Hindernisse entgegen, nämlich (1) ihr Rechtsbegriff, (2) ihr Systembegriff und (3) ihr verfehltes Verhältnis zur Rechtssoziologie. Vom Standpunkt der Rechtstheorie, wie sie im juristischen Positivismus bis auf den heutigen Tag vertreten wird, werden alle Vorstellungen vom Recht reduziert auf die Rechtsnorm, wird das Rechtssystem begriffen als ein System von Rechtsnormen und das Rechtswissenschaftssystem als ein System von Aussagen über Rechtsnormen[20]. Das macht es so schwierig, wenn nicht unmöglich, die Abhängigkeit des Rechts von den gesellschaftlichen Kräften voll in Rechnung zu stellen und das Rechtssystem als Teil des Gesellschaftssystems zu begreifen, zu dem es in wechselseitigen Abhängigkeiten steht[21]. Die Hauptschwierigkeit liegt jedoch in einer Fehleinschätzung des Verhältnisses zur Rechtssoziologie.

a) Folgt man in der Theorie des Rechts den Vorstellungen der analytischen Jurisprudenz, deren Ideal gegenwärtig wohl „am vollkommensten" von der *Wiener rechtstheoretischen Schule* Kelsens verkörpert wird[22], so erscheint eine Kooperation der Rechtstheorie mit der Systemtheorie und ihrer *soziologischen* Theorie des Rechts — zumindest für orthodoxe Kelsenianer — von vornherein ausgeschlossen. Auf die Rein-

---

[20] *Werner Krawietz*, Reinheit der Rechtslehre als Ideologie?, in: RECHTSTHEORIE Beiheft 4 (1982), S. 345—421, 386 f.

[21] *Friedman*, Rechtssystem (FN 16), S. 28 ff., 59 ff., 281 ff.

[22] So mit Bezug auf die Wiener und Brünner Schule: *Ota Weinberger*, Die Bedeutung der Brünner Schule der Reinen Rechtslehre für die Entwicklung der Normenlogik, in: Vladimir Kubeš/Ota Weinberger (Hrsg.), Die Brünner rechtstheoretische Schule, Wien 1980, S. 22—49, 34 f.

heit seiner „Theorie des positiven Rechts" bedacht, wollte Kelsen zwar das „positive Recht als Rechtswirklichkeit" begreifen, doch sah er es als schlechthin „unmöglich" an, die nach heutiger Auffassung für die Erfassung der Rechtswirklichkeit sicherlich nicht gänzlich unzuständige Rechtssoziologie beim Aufbau seiner Theorie des Rechts zu beteiligen, weil dies darauf hinausliefe, die Rechtswissenschaft „durch Rechtssoziologie zu ersetzen"[23]. Demgegenüber hat *René König*, einer der führenden westdeutschen Rechtssoziologen, sehr treffend eingewandt, daß eine derartige Rechtswirklichkeit „nur rein rechtswissenschaftlich relevant" sei, ohne überhaupt die „soziale Wirklichkeit des Rechts" zu erreichen[24].

b) In diametralem Gegensatz hierzu steht der juridische „Rechtsrealismus" von *Theodor Geiger*, der „auf der Suche nach erfahrungswissenschaftlichen Grundlagen einer allgemeinen Rechtslehre" in seiner Theorie des Rechts davon ausgeht, daß die allgemeine Rechtslehre „von soziologischen Ausgangspunkten her entwickelt werden muß, ja mit der theoretischen Rechtssoziologie zusammenfällt"[25]. Stehen wir somit vor der Notwendigkeit einer Wahl zwischen den beiden Extrempositionen? Und hängt von der getroffenen Wahl auch unsere Stellungnahme für oder gegen eine rechtstheoretische Beschäftigung mit der Systemtheorie ab?

c) Im folgenden werde ich einen *vermittelnden Standpunkt* zwischen diesen beiden Extrempositionen einnehmen und für eine *rechtstheoretische Beschäftigung mit Systemtheorie* plädieren. Ich benenne dafür drei Gründe: (i) In der jüngsten Entwicklung der heutigen Rechtstheorie zeichnet sich zwischen den beiden, von mir hier nur namentlich aufgeführten Extrempositionen eine ganze Reihe mehr oder weniger rechtsrealistischer Entwicklungsrichtungen ab, denen bereits eine wesentlich offenere, am Verhältnis von Recht und Gesellschaft orientierte Auffassung des Rechtssystems zugrunde liegt. Ich erwähne hier aus dem Bereich der analytisch-normativen Jurisprudenz die rechtstheoretischen Denkansätze von *Ota Weinberger*[26] und *Neil MacCormick*[27], die sich —

---

[23] *Hans Kelsen*, Reine Rechtslehre, 2. Aufl., Wien 1960, S. 111.

[24] *René König*, Das Recht im Zusammenhang der sozialen Normensysteme, in: Ernst E. Hirsch/Manfred Rehbinder (Hrsg.), Studien und Materialien zur Rechtssoziologie, 2. Aufl., Opladen 1971, S. 36—53, 48 f.

[25] *Geiger*, Vorstudien (FN 8), S. 39 f.

[26] Eingehend hierzu: *Ota Weinberger*, Logische Analyse als Basis der juristischen Argumentation, in: Werner Krawietz/Robert Alexy (Hrsg.), Metatheorie juristischer Argumentation, Berlin 1983, S. 159—232, 170 ff., 176 f., 214 ff., der seinen Denkansatz jedoch nach wie vor als einen „institutionalistischen Rechtspositivismus" charakterisiert.

[27] *Neil Mac Cormick*, Law As Institutional Fact, Edinburgh 1973; *ders.*, On Analytical Jurisprudence, in: Archiv für Rechts- und Sozialphilosophie Supplementa Vol. I Part 1 (1982), S. 29—41.

wenn auch nur bis zu einem gewissen Grade — einem institutionalistischen Rechtsdenken geöffnet haben. Sie bleiben allerdings ihrem eigenen Selbstverständnis nach dem Rechtspositivismus verhaftet[28], wenn auch in unterschiedlichem Maße. Ferner muß (ii) im Bereich einer eher normativ-realistischen Jurisprudenz, wie sie heute vor allem in Skandinavien, insbesondere in Dänemark[29] und Finnland[30] vertreten wird, auf den wiedererstarkten skandinavischen, insbesondere den neuen finnischen Rechtsrealismus hingewiesen werden. Diese jüngsten Entwicklungsrichtungen zeigen, daß der Rechtsrealismus *keine bloß historische*, sondern eine *systematische Position* ist, die in der Rechtstheorie nach wie vor grundlegende Bedeutung besitzt. Was schließlich (iii) die nordamerikanische Rechtstheorie angeht, so hat neuerdings *Robert S. Summers* mit Blick auf das Recht und das Rechtssystem eine „Theorie des pragmatischen Instrumentalismus" vorgelegt, die sich selbst in erster Linie als eine Verbindung von Rechtsrealismus und soziologischer Rechtslehre mit philosophischem Pragmatismus versteht[31]. Seine rechtstheoretischen Auffassungen decken sich sehr weitgehend mit einem sinnkritischen Rechtsrealismus, wie ich ihn vertrete. Jedoch erscheinen mir die verbleibenden Auffassungsunterschiede als so bedeutsam, daß ich Anlaß sehe, die Frage nach dem richtigen Namen[32] für seine Forschungsrichtung aufzuwerfen[33]. Auch wenn diese neueren Forschungsrichtungen bislang wenig Grund gesehen haben, sich mit der soziologischen Systemtheorie, insbesondere mit einer Theorie staatlich organisierter Rechtssysteme, auseinanderzusetzen und demzufolge auf letztere so gut wie gar nicht eingehen[34], belegen alle diese Untersuchungen — wenn auch unge-

[28] *Neil MacCormick/Ota Weinberger*, Studien zum institutionalistischen Rechtspositivismus, Berlin 1983.

[29] Zu der von mir hier zugrunde gelegten typisierenden Unterscheidung zwischen analytisch-normativer und normativ-realistischer Jurisprudenz vgl. auch: *Stig Jørgensen*, Pluralis Juris. Towards a Relativistic Theory of Law, Århus 1982, S. 9 f., 32 ff., 37 ff., 48 f., der gleichfalls zwischen „realistic and analytical theories" unterscheidet, letztlich jedoch für eine realistische Version des Rechtsbegriffs optiert.

[30] Eingehend hierzu: *Juha Tolonen*, Grundzüge der finnischen Rechtstheorie, in: RECHTSTHEORIE Beiheft 2 (1981), S. 11—27, 21 ff.

[31] *Robert S. Summers*, Pragmatischer Instrumentalismus und amerikanische Rechtstheorie, Freiburg — München 1983, S. 11 f., 15 ff., 48 ff.

[32] Gegen die Identifikation des im nordamerikanischen Rechtsdenken seit jeher geläufigen Ausdrucks „Rechtsrealismus" (Legal Realism) mit seiner „Theorie des pragmatischen Instrumentalismus" *Summers* (FN 31), S. 3 ff. mit einer m. E. nicht durchschlagenden Begründung.

[33] Für die Beibehaltung der Bezeichnung „Rechtsrealismus" schon: *Werner Krawietz*, Juristische Entscheidung und wissenschaftliche Erkenntnis, Wien — New York 1978, S. 115 ff., 122 ff., 141 ff.

[34] Eine erfreuliche Ausnahme machen die Untersuchungen von: *Ota Weinberger*, Institutionentheorie und Institutionalistischer Rechtspositivismus, in: Ders./Werner Krawietz (Hrsg.), Helmut Schelsky als Soziologe und politischer Denker, Grazer Gedächtnisschrift zum Andenken an den am 24. Fe-

wollt! — doch recht eindrucksvoll, daß es heute auf seiten hinreichend realistischer Rechtstheorien wohl keine unüberwindlichen Hindernisse mehr gibt, die einer möglichen Verbindung von Rechts- und Systemtheorie, wie ich sie verstehe[35], entgegenstünden.

2. In den letzten Jahren hat sich die Entwicklung der Rechtstheorie nicht nur in einem ungeahnten Ausmaß beschleunigt, sondern auch rascher gewandelt als uns heute vielleicht bewußt ist. Der sog. *Theorienpluralismus,* d. h. die vermeintliche Vielzahl und Vielfalt miteinander konkurrierender Rechtsauffassungen und Rechtstheorien, ist längst als mehr oder weniger illusionär durchschaut[36]. Im Rückblick erscheint der Theorienpluralismus sehr weitgehend als eine bloße *Inflationierung des Theorienangebots,* der kein entsprechender Erkenntniszuwachs gegenübersteht. Die übriggebliebenen, wirklich unterschiedlichen Theorieansätze bedürfen daher einer *Integration* oder, falls letztere sich als nicht angebracht erweist, einer *Substitution.*

a) Wo eine Theorieintegration nicht gelingen will oder wegen der Gegensätzlichkeit der rechtstheoretischen Denkansätze nicht gelingen kann, erscheint eine Theorie*substitution* angezeigt[37]. Es geht dabei darum, die weniger ‚guten' Theorien des Rechts so weit wie irgend möglich durch ‚bessere' zu substituieren. Wie im Leben ist auch in der Wissenschaft das Bessere stets der Feind des Guten!

b) Die Substitution der ‚guten' Vorgängertheorie durch eine ‚bessere' Nachfolgertheorie erscheint jedoch nur dann angebracht, wenn die Nachfolgertheorie für die Problemlösungs- und Erklärungsansätze ihrer Vorgängerin entsprechend (‚bessere') Ersatzvorschläge anbietet[38]. Voraussetzung sind somit in jedem Falle ein *Theorienvergleich*[39] und eine *Theorienbewertung*[40]. Die moderne Rechts- und Systemtheorie, wie ich sie im

---

bruar 1984 verstorbenen Gelehrten, Stuttgart 1985, S. 134—172, 162 ff., 170 f. Vgl. jetzt auch: *Ota Weinberger,* Soziologie und normative Institutionentheorie, in: Recht und Institution. Helmut Schelsky-Gedächtnissymposion Münster 1985, hrsg. von der Rechtswissenschaftlichen Fakultät der Universität Münster, Berlin 1985, S. 33—58, 52 ff.

[35] *Krawietz,* Recht als Regelsystem (FN 3), S. 110 ff., 115 ff.

[36] Ebd., S. 148 ff., 150 f., 153.

[37] *Werner Krawietz,* Theoriesubstitution in der Jurisprudenz, in: Dorothea Mayer-Maly/Peter M. Simons (Hrsg.), Das Naturrechtsdenken heute und morgen, Berlin 1983, S. 359—412.

[38] Ebd., S. 409 f.

[39] Zu den Möglichkeiten eines Theorienvergleichs in der Rechtstheorie: *Werner Krawietz,* Juristische Argumentation in rechtstheoretischer, rechtsphilosophischer und rechtssoziologischer Perspektive, in: Norbert Achterberg/Werner Krawietz/Dieter Wyduckel (Hrsg.), Recht und Staat im sozialen Wandel, Berlin 1983, S. 347—390, 389 f.

[40] *Gerhard Radnitzky,* Das Problem der Theoriebewertung, in: Zeitschrift für die Allgemeine Wissenschaftstheorie 10 (1979), S. 67—97, 68 f.

Anschluß an Friedman, Parsons, Luhmann u. a. verstehe, bietet ein geeignetes *Framework*, d. h. eine *Rahmentheorie des Rechts und der Gesellschaft*, welche es uns ermöglicht, die erforderlichen Theorienvergleiche anzustellen. Diese Leistungsfähigkeit und das analytische Potential der modernen Systemtheorie kann und sollte die Rechtstheorie sich beim Aufbau einer Strukturtheorie des Rechts zunutze machen.

III. Systemische Struktur staatlich organisierter Rechtssysteme

1. Während die analytische Jurisprudenz der Wiener rechtstheoretischen Schule das Rechtssystem als einen Stufenbau begreift, der auf einer letzten, fundamentalen Basis- oder Grundnorm allen Rechts aufruht, kann nach der hier vertretenen Auffassung, die auf einer Verbindung normativ-realistischer Jurisprudenz mit Rechts- und Systemtheorie basiert, eine derartige, auch nach Ansicht von Kelsen nicht politisch-rechtlich gesetzte, sondern nur im Rechtsdenken präsupponierte, d. h. bloß in mente vorausgesetzte Grundnorm wohl kaum der „archimedische Punkt" sein, von dem aus die Welt der juristischen Erkenntnis in Bewegung gesetzt wird[41]. In einer höchst eindrucksvollen, auf rechts- und systemtheoretischer Grundlage basierenden Untersuchung über „The Notion of Basic Norm(s) in Jurisprudence" sind *Torstein Eckhoff* und *Nils Kristian Sundby* zu dem Ergebnis gelangt, „that basic norms do not 'exist' and that, moreover, there is no need for them"[42]. Sie haben darüber hinaus sehr treffend nachgewiesen, daß die Verkettung von Rechtssystemen mit einer einzigen, wie auch immer beschaffenen Grundnorm im Sinne einer ‚reinen' Theorie des Rechts und des Rechtssystems „may easily give rise to illusions of a sort of unity, consistency and simplicity which is highly unrealistic with regard to complex modern law systems"[43]. Dem ist aus rechtsrealistischer sowie rechts- und systemtheoretischer Sicht, wie ich sie verstehe[44], nichts hinzuzufügen.

a) Die Rechts- und Systemtheorie legt ihren Rechtsvorstellungen einen sehr weiten Begriff des Rechts bzw. des Rechtssystems zugrunde, von dem ich im folgenden im Anschluß an *Friedman*[45], *Eckhoff/Sundby*[46],

---

[41] Eingehend hierzu: *Werner Krawietz*, Grundnorm, in: Joachim Ritter (Hrsg.), Historisches Wörterbuch der Philosophie 3 (1974), Sp. 918—922.

[42] *Torstein Eckhoff/Nils Kristian Sundby*, The Notion of Basic Norm(s) in Jurisprudence, in: Scandinavian Studies in Law 19 (1975), S. 121—151, 129 f.

[43] Ebd., S. 137.

[44] *Werner Krawietz*, Reinheit der Rechtslehre als Ideologie?, in: RECHTSTHEORIE Beiheft 4 (1982), S. 345—421, 415 f.

[45] *Friedman*, Rechtssystem (FN 16), S. 12 f., 16 ff., 21 f.

[46] *Eckhoff/Sundby*, Basic Norms (FN 42), S. 123 f.

Luhmann[47] u. a. ausgehe[48]. Das Rechtssystem ist danach nicht bloß ein — mehr oder weniger weitgehend in Rechtstexten verbrieftes — gedankliches Gebilde, sondern auch und vor allem ein soziales Gebilde, zu dem auch Personen und Sachen gehören, beispielsweise Parlaments- und Gerichtsgebäude, Behörden, Beamte, Staatsanwälte und Richter, aber auch die Verträge abschließenden Parteien im alltäglichen Rechtsverkehr[49]. Aus der Sicht einer normativ-realistischen Jurisprudenz wie der modernen Systemtheorie werden Rechtssysteme (legal systems) somit als mehr oder weniger unabhängig von ihrer rechtssprachlichen Symbolstruktur *realiter existierende*[50] Sozialgebilde angesehen, die mit den normativen Rechtsvorschriften[51], in denen sie formuliert und durch die sie symbolisch repräsentiert werden, nicht einfach identifiziert werden dürfen. Im Gegensatz zu der unter Juristen sonst üblichen Vorstellung geht es hier somit gar nicht um das Rechts*normen*system (legal norm-system), letzteres verstanden als System von Rechtsnormen bzw. Rechtssätzen, sondern um das in einem sehr weiten Sinne verstandene Rechtssystem als Regelsystem (legal system), das aus Rechtsnormen *und* den zugehörigen Rechtsaktivitäten nebst deren Umständen und Bedingungen besteht[52]. Die Regelsysteme des Rechts werden somit — ganz abgesehen von ihrer rechtssprachlichen Fixierung — als in der gesellschaftlichen Wirklichkeit realiter existierende soziale Gebilde betrachtet.

b) Im Hinblick auf diesen weiten Rechtsbegriff werden im folgenden — über die eigentlichen Staatsfunktionen hinausgehend — *alle* sozialen Kommunikationen, die sich mit Bezugnahme auf das Recht vollziehen, als zum Rechtssystem gehörig verstanden[53]. Eingeschlossen sind daher

---

[47] *Niklas Luhmann,* Die Funktion des Rechts: Erwartungssicherung oder Verhaltenssteuerung?, in: Archiv für Rechts- und Sozialphilosophie Beiheft 8 (1974), S. 31—45, 35.

[48] *Krawietz,* Rechtssystem und Rationalität (FN 11), S. 12 f.

[49] Dieses realistische Rechtsverständnis ist übrigens durchaus charakteristisch für die bereits am Ausgang des 19. Jhdts. in Deutschland von Ihering und Heck begründete Interessen- und Wertungsjurisprudenz, die in ihrer allgemeinen Rechtslehre auf einer soziologischen Auffassung des Rechts basiert. Vgl. *Philip Heck,* Grundlagen des Rechts, in: Adolf Bauser (Hrsg.), Deutsche Staatsbürgerkunde, Stuttgart 1922, S. 139—157, 140 f.

[50] Sehr treffend: *Herbert Hirsch/M. Donald Hancock,* Legislative Systems: Legislatures in Systemic Perspective, in: dies. (Hrsg.), Comparative Legislative Systems, New York — London 1971, S. 1—20, 2 f., die mit Grund zwischen dem „symbolic system" und dem „system operating in the 'real' world" unterscheiden.

[51] Ganz im Sinne des heutigen skandinavischen Rechtsrealismus: *Jørgensen,* Pluralis Juris (FN 29), S. 48 f., der mit Vorbedacht den Ausdruck „prescription" verwendet, „to use an expression which applies both to the behaviour and the underlying mental processes".

[52] *Eckhoff/Sundby,* Basic Norms (FN 42), S. 123 f.

[53] Eingehend hierzu: *Niklas Luhmann,* Communications about Law in Interaction Systems, in: Karin Knorr-Cetina/Aaron V. Cicourel (Hrsg.),

auch alle *ohne* Beteiligung der staatlichen Rechtserzeugungs- und Rechtsanwendungsorgane ablaufenden *Kommunikationen des täglichen Lebens*, sofern sie nur irgendeinen (zumindest impliziten!) Bezug zum Recht enthalten[54].

2. Hier ist weder Zeit noch Raum, eine allgemeine *Normentheorie* zu präsentieren, wie sie sich *aus rechts- und systemtheoretischer Perspektive* darstellt. Sie hätte selbstverständlich auch der Tatsache Rechnung zu tragen, daß die Theorie des Rechts es nicht nur mit dem Rechtssystem zu tun hat, sondern zugleich auch mit sonstigen Normensystemen[55], z. B. der Religion[56] oder der Moral[57], die ihrerseits sozial etabliert sind. Ich muß mich hier jedoch auf die Feststellung beschränken, daß aus der Sicht einer allgemeinen Theorie sozialer Systeme die diversen Rechtssysteme in den jeweiligen Regionalgesellschaften durchgängig als integrierender Bestandteil des Gesellschaftssystems anzusehen sind.

a) Auf die für die moderne Rechts- und Systemtheorie zentrale Frage, wie angesichts der Tatsache, daß inzwischen mehr als vier Milliarden Menschen auf der Erde leben, denn überhaupt soziale Ordnung, insbesondere eine mit Mitteln des Rechts gewährleistete Rechtsordnung möglich ist, lautet die Antwort: (1) nur durch fortlaufende Neubildung sozialer Handlungs- und Sinnsysteme, (2) durch Anknüpfung an den jeweils schon sozial etablierten normativen Sinn, insbesondere an das schon geltende Recht, und (3) durch soziokulturelle Evolution, in der das Recht den jeweiligen Lebensformen in den sozialen Systemen und der Gesellschaft angeglichen wird. Diesem *Anknüpfungspunkt* ihrer Theoriebildung bei den *sozialen Handlungs- und Sinnsystemen*, die in unserer erfahrbaren und beobachtbaren Lebenswelt faktisch schon existieren bzw. noch auszubilden sind, verdankt die soziologische Systemtheorie ihren Namen.

b) Gerade die moderne Systemforschung mußte jedoch die Erfahrung machen, daß die Regeln des Rechts, wie ich — in Abwandlung eines Ausspruchs von *David Hume* über die Regeln der Moral — formulieren möchte, „nicht Schlußfolgerungen der Vernunft“ sind, sondern das Er-

---

Advances in Social Theory and Methodology: Toward an Integration of Micro- and Macro-Sociologies, Boston 1981, S. 234—256.

[54] *Krawietz*, Recht als Regelsystem (FN 3), S. 52 f.

[55] *König*, Recht im Zusammenhang der sozialen Normensysteme (FN 24), S. 44 f.

[56] Hierzu auf systemtheoretischer Grundlage: *Herbert Kaefer*, Religion und Kirche als soziale Systeme, Freiburg — Basel 1977.

[57] Eingehend dazu: *Klaus A. Ziegert*, Nach der Emanzipation des Rechts von der Moral: gesellschaftliche Wirkungschancen der Moral, in: Niklas Luhmann/Stephan H. Pfürtner (Hrsg.), Theorietechnik und Moral, Frankfurt a. M. 1978, S. 146—175.

gebnis von weitgehend undurchschauten, wenn nicht gar undurchschaubaren geschichtlich-gesellschaftlichen Entwicklungen, die wir selbst nicht aus rationaler Einsicht geschaffen haben und auch selbst allenfalls partiell gestalten können. „Legal norms", so formulieren *Torstein Eckhoff* und *Nils Kristian Sundby* sehr treffend, „are connected with one another and with legal activities through complex and sometimes opaque functional relations"[58].

3. Was die mittel- und langfristige Rechtsentwicklung angeht, so kann ich in diesem Kreise die Theorie der Evolution des Rechts und der Gesellschaft, wie sie sich aus der Sicht der Rechts- und Systemtheorie darstellt[59], als bekannt voraussetzen[60]. Ich greife nur ihr Kernstück, die *Theorie gesellschaftlicher Differenzierung,* heraus, da sich die jüngsten Neuerungen in der Systemforschung auf eben dieses Kernstück beziehen.

a) Nach der Theorie gesellschaftlicher Differenzierung vollziehen sich im Verlaufe der Geschichte und der soziokulturellen Evolution mit dem fortgesetzten Wachstum der Gesellschaft zugleich tiefgreifende sozialstrukturelle Veränderungen[61]. Während die *archaische Gesellschaft* nur segmentär differenziert war, das heißt sich aus gleichen Teileinheiten oder Teilsystemen (Familien, Stämmen) zusammensetzte, sind in der *prämodernen Gesellschaft,* das heißt in den vorneuzeitlichen Hochkulturen im Wege einer fortschreitenden stratifikatorischen Binnendifferenzierung Formen gesellschaftlichen Zusammenlebens entstanden, die sich in sozialstruktureller Hinsicht aus Klassen oder Schichten (lat. strata) zusammensetzen, also aus ungleichen Teilen aufbauen. Letztere werden in ihrer bislang dominierenden Funktion in der *modernen Gesellschaft* aufgelöst und abgelöst durch eine Differenzierung in funktional unterschiedene *Teilsysteme der Gesellschaft* (Politik, Wirtschaft, Kultur usw.), die ihrerseits heute ganz maßgeblich die Lebensformen in den sozialen Teilbereichen prägen und mitbestimmen.

b) Diese neuartigen Lebensformen zeichnen sich in sozialstruktureller Hinsicht durch zwei Momente aus, nämlich (i) dadurch, daß innerhalb

---

[58] *Eckhoff/Sundby,* Basic Norms (FN 42), S. 137 f.

[59] *Niklas Luhmann,* Evolution des Rechts, in: RECHTSTHEORIE 1 (1979), S. 3—22; *Friedman,* Rechtssystem (FN 16), S. 290 ff., 300 ff.

[60] Zur Rechtsentwicklung im Kontext gesellschaftlicher Evolution neuerdings: *Gunther Teubner,* Reflexives Recht. Entwicklungsmodelle des Rechts in vergleichender Perspektive, in: Archiv für Rechts- und Sozialphilosophie 68 (1982), S. 13—59, 14 f., 35 f., der jedoch die neuesten Entwicklungen in der Systemtheorie ignoriert und die Evolution des Rechts zu einseitig unter dem Aspekt der „Anpassung von Rechtsstrukturen an Sozialstrukturen" beurteilt. Theoriebautechnisch gesehen, geht es heute um einen Umbau der Theorie adaptiver Systeme zu einer Theorie selbstreferenzieller Systeme.

[61] Dazu und zum folgenden: *Niklas Luhmann,* Geschichte als Prozeß und die Theorie sozio-kultureller Evolution, in: ders., Soziologische Aufklärung, Bd. 3: Soziales System, Gesellschaft, Organisation, S. 178—197, 190 f.

der Gesellschaft im Wege der Arbeitsteilung *gesellschaftliche Teilsysteme* ausgebildet, verselbständigt und institutionell auf Dauer gestellt werden, die sich jeweils *primär nur noch an einer, für sie spezifischen Funktion* orientieren. Auf diese Weise haben sich in der modernen Gesellschaft auch die *politischen*, mehr oder weniger weitgehend *staatlich organisierten Rechtssysteme* ausdifferenziert[62], die mit Mitteln, d. h. auf Grund und nach Maßgabe des jeweils geltenden Rechts der *Herstellung kollektiv bindender Entscheidungen* dienen. Auf die Ausbildung anderer Teilsysteme der Gesellschaft, wie beispielsweise diejenige des religiös-kulturellen oder diejenige des wirtschaftlichen Subsystems, kann ich hier ebensowenig eingehen wie auf die zwischen den Teilsystemen bestehenden Inter-Systembeziehungen. Funktionale Differenzierung setzt mit Bezug auf das politische, gewöhnlich staatlich organisierte Rechtssystem ferner (ii) voraus, daß bei weiterem Wachstum der Gesellschaft das jeweilige gesellschaftliche Teilsystem nur noch weiterwachsen kann, indem es sich *intern* ausdifferenziert, d. h. weitere *soziale Teil- und Untersysteme* ausbildet, die ebenfalls Systemgrenzen institutionell auf Dauer stellen müssen, innerhalb welcher auch sie eine gewisse Autonomie erlangen. Auf diese Weise haben sich *innerhalb der staatlich organisierten Rechtssysteme* auch soziale Unter- und Teilsysteme gebildet, die beispielsweise als Gesetzgebungssystem, Regierungssystem, Verwaltungssystem, Rechtsprechungssystem usf. — auch auf der Grundlage intern noch fortgesetzter sozialer Untersystembildungen, z. B. durch Ausbildung von Instanzenzügen! — in ihren jeweiligen Systemumwelten operieren.

c) Meine zentrale These besagt, daß nicht nur auf der Ebene des Gesellschaftssystems, sondern auch *auf der Ebene der* sich ausdifferenzierenden gesellschaftlichen *Teilsysteme* — und das heißt hier: des *staatlich organisierten* Rechtssystems! — die unerläßliche, laufende *Transformation der* das jeweilige Gesellschaftssystem strukturierenden *Rechtsordnung* nur durch fortlaufende *Selbstreproduktion und Selbstsubstitution* möglich ist[63]. Für alle funktional ausdifferenzierten Teilsysteme, insbesondere für das staatlich organisierte Rechtssystem, wird gewöhnlich schon von Verfassungs wegen gewährleistet, daß eine fortlaufende *Transformation des jeweils geltenden Rechts* stattfinden kann[64]. Sie ist

---

[62] *Luhmann*, Ausdifferenzierung des Rechts (FN 15), S. 35 f., 366 ff., 440 f.; *Krawietz*, Recht als Regelsystem (FN 3), S. 117 f., 174.

[63] *Niklas Luhmann*, Identitätsgebrauch in selbstsubstitutiven Ordnungen, besonders Gesellschaften, in: ders., Soziologische Aufklärung (FN 61), S. 198—117, 206 ff., 209 f.

[64] Genau hier liegt der Zugang zur *sozialen* Tiefenstruktur (deep justification) des Rechts, der in der Transformationsjurisprudenz von: *Aleksander Peczenik*, The Basis of Legal Justification, Lund 1983, S. 3 ff., 44 ff., 70 ff. allzu stiefmütterlich behandelt wird.

einerseits eine bloße *Selbstreproduktion der Rechtsordnung*, die sich in der Anwendung des bereits geltenden Rechts auf einzelne Fälle vollzieht, andererseits jedoch auch eine zumindest partielle *Selbstsubstitution des Rechtssystems* in dem Sinne, daß auf den hierfür vorgesehenen Wegen und in den dafür eigens eingerichteten Verfahren auch ‚altes' durch ‚neues' Recht ersetzt werden kann. Das staatlich organisierte Rechtssystem der modernen Gesellschaft verfügt unter den Bedingungen der Positivität allen Rechts, das heißt aufgrund der im Rechtssystem selbst institutionalisierten und organisierten *Strukturvorgaben* für Rechtserzeugung, über politisch-rechtliche Entscheidungsmechanismen, in denen Rechtsregeln nicht bloß produziert und reproduziert, sondern auch die tradierten Rechtsvorstellungen der jeweiligen gesamtgesellschaftlichen Entwicklung im Wege der Selbstsubstitution angepaßt und in neues Recht transformiert werden können. Alles wie auch immer institutionalisierte Recht ist somit eine selbstsubstitutive Ordnung genau in dem und nur in dem Sinne, daß von Verfassungs wegen *Recht jeweils nur durch Recht substituiert*, aber *nicht* etwa durch die Normen der Moral, durch Erziehung oder Wissenschaft *ersetzt* werden kann. Das Recht kann durch Moral, Erziehung oder Wissenschaft nicht ersetzt, sondern allenfalls unterstützt werden.

IV. Aktuelle Tendenzen in der Entwicklung der Systemtheorie und ihre Konsequenzen für eine Strukturtheorie des Rechts

1. Geht man davon aus, daß bei der Bildung von Rechtssystemen die Probleme rechtlicher Regelbildung mit denjenigen sozialer Systembildung korrespondieren, so stellt sich die Frage, welche Konsequenzen sich aus der jüngsten Entwicklung der Systemtheorie im Rahmen einer Integration von Rechts- und Systemtheorie für den *Aufbau einer Strukturtheorie des Rechts* ergeben. Eine Verschiebung der Forschungsschwerpunkte und Erkenntnisinteressen innerhalb der Systemtheorie hat nahezu zwangsläufig auch Folgen für die zugehörige Theorie sozialer Normen, insbesondere für die Theorie des Rechts. Dies gilt auch und vor allem für die Theorie staatlich organisierter Rechtssysteme, sofern man letztere — rechts- und systemtheoretisch betrachtet — als eine Theorie sozialer Institutionen, Organisationen und sonstiger Handlungs- und Sinnsysteme begreift, die mit Mitteln des Rechts Einfluß auf das menschliche Erleben und Handeln ausüben. Neue Entwicklungen in der Systemtheorie müssen infolgedessen auch Berücksichtigung finden beim Aufbau einer Strukturtheorie des Rechts.

a) Gegenwärtig ist noch umstritten, wie tiefgreifend die jüngsten Veränderungen und Auffassungsunterschiede in der aktuellen Entwicklung der Systemtheorie wirklich sind[65]. Auch steht eine zufriedenstellende Analyse der Voraussetzungen und Folgen dieser Entwicklung noch aus[66]. Immerhin lassen sich zumindest *drei Phasen* in der jüngsten Entwicklung der Systemtheorie unterscheiden, die auch Folgen für die Konzeption der Rechtstheorie zeitigen dürften:

(i) Ursprünglich hatte sich die allgemeine Systemtheorie und mit ihr die Theorie sozialer Systeme zunächst als *System/Umwelt-Theorie* etabliert. Die Folge davon war, daß in der systemtheoretischen Forschung lange Zeit vor allem Probleme der Anpassung sozialer Handlungs- und Sinnsysteme an ihre jeweiligen Umweltbedingungen im Vordergrund standen[67]. Demzufolge standen auch in der Normentheorie, insbesondere in der Theorie des Rechts, lange Zeit die *Anpassungsprobleme* im Zentrum, denen sich jede Rechtsordnung mit Bezug auf ihre jeweiligen Umweltbedingungen nur einmal ausgesetzt sieht. Diese Ausgangssituation hat sich inzwischen ganz radikal gewandelt.

(ii) In einem weiteren Entwicklungsschritt wurde in der letzten Dekade die System/Umwelt-Theorie ergänzt durch eine *Theorie der Selbstorganisation von Systemen*[68]. Im Vordergrund standen nun nicht mehr der Bestand oder die Bestandserhaltung von sozialen Handlungssystemen im Verhältnis zu ihrer Umwelt, sondern Probleme der *Strukturbildung in den Systemen* selbst. Hierzu zählen auch und vor allem die Probleme der *Selbstprogrammierung* und *Selbstkonditionierung* des systemischen Entscheidungshandelns, die zum Kernbereich jeder Normen- und Rechtstheorie gehören.

(iii) Der jüngste Entwicklungsschritt, dessen Konsequenzen für die Rechtstheorie und Systemtheorie sich bislang noch kaum abschätzen

[65] Sehr weitgehend: *Luhmann*, Soziale Systeme (FN 2), S. 15 ff., der in der zeitgenössischen Systemtheorie sogar einen „Paradigmawechsel" erkennen will. Vgl. hierzu aber die Kritik von: *Werner Krawietz*, Juridisch-institutionelle Rationalität des Rechts versus Rationalität der Wissenschaften?, in: RECHTSTHEORIE 15 (1984), S. 423—452, 442 f. Hier kann im Ergebnis dahingestellt bleiben, ob es sich wirklich um einen Paradigmawechsel handelt oder nur um längst fällige Reparaturen an den Fundamenten der Systemtheorie, die den Rahmen des bisherigen Theoriedesigns weder sprengen noch überschreiten.

[66] Dazu und zum folgenden: *Luhmann* (FN 2), S. 23 ff., 26 f.

[67] Exemplarisch: *Teubner*, Reflexives Recht (FN 60), S. 13 ff., 40 f., der wegen seines unreflektierten Festhaltens an der System/Umwelt-Perspektive die Relevanz bloßer „Anpassung" und „Integration" überschätzt. Rechtstheoretisch erscheint es mir auch verfehlt, die höchst unterschiedlichen Theorieansätze von Habermas und Luhmann „nicht als konkurrierend", sondern „als komplementär" zu behandeln! Eine Theorieintegration dürfte bei den vorhandenen Divergenzen wohl ausgeschlossen sein!

[68] *Gerhard Roth/Helmut Schwegler* (Hrsg.), Self-Organizing Systems: An Interdisciplinary Approach, Frankfurt 1981, S. 106—120.

lassen, verdankt sich vor allem der Biologie und Epistemologie der Kognition von *Maturana* und *Varela*, die mit bezug auf ‚Living Systems' und ihre Organisation die Systemtheorie auf einige weitere, bislang vernachlässigte, vor allem *epistemologische Aspekte systemischer Aktivitäten* aufmerksam gemacht und damit zugleich auf eine gewandelte, zumindest partiell neue Grundlage gestellt haben[69].

b) Die im Anschluß an Maturana so bezeichnete *Theorie autopoietischer Systeme*[70], wohl häufiger als *Theorie selbstreferenzieller Systeme*[71] bezeichnet, wird heute zunehmend auf soziale Handlungs- und Sinnsysteme angewandt. Sie ist — teils aus logischen, teils aus soziologischen Gründen — durch eine Reihe von Autoren auch auf das politische System, insbesondere *auf staatlich organisierte Rechtssysteme* oder Teile derselben übertragen worden, zunächst von *Alf Ross*[72], der wohl als einer der ersten das Problem der Selbstreferenz bei dem von Verfassungs wegen verfügten Normieren des Normierens aufmerksam gemacht hat, und neuerdings von *Dias*[73], *Hejl*[74], *Luhmann*[75] und *Krawietz*[76].

c) Stark vereinfacht besagt die *Theorie selbstreferenzieller Systeme* im Hinblick auf das Rechtssystem, daß dieses sich mit allen einschlägigen Operationen politisch-rechtlichen Entscheidens stets nicht bloß auf seine Umwelt bezieht, sondern zugleich immer auch *auf sich selbst*, weil es nur aufgrund dieses Selbstkontaktes und nach Maßgabe der Interaktion mit Teilen seiner systemeigenen Ordnungsstruktur auf seine Umwelt zu reagieren vermag[77]. Aber nicht nur das Rechtssystem als ganzes,

---

[69] Hierzu jetzt: *Humberto R. Maturana*, Erkennen: Die Organisation und Verkörperung von Wirklichkeit. Ausgewählte Arbeiten zur biologischen Epistemologie (mit Ko-Autoren: F. J. Varela, S. G. Frenk, G. Uribe), Braunschweig 1982.

[70] *Frank Benseler/Peter M. Hejl/Wolfgang K. Köck* (Hrsg.), Autopoiesis, Communication, and Society. The Theory of Autopoietic Systems in the Social Sciences, Frankfurt — New York 1980.

[71] *Peter M. Hejl*, Sozialwissenschaft als Theorie selbstreferenzieller Systeme, Frankfurt/Main 1982.

[72] *Alf Ross*, On Law and Justice, London 1958, S. 78—84; *ders.*, On Self-Reference and a Puzzle in Constitutional Law, in: Mind 1969, S. 1—24. Hierzu auch: *H. L. A. Hart*, Self-referring laws, in: Festskrift tillägnad Karl Olivecrona, Stockholm 1964, S. 307 ff.

[73] *R. W. M. Dias*, Autopoiesis and the Judicial Process, in: RECHTSTHEORIE 10 (1979), S. 1—24.

[74] *Peter M. Hejl*, Die Theorie autopoietischer Systeme: Perspektiven für die soziologische Systemtheorie, in: RECHTSTHEORIE 13 (1982), S. 45—88.

[75] *Niklas Luhmann*, Die Ausdifferenzierung von Erkenntnisgewinn: Zur Genese von Wissenschaft, in: Nico Stehr/Volker Meja (Hrsg.), Wissenssoziologie, Opladen 1980, S. 102—139, 127 ff., 129.

[76] *Krawietz*, Recht als Regelsystem (FN 3), S. 110 f., 119 f., 139 f., 186.

[77] Ebd., S. 110 ff., 115 ff.

sondern auch seine im Wege der Binnendifferenzierung gebildeten Unter- und Teilsysteme fungieren als *realiter existierende* selbstreferenzielle Systeme menschlichen Erlebens und Handelns. Diese rechts- und systemtheoretische Rekonstruktion vermittelt zugleich ein neues Bild von Art und Ausmaß der sich intern abspielenden Interdependenzen. Im Hinblick auf die jeweiligen System/Umwelt-Beziehungen des staatlich organisierten Rechtssystems als eines ganzen, aber auch aller Unter- und Teilsysteme, die Außenkontakte mit ihrem jeweiligen Publikum unterhalten, muß ferner unterschieden werden zwischen *internen* und *externen* Interdependenzen[78].

2. Für den Aufbau einer Strukturtheorie des Rechts ergeben sich aus diesen systemtheoretischen Neuerungen eine ganze Reihe von Konsequenzen, vor allem aber zwei sehr tiefgreifende Folgerungen, die ich wenigstens kurz skizzieren möchte, weil sie zwangsläufig zu einer Veränderung fest eingefahrener Rechtsvorstellungen führen müssen. Eine sehr weitgehende Aufgabe liebgewonnener rechtlicher Denkgewohnheiten wird fällig (1) mit Bezug auf die sogen. *Einheit der Rechtsordnung* sowie (2) mit Bezug auf den sogen. *Stufenbau des Rechts.*

a) Was die Identität oder Einheit des Rechtssystems angeht, so dürfte sich die tradierte, bloß konventionelle Vorstellung einer analytischen Jurisprudenz nicht länger halten lassen, die bis auf den heutigen Tag von der Annahme einer durch die Grundnorm[79] hergestellten Einheit der Rechtsordnung bzw. von einer mit Notwendigkeit existierenden Primärhierarchie des Rechts ausgeht, welche ihrerseits zugleich dessen Einheit gewährleistet[80]. Auch wenn man beide Vorstellungen aufgibt, nötigt dies gleichwohl nicht zu der Besorgnis, daß eine Desintegration und Fragmentierung der Rechtsordnung in unzusammenhängende Teile die Folge sein werde. Mit Bezug auf die stets prekäre *Einheit des Rechtssystems* hat *Luhmann* in einem im Juni 1983 in Madison gehaltenen, noch unveröffentlichten Vortrag über „Self-Reproduction of the Law and Its Limits“[81] und in einer weiteren, gleichfalls unveröffentlichten, in dieser

---

[78] Zu dem mit Blick auf den Output von Entscheidungssystemen interessanten Problem eines „feedback“ vgl. vor allem: *Torstein Eckhoff,* Feedback in Legal Reasoning and Rule Systems, in: Scandinavian Studies in Law 22 (1978), S. 39—51.

[79] Eingehend hierzu: *Krawietz,* Grundnorm (FN 41), Sp. 919 f.

[80] Kritisch gegenüber der vor allem von Merkl vertretenen Auffassung einer „jeder Rechtsordnung immanent(en)“, d. h. mit Notwendigkeit bestehenden „Rechtshierarchie“: *Werner Krawietz,* Die Lehre vom Stufenbau des Rechts — eine säkularisierte politische Theologie?, in: Ders./Helmut Schelsky (Hrsg.), Rechtssystem und gesellschaftliche Basis bei Hans Kelsen, Berlin 1984, S. 255—271, 263 ff.

[81] Jetzt abgedruckt unter dem Titel: *Niklas Luhmann,* The Self-reproduction of Law and its Limits, in: Gunther Teubner (Hrsg.), Dilemmas of Law in the Welfare State, Berlin — New York 1986, S. 111 ff.

Zeitschrift erscheinenden Untersuchung[82] vom Standpunkt der Theorie selbstreferenzieller Systeme den rechtstheoretisch außerordentlich interessanten Gedanken einer im Rechtssystem *mitlaufenden Selbstreferenz* („concurring selfreference") entwickelt. Er besagt, daß sich im Rechtssystem die Einheit durch eine permanente Autopoiese herstellt, das heißt sich ständig eine „Selbstreproduktion des Rechts" vollzieht[83]. Mitlaufende Selbstreferenz oder Autopoiese des Rechtssystems bedeutet somit — abweichend von geläufigen Theorievorstellungen — stets zweierlei, nämlich daß (i) jedes Rechtssystem „normativ geschlossen (ist) insofern, als nur das Rechtssystem seinen Elementen rechtsnormative Qualität verleihen und sie dadurch als Einheiten konstituieren kann", und zugleich (ii) in seinem Umweltbezug ein „kognitiv offenes System" ist, das sich auf Grund der Struktur seiner Rechtsregeln im Wege der Selbstprogrammierung von eingehenden Tatsacheninformationen abhängig machen, aber auch seine Normen ändern kann[84]. Der systemtheoretische Begriff *mitlaufender Selbstreferenz* bezieht sich somit auf das allenthalben zu beobachtende Phänomen ständiger „Rechtsänderung", in der sich „eine Übertragung der Qualität normativer Geltung auf partiell *neue Erwartungen* vollzieht". Das Recht befindet sich danach „in ständiger Bagatellvariation" — sei es „in der Form einer fast unmerklichen Evolution", sei es „in der Form geplanter Strukturänderung"[85]. Für Luhmann bildet somit alles Recht „ein *normativ geschlossenes, aber kognitiv offenes System*"[86]. Das wichtigste Resultat dieser „Wende zur Theorie selbstreferenzieller Systeme" liegt somit in der Einsicht, daß *nur das Rechtssystem selbst* den Einheiten, aus denen es sich zusammensetzt, „rechtsnormative Qualität verleihen" kann, das heißt „kein rechtlich relevantes Ereignis kann seine Normativität aus der Umwelt des Systems beziehen". Ich erblicke in dieser Auffassung auch gewisse Bezüge zu Weinbergers „Stammbaumtheorie der Rechtsgeltung"[87], die ich hier aber nicht weiter ausloten kann. Auch muß hier dahingestellt bleiben, ob es überhaupt angebracht ist, mit Bezug auf die *Identität eines Rechtssystems,* in der auch seine — freilich nur relative — Autonomie zum Ausdruck gelangt, und auf die laufend erforderliche *Identifikation und Selektion neuer Regeln,* die damit als Recht eben dieses System ausgewählt und ausgezeichnet werden, von einer

[82] Jetzt veröffentlicht unter dem Titel: *Niklas Luhmann,* Die Einheit des Rechtssystems, in: RECHTSTHEORIE 14 (1983), S. 129—154.

[83] Ebd., S. 140 f.

[84] Ebd., S. 135 f., 138 f.

[85] Ebd., S. 136.

[86] Ebd., S. 139.

[87] Zuletzt hierzu: *Ota Weinberger,* Logische Analyse als Basis der juristischen Argumentation, in: Werner Krawietz/Robert Alexy (Hrsg.), Metatheorie juristischer Argumentation, Berlin 1983, S. 159—232, 224.

normativen „Geschlossenheit" ein und desselben Rechtssystems zu reden[88], worüber sich durchaus streiten ließe.

b) Was den Stufenbau des Rechts oder genauer (und ohne metaphorische Verbrämung[89] des ihm zugrunde liegenden Sachverhalts!) formuliert: die *Hierarchisierung von Verfassungs-, Gesetzes- und sonstigen Rechtsbestimmungen* angeht, so entwirft die Theorie selbstreferenzieller Systeme ein sehr viel realistischeres Bild der im staatlich organisierten Rechtssystem möglichen *und* wirksamen Interdependenzen, indem sie auf die Wechselseitigkeit der Beziehungen zwischen den Teil- und Untersystembildungen, d. h. den jeweiligen Entscheidungsorganen und Rechtsgeltungsebenen in ihren jeweiligen Systemumwelten hinweist[90]. Rechtsrealistisch betrachtet, wird im Rechtssystem trotz unterschiedlicher Rechtsgeltungsebenen[91] nicht nur ‚von oben nach unten', sondern auch ‚von unten nach oben' gesteuert. Auch ist die Rationalität des Rechtssystems, wie *Eckhoff* und *Sundby* richtig bemerken[92], nicht in Gefahr, wenn obsolet gewordene Hierarchievorstellungen verabschiedet werden: „Abandonment of the hierarchical way of thinking does not lead to a vicious circle or other logical difficulties". Dies schließt *sekundäre Selbsthierarchisierungen*[93] des Rechtssystems, die von Verfassungs wegen im jeweiligen System der Rechtsquellen verankert werden, selbstverständlich nicht aus, sondern ein.

3. Vor dem Hintergrund der hier angestellten, auf einer Verbindung von sinnkritischem Rechtsrealismus und Systemtheorie basierenden Überlegungen dürfte schon hinreichend deutlich geworden sein, daß die geläufige, mit Blick auf die zentralstaatliche Herkunft und Geschichte einiger kontinentaleuropäischer Staaten vorgestellte Annahme einer staatlichen *Zentralmacht* und einer für sie verfügbaren, instrumentell vollständig disponiblen *Normativstruktur des Rechts*[94] sehr weitgehend illusionär ist. Dies gilt auch für die vornehmlich gesellschaftskritisch

---

[88] Hierzu schon: *Krawietz*, Recht als Regelsystem (FN 3), S. 74 f.

[89] *Krawietz*, Lehre vom Stufenbau des Rechts (FN 80), S. 256 f., 260 ff., 264 f.

[90] Ebd., S. 267 f., 270 f.

[91] *Krawietz*, Reinheit der Rechtslehre als Ideologie (FN 20), S. 416 ff., 419.

[92] *Eckhoff/Sundby*, Notion of Basic Norm(s) in Jurisprudence (FN 42), S. 130.

[93] *Krawietz*, Reinheit der Rechtslehre als Ideologie (FN 20), S. 419 f.

[94] Zu sehr europazentrisch: *Immanuel Wallerstein*, The Modern World-System. Capitalist Agriculture and the Origins of the European World-Economy in the Sixteenth Century, London 1974; *ders.*, The Modern World-System II. Mercantilism and the Consolidation of the European World-Economy, London 1980; *ders.*, The States in the Institutional Context of the Capitalist World Economy, in: International Social Science Journal 32 (1980), S. 743—751, 748 mit Blick auf das in Zentrum und Peripherie gegliederte „interstate system".

motivierte, hauptsächlich politisch-ökonomisch begründete Kritik an einer vermeintlich nach wie vor starken, zentralen Staatsmacht[95]. Derartige Annahmen setzen mehr oder weniger unreflektiert *das* noch voraus, was heute wohl kein Rechts- und Systemtheoretiker mehr behaupten würde.

a) Die zentrale Steuerung von irgendeiner einzigen Stelle im staatlich organisierten Rechtssystem bzw. im Rechtswissenschaftssystem scheidet schon allein deswegen aus, weil — vom Standpunkt einer normativrealistischen Betrachtungsweise aus gesehen — allein schon die bestehenden *internen*, durch Rechtsregeln vermittelten *Interdependenzen* sich im Entscheidungs- und Erkenntnisprozeß als so hochgradig und vielfältig erweisen, daß *nicht* einmal eine *interne Transparenz dieser Interdependenzen* als Voraussetzung für eine wirksame *Kontrolle von einer einzigen Stelle* her gegeben ist. Ebensowenig erscheint ein rationaler Nachvollzug der *externen* Interdependenzen von einer einzigen Stelle her möglich. Das staatlich organisierte Rechtssystem der modernen Gesellschaft, das in eine Vielzahl und Vielfalt einander zuarbeitender Kommunikations- und Funktionssysteme untergliedert ist, verfügt nun einmal weder über eine Spitze noch über ein Zentrum.

b) Angesichts des Fehlens eines eindeutigen Steuerungszentrums[96] erscheint es — makrotheoretisch gesehen — allenfalls möglich, aber auch nötig, die im staatlich organisierten Rechtssystem und seinen Unter- und Teilsystemen wirksamen Kräfte der *Selbststeuerung des Rechtssystems* in der Systemrationalität ihres Miteinanderfungierens zu studieren[97]. Ansatzpunkt dafür bietet eine rechts- und systemtheoretische Rekonstruktion der intern und extern wirksamen Interdependenzen sowie der wechselseitigen Intersystembeziehungen. Sie hätte deutlich zu machen, daß alle im Kontakt mit ihren jeweiligen Umwelten erfolgenden Selbststeuerungsprozesse des Rechtssystems und im Rechtssystem stets nur im *Selbstkontakt*, das heißt über Interaktionen mit Teilen der systemeigenen Struktur *und* demzufolge auch nur *über interne Interdependenzen hinweg* erfolgen können, so daß sie zwangsläufig zugleich auch andere Steuerungseffekte beeinträchtigen und stören müssen. Eine Zentralsteuerung, die von einer einzigen Stelle, beispielsweise einem territorialen Herrscher (Monarchen, Kaiser, Zaren o. ä.) im Zentrum und/oder

---

[95] Hierzu beispielsweise: *Andre Gunder Frank*, Die gegenwärtige Krise und die Perspektiven des Weltsystems, in: Jochen Blaschke (Hrsg.), Perspektiven des Weltsystems, Frankfurt am Main 1983, S. 230—255; *Ulrich Menzel/Dieter Senghaas*, Autozentrierte Entwicklung im Weltsystem — Versuch einer Typologie, ebd., S. 142—188.

[96] Eingehend hierzu: *Niklas Luhmann*, Politische Theorie im Wohlfahrtsstaat, München — Wien 1981, S. 22 ff., 121.

[97] Dazu und zum folgenden: *Krawietz*, Recht als Regelsystem (FN 3), S. 111 f., 117 ff., 140 f.

an der Spitze eines politischen Gemeinwesens noch ausgehen mochte, ist im modernen, staatlich organisierten Rechtssystem schon deswegen ausgeschlossen, weil dessen Unter- und Teilsysteme (z. B. das Gesetzgebungs-, Regierungs- oder Verwaltungssystem) als relativ autonome soziale Handlungssysteme füreinander nur bis zu einem bestimmten Grade einsehbar, das heißt im übrigen *black boxes* sind, so daß sie sich schon mangelns hinreichender Information auch nur sehr begrenzt als regierbar und steuerbar erweisen. In den staatlich organisierten Rechtssystemen der modernen Gesellschaft kann daher die Einheit der Rechtsordnung *nicht* mehr durch eine *intrasystemische Zentralsteuerung* gewährleistet werden, sondern es *muß* zumindest eine partielle *Selbststeuerung* zugelassen werden.

c) An mangelnder rechts- und systemtheoretischer Aufklärung leiden nach meinem Eindruck auch die vielfältigen, in den Vereinigten Staaten wie in der Bundesrepublik zu verzeichnenden Vorschläge über „delegalization“[98], d. h. über „Entrechtlichung“ bzw. „Verrechtlichung“[99], und über etwaige „Alternativen“ zum Recht. Sie beziehen sich, wie neuerdings *Ziegert* dargelegt hat, nur auf die „Oberflächenstruktur“ des Rechts oder Teile des Rechtssystems, jedoch nicht auf die „Tiefenstruktur“ des Rechts einer differenzierten Gesellschaft[100]. Auch wird nicht hinreichend zwischen Alternativen zu einzelnen Rechtseinrichtungen und Alternativen zum Recht selbst unterschieden. Zum *Recht* selbst gibt es, rechts- und systemtheoretisch gesehen, in der modernen Gesellschaft *keine Alternative.*

V. Juristischer Positivismus oder Systemtheorie?

1. Mir ist selbstverständlich nicht unbekannt, daß gegen die Verwendung soziologischer Systemtheorie im Bereich des Rechts und der Rechtstheorie allerlei Bedenken erhoben werden. Jedoch besteht für mich im Ergebnis kein Zweifel daran, daß die *Systemtheorie in Verbindung mit einem sinnkritischen Rechtsrealismus und Institutionalismus,* so wie ich ihn verstehe, schon jetzt (i) allen rechtspraktischen Aktivitäten als

---

[98] Hierzu die Kritik von: *Richard L. Abel,* Delegalization: A Critical Review of Its Ideology, Manifestations, and Social Consequences, in: Erhard Blankenburg et. al. (Hrsg.), Alternative Rechtsformen und Alternativen zum Recht, in: Jahrbuch für Rechtssoziologie und Rechtstheorie 6 (1980), S. 27—47.

[99] *Rüdiger Voigt* (Hrsg.), Verrechtlichung. Analysen zu Funktion und Wirkung von Parlamentarisierung, Bürokratisierung und Justizialisierung sozialer, politischer und ökonomischer Prozesse, Königstein/Ts. 1980; *ders.* (Hrsg.), Gegentendenzen zur Verrechtlichung, Opladen 1983.

[100] Dazu und zum folgenden: *Klaus A. Ziegert,* Unterstützungssystem Recht: Zur Programmstruktur des Rechts in der nach-industriellen Gesellschaft, in: Jahrbuch für Rechtssoziologie und Rechtstheorie 9 (1983), S. 266—289, 286 f.

Orientierungshilfe zu dienen vermag, (ii) durchaus in der Lage ist, allen praktischen *und* theoretischen Bemühungen im Bereich des Rechts und seiner Anwendung einen einheitlichen Begriffsrahmen und eine einheitliche Terminologie zur Verfügung zu stellen und (iii) es ermöglicht, auf der Grundlage dieses Frameworks die inter- und multidisziplinären Forschungsbemühungen von Rechtswissenschaft, Soziologie und Philosophie zu koordinieren bzw. zu integrieren. Es geht mir aber wohlgemerkt *nicht* um eine unkritische *Ersetzung der bisherigen Rechtstheorie durch soziologische Systemtheorie*, sondern um eine Verbindung, genauer: um eine Fusion von rechts- und systemtheoretischen Denkansätzen. Genau in diesem Punkt unterscheidet sich mein Approach von denjenigen rechtstheoretischen Ansätzen, welche die Berücksichtigung soziologischer Theoriebildung im Rahmen der Rechtstheorie für irrelevant halten, wie es jedenfalls in der Wiener rechtstheoretischen Schule Kelsens bis auf den heutigen Tag geschieht. Ich unterscheide mich in diesem Punkt aber auch von der soziologischen Theorie des Rechtssystems Luhmanns, der in seiner Rechtssoziologie die diversen rechtsrealistischen und institutionalistischen Rechtslehren ignoriert, weil er sie — m. E. zu Unrecht — für rechtssoziologisch irrelevant hält. Mein hier vorgetragenes *Plädoyer für eine Fusion von Rechts- und Systemtheorie* zielt somit auch darauf ab, bestimmte Defizite in der soziologischen Systemtheorie zu sanieren. Es geht mir hier jedoch nicht um eine detaillierte rechtstheoretische Auseinandersetzung mit der soziologischen Theorie des Rechtssystems, wie sie vor allem von *Parsons* und *Luhmann* konzipiert worden ist. Vielmehr möchte ich mein bisheriges Vorbringen abschließend gegen einige *typische Mißverständnisse* ihrer Theorien absichern, die gewöhnlich auftreten, wenn es darum geht, Rechts- und Systemtheorie zu integrieren. Sie sind teils wissenschaftstheoretischer, teils erkenntnistheoretischer Natur und beziehen sich vor allem auf die *Eigenart rechts- und systemtheoretischer Theoriebildung.*

a) Der am häufigsten zu hörende Einwand besteht darin, die Systemtheorie sei eine bloße Modellwissenschaft, die nur operative Modelle, hingegen gar keine Theorie auf erfahrungswissenschaftlicher Grundlage biete. Ich kann und will gar nicht bestreiten, daß eine ganze Reihe sogen. systemtheoretischer Denkansätze bloß mehr oder weniger fiktive Modellkonstruktionen beinhalten und daher als Modell nur Werkzeugcharakter besitzen. Dies gilt jedoch nicht für eine auf *erfahrungswissenschaftlicher* Grundlage betriebene bzw. zu betreibende Rechts- und Systemtheorie, die sich mit einer Theorie sozialer Systeme, insbes. staatlich organisierter Rechtssysteme, befaßt und daher im Sinne von *Bunge, Lenk* u. a. Wissenschaftstheoretikern als „substantive“ Theorie angesehen werden muß[101].

b) Ein ganz anderer, durchaus ernst zu nehmender Einwand bezieht sich auf die in der Tat nicht unproblematische Interaktionsbeziehung zwischen der sog. Außenwelt und dem erkennenden Subjekt bzw. dem erkennenden System. Die Systemtheorie bietet hier in der Tat ein *neues*, auf seine Grundlagen hin noch nicht hinreichend ausgelotetes *epistemologisches Forschungsparadigma.* Die zentrale Schwierigkeit besteht darin, daß soziale Handlungssysteme genau so, wie sie systemtheoretisch analysiert werden, als solche nicht zugleich auch in der ‚Realität' vorkommen. Im vorstehenden Zusammenhang geht es jedenfalls um realiter in der Außenwelt *existierende, konkrete* „Realsysteme". Der modernen Systemtheorie ist jedoch durchaus bewußt, daß auch solche *Realsysteme* sich nur durch mehr oder weniger modellartige Beschreibungen erfassen lassen. Die Theorie selbstreferenzieller Systeme ist jedoch — und dies macht gerade ihre Eigenart aus — bemüht, die real existierenden, für uns unmittelbar, d. h. ohne eine gewisse Modellbildung unerfaßbaren Entitäten der Außenwelt nicht mit den Systemmodellen zu identifizieren[102]. Daher erscheint der übliche Einwand, *die* Systemtheorie verfalle einem *ontologischen* Realismus, der seinen Systemmodellen verknüpfungstreue Abbilder in der Wirklichkeit unterstelle, jedenfalls gegenüber der Theorie selbstreferenzieller Systeme nicht angebracht. Die bleibende Fruchtbarkeit des Ansatzes der soziologischen Systemtheorie besteht darin, die Wechselbeziehungen zwischen sozialen Handlungssystemen und ihrer jeweiligen Systemumwelt zu analysieren und zu deuten.

c) Was den epistemologischen und den wissenschaftstheoretischen *Status der modernen Systemtheorie* angeht, so kann ich mich hier kurz fassen. Die verbreitete *Fehleinschätzung der soziologischen Systemtheorie* durch ihre Kritiker hängt vor allem mit einer sehr häufig zu beklagenden, mangelnden Differenzierung bzw. mit einer Verwechselung verschiedener Systemreferenzen zusammen, insbesondere mit dem Umstand, daß von diesen Kritikern mit Bezug auf das geltende Recht nicht zwischen (1) dem staatlich organisierten Rechtssystem und (2) dem mit seiner Beobachtung, Beschreibung und Analyse befaßten Wissenschaftssystem unterschieden wird. Es ist ferner wichtig, zu unterscheiden zwischen (a) dem juristischen Positivismus, das heißt dem Gesetzes- und Rechtspositivismus und (b) dem wissenschaftstheoretischen Positivismus, die häufig gleichfalls miteinander konfundiert werden[103]. Im deutschen

---

[101] *Mario Bunge*, Scientific Research, Berlin — Heidelberg — New York 1967, Bd. 1, S. 502 ff.; *Lenk*, Wissenschaftstheoretische und philosophische Bemerkungen zur Systemtheorie (FN 6), S. 251 ff., 254 f.

[102] Eingehend hierzu: *Luhmann*, Soziale Systeme (FN 2), S. 16, der ganz ausdrücklich „den Begriff (oder das Modell) eines Systems nicht wiederum System nennen" will und davor warnt, „Erkenntnismittel (Begriffe, Modelle usw.) mit der Gegenstandsterminologie zu belegen".

Sprachgebrauch versteht man unter juristischem Positivismus, der sowohl in der Form des Gesetzes- als auch des sonstigen Rechtspositivismus auftritt, nach ganz einhelliger Auffassung ein Rechtsdenken, welches das Recht aus den komplexen geschichtlichen und gesellschaftlichen Zusammenhängen herauszulösen suchte, in denen es seiner Struktur und Funktion nach nun einmal steht. In diesem Sinne ist die hier vertretene Fusion von westdeutschem Rechtsrealismus und Institutionalismus in Verbindung mit moderner Systemtheorie ganz sicherlich *kein juristischer Positivismus*, da die obigen Zusammenhänge hier gerade berücksichtigt werden. Es handelt sich daher nach meiner Auffassung um einen durchaus schon *nachpositivistischen Rechtsrealismus*, der zugleich als eine neue Form institutionalistischen Rechtsdenkens in Erscheinung tritt[104]. Er ist durchaus charakteristisch für die deutsche Theorie und Soziologie des Rechts seit Rudolph von Ihering über Max Weber bis hin zu Schelsky und Luhmann.

2. Offensichtlich dient das Recht heute weltweit zunehmend nicht mehr bloß einer schon institutionalisierten *Erwartungssicherung* durch Verteilung von Pflichten und Rechten, sondern vor allem auch der *Verhaltenssteuerung* nach Maßgabe der vom staatlichen Gesetzgeber durch Gebote, Verbote, Ermächtigungen, Erlaubnisse u.a.m. als verbindlich gesetzten bzw. zu setzenden Rechtsnormen, Ziele, Zwecke und Werte, deren *schrittweise Realisierung* auf allen Stufen der Rechtsordnung intendiert, geplant und sukzessive bewerkstelligt wird bis hin zur zwangsweisen Durchsetzung des Rechts[105]. Eine derartige Ordnungsbildung ist jedoch, rechtsrealistisch betrachtet, nur möglich im Rahmen der bereits bestehenden sozialen Institutionen, Organisationen und sonstigen sozialen Handlungs- und Sinnsysteme, von denen schon wiederholt die Rede war[106]. Erst aus der Sicht rechts- und staatstheoretischer, in gesellschaftstheoretische Überlegungen eingebetteter Analysen, welche das Recht — unbeschadet seiner variablen normativen Inhalte und der einzelnen Rechtssystemen jeweils zugrunde liegenden Rechtsideologie — in der

[103] Zur kritischen Würdigung des juristischen Positivismus: *Samuel J. Shuman*, Legal Positivism. Its Scope and Limitations, Detroit 1963; *Werner Krawietz*, Juristische Entscheidung und wissenschaftliche Erkenntnis, Wien — New York 1978, S. X f., 3 ff., 92 ff., 227 f.; *ders.*, Juridisch-institutionelle Rationalität des Rechts versus Rationalität der Wissenschaften (FN 65), S. 423 f., 426 f.

[104] *Werner Krawietz*, Rechtssystem als Institution?, in: RECHTSTHEORIE Beiheft 6 (1984), S. 209—243, 210 ff., 213 f.

[105] *Luhmann*, Ausdifferenzierung des Rechts (FN 15), S. 73 ff., 78 f.; *Werner Krawietz*, Das positive Recht und seine Funktion. Kategoriale und methodologische Überlegungen zu einer funktionalen Rechtstheorie, Berlin 1967.

[106] Dazu und zum folgenden: *Werner Krawietz*, Ansätze zu einem Neuen Institutionalismus in der modernen Rechtstheorie der Gegenwart, in: Juristen-Zeitung 40 (1985), S. 706—714, 707 f.

seinem Wesen gemäßen sozialen *Tiefenstruktur* zu erfassen und wissenschaftlich zu erforschen suchen, wird sehr schnell deutlich, daß in der modernen Gesellschaft alles Recht, über die politischen Systemgrenzen hinweg, auf der ganzen Welt seiner Struktur und Funktion nach durchaus einheitliche oder doch zumindest vergleichbare *Eigentümlichkeiten und charakteristische Züge* aufweist.

3. Ausgangspunkt einer rechts- und systemtheoretischen Rekonstruktion, die Auskunft darüber zu geben vermag, in welcher funktionellen Beziehung das staatlich organisierte *Rechtssystem* und das zugehörige *Wissenschaftssystem* innerhalb des beide umfassenden, wenn auch jeweils bloß regionalen Gesellschaftssystems im Verhältnis zueinander stehen, hat auszugehen von dem *Faktum der Selbstreferenz* dieser Systeme, das heißt von der Tatsache, daß sowohl das Rechtssystem als auch das Wissenschaftssystem nicht bloß als eine Struktur des subjektiven Bewußtseins oder als eine Struktur menschlicher Erkenntnis zu begreifen sind[107], sondern in der gesellschaftlich schon geordneten Realität mit einer jeweils spezialisierten Funktion als *soziale Systeme menschlichen Erlebens und Handelns* existieren[108].

a) Beide Systeme beziehen sich mit ihren jeweiligen Operationen (des politisch-rechtlichen Entscheidens bzw. des wissenschaftlichen Erkennens) stets zugleich nicht bloß auf ihre Umwelt, sondern auch auf sich selbst, weil sie nur aufgrund dieses Selbstkontaktes und nach Maßgabe der Interaktion mit Teilen ihrer systemeigenen Ordnungsstruktur auf ihre Umwelt zu reagieren vermögen. *Das Rechtssystem wie das Wissenschaftssystem fungieren somit als selbstreferenzielle Systeme.* In dem Maße, in dem sich, wie hier im Verhältnis von Rechtssystem und Wissenschaftssystem, ein selbstreferenzielles System auf ein anderes selbst-

---

[107] Das verkennt nicht eben selten die Kritik an der soziologischen Systemtheorie, insbesondere an derjenigen Niklas Luhmanns. Diese Kritik sucht die normative Struktur des rechtlichen Sinns irrig am subjektiven Bewußtsein bzw. an der symbolisch vermittelten, das heißt auf sprachliche Zeichen reduzierten, rationalen Erkenntnis des Subjekts festzumachen, wie beispielsweise *Andreas Zielcke*, Die symbolische Natur des Rechts, Berlin 1980, S. 9 ff., 33 ff., anstatt den stets sozial konstituierten rechtlichen Sinn am normativ gesteuerten Sozialverhalten abzulesen und als *soziale Systemleistung* zu begreifen, das heißt als eine normativ wirksame *Struktur von Gesellschaft.*

[108] Eine systemtheoretische Grundlage der Theorie selbstreferenzieller Systeme, insbesondere im Hinblick auf das Rechtssystem bzw. das Rechtswissenschaftssystem bietet: *Niklas Luhmann*, Subjektive Rechte: Zum Umbau des Rechtsbewußtseins für die moderne Gesellschaft, in: ders., Gesellschaftsstruktur und Semantik. Studien zur Wissenssoziologie der modernen Gesellschaft, Frankfurt a. M. 1981, Bd. 2, S. 45—104, 102 ff.; *ders.*, Selbstreferenz und Teleologie in gesellschaftstheoretischer Perspektive, ebd., S. 9—44, 29 f., 36 ff. Hierzu im Anschluß an Luhmann auch: *Werner Krawietz*, Zur Struktur von Entwicklung und Fortschritt in der Rechtstheorie, in: RECHTSTHEORIE Beiheft 3 (1981), S. 333—347, 344 f.

referenzielles System richtet, haben wir es bei der soziologischen Rekonstruktion der wechselseitigen Intersystembeziehungen auf *beiden* Seiten dieses Verhältnisses mit dem sozialen Phänomen der Selbstreferenz zu tun. Eine *Theorie des Rechts,* die sich selbst systemtheoretisch als *Theorie selbstreferenzieller Systeme* begreift, muß daher diese *Verdopplung der Selbstreferenz* in Betracht ziehen. Sie zieht ihrerseits eine Reihe von methodologischen und epistemologischen Folgeproblemen nach sich, die in der Theorie des Rechts bislang kaum erkannt, geschweige denn adäquat ausgearbeitet sind[109]. Beispielsweise müßte im Rahmen der Selbstreflexion, die im Wissenschaftssystem — sei es auf dem Level der allgemeinen Rechtslehre/Rechtstheorie, sei es auf dem Level einer Soziologie des Rechts — auf den jeweiligen Systemebenen stattfindet, zugleich eine Reflexion darauf geleistet werden, daß auch die Operationen innerhalb des staatlich organisierten Rechtssystems ihrerseits selbstreferenziell erfolgen. Über die im System der Rechtsprechung erfolgende Produktion kollektiv bindender, präjudizieller Entscheidungen kann nur unter Bezugnahme auf Entscheidungen entschieden werden, über die *vorgängig* im Regierungs- und Verwaltungssystem sowie im Gesetzgebungssystem als den hierfür gleichfalls mit einem funktionellen Teilbeitrag zuständigen *Unter- und Teilsystemen* des staatlichen, das heißt auf der Grundlage der Staatsverfassung organisierten Rechtssystems, in arbeitsteiligem Zusammenwirken entschieden wurde. Ferner muß bei allen selbstreferenziellen Systemen auch im Hinblick auf die für das Rechtssystem wie für das Wissenschaftssystem bestehenden jeweiligen System/Umwelt-Beziehungen unterschieden werden zwischen *interner* bzw. *externer Interdependenz.* Die Selbststeuerung des Rechtssystems wie die Selbststeuerung des Wissenschaftssystems können als Systemfunktionen nur dadurch gewährleistet werden, daß diese als selbstreferenzielle soziale Systeme alle im Kontakt mit ihrer jeweiligen Umwelt erfolgenden Operationen stets nur *im Selbstkontakt* vornehmen, das heißt nur über Interaktionen mit Teilen ihrer systemeigenen Ordnung und demzufolge *über interne Interdependenzen* hinweg, die sich zwischen den einzelnen Systemteilen bzw. Teilsystemen abspielen. Jedoch ist bisher eine zureichende Reflexion auf die Autonomie des Rechtssystems wie des Wissenschaftssystems vor allem dadurch behindert worden, daß das hier vorausgesetzte Selbstverständnis von Autonomie oder Selbststeuerung unter dem Einfluß des juristischen Positivismus[110]

---

[109] Vgl. hierzu auch: *Krawietz,* Recht als Regelsystem (FN 3), S. 110 ff., 115 ff.

[110] Dies gilt nur mit Einschränkung für bestimmte neuere Spielarten analytischer Jurisprudenz, wie beispielsweise für die Rechtstheorie von *Herbert Hart* und seiner Schule. In seiner Auseinandersetzung mit der analytischen Rechtstheorie Harts kommt beispielsweise *Neil MacCormick,* H. L. A. Hart, London 1981, Introduction, S. 1 dem Problem der Selbstreflexion des

den Zugang zu den sozialen Bezugsproblemen selbstreferenzieller Prozesse versperrte, die im Rechtssystem wie im Wissenschaftssystem nun einmal bestehen.

b) Die Autonomie des staatlich organisierten Rechtssystems wie diejenige des Wissenschaftssystems kann zureichend weder erfaßt noch begriffen werden, wenn man *ersteres* auf das System von Rechtsnormen, *letzteres* auf das System von Aussagen über Rechtsnormen reduziert, wie der juristische Positivismus dies üblicherweise tut. Ausgangspunkt muß vielmehr die *Differenz zwischen dem staatlich organisierten Rechtssystem und dem Wissenschaftssystem* sein, die sich daraus ergibt, daß *beide* in unserer Gesellschaft als mehr oder weniger *autonome Funktionssysteme* existieren, deren Miteinanderfungieren eine wechselseitige Orientierung und Abstimmung der beiderseitigen Kommunikationsleistungen erforderlich macht[111]. Es geht vor allem darum, nicht bloß die *Trennung*, sondern auch die *Verknüpfung* der verschiedenen Kommunikationsebenen zu erkennen, die durch eine rein rechtsimmanente bzw. rein logische Betrachtungsweise nicht zureichend erfaßt zu werden vermögen.

c) Rechts- und systemtheoretisch betrachtet, gibt es zwei Möglichkeiten, durch Systembildung und arbeitsteiliges Zusammenwirken zur Festlegung von normativen, insbesondere von rechtlichen Verhaltensprämissen zu gelangen, nämlich (1) durch Organisation und (2) durch Wissenschaft. In der *Organisation*, insbesondere in der staatlichen Organisation und Entscheidungsbürokratie des Rechtssystems, geht es um das *Entscheiden über Entscheidungsprämissen*, unabhängig davon, ob dieses Entscheiden durch Wissen gedeckt ist oder nicht, da im Rechtssystem bei Beschreiten des Klageweges keinesfalls die Entscheidung verweigert werden darf (sogen. *Entscheidungszwang*). In der Wissenschaft kommt es demgegenüber maßgeblich auf ein — hier nicht näher zu qualifizierendes — Wissen an. Die *Wissenschaften*, insbes. die Rechtswissenschaft, aber auch die Soziologie und die Philosophie befassen sich mit dem *Erkennen der rechtlichen Verhaltensprämissen*, die — wenn sie im Entscheidungswege gesetzt bzw. geändert werden — das Rechtsge-

---

Rechtssystems schon sehr nahe. „Juristic theories are available to, and tend to become part of the intellectual equipment of, those who have particular practical concerns in the law. Jurists contribute to practical debates, practitioners contribute to jurisprudence. The law in its practical working reflects practical men's understanding of law." Augenscheinlich hindert ihn jedoch die Befangenheit im juristischen Positivismus daran, die konventionelle Problemsicht des Verhältnisses von Theorie und Praxis durch normativ-realistische Systemanalysen zu ersetzen.

[111] Eingehend hierzu: *Niklas Luhmann*, Selbstreflexion des Rechtssystems: Rechtstheorie in gesellschaftstheoretischer Perspektive, in: RECHTSTHEORIE 10 (1979), S. 159—185. Vgl. ferner *Krawietz*, Recht als Regelsystem (FN 3), S. 93 f., 96 ff., 104 ff.

schehen in angebbarer Weise beeinflussen. Der *Differenz zwischen Organisation und Wissenschaft* entsprechend divergieren in beiden Fällen auch die jeweiligen Operationsgrundlagen. Während im Falle von Organisation alles Entscheiden auf politisch oder durch Mitgliederkonsens gedeckter *Macht* bzw. auf der Bereitstellung *physischer Gewalt* beruht, basieren im Falle von Wissenschaft alle einschlägigen Operationen auf (wie auch immer methodisch gesicherter) *Wahrheit*. Organisation *und* Wissenschaft erbringen infolgedessen im Verhältnis zueinander durchaus *komplementäre Leistungen* und ergänzen sich wechselseitig im Hinblick auf die Funktion des Rechtssystems als ganzen[112]. Jedoch werden weder die staatliche Organisation des Rechtssystems noch die — gleichfalls bis zu einem gewissen Grade organisierte — Wissenschaft jeweils mit der konkreten *Totalität* des im Rechtssystem als ganzen *faktisch ablaufenden Rechtsgeschehens* konfrontiert, sondern es handelt sich stets nur um ein hochgradig selektives Vorgehen, das zur Auswahl und vorläufigen (bis auf weiteres geltenden bzw. gültigen) Festlegung von Verhaltensprämissen führt. Es findet eine *Selektion von Prämissen* statt, die den Zugriff auf das menschliche Verhalten im Falle von Organisation *durch rechtliche Entscheidung*, im Falle von Wissenschaft *durch wissenschaftliche Erkenntnis* sichert.[113] Im vorstehenden Zusammenhang können infolgedessen *Organisation und Wissenschaft* als in sich jeweils mehrstufig differenzierte soziale Handlungssysteme begriffen werden, die infolge ihrer hochgradigen Innendifferenzierung in der Lage sind, durch bessere Organisation ihrer Selektivität auf der Ebene rechtlichen Entscheidens bzw. wissenschaftlicher Erkenntnis gesteigerte Selektionsleistungen zu erbringen, gleichzeitig jedoch in ihrem Verhältnis zueinander durch Miteinanderfungieren zur Funktionssteigerung des Rechtssystems als ganzen beizutragen.

---

[112] *Krawietz*, Recht als Regelsystem (FN 3), S. 116 f., 119 f.

[113] Diese Unterscheidung liegt demzufolge auch schon meiner Untersuchung des Verhältnisses von dogmatischer Rechtswissenschaft und rechtswissenschaftlicher Grundlagenforschung zugrunde. Vgl. *Werner Krawietz*, Juristische Entscheidung und wissenschaftliche Erkenntnis, Wien — New York 1978.

LAW AS A SYSTEM: SOME COMMENTS

By Lawrence M. Friedman, Stanford (U.S.A.)

In his interesting and informative paper, Professor Werner Krawietz begins by asking the question: is modern systems theory of any interest or use to jurists? His answer is an emphatic yes. No doubt, there are many legal scholars who would give a different answer; especially if "systems theory" is given its narrowest and most technical definition. If, however, one takes the concept of "system" in a broader, less technical way, then I think it is true that those students of the legal system who come from the world of the social sciences, or who use its language and habits of mind, would essentially agree with Professor Krawietz. The work of these scholars depends on some notion of system. This is implicit in the very phrase "legal system".

The core idea concerns the proper *subject-matter* of legal scholarship: whether the focus is or should be on legal behavior, or on rules, norms, and codes. In some ways, the concept of legal behavior (not always explicitly recognized) binds together most modern approaches to law, at least outside the law schools themselves. The exceptions are those approaches which are strictly normative, and are thus unconcerned with how the conceptual apparatus translates into social action. Most of the traditional (and current) work of scholars inside the law schools falls into this last category, unfortunately.

Arguably, however, "system" is a fundamental conception in the sociology of law. It is also fundamental to a whole range of theories about law, and approaches to law. Some of these make strange bedfellows indeed. An explicit or implicit notion of system underlies Marxist approaches to law; on the other side, those who argue that economic efficiency (in a neoclassical sense) is the ultimate goal of a legal order, are equally concerned with law as a system. What binds these approaches together is a conception of the legal order not as a catalogue of rules or norms, but as an operating unit, made up of parts, and with definite boundaries that set it off from other units within society. The central image is not the tablets that Moses brought down from the mountain, not a lawbook, nor a legislative code, but an organism or a machine: something that moves, works, behaves.

Of course, those who start off from this point of view do not ignore norms or deny their existence. Obviously there are norms, and they occupy an important place in every system of law. But the central question to be asked is the influence or effect of these norms on people's behavior; and on the quality of life and justice in a given society. And this influence or effect of norms on behavior can never be assumed or taken for granted. It is always an empirical question. Some norms have a more powerful reflection in behavior than others. Some are ethically persuasive; others have to be forced down the throats of the public through brute force. Some are vibrant, effective; others are completely inert: we speak of them as "dead". One of the core pursuits of legal research (at least research of the behavioral persuasion) is to discover which norms are living, which norms are dead; which are obeyed, which disregarded, and by whom, and why, and through what mechanisms.

This approach to law is, of course, not quite the same as the approach applied in formal systems theory. The exact relationship is one which such scholars as Professor Krawietz will no doubt work out. For now, I would like to point out simply that not all formal theories are actually "theories" in the sense of propositions from which one might derive predictions of behavior. Rather, some "theories" serve as frameworks of analysis, ways of looking at the legal world. The work of definition and framing is, perhaps, a first step toward developing real theory; and hence it is a stop on the road to a genuine science of prediction. At least one can hope so.

There is an aspect of the systems approach, as applied to the legal system, which is worth a further word. The approach, of course, focusses on the behavior of the legal system; and hence it inclines quite naturally to what we might call a social theory of law. By this I mean an emphasis on the way outside social forces (economic and other) affect the operation of the legal system; and a tendency to look on law as a dependent, rather than an independent variable. A legal system is a system operating *in* society. On the other hand, the whole idea of a system requires us to be able to define it as an entity; one has to be able to mark off its boundaries. A system is distinct from its environment; and indeed from other systems. In addition, systems in society are linked to each other; and it is an interesting and important question how they are linked, how tightly or how loosely, and so on. But linked they are.

My own inclinations are to stress that the links are quite tight. Other scholars, of course, differ; and there is a continuing debate over the general issue of the linkages between the legal system and its environment. This is the heart of the debate over the so-called autonomy of the legal system. Many legal scholars, of course, reject the idea of law as a self-contained system, hermetically sealed, and impervious to the outside world. But there is a certain tendency in recent scholarship to reassess the degree to which the legal system *is* independent; and "autonomy" is making something of a comeback. Not, of course, in its crude and unsophisticated 19th century form; but a comeback nonetheless.

The "new" autonomy, indeed, accepts the concept of a legal system, and builds outward from the systematic nature of the legal system. The general notion is roughly this: the legal order is coupled to the outside world, and cannot be understood except in terms of its social context. But it has strong and well-defined boundaries. It has a skin, a membrane, which allows material from outside to penetrate, but only in a special, patterned, characteristic way — on the law's own terms, in a sense. And *within* the legal system, there is a great deal of independence. In this regard, the legal system is like all the other major social sub-systems (religion, education, politics). Each of them develops its own norms, language, procedures. They become, each of them, little worlds; and the people who run them follow their own little sets of norms and laws.

The subsystems, then, exist *in* society; but as independent organisms. An animal — an ape, let us say — is completely dependent on the outside environment. It will die without food and water. It can inhabit only one special slot in the world. Outside its jungles and its trees, it cannot live. But *inside* the organism, underneath its skin, what comes in from the outside — food, or sense-perceptions — gets processed according to a code or program which is specific to the species, and follows rules that apply only to that kind of organism, and to no others. Thus the ape, like all other organisms, is both "autonomous" and totally dependent on the outside environment, and at one and the same time.

This, I gather, is the central argument of a group of scholars — a notable example is Gunther Teubner — who have begun to explore once more the idea of an "autonomous" legal system, and who have made the *relative* independence of this system the keystone of their theories. Obviously, there is a good deal of validity to the notion; and considerable force in the comparison between the legal system, and a living organism. The analogy is, perhaps, inherent in the very concept of a system. The question is, how far to carry this notion. My own inclination is to stop far short of the point to which Teubner, for example, would take it. It seems to me more sensible, and more fruitful, both as theory and as a guide to research, to *assume* a close connection between social forces and any given state of the law. There is, of course, an integrity to the legal system; it does have an outer skin. My feeling, however, is that this skin is extremely permeable; it is thin and porous, rather than tough like a suit of armor.

There is no way, of course, to resolve the question of autonomy. There are arguments to be made on both sides; any notion of "proof" is out of the question. I would like, however, to make one comment about the social meaning of the controversy. Some jurists favor the concept of autonomy on the grounds that it yields a more ethical vision of law. The assumption is that a legal system which is not autonomous will be unable to uphold what we understand as the rule of law. It will be unable to protect itself from the wishes and desires of the regime; it will be at the mercy of those people whose hands are on the levers of power. Only an autonomous legal system can preserve human rights, and seek justice in the particular case.

The argument has a good deal of plausibility, on the surface. Certainly, there is nothing "autonomous" about the legal systems in totalitarian countries; there was nothing "autonomous" about the legal system under Hitler. But the argument, I believe, tends to ignore an important distinction. There is a difference between an autonomous legal system, and an *independent* one. An autonomous system is by definition relatively free from the influence of the social system. An independent system, on the other hand, is a system which is not under the control of the regime, administration, or government; but it may be quite responsive to social forces for all that. In my view, the high courts of most Western countries are quite independent; judges cannot be persecuted for making decisions that the regime does not like. But this does not by any means make them autonomous. And an independent system has all the virtues that are claimed for autonomy, without the vices of conceptualism, logic-chopping, and insensitivity to social wants and needs.

There are, of course, many problems which beset the study of law as a system. One is the problem of finding and defining the boundaries or limits. The "modern" conception of law has a good deal of trouble with this issue of boundaries. Where does "law" begin and end? Certainly, we cannot simply accept without question the definitions of jurists, especially the old-fashioned ones. Law is not just what lawyers say it is. If we define the legal system (for example) as including all the actions of institutions in the modern state which lay down authoritative rules, or carry out such rules, then the legal system contains within it the vast administrative apparatus of the modern state, whether or not traditional legal education and scholarship paid any attention to parts of this apparatus or not. Law also must necessarily include most of what I like to call legal behavior — conduct which is causally influenced by law or the legal system. If I see a policeman on the highway, and slow down my car to avoid a traffic ticket, that is an example of "legal behavior". If I ask a lawyer to draw up a contract, if I file an income tax return, if I obey a no-smoking sign — all of this is legal behavior too.

But the trouble is, once one expands the conception of "law" beyond those boundaries that the traditional jurists are comfortable with, one runs the risk of losing all reasonable sense of limits. For example, suppose you were interested in the subject of education — suppose you wanted to write a history of education, in some society, or study education sociologically. At the outset there is the question: what do we mean by "education"? A fairly narrow definition would be one that confined "education" to actions and behaviors that go on inside school systems. But of course schools are not the only institutions concerned with "education". The family, the church, the government, friends and neighbors — all of these are concerned with "education". After all, education is the process of transferring the accumulated knowledge and culture from one generation to the next (among other things). But once you leave the snug harbor of an old-fashioned, conventional definition of the boundaries of education, there does not seem to be any reasonable or convenient stopping point; education swallows up everything in society. The same, of course, happens if we adopt an expanded concept of "law" or "the legal system".

How can this paradox be resolved? How can one preserve a meaningful concept of law, without at the same time blurring the boundaries so totally that law melts into everything else going on in society? This is a difficult question, and I am by no means sure what the answer is. But the issue must be resolved in any study or approach that takes the idea of law as a system seriously.

All this, of course, does not detract from the utility of a systems approach to law. That remains, in a sense, a pillar on which the modern study of law tends to rest. On that point Professor Krawietz and I am in perfect agreement.

SELBSTVERWALTUNGSRECHT ALS TEIL DES RECHTSSYSTEMS

Unter besonderer Berücksichtigung des jugoslawischen Rechtssystems

Von Marijan Pavčnik, Ljubljana

I.

Ein Teil der Theorie steht auf dem Standpunkt, daß das Selbstnormieren für das Selbstverwaltungsrecht bezeichnend sei. Bei Berücksichtigung dieser Meinung gibt es im Vergleich zum Staatsrecht einen wichtigen Unterschied. Für das Staatsrecht ist es typisch, daß immer eine Entfernung zwischen dem Gesetzgeber und dem Normenadressat besteht, weil Gesetzgeber und Normenadressat nicht identisch sind. Vom Umfang der Identität hängt es dann ab, wie unmittelbar die gesellschaftlichen Interessen in allgemeinen Rechtsakten enthalten sein können. Die Selbstnormierung an sich sichert noch keine bessere Qualität der Selbstverwaltungsakte. Ob eine Qualitätsverschiebung stattgefunden hat, zeigen uns erst Inhalt und Wirksamkeit der Rechtsnorm[1]. Zu dieser Qualitätsverschiebung trägt das Selbstnormierungsverfahren dann bei, wenn die Selbstverwaltungsakte solche gesellschaftlichen Verhältnisse regeln, die dem Selbstverwaltungsrecht immanent sind.

II.

Daraus folgt, daß erst der Gegenstand der Rechtsnormen[2] eine weitere Entwicklung des Selbstverwaltungsrechtes ermöglicht. Hier werden drei Arten von gesellschaftlichen Verhältnissen unterschieden. Einerseits

---

[1] *A. Perenič*, Nekaj pogledov na normativno dejavnost delovnih organizacij (Einige Ansichten auf die Rechtsgebungstätigkeit der Arbeitsorganisationen), in: Pravnik (Ljubljana), 7—9 (1969), S. 255.

[2] Prinzipiell siehe *A. Ross*, Theorie der Rechtsquellen, Leipzig-Wien 1929, S. 359. Was den Gegenstand des Selbstverwaltungsrechtes betrifft, siehe: *A. Igličar*, Interesni konflikt in samoupravno pravo (Interessenkonflikt und Selbstverwaltungsrecht), in: Zbornik znanstvenih razprav (Ljubljana), 39 (1979), S. 73—85; *R. Lukić*, Samoupravno pravo i pravo (Selbstverwaltungsrecht und Recht), in: Samoupravno pravo (Beograd), 2 (1975), S. 3—6; *M. Pavčnik*, Pravni viri v jugoslovanskem pravu (Rechtsquellen im jugoslawischen Recht), Ljubljana 1983, S. 78 ff.; *N. Visković*, Marksistička teorija prava i samoupravno pravo (Marxistische Theorie des Rechtes und Selbstverwaltungsrecht), in: Pojam prava (Begriff des Rechtes), Split 1981, S. 327—346.

sind es solche gesellschaftlichen Verhältnisse, die nur vom Staat geregelt werden. Zweitens gehören dazu diejenigen Verhältnisse, die nur dem Selbstverwaltungsrecht immanent sind. Und drittens sind es Verhältnisse, die gemeinsamer Zuständigkeit unterliegen.

Typischer Gegenstand des Staatsrechtes sind diejenigen gesellschaftlichen Verhältnisse, die Klassenkonflikte widerspiegeln oder mit ihnen eng verbunden sind. Der Staat muß sie so lange regeln, als sie noch so stark, scharf und ungelöst sind, daß nur der Staat als Zwangsorganisation sie beherrschen und bewältigen kann. Was die Klasseninteressenkonflikte betrifft, die auch in der sozialistischen Gesellschaft noch immer bestehen, so sind auch diese und mit ihnen verbundenen Interessen immer dann Gegenstand des Staatsrechts, wenn sie die Grundlagen des gesellschaftlich-ökonomischen und gesellschaftlich-politischen Systems bedrohen. Neben dieser Grenze hängt es besonders von Bedeutung und Breite des Konfliktes ab, durch welchen allgemeinen Rechtsakt die einzelnen Verhältnisse geregelt werden.

Im Sozialismus gibt es auch Konflikte, die aus den sozialistischen Verhältnissen herrühren. Diese Konflikte entstehen, wenn auch die Klassen-Interessenkonflikte beseitigt sind. Sie beziehen sich z. B. auf „die weitere Entwicklung der sozialistischen Gesellschaft, die Lösung aktueller ökonomischer, sozialer, kultureller und anderer gesellschaftlichen Problematik, die Richtung und die Schnelligkeit der weiteren Entwicklung gesellschaftlich-ökonomischer, politischer und anderer Verhältnisse, ideologische und politische Unterschiede, die im Zusammenhang mit der Behandlung konkreter Fragen entstehen“[3]. Solche Konflikte sind regelmäßig beruhigbar und können demokratisch gelöst werden. Soweit diese Verhältnisse auch für das Recht von Bedeutung sind, werden sie durch Selbstverwaltungsakte oder durch allgemeine Rechtsakte der gesellschaftlich-politischen Gemeinschaften, die als selbstverwaltende Gemeinschaften tätig sind, geregelt.

Das Recht greift auch in Gebiete ein, die von gemeinsamem und allgemeinem gesellschaftlichem Interesse sind. In solchen Fällen müssen gesellschaftliche Verhältnisse schon deshalb geregelt werden, weil das schon die spezifische Weise der menschlichen Behandlung fordert. Das bedeutet, daß die Aktivitäten des Menschen genau bestimmt und miteinander koordiniert werden müssen[4]. Diesmal hängt die Abgrenzung der Zuständigkeit zwischen dem Staat und den selbstverwaltenden

---

[3] *E. Kardelj*, Smeri razvoja političnega sistema socialističnega samoupravljanja (Richtungen der Entwicklung des politischen Systems der sozialistischen Selbstverwaltung), Ljubljana 1977, S. 88 und 94.

[4] Siehe *G. Gurvitch*, L'idée du droit social, Paris 1932, S. 103 ff. und *R. Lukić* (FN 2), S. 5—6.

Organen davon ab, auf welcher Ebene die gesellschaftlichen Verhältnisse normiert werden müssen.

Auf der Makroebene sind die Rechtsgeber entweder die selbstverwaltenden Subjekte, die sich miteinander abstimmen und vereinigen, oder der Staat, der territorial die allgemeinste gesellschaftliche Organisation darstellt. Im Hinblick auf die Selbstverwaltung bestehen beide Möglichkeiten. In der sozialen Wirklichkeit soll diejenige Möglichkeit gewählt werden, die eine qualitativ bessere Normierung sichert[5]. Das wird in der Praxis teilweise vergessen, das heißt, daß einzelne selbstverwaltende Subjekte auch darum Rechtsgeber sind, weil das angeblich mehr „selbstverwaltlich“ ist. Unter Beachtung unseres Ausgangspunktes sollen also einzelne selbstverwaltende Subjekte nur solche Fragen und Verhältnisse regeln, die für sie spezifisch und typisch sind. Das ist die sogenannte Normierung auf der Mikroebene, z. B. auf der Ebene der einzelnen Organisationen der assoziierten Arbeit. Auf dieser Ebene wird die Ausübung von Rechten, Pflichten und der Verantwortung in diesen Organisationen geregelt. Mit allgemeinen Selbstverwaltungsakten dieser Organisationen werden auch ihre Organe und die Art, wie sie ihre Funktionen auszuüben haben, sowie sonstige Fragen der internen Arbeitsorganisation und der Geschäftsführung geregelt[6].

III.

Mit Unterschieden im Rechtsgegenstand eng verbunden ist auch die Frage, ob den Rechtsnormen nur die Staatssanktionen eigen sind. Für das jugoslawische Recht ist es charakteristisch, daß die Verfassung und die einzelnen Gesetze (z. B. das Gesetz über die assoziierte Arbeit) schon Sanktionen ermöglichen, die von den selbstverwaltenden Subjekten zu gestalten und zu vollstrecken sind[7]. Das bedeutet, daß bei einer Änderung des Rechtsgegenstandes auch die Rechtssanktionen verändert wer-

[5] Prinzipiell siehe den Artikel von *W. Maihofer*, der auch für das jugoslawische Rechtssystem sehr bedeutsam ist: Gesetzgebungswissenschaft, in: G. Winkler/B. Schilcher (Hrsg.), Gesetzgebung — Kritische Überlegungen zur Gesetzgebungslehre und zur Gesetzgebungstechnik, Wien-New York 1981, S. 3 ff.

[6] Über den Gegenstand der einzelnen Selbstverwaltungsakte siehe genauer Das Gesetz über assoziierte Arbeit, Herausgeber: Das Informationssekretariat des Parlaments der SFR Jugoslawien, Beograd 1977, Art. 573 ff. Siehe auch: *V. Jovanović/B. Košutić*, Samoupravno pravo u pravnom sistemu SFRJ (Selbstverwaltungsrecht im Rechtssystem der SFRJ), Beograd 1981 und *A. Nikolić/M. Petrović*, Samoupravno pravo (Selbstverwaltungsrecht), Beograd 1980.

[7] Siehe *J. Goričar*, Sankcije v našem samoupravnem pravu (Die Sanktionen in unserem Selbstverwaltungsrecht), in: Teorija in praksa (Ljubljana), 1—2 (1978), S. 23—36.

den müssen. Der Zwang bleibe immer mehr dem Staat als allgemeinste gesellschaftliche Organisation vorbehalten, die Normierung und die Vollstreckung von Sanktionen dagegen würden immer mehr dezentralisiert und in die Zuständigkeit der einzelnen selbstverwaltenden Organisationen und Gemeinschaften überführt.

Ein Teil der Theorie vertritt den Standpunkt, daß damit das Selbstverwaltungsrecht die Eigenschaft als Recht verliere und sich zu Moral und Gewohnheit wandle. Diese Interpretation geht von dem Grundsatz aus, daß es insbesondere von der Staatssanktion abhänge, ob eine gesellschaftliche Norm auch eine Rechtsnorm sei. Man kann m. E. diese Theorie nicht bejahen, weil Zwang nur eine von mehreren Eigenschaften des Rechtes ist und weil die Staatsgebundenheit des Zwanges nur in einer bestimmten Phase der Rechtsentwicklung besteht.

Ich stimme vielmehr mit dem Konzept überein, daß rechtliche Sanktionen voraussehbar und normiert sind und sein müssen. Die Sanktion muß bereits gesetzlich festgelegt sein, und auch die Voraussetzungen für den Ausspruch der Sanktion müssen in einem Verfahren festgestellt werden, das gesetzlich im voraus geregelt sein muß. Wenn in einer Gesellschaft mehrere Sanktionssysteme bestehen (z. B. auf der Ebene der allgemeinen gesellschaftlichen Organisationen und auf der Ebene der einzelnen selbstverwaltenden Organisationen und Gemeinschaften), müssen Kompetenzkonflikte und Diskrepanzen zwischen einzelnen Systemen ausgeschlossen sein. In solchem Fall ist der Staat als allgemeinste gesellschaftliche Organisation zur Koordinierung aufgerufen, um zu sichern, daß Sanktionen nur in Übereinstimmung mit den Prinzipien der Verfassungsmäßigkeit und der Gesetzmäßigkeit verhängt werden[8].

Diese Feststellungen begründen eindeutig, daß Selbstverwaltungsrecht noch immer Recht ist. Daraus folgt, daß wir Besonderheiten des Selbstverwaltungsrechtes im Phänomen des Rechts und in der sozialen Wirklichkeit, die dem Recht zugrunde liegt, suchen müssen. Im Hinblick darauf ist wichtig, welche Stelle die selbstverwaltenden Subjekte im einzelnen Rechtsverhältnis einnehmen. Meiner Meinung nach müssen wir drei Arten von Rechtsverhältnissen unterscheiden: Erstens sind hier solche Verhältnisse zu nehmen, in denen die Rechtssubjekte gleichgeordnet und rechtlich gleichwertig sind. Das ist das Gebiet der Privatautonomie, traditionell als Privatrecht bezeichnet. Ferner gehören hierzu Verhältnisse, in denen die Subjekte über- und untergeordnet sind. Dieses Gebiet wird üblicherweise öffentliches Recht genannt. Obwohl die Unterscheidung theoretisch problematisch ist, muß man doch feststellen, daß in der

[8] Siehe *J. Djordjević*, Prilog za teoriju prava o samoupravnom pravu (Beitrag für die Theorie des Rechtes über Selbstverwaltungsrecht), in: Samoupravno pravo (Beograd), 1 (1974), S. 6.

sozialen Wirklichkeit diese zwei Arten der Rechtsverhältnisse tatsächlich bestehen; das gilt noch immer auch für das sozialistische Recht[9], wenn es auch Ziel des Sozialismus ist, die Kluft zwischen beiden Gebieten zu überwinden. Für unser Problem am wichtigsten jedoch ist die dritte Art von Rechtsverhältnissen, nämlich die Verhältnisse, für welche die organische Verbundenheit des subjektiven Rechtes mit den Rechtspflichten und der Rechtspflichten mit dem subjektiven Recht typisch ist. In diesem Fall sind die Subjekte gleichzeitig Träger sowohl der subjektiven Rechte als auch der Rechtspflichten. Das subjektive Recht und die Rechtspflichten sind so eng miteinander verbunden, daß sie eine unteilbare Einheit bilden. Diese Einheit ist typisch für jene Verhältnisse, in denen die Subjekte nicht nur im eigenen Interesse handeln müssen. Das bedeutet, daß das Rechtssubjekt die eigenen Interessen nur so weit verwirklichen kann, wie diese Interessen mit dem Zweck und der sozialen Gebundenheit der subjektiven Rechte übereinstimmen (die sogenannten „mit Pflichten verbundenen Rechte"). Hier können wir z. B. das Recht, mit gesellschaftlichen Mitteln zu arbeiten, erwähnen. In Ausübung dieses Rechtes haben „die Arbeiter in der assoziierten Arbeit das Recht, die Pflicht und die Verantwortung, die gesellschaftlichen Mittel in ihrem gemeinsamen und im allgemeinen gesellschaftlichen Interesse gesellschaftlich und ökonomisch zweckmäßig zu nutzen und diese Mittel ständig zu erneuern, zu mehren und zu verbessern"[10].

Eine so geforderte Verbundenheit zwischen Recht und Pflicht ist auch für Verhältnisse, die in den allgemeinen Selbstverwaltungsakten geregelt sind, bezeichnend. Wenn die empirische Analyse zeigt, daß die selbstverwaltenden Subjekte wirklich als Träger der „Pflichtsrechte" (mit Pflichten verbundene Rechte) tätig sind, dann wird die Aussicht bestätigt, welche die sogenannte Theorie der Vertragsnatur der allgemeinen Selbstverwaltungsakte völlig verneint. Nach dieser Theorie sind die allgemeinen Selbstverwaltungsakte dem Vertrag gleichgestellt, weil beide Rechtsakte erst dann rechtlich bindend sind, wenn Einstimmigkeit erreicht ist. Dieser Parallelismus ist schon formellrechtlich nicht überzeugend, denn allgemeine Selbstverwaltungsakte können auch durch Mehrheitsbeschluß erlassen werden. Er ist auch inhaltlich nicht begründet, weil er von der Voraussetzung ausgeht, daß ein durch Vertrag entstandenes Abkommen das Resultat von gemeinsamen und allgemeinen gesellschaftlichen Interessen ist.

---

[9] Siehe R. *Lukić*, Uvod u pravo (Einführung ins Recht), Beograd 1977, S. 402.

[10] Das Gesetz über assoziierte Arbeit, Art. 13/3 und Verfassung der Sozialistischen Föderativen Republik Jugoslawien, veröffentlicht vom Sekretariat für den Informationsdienst der Bundesversammlung, Beograd 1974, Art. 13.

Im Fall eines Vertrages streben beide Parteien danach, im Rahmen des Rechtes ausschließlich die eigenen Interessen zu verwirklichen. Der Vertrag ist also nur das Mittel, dieses Ziel zu erreichen. Die Teilnehmer an allgemeinen Selbstverwaltungsakten sind dagegen verpflichtet, ihre gegenseitigen Verhältnisse im Einklang mit der Natur und dem Zweck des gesellschaftlichen Eigentums und unter Berücksichtigung auch anderer gesellschaftlicher Interessen zu regeln. Wie schon erwähnt, dürfen die eigenen Interessen nur soweit zur Geltung kommen, wie sie mit den allgemeinen gesellschaftlichen Interessen und mit den Verfassungsgrundsätzen übereinstimmen.

IV.

Diese Art des Normierens (im Sinne der organischen Verbundenheit des subjektiven Rechtes mit der Rechtspflicht und umgekehrt) ist nicht nur für das Selbstverwaltungsrecht, sondern auch für die klassischen allgemeinen Rechtsakte (z. B. für die Gesetze) charakteristisch. Auf diese Weise sind auch das gesellschaftliche Eigentum, die selbstverwaltende Vereinigung der Arbeit und der Mittel, die wechselseitigen Arbeitsbeziehungen der Arbeiter (das Arbeitsrecht) und Gebiete von besonderem gesellschaftlichem Interesse (z. B. die Sozialversicherung) geregelt. Hierin liegt ein weiteres Argument, daß Selbstverwaltungsrecht und staatlich gesetztes Recht nicht streng voneinander zu trennen sind. Und nicht nur das: es begründet auch, daß Selbstverwaltungsrecht und staatlich gesetztes Recht so eng miteinander verbunden sind, daß sie ein einheitliches Rechtssystem bilden.

Ferner folgt daraus, daß das Selbstverwaltungsrecht kein selbständiger Rechtszweig (wie z. B. Verfassungsrecht, Arbeitsrecht, Familienrecht usw.) ist. Wenn der Begriff Rechtszweig definiert wird als die Gesamtheit der Rechtsnormen und Rechtsinstitute, die einen größeren und geschlossenen Komplex von gesellschaftlichen Verhältnissen in derselben Weise (was die Art des Normierens betrifft) regeln, dann ist klar, daß dem Selbstverwaltungsrecht das Element „geschlossener Gegenstand des Normierens" fehlt. Die Selbstverwaltungsakte regeln sehr unterschiedliche gesellschaftliche Verhältnisse (z. B. die Arbeitsbeziehungen; die Beziehungen zwischen den Organisationen der assoziierten Arbeit; die Art der Ausübung von Rechten, Pflichten und der Verantwortung und die Organisationsfragen in selbstverwaltenden Organisationen; das gesellschaftliche Eigentum usw.), und zwar nur in dem Umfang, der mit der Verfassung und mit dem Gesetz nicht im Widerspruch steht[11]. So gestaltete selbstverwaltende Rechtsnormen sind Bestandteil des einheitlichen

[11] Siehe Verfassung der SFRJ, Art. 206/2, 207/2 und das Gesetz über assoziierte Arbeit, Art. 575.

Systems von Normen, die den einzelnen Rechtsinstituten, den Rechtszweigen und den anderen Rechtseinheiten zugeordnet sind.

Abschließend kann gesagt werden, daß unter verschiedenen Gesichtspunkten eines deutlich geworden ist: Das Selbstverwaltungsrecht ist integraler Teil eines einheitlichen Rechtssystems, ein Teil, der zwar gewisse Besonderheiten aufweist, dessen Rechtsnormen sich aber nicht so weit von anderen Normen unterscheiden, daß man das Selbstverwaltungsrecht rechtssystematisch selbständig klassifizieren kann.

WAS IST EINE REGEL?

Von Gregorio Robles, Palma de Mallorca

I.

Eine (auf die Handlung ausgerichtete) Regel ist ein von jemandem gegebener sprachlicher Ausdruck. Dieser sprachliche Ausdruck kann auf verschiedene Weise verwirklicht werden (explizit oder implizit) und dieser Jemand kann persönlich oder unpersönlich sein. Wichtig ist dabei, zu verstehen, daß abgesehen von den Formfaktoren und dem Schöpfungssubjekt oder Empfänger die Regel als solche nur von dem Augenblick an besteht, in welchem sie sprachlichen Charakter annimmt. Dies soll jedoch nicht bedeuten, daß jemand sie mittels einer ausdrücklichen Sprachformulierung äußert oder erschafft. Es soll vielmehr heißen, es ist charakteristisch für eine Regel, sich ausdrücken zu lassen. Eine Regel ist somit die Bedeutung eines sprachlichen Ausdrucks. Sie ist eine *Proposition*.

Nun gilt aber nicht, daß jede Proposition eine Regel ist, vorausgesetzt, daß es sich versteht, daß eine Regel auf die Orientierung der menschlichen Handlung ausgerichtet ist. Es gibt jedoch auch Propositionen, die hiermit nichts zu tun haben. Die Regel ist eine Proposition mit besonderer Bedeutung. Diese Bedeutung ist nicht so einfach und selbstverständlich auf die Handlung ausgerichtet, wie wir es bis jetzt zu verstehen gaben. Die Regel wird in ein propositionelles System eingeführt, welches einen ontischen Bereich schafft, in welchem die Handlung stattfinden kann und muß. Nennen wir diesen ontischen Bereich der Handlung den ontisch-praktischen Bereich. Dann können wir sagen: eine Regel ist eine Proposition, welche in das definierende System des praktisch-ontischen Bereiches eingeführt wird. Die Regel hat keine Bedeutung als solche, also wenn sie vom System losgelöst wird.

Der praktisch-ontische Bereich ist das aus Konvention geschaffene Seiende, das die menschliche Handlung ermöglicht und reguliert. Zum Beispiel: das Spiel ist ein ontischer Bereich, da es ein Wesen ist; es ist praktisch, da es ein Wesen ist, das als Wesen die Handlungen des Spiels reguliert und ermöglicht. Eine Regel, die von dem Regelsystem losgelöst ist, das den ontisch-praktischen Bereich konstituiert, ist nicht wirklich eine Regel, da eine grundlegende Bestimmung der Regel ist, der Gesamtheit anzugehören, welche die Handlung reguliert.

Daß eine Regel nicht direkt auf die Handlung in Form einer Forderung ausgerichtet ist, bedeutet nicht, daß es sich um keine Regel des Systems handelt. Die ontischen Elemente des Systems wenden sich ja nicht an die Handlung, sondern sind Bedingungen oder Voraussetzungen derselben. Der entscheidende Punkt bei der Analyse der Regeln, welche ein System bilden, ist somit, daß sie sich nicht vom System selbst lösen können, da sie als Regel nur Bedeutung haben, wenn sie sich miteinander verbinden, um ein System zu bilden. Umgekehrt: man kann sich ein System ohne Regeln nicht vorstellen, da das System nichts anderes ist als eine Verbindung von sprachlichen Ausdrücken, welche direkt oder indirekt darauf ausgerichtet sind, die Handlung zu bilden und zu orientieren.

Das System konstituiert die Handlung in dem Sinne, daß diese nur möglich ist dank der vorausgehenden Existenz des praktisch-ontischen Bereiches; ohne das Vorherbestehen desselben ist die Handlung nicht denkbar. Das System bildet nicht nur die Handlung, sondern es orientiert sie zugleich, indem es von dem Subjekt, welches sie ausübt, eine bestimmte Verhaltensform verlangt. Aber das System bildet und orientiert die Handlung nur mittels der Regeln. Jede Theorie der praktisch-konventionellen Wesen ist eine Theorie des Regelsystems. Wenn, wie wir gesagt haben, die Regel eine Proposition ist, d. h. die Bedeutung eines sprachlichen Ausdrucks, ist geklärt, was wir meinen, wenn wir vom propositionellen System sprechen. Das System, welches den praktisch-ontischen Bereich bildet, ist eine Gesamtheit von Propositionen, deren Sinn nur durch die gegenseitige Verbindung derselben zu erklären ist. Die Bedeutungen der Regeln werden nur dann verständlich, wenn durch konstruktive philosophische Arbeit die Systemverbindung dieser Bedeutungen dargelegt wird. Es kann jedoch der Sinn einer Regel mittels einer sprachlichen Rekonstruktion formuliert werden, welche auf den konkreten Inhalt der Regel verzichtet, indem sie ihre bildenden Elemente formuliert und mittels einer sprachlich angebrachten Verbindung miteinander verbindet. Für den Augenblick ist es nur wichtig, darauf hinzuweisen, daß die allgemeine Konstruktion des Systems nur auf der Basis der vorherigen Formalisierung der Bedeutungen möglich ist, welche die Regeln bilden.

Wenn wir nicht in der Lage sind, zu bestimmen, welche Arten von Regeln in einem ontischen Bereich auftauchen und wie sie sich in das System eingliedern, was wiederum den Sinn dieses Bereiches ergibt, wird es uns schwerfallen, das genaue Verständnis für die Beziehung zwischen den Regeln und dem System aufzubringen. Wir befinden uns damit in einer Sackgasse, die uns daran hindert, das Grundproblem der Theorie des Rechts und, allgemein gesagt, der Theorie der praktisch-ontischen Bereiche zu lösen.

II.

Als bestimmendes Element des propositionalen Systems, welches den praktisch-ontischen Bereich ausdrückt, richtet sich die Regel an die Handlung oder orientiert sie. Was bedeutet das? In welchem Sinn ist die Orientierungsfunktion der Regel, um es so auszudrücken, ein Teil seiner Eigennatur? Wir haben schon erwähnt, daß die Regel *direkt* oder *indirekt* auf die Handlung orientiert ist. Verweilen wir zuerst bei der Analyse dieser zwei Adverbien.

Daß eine Regel die menschliche Handlung direkt orientiert, will sagen, daß ein bestimmtes Verhalten gefordert wird. Diese Forderung kann sehr unterschiedlichen Charakters sein: sie kann eine Notwendigkeit oder eine Möglichkeit ausdrücken. Man kann durch eine bestimmte Verhaltensforderung dem Subjekt nachweisen, daß dieses Verhalten unumgänglich ist, wenn das Subjekt an der Handlung des praktisch-ontischen Bereiches teilnehmen will; außerdem kann man ein umgängliches Verhalten fordern, und auch ein angemessenes oder wünschenswertes.

Die erste Forderung entspricht dem, was ich technische Regel nenne (etwa in dem von *von Wright* vorgeschlagenen Sinne; vgl. seine Abhandlung „Norm and Action", London 1963, z. B. S. 9 ff.); das zweite entspricht einer deontischen Regel oder einer Norm. Die technische Regel fordert ein Verhalten als notwendig (im Verhältnis zu einem gegebenen Ziel bzw. zu einer vorgegebenen Handlung). Deswegen ist sein charakteristischer verbaler Zusammenhang ein Müssen. Die technischen Regeln des praktisch-ontischen Bereiches sind Verfahrensregeln. Die Normen fordern ein Verhalten als wünschenswert (gesollt) und nicht als notwendig; daher ist der verbale Zusammenhang dabei ein Sollen.

Aber neben diesen Regeln, welche eine Forderung zu einem bestimmten Verhalten ausdrücken und somit direkt auf die Handlung ausgerichtet sind, gibt es auch Regeln, welche die notwendigen Elemente der Konvention aufweisen oder bestimmen. Sie richten sich nicht direkt auf die Handlung, da es vom logischen Standpunkt aus undenkbar ist, eine Handlung auszuführen, ohne vorher die räumlich-zeitlichen Elemente, die Subjekte und die Kompetenzen, aufzuzeigen. Diese Regeln werden ausgedrückt oder sind ausdrückbar mittels des Verbs „sein"; aus diesem Grund kann man sie als ontische Regeln bezeichnen. Dies mag einem unsinnig erscheinen, wenn man sich an die beim Studium der sogenannten normativen Systeme vorherrschende Auffassung hält. Zunächst einmal pflegt man nicht, eine Norm von einer technischen Regel zu unterscheiden, da Müssen und Sollen als Synonyme gebraucht werden. Aber dieses Mißverständnis — an sich ein Produkt des normalen Sprachgebrauchs, was extrem paradox erscheinen mag — berührt nicht die Existenz der ontischen Regeln. Jetzt ist es wichtig, klarzumachen, daß die ontischen Regeln nicht einfach, wie einige Autoren sagen, „die Regeln der Regeln" sind. Ihr wahrhaftiger Charakter besteht darin, daß sie sprachliche Propositionen sind, die die Bedingungen der Handlung schaffen. Sie sind die notwendigen Voraussetzungen der Handlung, die in einer propositionellen Form ausgedrückt werden. Auch wenn hier das Verb „sein" gebraucht wird, sind es keine beschreibenden oder voraussagenden Propositionen, sondern kreative. Die Regel, welche besagt, daß ein Schachbrett aus 64 Feldern besteht, beschreibt kein bestimmtes Spielfeld und sagt auch nichts über die Qualität des Schachbretts aus; es schafft einfach das Brett, d. h. das Handlungsfeld für das Spiel, welches als ein notwendiges Element die Konvention enthält.

In diesem Sinne kann die ontische Regel eine „Regel" genannt werden, da sie die notwendigen konventionellen Elemente reguliert, welche Voraussetzungen der Handlung sind. Nichtsdestoweniger bekommt hier das Wort ‚Regel' einen Sinn, der, obwohl er gleichstimmend und verbindend ist, von dem Sinn der eigentlichen Regeln, die ein Müssen oder ein Sollen ausdrücken, verschieden ist. Deswegen benutzen wir, wenn wir sagen, daß der praktisch-ontische Bereich aus Regeln zusammengesetzt ist, das Wort ‚Regel' in seinem weiten Sinn, d. h. sowohl für ontische Regeln als auch für Regeln in striktem Sinn, d. h. für technische Regeln und für Normen. Dies ist der Grund für unsere Bestimmung der Regel als eine sprachliche Proposition, die darauf ausgerichtet ist, die Handlung direkt oder indirekt zu orientieren. Somit ist der Sinn erklärt, welcher den Adverbien „direkt" und „indirekt" zukommt.

Außerdem ist es notwendig zu erklären, was es genau bedeutet, daß die Regel die Handlung orientiert; oder mit anderen Worten, welcher Wert dem Ausdruck „Orientierung der Handlung" beigemessen wird, wenn wir von Regeln sprechen, die einem praktisch-ontischen Bereich angehören.

Orientierung bedeutet nicht Beschreibung, Erklärung oder Voraussagung. Die Regeln beschreiben und erklären nicht die Handlung; sie liefern auch keine Voraussage; es ist einfach so, daß sie die Handlung orientieren. Dies will jedoch nicht heißen, daß ohne die Regeln eine Erklärung, Voraussagung oder Beschreibung möglich wäre. Eher geschieht das Gegenteil: die Beschreibung, die Erklärung und die Voraussagung einer Handlung sind nur dann möglich, wenn vorher ein praktisch-ontischer Bereich besteht, in welchem die Handlung stattfindet oder stattzufinden hat.

Die Regeln beschreiben nicht die Handlung. Es ist von vielen Autoren, ja sogar fast allgemein angenommen, daß die Regeln — oder wenigstens bestimmte Regeln — verschiedene Arten von Handlungen beschreiben. Zum Beispiel, wenn wir uns auf das Recht beziehen, wäre eine beschreibende Regel diejenige, welche beschreibt, was Mord ist oder Kauf, oder die alleinige Nutznießung von Aktien; auf die Spiele bezogen wären solche Regeln diejenigen, die beschreiben würden, was ein Tor im Fußball bedeutet, oder das Pferd im Schachspiel. Gemäß dieser Meinung, die ziemlich weit verbreitet ist, zeigt die Mordregel diejenigen Merkmale auf, die für dieses kriminelle Verhalten typisch sind; sie gibt zu verstehen, daß die besagten Merkmale schon vor der Beschreibung bestehen, denn man kann effektiv nichts beschreiben, was nicht besteht.

Obwohl diese traditionelle Auffassung allgemein genommen zutreffend sein mag, ist sie radikal widersprüchlich, da das kriminelle Verhalten oder, besser gesagt, der kriminelle Typus nur existiert, weil vorher die Regel existiert. Tatsächlich ist dieser Umstand genau das Gegenteil von dem, was normalerweise gedacht wird. Wenn es keine Regel gäbe, welche kriminelle Verbrechen als solche Tatbestände darstellten, wäre es erwiesen, daß es solche Typen nicht gibt und somit auch nicht diese kriminellen Verbrechen. Allgemein kann man sagen, und nicht nur in bezug auf strafbare Taten, daß es keine juristischen Tatsachen oder Handlungen geben würde ohne die vorhergehenden Regeln, die sie als solche erst erschaffen. Somit entsteht die Regel vor der Handlung, was bedeutet, daß die Regel kaum die Handlung beschreiben kann, wenn die Annahme gilt, daß logischerweise nur das vorher Existierende beschrieben werden kann. Das will heißen, daß das Wort Beschreibung, auf die Regeln angewandt, absolut keine Bedeutung hat. Es gibt keine beschreibenden Regeln.

Auch ist es nicht so, daß die Regeln die Handlung erklärten. Eine Handlung zu erklären ist möglich, wenn man ihre Ursachen finden kann. Die Handlung ist ein Ereignis, welches sich wie jedes andere räumlich-zeitliche Phänomen in den Rahmen der faktischen Realität einreiht. Auch wenn es kein sehr gelungener Ausdruck ist, könnte man sagen, daß die Handlung eine Tat ist, etwas, das geschieht. Wie bei allem, was geschieht, ist es möglich, seine Ursachen zu untersuchen.

Diese kausale Analyse ist die Eigenanalyse der Erklärung. Warum geschieht eine bestimmte Handlung? Welche sind die Ursachen (Motive) zur Verwirklichung einer Handlung? Eine Ursache ist eine vorhergehende Tat, welche die Handlung auslöst, die die Rolle des Wirkungseffekts spielt. Es wird vorausgesetzt, daß zwischen der auslösenden Ursache und der verwirklichten Handlung ein objektiver Zusammenhang besteht, welchen man mittels der Forschung ermitteln kann. Als Motiv kann die Ursache oder eines seiner bildenden Elemente gelten, sobald es subjektiv im Bewußtsein der Menschen erscheint.

III.

Viele Autoren (z. B. einige Vertreter des „Soziologismus" bzw. „Psychologismus", auch in der Rechtstheorie) verstehen die Regeln als ein Erklärungsschema für das menschliche Verhalten, indem sie alle deontischen Ausdrucksformen auf einfache Faktizität reduzieren, die durch das erklärende Kriterium preisgegeben werden. Besessen vom Prinzip einer warum auch immer notwendigen Einheit der Wissenschaft, sind diese Autoren nicht für die Erscheinungsvielfalt der sozialen Phänomene empfänglich, und aus diesem Grund versuchen sie, diese Phänomene in ein einziges Schema zu zwängen. Damit verteidigen diese Psychologisten und Soziologisten die Idee, daß die Regeln nur ein Ausdruck von *Regelmäßigkeiten* im Verhalten sind, unter welchem wohlgemerkt das normale Verhalten der Menschen zu verstehen ist. Die Gültigkeit der Regel wird somit auf ihre Wirksamkeit reduziert. Dies hat dann zur Folge, daß auch die Regel, wenn diese Wirksamkeit verschwindet, nicht mehr gültig ist und als solche verschwindet. Jedes Zugeständnis an das definitive Kriterium der Wirksamkeit der Regeln ist ein Zugeständnis an den Realismus, und jedes Zugeständnis an den Realismus ist meiner Meinung nach gleichbedeutend mit einer Unkenntnis dessen, was eine Regel wirklich (d. h. entsprechend seiner eigenen Natur) ist.

Eine Regel ist eine sprachliche Proposition, ausgerichtet auf ein Verhalten, d. h., sie ist die Bedeutung des sprachlichen Ausdrucks. Als solche ist sie keine Tat, obwohl es eine Tatsache ist, daß die Regel diktiert oder auferlegt wird (oder wie immer man es nennen möchte), und zwar durch jemanden und zu einem bestimmten Zeitpunkt.

Es muß ferner berücksichtigt werden, daß die Regel normalerweise von jemandem für irgendeinen Zweck geschaffen wird. Diese Beabsichtigung durch die schaffenden Subjekte der Regel ist vielleicht (zumindest teilweise) erklärlich unter Bezugnahme auf den sozialhistorischen Zusammenhang, auf die Sozialpsychologie und auf die individuelle Psychologie der Subjekte selbst. Alle diese — und viele andere Aspekte, die hier nicht behandelt werden können — sind „Tatsachen", genauso wie die physisch-natürlichen Ereignisse, die unmittelbare Voraussetzungen für die Entstehung einer Regel sein können (z. B. jemand diktiert sie wörtlich, schreibt sie nieder, usw.).

Für den Soziologisten ist die Regel nur eine soziale Tatsache mit besonderen Charakteristiken. Er geht davon aus, daß nichts existiert außer der psychologisch-sozialen Wirklichkeit; und jede andere diesbezügliche Haltung wird von ihm als metaphysisch abgetan. Das Regelkonzept, das in einer von dieser soziologistischen Denkweise abweichenden Form verstanden ist, erscheint damit als eine metaphysische Eingebung, eine „Idee-Vorstellung", die den Soziologisten als solche verachtenswert ist, da diese für sie keine Wirklichkeitsverankerung hat und somit keiner Untersuchung den Weg weisen kann.

Aber zugleich mit der Tatsache der Regelmäßigkeit einer bestimmten Verhaltensweise, welche für die Soziologisten eine Art Axiom ist, gibt es, ganz logischerweise, auch die Tatsache der Unregelmäßigkeit, der abweichenden Verhaltensweise (das „Abweichende" verstanden unter Bezug auf die „normale" Verhaltensweise). Die Unregelmäßigkeit ist eine Ausnahme im Zusammenhang mit der Regelmäßigkeit und deswegen bildet letztere sowohl die Regel als auch die Grundlage für die Wahrnehmung der Abweichung. Trotzdem wird auch abweichendes Verhalten in der soziologischen Forschung zum Problem, sobald es sich ergibt, daß „Regelmäßigkeiten bei den Unregelmäßigkeiten" vorkommen, wenn wir es so nennen dürfen. Auf diese Art kann die soziologische Analyse nicht die Regelmäßigkeit, welche die Regel bildet, in bezug auf die Abweichung bestimmen. Die Bestimmung kann nur dank der statistischen Daten erfolgen, welche beweisen, daß regelmäßiges Verhalten prozentmäßig höher liegt. Wichtiges Belegmaterial sind auch die psychologischen Daten, die bezeugen, daß die Mitglieder einer bestimmten Gesellschaft oder Gruppe im allgemeinen ein Verpflichtungsbedürfnis im Hinblick auf die Regel (oder die dominierende Regelmäßigkeit) und ein Gefühl der Ablehnung und Abscheu im Hinblick auf die abweichende Verhaltensweise (oder eine minderrangige Regelmäßigkeit) verspüren. Die „Soziologisten" bewegen sich also im Bannkreis der statistischen Daten, und alles dies geschieht auf der Grundlage empirischer Beobachtung.

Diese Theorien, abgesehen von ihren erkenntnistheoretischen Mängeln, versagen, wenn es um die präzise Begrenzung dessen geht, was eine Regel ist. Das Konzept der Regelmäßigkeit, bezogen auf die menschliche Verhaltensweise, kann nur als Instrument dienen, um zu beschreiben, wie sich die Menschen in bestimmten Situationen verhalten. Aber eine Verhaltensweise kann viele verschiedene Bedeutungen haben und somit in der Sache variieren, abhängig von der Auslegung, die ihren Erscheinungsformen zugeschrieben wird. Da die Handlung eine Einheit mit einem zu erarbeitenden Sinn bildet, und da dieser Sinn nur mittels eines Interpretationsprozesses zu schließen ist, der vorher die Existenz eines Diskurses voraussetzt, von welchem aus sie interpretiert wird, ist es offensichtlich, daß es ohne eine vorhergehende Regel nicht möglich ist, z. B. von einer rechtlichen Handlung oder von einer Spielhandlung zu sprechen — oder, allgemein gesagt, von einer Handlung, die einem bestimmten praktisch-ontischen Bereich angehört.

Genau hier, wo es darum geht, die Existenzbedingungen einer Handlung festzulegen, welche einem bestimmten praktisch-ontischen Bereich zugeschrieben wird, ist es unausweichlich, ihre vorherige Existenz als sprachliche Konstruktion zu unterstreichen, welche die Handlung ermöglicht, die wir vor uns haben. Wann können wir z. B. sagen, daß eine bestimmte menschliche Verhaltensweise eine Handlung des Spiels ist? Offensichtlich sagen wir das, wenn sich dieses Verhalten in den praktisch-ontischen Bereich einfügt, der das betreffende Spiel bildet. Wann kann man sagen, daß ein bestimmtes menschliches Verhalten ein juristisches Verhalten ist? In entsprechender Weise sagt man das nur, wenn die Handlung juristisch durch ihren praktisch-ontischen Bereich festgelegt ist, der das Recht bildet.

Die verschiedenen Bereiche zeigen durch ihre Regeln die notwendigen Elemente der Handlung auf, oder, was dasselbe ist, die Bedingungen derselben. Sie zeigen auch das Verfahren auf, mit welchem die Handlung verwirklicht werden soll, i. e. zeigen die Handlung an sich auf. Die Regeln des praktisch-ontischen Bereiches bilden einen praktisch-ontischen Diskurs, der als ein natürliches Element der Handlung — durch die Auslegung — angewandt werden kann. Damit zeigen sie an, daß die Handlung sich in die erwünschten Bedingungen einfügt und somit zu dem praktisch-ontischen Bereich gehört, um den es sich jeweils handelt.

Die „soziologistische" Betrachtungsweise mündet letzten Endes in Absurditäten: Weil sie darauf verzichtet, die Regeln als sprachliche Ausdrücke oder Propositionen zu betrachten, die in dem System verbunden sind, welches der praktisch-ontische Bereich ist, wird es ihr unmöglich, die Vorgänge in der gesellschaftlichen Wirklichkeit zu deuten. Was in der Wirklichkeit geschieht, kann nur mittels eines vorhergehenden Interpretationsschemas verstanden werden. Was geschieht, ist nicht unumstößlich. Ganz im Gegenteil: im Zusammenhang mit den „natürlichen" Phänomenen (Bewegungen, Vorgänge, Handlungen in ihrem äußeren Sinn) können die verschiedensten Dinge gleichzeitig geschehen. Einzig und allein mit Hilfe eines bestimmten Diskurses, der uns ein Interpretationsschema verschafft, können wir wissen, welche Art von Handlung stattfindet. Der Soziologismus und, allgemein gesagt, die ganze „realistische" Denkweise haben es nicht verstanden, daß die Handlung kein bloß physisch-naturhaftes Ereignis ist, obwohl es auch als solches interpretiert werden kann. Aber im letzteren Fall versteht man es nicht als eine eigentliche Handlung, da die naturhaften Ereignisse an sich jeglicher Bedeutung entbehren.

Wenn man davon ausgeht, daß die Handlung eine Einheit der Bedeutungen ist, die einer Bewegungsgesamtheit zugeschrieben werden, ist es leicht zu verstehen, warum gerade der praktisch-ontische Bereich den Diskurs verschafft, von dem aus die Interpretation und somit die im voraus bestehende Erkenntnis der Bedeutungen möglich werden. Der praktisch-ontische Bereich geht der bloßen Faktizität voran und kann außerdem unabhängig von dieser, also in einem Sinne durch sich selbst, „beschrieben" werden. Die „Beschreibung" eines Bereiches ist die Aufzählung seiner Regeln und der Verbindungen derselben im System. Der praktisch-ontische Bereich wird durch das Regelsystem ausgedrückt. Die Faktizität, auf die wir uns hier beziehen, kommt logischerweise später als der praktisch-ontische Bereich; sie also setzt die Existenz desselben voraus. Die Faktizität ist abhängig von diesem Bereich. Ohne die Regeln hört die Faktizität freilich nicht auf zu bestehen, aber ohne jeden Sinn würde sie dies bestimmt tun. Wie können wir z. B. wissen, was ein Tor ist, ohne die vorherige Regel und den durch sie vermittelten Sinn? Wie würden wir bei einem rechtswidrigen Verhalten vorgehen, wenn vorher nicht eine Regel bestünde, aufgrund deren wir ein Urteil über die Verhaltensweise abgeben können? Die Regeln auf mögliche Regelmäßigkeiten des Verhaltens herabzusetzen bedeutet die Auslöschung der Analyse der praktisch-ontischen Bereiche und letzten Endes die Unmöglichkeit zu verstehen, was eine Regel ist und was eine regelgemäße bzw. nicht-regelgemäße Handlung ist.

Eine Variante der psycho-soziologischen Denkrichtung ist besonders stark in den Vereinigten Staaten vertreten. Dieser Ansicht zufolge haben die Regeln die Aufgabe, das künftige Verhalten vorauszusagen (einige Autoren sprechen sogar von der „Prophezeiung"). Die Verwandtschaft dieser prediktionistischen Idee mit derjenigen, die besagt, daß die Regel hauptsächlich auf eine bloße Regelmäßigkeit im Verhalten zurückzuführen ist, ist offensichtlich: Wenn die Regel die Beschreibung eines möglichen, normalen Verhaltens ist, dient sie nicht nur dazu, zu ermitteln, was im Leben der Menschen geschieht, sondern auch dazu, zu erfahren, was möglicherweise geschehen kann. Im Lichte des Wissens, was bei bestimmten Sektoren des menschlichen Verhaltens bisher geschehen ist, könnten wir dann — gemäß dieser Denkweise — „prophezeien", was weiterhin geschehen wird, vorausgesetzt, daß die Umstände sich nicht ändern.

Während die anderen psycho-soziologistischen Denkrichtungen danach streben, ein Wissen zu erhalten, welches als wissenschaftlich bezeichnet werden könnte, beschäftigt sich die prediktionistische Richtung eher damit, den Juristen eine strategische Orientierungsweise in ihrem Berufsleben aufzuzeigen. Aber auch die prediktionistische Theorie setzt den Begriff der Regelmäßigkeit der psycho-soziologischen Denkweise voraus, und wir haben gesehen, daß die Regelmäßigkeit die vorhergehende Existenz der praktisch-ontischen Bereiche voraussetzt. Wir können somit feststellen, daß auch die prediktionistische Theorie von der Annahme, daß Bereiche dieser Art bestehen, abhängig ist. Man kann nur Voraussagen formulieren auf der Basis dessen, was bis jetzt wirklich geschehen ist (der Ausdruck „prophezeien" ist hier weniger angebracht, wenn man davon ausgeht, daß für die Propheten die Erfahrungsdaten im Prinzip überflüssig sind, welche die gewöhnlichen Sterblichen für ihre Voraussagungen heranziehen). Es kann passieren, daß sich die Tatsachen in der vorausgesagten Weise verbinden, aber es ist auch möglich, daß sie sich in Richtung Vergangenheit bewegen. Nun, das normale Verhalten ist nur dann in einen bestimmten praktisch-ontischen Bereich eingeschlossen, wenn es in Übereinstimmung mit den Regeln ist, welche diesen Bereich ausmachen. Aber außerdem, abgesehen von diesem Argument, das in sich selbst unabwendbar ist, setzt dieses Verhalten die vorherige Existenz des praktisch-ontischen Bereichs voraus und folglicherweise auch die Existenz der Regeln, die diesen Bereich bilden. Wie können wir das entsprechende Verhalten eines Richters voraussagen, wenn wir nicht voraussetzen, daß es einen praktisch-ontischen Bereich gibt als Konstitutionsbasis für eine bestimmte Kompetenz, der es dem Richter möglich macht, sich für ein bestimmtes Verfahren zu entscheiden? Was würde dies alles bedeuten ohne die vorherige Existenz von Regeln, welche alle diese Elemente des praktisch-ontischen Bereichs bilden? Damit ist bewiesen, daß die Voraussagungen die Regeln voraussetzen.

IV.

Auf der Grundlage der oben angeführten Gesichtspunkte können wir feststellen: Obwohl eine gewisse Übereinstimmung zwischen den intellektuellen Operationen (wie Beschreiben, Erklären und Voraussagen) besteht, die im Zusammenhang mit den Regeln stehen, welche den praktisch-ontischen Bereich ausmachen, setzt eine jede dieser Operationen die Existenz solcher Regeln voraus. Die Regeln an sich aber beschreiben weder das menschliche Verhalten, noch erklären sie es.

Nachfolgend werden wir versuchen, zu erklären, wie die Regeln selbst beschaffen sind, die die Handlung orientieren und dirigieren. Unsere definitive Aufgabe besteht darin, aufzuklären, welche Funktion die Regeln in bezug auf menschliche Verhaltensweisen haben, und spezifischer, ihren Zusammenhang mit der Handlung, die selbst einen „Moment" dieses Zusammenhanges darstellt, klarzumachen.

Die Regeln, die bestimmte praktisch-ontische Bereiche bilden, sind nicht homogen, sie sind nicht gleichartig beschaffen. Als Beispiele für diese Bereiche können wir — abermals — die Spiele und das Recht nennen. Aufgrund der Verschiedenheit der Regeln bei jedem dieser Bereiche wäre es vielleicht unlogisch, nach der „allgemeinen Funktion der Regeln" zu fragen. Es ist offensichtlich, daß jede Art von Regel ihre eigene Aufgabe in bezug auf die Handlung hat, ihre spezifische Funktion, die durch ihre unterschiedlichen Ausdrucksformen artikuliert wird. Vor einer solchen Verschiedenheit verspürt man die Lust, das Problem der Funktion der Regeln im allgemeinen durch die Frage nach den spezifischen Funktionen der verschiedenen Arten von Regeln zu ersetzen. Würden wir aber diese Haltung einnehmen, wäre das gleichbedeutend mit dem Verzicht darauf, die Frage nach der Funktion eines praktisch-ontischen Bereiches zu beantworten, der, wie wir schon festgestellt haben, eine Gesamtheit der Regeln ist. Außerdem, wenn wir das Wort „Regel" benutzen, wird das seinen Grund haben; damit unterstellen wir, daß die verschiedenen Arten von Regeln etwas gemeinsam haben. In der Tat gibt es ja viele solche übereinstimmenden allgemeinen Punkte, nicht zuletzt der wirkliche Ursprung der Regel, der in der Konvention liegt. Daß die Regeln ihren Ursprung in der Konvention haben, ist also gewissermaßen ein allen Regeln gemeinsamer Aspekt. Aber im Moment interessiert dieser Aspekt uns nicht, da es eher darum geht, herauszufinden, ob die Regeln in ihrem eigenen Sein gemeinsame Elemente aufweisen oder nicht.

Wenn man in Betracht zieht, daß die hier behandelten Regeln im Hinblick auf ihre praktisch-ontischen Bereiche keine logisch-sprachliche Eindeutigkeit haben, sondern daß es drei diesbezügliche Arten von Regeln gibt (Regeln des Seins bzw. des Müssens und des Sollens), ist es leicht festzustellen, daß in der syntaktischen Struktur der Regeln keine übereinstimmenden Elemente auftauchen, da diese drei Arten etwas ganz radikal anderes darstellen. Eine Besessenheit der Allgemeinen Rechtstheorie ist es, die angeblichen syntaktisch-sprachlichen Übereinstimmungen der verschiedenen Regeln zu finden. Aber dieses Vorhaben ist von vornherein zum Scheitern verurteilt, da die Regeln unter diesem Gesichtspunkt eben verschieden sind. Die verschiedenen Regeln an sich besitzen keine allgemeinen Elemente, welche sie, voneinander unabhängig betrachtet, als Regeln eines praktisch-ontischen Bereichs darstellten. Nur wenn wir sie als Teil des letzteren betrachten, intim miteinander verbunden und verschlungen, werden wir ihre Gemeinsamkeit finden: ihre Funktion als solche, die keine andere ist als der Bereich selbst.

Dies führt uns zu Überlegungen über die Funktion des praktisch-ontischen Bereichs. Warum werden solche Bereiche geschaffen, und warum werden die Regeln erstellt, die sie bilden? Die Antwort ist einfach: um die menschliche Handlung zu regulieren, d. h., sie zu dirigieren und zu orientieren. Das ist eine grundlegende allgemeine Bestimmung. Wir könnten sagen, daß es sich hier um ein analytisches Urteil handelt, denn im Sein des praktisch-ontischen Bereichs liegt seine Funktion. Die Bestimmung der durch Vereinbarungen entstehenden Konventionen ist es, menschliche Handlungen zu regulieren, zu orientieren und zu dirigieren. Dieses bringt uns erneut mit dem Begriff der Konvention in Verbindung. Eine Konvention ist ein Abkommen zwischen zwei oder mehreren Leuten, dem zufolge etwas von einem bestimmten Zeitpunkt an auf eine bestimmte Art sein oder gesollt werden soll. Aber dieses „etwas", eingeschlossen in die Beschreibung, ist nicht etwas ganz Beliebiges. In der generischen Konvention eines praktisch-ontischen Bereichs ist dieses „etwas" selbstverständlich die menschliche Handlung. Mittels der Konvention wird erklärt, wie die Handlung stattfinden muß oder soll und wie die ontischen Voraussetzungen, unter denen sie stattzufinden hat, festzulegen sind.

Die Funktion der Konvention muß in ihrer Verbindung mit der inneren Beschaffenheit des betreffenden Systems betrachtet werden; durch diese Funktion werden das System und seine Regeln mit dem Objekt selbst verbunden. Das Objekt des praktisch-ontischen Bereichs ist die menschliche Handlung, und zwar nicht jede beliebige, sondern genau die Handlung, die den besagten Bereich als solche schafft. Die Handlung ist eine konventionelle Schöpfung des praktisch-ontischen Bereichs; sie ist gleichzeitig „Objekt" und „Bestandteil" desselben. Es wird hiermit jede Möglichkeit von der Hand gewiesen, die Funktion in anderem Sinn aufzufassen, als gleichwertig mit den Absichten, die der Schöpfer eines praktisch-ontischen Bereichs unter Bezug auf die äußere Umgebung des Systems verfolgt.

Es ist natürlich möglich, daß z. B. die Schöpfer des Bereiches die Funktion der Konvention auch anders sehen. In diesem Fall beziehen sie ihre Funktion z. B. auf das Feld der Forschung des Ursache-Wirkung-Zusammenhanges, der den praktisch-ontischen Bereich mit der psychologisch-sozialen und wirtschaftlichen Welt verbindet. Die innere Funktion der Konvention jedoch bezieht sich — im Gegenteil — auf die immanente Finalität des praktisch-ontischen Bereichs und soll interpretiert werden als die bestehende Verbindung zwischen diesem und der Handlung als eines seiner Elemente. Dieses Element ist geradezu definitiv, wenn man in Betracht zieht, daß die Daseinsberechtigung des Bereichs durch die Notwendigkeit entsteht, die Handlung zu regulieren. Ganz einfach kann man in diesem Sinn behaupten, daß z. B. die Funktion des Spiels das Spielen ist, m. a. W., die Spielhandlungen möglich zu machen. Auf die gleiche Weise ist die Funktion des Rechts, juristische Handlungen durchzuführen. Neben diesen inneren Funktionen bestehen, ohne Zweifel, die äußeren. Das Objekt unserer Analyse sind aber die ersteren und nicht die letzteren; die äußeren Funktionen sind ein Gegenstand der Erforschung der Verbindungen, die zwischen dem praktisch-ontischen Bereich und der den empirischen Wissenschaften zugänglichen Außenwelt bestehen.

Mit der vorliegenden Analyse wollen wir uns also auf einer rein formalen Ebene bewegen. Das bedeutet, daß die Erforschung der Funktion der Konvention eine Verbindung zum logisch-linguistischen Studium der Propositionen haben muß; diese Propositionen machen ja den praktisch-ontischen Bereich aus. Die Funktion muß sich in der sprachlichen Natur der Propositionen widerspiegeln. Hier können wir von der vektorialen Funktion (um eine Begriffsübernahme aus der Physik zu verwenden) der praktischen Propositionen sprechen, die den Bereich ausmachen. Die Vektoren sind in der Physik die (formale) graphische Darstellung der Kräfte, die in der Natur wirken und die es ermöglichen, „daß sich die Sachen bewegen". Sie stellen eine Kraft in eine bestimmte Richtung dar. Analog können wir sagen, daß das gleiche mit den praktischen Propositionen geschieht.

Die Regeln, die den praktisch-ontischen Bereich bilden, sind praktische Propositionen, deren vektorielle Funktion genau darin besteht, die Handlung zu orientieren oder zu dirigieren. Mit den praktischen Propositionen wird nicht nur etwas gesagt, sondern auch getan. Dieses „etwas", was gemacht wird, ist nämlich die Schöpfung des praktisch-ontischen Bereichs. Dieser Bereich kann nur als ein sprachlicher verstanden werden, da es gerade die Regeln sind, die ihn ausmachen, d. h. die praktischen Propositionen. Diese Propositionen sind die Basiselemente, deren Verbindung untereinander uns den Schlüssel zur Analyse liefert. Durch die praktischen Propositionen werden die notwendigen Elemente des Bereiches geschaffen, d. h. die räumlich-zeitlichen, persönlichen und kompetenziellen Voraussetzungen der Handlung, das Handlungsverfahren selbst, sowie die gesollten Handlungsanforderungen. Diese sind respektiv die immanenten vektoriellen Funktionen der ontischen Propositionen, der technischen Propositionen und der deontischen Propositionen, welche den praktisch-ontischen Bereich ausmachen.

Es erweist sich also, daß die Regeln, die im Recht auftauchen, praktische Propositionen sind, untereinander verbunden und eine Einheit bildend, deren Ursprung in der Konvention liegt. Diese Propositionen sind als Bedeutungen aufzufassen — daher werden sie hier Propositionen genannt — und in der Tat als „praktische", d. h. zugehörend einem praktisch-ontischen Bereich, dessen immanentes Ziel ist, die Handlung zu dirigieren oder zu regulieren. Die Funktion der Regeln ist einfach zu verstehen, wenn man sie mit dem gesamten System des Bereiches in Verbindung bringt. Diese Funktion ist dem Bereich immanent, also nicht äußerlich zu ihm. Wir benutzen hier das Wort ‚Funktion' in einem anderen Sinn als dem normalen, aber es ist deswegen nicht weniger exakt.

Die logisch-sprachliche Analyse der praktisch-ontischen Bereiche führt somit zu einem strukturell-funktionellen Verständnis des Rechts. Strukturell, soweit es sich den Bereich als etwas durch verschiedene Arten von Regeln Artikuliertes vorstellt, deren Gesamtheit dieses Etwas bildet. Und funktionell, weil es die Regeln nicht nur als miteinander verbunden versteht (die Verbindung der Regeln miteinander macht ja genau die Struktur aus), sondern auch in Verbindung mit dem Objekt derselben. Dieses vektorielle Verhältnis drückt sich im sprachlichen Charakter der Regeln aus, indem es einen Teil ihrer Natur bildet. Die strukturelle Verbindung und die funktionelle Verbindung der Regeln sind zwei durch Sprache vermittelte Verbindungen, deren Analyse nur mittels eines linguistischen Ansatzes möglich ist.

Wir können somit eine Regel als eine praktische Proposition definieren, welche einem praktisch-ontischen Bereich angehört.

DER SYSTEMBEGRIFF IM RECHT

Von Marcelino Rodriguez Molinero, Salamanca

I.

Seit einigen Jahren vertiefe ich meine Studien insbesondere auf dem Gebiet einiger zentraler Themen der Rechtswissenschaft und Rechtstheorie. Im Augenblick beschäftigt mich vor allem die Problematik des Systembegriffs im Recht. Das Aufwerfen dieses Themas und den Stand seiner augenblicklichen Darlegung kann ich hier wie folgt zusammenfassen.

Ich gehe von der Voraussetzung aus, daß es vermutlich nur wenige Wörter gibt, die in den heutigen Tagen so schnell und ebenso leichtfertig von manchen wissenschaftlichen Autoren benutzt werden wie das Wort „System". Der begriffliche Inhalt aber, der diesem Wort innewohnt, ist weder klar noch unumstritten. Denn die meisten zeitgenössischen Bücher und Aufsätze auf dem Gebiet des Rechts, die mit dem Wort „System" betitelt sind, zeigen, daß es keine allgemein akzeptierte Deutung dieses Begriffs gibt, und daß dieser Begriff von den verschiedenen zeitgenössischen Forschungstraditionen in der Rechtstheorie entsprechenderweise sehr verschiedenartig interpretiert wird. Als leuchtenden Beweis dafür könnte man unter anderen das hier so viel zitierte Buch von *J. Raz*, „The Concept of a Legal System" nennen.

Bedauerlicherweise habe ich auch auf diesem Kongreß bemerkt — und das hatte ich wirklich vorher nicht vermutet —, daß hier kein Wort darüber gesagt wurde, was den lebhaften Streit und die Meinungsverschiedenheiten zwischen den Vertretern der systematischen und der problematischen Auffassung der Rechtsordnung betrifft. Dieser Streit ist vor allem im deutschen Rahmen (denken wir z. B. an *Th. Viehweg*) unter dem Einfluß der Philosophie *N. Hartmanns* sehr lebhaft gewesen und dauert auch immer noch an. Er hat auch in anderen Ländern, insbesondere im lateinamerikanischen Raum, ein großes Echo gefunden. Denken wir einmal an einen so bekannten Rechtsphilosophen wie den Uruguayer *J. Llambias de Azebedo*, der in seinem Buch „Eidética y Aporética del Derecho" sehr scharfsinnig fragt, ob es im Recht nicht nützlicher wäre, das systematische Denken durch das aporetische Denken zu ersetzen.

Unter diesen Prämissen und Voraussetzungen besteht der Leitgedanke meines Vortrags darin, festzustellen, bis zu welchem Punkt das positive Recht, nachdem es als Inbegriff von Normen und Entscheidungen studiert worden ist, als ein *System* dargestellt werden kann, und welchen praktischen Nutzen eine solche Darstellung bieten kann.

Um diese Aufgabe erfüllen zu können, müssen zuerst einige Gesichtspunkte behandelt werden, die ich als grundlegend betrachte. An erster Stelle, und als vorausgehende Frage, muß festgestellt werden, wie der *Systembegriff*, und ebenso das *Wort* als solches, im philosophischen und wissenschaftlichen Denken entstanden ist. An zweiter Stelle muß untersucht werden, wie der Systembegriff im Recht eingeführt wurde. An dritter Stelle müssen die verschiedenen Bedeutungen aufgezeigt werden, die der Ausdruck System im juristischen Denken des 19. und 20. Jahrhunderts angenommen hat. Und endlich sollen auch die gegenwärtigen Auffassungen des Systembegriffs im Recht behandelt werden.

II.

An erster Stelle also muß gezeigt werden, wie der *Systembegriff*, und ebenso das Wort als solches, im philosophischen und wissenschaftlichen Denken entstanden ist.

Hierbei ist zuerst aufzuzeigen, daß das Wort „System" ursprünglich ein griechisches Wort von kosmologischer Herkunft ist. Es hatte jahrhundertelang vor allem eine astronomische Bedeutung. Noch im Jahre 1632 veröffentlichte der weltberühmte Italiener *Galileo Galilei* seinen bekannten Essay unter dem Titel „Dialogo sopra i due massimi sistemi del mondo".

Der Gebrauch dieses Wortes im rein philosophischen Sinne begann erst an der Wende vom 16. zum 17. Jahrhundert, und zwar im logischen Rahmen, durch das Werk von *Bartholomäus Keckermann* „Systema Logicae tribus libris adornatum", veröffentlicht im Jahre 1600. Von da an wurde der Ausdruck „System" das am meisten bevorzugte Wort in vielen Werken über Logik, anstatt daß andere Wörter wie z. B. *Summa*, *Compendium* usw. benutzt worden wären.

Was aber den Begriff angeht, so finden wir schon im Jahre 1606 eine Typifizierung des Systems, die es unserer heutigen Vorstellung sehr nahe bringt. Es handelt sich um die Definition des Philosophen *Ch. Timpler* in seinem „Metaphysicae Systema methodicum", wo er ausdrücklich sagt, ein System sei so etwas wie ein „corpus doctrinae ex diversis partibus coagmentatum, non confusum et perturbatum, sed bene secundum leges methodi ordinatum et dispositum". Dabei finden wir schon die drei Elemente unseres heutigen Systembegriffes angedeutet, nämlich: die Verschiedenheit der Teile, die Ordnung und die Einheit.

Im Verlauf des 17. Jahrhunderts verbreitet sich allmählich der Gebrauch des Wortes „System" im rein philosophischen Raum. Es ist nicht möglich, hier die Entwicklung und Erweiterung dieses Gebrauchs weiter auszuführen. Auf jeden Fall werde ich mich in meiner entsprechenden Monographie sehr eingehend damit befassen.

III.

An zweiter Stelle, hatten wir gesagt, muß untersucht werden, wie der Systembegriff, insbesondere durch *Savigny*, im Recht eingeführt wurde. Wenn wir einige Besonderheiten beiseite lassen, und wenn wir unsere Aufmerksamkeit auf das Spätwerk von Savigny lenken, d. h. auf sein Hauptwerk „System des römischen Rechts" von 1840, werden wir zu unserem großen Erstaunen sehen, daß für ihn das System kein Inbegriff von Regeln oder Normen ist, sondern, was sehr bemerkenswert ist, der organische und lebendige Zusammenhang von allen *Rechtsinstituten*. Diese, die Rechtsinstitute, sind vor allem die typischen Lebensverhältnisse, wie z. B. die Ehe, das Eigentum, der Kauf, der Staat usw. Im besten Falle kommen die *Rechtsregeln* für Savigny nur an einer zweiten Stelle, und zwar allein als Ausdruck der lebendigen und naturhaften Wirklichkeit der Rechtsinstitute. Man kann dann legitimerweise denken, daß das System in diesem zweiten Sinne sich „auf den inneren Zusammenhang, welcher alle Rechtsinstitute und Rechtsregeln zu einer großen Einheit verknüpft", bezieht.

IV.

An dritter Stelle, so wurde anfangs bemerkt, müssen die verschiedenen Bedeutungen aufgezeigt werden, die der Ausdruck System im Verlauf des 19. und 20. Jahrhunderts im juristischen Denken angenommen hat. Darunter sind etwa als wichtigste Punkte die folgenden zu erwähnen:

1. Der Systembegriff als *Stufenpyramide*, bei welcher alle juristischen Begriffe und alle juristischen Sätze sich aus einem Oberbegriff ergeben und ableiten lassen, nach der Art der Begriffsjurisprudenz.

Der Hauptvertreter dieses juristischen Systembegriffes ist, wie wir alle wissen, *G. Puchta*. Wenn er die innere Dynamik der Begriffspyramide andeutet, spricht er von nichts mehr und nichts weniger als einer „Genealogie der Begriffe". Nun eben bildet die juristische Begriffspyramide in ihrer logischen Einheit gerade das juristische System. Demgemäß hat die Rechtswissenschaft als ihre eigene Aufgabe die Rechtssätze in diesem systematischen Zusammenhang „als einander bedingende und voneinander abstammende zu erkennen, um die Genealogie der einzelnen bis zu ihrem Prinzip hinauf verfolgen und ebenso von den Prinzipien bis zu ihren äußersten Sprossen herabsteigen zu können".

Das Rechtssystem ist also für Puchta, und nach ihm für die spätere Begriffsjurisprudenz, einfach ein *logisches System*. Die echte Erkenntnis dieses logischen Systems ergibt sich eben nur, wenn man an die Spitze der Pyramide den allgemeinsten der juristischen Begriffe, gerade den *Rechtsbegriff* selbst, setzt. Der Systembegriff im Recht ist dann eine Anwendung eines echten formal-logischen und rein deduktiven Systembegriffes.

2. Die Reaktion auf diese logisch-deduktive Vorstellung erfolgt durch eine Jurisprudenz pragmatischer Art, hauptsächlich durch *Ph. Heck*. Er führt in der Rechtswissenschaft die Teilung in ein *äußeres* und ein *inneres* System ein.

Das Hauptmerkmal jedes Systems ist für Heck die Idee der Ordnung. In dieser Hinsicht ist für ihn das „äußere System" nichts anderes als „die Ordnung, welcher eine Gedankenmasse im Darstellungsinteresse gegeben ist". Diese Ordnung bestimmt sich sowohl durch die Begriffsbildung als auch durch ihre Reihenfolge. Dann kommt noch die Teilung des zu ordnenden Stoffes. Das deutlichste Beispiel dafür ist gerade die Gliederung des deutschen BGB in fünf Bücher.

Bei dem „inneren System" dagegen handelt es sich um jene Ordnung, die sich aus dem sachlichen Zusammenhang desselben Stoffes ergibt. Demgemäß entsteht dieses System nicht durch die ordnende Tätigkeit, sondern, wie Heck ausdrücklich sagt, es wird „automatisch" von dem zu ordnenden Stoff gegeben. Es wird also nicht geschaffen, sondern nur erkannt. Da es sich aus einer „immanenten Ordnung" ergibt, könnte man auch hier — so fügt Heck hinzu — „von einem immanenten System reden".

3. Durch den Normativismus von *Hans Kelsen* kommt man jedoch wieder auf den pyramidenartigen Begriff des Systems zurück. Kelsen unterscheidet seinerseits zwischen einem *statischen* System, welches der Moral und dem Naturrecht eigen ist und das den Inhalt betrifft, und einem *dynamischen* System, das dem positiven Recht eigen ist und nur die Form betrifft, wie sich Normen von anderen Normen ableiten lassen.

War für Heck die Idee der „Ordnung" das Hauptmerkmal eines jeden Systembegriffes, so ist sie auch für Kelsen in strengster Verbindung mit dem *Geltungsgrund* dieser Ordnung das konstitutive Element sowohl des statischen wie auch des dynamischen Systems. „Eine Ordnung" — sagt

Kelsen an einer sehr typischen Stelle seiner „Reinen Rechtslehre" — „ist ein System von Normen, deren Einheit dadurch konstituiert wird, daß sie alle denselben Geltungsgrund haben; und der Geltungsgrund einer normativen Ordnung ist eine Grundnorm, aus der sich die Geltung aller zu der Ordnung gehörigen Normen ableitet."

V.

Kommen wir nun zum letzten Punkt unserer jetzigen Untersuchung: zu den gegenwärtigen Vorstellungsweisen des Systembegriffes im Recht. Man soll aber nicht in den Irrtum verfallen, daß es sich bei ihnen um eine bloße Weiterentwicklung der zuletzt vorgetragenen Systembegriffe handele.

1. Zuerst sind hier, im Anschluß an Kelsen, zwei Hauptrichtungen zu unterscheiden. Die eine ist die sogenannte *analytische* Richtung, die von *J. Austin* über Kelsen bis hin zu *H. L. A. Hart* reicht, und das Rechtssystem als ein System von primären und sekundären Regeln begreift. Sie hat in dem Hauptwerk von Hart, „The Concept of Law", ihren Höhepunkt erreicht. Was andere Autoren, ihm folgend, zu der Erklärung des Systembegriffes im Recht beigetragen haben, ist im besten Falle eine einfache Ausarbeitung seiner, bzw. der analytischen Rechtsauffassung. In dieser Hinsicht beurteile ich das schon erwähnte Buch von *J. Raz*, „The Concept of a Legal System", als das glänzendste Beispiel.

Die andere Richtung ist jene, welche mit der *deontischen Logik* in Verbindung steht. Sie versucht vor allem eine juristische Logik zu entwickeln, die ihrerseits auf dem Wege ist, eine exakte juristische Sprache zu schaffen, welche sich wiederum auf ein *Formalsystem* zurückführen läßt. Hier sind zu nennen, angefangen von den Werken von *G. H. von Wright*, insbesondere „Norm and Action", auch die Werke von *U. Klug*, „Juristische Logik", von *Alf Ross*, „Directives and Norms", und nicht zuletzt das interessante Buch der Argentinier *C. E. Alchourrón* und *E. Bulygin*, „Normative Systems".

2. Ein ganz anderes und gewiß heute sehr lebendiges Bild gewinnt man, wenn man die Anwendung der allgemeinen Systemtheorie (General Systems Theory) im Rechtsgebiet betrachtet. Voraussetzung dafür ist hier eine Stellungnahme zum Verhältnis der Rechtswissenschaft zu den Sozialwissenschaften und der Rechtstheorie zur Wissenschafts- und Sozialtheorie. Daraus ergeben sich eine Reihe von Fragestellungen, die sich vor allem auf die jüngste Entwicklung der Systemtheorie als Theorie sozialer Systeme beziehen. Insbesondere sind hier die neuesten Versuche *N. Luhmanns* und seiner Anhänger, sowie die Argumente ihrer Kritiker

zu prüfen. Das Unterfangen, diese neuen Entwicklungen des Systembegriffs im Recht zu erklären, ist heutzutage ohne Zweifel ebenso schwierig wie erforderlich. Unter anderem ist es einmal sehr schwierig und auch kompliziert, weil gerade heute die Sozialwissenschaften, und das besonders in diesem unserem Bereich, mit anderen Begriffen und Denkkategorien, und parallelerweise mit einer anderen Sprache als die Rechtswissenschaft arbeiten. Trotzdem ist aber dieses Unternehmen unbedingt erforderlich. Denn der Systembegriff der allgemeinen Systemtheorie hat ein großes Echo bei manchen Vertretern der heutigen rechtstheoretischen Grundlagenforschung gefunden.

VI.

Das wären in etwa die Hauptgesichtspunkte, die ich in diesem Beitrag eingehend darstellen und ausführen möchte.

Da die mir zur Verfügung stehende Zeit und der gegenwärtige Stand meiner Forschung mir nichts anderes ermöglicht, möchte ich nur noch einige für mich sehr bedeutende Ziele als provisorische und zugleich zusammenfassende Ergebnisse meiner Studien zum Systembegriff im Recht hervorheben, und zwar folgende:

(1) Es besteht kein Zweifel daran, daß hinsichtlich des Rechts und der Rechtswissenschaft verschiedene Systembegriffe unterschieden werden müssen.

(2) Theoretisch haben alle diese Systembegriffe dieselbe Fähigkeit, das Recht, oder wenn man will, die Rechtswissenschaft, als „System“ zu begreifen; eine ganz andere Frage wäre aber, ob in praktischer Hinsicht alle diese Systembegriffe geeignet sind, den Forderungen und Besonderheiten des Rechts, wie man es auch verstehen mag — z. B. als Inbegriff von Normen, oder von Normen und Entscheidungen usw. — Rechnung zu tragen.

(3) Endlich bleibt noch zu erklären, welche von diesen Systembegriffen am besten die latente und heute mehr als früher im praktischen Leben auftauchende Auseinandersetzung zwischen *System* und *Problem* zu lösen vermögen.

Eine Erweiterung und Wiederverarbeitung dieser meiner hier schematisch vorgetragenen Gedanken sind in meiner demnächst erscheinenden Monographie „Der Systembegriff im Recht“ zu finden.

SCIENCE AND TECHNIQUE IN JURISPRUDENCE

By José de Sousa e Brito, Lisbon

I. The Modern Idea of Science and How It Relates to Art or Technique

There is a theory about the relationship between art and science which I will call modern. It has strong roots in Bacon[1] and Hobbes[2] and a later exponent of it is John Stuart Mill. According to Mill "the imperative mood is the characteristic of art as distinguished from science. Whatever speaks in rules or precepts, not assertions respecting matters of fact is art."[3] He goes on to consider the relation between rules of art and the theorems of the corresponding science. He makes a distinction, which he illustrates with examples taken from the law: "in all branches of practical business, there are cases in which individuals are bound to conform their practice to a pre-established rule, while there are others in which it is part of their task to find or construct the rule by which they are to govern their conduct. The first, for example, is the case of a judge under a definite written code. The judge is not called to determine what course would be intrinsically the most advisable in the particular case in hand, but only within what rule of law it falls ... in order that our illustration of the opposite case may be taken from the same class of subjects as the former, we will suppose, in contrast with the situation of the judge, the position of the legislator. As the judge has laws for his guidance, so the legislator has rules and maxims of policy; but it would be a manifest error to suppose that the legislator is bound by these maxims in the same manner as the judge is bound by the laws, and that all he has to do is to argue down from them to the particular case, as the judge does from the laws. The legislator is bound to take into consideration the reasons or grounds of the maxim; the judge has nothing to do with those of the law, except so far as consideration of them may throw light upon the intention of the law-maker, where his words have left it doubtful. To the judge the rule once ascertained is final, but the legislator or other practitioner, who goes by rules rather

---

[1] The Works, ed. Spedding, I, 1858, p. 157 (Aphorismus III).

[2] De corpore, Pars I, c. I, 6 (Opera, ed. Molesworth 1838, I, p. 6): "theorema ... propter artem"; Leviathan, Part I, ch. V (ed. Macpherson, 1968, p. 115).

[3] A System of Logic, reimp. 1967, p. 616; cf. pp. 619—620.

than by their reasons, like the old-fashioned German tacticians who were vanquished by Napoleon, or the physician who preferred that his patient should die by rule than recover contrary to it, is rightly judged to be a mere pedant, and the slave of his formulas."

Of course, this account of judges as slaves of their formulas, would be much objected to. Even if there is an apparently clear statement of law, the judge still has to establish the features of the case which are relevant to the rule. It may well be that the case does not fit the legislative provision, however clear. If it does fit, the judge must still justify his selection of the features of the case that are relevant to the rule; and for this the judge has to look for reasons. So the judge often has both to find or construct the rule of the case and to consider the reasons of whatever rules he applies.

There remains however an important and much less disputable point to Mill's distinction: the legislator is not bound to affirm or maintain pre-existing laws. Some qualification is needed here, as the legislator may be bound by the constitution, and the judge may be allowed by law to use some discretion. (Some would even reject the last mentioned possibility.) In any event, the judge is legally bound in a way in which at least the constitution maker is not. The difference lies not in the need to consider the reasons for the rules, which applies to both, but in the legal position: only the judge has a legal duty to apply the law, including the reasons that govern it. Does it follow that the judge is not called upon to determine the best course to follow in the case at hand, that he must be ready to let a citizen die, if that is the consequence of applying the rule? The answer depends on the scope of the judge's duties in adjudication: do they allow him to deviate from an apparent rule, for good and sufficient reasons? And what kind of reasons are admitted? I will return later to these questions.

We come next to the main point: "Now" — says Mill — "the reasons of a maxim of policy, or of any other rule of art, can be no other than the theorem of the corresponding science." This sentence is rather strange from an author who began by stressing the distinction between scientific assertions and artistic rules or precepts. Mill has to show how a theorem may be a reason for a maxim without violating Hume's law, that is without deriving an ought from an is. He must further show that there can't be another reason than a theorem for a rule, so that no rule is a reason for another rule. The way he takes to demonstrate the first thesis reveals, I think, that the second is false.

"The relation" — so Mill — "in which rules of art stand to doctrines of science may be thus characterised. The art proposes to itself an end to be attained, defines the end and hands it over to the science. The science receives it, considers it as a phenomenon or effect to be studied, and having investigated its causes and conditions, sends it back to art with a theorem of the combination of circumstances by which it could be produced. Art then examines these combinations of circumstances, and according as any of them are not in human power, pronounces the end attainable or not. The only one of the premises, therefore, which Art supplies is the original major premise, which asserts that the attainment of the given end is desirable. Science then lends to Art the proposition (obtained by a series of inductions or of deductions) that the performance of certain actions will attain the end. From these premises Art concludes that the performance of these actions is desirable, and finding it also practicable, converts the theorem into a rule or precept."[4]

Mill's explanation is perhaps better understood if we imagine the following example of an Aristotelian practical syllogism of the technical kind:[5]

1. I should increase the production of corn.
2. To impose new corn laws will increase the production of corn.
3. I can impose new corn laws.
4. I should impose new corn laws.
5. I impose them.

1 and 4 are premises "of the good", 3 is a premise "of the possible". 2 is a premise of transition and is or should be according to Mill a scientific assertion or theorem of Political Economy as a kind of sociological enquiry.[6]

Mill here describes two classes of premises: propositions of science asserting matters of fact, and propositions peculiar to art, "of which the predicate is expressed by the words *ought* or *should be*". Why then restrict the word "reason" to only one kind of premises, the "speculative" propositions of science? Actually Mill implies the contrary, and so corrects his former statement, when he says: "Every art is thus a joint result of laws of nature disclosed by science, and of general principles of what has been called Teleology of the Doctrine of Ends; which, borrowing the language of the German metaphysicians, may also be termed, not improperly, the principles of Practical Reason." There are correspondingly two sources of error: unscientific laws of nature and irrational principles of practice. To eradicate each kind of error is a different kind of progress: in the first instance, progress will avoid "that some modifying cause may prevent the attainment of the given end by

[4] Op. cit., pp. 616—617.

[5] Cf. *A. Kenny*, Aristotle's Theory of the Will, 1979, p. 136 ff.

[6] So *Mill* (note 3), p. 594.

the means which the rule prescribes"; in the second instance, progress will avoid "that success itself may conflict with some other end, which may possibly chance to be more desirable".[7]

II. Jurisprudence as a Science and as an Art in the "Modern" View

If we take Mill as representative of the modern view of the relation between art and science, let us see, then, how this view applies to jurisprudence.

To the basic distinction between assertions of matters of fact and rules, corresponds Bentham's division of jurisprudence in expository or enunciative and censorial. The first addresses itself to the understanding and describes the law that exists, the second addresses to the will and proposes the law that should exist.[8] Both can consider either the general words, principles and rules of the law or the particular rule that applies to the individual case at hand. Bentham's peculiar terminology uses in the first case the appellatives "genicoscopic" or "theoretical", in the second "idioscopic" or "practical". But it is clear that the words "theoretical" and "practical" do not refer to the distinction between assertions and rules, but the greater or lesser proximity to the action which concludes the practical syllogism. So the administrative act that gives to the individual corn producer a right to a minimal selling price may be described as existing by jurisprudence of the expository and practical kind or proposed by the kind of jurisprudence called by Bentham censorial and practical. The earlier premises such as the rules that government can make agricultural laws or that government has the duty to promote welfare (as possible constitutional rules) as well as the argument of economic science, that price guarantees promote production, are described by the theoretico-expository or instead proposed by the theoretico-censorial jurisprudence.

Mill would say, as we may safely conclude from the foregoing, that expository jurisprudence is a science and censorial jurisprudence is an art. We have therefore in the view which I have called "modern", a science *de lege lata* and an art *de lege ferenda.*[9]

---

[7] Op. cit., p. 618.

[8] A Fragment on Government (Collected Works, ed. J. H. Burns/H. L. A. Hart), pp. 397—398.

[9] *Bentham,* An Introduction to the Principles of Morals and Legislation (Collected Works, ed. J. H. Burns and H. L. A. Hart), p. 298, opposes also ancient and living jurisprudence as "branches of science" to the "art of legislation", which he equates with "censorial jurisprudence" (p. 294). But he seems to have modified this view later, since in the Chrestomatia (Collected Works, ed. M. J. Smith/W. H. Burston), pp. 59—61, he holds that

III. Objections to the "Modern" View

I accept the idea that jurisprudence has at least two tasks, in so far as it deals with positive law:

— to formulate the rule of each case;

— to ascertain the meaning of concepts, the principles and rules which allow the rule in each case to be found in a systematic way.

It has certainly other tasks as well, but I presume a large consensus on these two.[10]

It is however arguable to say that such formulations are assertions of matters of fact. Some positivists, like Bentham[11] and Ross[12] maintain this because they claim to reduce the statements of jurisprudence to propositions about facts: either about some past actions of the legislator or of the judge and other people (so Bentham), or about the probability of future events, the application of sanctions (so sometimes Bentham) or "the actions of the courts under certain conditions" (so Ross).

This is a misinterpretation of the sentences that ascertain a rule of positive law. What is implied by such sentences, in their usual context, is simply that the rule is part of the *system* of positive law, that is, it should be recognized in the legal practice of a given society, by the law-applying agents, as a rule of positive law. Doctrine integrates the legal practice of society as it contributes to the social consciousness of existing rules and intends to play such a role in the jurisprudential activity of finding the rules. Actually the jurisprudential sentences are intended to guide people, to tell them how they *should* behave. Certainly other kinds of statement may be found in a text of jurisprudence, but they are not specific to it. Jurisprudential sentences do not tell how to behave in an authoritative manner, that is, from a position of authority. They tell how to behave from a position of counselling. I suggest that they are a kind of speech act which, following Kenny,[13] may be called a fiat. They intend to bring about a state of affairs not

---

there is "no determinate line of distinction between *art* and *science*". "As between *art* and *science*, in the whole field of *thought* and *action* no one spot will be found belonging to either, to the exclusion of the other" (ibid.).

[10] See *Ph. Heck*, Grundriß des Schuldrechts, 1929, p. 471 ff., who says that the first task poses "problems of regulation" (Normierungsprobleme), the second "problems of formulation".

[11] Cf. e. g. Fragment on Government (note 8), pp. 429—430, and Chrestomatia (note 9), p. 202.

[12] On Law and Justice, 1958, p. 40.

[13] Cf. *A. Kenny*, Will, Freedom and Power, 1975, p. 39, following the proposal of *A. Hofstadter/J. C. C. McKinsey*, On the Logic of Imperatives, in: Philosophy of Science 6 (1939), p. 446 ff.

merely because the speaker uttered them, but because they are part of the law.

If this is true, jurisprudence, in the sense of doctrine of positive law or legal dogmatics, should be conceived of as an art. It is searching for rules, like the art of legislation. The difference lies here, as between the judge and the legislator, in that jurisprudence is bound by the system; the rules are there to be justified or legitimated according to the rules of recognition of the legal system, which describe the formal and material conditions for those actions which create, modify or revoke the law (the "sources"), whereas the art of legislation is not bound in this way.

To confirm this, we might also consider the way we talk of progress in so-called legal science. "Progress" consists in avoiding errors in evaluation, in clarifying principles and in resolving conflicts between principles, rather than in avoiding errors in formulation of scientific laws. Take, for example, the distinction between justification and excuse in Criminal Law, which corresponds to the German contrast between "Rechtswidrigkeit" and "Schuld" as elements of crime, confused before under the concept of fault, "la faute" of French law.

Compare killing in self-defense and killing under the effect of insanity or of very strong coercion or necessity (to save one's own life, for example). In both cases one necessary condition for punishment is lacking. Both conditions exclude the existence of homicide, in contrast with the circumstances of acting in the national territory or of having citizenship, on which punishment may also depend. However, they exclude homicide on very different grounds. The conduct of someone who acts in selfdefense is approved by law and so there is no self-defense against him. To kill another person violates a cherished value in every system of law, the sanctity of life. But if a person is or is about to be illegally attacked, the law evaluates the values defended higher than it normally does, since the sanctity of law itself as an important value is also defended. The killing being then permitted, there is no reason for punishment, which is a sanction for deviant behaviour.

But the conduct of someone insane or under duress is nonetheless disapproved by law and so there is self-defense against him. It is simply that the offender cannot be disapproved. His conduct was not that of a free agent; he could not have done otherwise. The law orders him to act otherwise, but does not expect *him* to obey. There is here no reason for punishment, because of the nature of punishment as a specific sanction. Punishment would not be a fair retribution, because it would put on the same footing those who act with culpability and those who do not. Punishment would produce despair and revolt, and perhaps contribute to crime instead of preventing it, as it would conflict strongly with social morality. This would be particularly the case for the individual offender, who could never be sure of escaping punishment by trying honestly to comply with the law, and would therefore be less motivated to do so. The reasons mentioned here do not entirely apply to a person under duress, because he or she is still to some extent free to resist, able to respond to legal norms, and to understand the role of punisment in the situation. Thus, the excuse may understandably be not admitted with regard to some individuals in particular positions, like soldiers or firemen, or to some crimes. However, in this case these reasons are still the very principles of punishment that explain why the law desists from censuring what could only with exceptional force of mind be avoided.

This is not the place for a more detailed discussion of the principles at stake in justification and in excuses, but the above should be enough to show that it is a clearly progressive step to recognize that we are dealing in each type of case with characteristically different problems.

According to the modern view, this is not scientific progress but progress "peculiar to art", in other words technical or teleological progress. Scientific progress in this field would be a more precise definition of mental illness, which could serve to identify cases of insanity. This would usually be said to be progress *for* Criminal Law, as a branch of jurisprudence, rather than progress *of* the Criminal Law. The latter terminology would, however, probably be reserved for the first kind of progress. This again suggests that we deal with an art in Mill's terms, although progress by perfecting a system of principles is also said by lawyers, in spite of Mill's viewpoints, to be "scientific" rather than "technical". This may be a kind of Aristotelian usage, since Aristotle admitted not only practical reasonings, as did Mill, but also practical sciences.[14]

What are the boundaries between jurisprudence and other arts, and how does it relate to what Mill calls the Art of Life, Teleology or Doctrine of Ends, the art of practice in general? Mill seems to say that all other arts are subordinates of this last-mentioned, "since its principles are those which must determine whether the special aim of any particular art is worthy and desirable, and what is its place in the scale of desirable things."[15] Aristotle makes however a point here which is not of minor terminological interest, but crucial indeed for an understanding of the matter. He makes a sharp distinction between *techne* and

[14] Met. 1025 b 19.

[15] Op. cit., p. 620.

phronesis. Techne is the capacity to produce according to reason, using technical (or productive or "poetical") reasoning, which includes the rules that govern a practice that has an end, a particular good outside itself which is posited without demonstration or evidence at the beginning. *Phronesis* is the virtue of acting according to reason, which uses ethical or "practical" reasoning, including the rules that govern the whole practice of life, which has an end in itself, the general good of life, posited at the beginning and demonstrable.[16] Does jurisprudence belong to the realm of *techne*? Is it an art, or is it a field of practical wisdom? In the first case, the judge who convicts the accused person knowing why he or she should be acquitted, is a good lawyer, although he is committing a crime, just as the doctor who lets someone die while knowing how to save him is according to Aristotle a better doctor than the one who does the same thing without this knowledge, although the former is ethically worse.

Let us go back to the discussion on the aims of punishment. It is certainly important for the criminal lawyer, as far as he pursues jurisprudence, understood as doctrine of positive law or legal dogmatics, to discuss the reasons for punishing since they allow him to understand the system of criminal law and to find the relevant rules or to assess their meaning. I myself referred earlier to them in discussing the rationale of excuses. But what about the legitimacy of the institution as a whole, advocating for example, as the Italian criminalist Ferri did, the overall substitution of purely preventive measures of social defence for punishment? If jurisprudence is a part of practical wisdom or Teleology, then such arguments are in order. But if such arguments may be dismissed in the jurisprudence of a particular country by saying, for instance, that the constitution explicitly provides both for punishments and for measures of social security, so that the first can not be substituted by the latter, then jurisprudence is rather a technical discipline. I think that this is so, and that correct jurisprudential arguments are limited to those compatible with the system of positive law in a given society.

But we are still at the beginning. What are the relations between the rules that govern the practice of law — rules analyzed by jurisprudence — and rules of social morality, of normative politics, of ethics, and so on? Is law a merely technical restriction on social practices or is it a particular practice which both interferes with and (partially) absorbs social morality and ethics, and their rules? These are harder questions, which I leave for another occasion.

[16] Cf. Eth. Nic., 1094 a 5, 1140 a 2—5, b 21—22.

SYSTEME POLITIQUE / SYSTEME JURIDIQUE

Par Jean-Louis Vullierme, Paris

I.

Puisque le temps nous est compté, je commencerai par l'affirmation brutale d'une thèse qui, je le crains, est susceptible de heurter un sentiment très partagé. A la question: «La théorie des systèmes a-t-elle fourni jusqu'à présent une compréhension originale et satisfaisante de la politique et du droit, ainsi que de leur interface?», la réponse, au-delà de quelques indispensables nuances, sera «non». Je voudrai montrer que, sous couvert d'un nouveau paradigme, elle s'est contentée d'habiller la théorie classique de l'Etat d'un vêtement contemporain; que, sans rien modifier d'essentiel sur le fond, elle a traduit cette théorie en langage cybernétique; ce qui eut par conséquence, non de substituer une approche holistique à l'analyse, conformément à l'intention initiale, mais au contraire de renforcer sur certains points décisifs l'aspect analytique de la théorie, en alourdissant par ailleurs inutilement sa manipulation conceptuelle.

Ce que j'entends ici par «Théorie classique de l'Etat» ne renvoie pas à un auteur particulier, mais à une détermination du politique, qui commence de se constituer dès la fin du Moyen-Age et trouve son apogée dans la pensée moderne. D'après cette conception, le politique se confond avec la production dans le système social d'une unité intégrée, disposant du monopole des pouvoirs publics et de la force légitime. Son but est l'organisation des rapports sociaux, face aux périls naturels et extérieurs, et contre la tendance spontanée du système social à l'anarchie. Son moyen est une réglementation volontaire et impérative de l'ensemble du comportement des agents composant la société. L'Etat est le nom généralement donné à cette institution monopolistique intégrée. Par métonymie, le même nom finit par désigner aussi tout le système social qui lui est soumis. L'Etat est donc toute société humaine dotée d'un Etat, c'est-à-dire d'un complexe institutionnel appelé (1) à défendre son identité ou volonté contre celle des autres Etats, (2) à retirer aux individus et aux groupes la liberté de régler par eux-mêmes les conflits qui ne peuvent manquer de les opposer entre eux (du fait des tendances sociales à l'anarchie), et de réparer de leur propre chef les torts dont ils sont les victimes à l'occasion de ces conflits. La soustraction par l'Etat de la puissance vindicatoire individuelle ou associative marque ainsi le passage de l'état de nature à la société civile (ou état de droit). Elle vise à mettre fin à l'état de guerre intestine qui est censé corrompre toute société livrée à sa spontanéité propre. Pour ce faire, elle égalise face à l'Etat tous les individus, en dissolvant notamment les corps multiples ou «Etats» qui s'arrogeaient encore, dans les sociétés à caractère féodal, une certaine autonomie vis-à-vis de l'autorité centrale.

Or l'Etat ne se contente pas d'encadrer par les règles qu'il édicte les comportements sociaux, et d'y fixer des bornes. Il ne se contente pas davantage de trancher souverainement les litiges, même proprement individuels (ou «oikonomiques», c'est-à-dire concernant la prospérité matérielle des différents foyers). Mais il considère en outre les actes qui les ont occasionnés comme autant de violations de son autorité. C'est pourquoi il se subroge aux justiciables dans l'action contre les coupables, prenant à leur sujet les mesures qui lui conviennent; sauf dans les cas spéciaux qui relèvent strictement du domaine étroit qu'il octroye aux particuliers, auxquels cas ceux-ci sont associés à l'Etat dans le règlement du litige.

Le droit, dès lors, n'est plus l'ensemble des rapports justes dans lesquels les citoyens sont placés, comme il l'était naguère, mais l'instrument dont l'Etat dispose pour organiser la société et pour s'organiser lui-même. Il contient une procédure de modification autoritaire de toutes les situations dans lesquelles ses instructions ne sont pas exécutées, que l'acte violateur soit directement dirigé contre lui, ou qu'il ne le concerne qu'à l'occasion d'une lésion infligée à un particulier. Le droit est ainsi divisé fonctionnellement en deux parties principales, elles-mêmes subdivisées d'après les zones d'activité sociale auxquelles elles s'appliquent: (1) la loi formulaire positive, instaurée au nom de la société et à sa place par les instances représentatives de l'Etat, ainsi que les dispositions subalternes prises par ses instances exécutives; (2) le système judiciaire, partiellement doté des pouvoirs de police, pour garantir le respect de la loi positive.

II.

Cette doctrine bien connue, thématisée par Machiavel, Bodin, Hobbes, adaptée par Locke aux spécificités du libéralisme parlementaire, est précisément celle qui fut aussi adoptée naïvement, c'est-à-dire comme si elle était «neutre» ou la seule possible, par la théorie du système, lorsque, parvenue à l'âge cybernétique, celle-ci a étendu son intérêt aux phénomènes sociaux. L'analogie structurelle de l'approche cybernétique et de la théorie classique de l'Etat prédisposait, il est vrai, à une telle alliance.

Quoi, en effet, de plus foncièrement cybernétique que le politique conçu comme un système de commandement? Le mot même de «cybernétique» signifie, on le sait, «gouvernement». Le verbe «kubernao» désigne simultanément l'activité du pilote placé aux commandes du navire, et celle du prince placé à la barre étatique pour assurer le bien commun. D'après cette détermination, une machine cybernétique n'est rien d'autre que le mécanisme de contrôle d'un système complexe en interaction avec son environnement, pareillement à l'Etat qui réglemente l'activité de ses ressortissants dans leur rapport avec le monde.

En sorte que, malgré son extrême complexité microscopique, le système politique peut être décrit au niveau macroscopique comme une machine aux fonctions relativement simples. Un problème surgit toutefois dès qu'il s'agit de décider entre un modèle véritablement global, capable d'envisager la société politique en son entier, et un modèle polarisé sur l'Etat. Le premier modèle traite le système comme une unité sociale en interaction avec un environnement (la nature et les sociétés extérieures) par l'intermédiaire d'une commande centrale, l'Etat, qui collecte les informations périphériques, recense les ressources, coordonne les exigences; y réagit par des dispositions législatives à caractère organisationnel, et des mesures allocatives à caractère administratif. La difficulté est alors d'expliquer la formation de l'Etat. Force est donc d'introduire une fiction, la Volonté divine exprimée par un législateur ancestral ou la Volonté générale exprimée par un contrat primitif. Dans les deux cas, le système politique est renvoyé à une extériorité fondatrice qui joue un rôle comparable à celui de Papin ou de Watt à l'égard de la machine à vapeur. D'où un second modèle qui, pour éluder la question, referme la perspective globale, fait de l'Etat une donnée à laquelle se réduit le système politique tout entier, et rejette la société civile ... dans l'environnement! A cet environnement est accordé le nom particulièrement étrange mais très révélateur d' «environnement interne». Paradoxalement, cette expulsion de la société civile hors du politique, et la subordination consécutive du système social au système politique, permettent de décrire les interactions du social et du politique.

L'Etat n'est plus seulement une «boîte noire» à la structure insignifiante, qui reçoit les demandes du reste de la société, et les traite dans les limites imposées par les contraintes extérieures (naturelles et diplomatiques), conformément aux plans tracés par un architecte fictif.

Il devient une machine qui évolue au gré de la conjoncture formée par l'état des ressources, la nature des demandes intérieures, et la situation extérieure. Cette machine, engendrée d'abord par une concentration de force au sein de la société, puis séparée du reste de la société par une inertie propre, doit en effet posséder une «variété» suffisante, autrement dit une souplesse lui permettant de s'adapter notamment aux transformations des exigences intérieures qui lui parviennent. Faute de quoi l'Etat serait bientôt dissout, puis remplacé par une nouvelle concentration de force au sein de la société. La variété requise est obtenue par le jeu d'une série d'instances hiérarchiques dont la plus élevée est le législateur «permanent» (qu'il ne faut pas confondre avec le législateur primitif du premier modèle). Le législateur «permanent» est censé représenter les diverses demandes sociales, qu'il exprime en édictant une suite de règles positives dont certaines sont susceptibles de modifier l'organisation de l'Etat lui-même (d'où la variété), et dont les autres cherchent à établir un équilibre évolutif entre les diverses forces de la société. Le gouvernement met en oeuvre ces instructions pour ce qui le concerne, généralement en ayant d'abord coordonné l'activité législative; puis contrôle, par l'intermédiaire de l'appareil judiciaire, leur respect par les agents périphériques.

III.

Cette conception cybernétique du politique correspond, on le voit, à la vision moderne du droit comme instrument de la volonté étatique. Le droit est la forme que prennent les décisions politiques, qui sont les sorties (outputs) du système cybernétique dont les entrées (inputs) sont les demandes sociales. Or la théorie en question, qui relève entièrement du rationalisme volontariste moderne, est grevée de plusieurs défauts rédhibitoires. En confondant le politique avec l'Etat, elle exclut de l'ordre politique, non seulement une écrasante majorité de systèmes sociaux décrits par l'anthropologie, dans lesquels nulle instance centrale ne peut édicter des dispositions pour organiser le groupe, ou même formuler les règles qui y ont cours; mais, par desus tout, elle exclut du politique le système historique où le politique a été pensé pour la première fois, à savoir la Cité d'Athènes à l'âge classique. A la suite des historiens du 19ème siècle (notamment en France, Fustel de Coulanges), nous appelons Athènes une «Cité-Etat», alors même que ce qui est pour nous l'Etat était considéré par les penseurs grecs, soit comme une organisation archaïque, littéralement proto-politique, tout juste bonne pour les barbares et les Perses, soit comme une perversion particulièrement dangereuse de la politique: la tyrannie démagogique. Il n'y avait à Athènes nulle organisation monopolistique et intégrée, capable d'administrer à elle seule la Cité, de la défendre contre l'étranger, et d'inventer les lois, mais une série de pouvoirs publics distincts, sans connection directe l'un avec l'autre, et surtout sans autorité sur le comportement global des citoyens. Aristote considérait la cité comme un organisme naturel, une *physis,* composé de foyers séparés qui oeuvraient entre eux, au milieu d'eux, un espace public (symboliquement: une *agora*), où était discuté collectivement ce qui les concernait en commun, et où étaient tranchés les quelques litiges que les particuliers n'avaient pu résoudre par eux-mêmes, conformément à la loi, c'est-à-dire à l'ordre juste qui régnait *dans les choses* avant l'action coupable. Nul n'était autorisé à creer la loi, *nomos,* mais tout au plus pouvait-on en commun prendre des décrets *(psephismata)* destinés à la consolider ou à la rendre plus précise. Le droit était alors centré sur l'activité judiciaire, et non sur l'activité législative. La Cité fournissait à tous ceux qui s'estimaient lésés et impuissants à se défendre eux-mêmes, le tiers impartial, ou juge, qui rétablirait le droit en réparant la faute, et non en appliquant la volonté d'une quelconque autorité centrale. Ce n'était que dans les *périodes de crise,* lorsque l'ordre politique se corrompait, qu'un individu ou un groupe prétendait imposer son vouloir à la société, et substituait ses décrets à la loi, fort qu'il était, le cas échéant, d'un soutien majoritaire. Le juge exécutait les ordres publics qu'il recevait alors, devait trancher, non pas d'après la justice, mais d'après les vues législatives de qui dominait la Cité et formait un Etat.

La doctrine moderne, adoptant une conception réductrice en politique, et étatiste du droit, a perdu jusqu'au souvenir d'un semblable état des choses. Elle est devenue incapable de comprendre la place relative de l'Etat dans l'histoire politique, et moins encore de considérer le droit hors du fonctionalisme instrumental dans lequel il se trouve désormais enfermé.

La question est de savoir si la théorie des systèmes pour sa part est condamnée à soutenir cette théorie classique du politique; ou s'il lui est possible de s'en libérer, en passant à un point de vue plus large, qui ne ferait plus de l'étatisme moderne une norme conceptuelle absolue, mais simplement un cas particulier. Pour le savoir, il faut préalablement répondre à cette autre question: le lien historique entre le cybernétique et la théorie des systèmes est-il indéfectible?

S'il est vrai que la cybernétique est largement issue de la théorie des systèmes, c'est à tort, me semble-t-il, qu'elle passe pour son accomplissement. Bien qu'en un sens la cybernétique ait effectivement donné à la systémique la forme scientifique, ou plutôt le contenu technologique, qui lui faisait d'abord défaut, ce fut au prix d'un appauvrissement considérable qui l'empêcha, de réaliser jusqu'au bout la révolution holistique à laquelle L. von Bertalanffy avait imprimé une première impulsion.

Les systèmes cybernétiques ne sont pas moins que les objets de la science analytique traditionnelle des ensembles d'éléments. Leur particularité, et leur intérêt, est que ces ensembles ne sont pas traités comme des agrégats dont les propriétés seraient équivalentes à la somme des propriétés de leurs éléments, mais comme des unités en interaction globale avec un environnement, par l'intermédiaire d'un appareil de régulation. Il manque pourtant à ces systèmes, une dimension essentielle, manifestement caractéristique des systèmes naturels, que la science traditionnelle avait été incapable de reconnaître, et que la théorie des systèmes devrait avoir précisément pour tâche de décrire: l'*autonomie*. Il leur manque la faculté de croître et de se doter eux-mêmes de nouveaux organes, sans être préfabriqués par une source extérieure et hétérogène. Il leur manque, pour ce faire, la capacité de s'identifier eux-mêmes, de se différencier progressivement par eux-mêmes du reste du monde, et partant de se produire eux-mêmes, sans avoir à recourir aux services d'un démiurge, qu'il soit dieu créateur, législateur transcendant, ingénieur, ou artisan. Si les systèmes cybernétiques sont des «automates», c'est non pas parce qu'ils seraient autonomes, mais au contraire parce qu'ils se meuvent conformément à un programme inséré dans leurs plans. Bien qu'ils puisent dans l'environnement les ressources énergétiques et matérielles qu'ils consomment, bien qu'ils soient pourvus de mécanismes de stabilisation par rétroaction, ils n'en sont pas moins conditionnés par une source extrinsèque qui les «informe» au sens fort, c'est-à-dire qui leur fournit leur forme. Même lorsque cette source paraît intégrée au système, elle renvoit alors à une autre source extérieure de niveau supérieur, les systèmes cybernétiques étant foncièrement incapables d'être à eux-mêmes leur propre ingénieur (aumoins ace stade de la theorie).

Ce talon d'Achille de la cybernétique est précisément la cause de son isomorphie avec la conception mécanique du politique; que l'ingénieur politique soit Dieu, la Raison universelle, la Volonté générale, la Souveraineté nationale, toujours une extériorité vient fabriquer la commande étatique qui organise et contrôle la société. Un bref regard sur les doctrines contractualistes suffit à l'attester. Elles n'introduisent la fiction contractuelle que pour établir la domination de l'Etat, sans lequel le «libre jeu» social ne serait à leurs yeux qu'une épouvantable anarchie. Elles divisent la société en deux parties, la partie constituante et la partie gouvernée, la première n'exerçant jamais réellement son activité qu'en renonçant au profit de l'Etat à toute autorité.

Le temps manquant pour développer avec tout le soin nécessaire une théorie alternative du système politique, je me limiterai à quelques remarques très générales. La première est que la théorie des systèmes ne s'est pas arrêtée à la phase cybernétique. De nouveaux modèles ont été développés, qui décrivent des organisations autonomes (théorie de l'auto-poïèse), dépourvues de commande centrale (théorie des automates acentrés), et capables de modifier leur forme d'ensemble par le jeu de leur interaction avec le reste du monde (théorie de l'ordre à partir du désordre, ou de l'ordre à partir du bruit).

Il est dont (re-)devenu possible de forger des modèles non-classiques du politique, proches par exemple de la conception aristotélicienne. Le politique n'y est plus distingué de la société, il est la société elle-même en tant que chacun de ses agents se reconnaît membre d'une organisation qui délibère des intérêts communs et prend les dispositions jugées les plus favorables à la préservation de ces intérêts. La loi n'est pas constituée par les décrets émanant d'une autorité centrale, elle est l'organisation même de la société. Le droit n'est pas la loi, mais le système des situations reconnues comme justes (c'est-à-dire conformes à l'organisation de la société), et telles que chaque agent de la société peut exiger réparation devant un tiers impartial, incarnation de la loi, de tous les torts qu'il a subi de la part d'un autre agent.

Dès lors, le système juridique est bien centré sur l'activité judiciaire au lieu d'être centré sur l'activité législative. Il est un système d'autorégulation des situations mutuelles entre agents sociaux. Et il n'évolue que par le jeu de l'interprétation donnée par la société de sa propre organisation, non par des transformations extrinsèques de cette organisation. L'existence d'un Etat n'est plus dans ces conditions qu'un cas particulier, simplement possible au lieu d'être nécessaire. Un système politique *étatique* est un système dans lequel le système juridique est soumis à une autorité centrale, détachée du reste de la société. Un système politique *en général* est une organisation sociale entièrement déterminée par la composition des modèles que s'en fait chacun des agents qui la composent; et qui est capable de se différencier des autres systèmes, de poser son identité, en produisant ses propres règles. L'activité législative n'a jamais pour cette raison la puissance nécessaire pour vérifier toute l'organisation. Elle n'est qu'un processus subalterne d'auto-détermination de l'organisation formée par les relations qu'entretiennent des agents dont chacun (comme dans un système holographique) produit un modèle du système tout entier, et conforme ses actes à ce modèle.

La science moderne, cartésienne, avait pensé les phénomènes internes d'hétéronomie. La politique moderne s'était, de façon parallèle, présentée comme une technologie d'horloger. C'est la tâche spécifique de la science contemporaine que restaurer l'autonomie dans toute son importance; et ce sera notre responsabilité que de rendre à la théorie politique sa capacité originelle de penser l'auto-organisation, au lieu de se soumettre sans autre réflexion à l'idéologie étatiste des trois derniers siècles.

IV. Ökonomische Analyse des Rechts

VALUE CHOICES IN THE DEFINITION OF POVERTY

By June Axinn, Philadelphia

An analysis of the concept of equality and consequently of the just allocation of resources in any society requires as a social policy correlative a definition of what is to be taken as a minimally acceptable human standard of living. In the United States today, the Reagan administration's programmatic use of the phrase "truly needy" has made the question of the definition of poverty a particularly urgent one. One can hardly discuss the existence or extent of any of our social welfare programs without some clarity about the nature of the groups in society that are to be considered deprived. The first policy analysis step would appear to be an exploration of the meaning of poverty. What is poverty? More specifically, for programmatic purposes, who is to be counted as poor?

The paper analyzes the value assumptions of alternative ways of defining poverty.[1] The philosophical concern with definitions and the legal concern with fairness meet in a special way in the analysis of poverty. The laws that provide for assistance to the poor obviously presuppose some definition of those who are to be classed as poor. Different definitions of poverty can be viewed as allied to different legal philosophies. We shall analyze one definition that a natural law position finds comfortable, another definition of the poor that is suitable for legal positivism, and a third position that evolves easily from legal realism. This study will analyze the official poverty standard, along with the major suggested modifications, in use by the United States government[2] for the last twenty years — i. e. since the era of the "War on Poverty."

---

[1] This paper is based on my commentary which will appear as: Explorations of the Definition of Poverty (Comment), in: K. Kipnis/D. Meyers (eds.), Economic Justice: Private Rights and Public Interests, Rowman and Allanheld, Totowa, N. J. 1986.

[2] Weighted average poverty threshold, developed at the Social Security Administration in 1964, revised by Federal Interagency Committees in 1969 and 1980, published annually. Most recent citation, U.S. Bureau of the Census, Current Population Reports, Series P-60, No. 147, Characteristics of the Population Below the Poverty Level: 1983, GPO, U.S. 1985.

In traditional fashion we may distinguish relative and absolute poverty. Relative poverty is usually defined as the inability to reach an "acceptable," "average" standard of living, whereas for absolute poverty, the words used are "minimal" and "bare survival." To expand: In economic terms what we are discussing when we talk of relative poverty is economic distance. An individual or group is considered relatively poor if their standard of living does not keep pace with the average. Absolute poverty on the other hand refers to a fixed unchanging minimal market basket of goods. By relative poverty standards, if my neighbor acquired a new car and nothing else changed, I would be poorer; by an absolute definition, I would not. Thus, over time, if living standards rose for the population as a whole a relative poverty line would go up; an absolute line would remain constant.

The Federal government's poverty measure was developed in 1964 by the Social Security Administration. The government defined poverty first of all in terms of cash income (before taxes) for a family over the period of a year. The methodology involved basically pricing the cost of the Economy food plan of the Department of Agriculture (based on both Recommended Dietary Allowances and low income food consumption patterns of 1955). It was then assumed, based on a Household Consumption Survey of the general population, also 1955, that food expenditures were 1/3 of the total family budget. The minimum required income — the poverty line — was calculated at 3 times the Economy food plan, with some adjustments for family size, and a few other variables. This measure, priced in 1964 was adjusted backwards to 1959 for changes in the consumer price index and has been similarly adjusted forward with only minor changes.

It is of historical interest perhaps that this index was devised in part in response to a tremendous increase in relative poverty. World War II and the period right after that, the early 1950s, were times of a great deal of economic growth. The war itself was a period of major income redistribution. By the late 1950s however it was clear that the assumption that resource redistribution would continue, or even that everyone would benefit from economic growth, was not true. Poverty, the "invisible poor" who were not "keeping up," was "rediscovered" and measures were being designed to "bring the poor into mainstream." Relative poverty was the concern, but a market basket index was to be used for measurement. One result of using a fixed measure of poverty was that the poverty gap widened dramatically during the period. In 1959, the first year for which we have an official U.S. standard, a family of four was considered poor if it had less than $ 2,973 a year; median family income that same year was $ 5,417. Thus the poverty line was

55 % of median income. By last year, median family income had risen to $ 24,580 and the poverty line for a family of four was $ 10,178 or only 41 % of median family income. Economic distance between the poor and the average family has widened steadily.

The market basket of the poor's goods has remained the same over the years with only the dollar value changing, despite the increased standard of living of everyone else. But in at least one sense this can *not* be said to be an absolute standard. Consider how the market basket was selected in the first place. An absolute standard would be based on minimal nutrition and a maximum percentage of total income spent on food. But this index was based on the national average percentage of family food expenditure to total family income (after taxes) — the standard for the whole society, not the standard of the lowest income group. Thus, the general standard, the most accessible, not the minimum, became the base and indeed it is difficult to imagine a society constructing a minimum standard of living that would be completely context-free. It has been argued that the very notion of absolute poverty is a vaguely comparative one.[3] In this case it is more than that: it is in part truly relative.[4]

There are a host of other policy choice questions underlying statistical decisions in the construction of the official poverty cutoff figures. Originally a matrix of 124 separate poverty threshold figures was calculated. The size of the family unit (up to 7); the sex of the family head; the age of the family head (under or over 65); and the question of farm or non/farm residence were the selected categories for special indexes. Since 1964, the size of the family unit for which extra income is considered necessary has increased (to 9), the needs distinction between male and female headed families has been eliminated, as has the differential between farm and non/farm families.

These changes were made for political, social, and economic reasons. As an example: Initially, in 1964, the poverty line for those residing on farms was set at 70 % of that of families not on farms. The assumption was that farmers could (should?) grow their own food and had therefore less need for cash income. A readjustment of the indexes narrowed the difference to 85 % in 1969 and it was eliminated completely in 1981. The current poverty threshold assumes that the need for cash income

[3] For example the argument developed in *T. Airaksinen*, Hegel on Poverty and Violence, unpublished paper delivered at Ninth Plenary Conference, Amintaphil, Gainesville, Florida, January 14—16, 1983.

[4] There are many ideological inconsistencies in the design of the poverty index. It had one great political virtue. It gave a result which was the "appropriate" economic distance from the median income at that time and which fit the preconceived notion of the Council of Economic Advisors.

is the same city and country. The reasons were heavily political and involved the urgent wish of some officials to increase the eligibility for welfare programs of some farm state constituents. One might however argue the matter on ideological grounds ... i. e. those who live in cities have a personal desire for that type of life ... theirs is a choice which includes a choice of income possibilities and limitations. One might argue in a similar vein against special considerations for family size.

Interestingly, emphasis on the role of personal choice and personal needs did play a part in the early discussions of social insurance when it was decided that residency was a matter of personal taste and that therefore, despite dramatically different living costs in the different states, the United States would have one geographic standard of payment for old age benefits. It has not however generally played an explicit part in the debates in the poverty literature of the last 25 years. These issues are more apt to arise now that the role of non-cash income in the definition of poverty thresholds is being seriously considered.

The current Census Bureau definition is based only on cash income. And yet in the years since the introduction of the poverty measure the dollar value of the major non-cash or "in kind" transfer programs available to the poor — for food, housing and medical care — has grown rapidly and currently far exceeds public assistance in cost to the government.[5] The Bureau is now discussing the impact on our poverty count of including in the definition of income of the poor the value of some of these noncash benefits given to individuals, specifically, the value of food stamps, school lunches, housing subsidies, Medicaid, and Medicare. Clearly, which of these benefits is counted and how they are counted matters in both the poverty total and structure. Census estimates of poverty in 1979, for example, drop by amounts varying from 12.3 % to 42.3 % depending on which noncash benefits are included and how they are valued.

Three ways of valuing noncash benefits have been suggested.

1. Market Value — The private sector purchasing power of benefits is assumed to be the value of the in-kind transfer received by the individual. In the case of food stamps, for example, the dollar value of food coupons would be taken to be the value to the recipient of the food stamps. In the case of the free distribution of cheese, the market value would be determined by the market price of cheese. This technique puts the highest price tag on noncash transfers. The measure is objective,

[5] U.S. Bureau of the Census, Current Population Reports, Series P-60, No., 1361, Characteristics of Households Receiving Selected Noncash Benefits: 1981, GPO, U.S. 1982.

easily measurable. The difficulty is however that market price is determined by all consumers. This total group evaluation would in effect be counted as the individual value. Thus, the values of the lowest economic class would be taken as identical with those of the entire consumer class.

This definition, featuring an objective, easily measurable basis, seems to be attractive to the legal positivist position on the nature of law. It requires no personal qualitative judgements, no theory of what is natural or rational, apart from the clear and enforceable criteria of market price.

2. Recipient or Cash Equivalent Value — This valuation is defined as the amount of money that would make the recipient just as well off as the noncash transfer. In the case of the free distribution of cheese the cash equivalent value is the amount of cash the recipient would take instead of the cheese. Implied ordinarily is the notion that in-kind transfers need to be discounted because they are not as valuable to their recipients as cash income would be, (although one might hypothesize the reverse). When this "Hicksian variation" is calculated, a hybrid process is used which involves components of average budgets and poverty budgets. While it allows for more differences in expenditure preferences between low income groups and the population at large than does straight market evaluation, it is still a large group technique and assigns class values and choices to individuals. In any case it yields a lower value on noncash benefits than a straight market valuation.

This definition, making the poverty group's preferred behavior the measure, must be most attractive to those who take legal realism to be the proper view of law. It puts the largest weight on the actual budget choices made by people in poverty (and by a formula also using average situations). The legal realist and those holding that sociological jurisprudence is correct must find this position quite obvious.

3. Poverty Budget Share-Value — This valuation technique would limit the value assigned to a benefit to the proportional share it would normally assume in a poverty budget. In the case of the free distribution of cheese the poverty budget share value would be a function of the amount of money the recipient usually spends on cheese (or a cheese like commodity). The argument is that in setting the cash poverty line at a fixed multiple of the Economy food plan, a minimum level of other necessary commodities such as housing and medical care was implied. Therefore, this view holds, no value should be assigned to any one of these components which usurps the role of the other elements. Food, clothing, housing and medical care are not considered substitutes for each other. The views and values of a panel of experts are assumed. This

approach would put the lowest dollar value of the three on in-kind benefits and would thus have the smallest impact on the actual poverty count.

According to this definition, there is a natural balance of items in a rational budget, and the proportion of an item in such a rational budget is the basis for the value of that item. It takes a panel of experts to determine just what that rational balance is. Those who find the natural law theories most agreeable will also find this definition the most reasonable of the three.

Calculating these values for 1983,[6] poverty on a cash income basis (traditional Census definition) gave a poverty rate for the U.S. of 15.3 %; When food stamps, school lunches, housing subsidies, Medicare and Medicaid were added in, the rate dropped to 12.9 % at a poverty Budget Share Value; to 13.0 % at a Cash Equivalent Value; and to 10.2 % at Market Value. For the aged, who use Medicare and Medicaid very extensively, the impact is even more dramatic and their poverty rates for 1983 shift from 14.1 % to as low as 3.3 % depending on definitional variations. Note that under any valuation of in-kind benefits other than the third — poverty share value — one could define the poor out of existence just by insuring that they got sick enough!

But there is a still more basic question. If free school lunches are part of the income of the poor, is free tuition for their children part of the income of the professoriate? If Medicaid and Medicare, why not employer paid health and dental insurance benefits, paid vacations; if housing rent subsidies, why not tax deductions for mortgage payments? To the extent that poverty lines are relative — to the extent they measure economic distance — then shouldn't noncash income be measured for all involved?

Most of the current discussion of poverty lines deals with issues of income distribution and income measurement. But other analyses have raised the question of whether or not wealth as well as income should be counted in some fashion in the evaluation of poverty. If so, the number and structure of the poor might shift. The percentage of aged who are counted poor might be different from the number under current income definitions, because their accumulation of assets is quite different from that of other income-poor groups. And the loss of income can have dramatically different meaning under different poverty conditions.

---

[6] U.S. Bureau of the Census, Technical Paper, No. 50, Alternative Methods for Valuing Selected In-Kind Transfer Benefits and Measuring Their Effect on Poverty, GPO, U.S. 1982.

It can mean different things for different time spans as well. There are some female heads of families who are transitionally poor, students who are poor but who may have an expectation of income in the near future, and some for whom poverty may be a life-time phenomenon. For many reasons, an annual measure of poverty may be inadequate and we may require some measures of permanent income to incorporate the view that any standard of living is determined by accumulation over time of economic resources. This is particularly true if we make efforts to include less easily quantifiable factors.

In sum: Moving from a poverty index which is a cash measure to one which includes non-cash benefits, adjusting the measure to include wealth as well as income, and shifting the index from an annual to a life cycle scope is attractive. Conceptually, it increases the potential for measuring "well being." It offers the opportunity to include important factors in material satisfaction. Such diverse things as home ownership, the expectation of an eventual career, an individual's choice of solitary living, might all be discounted in the formula. With the current emphasis on locating the "truly needy" the political appeal of such a measure is apparent. For there is a temptation certainly to see all modifications in the definition as ways of solving the poverty problem. Instead of redistributing resources, distribution will be redefined. The difficulty is that all poverty indexes are relative in part and in the end the distribution problem will not disappear semantically.

While this paper has emphasized the role of definitions in formulating an institutional response to poverty, it has also indicated something of the underlying pattern of legal theories. Political pressures are certainly significant. However, the issues between legal positivism, legal realism, and natural law theories are also involved in the complete basis for choosing and rationalizing definitions of poverty.

LEGAL REASONING
AND ECONOMIC REASONING: INTERACTIONS

By Wahé H. Balekjian, Glasgow

Ideas, theories and ideologies of social welfare, social and economic justice, when considered at the level of policy formation and application, relate not only to the teleological question of maintaining, modifying and evolving the socio-economic fabric of society, but significantly touch the highly complex sphere where economic and legal reasoning meet. This is due to their relevant conceptual components and underlying assumptions which point to a *fundamental question* as to (i) *interaction* between legal and economic reasoning and (ii) the *quality* of such interaction in terms of desirability, necessity, inevitability.

In a historical, descriptive or analytic sense, "interaction" may stand for a mutually exerted influence and even possible conditioning in the past; it may also be used, as in the present paper, for a dimension of "ought" as to desirability and benefits which could accrue toward better economic law, if, for example, normative traits in *economic* and respectively legal reasoning could be relevantly identified, the extent to which economics and law can relate could be defined, and above all the basic question of how the normative quality and effectiveness of economic law could be tackled in the interest of economic objectives and policies. Interaction between legal and economic reasoning is a pragmatic and inevitable reality and necessity related to the implementation of socio-economic policies and objectives, and a better understanding of it could promote a more critical, i. e., reality oriented (German: wirklichkeitsnah) and hence more constructive approach (i) to the vital role of law in the service of economic aspirations, goals and policies, on the one hand, and (ii) to the essential function of (feasibility orientated) economic and/ or socio-economic (welfare) reasoning in generating (good) economic law and economic justice on the other.

It may dialectically be arguable that interaction between legal and economic reasoning cannot be a quantifiable and/or qualifiable matter deserving attention for practical legislative purposes; it may possibly be a purely theoretical matter dealing with details of conceptual constructions. Such an argument may be countered by referring to and considering developments in the last decades: significant expectations have been and continue to be attached to socio-economic objectives and socio-economic law in Western oriented as well as socialist systems. An almost explosion-like expansion of *economic law*[1] has taken place. This and the therewith created vast and continuously growing corpus of international and municipal legislative texts convincingly illustrate and establish how the normative dimension of legal rules has been called upon as an extensively used tool for achieving social and/or economic policy goals; law has been expected and continues to be expected to contribute to the consistency, stability and feasibility of the existing or evolving or emerging normative economic systems and to the respective consolidation of what can be best conceptualised with the German term "Wirtschaftsverfassung" (economic normative/normative economic system). The same developments also show, amply, how scathing existing gaps are; for example, the initially aspired and promised socio-economic goals and expectations, attached to economic law too as an instrument, do not find their corroboration in the lagging and limping socio-economic realities and shortcomings in both Western oriented welfare as well as socialist systems.

Such a fundamentally general situation, while variable from system to system as to discrepancy between expectations and achieved results, directs the enquiring mind to scrutinise the functional efficiency or deficiency of (economic) law in its contribution to socio-economic developments.[2] One may advocate that while the quality of law cannot have been but good, too many (unrealistic) expectations have been attached to the normative function of law in economic life, that the capability of law has been overtaxed in regulating economic behaviour and processes in otherwise reasonably normative situations related, for example, to income distribution, taxation, competition; or one may prefer to advocate that belief in a functional parity between legal rules and socio-economic goals and policies is a deficient proposition: it is a fundamentally wrong proposition to expect economic processes and law to match beyond an ascertainable level.[3]

---

[1] While aware of the semantics and conceptual differentiation between "economic law" and "the law of the economy", the author of the present paper will use the term "economic law".

[2] On the concept of *good law* in the light of technical criteria, see *H. J. M. Boukema*, Good Law, published as volume 2 in the series Salzburger Schriften zur Rechts-, Staats- und Sozialphilosophie, 1982; for examples of the concept applied to economic law, see particularly, pp. 82 ff.

[3] This point involves philosophical implications relating to the analysis of liberal, free market, mixed economy, planned economy theories as respective systems of economic law.

Whatever approach is adopted or applied, it is necessary to grapple with the reality that law is called upon to fulfill, however satisfactorily or unsatisfactorily, an important function in the economic life of modern society. It is hence purposeful to ask what pertinence economic reasoning and the logic of economic feasibility (and its limits) offer to legal theory and legislative drafting in the framework of economic goal and policy parameters, not least in the context of such basic concepts as "economic justice" and "economic distributive justice".

A survey of the related economic as well as legal literature does not facilitate the search for an adequate answer to the above raised question. Therewith the need for comprehensive inter-disciplinary research, discussion and comparison is indicated. Economic texts, with notable exceptions, lack even implicit references to the (anticipated) function of legal rules in the pursuit of economic objectives and policies while such objectives and policies seem to reflect the existence of definable normative assumptions. Maybe such normative elements are taken for granted as part of the behaviouristic nature which the abstract model of homo economicus may possess. On the side of legal literature, texts dealing with the concept of economic justice and its intricacies, or with the application of law to economic processes and economic behaviour, equally contain but notably few references to economic assumptions borrowed from the realm of economic reasoning and transferred as given to the sphere of law. For example, the objectives and contents of applied economic law cannot be realistically conceptualised without reference to the concept of economic feasibility. This concept is in many respects determined by economic behaviouristic, that is, non-legal (metajuridical) factors and is as such of essential importance when assessing the potential credibility of an economic normative (legal) rule, and is to be considered in association with lawyers' concepts of certainty and predictability in the context of economic law.

It may be argued that all what has been said above may be relevant and desirable with respect to ideal economic law, but it cannot be a practical proposition because the common basis of *normative reasoning* applicable to coordinated legal and economic thinking is weak and even frail; as economists tend to argue, particularly in times of economic crises or recession, too many factors influence economic processes and economic behaviour and thus make them very difficult to predict with reliability. This view may be countered with the argument that nonetheless economics is not a purely historical and as such retrospective or contemplative exercise, and that the concepts of economic goals and policies are not pure figments of the human intellect or of politicians. They presuppose and claim to have minimum standards of expectations and predictability and as such suggest some link with the concept of normativity in the sphere of law.

Obviously, it cannot be claimed that all aspects of economic reasoning involve normative elements. Econometrics, as an example, may be defined as a non-normative, descriptive, analytic area of enquiry. However, even as such it may be as relevant as legal statistics for gauging the effectiveness of operative or projected law. In other words, economic law and its functional, operative efficiency point to the integration of elements of both economic and legal reasoning in a coherent system of economic legal reasoning.[4]

An economic lawyer has to deal with two levels of economic reasoning (in analogy to Max Weber's two types of understanding, *Verstehen*): "Understanding" in the sense of grasping economic processes and facts with a dominantly descriptive or analytic economic dimension. At this level, the question of interaction with legal reasoning may not be practically relevant. At the level of "explanatory understanding" (erklärendes Verstehen),[5] however, for the purpose of economic law related to economic goals and policies, a consideration has to be faced in the sense that the "understanding" of economic processes and projections involves notions of expectations in terms of minimum predictability, and as such it may be qualified as "expectative" economic reasoning. Such reasoning cannot be devoid of normative elements, thus blending economics and law into a system of economic law. This law is, beyond behaviouristic, mechanistic and other factors on which economists rely for certain operative aspects of an economic system, essential for translating policies and goals from the stage of mental models into the world of socio-economic realities. This normative contribution of law is additionally necessary inter alia as a framework of reference for monitoring progress and assessing results and their normative impact on social and economic realities.

A *teleological* interaction and interdependence between legal and economic reasoning can be perceived with respect to "economic (distributive) justice". At the level of this comprehensive, ambitious and hence as yet but vaguely defined concept relating to a continuous process toward an ultimate objective (of justice), both economic and legal reasoning try to reconcile and balance two imperatives which affect

---

[4] For an example of such an approach, see *Lars Werin*, Ekonomi och rättssystem (2nd edn.), Stockholm 1982; see also the series Research in Law and Economics, Richard O. Zerbe, Jr. (ed.), with four volumes published since 1979 (JAI Press).

[5] *Max Weber*, Economy and Society (transl. by G. Roth and C. Wittich), New York 1968, p. 8.

society: (i) economic renewal or development for society as a whole, and (ii) constant or rising benefits thereof for individuals as members of that society. The two are not identical, as economic renewal or development has to do in the first place with the creation or generation of wealth, which thus far has been a strong dimension of capitalist economics and law, while the notion of economic benefits for individuals has in the first place to do with the distribution of wealth. In the context of social and economic justice, such distribution has been a dominant endeavour of welfare and socialist systems, obviously to the extent the economic dimension and capability of the given system has been able to serve as a foundation for effective distributive law and effective distributive justice. The imperatives of *renewal* of wealth and *distribution* of wealth are not identical but they overlap functionally: the quality and feasibility of applied distributive justice as well as the generation of wealth underlying the workability of such justice depend on the relevant qualitative aspects of economics as well as law.

John M. Keynes has implicitly but aptly referred to the inevitable interaction between economic and legal reasoning by looking at them as constitutive parts of a political reasoning underlying "the political problem of mankind". He has defined the latter as the need "to combine three things: economic efficiency, social justice and individual liberty". It cannot be denied that "social justice and individual liberty" involve eminently normative components of economic and legal thinking in Western oriented as well as socialist societies. The term "economic efficiency" too is not a purely economic or socio-economic proposition detached from any normative dimensions. Its transformation into reality is not a matter of isolated economic knowledge or skill; it is also a matter which is dependent on normative regulation with limits of feasibility inter alia through law for encouraging, promoting and also rewarding those who contribute to it. The promotion of economic efficiency with the assistance of normative tools serves a further purpose. It protects material as well as non-material essential economic values in society beyond the immediate pragmatic purpose of generating new wealth or maintaining the level of already existing wealth as a foundation for a reality oriented economic law and economic justice. In such a context reference may be made to what could be qualified as a "negative interaction" between economists and lawyers.[6] Both on the side of economic thinkers as well as lawyers there has been but insufficient marginal attention paid to the question whether "distributive economic justice" should not be matched or even conditioned with what one might call

[6] "The modern development of law has been guided largely by false economics." *F. A. Hayek*, Law, Legislation and Liberty, vols. 1—3, reprinted 1982, vol. 1, p. 67.

"generative distributive justice" implicitly hinted inter alia by John M. Keynes. Only such a comprehensive and integrative approach can lead to an optimal coordination and interaction between economics and law.

The state has in our times become a very powerful tool for influencing economic processes and for distributing income. A thorough analytic and comparative study between *economic* theories of the state and *legal* theories of state may yield highly revealing results with a possibly sobering impact on the manner in which economics and law have hitherto been related or neglected as to a margin of potential and useful interaction. Such a study may also prove to be highly valuable for the progressive definition and concretisation of the comprehensive concept of "distributive economic justice".[7] What socio-cultural, socio-economic, economic pragmatic (feasibility) criteria should be adopted at the level of sociological and economic considerations when dealing with the contribution which economics may make? To what extent should law normatively contribute when regulating economic behaviour and the concretisation of economic distributive justice? What immediate remedies should be considered for reducing the margin of increasing economic crime and ancillary economic criminal law? What lessons are to be learned from the growth of underground or black economies? There are as yet no constructive answers to these and many other related questions. Should we conclude that such questions are not relevant to applied economic and legal thought?

A further area where economists and lawyers do not seem to perceive the necessity of dialogue and interaction concerns the concept of the New International Economic Order (NIEO). A growing volume of publications deals with the economic dimensions and implications of the NIEO in terms of economic development planning, processes and policy options. These are terms which are also relevant for the purpose of normative reasoning, because such normative reasoning is either implied or taken for granted in the context of economic dimensions without clarifying, however, the function which development law as part of a new international economic law is expected to fulfill. A corresponding deficiency can be detected on the side of legal literature dealing with international economic and/or development law. As a result, it is dif-

[7] On distributive justice see *M. J. Sandel*, Liberalism and the Limits of Justice, 1982, pp. 66—103; on the morality and rationality of economic man, *David Gauthier*, in: B. Barry/R. Hardin (eds.), Rational Man and Irrational Society?, 1982, p. 105; on a discussion of a Marxian approach to distributive justice, see *Allen E. Buchanan*, Marx and Justice: The Radical Critique of Radicalism, 1982, pp. 57 ff. Within the limited scope of the present paper, no reference can be made to another challenging area related to economics, morals and ethics, on the one hand, and law, morals and ethics on the other.

ficult to consider the parameters of economic feasibility within which law is expected to function and make a concrete contribution as a vital component of the New Order (NIEO), that is, as a model beyond the confines of currently existing fragmentary international economic law dealing with contracts, foreign investment, concession agreements, dispute settlement etc. It should not be forgotten that the concept of the NIEO too implies and introduces the notion of economic distributive justice to the sphere of international economic relations, thus adding an axiological dimension to applied international economic law.

In conclusion, the following may be said with respect to the basic questions referred to in the present paper:

(i) Interaction between legal and economic reasoning is an inevitable necessity at the point where economics and law meet and touch the concept of justice. While justice may be defined as a concept related to fairness, in the context of economic justice it may be conditioned by existentialist dimensions of economic feasibility or non-feasibility. As a result, it is difficult to define economic justice in terms of a legal quantifiable constant; such a constant presupposes the existence of a quantifiable economic constant. A formal definition of economic justice may be possible with reference to deontological concepts;

(ii) At the level of economic policies and goals, as well as their implementation and achievement, economic reasoning involves normative dimensions. These dimensions may be fruitfully supplemented with the contribution which legal reasoning can make with law as an instrument serving economic policies and goals. This may in turn have a propitious effect on the quality of law, its effectiveness, predictability and certainty.

ECONOMY WITHOUT LAW: PASHUKANIS REVISITED

By Eugene E. Dais, Calgary

E. B. Pashukanis, in his *General Theory of Law and Marxism* (1924),[1] set out to explain what happens to law after the proletariat class takes the state away from the capitalist class. While he had both practical and theoretical reasons for doing that, this paper considers only the conceptual aspects of his interesting attempt to formulate a general theory of law.

A general theory that identifies law with the state poses no difficulty for Marxism. Law is then simply the coercive instrument the capitalist class uses to suppress and exploit the proletariat class. As such, law can be equally used by the proletariat to bring about the classless society, and thus do away with both the state and law. In a classless society which faces no external enemies, there is no need for the state, and since law is identified with the state it too disappears. However, in the transitional phase of communism, before the classless society in a secure world is attained, the state temporarily survives and it uses law to serve the cause of socialist advancement to fully developed communism.

Pashukanis's historical analysis, however, revealed that law in its true form developed and existed apart from the state. It has an autonomous life of its own, reaching its highest and final form in the protection of abstract rights in a bourgeois society. By its very nature, therefore, true law cannot serve the socialist cause of bringing about the classless society. For in its final form, law necessarily exploits the proletariat who by definition have no property to protect other than their labor. True law can serve only bourgeois interests. Consequently, when the proletariat state uses law to avoid anarchy, it uses an instrument that is a contradiction to its interests.

---

[1] *P. Beirne/Sharlet* (ed.), Pashukanis: Selected Writings on Marxism and Law, London 1980, pp. 37—131. The third edition in 1927 served as the basis for the first translation into English: *J. N. Hazard* (ed.), Soviet Legal Philosophy, Boston 1951, pp. 111—225. In the second edition (1926), Pashukanis emphasized that "the elements which chiefly provide the material for the development of the legal form can and should be segregated from the system of relationships which are responsive to the dominant class ..." *Beirne/Sharlet*, p. 38. Pashukanis's later revisions to his general theory of law are not considered. See *Beirne/Sharlet*, pp. 24—31.

Thus, a general theory of law presents a special problem for Marxism. Is socialist legality possible? Pashukanis insisted that the problem be squarely faced and that its theoretically sound solution not be compromised by expedient measures for avoiding anarchy. But in concluding that socialist legality is impossible, since true law is bourgeois law, Pashukanis had to face the conceptual problem. He had to clarify how law can become nonlaw in order to further the classless society. He had to define law clearly to show what it is exactly that must cease to exist. His general theory of law was not to defend or improve law as such. It was instead to do away with law altogether. That inversion of purpose is one reason why his thesis that all law is bourgeois law naturally appears bizarre to jusnaturalists and legal positivists alike. But it is precisely his asking the question, exactly what it is about law that if changed will cause law to cease to exist, that gives his Marxist analysis conceptual worth for legal theory generally.

Another reason for interest in his thesis is its paradoxical nature. The disappearance of true law, while it leaves the classless society without law, also leaves it well ordered. Not only will the classless society not be lawless or anarchical; but it will also have a more stable, enduring economic order. An economy without law will still be lawful. We can fully explain that paradox only after we critically review Pashukanis's commodity exchange thesis. For the moment it is important to recognize that the paradox arises only by defining law as narrowly as possible while rejecting as theoretically trivial its more inclusive definition which is the negation of the unexpected in social relations.

The narrow approach is the usual one in legal theory. Legal positivism reduces the essential element in law variously to authoritative commands, a system of rules, coercive enforcement, or the prediction of judicial decisions. Natural law narrows the definition even further to norms that nature or morality does not invalidate or rule out as nonlaw or improper law. In brief, legal theorists generally, not just Pashukanis, reject the inclusive definition of law as the negation of the socially unexpected. That definition covers too wide an area, not only all social relations but natural events as well, and thus cannot serve to differentiate law from other natural phenomena and social activities. A general theory of law in the wide sense risks becoming a theory of everything.

But in Pashukanis's case, because his theory is that law itself has to be negated, a wider definition is needed to make sense of the paradox of a well-ordered economy without law. While the inclusive view conceptually rules out only definitions of law that tolerate the unexpected in social relations, it does not preclude special definitions for distinguishing how different forms of social regulation differently define and negate the unexpected. In the inclusive sense, an economy and society are lawful or well ordered if they have a form of social regulation that assures that each person can reliably trust others to respect the expectations on which each should know that the other reasonably relies.[2] Such a condition is most clearly found in a network of intimates sharing a way of life over generations that mutually satisfies their basic human needs for survival and well being. We may call that the communal form of the social relation. Pashukanis viewed such a relation as the old society out of whose elements the new society would be constructed. That construction would take place when people think and understand that social relations be only "a means for their private purposes".[3]

In the communal form of the social relation, production and distribution are only for use value. Such processes satisfy concrete needs of intimates who by nature do not each count abstractly for one. Each counts as a concrete being with unique capacities and needs. A child, for example, with greater needs than an adult, would work less and receive more, while the adult, on whom the child is intimately dependent, would thus be socially related to the child in a way that obligates him morally to give up more than he receives, but only in the short run. In the long run, as Malinowski suggests,[4] such concrete equivalency in need satisfaction tends toward an equivalency of givings among a network of intimates over time, and not simply in an immediate sense between a giver and receiver. For example, a brother may for life take care of his sisters' families on the expectation that his wife's brother will likewise care for the needs of her and their children. Thus, what is typically

---

[2] For an elaboration of the idea of law negating the unexpected, see *Lon L. Fuller,* The Morality of Law, New Haven 1969, rev. ed., p. 9. I would, however, modify the following sentence: "Their (tort and contract principles) acceptance today represents the fruit of a centuries-old struggle to reduce the role of the irrational in human affairs", by substituting "unexpected" for "irrational", and stressing that "the struggle to reduce" is ideally a negation even though in practice the negation will always fall short of the ideal. In brief, law generally is the belief that the unexpected will not occur and if it does its harmful effects will be negated. Such belief appears essential in the sense that its absence disturbs complex, enduring social relations in primitive as well as modern societies. Negating the unexpected, it should be stressed, does not mean that expectations are always known in advance. In fact law is most relevant when reasonable expectations clash and there must be negation of the uncertainty for future reliance. Moreover, expectations once secured by law can over time socially change in which cases we have the well-known gap between law-in-books and law-in-action.

[3] *Beirne/Sharlet* (note 1), p. 89. For an example of such a society, see *Colin M. Turnbull,* The Forest People, New York 1962, but compare his, The Mountain People, New York 1972.

[4] *B. Malinowski,* Crime and Custom in Savage Society, London 1926, p. 41. For the concept of the stranger see p. 113.

called customary law (whether or not in fact it is really law) negates the unexpected as an essential element in the well-ordered society and economy, and it does so by the social or communal relation of concrete equivalency over time.

In conventional legal theory, customary law is not really law unless it can be made to fit the legal positivist conception of authoritative commands laying down general rules of conduct that are enforced by threats of harm which organized officials alone have the force to make good. But such a positivist conception, if it faithfully attended to the requirements for concrete equivalency in the communal relation among intimates, could not be abstract law. The authoritative commands could not be general but would have to be specific to each individual as to the contribution he is obligated to make to the common wealth in accordance with his capacities to produce, and equally specific in assessing his real needs to determine his rightful share of the common wealth. In brief, concrete equivalency requires obligation as the precondition of rights in the communal sense. Such rights and obligations must be concretely specific, and their social function is to assure equivalence in measuring the unique capacities to produce and needs to be satisfied of individuals whose actual capacities and needs over time may differ widely under varying circumstances.

In contrast, as Pashukanis claimed, the true form of law, as reflected in the ideology of the bourgeois society, is the social relation manifesting the idea of abstract equivalency.[5] The concrete capacities and needs unique to each individual are irrelevant. The individual relates to other individuals as strangers only. The relation is random and *ad hoc*, not an ongoing involvement. One has rights not to a share in the common wealth but only against other persons who like him are legal subjects or personalities as defined by law as having status to claim and enforce rights before impartial judges. To the extent one makes good his claim of rights, other persons have duties, or more properly are liable to return converted property, to pay damages for harm done to him or his property, or to perform promises. Property by nature is a necessity of abstract law since to have and claim rights as in claiming compensation or exchanging commodities each must know what things he may absolutely exclude everyone else from possessing or using irrespective of their concrete needs.

[5] *Beirne/Sharlet* (note 1), p. 192, fn. 44. "The intensification of the transcendence of the legal form would be reduced to the gradual transition from the (abstractly) equivalent method of distribution — definite quantities of products for definite quantities of labor — to the realization of the (concrete) formula of developed communism: "from each according to his abilities, to each according to his needs". (parentheses added)

Abstract rights by nature cannot be specific to certain individuals; they must be general and reversible among all persons equally. They are rights suitable among strangers who by definition cannot know the unique needs and capacities of each other and thus cannot have the mutual obligations that flow from a network of intimates living together over time. The negation of the unexpected among strangers is the assurance they have that each has the same rights as all others depending on their abstract status in law. The fact that a debtor concretely needs the money more than a creditor can make no legal difference. If a debtor owes the money as a legal duty, he must pay it. At the same time a debtor knows that if he had loaned the money, he would have the same right of repayment however harshly it may deny the other party the means he needs to live decently or at all. The rights of all legal subjects thus are abstractly equivalent and reversible while at the same time they are likely inequivalent in relation to their concrete needs.

Consequently, it is essential that strangers, if the socially unexpected is to be negated, maintain among themselves the social relation suitable in an alien condition in which each "person" treats every other "person" as abstractly equivalent. For this reason rights must determine duties, and the social function of both is to assure equivalence in measuring abstractly the claims to the protection of life, liberty and property of individuals whose possessions of such things are naturally unequal. Abstract rights by their very nature must ignore the inequality of possessions for satisfying concrete needs.

Thus, abstract law by its inherent nature exploits the proletariat, but that exploitation is not easily seen. In comparison with class law, the exploitation is indirect. When the dominant class excludes other classes by name from the protection of special laws conferring benefits on the powerful and burdens on the powerless, there can be no doubt but that the state is using its coercive sanctions to exploit the ruled for the advantage of the rulers. There is in that case no assurance for either concrete or abstract equivalency. Thus, class law cannot be true law. As Pashukanis would claim, class law inherently lacks abstract equivalency. The more basic reason is that class law, since it depends on arbitrary will, cannot negate the unexpected even for the dominant class. Although the unexpected in class law likely favors the rulers, randomness still disrupts the mutual reliance they require to dominate the exploited in a way that can be called law in the wider sense. Class law can unexpectedly benefit the powerless if the powerful choose that result, and changes in the ruling class always risk radical change in the substantive rights protected by law.

Less easily seen is the indirect exploitive effect of abstract law. Such effect depends on the results of equally protecting the same abstract rights for all subjects. Proletarians are equally subjects before the law the same as capitalists, and thus are entitled to the same rights and duties. But their entitlement and equivalency are purely abstract. Wage workers own little but their labor, and this they can often sell only for low wages. What they produce, however, is sold for profits which are protected by the law of abstract equivalency as the property of capitalists. What concretely belongs to wage workers is thus taken from them by an abstractly equivalent regime of rights and duties. They are exploited but their exploitation is lawful in the sense that it is not unexpected. Thus, while class law exploits lawlessly, abstract law exploits lawfully.

It thus follows, as Pashukanis argued, that converting the private ownership of the means of production into public ownership does not, by removing the exploitation of abstract law, transform it into socialist law. Abstract law in the absence of private property can continue under public ownership to give state officials and enterprises, as a bureaucratic class, the abstract rights to control the use of all property. State enterprises would claim ownership of property for contractual exchanges with other state enterprises. Moreover, workers would contract for employment and be paid abstractly according to the contribution they make, which may be less than the capacities of each and unrelated to each's uniquely concrete needs.[6] While these "quasi-private economic relationships"[7] remain during the transitional period, they must disappear as a precondition of the fully-developed communist economy. Bourgeois or abstract law, which is historically the only true law, must thus be negated by the proletariat state as an essential stage in the development of true communism. In brief, socialist legality contradicts itself.

Pashukanis's analysis consequently brings him squarely to face the key conceptual problem of an economy without law. When abstract law has disappeared, what form of social regulation can conceivably negate the unexpected in ensuring that production is according to each's unique capacities to work and that distribution of the common wealth is according to the concrete needs of everyone?

Pashukanis's response to this question is constrained by Marxist theory generally and specifically by the commodity exchange theory of value. True law dialectically had to be the other side of the coin.[8] It is thus not

[6] Ibid., p. 89.
[7] Ibid., p. 88.
[8] Ibid., p. 79.

surprising that he fails to clarify the difficulty of the problem to which his historical analysis leads. That difficulty had to be obscured for the analysis to remain consistent with dialectical materialism. Since bourgeois or abstract law is the final form of law, since as an ideology such law must radically change with radical change in the economy, and since the proletarian revolution is such radical change, then there must be the dialectical leap manifested by an economy without law. Such an economy is "a return to the elementary living relationship",[9] and that communal relation requires the socially unexpected to be negated by concretely measuring the equivalence of capacities to produce and needs to be satisfied.

We can now see that Pashukanis's paradox of a lawful economy without law is explainable first by distinguishing between the special definition of abstract law and the inclusive definition of negating the unexpected in social relations, and then by recognizing that abstract law is not the only way to negate the socially unexpected. But we further see that the paradox obscures the main point of inquiry: How can the "elementary living relationship" be recaptured in a modern economy and society that is obviously not elementary? Specifically, what form of social regulation implicit in such a relation can conceivably negate the unexpected in a complex, industrial economy that rejects abstract for concrete equivalency?

An economy that defines social relations by concrete equivalency may try to negate the unexpected by a central plan for production and distribution. But that is as if a primitive tribe planned its hunting by experts formulating a plan that officials carry out by coercively disciplining the conduct of hunters, and then authoritatively determining the concrete needs of the hunters and their families for distributing the food. Rules must be used for such purposes, but such rules cannot be true law. They are technical rules, and subordination to them is for the purposes of exacting contributions according to each individual's capacities and making distributions according to each individual's concrete needs. Consequently, it is movement away from true law to change the subordination of state enterprises from the dominance of the circulation of commodities and its form of exchange to the dominance of technical rules which are simple, rational and specific instructions constantly changing depending on changing circumstances. Such technical rules and the official discretion they require do in fact make impossible the legal art of negating the unexpected by abstract rights.[10]

---

[9] Ibid., pp. 87—88.

[10] Ibid., p. 88. Thus, for example, the constant tension in such countries as Canada and the United States between statutes affecting private property

As Pashukanis admits, however, such technical rules may appear as the public law of the state creating rights and duties dependent on the legislative fiat of the ruling class which alone can invoke coercive sanctions.[11] If that is the case in the transitional socialist period, then true communism is frustrated. For the simple, technical and rational instructions means that the state has adopted "the form of a power alienated from man and standing above him". The new society cannot emerge, to quote Marx, until "... the real individual man ... shall become a universal being in his empirical life, in his individual work, in his individual relations ..."[12] Only then can the "elementary living relationship" be recaptured and the economy escape the corruption of true law.

Thus, Pashukanis's response to the main point of inquiry is at best ambiguous. The form of social regulation that is to negate the unexpected in economic relations must not be abstractly but concretely equivalent. Technical rules, as exemplified in scheduling railroad service, are to replace the residue of abstract law governing state enterprises in employing labor and allocating resources. That assumes, of course, that expertise is as possible in planning an economy as a whole as it is for scheduling railroad service. But even then more is needed before economic life can fully flow from commodity categories into natural categories. That something more must be the concrete equivalency practiced by the "universal being" who apparently is a stranger to none and an intimate to all. Only then would the "universal being" be a part of a network of dependencies that naturally obligate production by unique capacities for satisfying unique needs despite the abstract inequivalency that is immediately involved.

If a "universal being" is not an abstraction of the communal being, in what social relation does he find himself? Unless he is in a communal relation, how can there be the concrete realization of the formula of developed communism: "from each according to his abilities, to each according to his needs."?[13] Can a central plan and technical regulations measure such needs without the knowledge available only to mutually dependent intimates? If such intimate knowledge is lacking, do not then the central plan and its technical regulations "adopt the form of a power

---

in the public interest, such as urban planning, and common law rights. Lawyers as lawyers would have little to do were such rights negated. They then would function as lobbyists.

[11] Thus, for example, in Canada the statutory rights, for example, of policemen and school superintendents to government jobs which courts will protect by reinstatement where at common law only notice or damages are available for wrongful dismissals.

[12] *Beirne/Sharlet* (note 1), p. 89.

[13] See note 5, supra.

alienated from man" by treating him as a stranger "and standing above him" as an alien force to which he must abstractly conform? What form of social regulation can possibly transform man into the "universal being" who recognizes no strangers but only intimates among the billions that populate the earth? In the event that man cannot become such a "universal being", is a well-ordered economy at all possible without a permanent residue of true law as abstract rights or pseudo-law as state domination? Such questions, I suggest, are the kind that require convincing answers before the issue of an economy without law can be more than the verbal dispute of refusing the name "law" to state domination. But even then, if the industrial economy of the modern society can be coordinated by the concrete equivalency of customary norms, a case can still be made for calling such sophisticated coordination "law". In intimate relations for living together, customary norms best negate the unexpected, and such negation is "law" in the wide sense. But it is not clear whether Pashukanis by his concept of nonlaw meant also to deny the name of law to customary norms.

Thus, despite his unclear response or perhaps because of it, Pashukanis poses the key conceptual question for a general theory of law. Assuming that the inclusive definition of negating the unexpected must be applied by special definitions competing for the title of law, the relevant question for each special definition is its limit. At what point does law as specially defined cease to exist conceptually? For John Austin, it would be the absence of a sovereign or the habitual disobedience of his commands.[14] For H. L. A. Hart, it would be the absence of a unified rule of recognition.[15] For Hans Kelsen, it would be the failure to presuppose a basic norm.[16] For Lon Fuller, it would be the absence of an enterprise for subjecting human conduct to the governance of rules or a gross departure from his eight canons of the inner morality of law.[17] But for Pashukanis, it would be the abolition of true law itself, and that is done by abolishing its abstract nature.

On the perennial problem of labeling, there is much to be said for Pashukanis's view that among the three forms of social regulation, governing human conduct by abstract equivalency, because it alone can negate the unexpected among strangers, is more deserving of the title of "law". Native peoples living in the communal relation typically view true law as a law for strangers, while we who live among strangers are

[14] *John Austin,* The Province of Jurisprudence Determined, H. L. A. Hart (ed.), New York 1954.

[15] *H. L. A. Hart,* The Concept of Law, Oxford 1961, p. 209.

[16] *Hans Kelsen,* The General Theory of Law and the State, Cambridge, Mass. 1946, and The Pure Theory of Law, Berkeley 1967.

[17] *Fuller* (note 2), p. 46, pp. 33—94. Also see *Lon L. Fuller,* The Principles of Social Order, K. I. Winston, ed., Durham, 1981.

more likely to call the "law" of concrete equivalency such things as equity, social justice or even welfare or human rights. Similarly, since the "law" of state domination, reducible to the interests of some ruling class, democratic or undemocratic, can only negate the unexpected to the extent there is social consensus in agreeing on the "public interest", such "law" is more accurately referred to as enacted rules reflecting the rational policy of calculated benefits and costs which can only impose at best, on the basis of some form of utilitarian or consensus theory, the social relation of constructed equivalency. It is abstract law alone that peculiarly stresses in social relations the autonomy and independent force of rules and rights for negating the unexpected with the greater logical force and predictability that lawyers and judges as a profession can bring about among strangers. Social relations based on concrete or constructed equivalency call for talents that judges and lawyers typically lack.

In addition to clarifying the problem of labeling, Pashukanis's analysis also has conceptual worth in revealing the social dimension of legal theory. His definition of true law as abstract equivalency distinguishes that form of negating the socially unexpected from customary norms and state domination, and makes it evident that abstract law not only exists independently of the society, the state and the economy but has its own history in shaping social relations for satisfying concrete needs. Abstract law is one form of response to the alien condition where man is not intimate to every other man, but is a stranger to many. He may in the Hobbesian conception be in atomistic collision with every man as nothing but a stranger to every other man. But, more realistically, the alien condition simply posits that in a complex society of any substantial size, man's emotional, linguistic and informational capacities cannot measure concrete equivalency beyond a certain limited number. For the state to assume the measuring task by technical regulation is to risk making its domination totalitarian. Man would then be governed by abstract equality that would have little relevancy to his concrete needs except as defined by officials in terms of another abstraction such as the "public interest".

In contrast, abstract law can respect man as an intimate among some and a stranger to many. It can afford the opportunity over time among new generations for enlarging and overlapping the plural circles of intimates. To be sure, the abstract person with abstract rights contributes to the erosion of communal bonds, especially among native peoples, and that erosion helps give rise to the major social problem of modernity, surplus peoples with nowhere to go.[18] Perhaps it is they who are to

[18] On the phenomenon of surplus people, see *Richard L. Rubenstein,* The Age of Triage, Boston 1983.

become "universal beings" in the limited sense of an openness to adapting their customary norms to the realities of the modern, plural society. For them and all others, abstract law can serve the useful purpose of helping to bring about, not by a dialectical leap, but by an incrementalism over generations, wider circles for measuring concrete equivalency among strangers who can be friendly to each other precisely because they can trust each other to claim no more rights than the rights to which each is abstractly entitled. The abstractness of the rule of law alone cannot achieve the wider circles, and, as Pashukanis argued, the same abstractness exploits classes who have no property for abstract rights to protect. But the longer history of the rule of law also shows that its abstractness is precisely what has enabled it to serve as a peaceful and productive, and even a relatively humane, alternative to the natural responses of intimate man to strangers in the alien condition: war, genocide and slavery.

Pashukanis would likely disagree that his analysis implies such a need for abstract law. But that only adds force to the view that, despite his Marxist presuppositions, his ideas independently have conceptual worth for the task of developing as a general theory of law, "the basic, i. e., the most abstract juridic concepts"[19] that have meaning for man.

---

[19] *Beirne/Sharlet* (note 1), p. 40.

METHODOLOGY OF RESEARCH INTO ECONOMIC LAW RELATIONS

By Vladimir Laptev, Moscow

In socialist society economic activity is based on public ownership of the means of production. In accordance with the 10th article of the USSR Constitution, two forms of socialist property constitute the foundations for the economic system of the country: state property and property held by collective farms and cooperatives. The property of trade unions and other public organisations is treated as socialist, but it is used for satisfying the needs of the members of corresponding organisations and not for economic activity.

The economic activity of the USSR is fixed by the state plan for economic and social development. In the process of exercising economic activity planned economic property relations are devised. The participants in these relations are working collectives-enterprises, units of enterprises, organs of economic management, but not private persons. These organs can be state, cooperative or public, depending on the form of property they are based on.

Economic relations are organised by the state through management, planning and control. Legal regulation of economic relations plays an important role in directing the economy. The economic law relations concerning economic management (vertical relations) are formed on this basis, as are also the relations emerging in the course of the economic activity (horizontal relations). Opinions differ as to the nature of these relations in the Soviet literature. Some scientists believe that horizontal relations belong to civil law, and vertical relations to administrative law. Others state that horizontal and vertical economic law relations constitute one united branch of law — economic law. The second point of view seems to be the more valid, and the ensuing problems of the methodology of research into economic law relations are considered on this basis.

First of all it is important to underline the fact that horizontal and vertical economic law relations form one united sphere of a socialist economy, which is an independent and important object of legal research. This idea is based on article 16 of the USSR Constitution, which states that the economy of the USSR is a united national economy complex comprising all branches of public production, distribution and exchange.

It is also important that the centralised management of economy is combined with the independence and initiative of enterprises. The economy is planned not only by directive orders but also with the help of economic contracts. Thus it is necessary to analyse horizontal and vertical relations in their combination. We need one single approach in studying economy-managing and economy-contracting relations.

At the same time it is essential to take into account the fact that in the sphere of economy there can be formed not only economic law relations, but also relations governed by labour, nature-protection and administrative and civil law. All these relations are involved with economic law relations, a fact that must be taken into consideration when studying various legal problems in the economic sphere. It is therefore necessary to undertake complex research into social economic relations. Such research is being carried out by composing the complex programs with the participation of scholars from different special fields.

At the same time the legal forms of economic phenomena should be studied in close association with the economic substance. Hence these research works must represent not only the legal, but also the economic viewpoint and must be conducted by lawyers and economists together.

Close attention is paid to complex economic and legal studies in our country, and results have been good.

Economic processes are mobile, economic legal relations are continually developing and they are highly dynamic. This makes it necessary to study them, not only on the basis of legal acts and juridical literature, but principally by examining the real phenomena of economic life. The result of this is the development of empirical studies of complex economic and legal relations, together with the application of sociological methods.

The direction of studies of economic and legal practice makes it possible not only to create the theoretical fundamentals of the legal regulation of economic relations, but also to prepare the proposals for using legal instruments for the promotion of efficiency of public production. Creation of both fundamental and applied problems of economic law requires that studies be undertaken in close connection with the state organs' practical activity. Contracts have recently been drawn up between scientific and state organs in order to strengthen the ties between science and practice. One such contract is that concluded between the Institute of State and Law and the State Arbitration attached to the Council of Ministers.

When researching the legal aspects of economic relations it is important to use also the comparative law method. It is highly productive for studying economic relations in countries with the same social and economic system. At the same time, the comparative law method can also be used for correlating the legal regulation of economy in countries with different social and economic systems, when studying the legal status of the enterprises and their units, their treaty relations and other questions that are important for economic and scientific cooperation. Thus, three symposiums have been held in recent years (in Moscow, Hamburg and Tbilisi) between lawyers from the USSR and West Germany on legal regulation of internal and bilateral economic relations. Such contacts also promote the development of economic and scientific cooperation between the USSR and West Germany.

ECONOMICS AND THE AUTONOMY OF LAW, LEGAL ANALYSIS AND LEGAL THEORY

By Robert S. Summers, Ithaca (New York)

I. Main Theses of This Paper

The main theses of this paper are:

1. Since about 1960 in the United States there has been an important movement in legal thought applying economic analysis to law (the "law and economics" movement).[1]

2. *Some* American proponents of economic analysis of law have expressly stated or implied that law, legal analysis, and legal theory have no genuine autonomy of any kind. Instead, law, legal analysis, and even legal theory can all be reduced, without loss, to economics and economic analysis.

3. Although nearly all legal theorists would ultimately reject the extreme view that law, legal analysis, and legal theory are all somehow reducible to economics and economic analysis, it can be instructive to take this view seriously and consider how it might be refuted.

II. The Recent American Movement Applying Economic Analysis to Law: Brief History

Long before 1960, various American laws incorporated economic theories about the proper workings of the American economy. The Sherman Act, adopted by the Congress in 1890 is the leading example. That Act was aimed at monopolistic practices and, as originally adopted, provided in section 1: "Every contract, combination in the form of trust or otherwise, or conspiracy, *in restraint of trade or commerce* among the several states, or with foreign nations, is hereby declared illegal. ..." (emphasis added). The Sherman Act is addressed to the *market behavior* of business firms, and generally seeks to require that those firms

---

[1] See, e.g. *R. Posner*, Economic Analysis of Law, 1977; *G. Calabresi*, The Costs of Accidents, 1970; *M. Polinsky*, An Introduction to Law and Economics, 1983.

compete without restraint. According to the neo-classical economic theory incorporated in the Sherman Act, noncompetitive behavior is usually "inefficient" (in one sense of that word). Under such a law, then, economic analysis is obviously relevant to defend the rationale of the law, and to determine its applicability to particular cases.

The American "law and economics" movement that began around 1960 did not (and still does not) focus on the Sherman Act or similar bodies of law incorporating economic theory directly. Instead, it turned to such common law fields as torts, property, and contract. Except in contracts, most such common law is addressed to *non-market behavior* such as driving cars, breathing clean air, and even running a court system. But most participants in the American law and economics movement assume that the core teachings of economics are not restricted to market behavior. They concur with the great British economist, Lord Robbins, who once stated: "... when time and means for achieving ends are limited and capable of alternative applications, and the ends are capable of being distinguished in order of importance, their behavior necessarily assumes the form of choice ... it has an economic aspect."[2] On this view, economics is not confined in its scope to market activities and the effects of competitive and noncompetitive behavior. Rather, economics is a more general *theory of rational choice*. The assumptions of the economic theory of rational choice are said to be generally applicable to nonmarket as well as to market behavior. These assumptions are: that only the individuals involved know what is best for them, that these individuals must choose between alternative courses of behavior (or make other value choices), that the levels or "quantities" of such behavior are divisible into commensurable units to which numerical weightings can be assigned to measure the benefits and costs of these alternatives, that individuals express their own comparative evaluations of alternatives by paying or by being willing to pay for one alternative over another, that individuals, over time, *seek* to maximize their total net benefits (value) by choosing those activities that secure for them the greatest benefits at lowest costs ("marginal benefits are equal to marginal costs"), that in the various discrete contexts of social life different individuals choose levels of activities in interaction with each other that may be said to "settle into stable equilibria", that such a state of equilibrium may either be efficient or inefficient,[3] and that

[2] *L. Robbins*, An Essay on the Nature and Significance of Economic Science, 1932.

[3] A chosen equilibrium which the participants have no incentive to alter may still be inefficient for a number of reasons. For example, one of the parties may not be required under the law to take into account all the costs attributable to his chosen level of activity, and therefore engage in a higher level of that activity than he would if he had to take all costs into account.

the efficiency of a given state of equilibrium may be partially attributable to existing legal rules applicable to the alternatives facing individuals, for such rules themselves have costs and benefits that individuals must take into account in choosing between alternatives.[4]

The essential aims of most *positive* economic analysis of law are to *explain* why law makers, including judges, have chosen to give legal rules the content they have, or to *predict* how actual or proposed laws will affect the behavioral choices of those subject to them. For example, the action of lawmakers in adopting our existing general rule that denies a plaintiff a right to require the defendant to perform his contract specifically rather than pay money damages for the breach might be explained on the ground that this denial of the remedy of "specific performance" is "economically efficient". At least it has been claimed that such a rule allows the breaching party to realize those gains from his breach that are left over after paying damages, and that this result represents a net social gain. In order for this *explanation* of our existing general rule against specific performance as adopted by our lawmakers (including judges) to be complete however, it must also be assumed that our *lawmakers* (and not just citizens subject to the rule) are themselves motivated by a desire to maximize net benefits of citizens. (Whether this assumption holds is an issue of "public choice" theory.)

The essential aim of most *normative* economic analysis is to determine whether a change *ought* to be made in an existing legal rule, or in a state of affairs in which there is no rule. We will return to this.

After about twenty years of research, the American "law and economics" movement now has numerous articles and several monographs to its credit. There are also several teaching books.

The claimed specific substantive contributions of this movement to the solutions of problems (either positive or normative) in particular branches of private law are numerous and wide-ranging. In contract law, for example, there are two dozen or so major articles on such topics as the right to specific performance, the measurement of money damages, the proper approach to issues of impossibility and frustration (excusing the duty to perform), the law of mistake, the validity of "penalty" clauses, etc. In tort law, there are many articles and a few books. In property law, there are articles and books. And so on.

Economic analysis of law also provides important contributions that transcend particular fields of law. For example, it reveals starkly how

---

[4] Cf. *P. Burrows/C. Veljanovski*, The Economic Approach to Law, 1981, p. 3—5; *R. Cooter*, Law and the Imperialism of Economics, in: U.C.L.A. L. Rev. 29 (1982), p. 1290.

there is no such thing as a "free lunch" (to impose a warranty of habitability on landlords costs money), that parties who ultimately bear the cost of a law may be quite different from those on whom the cost is initially imposed ("incidence analysis"), that those who benefit from the costs of certain activities can often be made by law to bear those costs (when not already doing so), that various costs can be imposed to reduce existing levels of an activity when this is desirable, that the future "incentive effects" of present legal decisions, in addition to "equities", are also of great importance in designing legal rules, that these "incentive effects" extend not only to "primary" out-of-court behavior, but also to such things as decisions to go to court, etc.

III. The Claimed Reducibility of Law, Legal Analysis and Legal Theory to Economics and Economic Analysis

Partly because of the successes, actual and claimed, of the "law and economics" movement since 1960, a few participants in this movement, including some of its most prominent figures, have asserted or implied that law, legal analysis, and legal theory or some combination of these are somehow essentially reducible to economics and economic analysis. Even quite explicit statements have been made to this effect.[5] One might explain these statements merely as the understandable exuberance of those who believe they have something entirely new to say. Or one might explain them as deliberate overstatements intended only to attract attention. Such explanations would suggest that the statements ought not to be taken seriously.

But in my view, the general thesis of the alleged ultimate reducibility of law, legal analysis, and legal theory merely to economics and economic analysis ought to be taken seriously. First, such radical reductionist theses in matters of law have been recurrent in American legal thought. For example, in the 1920's and 1930's in the United States there were various thinkers who, under the influence of behavioral social science, held that law is reducible to the behavior patterns of officials and that legal theory is somehow reducible to an empirical science of law.[6] Second, there is evidence that some modern day economic analysts of law do intend to be taken seriously when they advance some version of the reducibility thesis. Thus truth is at stake and has been for a long time. No doubt the truth varies somewhat,

[5] Professor, now Judge, Richard Posner is perhaps foremost here.

[6] *R. Summers*, Instrumentalism and American Legal Theory, 1982, p. 112—115. See also *R. Summers*, Pragmatischer Instrumentalismus und amerikanische Rechtstheorie, Karl Alber, 1983.

depending on to which subject matter law, legal analysis, or legal theory are said to be reducible: economics, or behavioral science, or philosophy or politics or whatever. Here I will address only possible reducibility to economics and economic analysis.

Even if the truth were not really in dispute, the reducibility thesis is, I suggest, a worthwhile one to refute systematically, for the effort can itself be instructive. Also, the extent to which law, legal analysis, and legal theory are relatively autonomous and thus not reducible to economics and economic analysis (or to any other discipline, for that matter) is an important question in its own right, for law, legal analysis, and legal theory are of immense practical and theoretical significance. If for example, law, legal analysis, and legal theory really are, in the end, little more than economics and economic analysis in disguise, profound reorientations would be required. Many books and articles might have to be revised. Even the existing curriculum of the American law school might have to be restructured. Judges might have to be retrained. Many laws might even to be changed! And so on.

Of course, limitations of space impose drastic limits on what can be said here about this large and complex topic. Often I can do little more than drop hints.

IV. Is Law Reducible to Economics?

The very question whether law is reducible to economics requires clarification. Several different forms of the reducibility thesis may be differentiated. In the space alloted I can take account of only a few of the relevant possibilities.

1. Possible Reducibility of Basic Goal or "Driving Force" of Law (legal system)

It might be thought that the essential character of social phenomena such as a legal system is to be found in its primary goal or its "driving force" or the like. Does an economic system have a primary goal or a driving force? Many American economic analysts would say, in rough terms, that the driving force of the American economic system is some form of economic "efficiency" such as wealth maximization. These analysts therefore assert that the primary goal or driving force of the American *legal* system must similarly be such efficiency.

But in my view any such description of "the" primary goal or driving force of a legal system must necessarily be inaccurate. No *single primary* goal can characterize anything so complex as a legal system. Lon L.

Fuller wrote that a system of law is an "enterprise" for subjecting society to the "governance of rules", i. e., the rule of law, which is itself to be analyzed into a complex cluster of inter-related goals.[7] Beyond such broadly procedural goals, legal systems typically have a number of fundamental substantive ends. For example, the *avowed* ends of the American system include freedom and justice. These ends are not meaningfully reducible to some form of economic "efficiency" such as wealth maximization. The same is true of other basic goals of that system such as fairness and legitimacy in the workings of ongoing legal processes.

2. Possible Reducibility of the Subject Matter to Which Law (mainly rules) Applies

The subject matter of those social phenomena traditionally characterized as economic consists essentially of human activities devoted mainly to the *production and consumption of material goods and services.*

It is undeniable that some of the subject matter to which law (mainly rules) applies consists of activities that are essentially economic in the foregoing sense. But not all social phenomena are thus essentially economic, and most of the law of American society applies to wholesome private activities of other kinds not essentially economic: social, familial, religious, educational, aesthetic, recreational, and more. Of course, some of our law applies to numerous unwholesome social activities such as crime and other antisocial behavior most of which is only metaphorically economic.

Also, some wholesome public activities within a society are essentially governmental and legal rather than economic in the sense of being concerned with the production and consumption of material goods and services. These include the recruitment and retention of personnel such as judges and officials, the creation and application of law, the exercise of official discretion, and the execution and enforcement of law. Vast bodies of law apply to such governmental and legal activities, too. Some of this law may be said to *constitute* these very activities. Court actions, for example, are *creatures* of law. Such essentially governmental and legal activities must not be equated with "economic" activity in the sense of the production and consumption of material goods and services.

In response, participants in the law and economics movement may argue that even though the subject matters to which much law is ad-

[7] *L. Fuller*, The Morality of Law, 1969.

dressed are not reducible to essentially economic phenomena, economic analysis nonetheless remains applicable because, as Lord Robbins has suggested, the core of economics is the theory of rational choice and all the social phenomena to which law applies consists of "choosing" activities. But the non-economic activities to which law applies are not all "choosing activities" in the respects required for the ready applicability of economic analysis. Also, once we move away from certain kinds of paradigmatic market activity, the conditions for the ready applicability of economic analysis are frequently much less evident. For example, such "goods and services" as the pleasures of viewing the countryside and the pleasures of family life are not, except metaphorically, divisible into equivalent and measurable units to which economic analysts can readily apply their theory of rational choice. At least, we may say that the reducibility of subject-matter thesis is "not proven", and that basic assumptions of the applicibility of the economist's theory of rational choice are thus in doubt. (Economists, of course, are aware of these problems.)

3. Possible Reducibility of Substantive Content of Law (mainly rules)

As we have seen, the substance of the laws of a particular society are addressed to social phenomena, non-economic as well as economic. Proponents of economic analysis might urge that, nonetheless, the substantive content of even those laws addressed to non-economic phenomena derives largely from the teachings of the academic discipline of economics, either directly or indirectly. For example, some economic analysts of law have claimed that the common law of negligence does not derive from a moral injunction requiring elemental due care and respect for others. Rather, a defendant is guilty of negligence only if the likely costs imposed by the accident, multiplied by the probability of its occurring, exceed the costs of precautions the defendant might have taken to avert it. This is said to be an economic test. It should be plain to historians that our law of negligence does not in fact *historically* derive from economic theory. Whether it so derives in some *logical* sense is another question.

But whether or not the foregoing example truly illustrates a rule the content of which derives from economics (historically or logically), I believe that few legal rules can be said to derive their essential content in any sense from the teachings of any particular academic discipline outside the law. Consider, for example, many of the rules constitutive of various judicial and legislative procedures. If their content derives mainly from any discipline, it derives from the law itself, including considerations of due process and of law-like governance. Moreover, insofar as the content of a legal rule can in some sense be said to derive mainly from a discipline external to law, that discipline will often be one other than economics such as political science, psychology, sociology, one of the health sciences or even that branch of philosophy called ethical theory. Even then, it will often be appropriate to say that the law's content derives (historically, logically or otherwise) only partially from one of these so-called "policy sciences", for that content will *almost always* also be partially attributable to the *interaction* between these teachings and available legal means (with all their limitations). For example, the shape of the substantive content of our anti-trust law reflects a concern not only for economic ends but also the limitations of the law's means of authoritatively finding facts about market behavior (by courts and other bodies).

4. Possible Reducibility of Basic Form of Law (mainly rules)

It should be plainly obvious that the basic form of legal rules is not reducible to that of positive economic "laws" such as the so-called laws of supply and demand. Legal rules and other such precepts are themselves *normative* and thus differ in fundamental type from *positive* economic laws. Most legal rules — civic laws — *bind* those subject to them but economic laws do not. Economic laws are invoked to *explain* and to *predict*. And despite several decades of American legal theory to the contrary, civic laws are not, essentially, predictions. They are legal *norms*. Of course, it is sometimes wise to try to predict what a judge or an official will do in light of factors other than applicable legal norms. When so, these other factors will typically also include factors that are not economic in character. And the resulting predictions will not, *as such*, qualify as legal norms.

Whether civic laws are reducible in any way to economic "laws" of a *normative* character cannot be decided. This is because within the discipline of economics there is no agreed meaning for the phrase "economic laws of a normative character".

5. Possible Reducibility of Legal Techniques

This cannot be considered here for lack of space.[8]

[8] Compare "the market" as an economist's social technique, with the law's techniques in *R. Summers*, The Technique Element in Law, in: Calif. L. Rev. 59 (1971), p. 733.

V. Is Legal Analysis Reducible to Economic Analysis?

In my view, there are several varieties of distinctively legal analysis. Similarly, there are several varieties of economic analysis of law. I can take account of only a few of these variations here.

1. "Positive" Analysis in Law and in Economics — Irreducible Differences

Much "positive" legal analysis is devoted to determining what the law *is* in the first place. It thus deals with the interpretation and application of statutes, of court opinions and of other sources of law. The primary purpose of such analysis (which includes much argumentation) is to establish, for the specific issues at hand, what the law *is*.

Most positive economic analysis *presupposes* that the analyst knows already what the applicable law is, and goes on to *explain* why that law is the way it is, or to *predict* how particular actors will behave under such a law. Thus the fundamental purposes of much positive legal analysis and much positive economic analysis of law are not at all the same. (Admittedly, some economic analysts have also argued for particular interpretations of rules as the ones most consistent with "efficiency", which they assume to be the "real driving force" behind all the legal "verbiage". This mode of positive economic analysis of the "real" content of legal rules has yet to prove itself.)

An economic analyst of law might hold that the lawyer, when determining what the law *is*, engages essentially in a process of prediction, and that the lawyer is therefore doing (albeit less perfectly) what the economic analyst does when he predicts. But in my view, the lawyer who interprets and applies authoritative sources is, typically, *not predicting*. He is *presupposing* that the judges will follow the law and is formulating a reasoned judgment about what that law is, in light of the content of the authoritative sources and in light of generally accepted techniques of interpretation and application.[9] (Not all analysis that is future regarding in some way qualifies as predictive.) This also helps explain an obvious difference between positive legal analysis and positive economic analysis. The lawyer's (and judge's and professor's) tools are simply not the same as the economic analyst's tools. The positive economic analyst uses a methodology drawn from positive economics (here, largely the assumptions and techniques of rational choice theory).

---

[9] *R. Summers*, Instrumentalism and American Legal Theory, 1982, ch. 5. See also *R. Summers*, Pragmatischer Instrumentalismus und amerikanische Rechtstheorie (note 6 above).

In some legal systems (all?) there is a further basic difference signifying the non-reducibility of positive legal analysis to positive economic analysis. Sophisticated legal observors would agree that no *sharp* line can be drawn between positive legal analysis and normative legal analysis, and many would also agree that it is unhealthy to try to draw such a line. Ideas and principles of what the law *ought to be* do (and should) help shape the determination of what the law *is* in various ways and respects. Lon L. Fuller was perhaps the most eloquent defender (and proponent) of this view in Anglo-American countries in this century.[10] But it is almost an article of faith with economic analysts that, in the interest of science, a sharp line *must* be drawn between positive and normative economic analysis. (Of course, economists recognize that once positive economic analysis is done, the analysis may then supply predictions that figure in normative reasons for decision or standards of criticism. For example, if by positive analysis a lower income group would likely bear a proposed tax, this might generate an argument against the proposal.)

2. "Normative" Analysis in Law and Economics — Irreducible Differences

Normative analysis in law may be defined as analysis that is concerned not with the construction of reasons that appeal to existing legal authority, but rather with the construction and evaluation of *substantive* reasons that appeal to social, moral, economic, institutional and other considerations of policy or principle. I have elsewhere published a study of substantive reasons that actually appear in American common law cases.[11] The substantive reasons fall into three main categories: "goal reasons" (the justificatory force of which depend on the predicted efficacy of projected decisions to serve good social goals), "rightness reasons" (the justificatory force of which depend not on the predicted effects of decisions but on the accordance of projected decisions with norms of right conduct applicable to past interactions of the parties or the results of those actions), and "institutional reasons" (which are either goal reasons or rightness reasons which relate peculiarly to the institutional roles and machinery of the law).

An example of a rightness reason would be one that says: "We should decide for the plaintiff because the defendant unjustifiably misled the plaintiff to rely to his detriment and must therefore be estopped." An

---

[10] *R. Summers*, Lon L. Fuller — An Introduction to His Life and Work, Stanford U. Press, 1984.

[11] *R. Summers*, Two Types of Substantive Reasons, in: Cornell L. Rev. 63 (1978), p. 707.

example of an institutional reason would be one that says: "We should decide for the defendant (the plaintiff's father) because courts have no way to measure damages for the social disgrace that the plaintiff claims resulted from being born illegitimate." (Some institutional reasons have to do with what is required to protect the integrity of the very institutions involved, e. g., proper participation by affected parties in adjudication). The basic types of substantive reasons are invoked by judges most often and most robustly in new cases posing novel issues, in cases overruling past decisions, and in cases of conflicting precedent.

Now, in their own normative analysis, economists often invoke two types of substantive reasons for decisions. I have also published a study of those reasons (jointly with Professor Leigh B. Kelley).[12] The general character of the two main types of "economists' reasons" can also be sketched briefly. The first may be called "Pareto superior" reasons. These derive what justificatory force they may have from the notion that if a change can be made in existing law that makes at least one person better off (by his own lights) and no one worse off (by their own lights) then such a change ought to be made, for it achieves a state that is "Pareto superior" to the status quo. The second type may be called "Kaldor-Hicks superior" reasons. These derive what justificatory force they may have from the notion that if a change can be made in existing law that makes one or more persons better off and some persons worse off but the former gain more than the latter lose, then such a change ought to be made (possibly with compensation to the losers), for it achieves a state that is "Kaldor-Hicks superior" to the status quo. (There are many variations on this.)

Now, the narrow issue I raise here is whether the normative analysis — the goal reasons, rightness reasons, and institutional reasons found in Anglo-American common law (and, if I am correct, in our law generally) — all can be reduced to economists' reasons of one of the two foregoing types. To date, no economic analyst has demonstrated as much, and in my view no such reduction is possible. Rather, if I am right, economists' reasons are merely two subclasses within the general category of *goal reasons*, a general category already recognized in the common law. As such, economists' reasons depend for their force on predicted effects of decisions to serve social goals.

Yet, *rightness reasons* make up the most common type of substantive reason in common law. And again, no economic analyst of law has demonstrated that these reasons collapse into economists' reasons. Unlike

[12] *R. Summers/L. Kelley*, Economists' Reasons, in: Oxford J. Legal Studies 1 (1981), p. 213. See also *R. Dworkin*, Is Wealth a Value?, in: J. Legal Studies (1980), p. 191.

economists' reasons and the whole category of goal reasons, rightness reasons do not depend for their justificatory force on predicted effects of decisions. Rightness reasons would have justificatory force even if there were no future (and therefore no predicted decisional effects). It is true that many reasons *are* consistent in their decisional implications with rightness reasons, but that is another matter.

Finally, institutional reasons arise from what is special to institutional roles and processes inside the law and almost certainly cannot be reduced to economists' reasons.

3. The Unavoidable Element of Fiat in Law and Its Bearing on Normative and Positive Analysis

Frequently there is some unavoidable element of "fiat" in the law. Substantive reasons cannot determine all of the "twists and turns" of the law. Substantive reasons may have no bearing, or they may conflict and be of roughly equal weight so that the matter must be decided by *mere authoritative choice, i. e. fiat.* Note that if an unavoidable element of fiat is involved, there is nothing necessarily pejorative about saying that the matter must be decided by fiat. (The word "arbitrary" is not a good word to use in place of "fiat" because "arbitrary" does have pejorative connotations.) Although I concede that some unavoidable element of fiat may be involved, I do not imply that this element can be sharply differentiated from all elements of reason. When one encounters an element of fiat, it is usually part of a "mix of reason and fiat", as, for example, in time periods in statutes of limitations.

When a new case arises posing novel issues, or an old case is to be overruled, or a choice made between conflicting precedent or some other creative decision is necessary, the problem for the lawmaker may be one that cannot be resolved in its entirety without resort to some element of fiat. I do not see how normative economic analysis can have anything to say that might be substituted for this element of fiat, yet this element is a significant part of the solution to some important legal problems. If normative economic analysis can have nothing to say here, there is nothing economic to which legal analysis could be "reduced". I concede that normative legal analysis may also have nothing to say here, as well. Still the law has had a good deal of experience with such problems on which to draw. Moreover, some elements of fiat are more readily accomodated within the law than are others. The normative legal analyst, but presumably less so the economic analyst, might have something to say about this (a complex matter I cannot treat here).

When an element of unavoidable fiat is already recognized in the law, the *positive* legal analyst will usually discern this and reason accordingly to determine and apply applicable law. Such "fiat" reasoning will be as near to the "purely authoritative" as is possible. But it is not clear that positive economic analysis has anything at all to say here, either. (Note that such "fiat" oriented reasoning is still not purely authoritative, for it implicitly invokes the ideal of governance according to the rule of law, and this ideal rests to some extent on substantive reasons of fairness and legitimacy.)

VI. Is Legal Theory Reducible to Economics?

Space remains only for the briefest general thoughts on the question: Is legal theory reducible to economics? Legal theory could not possibly be reducible to economics. At the very least, economic analysis of law (1) presupposes the answers to some fundamental questions of legal theory, (2) fails to address certain fundamental questions of legal theory, and (3) addresses, but in an unsatisfactory way, certain other fundamental questions of legal theory.

Economic analysis *presupposes* an answer to the most basic question of legal theory: What social phenomena are to count as legal in character (including what kinds of criteria or standards serve to identify valid law within particular societies)?

Economic analysis of law does not frontally address *numerous* basic issues of legal theory, including: In what senses are law, and life under law, normative in character? What items would a reasonably comprehensive inventory of the law's ways, means, and techniques include, and how should the distinctive uses and limits of these be described and characterized? Is any substantive content essential to the existence of law, or can a legal system have just any content? How are basic legal processes to be analyzed? How are fundamental legal concepts such as rule, right, duty, and sanction to be elucidated?

Of the traditional problems of legal theory that economic analysis (in this case, normative) does address, directly or indirectly, perhaps the most important is this: What general theory of value should inform the content of reasons for legal decisions (including decisions adopting rules)? This is probably the most significant problem in the entire field of legal theory, and the solution that American economic analysts today offer to this problem is very largely the solution put forward in the 19th century by Benthamite utilitarians. This solution has always been and continues to this day to be highly controversial. For one thing, it is not evident that utilitarian theory can accomodate the most common general justifying reasons to be found today in Anglo-American common law (and also in many statutory schemes), namely, rightness reasons. It may be that such reasons are, in significant ways, past-regarding and thus quite unlike the future-regarding reasons of consequentialist utilitarianism. Bentham was wrong to believe that "thank you" means "more please".

ECONOMICS AND THE AUTONOMY OF LAW: SOME COMMENTS

By Juha Tolonen, Vaasa

I. Introduction

The theme discussed by Prof. Summers in his paper is dealt with in the light of the American discussion of the last 10—20 years. The key concept has been that of "economic rationality" as interpreted, as Prof. Summers states, within the framework of neo-classical economics. While one can fully agree with all the criticisms made by Prof. Summers against the American Law and Economics movement, yet I want to maintain in this paper that the classical idea of economic rationality as a basis of law is defensible. One must bear in mind the existence of a certain weakness within the whole neo-classical school: these scholars did not show any particular respect toward classical English political economy. The neoclassical economists have omitted the intrinsically political element which was essential part in the doctrines of Smith, Ricardo, Mill and others.

Classical political economy in England was theoretically as well as politically very closely connected with Utilitarianism. Jeremy Bentham regarded himself as a pupil of Adam Smith, and David Ricardo, James Mill and later John Stuart Mill belonged to the inner circle of Bentham's adherents. These men were also politically active. They represented radicalism in those days in England, demanding radical legislative reforms in most branches of social life and opposing privileges and obstacles to free trade. Moreover, a vitally important thing is that they were politically democrats, their famous slogan being "Universal Suffrage, Annual Parliaments and Election by Ballot". All these requirements they argued for had a common source, the principle of utility. This principle is one of the forms of rational (economic) choice.

In the following I shall attempt to reconstruct the relevant essence of Utilitarianism (section II) and then to elaborate the Utilitarian idea of law as an instrument in contradistinction to the legal positivism that assumes the autonomous position of law (section III).

II. Utilitarianism and Its Essence

Utilitarian principles in concise form are elaborated by Bentham in his book *Fragment on Government*. These principles are summarised in the tenet: The greatest happiness of the greatest number. Happiness again is calculated as the sum of pleasure less the sum of pain. This method of calculation was according to the view of the Utilitarians applicable to individual as well as social action. The legitimacy of the whole social order and all its elements were held to be determinable according to this criterion.

This idea of a calculation of happiness is in many ways an oversimplification of the social reality, as many critics have stated. Nevertheless, the Utilitarians deduced from it some corollaries which seem quite plausible. The *first* corollary is that of equality, the *second* that of freedom and the *third* that of democracy.

First, in their calculation of social happiness the starting point was that every human being without exception was equally a subject capable of feeling pleasure and pain. Thus it was deduced that every human being should count as much as every other. There could be no rational basis for any privileged positions in the calculation of happiness. Hence there emerged a very radical egalitarianism which was reflected in the politics of the Utilitarians.

Second, pain and pleasure were considered to be subjective and individual feelings. Hence, every adult citizen had to have an opportunity to himself and independently define what his happiness was and act accordingly. From this derived the claim for *freedom* of choice and action for every adult citizen. The guardianship of the upper classes of society over the personal matters of the less fortunate was held to be irrational.

These two principles (equality and freedom) form, it should be noted, a holistic totality. There cannot be any real or rational freedom without equality and vice versa. The idea of *equal freedom for all* was the basic principle of the Utilitarians (Benthamites) in their programs for the reform of civil society (Bürgerliche Gesellschaft). If we look a little closer at the law of contract, the law of property or the law of torts, etc. as they stand now, we may note that this principle of equal freedom is the leading principle in these branches of law. This Utilitarian idea has thus had a tremendous success in all countries.

Third, originally Bentham was a Tory and passive in the politics of his time. But gradually he noticed that the privileged classes wielding political power were unwilling to implement the idea of equal freedom for all. This observation radicalised Bentham and his adherents. It was the ordinary people, they thought, who were interested in these kinds of reforms. So the Benthamites started to advocate parliamentary reform. The right to vote in parliamentary elections must be granted to every adult citizen. Universal suffrage would reveal the real will of the people. It was held self-evident by Bentham, James Mill and Ricardo that this real will of the people would be on their side. Thus democracy would help to maintain the social order which would guarantee equal freedom for all.

In summing up, I would like to point out that Utilitarianism (in the form articulated by Bentham and his radical followers) was not such a bad, unarticulated or naive idea as is very often maintained. On the contary, their doctrines define in a strikingly consequent way the three basic principles of liberal democracies. These principles, namely freedom, equality and democracy, are also the very fundaments of the law in liberal-democratic countries. It should be emphatically noted, however, that these principles have been defined by most post-Utilitarians in terms of one kind of principle of rational choice only (the economic one).

There is one more aspect in the ideology of Utilitarianism that is worth mentioning. This aspect is markedly present in the works of John Stuart Mill (e. g., *Principles of Political Economy* and *On Representative Government*).

The problem for John Stuart Mill was this: Why did the labouring classes of England not support the system of free enterprise (laissez-faire), but were more or less apt to vote for socialists? In his consideration of this state of affairs one can distinguish two lines of argument. On the one hand, Mill was of the opinion that the labouring classes were not yet conscious enough of the realities and possibilities of social life. Improvement in this respect could be achieved through education. On the other hand, Mill pointed out that in the classical free-market system implemented already in England by the middle of the last century there were laws and institutions that violated the principle of equal freedom for all. The law of inheritance was one example of this, and a system of private property in land that gave unearned income (rents) to the landlord was another. Due to laws of this kind some members of society were from the very beginning unjustifiably better off than others. We may generalise this point of Mill's and claim that up to now there have been no societies where these ideas of the Utilitarians would have been completely implemented. But the development of legal and social institutions over the last two hundred years can be interpreted as being a gradual realisation of the said ideas.

Everything that I have said above may be perhaps summarised in the following theses:

1. The whole Utilitarian doctrine was based on the calculation of happiness (a kind of cost-benefit analysis). Although the deduction of practical principles and rules from/through the calculation was in many ways far from correct and complete, there did exist nevertheless a meaningful connection between the theoretical starting points (maximum happiness for most people) and the practical reform program (equal freedom for all and political democracy).

2. The Utilitarian ideology has been generally accepted in the liberal democracies. Without knowing it we cannot understand the organisation, law or basic way of thinking in these democracies.

3. This ideology has, however, a progressive role to play even now. No liberal democracy has so far completely implemented the equality of freedom and the democracy provided by the Utilitarian ideology.

III. The Autonomy of Law

An inquiry into the problem of the autonomy of law has many different aspects. Here I am only concerned with this problem from the *de lege ferenda* (political) point of view. The basic question, as I see it, is this: Would it be advisable to consider legal rules to be a separate system of norms which should be applied without reference to the social, political or economic ideas which have generated the said norms? It is impossible to answer this question in a way that would be valid in all possible circumstances. In the paper by Prof. Summers where this question comes up as a theoretical problem (is the law autonomous?) one may sense an attitude favouring, more or less, the autonomy of law. This attitude corresponds, I think, to the majority view among lawyers. In the following I shall try, however, to defend the opposite view.

If we compare the Utilitarian scholars (Bentham, Ricardo, the Mills, etc.) with the lawyers or economists of today, one remarkable difference may be noticed. The Utilitarians were not specialists, while the modern scholars are. The tendency to make law (or economics) an autonomous field of intellectual activity can be seen to have emerged as a result of specialisation.

There is one very real danger in this tendency towards a growing specialisation in all branches of social life: every particular branch (law, economics, etc.) applies its own concept of rationality, but in society as a whole there isn't one. In the case of law this means that lawyers are getting specialised to an ever-increasing degree. This leads to a vicious circle: as the result, they may from the technical point of view do their job more effectively than earlier, but the social function of the whole legal machinery will be worse and worse fulfilled. The same holds for economics. The more the economists are "scientifically" qualified, the more there will be a sheer social waste of resources. Specialised rationalities thus tend to result in social anarchy.

The Utilitiarians' view of society was in many ways rude and erroneous, due to their concept of social rationality as a whole. Nevertheless they created a holistic ideology for the society of their time. This ideology has kept the liberal democracies organised in a meaningful way. As Dicey has evidenced in his excellent book *Law and Public Opinion in England*, this ideology created the whole public spirit in England in the nineteenth century. Kelsen, on the other hand, has written excellent books arguing for the autonomy of law. He also created through his books an ideology. However, it was not a general ideology for society as a whole, but an ideology for a certain interest-group called lawyers. It is this ideology that the privileges of the lawyers are based on.

ECOLOGY VERSUS ECONOMY IN LAW

Study of a Basic Problem

By Robert Weimar, Siegen

The problematic triangle of *Law* — *Economics* — *Ecology* has not as yet been sufficiently comprehended. One of the reasons for this may be the imperfect translation of economic and ecological patterns of thought and principles into jurisprudential reflection.

The implementation of an economic method for arriving at a settlement in the case of an encroachment on the environment can hardly be expected to bring about a solution serving the interest of all parties concerned unless restrictions are brought to bear on market-related forces. Moreover, as it is assumed that differing predominances cannot be simply adjusted evenly, effective rules of law that take into account both economics and ecology will be required for bringing about a suitable balance.

Any such rules, if they are to serve the purpose effectively, must rely on an analysis of the underlying economic and ecological data in the light of a new jurisprudential paradigm.

I. Aspects of the Interrelations between Ecology and Economics in Jurisprudence

1. The Exchange of Rights

Just as a producer has the right to influence and make demands on the environment (although not necessarily to damage it), the individual citizen may claim that his habitat should be protected against harmful influences (although not necessarily demand an "unimpaired" environment).

These rights may be understood in the sense of sound conformity with economic laws. Just as goods are subject to exchange, such rights may also be exchanged up to the point at which they will achieve the highest degree of utilization. The final stage of such an exchange process is reached where parity is optimized. This is a situation of balance in which no person (or owner of a right) can improve his position without simultaneously impairing that of the other persons. The idea underlying this concept is that of an established distribution of goods, for each of which the best possible condition is to be created. No indication is given as to whether the welfare of society as a whole may be improved by another, more efficient, utilization of right.

This principle of "efficient" distribution of goods or rights does not therefore appear to contribute significantly to maximum welfare, but far more so to maximum individual utilization. *Coase*[1] maintains that, in the case of an award of rights, the parties concerned have entered into a process of "exchange in kind" which offers maximum utilization to both. If a subsequent change in the allocation of resources is made on the strength of an award of title by law, it may be asserted that economic logic has enforced its rights "behind the back" of the Law. An effective solution to the conflict has been achieved in a manner which, while improving values,[2] will be neglecting social issues.[3]

2. The Problem of Costs of Transaction

These considerations are of no consequence when the assumption of non-existent costs of transaction is not applied, i. e. if these, on the contrary, are taken for granted, and at a significant level. In this case, in spite of the fact that they offer an advantage to both parties, transactions will not be made because the costs of the transaction would exceed the potential gains expected by the parties involved. The distribution of rights (including indemnities) would, in this case, have an allocating effect.

In the case of potentially high costs of transaction, the title would have to be passed to the party that would profit more from the utilization of such a title. This method produces an anticipation of expensive market transactions; the costs involved would be incurred in the absence of any interference by the authorities for achieving the state of affairs which would come about in any case under the compulsive forces exerted by economics. The argument that the ecological issue does not enter into consideration in the award of rights also holds true for this case.

---

[1] *R. H. Coase*, The Problem of Social Cost, in: Journal of Law and Economics (1960), p. 1 pp.

[2] *M. Prisching*, Ökonomische Rechtslehre?, in: Rechtswissenschaftliche Fakultät der Universität Graz (ed.), Reform des Rechts. Festschrift zur 200-Jahr-Feier der Rechtswissenschaftlichen Fakultät der Universität Graz 1979, p. 1000 pp.; *P. Behrens*, Aspekte einer ökonomischen Theorie des Rechts, in: RECHTSTHEORIE 12 (1981), p. 472 pp.; *H. J. M. Boukema*, A Philosophical View of Ecology, in: RECHTSTHEORIE 13 (1982), p. 337 pp.

[3] Cf. *R. A. Posner*, Economic Analysis of Law, second edition, Boston-Toronto 1977.

3. The Approach to Maximum Welfare with Respect to the Relations between Ecology and Economics

A point of departure is offered here for arriving at an ideal balance between economic and ecological welfare through maximum individual benefit. Decisions relating to environmental situations have an influence on future conditions, recognizing that they support and/or influence human behaviour. Moreover, a qualitative change with regard to the legal award for the consequences of actions affecting environment can be achieved in the course of judicial decision making. Hence, courts of law can screen and give adequate consideration to the complexity of problems of settlement by carefully scrutinizing decisions and consequences. This approach would not produce any direct change in the legal system, although it would generate a means of settling existing and potential future conflicts in the shape of judge-made law as well as give rise to an environmental jurisprudence.

In a case of precedent the judge should measure the possible effects of all potential decisions on the future behaviour of individuals or groups, or both, whose activities may have a similar effect on the environment. In this case, the measures enforced for remedying the damage to the environment could also rely on judge-made decisions rather than on an approach based on environmental legislation; this would finally be less expensive. When considering these aspects, it becomes obvious that the maximum welfare issue and maximum individual benefit may be brought into agreement.

II. Interlacing of Economics and Ecology: A Point of Efficiency

1. The Criteria of Efficiency

If, on the strength of an exchange process, resources (or title) are employed to the extent that their value attains its highest degree, this will represent efficient utilization. In this case, the meaning of efficiency should be interpreted as the utilization of economic resources in a manner which aims at the achievement of maximum benefit, which is understood to be the satisfaction of human needs in relation to the communal desire of consumers to acquire goods and services.

In the light of the efficiency concept, the willingness to pay depends on various factors, e. g. income, capital and their distribution. Since economists have no answer to the question of whether a given pattern of distribution is good or bad, that is, whether it is just or injust, they cannot be expected to say whether an efficient allocation of resources is good, just, or in some such way desirable. Only the effects of legal provisions are supposed to have a value and efficiency (in the technical understanding of these terms) and only the effects of the distribution of income and/or capital can be predicted on the strength of this conception. Therefore, it cannot be regarded as a point of departure for social change.

In principle it may be stated that an exchange of resources and/or title on voluntary grounds increases efficiency. The point that still remains unsolved is whether (and to what extent) an involuntary exchange such as an award of rights may also, in this context, be considered to be efficient or to increase efficiency. The consequences of such transactions cannot be adequately evaluated with regard to their efficiency, as this would require comparing the benefits gained by the individual parties concerned. It does, however, remain possible to investigate whether a feasible voluntary exchange might have occurred as a matter of course.

Evidence of the increase, or decrease, or both, of efficiency will only be produced at this rate by the legal system after the exchange has already taken place. The probable conditions of a voluntary transaction negotiated on the market are in this case reproduced. When seen in this light, enforced exchange "in kind" (as compared with that of a voluntary nature, provided it is feasible) does not represent a truly efficient mechanism for awarding resources. Should the former not be possible, there only remains the introduction of a system of legal settlement of transactions.

2. Efficiency in the Case of Environmental Problems

These considerations can be applied to problems of the environment. The significant point in this context is that this topic is approached while rather unrealistically assuming that the party encroaching and the party encroached on would buy each other's rights by means of an exchange process. The point of departure for further reflection is the fact that market mechanisms will necessarily fail if goods are of such a nature that will disallow reservation of their use to a selected few. It is not only some particular persons who will pay for the benefit of using such a good (e. g., an unpolluted environment) but the entire population of a region. Now, if the damage to the environment by the enterprises causing the pollution is reduced by means of adequate protective measures, nobody can or will be excluded from benefiting from the clean air, grounds or waters. In the economist's understanding of the law, this signifies that, by way of ruling the responsibilities, the results of the market can be anticipated in cases of this sort. This anticipation, of course, requires all relevant things, such as the preferences of individual persons, to be known and to be taken into consideration when the respective decisions are made.

Different approaches to the award of resources and rights exist for the transfer of market-oriented relations in settling problems of the environment. By this means, the polluting enterprise can be made to instal filter units. The proprietors in the neighbourhood can themselves apply appropriate measures, or may even move to another district. The parties concerned will invariably encounter costs, and the enterprise causing the pollution may even have to shoulder the additional costs generated by a demand to restrict production.

3. Efficiency of an Overall-Welfare Nature

Rules governing responsibilities which are not restricted to maximum individual conditions, but moreover, also take the social issues into consideration, must be adapted to the criteria prompted by overall welfare efficiency. In this case, the matter of who is placing a burden on the environment is of secondary importance. The focus here is on investigating the permissible extent of environmental burdening from the ecological point of view. This would be the degree of encroachment at which the resulting issue is balanced or is at least no greater than the costs incurred by its victims.

This may be looked upon as a sensible rule for arriving at a compromise between the interests of the parties concerned,[4] which needs to be reconciled with the economic and ecological context underlying the conflict. It is not possible to predict the various circumstances related to the yield and costs in every conceivable case. The assumption that both the damaging and the damaged parties would (after the establishment of their individual preferences and the degree of damage caused) agree to enter into round-the-table negotiations about their rights would appear to be an "hypostasis of the general freedom of negotiation that is far removed from reality".[5] It should therefore be rejected in this form, irrespective of its social relevance, at least in so far as environment is concerned.

---

[4] Cf. *Prisching* (note 2), p. 1002.

[5] Cf. *Prisching* (note 2), and *G. Calabresi*, The Decision for Accidents: An Approach to Nonfault Allocation of Costs, in: Harvard Law Review (1965), p. 713 pp.

By the expression "effective legal provisions with regard to economic and ecological interlacing", we should therefore understand those legal provisions that lead to the best possible utilization of the value of resources by taking into consideration both the economic and the ecological aspects related to this. The idea here is to balance economic requirements and the ecological offence that remains within reasonable limits, in order to arrive at environment-oriented forms of propriety, justice and reasonable behaviour. These take the form, for example, of the observance of ecological restrictions for ensuring the overall social applications of resources which offer the highest yield in value as determined by a well-reflected cost/benefit analysis.

III. The Necessity of Scientific Cooperation at Various Levels

Integrated research at various levels is required for tackling these problems. An economic analysis of law would also have to cover the relevant aspects of ecology. From this point of view, an analysis of law focusing on the interlacing of economics and ecology would be appropriate at the intersections where extra-economic and extra-ecological factors may be neglected. This requires a reversal of the present trend which shows a wide-spread neglect of ecological issues in legislation, administration and jurisdiction, particularly in terms of planning and economic law. There is also neglect at the point of the interlacing between economic and ecological efficiency. This, too, must be reversed in order to achieve a reasonable approach to economics and ecology which sets out to improve welfare in general.

The one-dimensional approach prevailing at present in jurisprudence, which excluded these aspects, may lead to faulty developments and should therefore be abandoned in favour of integrating methods of decision-making. Only then will the law rise to its task of promoting adequate reconciliation in a complex civilization. The aim should therefore be to bridge the gap between academic university disciplines so as to end the isolation into which jurisprudence has worked its way through its overly unilateral orientation. The transdisciplinary efforts may involve penetrations into other scientific fields. This certainly does not imply a political ecology in law, but rather an ecology-oriented approach (in the same way as there is an economy-oriented approach) to a jurisprudence focused on handling the specific problems of environment in a world undergoing continuous development. "Decisive measures need to be taken worldwide in order to prevent even more damage to an environment that has already been severely maligned." "Wasteful exploitation of natural resources must stop." "The giving over of life to wastefulness must be checked." These are the postulates *Tammelo*[6] expresses as a warning to mankind in his "fundamental commands of justice pro futuro", the observation of which is a conditio sine qua non for ensuring that "future generations will neither curse nor deride us".[7] A jurisprudence disposed to both ecology and economics is under obligation to these principles. Can it be assumed that this is the next step to be taken in the development of jurisprudence?

---

[6] *I. Tammelo*, Über die Zeitdimension der Gerechtigkeit, in: Jus Humanitatis — Festschrift zum 90. Geburtstag von Alfred Verdross, Berlin 1980, p. 269 pp.; cf. also *E. Mock*, Die Erschließung der materialen Rechtsphilosophie durch A. Verdross, in: ibid., p. 21.

[7] Cf. *Tammelo* (note 6), p. 269; for details see *Tammelo*, Zur Philosophie des Überlebens, Freiburg/Brsg. 1975.

Personenregister

Verzeichnis der Mitarbeiter

(einschl. des Beirats der Herausgeber)

Aarnio, Aulis, Prof. Dr., Institut für Privatrecht, Universität Helsinki, Vuorikatu 5 C, SF-00100 Helsinki.

Alchourrón, Carlos E., Professor of Philosophy of Law, Faculty of Law, University of Buenos Aires. Home: Junin 1533, 1113 Buenos Aires, Argentina.

Aomi, Junichi, Prof. Dr., Rechtswissenschaftliche Fakultät, Universität Tokio, 3-1 Hongo 7-chome, Bunkyo-ku, Tokio, Japan.

Axinn, June, Professor of Social Welfare, Ph. D., School of Social Work, University of Pennsylvania, 3701 Locust Walk/C3, 19104 Philadelphia PA, U.S.A.

Balekjian, Wahé H., Dr., Dept. of European Law, University of Glasgow, G12 8QQ Glasgow, Scotland, United Kingdom.

Bax, Cees J., Mr., Dept. of Constitutional Law, Erasmus University Rotterdam, P.O. Box 1738, 3000 DR Rotterdam, The Netherlands.

Boguszak, Jiří, Professor, Jur. Dr., Dr. Sc., Ústav státni správy (Institut für staatliche Verwaltung), Jungmannova ul. 29, P.O.B. 45, 110-01 Praha 1, ČSSR.

Boukema, Henk Jan M., Prof. Dr., 376 Herengracht, 1016 CH Amsterdam, The Netherlands.

Bulygin, Eugenio, Professor, University of Buenos Aires. Home: Arroyo 963, 1007 Buenos Aires, Argentina.

Conte, Amedeo G., Professor Dr., Università degli studi, Strada nuova 65, I-27100 Pavia PV, Italia.

Dais, Eugene E., Professor of Law, The University of Calgary, Faculty of Law, 2500 University Drive N.W., Calgary, Alberta, Canada T2N 1N4.

Dauchy, Pierre, Professor, 8 Rue Louis Christiaens, F-59800 Lille, France.

van Dunné, Jan M., Prof. Dr., Institute of Legal Decision Making, Faculty of Law, Erasmus University Rotterdam, P.O. Box 1738, 3000 DR Rotterdam, The Netherlands.

Eckhoff, Torstein, Prof. Dr., Institutt for Offentlig Rett, Universitetet i Oslo, Karl Johans gt. 47, N-Oslo 1.

Fenge, Hilmar, Prof. Dr., Lehrgebiet B für Zivilrecht und Zivilprozeßrecht, Universität Hannover, Hanomagstraße 8, D-3000 Hannover 91.

Flower, Elizabeth, Professor of Philosophy, University of Pennsylvania, 305 Logan Hall C/N, 19104 Philadelphia Pa., U.S.A.

Friedman, Lawrence M., Marion Rice Kirkwood Professor of Law, Stanford University, School of Law, Crown Quadrangle, Stanford, California 94305, U.S.A.

Galligan, Denis J., Professor of Jurisprudence, Law Faculty, University of Southampton, Southampton S09 5HN, England.

Gianformaggio, Letizia, Prof. associato, Istituto di Filosofia e Scienze Politiche, Università di Siena, Via Colleverde 1, I-53100 Siena.

Graver, Hans Petter, Cand. jur., Institute for Sociology of Law, University of Oslo, Sporveisgt. 35, N-Oslo 3.

Guastini, Riccardo, Prof. Dr., Università di Genova, Istituto di Filosofia e Sociologia del Diritto. Home: Corso Carbonara 5, I-16125 Genova, Italy.

Intzessiloglou, Nikolaos, Docteur d'Etat en Droit, Agregé de Sociologie, Prof. Ass. au Département d'Histoire, de Philosophie et de Sociologie Juridique de la Faculté de Droit à l'Université d'Aristote, Thessaloniki. Kastritsiou 3, 54623 Thessaloniki, Grèce.

Klenner, Hermann, Prof. Dr., Zentralinstitut für Philosophie, Akademie der Wissenschaften der DDR, Otto-Nuschke-Straße 10/11, DDR-108 Berlin.

Krawietz, Werner, Prof. Dr. Dr., Lehrstuhl für Rechtssoziologie, Rechts- und Sozialphilosophie, Rechtswissenschaftliche Fakultät, Universität Münster, Bispinghof 24/25, D-4400 Münster i. W.

Laclau, Martín, Professor, Lawyer, University of Buenos Aires. Home: Santa Fe 1731, Piso 5, Dep. 17, 1060 Buenos Aires, Argentina.

Laptev, Vladimir, Professor, Institute of State and Law, USSR Academy of Sciences, Frunze Str. 10, Moscow 119841, U.S.S.R.

Łopatka, Adam, Professor, Institute of State and Law, Polish Academy of Sciences. Partyzantów 4 m. 2, 00-629 Warsaw, Poland.

López Calera, Nicolás, Prof. Dr., Institut für Rechtsphilosophie, Universität Granada, Plaza de la Universidad no. 1, Granada, Spanien.

Maihofer, Werner, Prof. Dr. Dr., Präsident des Europäischen Hochschulinstituts, Badia Fiesolana, Via dei Roccettini, I-50016 S. Domenico di Fiesole, Florenz, Italien.

Martin, Rex, Professor of Philosophy, Dept. of Philosophy, University of Kansas, Lawrence, Kansas 66045, U.S.A.

Moutsopoulos, Evanghelos A., Professor, 40 Hypsilanou street, 140 Athens, Greece.

Pattaro, Enrico, Professor, Istituto Giuridico A. Cicu, University of Bologna, Via Zamboni 27/29, I-40127 Bologna.

Pavčnik, Marijan, Dr., Dozent für Staats- und Rechtstheorie, Pravna fakulteta, Trg osvoboditve 11, 61000 Ljubljana, Jugoslavija.

Peczenik, Aleksander, Professor of Jurisprudence, Lund University, Juridicum, Box 1165, S-221 05 Lund.

Peschka, Vilmos, Prof. Dr., Institute for Legal and Administrative Sciences, Hungarian Academy of Sciences, Országház utca 30, H-1250 Budapest 1.

Raz, Joseph, D. Phil. (Oxon), Balliol College, Oxford, United Kingdom.

Robles, Gregorio, Prof. Dr., Institut für Rechtsphilosophie, Rechtswissenschaftliche Fakultät, Universität Palma de Mallorca, Miguel de los Santos Oliver 2, Palma de Mallorca, Spanien.

Rodriguez Molinero, Marcelino, Ordentl. Professor, Rechtsfakultät der Universität Salamanca, 37071 Salamanca, Spanien.

Sajó, Andras, Associate Professor, Institute for Political and Legal Sciences, Hungarian Academy of Sciences, P. O. Box 25, H-1250 Budapest.

Sampaio Ferraz Jr., Tércio, Prof. Dr., Titular da facultade de direito da Universidade de São Paulo. Home: Av. Paulista 21, apt. 171, 01311 São Paulo, Brasilien.

Sharma, Gyan, Professor, University/Studies in Law, B-39 Sector "A" Mahanagar, Lucknow 226006, Uttar Pradesh, India.

Sintonen, Matti, Ph. D., Research Fellow at the Academy of Finland, Dept. of Philosophy, University of Helsinki, Unionink. 40 B, SF-00170 Helsinki.

Soaje Ramos, Guido, Prof. Dr., Instituto de Filosofia Practica, Viamonte 1596, 1055 Buenos Aires, Argentina.

de Sousa e Brito, José, Professor, Universidade Livre, Lisboa, Avenida da República 14-7°, P-1000 Lisboa, Portugal.

Strangas, Johannes, Prof. Dr., Lehrstuhl für Einführung in die Rechtswissenschaft, für Rechtsphilosophie und Juristische Methodenlehre, Juristische Fakultät, Demokritos-Universität Thrazien. Privat: A. Metaxa Str. 2, 10681 Athen, Griechenland.

Summers, Robert S., McRoberts Professor of Law, Cornell Law School, Myron Taylor Hall, Ithaca, New York 14853, U.S.A.

Tamayo y Salmoran, Rolando, Dr. jur., Research Fellow, Instituto de Investigaciones Jurídicas, Torre 2 de Humanidades, 4 piso, Cd. Universitaria, Coyoacán 04510, México D.F., Mexico.

Tay, Alice Erh-Soon, Challis Professor and Head, Dept. of Jurisprudence, Faculty of Law, The University of Sydney, 173-175 Phillip Street, Sydney, NSW 2000, Australia.

Terré, François, Professeur, Université de droit, d'économie et de sciences sociales, 10 square de l'Alboni, F-75016 Paris.

Tolonen, Juha, Prof. Dr., University of Vaasa, P.O. Box 297, SF-65101 Vaasa.

Uusitalo, Jyrki, Research Associate at the Academy of Finland, Dept. of Private Law, Helsinki University, Vuorikatu 5 C, SF-00100 Helsinki.

Vanderlinden, Jacques, Professeur, Faculté de droit, Université Libre de Bruxelles, Avenue F.D. Roosevelt 50, B-1050 Bruxelles.

Van Hoecke, Mark, Chargé de cours, Faculté de droit, Universitaire Faculteiten Sint-Aloysius (UFSAL), Vrijheidslaan 17, B-1080 Bruxelles.

Vernengo, Roberto J., Prof. Dr., University of Buenos Aires, Faculty of Law and Social Sciences. Home: Teodoro García 3030, 1426 Buenos Aires, Argentina.

Visser't Hooft, Hendrik Ph., Prof. Dr., Maliebaan 135, 3581 CL Utrecht, The Netherlands.

Vullierme, Jean-Louis, Dr., Directeur du Groupe de Politique Théorique (C.N.R.S.). 194 rue de Rivoli, F-75001 Paris.

Weimar, Robert, Prof. Dr. Dr., Institut für Wirtschaftsrecht und Wirtschaftsgesetzgebung, Universität Siegen, Postfach 10 03 18, D-5900 Siegen 1.

Weinberger, Ota, Prof. Dr. Dr., Institut für Rechtsphilosophie, Universität Graz, Universitätsstraße 27, A-8010 Graz.

Wellman, Carl, Professor of Philosophy, Dept. of Philosophy, Washington University, Campus Box 1073, St. Louis, MO 63130, U.S.A.

von Wright, Georg Henrik, Prof. Dr. Dr., Institut für Philosophie, Universität Helsinki, Unioninkatu 40 B, SF-00170 Helsinki.

Yasaki, Mitsukuni, Prof. Dr., Faculty of Law, Osaka University, Machikaneyama, Toyonaka-shi, Osaka-fu, Japan.

Zuleta Puceiro, Enrique, Prof. Dr., University of Buenos Aires. Home: Rodriguez Peña 1405, 10° "B", 1021 Buenos Aires, Argentina.

Beiträge des 11. Weltkongresses für Rechts- und Sozialphilosophie Gesamtverzeichnis

1. Verlag Duncker & Humblot: Beihefte von RECHTSTHEORIE, 1985

Beiheft 8: **Juristische Logik, Rationalität und Irrationalität im Recht.** Hrsg. von A.-J. Arnaud, R. Hilpinen und J. Wróblewski. Mit einem Vorwort von R. J. Vernengo.

I. Logik im Dienste des Rechts: J.-L. Gardies / M. P. Golding / S. Gram Jensen / V. Knapp / A. A. Martino / A. Menne / H. Schreiner / R. Sève / L. Åqvist; *II. Grundlagen und Grenzen der Rationalität im Rechtsdenken:* V. Arévalo / R. Dreier / A. Edel / M. D. Farrell / Å. Frändberg / U. Lohmann / N. MacCormick / E. Pattaro / D. A. J. Richards / N. Roos / A. Sajó / L. S. Sheleff / F. Terré / H. Ph. Visser't Hooft / R. Weimar / E. Zalten / Z. Ziembiński / M. Zirk-Sadowski; *III. Menschenrechte, Bürgerrechte und ziviler Ungehorsam:* M. D. Bayles / J. Ellin / L. D. Eriksson / V. Gulyev / J. Kleinig / T. Laker / A. Łopatka / B. J. Narain / D. Nazarov / J. Paust / R. Tamayo / K. E. Tranøy.

Beiheft 9: **Soziologische Jurisprudenz und realistische Theorien des Rechts.** Hrsg. von E. Kamenka, R. S. Summers und W. L. Twining. Mit einem Vorwort von A. Peczenik.

I. Recht und Gesellschaft in rechtsphilosophischer Perspektive: N. Ananieva / A. J. Arístegui / E. Backman / W. Eichhorn / K. Fabian /Ph. Gérard / H. Klenner / V. Luizzi / V. Nersesyants / J. B. Oakley / K. Penegar / P. Popoff / A. Visegrády / T. Wilhelmsson; *II. Theorien des Rechts in rechtssoziologischer Perspektive:* M. Borucka-Arctowa / K. Liebl / L. Mazor / M. Mikkola / K. Mollnau / D. Nelken / H. Rottleuthner / S. Sariola / C. Varga / E. Zalten; *Voraussetzungen und Folgen des Rechtsrealismus:* J. Bjarup / S. Castignone / C. Faralli / S. Jørgensen / A. Lagerqvist Almé / F. Michaut / E. Pattaro / J. W. F. Sundberg / D. Wyduckel.

Beiheft 10: **Vernunft und Erfahrung im Rechtsdenken der Gegenwart.** Hrsg. von T. Eckhoff, L. M. Friedman und J. Uusitalo. Mit einem Vorwort von O. Weinberger.

I. Systemische Grundlagen der Rechtsvernunft: C. J. Bax / H. J. M. Boukema / J. M. van Dunné / E. Flower / D. J. Galligan / L. Gianformaggio / H. P. Graver / M. Laclau / A. Peczenik / J. Raz / A. Sajó / M. Sintonen / J. Strangas / R. Tamayo / J. Uusitalo / J. Vanderlinden; *II. Systematisierung in Rechtsdogmatik und Rechtswissenschaft:* A. Aarnio / C.

Alchourrón / J. Boguszak / E. Bulygin / P. Dauchy / M. Van Hoecke / R. J. Vernengo; *III. Das Rechtssystem und seine gesellschaftliche Basis:* A. Conte / H. Fenge / L. M. Friedman / R. Guastini / N. Intzessiloglou / W. Krawietz / M. Pavčnik / G. Robles / M. Rodriguez Molinero / J. de Sousa e Brito / J.-L. Vullierme; *IV. Ökonomische Analyse des Rechts:* J. Axinn / W. Balekjian / E. E. Dais / V. Laptev / R. S. Summers / J. Tolonen / R. Weimar.

2. Verlag Franz Steiner Wiesbaden GmbH: Beihefte von *Archiv für Rechts- und Sozialphilosophie*, 1985

Beiheft 23: **Tradition und Fortschritt in den modernen Rechtskulturen.** Hrsg. von S. Jørgensen, J. Pöyhönen und C. Varga. Mit einem Vorwort von J. Llompart.

I. Genese und Geltungsgrundlagen des zeitgenössischen Naturrechtsdenkens: C. D. Johnson / A. Kaufmann / G. Lanata / J. López Medel / G. Lübbe-Wolff / R. Lukic / G. Soaje Ramos / R. Tokarczyk / F. Viola / S. O. Welding; *II. Strukturen moderner Rechts- und Staatstheorien:* G. Antalffy / C. Despotopoulos / A. Levine / W. Maihofer / N. Nenovski / W. Weichelt; *III. Begriff, Grundlagen und Entwicklung der Rechtskulturen in vergleichender Perspektive:* G. Haney / J. Ojwang / B. Ranchod / N. Sanajaoba / A. Tay / V. Tumanow / F. Wieacker / M. Yasaki; *IV. Menschen- und Bürgerrechte als Erfindung gegen den Machtmißbrauch:* P. Bénéton / J. Blahož / J. Feinberg / S. Cotta / M. Villey / N. Kobayashi / S. Leader / E. Moutsopoulos.

Beiheft 24: **Soziale Gerechtigkeit und individuelle Verantwortlichkeit im Wohlfahrtsstaat.** Hrsg. von J. M. Broekman, K. Opałek und D. A. Kerimow. Mit einem Vorwort von C. Wellman.

I. Moralische und rechtliche Prämissen materialer Gerechtigkeit: L. Garcia Alonso / J. R. Lucas / A. Macleod / S. Panou / J. Parain-Vial / V. Peschka / V. Petev / T. Sampaio Ferraz Jr. / D. Scheltens / O. Weinberger; *II. Mensch und Menschenbild im Recht:* M. Alliot / A.-J. Arnaud / P. Braun / B. Edelman / F. Lachmayer / E.-J. Lampe / S. Latouche / E. Mock / A. Oldenquist & M. Lynn / J. Van Peteghem / H. Rodingen / K. S. Tollett / W. Zitscher; *III. Recht und Rechtsstaat in wohlfahrtsstaatlicher Perspektive:* J. Bell / E. Kamenka / L. Lombardi Vallauri / N. B. Reynolds / L. Tower Sargent / M. Urso / R. Voigt; *IV. Soziale Verantwortung und strafrechtliche Zurechnung:* R. W. Burgh / S. Gbadegesin / N. Jareborg / N. Lacey / R. Lahti / W. Lang / A. Mabe / R. Martin / A. Papsthart / Ch. Sharma.

Beiheft 25: **Geltungs- und Erkenntnisbedingungen im modernen Rechtsdenken.** Hrsg. von N. MacCormick, S. Panou und L. Lombardi Vallauri. Mit einem Vorwort von R. Dreier.

I. Prinzipien und Regeln im Recht: R. Alexy / S. Axinn / M. Henket / J. Llompart / J. W. Murphy / Th. Schramm / R. A. Shiner / C. Wellman; *II. Wachstumsbedingungen des Erkenntnisfortschritts im Recht:* J. Dalberg-Larsen / E. V. Heyen / T. Sampaio Ferraz Jr. / D. Töllborg / V. Villa / A. H. de Wild / E. Zuleta Puceiro; *III. Modernes Recht und Wahrheitstheorien:* H. Aoi / O. A. Ghirardi / T. Gizbert-Studnicki / D. Lyons / I. Niiniluoto / F. Ost / J. Woleński.

3. D. Reidel Publishing Company: *Law and Philosophy Library*, 1985

Man, Law and Modern Forms of Life. Edited by E. Bulygin, J. L. Gardies and I. Niiniluoto. With an introduction by M. D. Bayles.

I. Anthropological and Epistemological Dimensions of Law and Ethics: T. Airaksinen / E. Bodenheimer / J. M. Broekman / J. B. Oakley / A. Oldenquist / P. G. Sack / M. Saltman / T. Stroup; *II. Schools and Perspectives in Legal Theory:* J. H. Crabb / M. M. Karlsson / R. Kevelson / H. T. Klami / K. Opałek / M. Samu; *III. Is and Ought: Present Issues in Argumentation and Legal Thinking:* J. Aomi / A. de Cervera / R. Hilpinen / J. Hintikka / N. Jääskinen / G.-F. Malt / A. Stening / L. Vandervort / G. H. von Wright / J. Wróblewski.

FSC
www.fsc.org
MIX
Papier | Fördert
gute Waldnutzung
FSC® C083411

Kolibri 360 GmbH
Ferdinand-Jühlke-Straße 7
99095 Erfurt, Deutschland
produktsicherheit@kolibri360.de

Druck:
CPI Druckdienstleistungen GmbH
im Auftrag der
Kolibri 360 GmbH
Ferdinand-Jühlke-Str. 7
99095 Erfurt